International Financial Management

An Analytical Framework

International Financial Management

An Analytical Framework

Second Edition

Thummuluri Siddaiah

Formerly Professor of Management and Dean
Sri Venkateswara University
Tirupati, Andhra Pradesh

Editor—Acquisitions: Pradeep Kumar Bhattacharjee
Senior Editor—Production: C. Purushothaman

ISBN 978-93-325-4137-5

First Impression, 2016
Third Impression, 2017
Fourth Impression, 2018

Published by Pearson India Education Services Pvt. Ltd, CIN: U72200TN2005PTC057128

Head Office: 15th Floor, Tower-B, World Trade Tower, Plot No. 1, Block-C,Sector-16, Noida 201 301, Uttar Pradesh, India.

Registered Office: 4th Floor, Software Block, Elnet Software City, TS-140, Block 2 & 9, Rajiv Gandhi Salai, Taramani, Chennai 600 113, Tamil Nadu, India.
Fax: 080-30461003,Phone: 080-30461060
Website : in.pearson.com , Email: companysecretary.india@pearson.com

Compositor:Cameo Corporate Services, Coimbatore.
Printed in India. Sai Printo Pack Pvt. Ltd.

In memory of
my late parents,
Thummuluri Nagamma and
Thummuluri Narayana
and
my late daughter *Haritha*

About the Author

Thummuluri Siddaiah was a Professor of Management at Sri Venkateswara University, Tirupati, Andhra Pradesh. He received master's degrees in commerce and economics from Sri Venkateswara University, and went on to receive M.Phil. degree from the Delhi School of Economics. He received his Ph.D. in banking in 1984.

Professor Siddaiah's academic interests include finance and information systems. He has taught courses in finance and information systems at the master's level for over 35 years, and has over 25 years of experience in teaching international finance to students pursuing MBA and other master's programmes.

Besides teaching and research, Professor Siddaiah is involved in executive development programmes and various administrative and advisory roles. He was the Principal of Sri Venkateswara University College of Commerce, Management and Computer Science, and also the Faculty Dean for a full term. He has also served as the Registrar of Sri Venkateswara University. He has been a member of the Expert Committee of the All India Council for Technical Education (AICTE) and Chairperson of the Peer Team of the National Assessment and Accreditation Council (NAAC). Professor Siddaiah is associated with the Institute of Chartered Accountants of India (ICAI) as an examiner, and was the vice-president of the Indian Association for Management Development. Professor Siddaiah has presented papers on contemporary issues in finance at several seminars and conferences. His columns have appeared in newspapers, magazines, and journals. He is the author of *Financial Services*, published by Pearson Education.

Contents

Preface to Second Edition

The book is intended as a text for both undergraduate and master's courses in international financial management. It can also be used in management/executive development programs. Apart from using it as a full text on each of the concepts and techniques of international finance presented in a lucid style with a number of live examples, a student can attempt challenging exercises and cases at the end of each chapter. The multiple-choice questions at the end of each chapter involve the thought process to choose the right answer. The Instructor Manual which accompanies this book provides a right direction of teaching the subject. The PowerPoint slides will come in handy for teachers to make interactive learning easy and effective in the classroom, whether real or virtual.

Many developments have taken place in the world economy after the global financial crisis (2007–09). The economies of the U.S., the U.K., Japan, and many of the euro-area countries were more deeply doused in the crisis. To come out of the crisis and boost the economies, central banks such as the Federal Reserve, the Bank of England, the Bank of Japan, etc. slashed their interest rates. But even reducing the interest rates as far as they could go, to almost zero, did not yield the desired result. Therefore, the central banks, especially the Federal Reserve began to pump money into the economy by a monetary tool called quantitative easing (QE). The QE entails the central bank buying assets in the form of government bonds, equities, or corporate bonds from commercial banks or other financing companies. The central bank is thus able to increase the spending power of the people and create more demand, pulling the economy out of recession. By purchasing bonds from the public, the central bank can increase the amount of currency and bank reserves in the economy which in turn affect asset prices including stock prices, exchange rates, etc. Higher asset prices can directly stimulate consumption and investment, leading to higher growth of the economy. But, if the economy is not vibrant, people may not spend much. Therefore, the excess money created by QE may go into the stock market, real estate, etc. Further, if the economy is bereft of sufficient entrepreneurial class, the excess money may not get into real investment. In other words, the growth of the economy may not become faster with the excess money created by QE, unless there is a potential entrepreneurial class to take advantage of the lower cost of capital.

To come out of a deep recession due to the housing market bubble, the Federal Reserve lowered the headline interest rate, also known as the Fed Funds rate, to the zero bound in December 2008. As the Federal Reserve could no longer control the money supply in the economy by cutting the interest rates, it decided to use a conventional monetary tool, quantitative easing. On 25 November 2008, the Federal Reserve announced that it would purchase USD 800 billion in bank debt, mortgage-backed securities (MBS), and Treasury securities from member banks. In fact, the Fed aggressively purchased the corporate securities and long-term Treasuries in a bigger volume than what it announced initially. As a result, the value of securities held by the Fed increased from USD 0.5 trillion in November 2008 to USD 2 trillion in March 2010. On 3 November 2010, the Fed again announced that it would increase QE, buying USD 600 billion of Treasury securities by the end of the second quarter of 2011 as the global recovery faltered with the euro crisis. This second round of easing was colloquially known as QE2. On 13 September 2012, the Fed announced QE3 which entailed buying USD 40 billion in MBS, adding a total USD 85 billion of liquidity a month. It was also decided to continue the extremely low rates policy until at least mid-2015. The policy was aimed at lowering borrowing costs and easing credit so that the business sector would promote growth and employment.

Having got three economic targets met: unemployment rate at 7 percent, GDP growth rate at 2–3 percent, and the core inflation rate not exceeding 2 percent, the president of the Fed announced on 19 June 2013 that the Fed would soon move to scale back QE from the USD 85 billion per month pace of purchases at the time. The announcement of early tapering sent tremors through global markets. Many emerging markets, including India were the most affected. The FIIs across the world shorted their position in most of the developing markets in the expectation that the liquidity in the U.S. economy would dry up and interest rates would harden. Between June and August 2013, the FIIs pulled out more than USD 3.7 billion from the Indian stock markets, dragging the Sensex down by more than 10 percent. The INR also touched an all-time low of 68.85 against the USD on 28 August 2013. Subsequently, tapering was postponed although the intention to taper was not abandoned. Ending the speculation, the Federal Open Market Committee (FOMC) – the Fed's policy-setting committee – took the decision on QE at its October (2013) policy meeting to conclude its asset purchase programme. Accordingly, the taper began in December 2013 and ended with a final USD 15 billion purchase in October 2014. Meanwhile, the European Central Bank (ECB) announced an expanded QE programme. Starting in March 2015, the ECB would buy, on a monthly basis, EUR 60 billion worth of euro-area sovereign bonds and private sector securities to boost the euro-area economy, where high unemployment is contributing to a prolonged spell of 'low inflation'. The Bank of Japan created a precursor to the Fed's QE programme when it announced in March 2001 that it was increasing the target for bank reserves from JPY 4 trillion to JPY 5 trillion to drive the overnight call rate from 0.15 percent to zero. By 2004, the Bank of Japan had incrementally increased the target for bank reserves from JPY 30 trillion to JPY 35 trillion, while simultaneously purchasing public and private debt. Although the Bank of Japan ended its official QE programme in March 2006, it continues to pursue easy monetary policy to stave off deflation in the economy.

The economic slow-down or recession in Japan as well as in euro-area continues to be deep even in the early part of 2015, despite loose monetary policies adopted by the Bank of Japan and the European Central Bank. As the investors pulled back funds from the emerging economies expecting higher interest rates in the U.S. after the Fed ended its QE of USD 85 billion of monthly bond purchases, many key exchanges rates have fallen against the USD. For example, the Russian ruble lost its value by about 38 percent against the USD in 2014. The JPY recorded a more than seven-year low against the USD in 2014. One may welcome a weaker currency because it makes the country's exports more competitive. But the pace of decline of the currency may destabilize the economy by fueling inflation and shattering investor confidence. Another development is shifting of base currencies from US dollar and Swiss franc to euro and Japanese yen. That is, the traders and investors are using the euro and Japanese yen as base currencies to acquire emerging market currencies such as the South African rand, Mexican peso, Brazilian real, Turkey's lira, Indian rupee, etc.

In contrast to 2013 when the INR was the worst performer, the Indian rupee was better off in 2014 against most currencies including the USD on expectation of reforms and carry trade opportunities. India offers more than 5 percent interest rate as against near-zero percent interest rates in countries such as Japan, the U.S., and countries in the euro area. Under the carry trade, the investors borrow from countries where the interest rates are low and invest in countries with higher interest rates. Since India is a net importer of crude oil, a steep fall in prices of crude oil has also supported the INR to be the best performer among 24 emerging market currencies in the first quarter of 2015. The INR had also a support in a record amount of USD 40.32 billion foreign investments received by India in 2014. The increase of overseas investment limit for resident individuals under the Liberalized Remittance Scheme (LRS) to USD 250,000 from USD 125,000 has not deterred the Indian rupee from rising against many currencies including the JPY and EUR in 2014. In the words of the RBI Governor, Raghuram Rajan, India will see a lot of money looking for returns. However, falling oil prices, slow growth in China, surging demand for USD on the speculation that the interest rates in the U.S. would rise, and impact of sanctions against Russia for its incursion into Ukraine, are the major challenges the world economy is facing in 2015.

In the light of several changes taking place in the world economy, it is felt necessary to revise the book with updated policy changes and data. A new chapter on Interest Rate Futures is added with extensive coverage of various dimensions and implications of changes in interest rates. In the revised edition, concepts like credit default swaps, real effective exchange rates, etc. are extensively covered with practical examples. A variety of real-life examples are added as practical application of concepts and techniques. The emphasis throughout this book is on providing a comprehensive knowledge of the subject with application, but in a lucid style to make even an average student to understand.

Organization of the Book

This book is organized into 17 chapters. The topics in each chapter are discussed from the perspective of the finance manager in the international context, with a special focus on India.

Chapter 1, "The Foreign Exchange Market: Structure and Operations," discusses the structure and operations of the foreign exchange market and introduces the reader to foreign exchange rates. This chapter acts as the foundation for the concepts dealt with in the following chapters.

Chapter 2, "The International Monetary System," focuses on different exchange rate regimes in the world and their implications. The chapter also highlights the developments in the exchange rate system of India.

Chapter 3, "The Balance of Payments: Implications for Exchange Rates," deals with the balance of payments and discusses its impact on exchange rates. Students of international finance usually find it difficult to understand how international transactions are recorded and what their implications for exchange rates are. This chapter deals with these issues by providing various solved examples, and it also discusses the convertibility of currency and its implications.

Chapter 4, "International Parity Relationship," discusses various parity conditions such as purchasing power parity, interest rate parity, forward rate parity, and the international Fisher effect. The basic concept of exchange rate determination leads the discussion on international parity.

Chapter 5, "Management of Foreign Exchange Exposure and Risk," highlights different kinds of foreign exchange exposures and risks faced by firms and discusses how such risks can be managed.

Chapter 6, "Currency Forwards and Futures," Chapter 7, "Currency Options," and Chapter 8, "Financial Swaps," deal with derivatives. Chapter 6 highlights how the forward and futures markets operate and elaborates on the trading strategies associated with futures. The chapter also introduces the concept of interest rate futures to readers. Chapter 7 explains various currency option trading strategies. Option pricing is the focus of this chapter. A comparison of options, forwards, and futures provides an overview of the various currency derivatives. Chapter 8 discusses financial swaps as risk-management tools and profit-generating strategies. The chapter focuses on interest rate swaps and currency swaps.

Chapter 9, Interest Rate Futures, dwells on various aspects of interest rate futures including Forward Rate Agreement.

Chapter 10, "Cross-border Investment Decisions," deals with the evaluation of investment projects from an international perspective. The concept of real options is also explained here.

Chapter 11, "Financing Decisions of MNCs," provides insights into the financing decisions of multinational corporations. It explains how the cost of capital and capital structure decisions of MNCs are different from those of domestic firms. It also discusses various methods of raising capital funds for foreign projects.

Chapter 12, "Management of Working Capital: An International Perspective," discusses the four major variables of working capital—cash, receivables, inventory, and trade credit—from the perspective of international working capital management.

Chapter 13, "International Trade," begins with an introduction of the major theories of international trade and goes on to discuss various developments in world trade. India's performance in international trade is a major highlight of this chapter.

Chapter 14, "Foreign Investments," discusses foreign direct investments (FDIs) and foreign institutional investments (FIIs) at length. India's policy towards FDIs and FIIs are also discussed in this chapter.

Chapter 15, "Portfolio Theory: An International Perspective," focuses on the capital asset pricing model (CAPM) from an international perspective. The chapter also discusses the scope for reducing investment risk through international portfolio diversification.

Chapter 16, "The Indian Accounting and Taxation System," discusses accounting and taxation systems at the international level and focuses on India's accounting and taxation system. It also provides a glimpse of the treaties between India and its neighbouring countries for the avoidance of double taxation.

Chapter 17, "Multilateral Financial Institutions," is the final chapter in the book. It provides a brief overview of significant multilateral institutions such as the World Bank, the International Monetary Fund (IMF), the Asian Development Bank (ADB), the International Development Association (IDA), and the International Finance Corporation (IFC).

Features

To enable students to understand the complex concepts of international financial management, the following pedagogical features have been incorporated into each chapter:

CHAPTER OBJECTIVES

After studying this chapter, you should be able to:

1 Gain insight into developments in the world economy that have influenced the foreign exchange market.
2 Delve into the nature and functions of the foreign exchange market.
3 Understand the dynamics of foreign exchange rates.
4 Gain knowledge in the trading mechanism in the foreign exchange market.
5 Understand the implications of cross rates.
6 Explain the process of arbitraging.
7 Explain the concept of foreign exchange swaps.
8 Understand the relationship between forward rates and future spot rates.

Chapter objectives define the key points that need to be focused on while studying each chapter.

The institutional setup that facilitates the trading of currencies is known as the ***foreign exchange market****. It is also referred to as the forex market, or the FX market.*

According to the Foreign Exchange Management Act (FEMA) Act, 1999, foreign exchange means foreign currency that includes deposits, credits, and balance in any foreign currency. Drafts, traveller's cheques, letters of credit or bills of exchange, expressed or drawn in Indian currency but payable in any foreign currency, are also considered as foreign exchange. A *foreign exchange transaction* is a trade of one currency for another currency. The institutional set-up that facilitates the trading of currencies is known as the **foreign exchange market**, or the *forex market* or *FX market*. The foreign exchange market is not located in a physical space and does not have a central exchange. Rather, it is an electronically linked network of a large number of individual foreign exchange trading centres, in which the market participants deal directly with each other. In other words, the foreign exchange trades are over-

The **margin notes** in each chapter define important terms and highlight significant facts.

Example 1.3

A trader purchased 200,000 units of EUR/JPY at 135.32 and sold at 135.34. What is the profit the trader has made in JPY and EUR? What is the profit in USD given the exchange rate of USD/JPY: 107.168 and JPY/USD: 0.00933?

Solution

Number of pips: 135.34 − 135.32 = 0.02 = 2 pips
Total pips in the transaction: 200,000 × 2 = 400,000 pips
Profit in yen: 400,000 × 0.01 = JPY 4000; (since a pip is worth 1% of the yen)
Profit in euro : 4000 ÷ 135.34 = EUR 29.5552
Profit in USD: 4000 ÷ 107.168 = USD 37.32 (given USD/JPY: 107.168)
Profit in USD: 4000 × 0.00933 = USD 37.32 (given JPY/USD: 0.00933)

The solved **examples** are designed to help students in solving complex problems and applying the concepts discussed in the chapter.

Real-world data from organizations such as the RBI, UNCTAD, and IMF help students and managers relate financial concepts to real-world events.

Table 1.9 Exchange-traded Currency Derivatives Market in India

Year	*Currency futures turnover (INR crore)*	*Currency options turnover (INR crore)*	*Total turnover (INR crore)*	*Average daily turnover (INR crore)*
2013–14	29,40,885.92	10,71,627.54	40,12,513.45	16,444.73
2012–13	37,65,105.33	15,09,359.32	52,74,464.65	21,705.62
2011–12	33,78,488.92	12,96,500.98	46,74,989.91	19,479.12
2010–11	32,79,002.13	1,70,785.59	34,49,787.72	13,854.57
2009–10	17,82,608.04	—	17,82,608.04	7,427.53
2008–09	1,62,272.43	—	1,62,272.43	1,167.43

The chapter **summaries** present a quick recapitulation of the key concepts discussed in each chapter. This acts as a ready reference for students who want to revise the concepts learned in the chapter.

Summary

1. Over the last two–three decades, the foreign exchange market has witnessed unprecedented growth following developments in the world economy.
2. The institutional set-up that facilitates the exchange of currencies is known as the *foreign exchange market.*
3. The rate at which the home currency is exchanged for a foreign currency is known as the rate of foreign exchange or the *foreign exchange rate.*
4. The foreign exchange market has two segments—the *wholesale segment* and the *retail segment*. The wholesale segment is also known as the *interdealer market.*
5. There are two kinds of exchange rate quotations—direct quotations and indirect quotations. A *direct quote* refers to the number of units of home currency that can be exchanged for one unit of a foreign currency, while an *indirect quote* refers to the number of units of a foreign currency that can be exchanged for one unit of home currency.

The **questions and problems** at the end of each chapter test the readers' understanding of concepts and their ability to critically analyse and apply these concepts. The numerical problems are designed to help students practice the solved examples, equations, and concepts discussed in the chapter.

Questions and Problems

1. Explain the structure of the foreign exchange market.
2. What is foreign exchange rate? How is the exchange rate of a currency determined?
3. Who are the participants in the foreign exchange market? What are their motives?
4. Distinguish between spot transactions and forward transactions.
5. What is arbitrage? How does arbitrage yield profit? How

12. The 180-day forward rate on the British pound is INR 87.79. A trader expects that the spot rate of the British pound will be INR 86.50 in six months. What is the expected profit on a forward sale of GBP 1 million?
13. If exchange rates are GBP/USD 1.92 and USD/JPY 116, what is the exchange rate between the yen and the British pound?
14. Show how one can make a triangular arbitrage profit by trading at the following rates:

The **case studies** at the end of relevant chapters provide real as well as hypothetical financial data and require students to analyse the data and draw conclusions from the perspective of a financial manager.

Case Study

Ravi Nikethan is a Mumbai-based tax consultant and his customers are mostly multinational firms. A London-based MNC has its subsidiary unit in Mumbai, engaged in manufacturing textiles. The subsidiary unit has earned a net profit of INR 130 million for the financial year 2013–14.

The company has requested Ravi to assist the subsidiary unit to compute its taxable income after taking note of the following:

1. Other income credited to profit and loss account includes the following:

- Payment of interest on overdraft utilized for payment of dividend: INR 1 million.

3. Repairs and maintenance include the following:
   - Expenditure incurred on replacement of worn out asbestos sheets of the factory shed with new sheets: INR 50,000.
   - Repairs to the compound wall that collapsed due to heavy rain: INR 0.5 million.

Multiple-choice Questions

1. Stakeholders of a company include ———.
   (a) Creditors (b) Employees
   (c) Customers (d) All the above
2. Accounting standards would ensure ——— of financial reports prepared by different enterprises.
   (a) Comparability (b) Consistency
   (c) Equality (d) None of these
3. Shifting to IFRS would enable Indian companies to have

8. Indian income is taxable, irrespective of the ——— of recipient.
   (a) Residential status (b) Country of origin
   (c) Economic status (d) None of these
9. The year in which the income is earned is known as the ———.
   (a) Previous year (b) Assessment year
   (c) Financial year (d) None of these

Multiple-choice questions enable the students to get deeper insights of the concepts.

The Teaching and Learning Package

The teaching and learning package includes an instructors' manual and PowerPoint lecture slides, which can be downloaded from www.pearsoned.co.in/thummulurisiddaiah, the book's companion Web site.

- *Instructors' Manual:* Chapter overviews and hints to relevant chapter-end questions and problems are provided in the instructors' manual.
- *PowerPoint Presentations:* PowerPoint lecture slides are designed to provide an overview of the important concepts and equations discussed in each chapter.
- *Additional Material:* In addition to the PowerPoint presentations and the instructors' manual, the companion Web site can also be used to access data on additional topics such as external commercial borrowings (ECBs), euro issues, and India's FDI policy. With rapid developments at the global level, some of the information provided in this book, like all other books on contemporary issues, is bound to require revision despite our best efforts to provide current data. Readers can refer to the companion Web site for updated information as such developments take place.

A Note on the Terms and the Currency System Used in this Book

- The ISO 4217 code for currencies has been used in this book. So, readers will find that INR has been used in place of Rs, GBP in place of £, USD in place of $, and JPY in place of ¥. Table 1.1 in Chapter 1 provides a list of the major currencies in the world and their symbols and ISO 4217 codes.
- As far as possible, million and billion have been used to represent large numbers in place of lakh and crore, which are commonly used in Indian books. However, where the primary data was available in lakh and crore (most of the RBI data, for instance), the information has been retained in the original style. The following table will help readers convert amounts in lakh/crore to amounts in million/billion in the same currency:

Amount in lakh/crore	*Amount in figures*	*Amount in million/billion*
1 lakh	100,000	100 thousand
10 lakh	1,000,000	1 million
1 crore	10,000,000	10 million
10 crore	100,000,000	100 million
100 crore	1,000,000,000	1 billion

Acknowledgements

For this edition too, I owe a debt of gratitude to those who helped in updating and revising this book. I thank my family members, more particularly my grand-children, Chi. Guruji and Chi. Baba for being a source of renewed strength whenever I am overused.

I am also thankful to Pradeep Kumar Bhattacharjee and C. Purushothaman of Pearson India Education Services Pvt. Ltd, Chennai, for their unstinted cooperation in bringing out this edition.

Thummuluri Siddaiah

Foreword to First Edition

Since around 1970, the world is said to have left behind modernity and entered the postmodern phase, which is marked by the spread of globalization. In this postmodern era, finance was the fastest growing area until the end of the twentieth century, when it was overtaken by the information technology (IT) and business process outsourcing (BPO) industries. The onward march of the savings-investment process has been affected lately by the economic recession, manifestations of which first appeared in mid-2007. The so-called global village is now going through a period of economic gloom, and normalcy does not seem foreseeable in the near future despite various bailout and stimulus measures. Writing on the subject of international finance against the backdrop of the present turbulence, when almost all major economic chips are down the world over, is a formidable task, but Professor Siddaiah has done an outstanding job.

Divided into 16 chapters, *International Financial Management* focuses on financial decision-making in terms of investment, financing, and distribution of profits and working capital from a cross-border perspective. The variety of topics included makes this an authoritative text on international trade and financial systems.

The progression of chapters shows the depth of Professor Siddaiah's scholarship. His arguments are well substantiated and moderately mathematical. Other merits of this text are the balanced treatment of the subject with a sound conceptual framework, market-related wisdom, solved numerical examples, practice problems and case studies, updated facts and figures, and a thorough analysis of financial-sector reforms in India and overseas.

The book will be a valuable resource for students aspiring to specialize in international finance. Also, for those taking the course as an elective, it will be an excellent introductory text. Teachers will also benefit immensely from this text as it provides state-of-the-art material.

Dr B. M. Lall Nigam
Former Professor
Delhi School of Economics

Preface to First Edition

This book comes at a time when we are grappling with the challenges of a global economic crisis, the ramifications of which are as severe as that of the Great Depression of the 1930s. In a world where economies are increasingly integrated and open to cross-border trade and investments, we have experienced the benefits of globalization, be it in small or large measure. And now, we are witness to the other side of globalization and can see how fast the economic ills of one country can spread throughout the globe and affect people and institutions the world over. An overview of the developments that led to this crisis and its aftermath will help us appreciate the integration of world economies.

Recent Developments in the Financial World

The subprime crisis in the United States and the subsequent collapse of several financial institutions, the increased volatility in foreign exchange rates, and the bailout and stimulus measures adopted by the governments of various nations to control the crisis are some of the most important developments in the global financial world in recent times.

The U.S. Subprime Crisis

The present world economic turmoil can be traced back to the subprime lending crisis in one of the largest economies in the world, the United States. Lending to those who don't qualify for the best market interest rates because of their deficient credit record is referred to as subprime lending. The subprime lending debacle, which started in mid-2007 in the United States, has become a financial contagion and sent shock waves throughout the world economy. Several financial institutions, such as Fannie Mae; Freddie Mac; Lehman Brothers; American International Group, Inc. (AIG); and Washington Mutual in the United States, and Fortis, the Dutch-Belgian Bank; Dexia, the French-Belgian bank; Bradford & Bingley; Aegon; and Hypo Real Estate in Europe, were declared bankrupt. Some, of course, were bailed out when they were on the verge of collapse. According to the United Nations Conference for Trade and Development (UNCTAD), between September 2007 and October 2008, 16 banks in the United States filed for bankruptcy and more than 100 were on the watchlist of the Federal Reserve. In addition to this, stock markets, along with commodity prices, collapsed. For instance, the Bombay Stock Exchange (BSE) Sensex reached its peak of 20,812.65 in January 2008, but rapidly came down to 8451.01—the lowest in the year— in October 2008. The high volatility in stock prices as well as commodity prices has shattered the confidence of market participants. The exports of several countries have been hit badly, which has further increased their current account deficits. The spread between interbank interest rates and treasury bills has increased tremendously because of increasing interbank interest rates and decreasing yields on treasury bills. In this scenario, banks have become extremely reluctant to participate in the interbank market as they have lost confidence in the creditworthiness of counterparties. In view of their bad loans, particularly sub-prime mortgage loans, financial institutions including banks worldwide had written down about USD 700 billion worth of asset-backed securities by the end of September 2008. This indicates that their capital base has been eroded and, consequently, their capacity to lend has been reduced. The contagion effect of the crisis has also resulted in reversals in private capital flows to developing economies. The cost of external borrowing has increased phenomenally. These developments will have far-reaching implications for the development of emerging economies.

Volatility in Foreign Exchange Markets

The turbulence in global financial markets has also increased the volatility in foreign exchange markets. The U.S. dollar depreciated substantially against other major currencies in the beginning of 2008, but subsequently reversed its direction in late 2008. Many currencies, including the currencies of developing nations, have depreciated considerably against the U.S. dollar. For example, the exchange rate of the Indian rupee against the U.S. dollar appreciated to 34.48 in March 2008 from 39.28 in January 2008. Large foreign capital inflows resulted in the appreciation of the Indian rupee against the U.S. dollar. But, following this, the Indian rupee depreciated and recorded a historic low of 50.58 in October 2008, mainly because of large outflows of foreign institutional investments. The Indian rupee's previous historic low was recorded in 2002, when it touched 49.07 against the USD. As a result of the depreciation of major currencies against the U.S. dollar, current account imbalances across the world have narrowed. For example, the current account deficit of the United States reduced to some extent in 2008. The official foreign exchange reserves of many countries are expected to either stagnate or decline, as they are likely to experience a weakening of the current and/or capital accounts.

The Need for Adequate Control Mechanisms

The global financial crisis is considered to be a systemic crisis because it has affected all financial institutions and markets and, moreover, has spread to the real economy. The lack of an institutional mechanism along the lines of the World Trade Organization (WTO) to monitor and coordinate the activities of financial institutions, including banks and financial markets, is a major shortcoming of the international financial system. Further, there is no mechanism or institution that can integrate the functioning of the international trading system and the international financial system (including the international monetary and fiscal system). Unfettered financial markets, including foreign exchange markets, have proved wanting in their self-regulatory capacity.

According to UNCTAD, most developed countries entered an economic recession during the latter part of 2008. The economic slowdown has also gripped developing economies and economies in transition. The United Nations' baseline forecast says that the world's gross product would come down to just 1 per cent in 2009 as against the 2.5 per cent growth estimated for 2008. The income per capita for the world as a whole is expected to decline in 2009. The per capita income growth in many nations will be negative, as compared to the robust growth registered during the period 2002-2007. The report further states that it will take six to nine months for financial markets in developed countries to return to normalcy, provided certain stimulus measures are introduced. The governments of many countries have now initiated both bailout and stimulus measures. For instance, the Government of India, in its efforts to minimize the impact of the global economic slowdown, has announced a stimulus package, which includes a 4 per cent across-the-board cut in excise duty, a hike in public expenditure on infrastructure projects, and an increase in public expenditure by INR 1.47 lakh crore, which would be over and above the INR 7.5 lakh crore already provided in the budget for 2008-09. In September 2008, the Reserve Bank of India (RBI) reduced the repo rate from 9 per cent to 6.5 per cent and the reverse repo rate from 6 per cent to 5 per cent. The cash reserve ratio (CRR) was reduced from 9 per cent to 5.5 per cent. In the second stimulus package announced on 2 January 2009, the RBI further reduced the repo and reverse repo rates by 100 basis points each, from 6.5 per cent to 5.5 per cent and from 5 per cent to 4 per cent. The *repo rate* is the rate at which banks can borrow from the RBI, and the *reverse repo rate* is the rate at which banks can park their funds with the RBI. The second stimulus package includes the reduction of CRR from 5.5 per cent to 5 per cent. The *cash reserve ratio* refers to the portion of deposits that banks have to maintain with the RBI. A reduction in CRR infuses additional liquidity into the economy. Following the reduction of repo rates by the RBI, several banks in India have announced lower lending and deposit rates.

Dealing with Corporate Finance from the International Perspective

The phenomenal growth of international trade, cross-border investments, and the recent economic crisis have made it necessary for finance managers and students of finance to understand the dynamics of financial decisions, especially those that involve foreign exchange rates and markets. *International Financial Management* seeks to provide finance managers and students with the knowledge and skills required for managing business operations in the international arena. The book also aims to help them take advantage of the opportunities available in the global environment and, at the same time, protect their businesses from the vagaries of exchange rates. The framework of international finance will also be useful for policymakers and executives in government and non-governmental (not-for-profit) organizations.

With its numerous solved examples, practice problems, and case studies and its focus on financial practices and policy, the book is designed to help students who aspire to become finance managers, executives, financial analysts, or financial consultants to apply the concepts of international finance to real-world events and situations. As the book provides the conceptual framework and analytical tools necessary to make financial decisions from an international perspective, it is also suitable for executive development programmes and management development programmes.

Testimonials

The scheme of chapters has been done excellently. All important and relevant topics have been covered with due diligence. All the concepts have started with the previous knowledge of the students. This is the USP of the book.

Shegorika Rajwani
Assistant Professor
IILM Institute for Higher Education

The chapters are logically and appropriately organized. Concepts and topics are well explained from student's point of view. The important topics have been explained in sufficient.

Sonali N. Parchure
Assistant Professor
Smt. Hiraben Nanavati Institute of Management and Research for Women

All the topics are presented in a simplified manner and hence student friendly. The level of the book seems to be appropriate for student community. Recent developments in the area of International Financial Management are covered adequately.

A. Narasimha Rao
Professor
Department of Commerce and Management Studies
Andhra University

The book is student friendly, and cases used in the book are good and unique. As we know that in this area of International Finance there are less number of cases available and this book fulfils that gap.

Dr Sunita Rani (Jindal)
Associate Professor
Guru Gobind Singh Indraprastha University

Adequate numbers of good examples help in understanding the concepts better and the book has good pedagogical features. The book blends theory and practice with real-world data analysis.

Swati Shukla
Assistant Professor
Symbiosis Centre for Management Studies

CHAPTER 1

The Foreign Exchange Market: Structure and Operations

CHAPTER OBJECTIVES

After studying this chapter, you should be able to:

1. Gain insight into developments in the world economy that have influenced the foreign exchange market.
2. Delve into the nature and functions of the foreign exchange market.
3. Understand the dynamics of foreign exchange rates.
4. Gain knowledge in the trading mechanism in the foreign exchange market.
5. Understand the implications of cross rates.
6. Explain the process of arbitraging.
7. Explain the concept of foreign exchange swaps.
8. Understand the relationship between forward rates and future spot rates.
9. Know the major communication networks for foreign exchange transactions.
10. Gain an overview of the foreign exchange market in India.

Introduction

The foreign exchange market is a key economic process that affects many facets of life of people wherever they dwell. It is the largest market in the world in terms of turnover. It is estimated that the foreign exchange market turnover is more than ten times the value of world trade in goods and services. As a world-wide network of traders, the foreign exchange market, colloquially known as forex market, has witnessed unprecedented growth and changes following developments that have taken place in the world economy over the last two or three decades. The developments, such as launching of the World Trade Organization (WTO), globalization of trade, growth in international investments, and expansion of international trade, along with explosive pace of deregulations and liberalizations have brought about a perceptible transformation in the size, structure, coverage, and operations of the foreign exchange market. No lesser than these is the information and computing technology, which has had a great impact on the development of the foreign exchange market.

The General Agreement on Tariffs and Trade (GATT) and subsequent creation of the WTO have brought about a surge in international trade and cross-border investments.

The WTO has been reasonably successful in dismantling many international trade barriers and in extending the scope of international trade to include a variety of commodities and services. Reductions in tariffs, controls, and quotas, and removal of other impediments have resulted in a phenomenal increase in international trade. With the entry of many commodities into the international market and increasing proportion of services in international trade, the depth and breadth of international trade have improved tremendously over the last twenty–thirty years.

Globalization of trade, which is based on the *theory of comparative advantage*, propounded by David Ricardo, is another factor that influences the foreign exchange market to a great extent. According to Ricardo, countries can benefit by exploiting the comparative advantages in efficiency that arise from specialized production and economies of scale. Although globalization benefits every nation, countries with dynamic leadership, wide entrepreneurial class, and discerning buyers can gain a competitive advantage in the globalization process.

Parallel to international trade, there has been a tremendous increase in international investments. Foreign investments have even exceeded domestic investments in some of the countries. The growth and development of multinational corporations (MNCs) are the cause and consequence of a substantial rise in foreign direct investments. In earlier periods, MNCs aimed at exploiting raw materials found overseas. Later, they began investing in countries with potential markets for their products. These days, MNCs seek out and invest in countries where they can create and maintain a competitive advantage, which provides a fillip to the development of the global foreign exchange market.

The liberalization and privatization policies of some countries, the former socialist countries in particular, have spurred a tremendous increase in cross-border investments. Formal arrangements among countries of various regions, such as the European Union (EU), the North American Free Trade Agreement (NAFTA), the Association of South-East Asian Nations (ASEAN), Mercosur Group (MC), and the Asia-Pacific Economic Cooperation (APEC), have also promoted economic integration. The introduction of the euro has had a profound effect on the world economy. Major developments such as financial disintermediation at an increasing pace, a surge in mergers and acquisitions (M&A), and multiplicity of cross-border alliances have brought about revolutionary changes in the world economy, particularly in financial markets. Many countries have relaxed or repealed acts that restricted the activities and operations of financial institutions, including commercial banks and investment banks. The easing of barriers in cross-border capital flows has enabled corporates to raise capital in markets and currencies they find attractive. Financial service providers have thus been able to go global and bring about robust changes in the world of finance.

International trade and investments have a profound effect on the foreign exchange market, but the reverse is also true. An example will help illustrate this relationship. International trade and investments cause a large flow of foreign currencies across countries, influencing the breadth and depth of the global foreign exchange market. Along the same vein, the foreign exchange market also influences international trade and international investments. For example, stability in exchange rates can facilitate robust growth in international trade and investments, while exchange-rate volatility can have an adverse effect on both trade and investments. This is thus a two-way relationship.

We shall discuss some of the developments outlined here in greater detail throughout the book. This chapter mainly describes the instruments and mechanics of the foreign exchange market. Some recent trends in the foreign exchange market and the structure of the Indian foreign exchange market are also discussed in this chapter. The differences between domestic financial management and international financial management are also outlined towards the end of the chapter.

Money as a Medium of Exchange

In the past, the value of a commodity or service used to be expressed in terms of some other commodity or service. It was a barter system on a global scale. Under the barter system, the value of a commodity like paddy could be expressed in terms of say, pulses; the value of apples could be measured in terms of a certain number of oranges; and so on. In the monetary world, where we are now, the value of every commodity or service is expressed in terms of money. Money is a measure of value for all goods and services and thus becomes a medium of exchange for most things in the world.

Different countries have different currencies as their monetary unit. For example, the Indian rupee is the currency or monetary unit in India, and the value of all goods and services in India is measured and expressed in terms of Indian rupees. Similarly, the US dollar is the currency in the United States, and the value of all goods and services in the United States is measured and expressed in terms of this currency. Although the terms *money* and *currency* have different connotations in economics, no distinction is observed between them in common parlance.

People in different countries can use their respective currencies as the medium of exchange for all goods and services within the geographical borders of their country. However, when people from one country intend to buy goods from a foreign country or engage in financial transactions abroad, they usually need the currency of that country. In such situations, it should be possible to acquire the required amount of the foreign currency by exchanging a specific amount of domestic currency for it. There would be no need for foreign currency and the foreign exchange market if all the nations in the world were to have a single currency. However, since it is not practical to have a single currency for all nations (although the introduction of the euro is a step towards this direction), it is imperative to have a foreign exchange market.

The International Organization for Standardization (ISO) has developed a system of three-character codes or abbreviations for all the currencies in the world to facilitate easy and efficient currency trading. The codes under this standard are referred to as ISO 4217; the first two characters indicate the name of the country and the third designates the currency. However, there are some variations. For example, the symbol of Swiss franc is CHF, where CH stands for Confederation Helvetica, which refers to Switzerland, and F stands for franc. Similarly, MXN represents Mexican currency, where MXN stand for Mexican Nuevo peso, even though the Mexico's currency is simply the peso. An illustrative list of some currencies and their codes is presented in Table 1.1.

Table 1.1 List of Select Currencies with Codes and Symbols

Country/region	*Currency*	*Currency code*	*Currency symbol*
United States of America	US dollar	USD	$
United Kingdom	British pound	GBP	£
European Union	European Union euro	EUR	€
Switzerland	Swiss franc	CHF	CHF
Australia	Australian dollar	AUD	$
Canada	Canadian dollar	CAD	$
Japan	Yen	JPY	¥

(Continued)

Table 1.1 ***(Continued)***

Country/region	*Currency*	*Currency code*	*Currency symbol*
China	Yuan Renminbi	CNY	¥
Malaysia	Malaysian ringgit	MYR	RM
Mauritius	Mauritius rupee	MUR	Rs
Pakistan	Pakistan rupee	PKR	Rs
Singapore	Singapore dollar	SGD	$
Sri Lanka	Sri Lanka rupee	LKR	Rs
India	Indian rupee	INR	₹

The Foreign Exchange Market

The institutional setup that facilitates the trading of currencies is known as the ***foreign exchange market****. It is also referred to as the forex market, or the FX market.*

According to the Foreign Exchange Management Act (FEMA) Act, 1999, foreign exchange means foreign currency that includes deposits, credits, and balance in any foreign currency. Drafts, traveller's cheques, letters of credit or bills of exchange, expressed or drawn in Indian currency but payable in any foreign currency, are also considered as foreign exchange. A *foreign exchange transaction* is a trade of one currency for another currency. The institutional set-up that facilitates the trading of currencies is known as the **foreign exchange market**, or the *forex market* or *FX market*. The foreign exchange market is not located in a physical space and does not have a central exchange. Rather, it is an electronically linked network of a large number of individual foreign exchange trading centres, in which the market participants deal directly with each other. In other words, the foreign exchange trades are over-the-counter deals agreed and settled by counterparties. Thus, the forex market provides a single, cohesive, integrated, and world-wide market by linking various individual foreign exchange trading centres or markets spread all over the globe.

The currencies of developed economies that are most actively traded (e.g. euro, British pound, US dollar, Swiss franc, Japanese yen, etc.) are considered to be the major currencies, and are referred to as majors, while all other currencies are considered to be minor currencies, and are referred to as minors.

There are a large number of foreign exchange trading centres in the world as each country has its own centre(s). The functioning of each trading centre is governed by the respective country's laws, tax code, banking regulations, accounting rules, and financial system. Unlike the trading on stock exchanges or commodity exchanges, foreign exchange trading is not governed by any unified body.

Electronic trading, or e-trading, is a method of trading in which market participants can see the bid–ask rates quoted by potential counterparties on their computer screens, match orders, and make deals electronically.

Foreign exchange traders carry out their business through a network of communications. Although market participants are geographically far away from each other, high-speed communication systems have an instantaneous impact on market movements, making the foreign exchange market as efficient as other markets. Banks and dealers, who largely constitute the foreign exchange market, are connected by communication networks provided by the Society for Worldwide Interbank Financial Telecommunication (SWIFT). The Clearing House Interbank Payment System (CHIPS) links several banks and dealers involved in dollar currency transactions. The profiles of these two networks are briefly presented in Section 1.9.

In the past, forex transactions were conducted primarily by telegram, telephone, or telex. But several changes have taken place in every walk of life with advances in information and communication technology, and foreign exchange trading is no exception. The latest development in foreign exchange trading is **electronic trading**—a method of trading that enables market participants, particularly large financial institutions, to set up algorithmic trading systems and provide trading facilities to retail investors. Participants in the foreign exchange market can see bid–ask rates quoted by potential counterparties on their computer screens, match their orders, and make deals electronically. The electronic trading system has all the advantages of voice trading, besides being faster and more reliable. Electronic trading also manages credit lines.

With the advent of high-speed digital data lines and satellite-based communication systems, foreign exchange transactions are now carried out rapidly and in real time. In fact, in most cases of currency trading, there is no physical transfer of paper notes and coins, but a series of book or digital entries made in the accounts of the two parties—the buyer of the currency and the seller of the currency—to record their new positions. In view of developments in computing and communication technologies, particularly in international communications networks, foreign exchange markets all over the world have virtually become one sophisticated global market with more than USD 5 trillion worth of trade taking place every day.

Foreign exchange markets were originally conceived to facilitate international trade. Over the years, these markets have become an integral organ of the world economy. Now, foreign exchange markets are indispensable institutional machinery that facilitates not only cross-border payments but also cross-border capital flows and overseas investments.

The global foreign exchange market is a twenty-four-hour (around-the-clock) non-stop market. It has no fixed trading floor, no prescribed working hours, and no single governing authority. It is an over-the-counter (OTC) market with a world-wide network of participants such as banks, corporates, etc. Currency trading is carried out around the clock and around the globe. As foreign exchange centres are spread throughout the world, at any given point in time, some centres are closed while others are open for trade. For instance, Europe's morning hours overlap with the late hours in Asia, and Europe's afternoon hours correspond to the morning hours in North America. The different time zones make the global foreign exchange market a real-time market. Some centres are characterized by very heavy trading during certain times when their business hours overlap with those of many other trading centres. For example, the morning business hours of New York and the afternoon business hours of London overlap, and therefore very heavy trading takes place during these hours at these two centres. This happens because participants can have access to the maximum number of potential buyers and sellers when many trading centres are open. London has become the largest foreign exchange trading centre, mainly because of the unique advantage of its business hours overlapping with those of many major foreign exchange trading centres such as New York, Frankfurt, Tokyo, and Singapore. During these overlapping hours, the largest number of potential foreign exchange traders is available on a global basis. This also provides traders the best prices, in addition to greater market liquidity. Trading in the foreign exchange market takes place in currency pairs. In a pair of currencies, if one currency is considered to be up, the other currency is considered to be down. Therefore, the ups and downs in the foreign exchange market are seen only in trading volumes but not in prices.

Characteristics of the global foreign exchange market:

- *Twenty-four hour, non-stop operations.*
- *Real-time market.*
- *Heavy trading during overlapping hours.*
- *Major trading centres in London, New York, Frankfurt, Tokyo, and Singapore.*

Market Participants

Who requires foreign exchange? At the primary level, individuals who receive remittances denominated in a foreign currency may sell their foreign currency for domestic currency, and those who travel abroad may buy foreign currency. At the next level, businesses, including corporations engaged in international trade, may buy or sell foreign currency. Governments and other organizations such as banks may also buy or sell foreign currency to carry out their international transactions. Investors, including institutional investors, may also require foreign currency. To facilitate the individuals and organizations including governments to buy or sell foreign exchange, certain other organizations and individuals, called *facilitators,* have come to play a role. In market terminology, these facilitators are categorized as primary dealers and brokers. *Primary dealers* act as a principal in a transaction and conduct business in their own account by committing their own funds, while *brokers* act as an agent for an actual buyer/seller of foreign exchange and do not commit their own funds. Brokers do not take positions and, therefore, are not exposed to foreign exchange risks. They rely on the brokerage commission or fees that they receive from their clients. Dealers, on the other hand, rely on their bid–ask spread.

Dealers may seek the help of *foreign exchange brokers* who have access to specific information and possess specialized knowledge in the fundamentals and market movements of different currencies. As each broker specializes in a particular currency or a set of currencies, dealers may seek the services of a particular broker(s) according to their requirement. Besides bringing the buyer and seller together, brokers provide quick access to information and a wide choice of counterparties. In other words, the market participants can save time and effort by using brokers in their foreign exchange trading. Brokers are also organized as firms or corporates with branches in different countries, or be affiliated with broking houses in other countries.

Individuals and organizations that participate in the foreign exchange market may also be classified as hedgers, arbitrageurs, and speculators. *Hedgers* are those who participate in the foreign exchange market to reduce the foreign exchange risk that they already face. They try to insure themselves against adverse foreign exchange rate movements while benefiting from favourable movements. *Arbitrageurs* attempt to make risk-less profits by entering into foreign exchange transactions simultaneously in two or more market centres. *Speculators* are those who take positions in the foreign exchange market by anticipating whether the exchange rate will go up or down. They take positions to profit from exchange rate fluctuations. It may sometimes be difficult to distinguish between a speculative activity and a prudent business activity. This is because even firms that restrict their foreign currency operations to their normal business needs may not hedge their foreign exchange exposure at times. So, their uncovered positions in the foreign exchange market may yield profits on the movement of exchange rates. Even other market participants including banks and other financial service providers seek to derive gains out of fluctuations in foreign exchange rates.

According to the BIS Triennial Central Bank Survey, market participants may be dealers, other financial institutions, or non-financial customers. *Dealers* are financial institutions that actively participate in local and global foreign exchange and derivatives markets. These are mainly large commercial banks, investment banks, and securities houses. They participate in the interdealer market and/or have an active business with large customers such as corporate firms and governments. *Other financial institutions* comprise smaller commercial banks, investments banks, securities houses, mutual funds, pension funds, hedge funds, currency funds, money-market funds, building societies, leasing companies, insurance companies, and other financial subsidiaries of corporate firms and central banks. The category of *non-financial customers* covers any market participant other than those described in the preceding definition (corporations and governments, for example).

The global foreign exchange market is always dominated by interbank trading with a share of about 43 percent; followed by trading between dealers and other financial institutions (40%); and between dealers and non-financial customers (17%). There are about 10 major international banks that account for more than 70 percent of currency trading in the world. Money transfer companies or remittance companies (e.g. Western Union) are also high-volume performers in the foreign exchange market.

Market Makers

Many dealers in the foreign exchange market act as **market makers** by offering two quotes—*bid* and *ask*, or *price to buy* and *price to sell*—for the currencies in which they are dealing. Such quotations are known as *double-barrelled quotations*. Market makers stand ready to buy and sell standard amounts of the currencies for which they are making a market, and seek to make a profit on the spread between the two prices. Thus, market makers contribute to liquidity, price discovery, and price stability in the foreign exchange market by providing a continuous market and price-sensitive information.

__Market makers__ stand ready to buy and sell standard amounts of the currencies for which they are making a market, and seek to profit on the spread between the two prices.

Market Segments

The foreign exchange market may be divided into the wholesale segment and the retail segment. The interdealer trading dominates the **wholesale segment** of the foreign exchange market. The size of each transaction in the wholesale market is very large. Because of its size and intensity, the wholesale market remains the focus of study in international finance.

The foreign exchange market may be divided into the wholesale segment and the retail segment. The __wholesale segment__ is also known as the interdealer market, as the exchange transactions take place between banks that are the primary dealers. The __retail segment__ of the foreign exchange market consists of tourists, restaurants, hotels, shops, banks, and other bodies and individuals.

The market participants in the wholesale segment are commercial banks, investment banks, central banks, corporations, and high-net-worth individuals. Let us discuss these entities briefly.

- *Commercial banks*: Originally, commercial banks used to buy and sell foreign currencies for their customers as a part of their financial services. They later took on foreign exchange trading as their principal business. Commercial banks have also found it useful to trade with each other. As commercial banks trade in large volumes of foreign exchange, the wholesale segment of the foreign exchange market has become an interbank market.
- *Investment banks and other financial institutions*: Although the interbank foreign exchange market was the exclusive domain of commercial banks for a long time, over the last two decades, investment banks, insurance companies, pension funds, mutual funds, hedge funds, and other financial institutions have also entered the foreign exchange market and have become direct competitors to commercial banks. These new institutions have emerged as important foreign exchange service providers to a variety of customers in competition with commercial banks. Hedge funds, in particular, have become more aggressive in currency speculation. With their dealings in many millions of US dollars every day, hedge funds can influence foreign exchange rates.
- *Corporations and high-net-worth individuals*: Domestic as well as multinational corporations participate in the foreign exchange market to convert their foreign currency-denominated export receipts, foreign borrowings, and foreign remittances into their home currency. They may also buy foreign currency to make import payments, interest payments, and loan repayments, and to invest funds abroad. Some high-net-worth individuals also participate in the foreign exchange market to meet their investment needs.
- *Central banks*: The central banks of countries (e.g. the Reserve Bank of India; RBI) may also participate in the foreign exchange market in order to control factors such as money supply, inflation, and interest rates by influencing exchange rate movements in a particular direction. In other words, the intervention of a central bank is warranted when the respective government wants to maintain target exchange rates or avoid violent fluctuations in exchange rates. Even a talk of possible central bank intervention may sometimes lead to stabilization of the exchange rate. The central banks may use their foreign exchange reserves to intervene in the foreign exchange market.

In the interbank market, currency notes and coins rarely change hands. The buying/selling of a particular currency is actually the buying/selling of a demand deposit denominated in that currency. Thus, the exchange of currencies is, in reality, the exchange of a bank deposit denominated in one currency for a bank deposit denominated in another currency. For example, a dealer buying yen, no matter where the transaction takes place, is actually buying a yen-denominated deposit in a bank located in Japan or the claim of a bank located outside Japan on a yen-denominated deposit in a bank located in Japan.

The **retail segment** of the foreign exchange market consists of tourists, restaurants, hotels, shops, banks, and other bodies and individuals. Travellers and other individuals exchange one currency for another in order to meet their specific requirements. Currency notes, traveller's cheques, and bank drafts are the common instruments in the retail segment of the foreign exchange market. Authorized restaurants, hotels, shops, banks, and other entities buy and sell foreign currencies, bank drafts, and traveller's cheques to provide easy access to foreign exchange for individual customers, and also to convert their foreign currency into their home currency. Individuals who receive foreign remittances and those who send foreign currencies abroad may also participate in the retail segment of the foreign exchange market.

Although the foreign exchange needs of retail customers are usually small and account for a small fraction of the turnover in the foreign exchange market, the retail market assumes great importance, especially for people of small means. This is the reason behind the growing importance of the retail segment. The transaction costs, however, are higher because of the small size of the retail segment.

Foreign Exchange Rates

*The price of one currency in terms of another currency is known as the **foreign exchange rate**.*

Depending on the perspective of the participant, a currency is identified as the *domestic* or *home currency*, or as a *foreign currency*. For example, from the perspective of an Indian participant, the Indian rupee is the home currency, and any other currency is a foreign currency. Similarly, for a US participant, the US dollar is the home currency and any other currency is a foreign currency. The rate at which the home currency is exchanged for a foreign currency is known as the **foreign exchange rate**. In general, the foreign exchange rate is the price of one currency quoted in terms of another currency. The foreign exchange rate is also known as the *forex rate* or *FX rate*.

Currencies are always traded in pairs. A foreign exchange trade involves buying of one currency and selling of another currency. With reference to a pair of currencies, buying of one currency (*long position*) always involves selling of the other currency (*shorting*). Traditionally, currency pairs are separated by a solidus (e.g. USD/INR) or a hyphen (e.g. USD-INR). According to established convention, the first currency in the pair is the **base currency** or **primary currency**, and the second currency is referred to as the **quote currency** or **counter currency** or **secondary currency**. The base currency, also known as fixed currency or underlying currency is always one unit. That is, one unit of the base currency is traded for a variable amount of the quote currency. Quote or counter currency is the amount of the currency equal to one unit of the base currency. For example, in the currency pair USD/INR, USD is the base currency and INR is the quote currency. The rate of exchange between these two currencies is expressed in terms of the amount of INR to be received or paid per US dollar. If USD/INR is 61.2345, it means that INR 61.2345 can be exchanged for one unit of USD. Conventionally, stronger currency is used as the base currency in a pair of currencies. Thus, a foreign exchange rate is always quoted for a pair of currencies.

*When considering an exchange between a pair of currencies, the first currency is the **base currency** and the second currency is the **counter** or **quote currency**. This implies that one unit of the base currency is traded for a variable amount of the counter currency.*

The relationship of a pair of currencies may also be stated as:

Quote currency/Base currency = 1/(Base currency/Quote currency)

In mathematical functions, X/Y (i.e. amount of X divided by amount of Y) represents the number of units of X per unit of Y. But in foreign exchange transactions, X/Y represents the number of units of Y per unit of X.

Forex trading in a currency pair always implies simultaneous buying of one currency and selling of the other currency. When a currency trader buys a pair of currencies, it means that he is buying the base currency and selling the quote currency. He buys the base currency when he expects that its value to increase in terms of the quote currency or exchange rate rises in future; and sells the base currency when he expects that the value of the base currency to decrease in terms of the quote currency or exchange rate decreases in future. A lower quote means that the value of the base currency is weakening.

American Terms and European Terms Rates quoted in amounts of US dollar per unit of foreign currency are known as quotes in *American terms,* while rates quoted in amounts of foreign currency per US dollar are known as quotes in *European terms.* For example, USD 1.6183/GBP, read as "1.6183 US dollars per British pound," is a quotation in American terms. Thus, in American terms, the foreign exchange quotation gives the US dollar price of one unit of the foreign currency. In contrast, quotations in European terms state the foreign currency price of one US dollar. For example, GBP 0.6180/USD, read as "0.6180 British pounds per US dollar," is a quotation in European terms. As most Asian and European currencies are quoted in European terms (a certain number of units per US dollar), the USD is the most widely used base currency in the global foreign exchange market. Of late, the euro has also become a base currency against many currencies, particularly for European countries. It should be noted that American terms and European terms are reciprocals.

Direct Quotes and Indirect Quotes There are two kinds of exchange rate quotations: direct and indirect. A **direct quote** is the number of units of home currency that can be exchanged for one unit of a foreign currency, i.e. foreign currency is used as the base currency and domestic currency is used as the quote currency. An **indirect quote** is the number of units of a foreign currency that can be exchanged for one unit of the home currency. In an indirect quote, the home currency is used as the base currency and the foreign currency is used as the quote currency. For example, the exchange rate between the Indian rupee and the US dollar can be stated as either INR/USD or USD/INR. If INR is used as the quote currency, then USD/INR is a direct quote with reference to India. Alternatively, if INR is used as the base currency, INR/USD is an indirect quote with reference to India. For an Indian participant, USD/INR 60.53 is a direct quote, and INR/USD 0.01652 is an indirect quote. As the indirect quote is the reciprocal of the direct quote, one can obtain an indirect quote, given a direct quote and vice versa. A direct quote is known as the price quote, whereas an indirect quote is known as the quantity quote.

*A **direct quote** is the number of units of home currency that can be exchanged for one unit of a foreign currency. An **indirect quote** is the number of units of a foreign currency that can be exchanged for one unit of the home currency.*

Bid/ask Rates In the foreign exchange market, market makers are always ready to buy or sell currencies by quoting two rates—the bid rate and the ask rate. For example, a bank may quote USD/INR: 61.5410/61.5499. The component before the solidus is the bid rate and the one after the solidus is the ask rate or the *offer.* Quotes are thus expressed as bid/ask in terms of the quote currency. However, in the London foreign exchange market, the rates are quoted as ask/bid (or offer/bid). The **bid rate** is the rate at which the market maker giving the quotation is ready to *buy* one unit of the base currency against the quote currency, while the **ask rate** is the rate at which the market maker is ready to *sell* one unit of the base currency for the quote currency. In the USD/INR example discussed here, the market maker is ready to buy one US dollar by paying INR 61.5470, and to sell one US dollar, the market maker wants to be paid INR 61.5499. Considering the same example, if you want to buy a US dollar, you have to pay INR 61.5499 and if you want to sell a US dollar, you have to sell it at INR 61.5470. Thus, you would lose money and the dealer would make money. The difference between the bid rate and the ask rate is known as the *spread*. Thus, the spread represents the transaction cost and it is also a margin for the forex dealer.

*The **bid rate** is the rate at which the bank giving the quotation is ready to buy one unit of the base currency by paying the quoted currency. The **ask rate** is the rate at which the bank giving the quotation is ready to sell one unit of the base currency for the quoted currency.*

The quotations are conventionally shortened as, for example, USD/INR: 61.5410/99 or 10/99. The bid–ask spread is obtained in *points* or *pips* (price interest point). The currency quotes are displayed in two parts, viz. the big figure and the dealing price. The big figure, being the main price, is usually the same for both the bid and offer quotes. But the dealing price, also known as handle, is the last two digits in a quote and it is different for the bid and ask quotes.

Direct quotations can be converted into indirect quotations and vice versa.

Direct quote: Bid --- Ask
Indirect quote: 1/Ask ---- 1/Bid

For example, the USD is quoted at INR 61.5410/61.5499. The reciprocal of the bid (direct) of 61.5410 becomes the ask (indirect) of USD 0.01625, and the reciprocal of the ask (direct) of INR 61.5495 becomes the bid (indirect) of 0.01624, resulting in an indirect quotation of USD 0.01624/0.01625. Thus, when direct quotations are converted into indirect quotations, the bid and ask quotes are reversed.

Banks and dealers always follow the old adage: "Buy low, sell high." The ask rate is always more than the bid rate because banks and dealers want to earn a profit on currency dealings. The spreads are generally based on the currency's volatility as well as on the breadth and depth of the market for a given currency. Currencies with volatile foreign exchange rates may have higher spreads. Similarly, spreads tend to widen for currencies that are not widely traded. The spread of select currencies in a spot market is given in Table 1.2. It can be observed that the spread depends on how actively the currency pairs are traded. The spread of a currency pair with both the currencies being hard (e.g. USD, GBP, etc.) is narrow, it is larger for the others.

Spreads include commissions, which, in turn, depend on the size of the transactions. Therefore, the larger the transaction, the lower is the spread. Bid–ask spreads are more pronounced in the retail segment than in the wholesale segment. In the retail segment of the foreign exchange market, banks sell foreign currency at a rate higher than the interbank ask rate, and buy foreign currency from customers at a rate lower than the interbank bid

Table 1.2 Spread of Select Currencies—Spot Market (15 October 2014)

Currency pair	*Bid*	*Offer*	*Spread*
EUR/USD	1.26396	1.26408	0.00012
USD/EUR	0.79103	0.79114	0.00013
GBP/USD	1.59019	1.59038	0.00019
USD/GBP	0.62878	0.62887	0.00009
USD/CAD	1.13294	1.13311	0.00017
CAD/USD	0.88254	0.88266	0.00012
USD/CHF	0.95484	0.95506	0.00022
CHF/USD	1.04705	1.04730	0.00025
USD/JPY	107.076	107.339	0.263
JPY/USD	0.00934	0.00934	0.000
GBP/JPY	170.296	170.339	0.043

(Continued)

Table 1.2 ***(Continued)***

Currency pair	*Bid*	*Offer*	*Spread*
JPY/GBP	0.00587	0.00587	0.000
USD/CNY	6.14242	6.14492	0.00250
CNY/USD	0.16274	0.16280	0.00006
USD/INR	61.353	61.493	0.140
INR/USD	0.01626	0.01630	0.00004
USD/SGD	1.27642	1.27676	0.00034
SGD/USD	0.78323	0.78345	0.00022

rate. The bid–ask spread is large in the retail segment because of higher average costs of retail transactions. For the most actively traded currency pairs, the spread is generally at 3 pips. But sometimes, the spread can be at 1 pip or 2 pips because of competition. The bid–ask rates are reviewed and revised from time to time, keeping in view the market factors.

Pip and Lot A pip measures the amount of change in the exchange rate of a pair of currencies. That is, a *pip* is the smallest price increment a currency can make against the other currency in the trading of a currency pair. Conventionally, a pip has a value of 0.0001 of the base currency. For example, a pip is 1/100 of a cent in case USD is the base currency. Thus, 10,000 pips are equivalent to 1 USD. A pip value is 0.01, if the currencies are quoted to two decimal places. As Japanese yen has a much lower value than many of the currencies, a pip is considered only 1 percent of the yen. All yen-based currency pairs are generally quoted to two decimal places and therefore the pip value is 0.01. As most currency quotes are expressed to four decimal places, the pip value generally is 0.0001 of the base currency. The market participants may also offer fractional pips, known as 'pipettes', to provide extra precision. In such cases, the quotes are in five or six decimal places, where the last digit would represent 1/10 or 1/100 of a pip. In the case of the Japanese yen, the quote may be expressed to three decimal places instead of the default two places. A pip may seem small, but a movement of 1 pip in either direction can result in substantial gains or losses to the parties.

The value of the pip varies from currency pair to currency pair. For example, the pip value for EUR/USD is fixed at USD 10 for standard lots; USD 1 for mini lots; and

Example 1.1

The currency pair of EUR/USD has closed on a particular day at 1.2626 by gaining 30 pips for a market participant with a trade of EUR 100,000. What is the profit in EUR?

Solution

Total pips in the transaction: 100,000 × 30 = 3,000,000
Number of pips in USD: 3,000,000 × 0.0001 = USD 300
Profit in euro: 300 ÷ 1.2626 = EUR 237.6049

Example 1.2

The currency pair of USD/JPY has closed on a particular day at 107.65 by losing 20 pips for a market participant with a trade of USD 500,000. What is the profit/loss in USD?

Solution

Total pips in the transaction: $500,000 \times 20 = 10,000,000$
Loss in yen: $10,000,000 \times 0.01 =$ (JPY 100,000)
Loss in USD: $100,000 \div 107.65 =$ (USD 928.94)

Example 1.3

A trader purchased 200,000 units of EUR/JPY at 135.32 and sold at 135.34. What is the profit the trader has made in JPY and EUR? What is the profit in USD given the exchange rate of USD/JPY: 107.168 and JPY/USD: 0.00933?

Solution

Number of pips: $135.34 - 135.32 = 0.02 = 2$ pips
Total pips in the transaction: $200,000 \times 2 = 400,000$ pips
Profit in yen: $400,000 \times 0.01 =$ JPY 4000; (since a pip is worth 1% of the yen)
Profit in euro : $4000 \div 135.34 =$ EUR 29.5552
Profit in USD: $4000 \div 107.168 =$ USD 37.32 (given USD/JPY: 107.168)
Profit in USD: $4000 \times 0.00933 =$ USD 37.32 (given JPY/USD: 0.00933)

USD 0.10 for micro lots. A *lot* is the standard unit size of a foreign exchange transaction. Typically, one standard lot is equal to 100,000 units of the base currency; one mini lot is equal to 10,000 units of the base currency; and one micro lot is equal to 1,000 units of the base currency.

Spot and Forward Transactions

When two parties enter into a foreign exchange transaction, there are two dates that are to be reckoned with. One is the trade date or entry date, which refers to the day that a currency pair is traded and accepted by both the parties. The other date is the value date or settlement date that the actual settlement takes place. The settlement date may be any date after the deal or trade date. Depending on the time period between the trade date and the settlement date, foreign exchange transactions can be classified as spot transactions and forward transactions. In a **spot transaction** the trade is considered to have been completed once the buyer and seller agree to the terms of the trade but the settlement of the transaction takes place in two business days. In trade parlance, it is known as T+2 (trade day plus two days). During the two-day period, the concerned parties arrange to effect the exchange of a deposit denominated in one currency for a deposit denominated in the other currency. In other words, necessary debiting and crediting of accounts with banks located in different places are carried out during this two-day period. In certain cases, the settlement is done the day after the deal. In some cases, it may even be possible to settle the transaction on the day of the deal, particularly if the foreign exchange trading centres are located in the same time zone. Such transactions are known as *short-date transactions* or *cash transactions* as they can result in immediate exchange of currencies involved in the transaction. The *spot rate* is the exchange rate at which spot transactions are carried out. Spot transactions can also be rolled over (even indefinitely) at a cost. The cost of rolling over a transaction is based on the interest rate differential between the two currencies. If a trader is long in the currency with a higher rate of interest, they will earn interest. On the contrary, if a trader is short in the currency with a higher rate of interest, they will pay interest.

Foreign exchange transactions can be categorized into spot transactions and forward transactions. Although ***spot transactions*** *are considered to be immediate, their settlement occurs within two days of the transaction date.* ***Forward transactions*** *permit the purchase or sale of a specified amount of a foreign currency at an agreed-upon exchange rate at a specified future date.*

In a **forward transaction**, the parties enter into a contract called the *forward contract*, which permits the purchase or sale of a specified amount of a foreign currency at an agreed-upon exchange rate on a specified date in future (more than two business days later). Thus, forward transactions do not require immediate settlement. They are settled on any predetermined date after the transaction date. By convention, the settlement date of forward transactions may be 30, 60, 90, 120, or 180 days after the deal date. Depending on the number of days in which a forward transaction may be settled, it may be referred to as a 30-day forward, 60-day forward, and so on. There are also cases in which the forward period is for a broken period, that is, it is not in whole months. Such transactions are known as *broken-date* or *odd-date transactions*. Sometimes, the forward contract period may be longer than 180 days. The market for forward transactions is known as the *forward market*. The rate at which forward transactions are settled at a future date is called the *forward exchange rate* or the *forward rate*. Thus, a forward contract is similar to a spot contract except that the settlement is on a specified date in future.

Forward contracts have gained much popularity in view of increasing foreign exchange exposure of organizations. For example, an Indian firm may enter into a contract with a firm in the United States, agreeing to sell its product at a specified price in USD for, say, one year. The Indian firm must meet its expenditure in INR, but it will receive a fixed flow of revenue in USD. If the Indian rupee appreciates over the year, the Indian firm's USD-denominated revenue will fall in value vis-à-vis its INR-denominated expenditure. Sometimes, the appreciation of the Indian rupee may make such a firm unsuccessful in breaking even. If the firm has no way to cover this risk, it may be unable to supply its product to the US firm. Such issues affect even international trade. In this context, forward contracts come in handy as effective hedgers. Forward contracts can thus be used to hedge foreign exchange exposure. Traders in the foreign exchange market may also enter into forward contracts for purpose of speculation or investment. A variant of conventional forward contract is the option forward wherein one of the parties will have an option to make or take delivery of the foreign currency on any day within a specified time interval, say, on any day from the end of three months to the end of six months.

Foreign Exchange Swaps

Forward contracts are very flexible and can be tailored to meet the specific needs of a trader with regard to currency, amount, and settlement date. Sometimes, a trader may strike a deal to exchange one currency for another currency immediately, with an obligation to reverse the exchange at a specified future date. Such a transaction is also known as a foreign exchange *swap*. Foreign exchange swaps are the transactions involving the actual exchange of two currencies (principal amounts only) on a specific date at a rate agreed at the time of the contract (short leg), and a reverse exchange of the same two currencies at a date further in the future at a rate agreed at the time of the contract (long leg). Thus, a foreign exchange swap is a combination of two transactions between the same two parties with the same two currencies. However, the maturity dates of both the transactions are different. They may be spot–forward or forward–forward. For example, a trader enters a forward contract with a bank to buy USD three months forward against the Indian Rupee. To neutralize the exchange rate risk in the trade, the bank sells the Indian Rupee spot against the USD and lends the USD for three months until they are needed to deliver to the trader. In a forward–forward foreign exchange swap, both transactions are forward contracts.

Cross Rates

There are thousands of pairs of exchange rates with more than 150 currencies in the world, but one does not need to know all these pairs of exchange rates when there is parity in the exchange rates. To explain, a foreign currency can be purchased with a home currency or with another foreign currency. For example, the US dollar can be purchased directly with Indian rupees and it can also be purchased indirectly by using Indian rupees to buy British pounds and then using British pounds to buy US dollars. When there are no transaction costs, there is no difference between buying a foreign currency with a home currency directly and buying it indirectly through another foreign currency. However, to buy a currency indirectly, there should be parity in cross-exchange rates between currencies. That is, in the present example, the market should offer exchange rates between the US dollar and the Indian rupee, between the Indian rupee and the British pound, and between the British pound and the US dollar such that one receives the same amount in US dollars whether they are purchased directly with Indian rupees, or indirectly via British pounds. With zero transaction costs, this implies that (USD/INR) = (GBP/INR) × (USD/GBP).

The rate of exchange between any two currencies as determined through the medium of some other currency is known as a ***cross rate****.*

The rate of exchange between any two currencies (say, *i* and *j*) as determined through the medium of some other currency (say, *k*) is known as a **cross rate**. This can be expressed as follows:

$$(i/j) = (i/k) \times (k/j) \tag{1.1}$$

From Eq. 1.1, since $(k/j) = 1/(j/k)$, the cross rate of (i/j) can be calculated from the following equation:

$$(i/j) = \frac{(i/k)}{(j/k)} \tag{1.2}$$

Analogously,

$$(j/i) = \frac{(k/i)}{(k/j)}$$

Now, if *i* stands for USD, *j* stands for INR, and *k* stands for GBP, then from Eq. 1.1,

$$(\text{USD/INR}) = \frac{(\text{USD/GBP})}{(\text{INR/GBP})} \tag{1.3}$$

Analogously,

$$(\text{INR/USD}) = \frac{(\text{GBP/USD})}{(\text{GBP/INR})}$$

If the GBP/INR and the GBP/USD exchange rates are known, the /USD/INR exchange rates can be calculated. For example, given GBP/INR: 98.8724 and GBP/USD: 1.6183, we can calculate the spot exchange rate between the Indian rupee and the US dollar using Eq. 1.3 in the following way:

$$(USD/INR) = \frac{(1/1.6183)}{\left(\frac{1}{98.8724}\right)}$$

$$(USD/INR) = \frac{98.8724}{1.6183}$$
$$= \text{INR } 61.0965$$

The cross rates can also be calculated by means of a chain rule. This can be understood with a simple problem: *if* USD = GBP 0.6180 and GBP = INR 98.8724, what is the price of the US dollar in terms of INR?

The given problem can be represented as follows:

USD 1 = GBP 0.6180

GBP 1 = INR 98.8724

INR x = USD 1

Dividing the product of the right-hand side of the equations by the product of the left-hand side of the equations, we get the following value of x:

$$= \frac{0.6180 \times 98.8724 \times 1}{1}$$
$$= \text{INR}61.1031$$

The Indian currency price of the US dollar arrived at by using the chain rule is INR 61.1031. It is the same as that computed earlier by Eq. 1.2.

In the examples as just discussed, it is assumed that there are no transaction costs. In practice, however, such an assumption is unrealistic as there cannot be any business without transaction costs. Transaction costs, which include commissions, brokerage charges, and communication charges, play an important role in the determination of exchange rates. Banks quote bid and ask rates keeping in view the various transaction costs and the return required to compensate for the risks associated with the foreign exchange business. Therefore, bid–ask spreads vary greatly for different pairs of currencies. Further, different banks may quote different rates, depending upon their exchange rate risk perceptions. Thus, the direct exchange rate between two currencies may be different from the exchange rate derived indirectly via another currency. This makes the calculation of cross rates imprecise. However, it is possible to compute a range within which cross rates must be quoted.

Here, we shall briefly discuss the rules underlying the calculation of cross rates with transaction costs. As stated earlier, a market participant can buy a currency either directly or indirectly. For example, if someone wants to buy US dollars with Indian rupees, they can buy US dollars at a quote of $(USD/INR)_{ask}$ from a dealer. Alternatively, they can first buy, say, British pounds with Indian rupees and then buy US dollars with British pounds. At the first instance, they buy pounds at $(GBP/INR)_{ask}$. $(GBP/INR)_{ask}$ is the dealer's asking rate for GBP or bid rate for INR in terms of GBP. Next, they would buy US dollars at $(USD/GBP)_{ask}$. $(USD/GBP)_{ask}$ is the dealer's asking rate for USD or bid rate on GBP for USD. Indirectly, a market participant can get $(GBP/INR)_{ask} \times (USD/GBP)_{ask}$ per INR. Thus, by going indirectly from INR

Example 1.4

Given exchange rates as of USD/EUR: 0.7736 and USD/GBP: 0.6180, what would be the exchange rate between GBP and EUR?

Solution

Reciprocals:

EUR/USD: 1/0.7736 = 1.2927

GBP/USD: 1/0.6180 = 1.6181

$$GBP/EUR = \frac{GBP}{USD} \times \frac{USD}{EUR}$$
$$= 1.6181 \times 0.7736$$
$$= 1.2518$$

to GBP to USD, the market participant should get at least the amount they would get directly. This can be expressed as:

$$(USD/INR)_{ask} \geq (GBP/INR)_{ask} \times (USD/GBP)_{ask}$$

Suppose the market participant wants to convert US dollars into Indian rupees. They can buy Indian rupees with US dollars directly at $(INR/USD)_{ask}$ or exchange it through British pounds. If they choose the indirect route, they would receive $(GBP/USD)_{ask} \times (INR/GBP)_{ask}$. Therefore, it is required that

$$(INR/USD)_{ask} \geq (GBP/USD)_{ask} \times (INR/GBP)_{ask} \quad (1.4)$$

By taking the inverse of Eq. 1.4,

$$\frac{1}{(INR/USD)_{bid}} \geq \frac{1}{(INR/GBP)_{bid}} \times \frac{1}{(GBP/USD)_{bid}}$$

$$(INR/USD)_{bid} \leq (INR/GBP)_{bid} \times (GBP/USD)_{bid}$$

The cross rates of select currencies on 16 September 2014 are presented in Table 1.3. Whenever direct quotes are not available for a particular pair of currencies, banks may create a quote based on the available direct quotes for pairs of other currencies. For instance, a quote for Indian rupees against Singapore dollars may not be available in the Indian inter-bank market. In such a case, the bank may base its quotation on rates available in other

Table 1.3 Currency Cross Rates (16 September 2014)

Currency	*British pound*	*Canadian dollar*	*Euro*	*Japanese yen*	*Swiss franc*	*US dollar*	*Australian dollar*	*Indian rupee*
British pound	1.0000	0.5582	0.77987	0.0058	0.6603	0.6180	0.5560	0.010114
Canadian dollar	1.7909	1.0000	1.4307	0.0103	1.1827	1.1068	0.9957	0.01812
Euro	1.2520	0.6989	1.0000	0.0072	0.8267	0.7736	0.6960	0.01266
Japanese yen	173.6350	96.9420	138.7000	1.0000	114.6460	107.3000	96.5290	1.7564
Swiss franc	1.5145	0.8455	1.2097	0.0087	1.0000	0.9359	0.8420	0.0153
US dollar	1.6183	0.9034	1.2926	0.0093	1.0686	1.0000	0.8994	0.01637
Australian dollar	1.7993	1.0042	1.4368	0.0104	1.1877	1.1118	1.0000	0.01819
Indian rupee	98.8724	55.1888	78.9717	0.5693	65.2853	61.0819	54.9520	1.0000

Source: © OANDA Corp. Reproduced with permission.

Example 1.5

The direct quote for GBP in New York is USD 1.9031, and the transaction costs are 0.2 percent. What are the minimum and maximum possible direct quotes for US dollars in London?

Solution

A trader who converts 1 British pound into US dollars would receive USD (1.9031 × 0.998) after paying transaction costs of 0.2 percent. Converting these dollars into pounds in London at a direct quote of x, the trader will have GBP ($1.9031 \times 0.998 \times x \times 0.998$). This quantity must be less than or equal to GBP 1 in equilibrium. That is, GBP ($1.9031 \times 0.998 \times x \times 0.998$) $\leq$ GBP 1, or $x \leq$ GBP $1/[1.9031(0.998)^2]$ (i.e. GBP 0.5276). Alternatively, the trader can convert 1 pound into US dollars in London at a rate of x, take those US dollars to New York, and exchange them for pounds. The trader will have GBP ($1/x \times 0.998 \times 1/1.9031 \times 0.998$), which must be less than or equal to 1 British pound. Therefore, $(0.998)^2 \times 1/1.9031x \leq 1$, or $x \geq 0.5234$. In other words, the direct quotes for the US dollar in London are in the range of GBP $0.5234 < x <$ GBP 0.5276.

centres for, say, INR/USD and USD/SGD. Therefore, when direct quotes are not available for two currencies, they can be computed through a vehicle currency. Let us assume there are no market quotes between the Canadian dollar and the Japanese yen. But quotes for USD/CAD and USD/JPY are available. So, one can compute a synthetic quote for JPY/CAD by using the following formula:

$$\text{JPY/CAD} = \frac{(\text{USD/CAD})}{(\text{USD/JPY})}$$

The synthetic cross rates would serve as proxies for the unknown direct rates.

Arbitrage

Arbitrage refers to the selling and buying of the same currency to profit from exchange rate discrepancies within a market centre or across market centres.

Arbitrage refers to the selling and buying of the same currency to profit from exchange rate discrepancies within a market centre or across market centres. Arbitrage transactions are carried out without any risk or commitment of capital. A market participant may therefore buy a currency in one market centre and simultaneously sell it in another market centre, thereby making a profit. This is called *two-point simple arbitrage* or *direct arbitrage.*

Two-point Arbitrage

Let us consider an example to understand the concept of two-point arbitrage.

Assume, Bank X quotes the rates USD/INR: 61.1234/61.1260. At the same time, the quote from Bank Y is USD/INR: 61.0825/61.1000.

This scenario provides an arbitrage opportunity. A market participant can buy U.S. dollars at INR 61.1000 from Bank Y and sell them to Bank X at INR 61.1234. These two transactions provide a profit of INR 0.0234 per US dollar. This profit is known as *arbitrage profit,* and it is made without any risk or commitment of capital.

While discussing two-point arbitrage, it is important to understand the concept of *implied inverse quotes.* Let us consider an example to understand this. Assume that the quote between two currencies, say, USD/INR, is 61.5821/61.9560. In other words, INR 61.5821 is the rate at which the bank is ready to buy US dollars and INR 61.9560 is the rate at which the bank is ready to sell US dollars. It is implied that the bid rate is also the rate at which the

Example 1.6

The USD is quoted at AUD 1.1197/1.2135 and the GBP is quoted at AUD 2.1920/2.2500. What is the direct quote between the USD and the GBP?

Solution

The following steps may be followed to obtain the direct quote:

1. Sell one USD for AUD 1.1197.
2. Convert AUD 1.1197 into GBP (1.1197/2.2500 = 0.4976). Thus, the bid rate for the USD is GBP 0.4976.
3. Buy AUD 1.2135 with GBP 0.5125 (i.e. 1.1235/2.1920). Buying AUD with GBP is equivalent to selling GBP for AUD at the bid rate of AUD 2.1920.
4. Buy one USD with AUD 1.2135.

Thus, the direct quote for USD is GBP 0.4976/0.5125.

bank is ready to sell Indian rupees. That is, the bid rate would correspond to the ask rate in the INR/USD quote. The ask rate in the quote INR/USD is 1/61.5821, which is equal to USD 0.01624. Similarly, the (USD/INR) ask rate would correspond to the (INR/USD) bid rate. In the example, the ask rate INR 61.9560 is equal to the bid rate 1/61.9560 (i.e., 0.01614) in the INR/USD quote. Thus, it can be stated that

$$\text{Implied (INR/USD)}_{bid} = 1/\text{(USD/INR)}_{ask}$$
$$\text{Implied (INR/USD)}_{ask} = 1/\text{(USD/INR)}_{bid}$$

The implied inverse quote (synthetic) in this example is:

INR/USD: 0.01614/0.01624

The implied inverse quote can also be stated as

$$\frac{1/\text{(USD/INR)}_{ask}}{1/\text{(USD/INR)}_{bid}}$$

If the actual quote in the foreign exchange market differs from the implied inverse quote, it may result in arbitrage opportunity. For example, suppose the exchange rate quote in New York is INR/USD: 0.0150/0.0155. A market participant can buy Indian rupees at USD 0.0155 in New York and sell them in Mumbai for USD 0.01614, thus making a riskless profit of USD 0.00064 for every Indian rupee. Such arbitrage opportunities, however, will soon disappear as arbitrageurs continue to earn profits.

If arbitrage opportunities are to be avoided, the ask rate of the actual USD/INR quote should be higher than the bid rate of the implied USD/INR quote, and the bid rate of the actual USD/INR quote should be lower than the ask rate of the implied USD/INR quote. The same can be stated as follows:

$$\text{Actual (USD/INR)}_{bid} < \text{Synthetic (USD/INR)}_{ask}, \text{ and}$$
$$\text{Synthetic (USD/INR)}_{bid} < \text{Actual (USD/INR)}_{ask}$$

The actual quote and the synthetic inverse quote must overlap (i.e. the bid rate in one quote should be lower than the ask rate in another) in order to avoid arbitrage opportunity.

Consider another example: The spot quotation in Mumbai is USD/INR: 59.8565/60.0000. At the same time, the quotation of a bank in New York is INR/USD: 0.0165/0.0170. In this case,

$$(USD/INR)_{bid} = 1/(INR/USD)_{ask}$$
$$= 1/0.0170$$
$$= 58.8235$$

$$(USD/INR)_{ask} = 1/(INR/USD)_{bid}$$
$$= 1/0.0165$$
$$= 60.6060$$

Thus, the synthetic inverse quote for USD/INR is 58.8235/60.6060. Since actual $(USD/INR)_{bid}$ < synthetic $(USD/INR)_{ask}$ and synthetic $(USD/INR)_{bid}$ < actual $(USD/INR)_{ask}$, there is no arbitrage opportunity.

The *inverse quote* is the reciprocal of the direct quote between two currencies. For example, the inverse quote for USD/INR is INR/USD. The *actual inverse quotes* may differ from *synthetic inverse quotes* by the amount of transaction costs. In the absence of transaction costs and spread (difference between bid and ask rates), the exchange rate in one country would have to be the exact reciprocal of the exchange rate in another country for the same pair of currencies. For example, if the exchange rate in New York is INR/USD 0.0165, then the exchange rate in Mumbai would be 1/0.0165, or USD/INR 60.6060. Otherwise, an arbitrage opportunity may arise.

Triangular Arbitrage

If three currencies are involved in an arbitrage operation, it is called a *three-point arbitrage* or a *triangular arbitrage.* In a triangular arbitrage, one currency is traded for another currency, which is traded for a third currency, which, in turn, is traded for the first currency. For example, assume a firm wants to convert INR to GBP. It can do so directly. The number of British pounds to be received per unit of INR is given as INR/GBP. The firm can also get pounds indirectly from INR to USD and then from USD to GBP. This is diagrammatically represented in Figure 1.1.

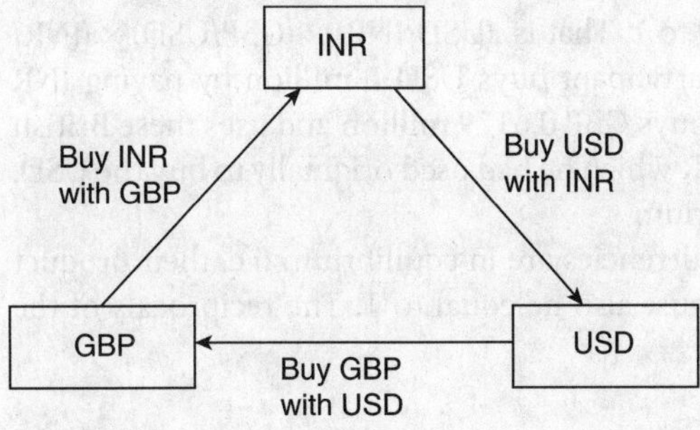

Figure 1.1

Triangular Trading

Example 1.7

A firm in England has to make a payment of SGD 1 million to its supplier in Singapore. The currency quotes available are as follows:
GBP 0.0117/0.0119 for INR
SGD 0.03510/0.03520 for INR

What is the amount to be paid in British pounds by the importer?

Solution

It is given that INR/GBP: 0.0117/0.0119 and INR/SGD: 0.03510/0.03520. The cross rates will be as follows:

$$\begin{aligned}(SGD/GBP)_{bid} &= (INR/GBP)_{bid} \times (SGD/INR)_{bid} \\ &= (INR/GBP)_{bid} \times 1/(INR/SGD)_{ask} \\ &= 0.0117 \times 1/0.03520 \\ &= 0.3324\end{aligned}$$

and

$$\begin{aligned}(SGD/GBP)_{ask} &= (INR/GBP)_{ask} \times (SGD/INR)_{ask} \\ &= (INR/GBP)_{ask} \times 1/(INR/SGD)_{bid} \\ &= 0.0119 \times 1/0.03510 \\ &= 0.3390 \\ SGD/GBP &= 0.3324/0.3390\end{aligned}$$

Therefore, the importer has to pay GBP 339,000 to get SGD 1 million to settle the dues to its supplier in Singapore.

For arbitrage profit in triangular trading to be zero, the product of the exchange rates should be equal to 1. For example, the following are exchange rate quotations in the market with zero transaction costs:

USD/INR: 60.7925
GBP/USD: 1.6183
INR/GBP: 0.01015

The product of these exchange rates is equal to 1. That is, (USD/INR) × (GBP/USD) × (INR/GBP) = 1. For instance, assume a market participant buys USD 1 million by paying INR 60.7925 million, with the USD 1 million he buys GBP 0.6179 million and uses these British pounds to get almost the same amount of INR which he had used originally to buy the USD. The exchange rates in this case are in equilibrium.

When the exchange rates of the given currencies are in equilibrium (i.e. their product is 1), the product of their reciprocal rates must also be equal to 1. The reciprocals of the exchange rates in this example are as follows:

INR/USD: 0.01645
USD/GBP: 0.6179
GBP/INR: 98.5222

Therefore, (INR/USD) × (USD/GBP) × (GBP/INR) = 1.

Triangular arbitrage opportunity arises when the currency direct quotes are not in alignment with the cross exchange rates. Taking another example, three currencies are quoted as follows:

GBP/USD: 2.0592
AUD/GBP: 0.4256
USD/AUD: 1.1310

If the rates are to be in equilibrium, the product of these rates should be equal to 1. But the product of the above rates is less than one. In other words, there is an arbitrage opportunity.

When there is an arbitrage opportunity, what can be done to make an arbitrage profit? That is, which currencies should be purchased and which ones should be sold to make a profit? In the current example, the arbitrageur should buy GBP with US dollars at a spot rate of 2.0592, buy Australian dollars with pounds at 0.4256, and then buy US dollars with Australian dollars at the spot rate of 1.1310. By doing so, the arbitrageur makes a riskless profit of [1 — (GBP/USD) × (AUD/GBP) × (USD/AUD] percent = 0.88 percent. If such a situation were to exist in reality, the arbitrage transactions would tend to cause the GBP to appreciate against the USD and to depreciate against the AUD. Further, the AUD would fall against the US dollar. Thus, the exchange rates would ultimately be in equilibrium and provide little scope for arbitrage profit.

In the example we just discussed, the product of the exchange rates is less than 1. If the product is greater than 1, which is also possible, then the arbitrageur should engage in triangular arbitrage by selling the currencies in the numerator for respective currencies in the denominator at their respective spot rates. For example, consider the following exchange rates:

GBP/USD: 2.1620
AUD/GBP: 0.4240
USD/AUD: 1.1425

Here, the product of the exchange rates is greater than 1. In such a situation, one can sell the numerator currencies to make an arbitrage profit. An astute investor can sell, say, GBP 1,000 to get USD 2,162, sell the US dollars to get AUD 2,470, and finally sell the Australian dollars to get GBP 1,047.32. Thus, the investor can make a riskless profit of GBP 47.32 by simultaneously executing the trades.

If the product of the cross rates is less than 1, at least one of these rates should rise and if the product is greater than 1, at least one of the rates must fall. The arbitrageurs will bring the exchange rates back into equilibrium through the buying and selling of currencies. Buying a currency raises the exchange rate of that currency, and selling a currency lowers the exchange rate of that currency. Therefore, arbitrage activities continue to affect changes in exchange rates until equilibrium is restored.

In these days of highly advanced communication networks, arbitrage opportunities very rarely exist. If at all they exist, they will disappear very soon as every market participant is vigilant and would revise the rates as frequently as necessary. Further, in view of the transaction costs, market participants may not bother about small variations in the quotes of different banks as the trading of currencies on such small differences in exchange rates will not yield a net profit. Nevertheless, the role of arbitrageurs is very important, particularly in ensuring equilibrium or parity in exchange rates.

Nostro, Vostro, and Loro Accounts

In interbank transactions, foreign exchange is transferred from one account to another account and from one centre to another. In order to facilitate easy and swift transfer of funds in different currencies, banks that are *authorized dealers* (AD) in foreign exchange maintain current accounts in different foreign currencies with overseas branches/correspondent banks located at different centres. Such a foreign currency account maintained by a bank at a foreign centre is known as a *nostro account,* or "our account with you." All sales of a particular foreign currency would result in debits to the nostro accounts, and all purchases of that particular currency would result in credits to the nostro accounts.

Foreign branches/correspondent banks also maintain accounts in their own currencies with this particular bank (the bank which maintains the nostro account). Such an account is known as a *vostro account*, or "your account with us." There is a third type of account, known as a *loro account,* wherein a bank remits funds in foreign currency to another bank for credit to an account of a third bank. *Nostro, vostro,* and *loro* are Italian terms meaning "our," "your," and "their," respectively.

Forward Rates and Future Spot Rates

The **forward exchange rate** is the rate at which the actual exchange of currencies takes place at a specified date in the future. The gain or loss from a forward contract depends on the actual future spot rate of the currency. In this section, we shall look at forward exchange rates and future spot rates in greater detail.

Example 1.8

The following quotes are available in the foreign exchange market:

GBP/INR: 85.16
USD/INR: 45
GBP/USD: 1.85

Are there any arbitrage gains possible from the spot exchange rates quoted in the three foreign exchange trading centres?

Solution

The arbitrageur can make a profit through the following steps:

1. Buy Indian rupees with, say, GBP 1 million to get INR 85.16 million.
2. Convert the Indian rupees into US dollars:

$$\frac{85.16 \text{ million}}{45} = \text{USD } 1.8924 \text{ million}$$

3. Sell these US dollars to get British pounds:

$$\frac{1.8924 \text{ million}}{1.85} = \text{GBP } 1.0229 \text{ million}$$

Thus, the arbitrageur gets a net gain of GBP 22,900. This is possible because the exchange rates in the three trading centres are not in parity.

Example 1.9

The spot rate of the Singapore dollar in the United States is USD 0.64 and that of the INR is USD 0.0224. What is the exchange rate of the Singapore dollar in India? If the Singapore dollar is quoted in India at SGD/INR: 29, how can an arbitrageur make a profit in this situation?

Solution

In the United States, the spot rates are:

SGD/USD: 0.64
INR/USD: 0.0224

So, the spot rate of the Singapore dollar in India should be:

$$(\text{USD/INR}) \times (\text{SGD/USD}) = 44.64 \times 0.64$$

Therefore, SGD/INR: 28.57

As the Singapore dollar quoted in India is higher, the arbitrageur can engage in the following steps in order to make a profit:

1. Buy USD 0.112 million by paying INR 5 million.
2. Convert these US dollars into Singapore dollars:

$$\frac{0.112 \text{ million}}{0.64} = \text{SGD } 175{,}000$$

3. Sell the Singapore dollars in India to receive INR 5.075 million.

The arbitrageur can thus make a net gain of INR 75,000.

Forward Premium and Forward Discount

The forward contract calls for the delivery of specified amounts of currencies at a specified rate of exchange on a specified future date. If a forward rate in home currency is more than the spot rate, the foreign currency is said to be at a *forward premium,* and if it is less than the spot rate, the foreign currency is at a *forward discount.* If the forward rate is equal to the spot rate, the foreign currency is said to be *flat.*

*The **forward exchange rate** is the rate at which the actual exchange of currencies takes place at a specified date in the future. If a forward rate in home currency is more than the spot rate, the foreign currency is at a forward premium, and if it is less than the spot rate, the foreign currency is at a forward discount. If the forward rate is equal to the spot rate, the foreign currency is said to be flat.*

As stated earlier, a *swap transaction* between any two currencies consists of a spot purchase (or sale) and a forward sale (or purchase) of a foreign currency. In other words, a swap transaction combines a spot and a forward in opposite directions. For example, consider a trader who buys US dollars spot against INR and simultaneously enters into a forward transaction with the same counterparty to sell US dollars against INR. The amount of the foreign currency is the same in both transactions. The difference between the spot and the forward exchange rates is known as the *swap margin,* and this margin corresponds to the forward premium or discount. A forward contract without an accompanying spot transaction is called an *outright forward contract.*

Forward rates are either quoted as outright rates or as a discount/premium on the spot rate. The forward premium or discount is known as the *forward differential* or *swap rate.* It is also common to state the premium or discount in points known as *swap points.* Usually, outright rates are quoted in the retail segment of the foreign exchange market. In the wholesale or interbank market, the forward rates are quoted as a discount or premium on the spot rate. The forward premium or discount can be expressed as follows:

$$\text{Forward premium/discount} = \frac{\text{Forward rate} - \text{Spot rate}}{\text{Spot rate}} \tag{1.5}$$

The forward premium or discount can also be expressed as an annualized percentage deviation from the spot rate:

$$\text{Annualized percentage forward premium/discount} = \frac{\text{Forward rate} - \text{Spot rate}}{\text{Spot rate}} \times \frac{360}{\text{Number of days of forward contract}}$$

Let us assume that the spot exchange rate between INR and USD is 61/USD and the one-month forward rate is 61.75/USD. The forward premium or discount as per Eq. 1.5 is:

$$\frac{43.75 - 43}{43} \times 12 = 0.2093$$

$$= \frac{61.75 - 61}{61} \times 12$$
$$= 0.1475$$

The US dollar is thus at an annualized forward premium of 14.753 per cent.

The forward rates are expressed in forward points which represent the difference between the forward rate and the spot rate. A currency with a higher interest rate trades at a forward discount and a currency with a lower interest rate trades at a forward premium.

As a matter of convention, the swap points are added to the spot bid–ask rates if the swap points are in ascending order ('bid swap point' is smaller than 'ask swap point'), and subtracted from the spot rate if the swap points are in descending order ('ask swap point' is smaller than 'bid swap point'). For example, the spot and forward quotations for INR/USD can be stated as follows:

Spot: 61.75/61.80
90-days forward: 20/25

In this example, as the swap points are in ascending order (20/25), the 90-days forward outright quotations can be represented as 61.95/62.05. This implies that the bank is ready to buy 90-days forward USD at INR 61.95 and sell at INR 62.05.

Similarly, assume that the US dollar is quoted as follows:

Spot: INR 61.75/61.80
90-days forward: 25/20

In this case, the swap points are in descending order and should therefore be subtracted from the spot bid–ask rates. The 90-days outright forward quotation shall be INR 61.50/61.60. This implies that the bank is willing to buy US dollars at INR 61.50 and sell at INR 61.60. Thus, the interbank forward rates may be quoted as the spot rate plus or minus the swap points.

The convention of adding or subtracting swap points is followed in direct quotations as well as indirect quotations. In a direct quotation (expressed in terms of the number of units of home currency per unit of foreign currency), if the swap points are added to the spot bid–ask rates, it will result in a forward premium (i.e. the foreign currency will be at a forward premium). If, however, the swap points are subtracted from the spot bid–ask rates in a direct quotation, it will result in the foreign currency being at a forward discount. In the case of indirect quotations (expressed in terms of the number of units of foreign currency per unit of home currency), the foreign currency will be at a forward discount if the swap points are added to the spot bid–ask rates; it will be at a forward premium if the swap points are subtracted from the spot bid–ask rates.

The (indirect) spot and forward quotations between INR (unit of 100) and USD can be stated as follows:

Spot:1.6371/1.6351
90-days forward: 20/25

The outright forward quotations can be stated as follows:

90-days forward: 1.6391/1.6376

This implies that the foreign currency (in this example, the US dollar) is at a forward discount. Similarly, when the swap points are in descending order, as in, say,

90-days forward: 25/20,

the outright forward quotation would be

90-days forward: 1.6366/1.6356

The foreign currency is at a forward premium.

When two-way quotations are given, one can compute the percentage forward discount or forward premium by taking the arithmetic average of the bid and ask rates.

The bid–ask spread in the forward market is usually more than that of the spot market and widens with increases in the forward contract period. The bid–ask spread in spot rates is lower than in forward rates because of the greater risk involved in forward contracts. The longer the period of the forward contract, the more is the risk involved. As the gain or loss from the forward contract depends on the future spot rate of the currency—the spot rate to be realized on the date of maturity or settlement of the forward contract—any uncertainty in future spot rates results in increased risk. The risk may arise if there are fluctuations in the future spot rate, or if the forward contracts are carried out by dishonest parties. Further, the bid–ask spread is wide for currencies that are widely traded. The bid–ask spread for the Indian rupee against the US dollar can be observed from Table 1.4. The data in the table indicate that the bid–ask spread is larger for contracts for the distant future than for the near future. It may be noted that the forward market in India is active up to six months. However, there are also quotes available up to one year. The link between forward premiums and interest rate differentials works largely through leads and lags. Importers and exporters influence the forward markets by making credit available from overseas parties or by granting credit to overseas parties.

Example 1.10

A bank in India gives the following 3-month forward quotation.

USD/INR: 61.6000/99

What are the inverse rates?

Solution

3-month forward rates of INR/USD are calculated as follows:

$$\frac{1}{(USD/INR)_{ask}} \div \frac{1}{(USD/INR)_{bid}}$$

$= (1/61.6095)/(1/61.6759) = 0.016231/0.016234$

Example 1.11

The following are the quotations given by a bank. Calculate the 3-month forward implied rate for GBP/EUR.

USD/EUR 3-month forward: 0.7736/0.7789

USD/GBP 3-month forward: 0.6180/0.6198

Solution:

3-month forward $(GBP/EUR)_{bid} = (GBP/USD)_{bid} \times (USD/EUR)_{bid}$

$= [1/(USD/GBP)_{ask}] \times (USD/EUR)_{bid}$

$(1/0.6198) \times 0.7736 = 1.2482$

3-month forward $(GBP/EUR)_{ask} = (GBP/USD)_{ask} \times (USD/EUR)_{ask}$

$= [1/(USD/GBP)_{bid}] \times (USD/EUR)_{ask}$

$(1/0.6180) \times 0.7789 = 1.2694$

Table 1.4 Forward Rates—USD/INR (19 September 2014)

Month	*Bid rate*	*Ask rate*	*Bid–ask spread*	*% Annualized premium/discount*
30 Sep 2014	60.865	60.8825	0.017498	3.815073
31 Oct 2014	61.295	61.325	0.030003	6.775193
30 Nov 2014	61.69	61.7125	0.022503	7.420656
31 Dec 2014	62.15	62.1775	0.0275	6.746425
31 Jan 2015	62.585	62.615	0.030003	5.936525
28 Feb 2015	62.98	63.01	0.029999	7.235642
31 Mar 2015	63.425	63.44	0.014999	4.324942
30 Apr 2015	63.915	63.93	0.014999	5.130733
31 May 2015	64.31	64.3375	0.027504	5.800855
30 Jun 2015	64.74	64.7675	0.027504	6.507977
31 Jul 2015	65.15	65.1775	0.027496	7.182201
31 Aug 2015	65.54	65.565	0.025002	7.819439

Source: The Economic Times (20 September 2014).

Future Spot Rates

Foreign exchange rates are influenced by several factors, including certain macroeconomic factors. Market participants predict future spot rates by keeping track of the various factors that influence exchange rates. Accordingly, they buy or sell currencies in the spot and forward markets. Spot rates and forward rates are expected to move in tandem so that they assume the same figure on the date of maturity of the forward contract. Theoretically, therefore, the forward rate should exactly reflect the expected future spot rate. For example, let us assume that a depreciation of the US dollar against the Indian rupee is anticipated. Indian traders who expect US dollar receipts in the future will sell these forward, while the future recipients of proceeds in Indian rupees will slow their sales of INR for US dollars in the forward market. In other words, those who hold INR will delay the conversion of INR into US dollars, and those who hold US dollars will speed up the conversion of their US dollars. This buying and selling of currencies in the forward market will have implications for spot rates. The pressure from the forward market is thus transmitted to the spot market and vice versa. As long as the expected future spot rate is greater than or less than the forward rate, market participants can make speculative profit. However, such profits will disappear once these two rates coincide with each other. In reality, the presence of transaction costs and risk premiums keeps the forward rate and the expected future spot rate different.

Closing of Positions

The main aim of any market participant in the foreign exchange market is to make a profit by buying and selling of currencies. For example, a market participant has purchased US dollars with Great Britain pounds. It amounts to exchanging of GBP for USD, which is the same as selling GBP for USD. Buying a currency pair is termed as 'going long' and selling a currency pair is termed as 'going short'. Because of the symmetry of currency transactions, a trader is always simultaneously long in one currency and short in another currency. By going long in the currency pair of USD/GBP (for example), the trader is purchasing the USD (base currency) and simultaneously is going short the same sum in the quote currency (GBP). Suppose there is a quote of USD/GBP 0.62963/0.62970. If a trader wants to buy USD 10,000, he has to pay GBP 62970. In other words, the trader sells GBP 62970 for USD 10,000.

Once a transaction is done (either buying or selling), the position is open. That is, an open position is one that is live and ongoing. As long as a position is open, the value of the trade fluctuates in accordance with the relevant exchange rate in the market. To realize profit or loss, the trader has to close out his position. To close out a position, the trader has to make an equal and opposite trade in the same currency pair. For example, suppose a trader has gone long in one lot of USD/EUR, he can close out that position by subsequently going short in one lot of USD/EUR. A currency that was originally bought is sold back, and the currency that was primarily sold is bought. The traders can also partially close an open position by only selling or buying enough to partly offset his open position in a currency pair. For example, a trader has an open position of USD 10,000 as having purchased against euro. He can close three-fourths of the original position, leaving open USD 2,500. A trader makes a profit in a short position when the base currency loses value against the quote currency and incurs a loss when it, on the contrary, goes up. The profit or loss is determined by the relative purchase and sale exchange rates in opening and closing positions.

In currency trading, particularly in interbank transactions, squaring is very common. For example, the State Bank of India buys Canadian dollars in exchange of U.S. dollars from a dealer, and Punjab National Bank buys U.S. dollars from another dealer in exchange for Canadian dollars. Suppose the State Bank of India sells Canadian dollars to Punjab National Bank in exchange for U.S. dollars. It means that both the banks have squared their earlier transactions.

If an open position is not closed out by the settlement or value date, the trades are rolled over from one value date to the next value date. By rollover, the open position at the end of the value date is closed, while simultaneously opening an identical position for the following value date. It means that the rollover postpones the actual settlement of the trade until the trader closes their position. In case a position remains open, the trader gets interest on the long currency and pays interest on the short currency every time the position is rolled over. When there is interest rate differential between the currencies, it may result in a net earning or payment of interest. If the interest rate of the base currency is higher than that of quote currency, then the trader earns the interest rate differential; otherwise he has to pay the interest rate differential.

Types of Orders Investors need to know different kinds of orders from which they can choose to make best use of the foreign exchange market. They may place an appropriate order with their broker to open or close a position.

Market order: An investor places a market order to buy or sell a currency at the spot rate. The market order is executed immediately and it becomes an open position. If the market order is to close out a position, the investor may realize a profit or loss on execution of the market order. The major problem with the market order is that the investor loses control over the exchange rate once the order is placed.

Limit order: As the name indicates, the investor may prescribe some limits for the order to be executed. The limits are stated by the investor with regard to the exchange rate and duration. That is, the investor may specify the exchange rate at which he wishes to buy or sell a currency pair and also specify the duration that the order should remain live or active. Until the conditions or limits as specified by the investor are met, the order is considered a pending limit order. Once the conditions are met, the limit order becomes an active market order.

Stop-loss order: This kind of order is used to limit loss potential of a position. For example, a trader has bought USD/GBP at 0.62970. His expectation is that the USD will appreciate against the British pound in the near future. But at the same time he is pessimistic about the US dollar value. So, a stop-loss order is placed to sell USD/GBP at 0.62940. If the bid rate of USD/GBP falls to this level, the open position is automatically closed, thereby capping the loss.

The US Dollar as a Vehicle Currency

A substantial proportion of foreign exchange trading takes place through an intermediate currency known as the *vehicle currency.* Vehicle currencies reduce transaction costs in the foreign exchange market as they eliminate the need for dealers to keep a large number of currencies in hand. In the presence of a vehicle currency, foreign exchange dealers need to simply maintain their domestic currency and one or more vehicle currencies.

The British pound, which was once the dominant global currency, has now been replaced by the US dollar, which is the most widely used currency in the world. It is used as an investment currency, a reserve currency, an invoice currency, and a transaction currency. A substantial share of foreign exchange trading involves the US dollar, and it is the invoice currency for foreign trade in many commodities, such as petroleum and gold. Investors also prefer USD-denominated investments. Many countries hold a large chunk of their external reserves in the US dollar. In view of its importance in the global economy, the US dollar is also used as a vehicle currency, or a common third currency for most pairs of currencies in the foreign exchange market. For instance, participants who want to convert their funds from Mexican peso to Thai baht may sell their Mexican pesos for US dollars and then sell the U.S. dollars for Thai baht. Such a transaction is necessitated by the fact that the USD/peso market and the USD/baht markets are more active and liquid than a market for peso/baht. In other words, the US market is considered to be more liquid and less volatile than other markets.

The dominance of USD in the world financial markets dates back to 1944 when the Bretton Woods Institutions, such as IBRD and IMF, were established. The British pound had reigned supreme in the world trade till the British empire collapsed in early 1990s. When the British pound slipped following severe financial and political crises in the west, the USD emerged as the dominant currency. Since then the USD has never looked back. Even after devaluation of USD in 1970s and without having been backed by gold, the dominance of USD has not diminished at all. That is, the USD continues to maintain its position as dominant reserve currency and as the chief currency for settling international transactions. What made the USD dominant among some hundreds of currencies in the world? The straight answer is that there is no alternative to the USD. To reduce the dominance of the USD, some of the European countries have joined together to launch their own common currency called euro. But the euro never emerged as a serious challenge to the USD. The financial crisis of the 2000s exposed the problems of the U.S. financial system as the people of the U.S. spent well beyond their means. The collapse of some of U.S.-based financial institutions and breaking state of some international banks in 2008 led to the expectation that the USD would collapse. Contrary to all expectations, the USD gained in value following the financial crisis. After the latest world financial crisis, nations such as Brazil, Russia, India, China and South Africa (BRICS) have intensified their efforts to bring about structural changes in the world economy. These nations along with others

Table 1.5 Global Foreign Exchange Market Turnover—Daily Average (Select Currencies) (Percentage)

Currency	*April 1998*		*April 2001*		*April 2004*		*April 2007*		*April 2010*		*April 2013*	
	Share	*Rank*	*Share*	*Rank*	*Share*	*Rank*	*Share*	*Rank*	*Share*	*Rank*	*Share*	*Rank*
USD	86.8	1	89.9	1	88.0	1	85.6	1	84.9	1	87.0	1
EUR	—	32	37.9	2	37.4	2	37.0	2	39.1	2	33.4	2
JPY	21.7	2	23.5	3	20.8	3	17.2	3	19.0	3	23.0	3
GBP	11.0	3	13.0	4	16.5	4	14.9	4	12.9	4	11.8	4
AUD	3.0	6	4.3	7	6.0	6	6.6	6	7.6	5	8.6	5
CHF	7.1	4	6.0	5	6.0	5	6.8	5	6.3	6	5.2	6
CAD	3.5	5	4.5	6	4.2	7	4.3	7	5.3	7	4.6	7
CNY	0.0	30	0.0	35	0.1	29	0.5	20	0.9	17	2.2	9
INR	0.1	22	0.2	21	0.3	20	0.7	19	1.0	15	1.0	20

Source: BIS Triennial Central Bank Survey of Foreign Exchange and Derivatives Market Activity in 2013.

have expressed their willingness to accept Chinese renminbi (RMB) as a reserve currency. But there is a lot of skepticism about the Chinese economy. The most important requirement of any country to become the anchor country is that it should run continuous current account deficits in order to provide more and more liquidity needed by the growing world economy. This necessitates significant reforms to political, institutional, and legal framework in the country, which no country is able to undertake. Therefore, the USD continues to remain the dominant global currency despite many odds against it. As can be observed from Table 1.5, no currency is anywhere near the USD to replace it as the dominant currency.

Trends in Foreign Exchange Trading

According to the BIS Triennial Central Bank Survey (2013), the average daily foreign exchange turnover increased to USD 5.3 trillion in April 2013, from USD 4.00 trillion in April 2010, and USD 3.3 trillion in April 2007. As discussed earlier, the USD remains to be the dominant vehicle currency by accounting for 87 percent of daily average foreign exchange turnover in April 2013. The euro, the second most traded currency, registered its share in foreign exchange turnover having been declined from 39 percent in April 2010 to 33 percent in April 2013. But the Japanese yen along with currencies of several emerging economies including the Indian rupee has registered an increase in its share in turnover between April 2010 and April 2013. Another noticeable feature is that the Mexican peso and Chinese renminbi entered the list of the top 10 most traded currencies. Countries such as the UK, the USA, Japan, Switzerland, Singapore, Hong Kong, and Australia accounted for about 80 percent of foreign exchange trading in April 2013, up by more than 5 percent since the BIS earlier survey (2010). Foreign exchange swaps are the most actively traded instruments in April 2013 at USD 2.227 trillion per day, accounting for 42 percent of the global foreign exchange turnover, followed by spot trading at USD 2.046 trillion per day with 38 percent market share. Table 1.6 depicts the daily average foreign exchange turnover by currency and instrument.

Table 1.6 Foreign Exchange Turnover—Daily Average in April 2013 (Select Currencies) (Billions of USD)

	Total	*Spot transactions*	*Out right forwards*	*Foreign exchange swaps*	*Currency swaps*	*FX options*
Total,"net–net"basis	5,345	2,046	680	2,228	54	337
By currency						
USD	4,652	1,691	588	2,030	50	293
EUR	1,786	754	178	766	18	70
JPY	1,231	612	123	332	11	153
GBP	631	227	69	301	5	29
AUD	462	196	50	183	6	27
CHF	275	84	27	149	1	14
CAD	244	93	36	101	2	12
MXN	135	57	14	58	1	6
CNY	120	34	28	40	1	17
RUB	85	37	9	37	0	3
ZAR	60	19	7	31	0	2
BRL	59	11	34	1	3	11
INR	53	15	24	10	0	3

Source: BIS Triennial Central Bank Survey of Foreign Exchange and Derivatives Market Activity in 2013.

Networks for International Transactions

The Society for Worldwide Interbank Financial Telecommunication (SWIFT) and the Clearing House Interbank Payment System (CHIPS) are the dominant networks used for international transactions and settlements. We shall take a look at each of these communication networks in this section.

SWIFT

SWIFT is a cooperative owned by its members to facilitate the exchange of proprietary data while ensuring its confidentiality and integrity. SWIFT was founded in Brussels in 1973 by a group of European bankers as a non-profit cooperative organization for processing securities trades and transferring international messages. Financial messages may include letters of credit, payments, and securities transactions.

SWIFT provides the proprietary communication platform, products, and services that allow its customers to connect and exchange financial information securely and reliably. It also acts as the catalyst that brings financial agencies together to work collaboratively and finds solutions to issues of mutual interest. SWIFT enables its customers to automate and standardize financial transactions, thereby eliminating operational inefficiencies through reduction in reduces telecommunication costs as well as in operational risk. The SWIFT mechanism also ensures full back-up and recovery capabilities. SWIFT facilitates payments between members through domestic funds clearing systems like the Fedwire and the CHIPS in the United States.

SWIFT services are classified into four key areas: securities, treasury and derivatives, trade services, and payments and cash management. SWIFT has different message codes for different services. For example, a funds transfer message is coded as MT 103. This is a customer payment message and relates to the transfer of funds in payment for goods received. Similarly, MT 799 is a free-format text message sent between banks and is treated much like a secure form of e-mail. SWIFT enables its customers to have direct access to confirmations of foreign exchange and money market securities trades and derivative securities transactions. SWIFTNet Mail provides a secure and reliable messaging service for transferring sensitive business documents, such as invoices, contracts, and signatures. SWIFT's customers can e-mail their messages through the highly secure and reliable SWIFTNet Mail instead of the open Internet. As of September 2014, SWIFT had more than 10,500 financial institutions and corporations spread over 215 countries in its network.

CHIPS

The Clearing House Interbank Payments System (CHIPS) is a funds-transfer system that transmits and settles payment orders in U.S. dollars for some of the largest and most active banks in the world. CHIPS transmits and settles over 400,000 payment messages worth an aggregate of USD 1.51 trillion on an average per day. Any banking organization with a regulated U.S. presence can have a share in the ownership of CHIPS and participate in the network. As a real-time clearing and settlement system, it continuously matches, nets, and settles payment orders. It facilitates not only trade-related payments but also foreign exchange trade. CHIPS maintains a database of more than 45,000 accounts of its participants' customers. The participants include U.S. commercial banks and foreign banks with offices in the United States. It settles transactions through adjustments in special account balances at the Federal Reserve Bank of New York City. It continuously reviews and monitors the increasing needs of the participants in order to match their needs with the state-of-the- art funds transfer technology.

The Indian Foreign Exchange Market

India has a long history in foreign exchange trading. In this section, we shall discuss the developments in the Indian foreign exchange market.

Landmark Regulations

Foreign exchange regulations came into being for the first time in India under the Defence of India Act, 1939, to conserve foreign exchange and to ensure its utilization for essential imports. Soon after independence, a complex set of controls were imposed on all external transactions through the Foreign Exchange Regulation Act (FERA), 1947. The FERA, 1947, gave a wide range of powers to the Government of India to control and regulate foreign exchange inflows and outflows. When international transactions (exports, imports, remittances, etc.) involving foreign exchange increased phenomenally, the Government of India had to bring out a comprehensive new legislation. The new legislation which became the FERA, 1973, mainly aimed at conserving foreign exchange and ensuring its utilization for national priorities. The Act also envisaged the control and surveillance of foreign capital and the activities financed by it.

According to FERA, 1973, all transactions in foreign exchange, including those between residents and non-residents, were prohibited unless specifically permitted. Strict controls were imposed even on current account transactions. The provisions of FERA were so strict and rigorous, and a minor violation would attract severe penalties. As years rolled by, the need had been felt to remove the drastic measures of FERA and to make the Act people, institutions, or economy friendly. It was against this backdrop that the High-Level Committee on Balance of Payments headed by Dr C. Rangarajan made far-reaching recommendations in its report submitted in 1993. The Committee made, among others, the following recommendations:

- Introduction of a market-determined exchange rate regime within limits.
- Liberalization of current account transactions, leading to current account convertibility.

In line with the recommendations of the Committee, and also in accordance with Article VIII of the Articles of Agreement of the International Monetary Fund (IMF), the Government of India announced current account convertibility with effect from August 1994 and relaxed the restrictions on current account transactions. Even earlier to these measures, as a step in the liberalization process of the Indian economy, the Indian rupee, which had earlier been pegged, was allowed to float partially with effect from March 1992 and subsequently was allowed to be fully floated with effect from March 1993.

In order to remove certain market distortions, the Government of India appointed the Sodhani Committee in 1994. The Committee, which submitted its report in 1995, recommended several measures to relax foreign exchange regulations. It recommended that corporations be permitted to take a hedge upon declaring the existence of an exposure. It also recommended that exporters be allowed to retain 100 percent of their export earnings in any foreign currency with an authorized dealer in India, subject to liquidation of outstanding advances against export bills. The Committee recommended various other measures to activate the foreign exchange market and to promote the development of a vibrant derivatives market.

In 1997, the Tarapore Committee on Capital Account Convertibility (CAC) recommended several changes in the legislative framework governing foreign exchange transactions. Following the recommendations of the High-Level Committee (Dr C. Rangarajan Committee) as well as the Tarapore Committee, the FERA, which had formed the statutory basis for exchange control, was repealed and replaced by the new Foreign Exchange Management Act (FEMA), 1999. With the enactment of FEMA, the philosophical focus has shifted from conservation of foreign exchange to facilitating trade and developing an orderly foreign exchange market. The FEMA has also diluted the rigorous enforcement provisions that were the hallmark of FERA, 1993.

On the recommendations of the Sodhani Committee, the Clearing Corporation of India Ltd (CCIL) was established in 2001, which makes the foreign exchange market more liquid and vibrant. The RBI has also made significant changes in its external sector policy. The focus of all the new measures has been to dismantle controls and provide an enabling environment to all entities engaged in external transactions. Although India is yet to move completely to CAC, the process of capital account liberalization, which aims at removing controls that hinder the integration of economies, has already started. Some of such measures are mentioned below in brief.

Under the Foreign Exchange Management Act, 1999 (FEMA), which came into force with effect from 1 June 2000, all transactions involving foreign exchange have been classified either as capital or current account transactions. All transactions undertaken by a resident that do not alter his/her assets or liabilities, including contingent liabilities, outside India are current account transactions. In terms of Section 5 of the FEMA, persons resident in India are free to buy or sell foreign exchange for any current account transaction except for those transactions for which drawal of foreign exchange has been prohibited by the Central Government.

A resident individual may open, hold, and maintain a Resident Foreign Currency (Domestic) Account out of foreign exchange acquired in the form of currency notes, bank notes, and traveller's cheques, from any of the sources like payment for services rendered abroad, as honorarium, gift, services rendered, or in settlement of any lawful obligation from any person not resident in India. The account may also be credited with/opened out of foreign exchange earned abroad like proceeds of export of goods and/or services, royalty, honorarium, etc. and/or gifts received from close relatives and repatriated to India through normal banking channels. The account shall be maintained in the form of a current account and shall not bear any interest. There is no ceiling on the balances in the account. The account may be debited for payments made towards permissible current and capital account transactions. Further, a person resident in India is free to hold, own, transfer or invest in foreign currency, foreign security, or any immovable property situated outside India if such currency, security, or property was acquired, held, or owned by such person when he or she was resident outside India or inherited from a person who was resident outside India. Under the Liberalised Remittance Scheme, all resident individuals are allowed to freely remit up to USD 2,50,000 per financial year (April–March) for any permissible current or capital account transaction or a combination of both. Under the Scheme, resident individuals can acquire and hold shares or debt instruments or any other assets including immovable property outside India, without prior approval of the RBI. Individuals can also open, maintain, and hold foreign currency accounts with banks outside India for carrying out transactions permitted under the Scheme.

In terms of the extant provisions under the FEMA, 1999, on overseas direct investments (ODIs), the total ODIs of an Indian Party in all its Joint Ventures (JVs) and/or Wholly Owned Subsidiaries (WOSs) abroad engaged in any bonafide business activity should not exceed 100 percent of the net worth of the Indian Party as on the date of the last audited balance sheet under the Automatic Route. Any ODI in excess of 100% of the net worth shall be considered under the Approval Route by the RBI. Listed Indian companies can invest up to 50 percent of their net worth as on the date of the last audited Balance Sheet in overseas companies, listed on a recognized stock exchange, or in the rated debt securities issued by such companies. Partnership firms registered under the Indian Partnership Act, 1932, can make ODIs subject to the same terms and conditions as applicable to corporate entities. Indian Mutual Funds registered with SEBI are permitted to invest within the overall cap of USD 7 billion in: (a) ADRs/GDRs of the Indian and foreign companies; (b) equity of overseas companies listed on recognized overseas stock exchanges; initial and follow on public offerings for listing at recognized overseas stock exchanges; (c) foreign debt securities—short term as well as long term with rating not below investment grade—in the countries with fully convertible currencies; (d) money market investments not below investment grade; repos where the counter party is not below investment grade; (e) government securities where countries are not rated below investment grade; (f) derivatives traded on recognized stock exchanges overseas only for hedging and portfolio balancing with underlying as securities; (g) short term deposits with banks overseas where the issuer is rated not below investment grade; and (h) units/securities issued by overseas Mutual Funds or Unit Trusts registered with overseas regulators.

A person resident outside India or an entity incorporated outside India can invest in India, subject to the FDI Policy of the Government of India. Indian companies can issue equity shares, fully and mandatorily convertible debentures, and fully and mandatorily convertible preference shares subject to the pricing guidelines/valuation norms and reporting requirements amongst other requirements as prescribed under FEMA Regulations. Foreign Institutional Investors (FIIs) registered with SEBI are eligible to purchase shares and convertible debentures issued by Indian companies under the Portfolio Investment Scheme (PIS). To increase the depth of the foreign exchange market, the RBI has permitted foreign institutional investors to access the currency futures or exchange traded currency options for the purpose of hedging the currency risk arising out of the market value of their exposure to Indian debt and equity securities.

Structure

As far as the structure of the foreign exchange market is concerned, the RBI is the administrative authority of foreign exchange regulations in India. In this capacity, it regularly issues the *Exchange Control Manual*, which outlines the exchange controls and the procedures thereof. Amendments to exchange controls are also notified by the RBI through circulars.

In India, foreign exchange transactions are carried out in three segments:

1. transactions between the RBI and ADs;
2. the interbank market, where ADs deal with each other; and
3. the retail segment, where ADs and money changers deal with forex customers.

In the first segment, transactions take place between the RBI and ADs. ADs—mostly commercial banks and other financial institutions—are categorized into Category I, Category II, and Category III. All scheduled commercial banks including foreign banks operating in India belong to Category I. They are permitted to maintain foreign currency accounts, known as nostro accounts, and engage in foreign exchange transactions outside forex markets. They are also authorized to act as market makers. All full-fledged money changers and select regional rural banks and cooperative banks belong to Category II. This category of ADs can open lines of credit (LCs) for their customers, make payments, and provide bank guarantees for imports. However, they are not authorized to maintain nostro accounts. Select financial institutions such as the Export–Import (EXIM) Bank belong to Category III. ADs under Category III are permitted restricted functions. There are also foreign exchange brokers who act as intermediaries. Licences for ADs and brokers are issued on request under Section 10(1) of the FEMA, 1999. Transactions between the RBI and ADs generally take place in the process of influencing the foreign exchange market by the RBI. The intervention of the RBI is necessary to maintain stability in the market and also to influence the exchange rate in a desired direction.

The second segment consists of the interbank or interdealer market, where ADs deal with each other. ADs have formed the Foreign Exchange Dealers' Association of India (FEDAI), which frames rules and guidelines for proper functioning of ADs. The Association also coordinates with the RBI for effective control over foreign exchange operations in the country. Although ADs are permitted to operate in any foreign exchange trading centre in the world, they normally do so within the country. Their dealings with foreign agencies are restricted to genuine transactions, including the squaring of currency positions. Forward trading by ADs with overseas agencies is also permitted for covering genuine transactions.

The third segment, known as the retail segment or the primary segment consists of ADs and money changers who deal with foreign exchange customers. Money changers are also authorized to buy and sell foreign exchange in a limited way. Some entities such as travel agents, hotels, and select government establishments are also licensed to buy, but not sell, foreign exchange. Tourists may go to money changers to encash their traveller's cheques and currency notes. The retail segment generates the primary business of foreign exchange, as all foreign exchange transactions of residents as well as tourists take place through this segment. The customer segment of the foreign exchange market mainly comprises of public sector companies including the Government of India, private firms, etc. In recent years, the foreign institutional investors (FIIs) have also emerged as major participants in the foreign exchange market.

The important foreign exchange market centres in India are Mumbai, New Delhi, Kolkata, Chennai, Bangalore, and Kochi. Mumbai is the main centre of foreign exchange business in the country as a large volume of foreign exchange transactions takes place through this centre. Moreover, the RBI is also headquartered in Mumbai.

Trading Platforms and Settlements

In India, there are four important platforms for trading of currencies:

1. FX-CLEAR of CCIL, set up in August 2003.
2. FX Direct launched by IBS Forex (P) Ltd in 2002 in collaboration with Financial Technologies (India) Ltd.
3. Reuters D2.
4. Reuters Market Data System (RMDS).

FX-CLEAR and FX Direct offer both real-time order matching and negotiation modes for trading. FX-CLEAR is the most widely used trading platform in India. Its main advantage is that it has straight-through processing capabilities as it is linked to CCIL's settlement platform. Reuters D2 and RMDS are robust platforms that can support huge throughputs of data. They bring unprecedented speed, resilience, and flexibility to data operations. They have a minimum trading amount limit of USD 1 million.

The Clearing Corporation of India Ltd, established in 2001, plays a very important role in the settlement of foreign exchange transactions. It undertakes settlement of foreign exchange transactions on a multilateral net basis through a process of novation. Accordingly, every eligible foreign exchange contract between members gets replaced by two new contracts—between CCIL and each of the two parties. The net amount payable to or receivable from CCIL in each currency is arrived at member-wise. CCIL thus provides the benefits of risk mitigation, improved efficiency, and easier reconciliation of accounts to market participants.

Telegraphic Transfer (TT) Rates and Bill Rates

Telegraphic transfer, or **TT**, is an order for payment of money notified through a telegram, cable, or other electronic media. In foreign exchange parlance, "telegraphic transfer" means immediate exchange of one currency for another currency. TT is the quickest mode of transfer of funds, involving no loss of interest and no risk.

TT, which stands for ***telegraphic transfer****, is an order for payment of money notified through a telegram, cable, or other electronic media.*

Banks quote TT rates and bill rates to their non-bank customers. Such rates are also called *merchant rates.* TT rates are of two types—*TT buying rates* and *TT selling rates.* The TT buying rate is the rate at which a bank makes payments for demand drafts, mail transfers, etc. drawn on it. TT rates are also applied to the collection of foreign bills and cancellation of foreign exchange sold earlier. Banks quote TT selling rates for issuing demand drafts, mail transfers, etc. and also for the cancellation of foreign exchange purchased earlier.

Bill rates are also of two types—*bill buying rates* and *bill selling rates.* Banks quote bill buying rates for purchasing a foreign bill, which may be a usance bill or a sight bill. Similarly, the bill selling rate applies to all transactions where the bank handles documents such as payment against import bills.

TT rates apply to transactions that entail currency transfers that do not require the handling of documents. For example, if a bank pays a demand draft drawn on it, there is no delay in the remittance to the bank because the foreign bank that issued the demand draft would have already credited the amount to the nostro account of the bank. TT rates, however, do not apply to bills to be purchased by a bank from a customer, as the bank has to wait till the drawee makes a payment against the bill. Moreover, such bills also involve the handling of certain documents. Hence, TT rates are usually lower than bill rates.

The bid–ask spread in the Indian foreign exchange market was high till the mid-1990s due to low exchange rate volatility and thin volumes. In subsequent years, however, the bid–ask spread has declined sharply and has remained low due to high liquidity in the market.

In the spot market, the bid–ask spread ranges between 0.25 of a paisa to1 paisa, while swap quotes are available at a 1- to 2-paisa spread.

Market Turnover

The Indian foreign exchange market has witnessed a phased transition from a pegged exchange rate regime to a market-determined exchange rate regime. The government has permitted current account convertibility since 1994 and there has been substantial liberalization in capital account transactions. It has progressively liberalized foreign exchange-related transactions by removing restrictions and simplifying procedures. There has been significant liberalization of outflows, especially foreign investments made by individuals, corporations, and mutual funds. Indian companies are permitted to invest up to 35 percent of their net worth in portfolio investments abroad. Mutual funds are permitted to invest up to USD 4 billion (aggregate) overseas. Individuals can remit up to USD 100,000 in a financial year for any permitted current or capital account transaction, or a combination thereof. Market participants have greater flexibility in undertaking foreign exchange operations. Besides participating in the spot market, market participants can trade in derivatives such as forwards, swaps, and options. The typical forward contract is for 1 month, 3 months, or 6 months. A swap transaction in the foreign exchange market is a combination of a spot and a forward in opposite directions. Exporters and importers are permitted to hedge their foreign exchange exposures. Resident individuals are also allowed to hedge their foreign exchange exposures, including anticipated exposures up to an annual limit of USD 100,000, which can be freely cancelled and rebooked. The availability of derivatives thus helps domestic entities and foreign investors in their foreign exchange risk management. The foreign exchange rate policy of the government is guided by the principles of careful monitoring and flexible management of exchanges rates.

As a result of various measures, particularly full convertibility under current account and limited convertibility under capital account, the foreign exchange market in India has become a mature market with greater depth and liquidity. The daily average foreign exchange market turnover has increased from USD 2 billion in April 1998 to USD 3 billion in April 2001, to USD 7 billion in April 2004, and to USD 38 billion in April 2007. The daily average turnover declined to USD 27 billion in April 2010 but increased to USD 31 billion in April 2013. A glance at Table 1.7 reveals that the UK tops the list of the countries with 41 percent share in the global foreign exchange market turnover followed by the US (19%); Japan (6%); Switzerland (3%); Singapore (6%); Hong Kong (4%); and Australia (3%). Although India has registered a substantial increase in the daily average foreign exchange market turnover over the period since 1998, its share in the global foreign exchange market turnover is miniscule i.e. less than 1 percent. Even some of the BRICS nations, viz. China and Russia are ahead of India in terms of daily average foreign exchange market turnover. In terms of currency pairs, as it can be seen from Table 1.8 that USD/EUR is the dominant pair, followed by USD/JPY, and USD/GBP. The USD/INR pair has a miniscule role in the global foreign exchange market. While INR trades account for just about 1 percent of the global foreign exchange market turnover, nearly half of these trades take place outside India and in jurisdictions outside the direct regulatory supervision of regulators like the RBI and the SEBI. The US dollar–Indian rupee trading accounts for about 60 percent of total currency trading turnover on Dubai Gold and Commodity Exchange (DGCX). Indian rupee–US dollar currency futures are also actively traded on DGCX.

Currency Derivatives Trading in India

Although foreign exchange derivatives had existed in an informal form for a long time in India, their formal introduction took place only in the mid-1990s. That is, a structured

Table 1.7 Select Country-wise Global Forex Market Turnover (Daily Average) (Amount in Billion USD)

Country	*April 1998*		*April 2001*		*April 2004*		*April 2007*		*April 2010*		*April 2013*	
	Amount	*%*	*Amount*	*%*	*Amount*	*%*	*Amount*	*%*	*Amount*	*%*	*Amount*	*%*
UK	685	32.6	542	31.8	835	32.0	1483	34.6	1,854	36.8	2,726	40.9
US	383	18.3	273	16.0	499	19.1	745	17.4	904	17.9	1,263	18.9
Australia	48	2.3	54	3.2	107	4.1	176	4.1	192	3.8	182	2.7
Brazil	5	0.2	6	0.3	4	0.1	6	0.1	14	0.3	17	0.3
Canada	38	1.8	44	2.6	59	2.3	64	1.5	62	1.2	65	1.0
China	—	—	—	—	1	0.0	9	0.2	20	0.4	44	0.7
France	77	3.7	50	2.9	67	2.6	127	3.0	152	3.0	190	2.8
Hong Kong	80	3.8	68	4.0	106	4.1	181	4.2	238	4.7	275	4.1
India	2	0.1	3	0.2	7	0.3	38	0.9	27	0.5	31	0.5
Japan	146	7.0	153	9.0	207	8.0	250	5.8	312	6.2	374	5.6
Russia	7	0.3	10	0.6	30	1.1	50	1.2	42	0.8	61	0.9
Singapore	145	6.9	104	6.1	134	5.1	242	5.6	266	5.3	383	5.7
South Africa	9	0.4	10	0.6	10	0.4	14	0.3	14	0.3	21	0.3
Switzerland	92	4.4	76	4.5	85	3.3	254	5.9	249	4.9	216	3.2
All countries	2,099	100.0	1,705	100.0	2,608	100.0	4,281	100.0	5,043	100.0	6,671	100.0

Table 1.8 Global Foreign Exchange Market Turnover (Daily Average) by Select Currency Pair (Amount in Billion USD)

Currency pair	*2001*		*2004*		*2007*		*2010*		*2013*	
	Amount	*%*	*Amount*	*%*	*Amount*	*%*	*Amount*	*%*	*Amount*	*%*
USD/EUR	372	30.0	541	28.0	892	26.8	1,098	27.7	1,289	24.1
USD/JPY	250	20.2	328	17.0	438	13.2	567	14.3	978	18.3
USD/GBP	129	10.4	259	13.4	384	11.6	360	9.1	472	8.8
USD/AUD	51	4.1	107	5.5	185	5.6	248	6.3	364	6.8
USD/CAD	54	4.3	77	4.0	126	3.8	182	4.6	200	3.7
USD/CHF	59	4.8	83	4.3	151	4.5	166	4.2	184	3.4
USD/CNY	—		—		—		31	0.8	113	2.1
USD/INR	—		—		—		36	0.9	50	0.9

derivatives market is a recent origin in India. Before the Indian economy was opened up for foreign investments and accelerated international trade, the Indian business had been in an insular economic environment without facing global completion. The limited number of financial products and stringent financial regulations also restricted the scope for risk taking. The businesses having international transactions with foreign exchange exposure and risk were also limited. Therefore, the foreign exchange forward contracts were the only hedging instruments available, that too in a restricted way, to those who were averse to risk. But after liberalization of the Indian economy in early 1990s, the entire economic scenario in the country has changed. There has been a lot of investment flows and trade flows happening across the borders which made Indian businesses vulnerable to all kinds of risks. It is in this globalization era that the Government of India has made some initiatives to help businesses and others manage their risks. The first initiative of the government in the post-liberalization era was to develop the conventional forward market by liberalizing some restrictions and introducing a derivative product called the cross currency forward contract. This was followed by the launch of much-awaited derivative products like foreign exchange swaps, currency swaps, currency futures, and currency options. The advances in technology, particularly information technology have also facilitated the introduction of several exotic financial products and brought sophistication to the markets. Thus, the derivatives market in India is rapidly evolving, but it has to still traverse a long way to match with the markets in developed nations in terms of market sophistication, liquidity, depth and width of products, etc. A developed derivatives market can change the overall risk profile of market participants and contribute to the growth of the foreign exchange market.

There are two major organizations in India, viz. the Reserve Bank of India (RBI) and the Securities and Exchange Board of India (SEBI) which regulate, guide, and facilitate the development of derivatives market in India. Their roles are well defined to avoid any scope for duplication of efforts and confrontation. The complementary roles of RBI and SEBI have also contributed to the development of derivatives markets in the country.

According to Foreign Exchange Management (Foreign Exchange Derivative Contracts) Regulations, 2000, a foreign exchange derivative contract means a financial transaction or an arrangement in whatever form and by whatever name called, whose value is derived from price movement in one or more underlying assets, and includes,

(a) a transaction which involves at least one foreign currency other than the currency of Nepal or Bhutan, or

(b) a transaction which involves at least one interest rate applicable to a foreign currency not being a currency of Nepal or Bhutan, or

(c) a forward contract.

but does not include foreign exchange transaction for cash or tom or spot deliveries.

There are two distinct groups of derivative contracts: over-the-counter (OTC) derivatives and exchange-traded derivatives. *OTC derivatives* are contracts that are traded directly between two eligible parties, with or without the use of an intermediary and without going through an exchange. *Exchange-traded derivatives* are traded on an exchange.

The participants in the derivatives market are classified into two functional categories: market makers and users. *Users* enter derivative transactions to hedge an existing identified risk, whereas *market makers* act as counterparties in derivative transactions with users and also amongst themselves. Scheduled commercial banks (excluding Regional Rural Banks) and primary dealers can act as market makers with approval from the RBI. Users are scheduled commercial banks, primary dealers, specified all-India financial institutions, and corporate entities including mutual funds.

As per RBI guidelines, market makers may undertake any derivative structured product (a combination of permitted cash and generic derivative instruments), as long as it is a combination of two or more of the generic instruments permitted by the RBI. Market makers should be in a position to mark to market or demonstrate valuation of these constituent products based on observable market prices. Second-order derivatives like swaptions, options on futures, compound options, and so on are not permitted. A user should not have a net short options position, either on a standalone basis or in a structured product, except to the extent of permitted covered calls and puts. Users can contract all permitted derivative transactions, including roll over, restructuring, and novation, only at prevailing market rates. Mark-to-market gains/losses on roll over, restructuring, novation, and so on shall be cash settled.

The foreign exchange derivatives available in India are as follows:

- *Foreign exchange forwards*: Foreign exchange forwards are permitted to be used by residents in India and residents outside India. The resident Indian can participate in forward market to hedge crystallized foreign currency/foreign interest rate exposure and to transform exposure in one currency to another permitted currency. A registered foreign institutional investor (FII) may enter into a forward contract with rupee as one of the currencies with an AD in India to hedge its exposure in India. A non-resident Indian or overseas corporate body may enter into forward contract with rupee as one of the currencies with an AD in India to hedge the amount of dividend due to him/it on shares held in an Indian company, the balance held in foreign currency non-resident (FCNR) account or non-resident external rupee (NRE) account, and the amount of investment made under portfolio scheme.
- *Currency futures*: In the process of developing Indian derivatives market to international standards, currency futures trading was introduced in August 2008, initially with a pair of USD–INR. Later, the currency futures trading has been extended to include the currency pairs such as EUR–INR, GBP–INR, and JPY–INR. The futures contract is quoted in rupee terms but the outstanding positions would be in the respective foreign currency. All futures contracts have monthly maturities from 1 to 12 months. Persons resident in India may purchase or sell currency futures to hedge an exposure to foreign exchange rate risk or otherwise. Further, persons resident outside India who are eligible to invest in securities as per Foreign Exchange Management (Transfer or issue of Security by a person resident outside India) Regulations, 2000, may purchase or sell currency futures to hedge an exposure to foreign exchange rate risk or otherwise. Foreign Portfolio Investors (FPIs) are also permitted to enter into currency futures contracts, subject to certain terms and conditions.
- *Exchange-traded currency options*: As the globalization has intensified, the volatility of exchange rates has increased affecting the value of businesses particularly. This has led to a requirement of making foreign exchange derivatives market more broad based and liquid. Therefore, the Government of India introduced exchange-traded currency options in October 2010 to provide more number of foreign exchange derivative instruments to the participants. The underlying for the currency option is USD–INR spot rate. The options are premium-styled European call and put options. The size of each contract is USD 1,000. The option premium is quoted in INR terms but the outstanding position is in USD. The maturity of the option does not exceed 12 months. The contract is settled in cash in INR terms. Initially, only persons resident in India were permitted to buy or sell exchange-traded currency options to hedge an exposure to foreign exchange rate risk or otherwise. Later, FPIs are also permitted to enter into exchange-traded currency options, subject to certain terms and conditions. The trading of exchange-traded currency options is subject to position limits and to maintaining margins as per the guidelines issued by the SEBI.

- *Foreign currency–INR swaps*: Indian residents who have a long-term foreign currency or INR liability are permitted to enter into foreign currency–INR swap transactions with Category I ADs to hedge or transform exposure in foreign currency/foreign interest rate to INR/INR interest rate.
- *Foreign currency–INR options*: Category I ADs approved by the RBI and Category I ADs who are not market makers are allowed to sell foreign currency–INR options to their customers on a back-to-back basis, provided they have a capital to risk-weighted assets ratio (CRAR) of 9 percent or above. These options are used by customers who have genuine foreign currency exposures, as permitted by the RBI, and by Category I ADs for the purpose of hedging trading and balance sheet exposures.
- *Cross-currency options*: Cross-currency options can be used by residents in India to hedge or transform foreign currency exposure arising out of currency account transactions. The market makers (Category I ADs) can also use this instrument to cover risks arising out of market making in foreign currency rupee options as well as cross-currency options, as permitted by RBI. Cross-currency transaction refers to transaction of a pair of currencies traded without involving the domestic currency. That is, one foreign currency is traded for another foreign currency without having to first exchange the foreign currencies into domestic currency.
- *Cross-currency swaps*: Persons or entities with borrowings in foreign currency under external commercial borrowing (ECB) are permitted to use cross-currency swaps for transformation and/or hedging of foreign currency and interest rate risks.

The derivatives trading market in India has matured over time, acquiring greater flexibility and depth. For example, earlier, forward contracts could not be re-booked once cancelled. These days, however, booking, cancellation, and re-booking of forward contracts is allowed. ADs are also given powers to allow residents engaged in import and export trade to hedge the price risk on all commodities in international commodity exchanges, with a few exceptions like gold, silver, and petroleum. Foreign institutional investors can hedge currency risk on the market value of the entire investment in equity and/or debt in India as on a particular date, using forward contracts. As far as FDIs are concerned, investors can access the forward market to hedge foreign exchange rate risk on the market value of investments and on dividend receivable on investments in Indian companies. They can also hedge exchange rate risk on proposed investments in India. Non-resident Indians (NRIs) can hedge balances/amounts in non-resident external rupee accounts (NRE Accounts) using forwards and foreign currency (non-resident) accounts (Banks) [FCNR (B)] using INR forwards as well as cross-currency forwards.

After the introduction of exchange-traded currency derivatives, the foreign exchange trading scenario in India has remarkably changed. The daily average foreign exchange market turnover in India has increased from USD 27 billion in April 2010 to USD 31 billion in April 2013. This phenomenal increase in the daily average turnover would have been facilitated or made possible by the growth and maturity of the Indian foreign exchange derivatives market. As can be observed from Table 1.9, the average daily turnover in the exchange-traded derivatives market has increased phenomenally from ₹1,167.43 crore in 2008–09 to ₹2,1705.62 crore in 2012–13 but declined to ₹16,444.73 crore in 2013–14. The daily average turnover in the derivatives market declined in 2013–2014 due to curbs such as doubling of margin requirements and a ceiling on position limits on exchange-traded currency derivatives imposed by the RBI. Nevertheless, the Indian currency derivatives have registered a significant increase in the average daily turnover over time due to increased volatility in the rupee against the US dollar. Arbitrage volumes have also increased between OTC and the exchange due to increase in volatility.

Table 1.9 Exchange-traded Currency Derivatives Market in India

Year	*Currency futures turnover (INR crore)*	*Currency options turnover (INR crore)*	*Total turnover (INR crore)*	*Average daily turnover (INR crore)*
2013–14	29,40,885.92	10,71,627.54	40,12,513.45	16,444.73
2012–13	37,65,105.33	15,09,359.32	52,74,464.65	21,705.62
2011–12	33,78,488.92	12,96,500.98	46,74,989.91	19,479.12
2010–11	32,79,002.13	1,70,785.59	34,49,787.72	13,854.57
2009–10	17,82,608.04	—	17,82,608.04	7,427.53
2008–09	1,62,272.43	—	1,62,272.43	1,167.43

Source: National Stock Exchange (NSE).

The Non-deliverable Forward Market (NDF)

Another market segment that is quickly picking up is the offshore non-deliverable forward (NDF) market, which has emerged out of the regulatory controls on the currencies in the onshore markets. A *non-deliverable forward* is a forward contract on a thinly traded or non-convertible foreign currency. NDFs are cash-settled and OTC forwards. Such transactions are settled not by delivering the underlying pair of currencies, but by making a net payment, in a convertible currency, equal to the difference between the forward rate and the spot rate on the date of settlement. NDFs are usually quoted for time periods ranging from 1 month up to 1 year, and they are normally quoted and settled in US dollars. They have become a popular instrument for corporations seeking to hedge exposure to foreign currencies that are not internationally traded. MNCs, portfolio investors, hedge funds, and proprietary foreign exchange accounts of commercial and investment banks use NDFs to hedge or take speculative positions in local currencies. The currencies that are traded in Asian NDF markets are the Chinese yuan renminbi, the Korean won, the Taiwan dollar, the Philippine peso, the Indonesian rupiah, the Malaysian ringgit, the Thai baht, the Pakistan rupee, and the Indian rupee. The NDF market for US dollar–Indian rupee contracts in Singapore, the US, and Europe accounts for about 45 percent of the entire trading in Indian rupee. However, the turnover in INR NDF is much smaller as compared to other Asian currencies such as Korean won, Chinese yuan, and Taiwanese dollar traded in the NDF market. As there is a strong correlation between the rupee and dollar spot, forward and NDF rates, the NDF market has a high impact on the exchange rate of INR, especially in volatile market conditions. The main participants in INR NDF market are MNCs, portfolio investors, hedge funds, and others who have genuine exposure to INR but not able to adequately hedge their exposure in the onshore market due to prevailing controls. There are also non-residents who wish to speculate on INR without having any exposure. The arbitrageurs also try to exploit the differences in exchanges rates in the onshore market and offshore market. Notwithstanding some issues that adversely affect the onshore market, the NDF market facilitates the foreign investments to take place in the domestic economy by providing hedging facilities or products that are not available in the onshore market.

Finance Function in a Multinational Context

The finance function in an organization consists of several activities and some of them are very important and crucial from the point of view of organization survival. Broadly stated, there are four major decisions that constitute finance function in an organization.

They are: investment decision, financing decision, dividend decision, and liquidity decision. Very closely related or ancillary to these decisions are accounting and transaction processing, control and risk management, and decision support systems. Finance function is the same in a multinational firm as in the case of a purely domestic firm. However, the decision choices and the associated risks become different in a multinational context. An MNC can have more choices because of more number of opportunities across the world, accompanied by varied risks of different magnitude. It can be said that decision making in a multinational context is very complex.

In a purely domestic firm as well as in an MNC, the basic objective of financial management is the same, viz. to maximize the value of the firm. But the valuation model is different. The basic valuation model is as follows:

$$V = \sum_{t=1}^{n} \frac{[E(CF_t)]}{(1+K)^n}$$

$E(CF_t)$ = Expected cash flows at the end of period, t

N = Number of periods
K = Required rate of return
If the firm has cash flows in foreign currency, then

$$E(CF_t) = \sum_{j=1}^{m} [E(CF_{j,t}) \times (S_{j,t})]$$

$[E(CF_{j,t}) \times (S_{j,t})]$ = Expected cash flows denominated in a foreign currency, j at the end of period, t being converted into domestic currency at the spot rate.

The two all-inclusive parameters that determine the value of a firm are expected cash flows and required rate of return. The expected cash flows are estimated on the basis of cash flows to be generated by a firm in future periods. A firm's decisions with regard to investment, business operations, etc. can affect the firm's expected cash flows. Assuming that other factors are constant, any increase in expected cash flows would increase the value of the firm. The required rate of return is the weighted average cost of capital based on all of a firm's investment projects. Keeping other factors constant, any increase in a firm's required rate of return will reduce the value of the firm.

In the case of a multinational firm, these two parameters have different dimensions and dynamics. The expected cash flows of an MNC may come from projects located in different countries, and such cash flows are obviously denominated in the functional currency of the host country. Therefore, the expected cash flows of an MNC are the sum of the products of cash flows in every future period denominated in each functional currency times the expected spot exchange rate at which a functional currency could be converted into a domestic currency of the parent firm of the MNC at the end of the period. As the MNCs are exposed to risks like political risk, economic risk, etc. in every country of their operations, the expected cash flows of MNCs are subject to a lot of uncertainty. The required rate of return increases with the increase in uncertainty associated with expected cash flows. In other words, the return required by the investors tends to increase with international exposure of an MNC.

The factors that differentiate a purely domestic firm from an international firm with respect to financial management are those that govern the valuation model. The expected cash flows of a domestic firm are those which emanate from domestic operations of the firm. But in the case of an international firm the expected cash flows come from all its operations across geographical borders. Another important feature of an international firm is that the amount of cash flows also depends on the spot exchange rate of foreign currency in which the cash flows are denominated. The required rate of return, being a significant factor in determining the value of a firm, is also different in the case of an international firm. Thus, the value of a domestic firm and the value of an international firm differ as they are influenced by different factors. A brief note on each of them is given below.

Exchange rate: As the purely domestic firm does not have any international operations, it is not affected directly by any change in exchange rate of domestic currency. But an international firm has foreign exchange exposure; and if the firm is an MNC with operational presence in many countries, it will have a lot of foreign exchange exposure with multiple functional currencies. The foreign exchange exposure influences both the expected cash flows as well as the required rate of return.

Macro-environment: The operations and performance of a purely domestic firm are influenced by the domestic macro-environment, which includes political environment, economic environment, social environment, etc. But an MNC is exposed to multiplicity of regulatory environments in terms of political, economic, legal, tax, etc. in each country of its operations that influence the expected cash flows and the required rate of return. Exchange rate risk and political risk are the two additional major risks which an MNC faces in its operations. But many cross-border hedging techniques are available to an MNC to avoid or reduce such risks.

Business risk: An international firm may have a business diversified into many parts of the world. This, apart from enhancing the business opportunities, diversifies the overall business risks of a firm. But a purely domestic firm has limited opportunities to diversify its business and thereby reduce its business risk. The business risk combined with financial risk will have a deleterious effect on the overall cost of capital of the firm.

Capital structure: An international firm has several options to raise capital across the globe. The financial management of an MNC has many funding choices in terms of markets, instruments, and currencies. In other words, the financial management of an MNC can lower its overall cost of capital by tapping the international financial markets with a right mix of financial instruments and currencies. The financial management of an MNC can also enjoy more flexibility in their capital structure because of their access to international financial markets and instruments. Notwithstanding that the capital structure of an MNC is always governed by social, economic, political, legal, tax, and other factors prevailing in each country in which an MNC has operations, the overall cost of capital of an MNC is always lower than that of a purely domestic firm because of international diversification.

Investments: Financial management of an MNC has ample opportunities to invest its surplus funds both short term and long term. International financial management can invest its surplus funds in a variety of money market financial instruments including currencies and treasury securities. The foreign bonds, euro bonds, international equities, etc. can also be attractive long-term options for international financial management to invest. Financial management of an MNC can also hedge the risks by participating in international derivative markets. Such opportunities may not be available for a purely domestic company.

Summary

1. Over the last two–three decades, the foreign exchange market has witnessed unprecedented growth following developments in the world economy.
2. The institutional set-up that facilitates the exchange of currencies is known as the *foreign exchange market.*
3. The rate at which the home currency is exchanged for a foreign currency is known as the rate of foreign exchange or the *foreign exchange rate.*
4. The foreign exchange market has two segments—the *wholesale segment* and the *retail segment*. The wholesale segment is also known as the *interdealer market.*
5. There are two kinds of exchange rate quotations—direct quotations and indirect quotations. A *direct quote* refers to the number of units of home currency that can be exchanged for one unit of a foreign currency, while an *indirect quote* refers to the number of units of a foreign currency that can be exchanged for one unit of home currency.

6. Depending on the time gap between the transaction date and the settlement date, foreign exchange transactions can be categorized into spot transactions and forward transactions. *Spot transactions are* for immediate delivery. *Forward transactions* involve settlement at a certain date in the future.

7. Banks always quote two rates—the *bid rate* and the *ask rate.* In the case of direct quotations, banks follow the rule of buying high and selling low, and in indirect quotations, they follow the rule of buying low and selling high.

8. *Arbitrage* is a process in which a market participant sells and buys a currency to profit from exchange rate discrepancies within a market centre or across market centres. Arbitrage may be a *two-point simple arbitrage* or a *triangular arbitrage.*

9. If a forward foreign exchange rate in terms of home currency is greater than the spot rate, the foreign currency is at a *forward premium.* If it is less than the spot rate, the foreign currency is at a *forward discount.*

10. The forward foreign exchange rate is based on certain expectations about the future spot rate. Depending on the actual movement of the spot rate of a currency, the participants in the forward market may make a gain or a loss. The forward rate is considered to be an unbiased predictor of the future spot rate of a currency.

11. The *foreign exchange derivatives* available in India are currency forwards, foreign currency–INR swaps, exchange-traded currency options, cross-currency swaps, and currency futures.

Questions and Problems

1. Explain the structure of the foreign exchange market.

2. What is foreign exchange rate? How is the exchange rate of a currency determined?

3. Who are the participants in the foreign exchange market? What are their motives?

4. Distinguish between spot transactions and forward transactions.

5. What is arbitrage? How does arbitrage yield profit? How does it get eliminated?

6. Describe the structure of the Indian foreign exchange market. Critically evaluate the foreign exchange regulations in India.

7. The spot rate of the US dollar is INR 45 and the 90-day forward rate is INR 45.60. Why do these rates differ?

8. Suppose a bank in India quotes spot rates of USD/INR 45 and GBP/INR 87.5. What is the direct spot quote for the British pound in New York?

9. Suppose that the direct spot quotations in New York and London are 1.9031/35 and 0.50/03, respectively. Calculate arbitrage profit per USD 10 million.

10. If GBP 1 = USD 1.9031 in New York, USD 1 = EUR 0.7830 in euroland, and EUR 1 = GBP 0.6710 in London, how can a market participant take profitable advantage of these rates?

11. Discuss forward rate and future spot rate parity. What are the causes of deviation?

12. The 180-day forward rate on the British pound is INR 87.79. A trader expects that the spot rate of the British pound will be INR 86.50 in six months. What is the expected profit on a forward sale of GBP 1 million?

13. If exchange rates are GBP/USD 1.92 and USD/JPY 116, what is the exchange rate between the yen and the British pound?

14. Show how one can make a triangular arbitrage profit by trading at the following rates:
USD/GBP 0.525
USD/AUD 1.303
GBP/AUD 2.400
What rate of USD/GBP can eliminate triangular arbitrage?

15. The current spot exchange rate is GBP/USD 1.92 and the 3-month forward rate is GBP/USD 1.95. It is expected that the spot exchange rate will be GBP/USD 1.92 in 3 months. Mr Mehra would like to buy or sell GBP 1 million. How much profit can he make on speculation? What would be the speculative profit/loss if the spot rate actually turns out to be GBP/USD 1.90 in 3 months?

16. Express the following quotations on an outright basis:

	Spot	*1-month forward*	*3-month forward*
USD/EUR	0.7736	25–45	75–90
USD/JPY	107.3000	520–549	825–897
USD/GBP	0.6180	40–52	75–89

What is the 3-month forward rate of EUR/GBP?

Multiple-choice Questions

1. CHIPS stands for ________.
   (a) Chinese International Payments System
   (b) Clearing House Interbank Payments System
   (c) Central House of Interbank Payments System
   (d) none of the above
2. Eurocurrency deposit is a ________.
   (a) deposit made in Europe
   (b) deposit in euro currency
   (c) deposit in the currency with a bank outside the home country of the currency
   (d) US dollar deposit with a bank in the US
3. Eurodollar loan is a ________.
   (a) loan made by an European bank
   (b) loan made by European Central Bank
   (c) loan made in euro currency
   (d) dollar loan made by a bank outside the US
4. Foreign exchange market is ________.
   (a) an over-the-counter market
   (b) a market located in a foreign country
   (c) a market for foreign goods and services
   (d) an organized exchange with a central clearing house
5. Global foreign exchange market functions virtually ________.
   (a) 12-hours-a-day (b) 9-hours-a-day
   (c) round the clock (d) none of the above
6. Foreign exchange market is dominated by ________.
   (a) central banks (b) interbank transactions
   (c) retail segment (d) investment banks
7. Market makers offer ________.
   (a) two-way quotes (b) single quote
   (c) discount (d) none of the above
8. Bid rate is the rate at which a bank ________.
   (a) buys the base currency
   (b) sells the base currency
   (c) lends the base currency
   (d) borrows the base currency
9. In retail segment of foreign exchange market, the bid–ask spread is ________.
   (a) small (b) large
   (c) zero (d) infinite
10. The most widely traded currency is ________.
    (a) British pound (b) Euro
    (c) US dollar (d) Japanese yen
11. Largest foreign exchange trading centre in the world ________.
    (a) New York (b) Tokyo
    (c) London (d) Frankfurt
12. Swaps are ________.
    (a) spot trades
    (b) forward trades
    (c) combination of spot and forward transactions
    (d) speculative trades
13. SWIFT is a ________.
    (a) clearing house
    (b) communications network
    (c) brokerage house
    (d) organized exchange
14. In a spot transaction, the settlement date is usually ________.
    (a) 1 business day (b) 2 business days
    (c) 3 business days (d) 1 business week
15. Forward contract without accompanying spot deal is known as ________.
    (a) swap
    (b) futures
    (c) outright forward contract
    (d) interbank forward deal
16. Arbitrage is a process to make profit ________.
    (a) with a certain amount of risk
    (b) with a certain amount of capital
    (c) without any risk or commitment of capital
    (d) with a speculative trade
17. Arbitrage opportunities disappear when ________.
    (a) there are no speculators
    (b) markets are efficient
    (c) markets are well regulated
    (d) none of the above
18. The rate between two currencies determined through the medium of some other currency is known as ________.
    (a) spot rate (b) cross rate
    (c) bid rate (d) forward rate

19. The rate quoted for transactions that call for delivery after 2 business days is known as _________.

    (a) spot rate (b) forward rate
    (c) ask rate (d) cross rate

20. If the forward rate is less than the spot rate, the foreign currency is selling at _________.

    (a) a forward premium (b) a forward discount
    (c) an ask rate (d) a bid rate

21. If the forward rate is greater than the spot rate, the foreign currency is selling at _________.

    (a) a forward discount (b) a forward premium
    (c) a cross rate (d) forward rate

22. A transaction made to profit from price discrepancy is known as _________.

    (a) arbitrage (b) speculation
    (c) spot transaction (d) forward transaction

23. The price of one currency in terms of another currency is known as _________

    (a) foreign exchange rate.
    (b) spot rate
    (c) forward rate
    (d) cross rate

24. Direct quote is the number of units of _________.

    (a) home currency for one unit of foreign currency
    (b) foreign currency for one unit of home currency
    (c) foreign currency for one unit of SDR
    (d) none of the above

Further Reading

1. K. Alec Chrystal, "A Guide to Foreign Exchange Markets," *Federal Reserve Bank of St. Louis Review* (March 1984): 5–18.
2. R. Dornbusch, "Expectations and Exchange Rate Dynamics," *Journal of Political Economy* (1986) 84, 1161–76.
3. Paul R. Krugman and Maurice Obstfeld, *International Economics: Theory and Policy* (Massachusetts: Addison-Wesley, 2002).
4. Michael E. Porter, *The Competitive Advantage of Nations* (Massachusetts: Harvard University Press, 1989).
5. J. Walmsley, *Foreign Exchange Handbook: A User's Guide* (New York: John Wiley, 1983).

CHAPTER 2

The International Monetary System

CHAPTER OBJECTIVES

After studying this chapter, you should be able to:

1 Describe various monetary systems.
2 Understand different exchange rate regimes and their implications.
3 Trace the origin of the euro.
4 Discuss the chronological developments in the exchange rates of the Indian rupee.
5 Highlight the implications of appreciation/revaluation and depreciation/devaluation of currency.
6 Understand the concept of international liquidity.
7 Discuss the concept of sterilization.

Introduction

A *system*, in general, is defined as a group of elements that are integrated with the common purpose of achieving certain objective(s). The **international monetary system** consists of the laws, rules, monetary standards, instruments, and institutions that facilitate international trade and cross-border flow of funds. Every nation has its own monetary system, which guides the monetary policy and economic framework of the government. A *monetary standard* refers to the principal method of regulating the quantity and the exchange value of standard money. Standard money is defined as a monetary unit adopted by a government to serve as the basis of its monetary system. Standard money, simply known as money, is supposed to perform certain functions: unit of account, measure of value, medium of exchange, means of payment, and store of value. In the beginning of human civilization, there was no money. People engaged in barter, the exchange of one commodity or item for another without value equivalence. As there was no common measure of value among the items bartered, the barter system was found to be inadequate. Then the commodity money came into existence. Some commodities like beads, cowries, feathers, ivory, mats, nails, leather, bovine , quartz, cocoa, salt, yarn, gold, silver, copper, and tobacco, etc. were introduced as the medium of exchange at different times and in different places in the world. Coins made of a metal with fixed weight and value, and bearing a mark or effigy of who had minted them, appeared as far back as the 7th century BC. No two coins were absolutely equal to one another as they had been made by hand in a very coarse way. Gold and silver were extensively used in coinage as they had some special features like rarity, beauty, immunity to corrosion, and economic value. People also used to ascribe sentimental or religious value to these metals. They found a relationship between gold and the sun, and silver and the moon. Copper was also used for lesser value coins. Coins made of cupronickel and other metallic alloys were also in circulation. Such coins had their extrinsic value or face value, independent of the value of their metal content. When only one metal is adopted as the standard money, it is known as monometallism or single standard. For example, Britain was on silver standard until 1816. If two metals are adopted as standard money, then it is called bimetallism or double standard. For example, many governments adopted gold and silver as their legal tender money with a fixed ratio of exchange between them. Bimetallism was introduced in France in 1803, followed by other countries like Belgium, Holland, Switzerland, etc.

Chinese were the first to use paper money way back in 1300 AD. They placed the emperor's seal and signatures of treasurers on crude paper made from mulberry bark. In Brazil, the first bank notes were issued by Banco do Brasil in 1810. They had their value written by hand, almost similar to cheques of today. As time passed, many governments adopted paper currency standard. As it is managed by the monetary authority of the country, it is also known as managed currency standard. Though it can function very effectively as money, there is a danger of over-issue of paper money, resulting in a rise in prices, adverse foreign exchange rates and many other bad effects on the economy.

*The **international monetary system** consists of the laws, rules, monetary standards, instruments, and institutions that facilitate international trade and cross-border flow of funds.*

Paper currency standard refers to paper money that has legal sanction for acceptance. Paper currency standard consists of paper money and a certain quantity of token coins made of cheap metal. Paper money is the main currency, and is unlimited legal tender. Even if paper money is not convertible into any metal, people accept it because it is the legal tender, and this is why paper money is known *as fiat money*. The value of paper money is determined by the government or public order, and it is not related to the intrinsic value of that paper. Along with paper money, token coins may also be in circulation to meet smaller requirements.

As various nations may have varying monetary standards, the international monetary system is required to define a common standard of value for various currencies, as the monetary standard of a nation influences national as well as international economic operations. The international monetary system has gone through several changes over the years. In the following sections, we shall take a look at some of these developments.

The Gold Standard

Gold has been used as a medium of exchange since time immemorial because of its special qualities. According to the rules of the **gold standard**, the value of the monetary unit of a country (e.g. paper money) was fixed in terms of a specified quantity and fineness of gold. Governments were committed to a policy of converting gold into paper currency and paper currency into gold, by buying and selling gold at specified rates. The issue or circulation of paper money in a country was backed by its gold reserve at a specified ratio. Thus, the stock of money in a country would increase or decrease with changes in its gold reserves. The exchange rate between any two currencies was determined by the ratio of the price of a unit of gold, in terms of the respective units of each currency. For example, during the period 1821–1914, the United Kingdom had maintained a fixed price of gold at GBP 3.17 per ounce, while the United States maintained it at USD 20.67 per ounce of gold. Accordingly, the U.S. dollar and British pound exchange rate was fixed at GBP/USD 6.5205, which was considered to be the par exchange rate. The other countries that had agreed to the gold standard, fixed the value of their respective currency in terms of gold and, accordingly, they had fixed exchange rates with respect to each other's currency.

*Under the **gold standard**, governments were committed to a policy of converting gold into paper currency and paper currency into gold, by buying and selling gold at specified rates.*

When the value of the monetary unit of each country is fixed in terms of gold, the exchange rate is also automatically fixed by the mint parity or gold parity. In reality, the exchange rate may be different from the mint parity, leading to arbitrage opportunities. However, arbitrage operations will soon exhaust such opportunities and ultimately bring the exchange rates in line with the mint parity. For example, if the gold rate is fixed at INR 2,150 per ounce in India and at USD 35 in the United States, the exchange rate between the Indian rupee and the U.S. dollar will be USD/INR 61.4286. If the actual exchange rate at any time is not INR 61.4286, arbitrageurs will bring it to that level through their buying and selling operations. An example will illustrate how this is possible. Let us assume that the actual exchange rate is USD/INR 62.2897. If arbitrageurs buy gold in India at INR 2,150 per ounce, ship it to the United States, sell it at USD 35, and convert the U.S. dollars to Indian rupees, they can make an arbitrage profit of INR 30.14 per ounce of gold. Conversely, if the exchange rate is INR 60.0000, then arbitrageurs can buy gold in the United States at USD 35 per ounce, ship it to India, sell it at INR 2,150, convert Indian rupees to U.S. dollars, and make an arbitrage profit of USD 0.8333 per ounce of gold. However, such arbitrage profits will disappear very soon and the exchange rate will come to the mint parity level of USD/INR 61.4286. The storage, transportation, and transaction costs are ignored here to make the example simple.

Under the gold standard, any disequilibrium in the balance of payments of a country is adjusted through a mechanism called the *price-specie automatic adjustment mechanism*. A deficit in the balance of payments means that there is an excess demand for gold. It implies that the country should sell gold from its reserves, which has the effect of reducing the money supply in the economy. This, in turn, will cause a fall in general prices. Consequently, the exports of the country will become more competitive (i.e. exports will increase), leading to a decline in the balance of payments deficit of the country. For example, suppose people in the United States buy more goods and services from India than Indians buy from the United States. Net exports from India to the United States will be accompanied by a net flow of gold from the United States to India. As more gold leaves the United States than arrives, money supply in the economy decreases, causing the general prices in the U.S. economy to fall. At the same time, general prices in India will increase consequent to an increase in gold supplies and increase in money supply in the economy. Lower prices in the United States will make U.S. goods relatively cheaper and Indian goods relatively more expensive. So, the demand for U.S. goods in India will increase, ultimately leading to a reduction in the U.S. balance of payments deficit. The reverse process will occur for India, which has a balance of payments surplus.

To generalize, a country having a favourable balance of payments will receive gold from other countries because it has excess foreign exchange receipts over foreign exchange payments. Conversely, a country with a balance of payments deficit will have an outflow of gold on account of excess foreign exchange payments over foreign exchange receipts. The inflow of gold increases the monetary reserves of the country, which, in turn, leads to an increase in the money supply. According to the *quantity theory of money*, other things remaining unchanged, an increase in money supply implies an increase in demand and a rise in the prices of goods and services. Higher prices would make the country's goods and services relatively more expensive in the international market. This would result in a fall in exports, leading to a balance of payments deficit. Thus, a favourable balance of payments caused by a surplus in the country's balance of trade would be automatically corrected. The reverse process would occur with a balance of payments deficit and outflow of gold.

In sum, a country having a balance of payments surplus receives gold and a country having a balance of payments deficit surrenders gold under the gold standard system. The movement of gold from one country to another country influences the money supply in both the countries. As the money supply in an economy is linked to the gold reserves of the country's central bank, any increase (or reduction) in gold reserves will lead to the expansion (or contraction) of money supply in the economy. In other words, if the volume of gold reserves increases, the supply of money in the economy can be increased in the same proportion, and if the volume of gold reserves falls, the supply of money can be reduced in the same proportion. As a result of changes in money supply, the price levels in the economy would change. This, in turn, affects the foreign exchange rates.

From different types of gold standards, such as the gold currency standard, gold bullion standard, gold exchange standard, gold reserve standard, and gold parity standard, each country adopted its own standard, keeping in view its domestic factors. Though each country was free to adopt its own form of the gold standard, it had to adhere to the rules of the standard. Whatever form the gold standard took, the essential feature was that the currency was directly linked to gold, either in volume or in value. For example, the monetary standard that prevailed prior to 1914 in the United States, the United Kingdom, and in certain other countries was known as the *gold standard*. Accordingly, gold coins of a fixed weight and fineness circulated within the country. In the United Kingdom, for instance, the sovereign was the gold coin which contained 123.17447 grains of gold of 11/12 fineness. Although other metallic coins and paper currency notes were also in circulation side by side, they were convertible into gold coins on demand at fixed rates. Similarly, under the *gold bullion standard*, the legal tender in circulation consisted of paper currency notes and token coins of some metal, but they were all convertible into gold bars or bullion at fixed rates. The governments were, of course, required to keep gold bars in reserve to facilitate easy conversion. When the gold bullion standard was in operation in India in 1927, the Indian paper money, the rupee, was convertible into gold bars containing 40 *tolas* at the rate of INR 27-7-10. Thus, the gold standard is a fixed exchange rate system as the exchange rate was determined in terms of gold, and the government was standing ready to freely and readily exchange currency for gold on demand.

The gold standard was widely appreciated because of certain inherent characteristics of gold as well as the rules governing the standard. Under the gold standard, any disequilibrium in the balance of payments of a country gets corrected automatically. As gold is the base for the creation of money in the economy, politicians cannot indulge in unrestrained money creation. Thus, countries can maintain stability in prices as well as exchange rates when they are under the gold standard. Notwithstanding these merits, the gold standard is criticized mainly because of its inflexibility. The rules of the gold standard do not allow the government to increase the money supply in the country without increasing gold reserves, even when the expansion of money supply is necessary to tide over serious situations. Besides, the gold standard cannot bring automatic correction of disequilibrium in the balance of payments unless all the countries follow the rules of the gold standard. For example, the government of a country may think that a reduction in money supply consequent of a balance of payments deficit will raise interest rates and unemployment. At the same time, the government of another country having a balance of payment surplus would not allow its money supply to increase because of the fear of inflation. Further, there may be parallel movement of prices in countries having a balance of payment surplus and in countries having a balance of payments deficit. In all such cases, there would not be an automatic correction of disequilibrium in the balance of payments. Further, the supply of gold cannot be increased at will because of its natural scarcity.

The gold standard that existed till 1914 was called the *classical gold standard* and it was embraced by most nations. The international business of most nations was therefore governed by the classical gold standard. More particularly, during the period 1880–1914, there was a rapid expansion of international trade with stable domestic prices and foreign exchange rates. The cost-price structures of different countries were in line. Along with the free flow of goods, there was also a free flow of labour and capital across countries.

When World War I broke out in 1914, the belligerent countries particularly suffered from high inflation, which made it difficult to fix the values of currencies in terms of gold. Some countries even prohibited making payments to other countries in gold. Since the value of domestic currencies was indeterminate in terms of gold, the par exchange rates could not be determined. This had an adverse effect on the exports and imports of many countries, throwing the international monetary system into turmoil. Further, as there was no inbuilt mechanism to make each country abide by the rules of the gold standard, some countries imposed high tariffs. They also failed to follow the principle of expanding credit when gold flowed into the country, and contracting credit when gold flowed out of the country. Thus, the countries failed to adhere to the rules of the gold standard, contributing to the end of the classical gold standard.

The Gold Exchange Standard

During the postwar period, each country followed its own exchange rate system keeping in view its own domestic compulsions. It was a period of flexible exchange rates that lasted until 1926. Revaluation and devaluation of currencies was undertaken indiscriminately by many countries to serve their own objectives. For example, France devalued its currency to stimulate its own economy, but this was detrimental to Britain. Many countries followed a policy of sterilization of gold by neutralizing the effects of gold flows on the domestic money supply. It was against this backdrop that some major countries, including the United Kingdom and the United States, made efforts to restore the gold standard, which later came to be known as the **gold exchange standard**. According to the new system, which came into effect in 1925, only the United States and the United Kingdom could hold gold reserves, while other countries could hold both gold and U.S. dollars or British pounds as reserves These reserves were meant for managing the balance of payments and thus the foreign exchange rates. Thus, the US dollar and the pound sterling were considered to be reserve currencies, and the other countries on the gold exchange standard had to relate the value of their paper currency to the value of any of the two reserve currencies. The reserve currency country also fixed its currency value to a weight in gold, and got ready to exchange gold for its own currency with other countries. For example, India had chosen British pound sterling as its reserve currency. So it would fix its exchange rate to the reserve currency (pound sterling) and hold a stockpile of reserve currency assets to maintain the exchange rate. It could also get its reserve currency assets converted into gold at any time as the British government was obligated to exchange gold for its currency. In effect, the gold reserves would flow back and forth between the reserve currency country and other countries.

*According to the **gold exchange standard**, only the United States and the United Kingdom could hold gold reserves, while other countries could hold both gold and U.S. dollars or British pound sterling as reserves.*

With the onset of the great depression in 1929, countries failed to follow the rules of the gold exchange standard. Many countries had a balance of payments deficit, resulting in massive outflow of gold. Consequently, the gold reserves of several countries including the United Kingdom and the United States continued to fall to a level where it was very difficult to maintain the gold exchange standard. They also found it very difficult to repay their international borrowings. Further, there was a beggar-thy-neighbour trade war in which nations devalued their currencies to maintain trade competitiveness. As a result, exchange rates fluctuated wildly. Speculators also played havoc with the foreign exchange market. The export earnings of many countries declined considerably, leading to depletion of their gold reserves. Following the stock market crash in 1929, many financial institutions, including commercial banks and investment banks, suffered sharp declines in their asset values. Some countries even experienced a spate of bank failures. Because of the adverse situations faced during such times, countries started getting off gold, one after another. Countries such as the United Kingdom, Canada, Sweden, Austria, and Japan got off gold in 1931. The United States pulled out from the gold exchange standard in 1933, and many other countries followed suit. France abandoned the gold exchange standard in 1936.

All these developments hindered international trade and, consequently, had an adverse effect on global economic growth. It was against this backdrop that the representatives of some major countries met at the Mount Washington Hotel in Bretton Woods, New Hampshire, in July 1944.

The Bretton Woods System

The main aim of the meeting of the representatives of 44 countries at Bretton Woods was to bring about international financial order through an effective monetary system. At the first instance, the representative members reviewed the working of the gold standard and identified the ills of the fixed exchange rate system. They were of the opinion that inadequate international monetary arrangements had contributed to the Great Depression of 1929. Therefore, they felt it necessary to have a system which could provide stable exchange rates under the surveillance of an independent international body. The representatives also proposed that the international body should provide credit facilities to member nations and establish arrangements for international liquidity. So, after a series of deliberations and negotiations, the representatives of 44 nations agreed to have an *adjustable peg exchange rate system* under the gold exchange standard, with currencies convertible into the U.S. dollar, and the U.S. dollar, in turn, convertible into gold. The U.S. dollar was the only currency that would be freely convertible into gold. According to the agreement signed by the representatives, each country would fix a par value of its currency in relation to the U.S. dollar, which was pegged to gold at USD 35 per ounce. For example, the British pound was set at GBP 12.0 per ounce of gold. In other words, the exchange rate between the U.S. dollar and the British pound was set at GBP/USD 2.92. Member countries were expected to maintain their exchange rates within a margin of 1 percent on either side of the par value. In the example given here, the upper and lower support points that the United Kingdom needed to maintain were USD 2.949 and USD 2.891, respectively. The exchange rates were thus allowed to fluctuate only within ±1 percent of the stated par value. Whenever the demand and supply factors in the market caused exchange rates to go outside the permissible limits, countries other than the United States would buy and sell U.S. dollars in the market in order to keep the exchange rates within ±1 percent limits. In case of disequilibrium in the balance of payments of any country, an adjustment process similar to the process under the gold standard would take place.

*The **Bretton Woods system** required that each country should fix a par value of its currency in relation to the U.S. dollar, which was pegged to gold at USD 35 per ounce.*

The United States on its part would stand ready to meet the requests of other nations to buy or sell gold or U.S. dollars. As there was a guarantee of the convertibility of the U.S. dollar into gold, other countries would hold reserves in U.S. dollars as well as in gold. The U.S. dollar thus became the world's reserve currency, and international liquidity came to be governed by the U.S. monetary policy. The new *adjustable peg exchange rate system* came to be popularly known as the **Bretton Woods system**. The new system also limited the scope of governments (other than the U.S. Government) in changing their monetary policy as they wished.

The Articles of Agreement adopted at Bretton Woods also envisaged the creation of two new institutions at the international level—the *International Monetary Fund (IMF)*, and the *International Bank for Reconstruction and Development (IBRD)*, popularly known as the *World Bank*. The chief objective of the IMF is to promote international monetary cooperation and facilitate the balanced growth of international trade. The IMF is also expected to enforce the set of rules governing the international monetary system.

Under the Bretton Woods system, if any country repeatedly faced a balance of payments disequilibrium, which was known as a fundamental disequilibrium, it could change the parity of its currency against the U.S. dollar up to 10 percent in either direction without the prior approval of the IMF. If a country wanted to effect changes larger than 10 percent in the parity rate, it had to obtain prior approval from the IMF. However, this facility was not available to the United States. In other words, the U.S. did not enjoy the privilege of changing the parity of its currency against gold or any other currency. On the contrary, the United States had the responsibility of maintaining the gold value of the U.S. dollar and price stability around the world. Further, whenever other nations wanted to convert their U.S. dollar balances into gold, the United States had to facilitate such conversion. For this, it was also required to maintain enough gold reserves to facilitate the conversion of dollars into gold at any time. As a reward for shouldering such onerous responsibility, the United States was permitted to print more dollars, and thereby derive seigniorage gains. Although the United States was not officially prevented from printing more U.S. dollars, it had to keep in view the world prices, because the printing of more U.S. dollars would lead to spiraling prices at the global level.

In order to partially alleviate the pressure on the U.S. dollar as the central reserve currency, the IMF created *Special Drawing Rights (SDRs),* which represented a basket of major currencies in the world. SDRs were allotted to member countries which, in turn, would use them for transactions among themselves or with the IMF. These SDRs could also be used as reserve assets.

Post-Bretton Woods Systems

The Bretton Woods system worked almost smoothly till the 1960s. There was stability in exchange rates, which effectively promoted international trade and investment. The system also brought about some sort of discipline on the part of member countries as far as their economic policies were concerned. In the early 1970s, however, it was realized that Bretton Woods system was not working as expected. Because of spiraling prices, many countries devalued their currencies by more than 30 percent against the U.S. dollar. A few countries revalued their currencies. Many countries were unable to maintain the par value of their currencies against the U.S. dollar. Further, as these countries recovered from the Great Depression and started reconstructing the devastation caused by World War II, the world economy progressively improved. This led to an increased level of world reserves, which consisted essentially of gold and the U.S. dollar. Since gold production was stagnant, world reserves could be further increased only on increase of U.S. dollar holdings. Moreover, dollar reserves could be kept in securities such as Treasury bills which would yield interest, while gold reserves would not carry any interest. All these factors culminated in mounting of U.S. balance of payments deficit.

Initially, the U.S. balance of payments deficit was not viewed as a problem. However, as the U.S. gold reserves progressively came down and other countries' holdings of U.S. dollar balances increased, countries started doubting the ability of the United States to maintain the gold convertibility of the dollar. The expansionary monetary policy and rising inflation in the United States resulting from financing the Vietnam War, also contributed to the woes of the U.S. economy. Even as the dominance of the United States over the world monetary system weakened, the strength of the European and the Japanese economies progressively improved.

Many countries started putting pressure on the United States to convert U.S. dollar resources into gold, but the U.S. did not have enough gold to honour its commitment to the other nations. Adding fuel to the fire, participating nations did not make necessary economic adjustments to maintain the par values of their currencies. Many countries devalued their currencies against the U.S. dollar at a high rate. The U.S. Government was also unable to manage its economy to keep the gold price at USD 35. It initiated certain measures to slow down the outflow of gold and reduce the mounting pressure to convert U.S. dollars into gold. But all these efforts of the United States failed to stop the run on the U.S. dollar from reaching alarming proportions. Therefore, in mid-1971, the United States decided to give up its role as the anchor of the international monetary system, and devalued the U.S. dollar to deal with the mounting trade deficit. But this did not restore stability to the international monetary system.

Notwithstanding the out-of-control situation, efforts were made to resurrect the gold exchange standard. A group of 10 countries—West Germany, Belgium, Canada, France, Italy, Japan, the Netherlands, the United States, the United Kingdom, and Sweden—met at the Smithsonian Institution in Washington DC in December 1971, and signed an agreement, that came to be known as the *Smithsonian Agreement.* According to the terms of the Agreement, the par value of gold was raised to USD 38 per ounce. Other countries were allowed to revalue their respective currencies against the U.S. dollar by up to 10 percent, and the band within which exchange rates were allowed to move was broadened from 1 percent to 2.25 percent in either direction.

The Smithsonian Agreement, however, did not last long. A few months after signing the Agreement, the foreign exchange rates of major currencies, including the U.S. dollar, became volatile. The U.S. dollar was devalued for a second time and the par value was reduced by an additional 10 percent, that is, from USD 38 to USD 42.22 per ounce of gold. But such measures were not sufficient to stabilize the situation and the U.S. trade deficit continued to rise. The U.S. dollar and the British pound became weak. As a result, there was a massive flow of capital towards countries with strong currencies, such as Germany, Switzerland, the Netherlands, France, and Japan. Therefore, in March 1973, the group of 10 nations announced that they would allow their currencies to float, dealing a death blow to the Bretton Woods system.

The inevitable collapse of the Bretton Woods system was recognized by a noted economist, Professor Triffin. According to the Bretton Woods system, the U.S. dollar could be used as a reserve currency along with gold for making international payments. The U.S. dollar was, therefore, the key currency in the foreign exchange market. As gold is a naturally scarce commodity, an increase in U.S. dollar holdings was the only way for the stock of world reserves to grow along with the increasing international trade. As a result, the United States had to face balance of payments deficits, so that the other nations could accumulate U.S. dollar reserves. However, with the increasing U.S. balance of payments deficits, the confidence of other nations in the ability of the United States to convert U.S. dollars into gold at the par value, diminished. This inherent contradiction, known as the *Triffin paradox* or the *Triffin dilemma,* doomed the Bretton Woods system.

In April 1972, the members of the European Economic Community (EEC) established a *pegged exchange rate system,* called the *snake within the tunnel.* The new system involved fixing the par exchange rate of the currencies of the European Economic Community against each other, and floating these currencies jointly against the US dollar. It allowed for a ±2.25 percent fluctuation of member currencies against the U.S. dollar, but only for a ±1.125 percent fluctuation around a central rate with each of the other member currencies. The 'tunnel' was the band around the U.S. dollar; and the 'snake' referred to the narrower band within which the member countries had to maintain their exchange rate against each other.

The purpose of fixing the band was to narrow down the fluctuation margin in the exchange rates. Although the "snake within the tunnel" was successful in the beginning, it became fragile in the volatile international economic environment. Many hurdles came in the way of the smooth functioning of the snake.

Given the uncertainty in exchange rates, academic discussions began at higher levels on possible reforms of the international monetary system. As the discussions continued, many countries opted for *a floating exchange rate system.* The first major oil crisis in 1973, followed by hyperinflation in many countries also added to the exchange rate crisis.

The IMF convened a monetary summit in Jamaica in January 1976, to approve the following broad options suggested by a committee constituted to evolve an exchange rate system:

1. Floating regimes;
2. Pegging of currencies
   - to a single currency,
   - to a basket of currencies, and
   - to SDRs; and
3. Crawling pegs.

We shall discuss these systems in detail in the following sections. The IMF Articles of Agreement were amended in 1978 to allow each member nation to choose an exchange rate system best suited to its needs, subject to firm surveillance of the member's policies by the IMF. Member countries, individually or in groups, have thus adopted different exchange rate approaches within the broader framework given by the IMF. As these countries were able to choose from a variety of exchange rate regimes, they pegged their currency exchange rates either to the U.S. dollar, the French franc, some other currency, or to some basket or composite currency such as the SDR. Some countries like the United States have allowed their currencies to float independently. The crawling peg was also adopted by a few developing countries. Some countries that had initially opted for a particular exchange rate system, subsequently switched over to a floating exchange rate system. The *floating exchange rate system* has gradually become widely accepted across the countries.

Since 1978, the exchange rate systems of various countries have gone through several modifications. However, the trend has been towards the adoption of more flexible exchange rate systems. Further, with the introduction of the euro, development of emerging markets, evolution of transnational economies, advancement of technologies, and the integration of economies through globalization, many changes have taken place in the international financial structure.

Alternative Exchange Rate Regimes

The international monetary system plays a vital role in the flow of goods, services, and capital across countries. It influences international trade and investments to a great extent. There is a wide choice of exchange rate regimes to choose from, ranging from completely fixed to freely floating, with a number of options in between. A country can choose an exchange rate regime depending on the long-term goals of its economic policy. Countries differ not only in terms of the exchange rate regime they choose, but also in their approach to maintaining the value of their currency in the foreign exchange market.

Foreign exchange rate regimes can be categorized into fixed, intermediate, and floating systems, as shown in Figure 2.1. The spectrum of exchange rate regimes has independent floating exchange rate regime at one end and fixed exchange rate regime at the other end. Intermediate regimes exist between these two extremes. Here, we shall discuss each one of them.

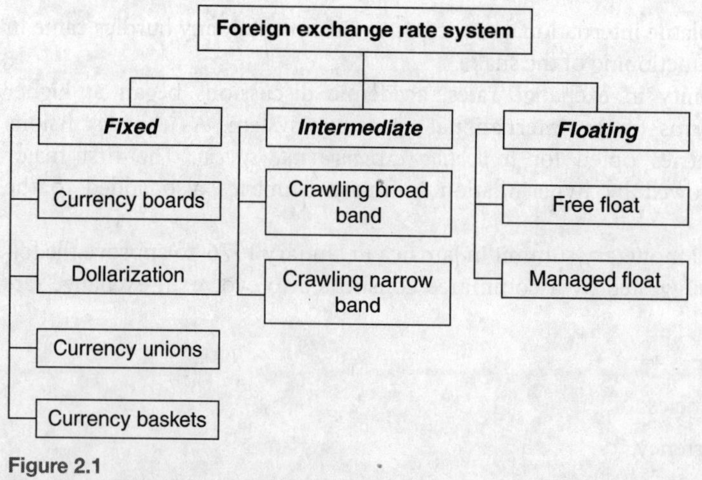

Figure 2.1

Foreign Exchange Rate Systems

Fixed Exchange Rate Under the fixed exchange rate regime, the government of a country is committed to maintaining a fixed exchange rate for its domestic currency against something else, which may be gold or any other currency. To maintain the exchange rate, the government is always ready to buy or sell unlimited quantities of gold or a foreign currency, as the case may be, at a fixed rate. To prevent the exchange rate from appreciating, the government buys gold or a foreign currency in exchange for domestic currency. The increased supply of the domestic currency lowers its value. Similarly, to prevent the exchange rate from depreciating, the government buys domestic currency using gold or a foreign currency. To make such transactions, the government must have sufficient quantities of gold or a foreign currency as well as domestic currency. When the government is not able to maintain sufficient supplies of these currencies, it fails to maintain the exchange rate. Thus, countries which adopt this exchange rate regime must strive to keep exchange rates stable even if the rates they choose deviate from the equilibrium. However, the monetary authority may change its fixed exchange rate by either devaluing or revaluing the domestic currency when the fixed exchange rate is untenable. The gold standard and the gold exchange standard are two classical examples of the fixed exchange rate system.

__A fixed exchange rate system__ is an exchange rate regime in which the government of a country is committed to maintaining a fixed exchange rate for its domestic currency.

The fixed exchange rate system has certain advantages. The main ones are:

- It ensures stability and certainty in exchange rates and thereby eliminates foreign exchange risk.
- It creates confidence in the currency, which promotes international trade and investments.
- It facilitates domestic economic stabilization.
- Countries with fixed exchange rates may have lower sovereign risk and inflation rates.
- Borrowing costs may become less because of lower risks. This may propel the economic development of a country through increasing investments and consumption.
- A country under the fixed exchange rate regime can maintain competitiveness in the world markets, if the peg is credible.

The major deficiencies of fixed exchange rate regime are:

- Exchange rate is determined by the monetary authority without taking into consideration the demand for and supply of the currency.

- Sometimes, the exchange rate is determined by a government on the basis of certain extraneous considerations, leading to trade wars in the international market.
- Although each fixed exchange rate regime has certain rules, a government may bypass those rules for short-term gains.
- Exchange rate determined at the discretion of the monetary authority may also cause uncertainty about the future exchange rates.
- As there is a free flow of goods, services, and investments across the countries, it may not be possible for a country to manage its own economy without independent monetary policy.
- System is inflexible, and therefore leads to slow growth of international trade.
- The countries that were under a fixed exchange regime had to enact laws to control capital flows across the borders.
- High international reserves are required to maintain the exchange rate.
- Prone to currency crisis.
- A fixed exchange rate regime was relevant when there was far less global trade and exchange of currencies.

Floating Exchange Rate At the other end of the spectrum of exchange rate regimes is the pure floating exchange rate. Under the pure floating exchange rate regime, the exchange rate is determined by the forces of demand and supply of a currency vis-à-vis another currency. In other words, the exchange rate is market determined, as there is free flow of goods, services, and capital across the nations. Changes in exchange rates occur continuously and automatically as the exchange rate is free to move according to the changes in demand and supply. The central bank of a country may intervene in the foreign exchange market through purchases or sales of foreign currency in exchange of domestic currency to limit short-term exchange rate fluctuations. But in countries such as the U.S., New Zealand, Sweden, and Iceland the central banks generally never intervene to manage the exchange rates. The countries in the euro zone also fall in the same category.

***The floating exchange rate system** has an exchange rate between two currencies that is determined by market forces.*

The major advantages of the floating exchange rate regime are:

- The floating exchange rate system allows the foreign exchange market to determine what a currency is worth. In the long run, it keeps the balance of payments of all countries in equilibrium through an automatic adjustment mechanism. For example, if a country has a deficit in its balance of payments, the exchange rate of its currency depreciates. This makes the country's exports cheaper and its imports dearer. In other words, the depreciation of the home currency encourages exports and discourages imports, adjusting the country's balance of payments deficit. Conversely, if a country has a balance of payments surplus, the exchange rate of its currency appreciates. Its exports become dearer and its imports become cheaper as a consequence. This ultimately results in adjustments in the country's balance of payments. It has been observed that the disequilibrium in balance of payments can be corrected with fewer disruptions to the domestic economy through a floating exchange rate system than through the fixed exchange rate system.
- If a country is able to control its trade deficit through the floating exchange rate system, it implies that it has a strong economic system.
- A country can boost its image and attract foreign investments by adopting a floating exchange rate system. This can further help the country by indicating to its

stakeholders that its financial system and its treasury management, in particular, are sound.

- Under the floating exchange rate regime, there is no need to bother about tariffs, subsidies, and quotas, etc. as they are automatically taken care of by market forces and, consequently, by the exchange rates.
- Different countries follow different economic policies and, therefore, different cost–price relationships exist. The floating exchange rate reflects the true cost–price relationship between any two countries.
- Another great advantage of the floating exchange rate is that it allows countries to pursue their own economic policies and to maintain their economicsovereignty.
- It allows the flow of investments to their most efficient uses in the world.
- A country may not be required to maintain high international reserves.
- A country may be able to absorb any currency crisis.
- If a country is under the floating exchange rate regime, it can maintain competitiveness in the world markets.

Like most systems, the floating exchange rate system also suffers from certain limitations, some of which are:

- The floating exchange rate system cannot ensure stability in exchange rates, which results in uncertainty and speculation. It is argued that the floating exchange rate system creates uncertainty for activities involving the inflow and outflow of foreign exchange. This uncertainty throws business planning out of gear, leading to economic instability and slow growth of the world economy.
- The floating exchange rate system may encourage speculation in the foreign exchange market and cause violent fluctuations in the exchange rates. This constitutes an additional risk to international trade and investment.
- Countries under the floating exchange rate regime may also witness a high rate of inflation. Countries have to keep their money supply and inflation under control in a fixed exchange rate system, but countries with a floating exchange rate system face no such compulsions. This may result in a high rate of inflation.
- The exchange rates may witness high short-term volatility.
- Unless monetary policy is properly handled, the economy may see many bumps.
- The markets in the economy must be deep enough to absorb shocks without large exchange rate fluctuations.
- The country should also have a developed derivatives market to offer a wide variety of instruments to hedge the risks arising from the exchange rate fluctuations.

Having discussed the two broad exchange rate regimes, viz. fixed exchange rate regime at one end of the spectrum and pure floating exchange rate regime at the other end of the spectrum, let us take a look at the various forms of these two exchange rate regimes.

Currency Board A currency board is a country's monetary authority that issues its base money (notes and coins) convertible into an anchor currency (a stable and internationally acceptable foreign currency) at a fixed exchange rate. The anchor currency is also known as the reserve currency. Although it is possible to fix the exchange rate in terms of a basket of currencies rather than one currency, the currency board may rigidly fix the exchange rate in terms of a single currency. The value and stability of the local currency is directly linked to the value and stability of the anchor currency. A typical currency board has the following features:

- A currency board is a monetary authority that issues notes and coins convertible on demand into a foreign anchor currency at a fixed exchange rate.
- To honour its commitment, it holds reserves of foreign currency (or gold or some other liquid asset) equal at the fixed rate to at least 100 percent of the domestic currency issued.
- Reserve levels are set by law, and are equal to 100%, or slightly more of its monetary liabilities (notes, coins, etc.).
- If it accumulates reserves exceeding 100 percent, it cannot use the surplus in a discretionary manner.
- It has no discretionary monetary policy. The quantity of domestic currency in circulation is determined solely by demand for domestic currency.
- It can issue domestic currency only when it has foreign exchange reserves to back it.

The currency board being protected from political pressures, conducts all affairs transparently, and commands credibility among the national and international community. Thus, the currency board provides a highly credible mechanism for defending a fixed exchange rate, but at the cost of losing its monetary sovereignty. According to IMF, countries such as Hong Kong, Brunei, Bosnia and Herzegovina, Bulgaria, Djibouti, Estonia, and Lithuania are under the currency board.

__A currency board__ is a country's monetary authority that issues its base money (notes and coins). The currency board system requires that the domestic currency be anchored to a foreign currency, which is also known as the reserve currency.

The exchange rate in a currency board system is strictly fixed. For example, the Hong Kong dollar has been officially fixed at USD/HKD 7.80 since the currency board was introduced in 1983. A currency board can function alone or work in parallel to the central bank of the country. If it functions along with the central bank, the central bank virtually loses its monetary autonomy. It cannot set interest rates and inject liquidity into the economy. A currency board is fully committed to the complete convertibility of the local currency into the anchor currency. There are no restrictions on individuals and businesses exchanging the locally issued currency with the anchor currency at a fixed rate, on both current account and capital account. Countries such as Lithuania, Estonia, and Bosnia have their local currencies anchored to the euro. Argentina had a currency board system (anchored to the U.S. dollar), which ended in an economic crash in 2002.

The main advantages of the currency board system are:

- It offers the prospect of a stable exchange rate.
- Besides ensuring monetary discipline in the economy, it generates fiscal discipline by preventing governments from direct monetary financing of government expenditure.
- Exchange rates under the currency board system are less volatile and, thus, less prone to speculative attacks.

However, the major problem with the currency board system is the loss of monetary independence. A country under the currency board system may not be able to respond effectively to external shocks without having an independent monetary policy.

The traditional currency board system had its roots in the English Bank Act of 1844. However, the currency board system no longer exists in its pure form today. These days, currency board-like systems exist instead. Present-day currency boards, for example, may not maintain 100 percent reserves. They are also allowed to use their surplus reserves in a discretionary manner. They are also permitted to accumulate profits unchecked. Further, a central bank may be in place, but with specific rules dictating the level of the reserves it should maintain.

Dollarization Dollarization is a generic term that refers to the use of any other currency (dollar or not) in place of a domestic currency as the legal tender. Some nations abandon their domestic currency and use one of the major reserve currencies. Panama has been using the U.S. dollar as the legal tender since 1904. There are as many as ten countries using the U.S. dollar exclusively. They include countries such as Ecuador, British Virginia Islands, East Timor, and El Salvador. These countries have adopted the U.S. dollar as their national currency of circulation. Countries such as Lesotho, Namibia, and Swaziland use South African rand as their currency of circulation. Some countries use two or more currencies. For example, Lebanon uses the U.S. dollar along with the Lebanese pound. North Korea uses euro along with the Chinese yuan, USD, and North Korean won. There are also countries using the U.S. dollar or euro alongside other currencies. Nauru has adopted Australian dollar as its currency but it also uses New Zealand dollar alongside.

When a country is unable to manage its own economic affairs, it may become an adjunct to the country issuing the currency. The dollarized country does not have its own monetary policy as its money supply is tied to the money supply of the country whose currency it has adopted. For example, the interest rates in the dollarized country must be the same as those prevailing in the anchor-currency country. Otherwise, the investments would flow into or out of the country as investors always seek higher returns. The prices of goods and services must also be almost equal with those of the reserve currency country. Otherwise, the arbitrage comes in to play. But the reserve currency country never considers the monetary needs of the dollarized country, as dollarization is not the same as the monetary union like the euro zone.

The system of adopting the currency of another nation as the legal tender is known as ***dollarization****.*

Currency Union Presently, there are four regional currency unions in the world. A currency union is an agreement among the member countries of the union to share a common currency, and a single foreign exchange policy. When some countries feel that multiple currencies and exchange rate fluctuations are seriously affecting their trade, they may adopt an exchange rate regime known as a *currency union*. In such a regime, countries decide to adopt a common currency so that, by definition, exchange rates between the member countries of the union disappear. The largest currency union in the world has been formed by 24 countries, using the euro as its common currency. The euro is managed by the European Central Bank that has a mandate to implement a common monetary policy and maintain price stability in the euro zone. The initial exchange rate between the euro and the US dollar was EUR/USD 1.18.

Eight member countries of IMF such as Antigua and Barbuda, Dominica, Grenada, Montserrat, St. Kitts and Nevis, St. Lucia, St. Vincent, and Grenadines, and two overseas territories of United Kingdom—Anguilla and Montserrat formed the Organization of Eastern Caribbean States with the Treaty of Basseterre in 1981. Later, they formed the Eastern Caribbean Currency Union (ECCU) under the monetary authority of the Eastern Caribbean Central Bank. They also agreed to share a common currency called the Eastern Caribbean dollar (EC dollar), which has been pegged to the US dollar since 1976 at USD/ECD 2.70. The EC dollar was pegged to pound sterling at an exchange rate of GBP/EC 4.80 from 1950 to 1976. The rationale for pegging the ECD to USD is that most of the external trade and financial flows are carried out with the US.

Countries such as Benin, Burkina Faso, Cote d'Ivoire, Guinea-Bissau, Mali, Niger, Senegal, and Togo formed the West African Economic and Monetary Union (also known by its French acronym, UEMOA) and agreed to share a common currency called the CFA franc.

The Central African Economic and Monetary Community (CEMAC) was formed in March 1994 by five former French colonies in Central Africa such as Cameroon, Central African Republic, Chad, Congo Republic, Gabon, and a former Spanish colony, Equatorial Guinea. The CEMAC was set up for sub-regional integration through the formation of a monetary union, with the Central African CFA franc as the common currency.

The CFA franc zone is a monetary union of countries in West and Central Africa that grew out of the financial arrangements between France and some of its colonies. Way back in 1947, the CFA franc was initially fixed to the French franc (FF) at one CFA franc as equivalent to FF 0.02. Later, in January 1994, the CFA franc was devalued to one CFA franc as equivalent to FF 0.01. When the euro came into existence, the peg of the CFA franc was changed from the French franc to euro at the rate of EUR/CFA franc 655.957 with effect from 1 January 1999.

Although, both UEMOA and CEMAC are in the CFA franc zone, each has a separate central bank, which issues CFA coins and banknotes. The CFA coins and banknotes issued in the UEMOA zone are not accepted in the CEMAC zone and vice versa. In other words, there is no direct convertibility between the two African CFA francs. The countries using the CFA franc have a formal understanding with the Government of France to maintain their currency peg and to take the sole responsibility of guaranteeing convertibility of CFA francs into euros.

Currency Baskets When a country has many major trading partners, or pegging its currency to another single currency might be risky at times, the country might peg its currency to a basket consisting of a certain number of foreign currencies. When the currencies are not equally important, weights should be assigned to each currency in accordance with the economic power of the nations whose currencies are included in the basket. Generally, currency baskets often include a small number of major currencies.

A basket of currencies is likely to be less volatile than a single currency. If the currencies for a basket are chosen correctly, the resulting peg will be more stable, and thereby reduce the exchange rate risk. By fixing the domestic currency value to a basket of currencies, a country can reduce wide fluctuations in the exchange rate, which will ultimately benefit many market participants, particularly those who have taken an open position in the currencies included in the basket. Pegging to a trade-weighted basket of currencies is also preferred when a country's trade is highly diversified and the exchange rates among the major trading partners tend to undergo large fluctuations. But, if a country's predominant share of trade is in one major currency, pegging to that major currency is desirable. Managing of currency baskets can be quite cumbersome. Therefore, a composite currency like SDR is used by some of the countries to peg their currencies. For example, Saudi Arabia has pegged its currency to the SDR and Botswana has pegged its currency to a basket consisting of the SDR and the South African rand. Such an arrangement would be simple to operate and, moreover, it would provide a more transparent system of currency management.

*There is no intervention by the monetary authority of a country in exchange rate determination when the domestic currency is **freely floated** against the foreign currency.*

Free Float In a **free float**, the government does not announce a parity rate; therefore, there is no intervention by the monetary authority in the foreign exchange market. Exchange rates vary in accordance with changes in the demand and supply of a currency. Demand and supply are influenced by several factors, which may include economic factors, social factors, political factors, and technological factors. In other words, any change in environmental factors may result in a change in the demand or supply of a currency. As the changes in environmental factors occur at random, the demand or supply of a currency may follow irregular patterns. Further, as market participants respond to new information instantaneously, the exchange rates keep changing. The free float is also known as the *pure float* or the *clean float*.

Managed Float In a free float, exchange rates may change so violently as to make international financial transactions very risky. The violent fluctuations in exchange rates can cause a lot of uncertainty about the future spot rates for market participants. This will vitiate the investment climate and international financial transactions. Therefore, a country may adopt a managed float system to guard against such untoward or uncertain situations. Under a managed float, the monetary authority of the country may occasionally intervene in the foreign exchange market, and buy or sell the domestic currency or foreign currency as per the requirement.

*Under a **managed float** system, the government intervenes in the foreign exchange market whenever it wants the exchange rate to move in a particular direction or to stabilize at a target level.*

Intervention by the government in the foreign exchange market to smooth out exchange rate fluctuations is known as a **managed float** or a **dirty float**. The managed float is primarily aimed at eliminating excess volatility and reducing uncertainty. When a government does not make an upward or downward change in its exchange rate when such a change is warranted, it also amounts to a managed float. This is because a managed float is not only for smoothing out daily fluctuations, but also for moderating or preventing short-term or medium-term fluctuations. Where there is light intervention by the monetary authority in the foreign exchange market to moderate excessive fluctuations, the float is a lightly managed one, and in such cases the foreign exchange rate is essentially determined by the market forces.

Currency Pegging **Currency pegging** involves fixing the value of a currency in relation to the value of another currency. A currency can be pegged to another currency, to a basket of currencies, or to SDRs. A country with a pegged exchange rate establishes a fixed exchange rate with another currency or a basket of currencies. So, the values of the pegged currencies move together over time. Generally, a country may peg its currency to the currency of its major trading partner in order to stabilize its trade receipts and payments. If a particular country's currency is not pegged, any change in the value of the currency of the country with which it has major trade relations, will adversely affect the cash flows of the country. Further, pegging may avoid the risk of taking a wrong decision with regard to devaluation or revaluation of the currency. The effort required for making changes in exchange rates can be minimized when a currency is pegged to another strong currency, because the value of the currency will automatically move with the value of the other currency, regarding which the other country has made a thorough analysis.

***Currency pegging** involves fixing the value of a currency in relation to the value of another currency or a basket of currencies.*

A currency may also be pegged to a basket of currencies, which will give more stability to the exchange rate. Similarly, a currency may also be pegged to the SDR, which itself is pegged to a basket of four currencies—the euro, the Japanese yen, the British pound, and the U.S. dollar—at present.

The pegging of a currency may take a form of hard pegging, adjustable pegging, or soft pegging. In the case of *hard pegging,* exchange rates are fixed and the government has no plans to change them. Currency boards and dollarization are examples of hard pegging. In reality, hard pegging corresponds to fixing the exchange rate to a hard currency, and holding enough reserves to back up the peg. Hard pegs are successful in countries with sound fiscal policy and low inflation. The countries with hard pegs cannot have an independent monetary policy as their interest rates are tied with those of the anchor-currency country. Thailand can be an example of disastrous currency pegging, and Zimbabwe can be an example in the success stories of currency pegging. The *adjustable pegging* system allows the government to revise or adjust exchange rates periodically. The Bretton Woods system is a case in point. *Soft pegging* involves frequent adjustment of exchange rates. This may be high-frequency pegging (day-to-day or week-to-week pegging) or low-frequency pegging (month-to-month or quarter-to-quarter pegging). Soft pegs are generally vulnerable to financial crises, which may lead to abandonment of the peg.

The **crawling peg** is a hybrid system with some features of the floating exchange rate system and some features of the fixed exchange rate system. It involves fixing a par value of a currency and allowing the exchange rate to move within a given percentage. If the actual exchange rate approaches a certain limit, the central bank intervenes by buying or selling home currency for the required foreign currency. In other words, a country which adopts this system is committed to maintaining its exchange rate within a certain margin at any point in time. For example, Mexico pegged its currency (peso) to the U.S. dollar. In the 1990s, when the inflation differential between the two countries increased considerably, Mexico adopted a crawling peg to devalue the Mexican peso drastically. Under the crawling peg system, however, governments are at liberty to revise the par value, as well as the limits in response to changes in the macroeconomic environment. Thus, the crawling peg system avoids violent fluctuations in the exchange rate without being purely flexible.

__A crawling peg__ may contain some features of the floating exchange rate system and some features of the fixed exchange rate system.

A crawling peg may take the form of a crawling broad band or a crawling narrow band. In a *crawling broad band,* the limits around the central parity are wide enough (say, ±20 percent) to provide more flexibility. Thus, the exchange rates are fixed, but considerable fluctuation is permitted around the central parity rate. It provides more flexibility and is closer to a floating system in terms of its merits and shortcomings. On the other hand, the *crawling narrow band* (e.g. the Bretton Woods system) is almost equivalent to the fixed exchange rate regime.

The IMF Classification of Exchange Rate Regimes

The IMF has classified exchange rate regimes in the following way:

- *Exchange arrangements with no separate legal tender*: A country adopts the currency of another country as the sole legal tender by giving up its own currency. This includes currency unions and dollarization.
- *Currency board arrangements*: These are regimes in which a nation commits to exchanging its currency for a foreign currency at a pre-specified rate.
- *Conventional fixed peg arrangements*: These exchange rate regimes differ from currency board arrangements only in the legal structure of the regime.
- *Pegged exchange rates within horizontal bands*: These are regimes in which a country allows only limited movement in exchange rates.
- *Crawling pegs*: Crawling pegs are essentially the same as pegged exchange rates, except that the price at which the currency is traded changes over time but in small amounts.
- *Exchange rates within crawling bands*: These are a combination of crawling pegs and pegged exchange rates with horizontal bands (wider bands).
- *Independently floating*: These are systems where the exchange rate is independently determined by market forces.
- *Managed floating*: Although the exchange rate in managed floats is determined by market forces, occasionally, the government seeks to influence the exchange rate through purchase or sale of the currency.

The distribution of the IMF member countries as per their exchange rate regimes is presented in Table 2.1. As shown in the table, there were more soft pegs at the end of April 2013 than others. Further, there has been a shift from floating to soft pegs or hard pegs over the period from 2008 to 2013. The preference for hard pegs has increased, perhaps because of strong external demand. Countries may shift from one regime to another due to various reasons. For instance, during the East Asian crisis (1997–98), the affected countries allowed their currencies to float when they could no longer defend their pegs. In moving from one regime to another, nations must exercise caution to avoid economic disruption.

Table 2.1 Exchange Rate Arrangements, 2008–2013 (percent of IMF members)

Exchange rate arrangement	*30 April 2008*	*30 April 2013*
Hard pegs	**12.2**	**13.1**
No separate legal tender	5.3	6.8
Currency board	6.9	6.3
Soft Pegs	**39.9**	**42.9**
Conventional peg	22.3	23.6
Stabilized arrangement	12.8	9.9
Crawling peg	2.7	1.0
Crawl-like arrangement	1.1	7.9
Pegged exchange rate within horizontal bands	1.1	0.5
Floating	**39.9**	**34.0**
Floating	20.2	18.3
Free floating	19.7	15.7
Residual (Other managed arrangement)	**8.0**	**9.9**

Source: IMF Annual Report on Exchange Arrangements and Exchange Restrictions (2013).

The U.S. dollar remains the currency of choice for countries with hard pegs as well as soft pegs. This reflects the importance of the U.S. dollar as an invoicing currency. It also reflects the high share of trade of many countries with the United States or with countries that have pegged their currency to the U.S. dollar. The euro is the next important currency and serves as an exchange rate anchor for countries in Europe and the CFA franc zone in Africa.

Selection and Management of Exchange Rate Regimes

Both the floating exchange rate system and the fixed exchange rate system have their own advantages and limitations. No country can afford to allow its exchange rate to float continuously, as a fluctuating exchange rate is not favourable for domestic economic stability. Volatile exchange rates disrupt the smooth flow of goods, services, and capital across political borders. At the same time, no country can follow a rigid fixed exchange rate system, particularly in an era of globalization of trade and investments. Therefore, a country may adopt a system that combines the advantages of the two systems. The extent to which the exchange rate should be floating and the extent to which it should be fixed, cannot be generalized. Depending upon the needs of its economy and other factors, a country can design its own exchange rate regime or adopt a regime that already exists elsewhere in the world.

Each nation chooses an exchange rate regime that will enable it to achieve its economic objectives. A large number of countries including the United States, the United Kingdom, Canada, Japan, New Zealand, and Australia allow their currencies to float independently in the foreign exchange market. The exchange rates of these currencies are essentially determined by market forces. Under the floating exchange rate regime, the monetary and fiscal policies of a country do not have to be subordinated to the needs of defending the exchange rate. The supporting policies (monetary policy and fiscal policy) can be guided by nominal anchors such as the target inflation rate and the target growth rate. Thus, the floating exchange rate regime allows greater autonomy to the monetary authority in pursuing the objectives of the economy (e.g., price stability and growth), while leaving the exchange rate adjustment to the market forces.

Countries such as Russia, Singapore, Pakistan, India, and Vietnam are under the managed floating system. Some countries may also have a mixture of fixed and floating exchange rate regimes. A few countries including Hong Kong have pegged the value of their currencies to hard currencies like the U.S. dollar or the euro. Some countries do not have their own national currencies. They use the currencies of other countries. Some countries jointly use a particular currency. For example, some African countries jointly use the CFA franc, which is fixed to the euro through the French franc. Foreign exchange rates significantly influence the flow of goods, services, and capital across countries and exert strong pressure on the balance of payments, inflation, and other macroeconomic variables. Therefore, the choice and management of exchange rate regimes is a critical aspect of the economic development of a country. Ideally, a country needs a regime that gives rise to three policy goals, viz. stable exchange rates, independent monetary policy, and open capital account. Stability of the exchange rates is required to avoid uncertainties and currency risk. An independent monetary policy provides considerable flexibility to cope with external shocks in an orderly way without affecting the economic objectives of the country. An open capital account enables the economy to get integrated with the world economy. A fixed exchange rate regime avoids volatility in the exchange rates, and thereby brings stability to the exchange rates. The floating exchange rate regime places no restrictions on the monetary policy of the country but causes volatility in the exchange rates. An open capital account cannot go concurrently with the other two policy goals. These three policy goals cannot be achieved together and, therefore, they are known as the 'impossible trinity'. For example, the main monetary policy objective of India is to maintain price stability. When inflation starts increasing, India raises the interest rates. Suppose the Indian rupee is pegged to the U.S. dollar, the U.S. investors will find an incentive to convert their dollars into Indian currency to earn a higher interest in India than what they could earn in the U.S. This would increase the demand for Indian rupee and decrease the demand for the U.S. dollar. Therefore, the Indian government would have to increase the supply of rupee to keep the exchange rate pegged. But increasing the supply of rupee will increase the money supply in the economy, leading to higher inflation. This goes against the monetary policy objective of the country. In view of these conflicting impacts, a country should balance all these three policy frameworks. The current policy framework of India comprises partial convertibility under the capital account and a floating exchange rate policy with the Reserve Bank of India having to intervene in the foreign exchange market to curb volatility arising due to demand–supply mismatch in the foreign exchange market. However, a country requires consistent and supportive monetary and fiscal policies to maintain a stable and competitive real exchange rate.

Exchange Rate Policy and Monetary Policy

A country's choice of exchange rate system has implications for its monetary policy. Monetary policy is the policy that controls the money supply in the economy. Under a fixed exchange rate regime, the government of a country fixes the exchange rate and controls the money supply in the economy to defend the exchange rate. The monetary policy of such a country is dedicated to maintaining the exchange rate, and it cannot be used simultaneously for controlling domestic prices (inflation) and interest rates. For example, to maintain the exchange rate, the government may have to print unlimited quantities of its own currency. This may lead to an increase in prices and inflation in the country.

A close relationship also exists between interest rates and the inflation rate. Further, interest rates influence the flow of funds from foreign countries to the domestic country, and vice versa. Any policy that restricts the free flow of funds, will lower the value of its currency. This is likely to have an impact on the money supply as well as the interest rates in the economy. In view of such cause-and-effect relationships, the monetary policy of a country that adopts a fixed exchange rate regime is likely to be quite different from one that has not adopted such a system. By pegging its currency to another currency, a country loses its monetary autonomy, because it essentially adopts the monetary policy of a foreign country.

The Par Rate of Exchange

*The **par rate of exchange** is the ratio between two currencies that would equalize their relative purchasing power.*

The value of a currency in terms of the value of another currency is determined by the forces of demand and supply of that currency. As demand and supply are susceptible to many changes in the domestic and international environment, the exchange rate of a currency is subject to variations, and, at times to violent movements. Market sentiment and speculative forces may also cause sudden changes in exchange rates. All such changes, however, are temporary or day-to-day fluctuations. In the long run, the exchange rate of a currency is determined by the relative purchasing power of the two currencies in terms of goods and services. The **par rate of exchange** is thus the ratio between two currencies that would equalize their relative purchasing power. The par rate of exchange is known as a *standard rate of exchange* between two currencies, and it is used as a reference rate in various contexts.

Regional Monetary Integration—A Case of European Union

The formation of the *European Economic Community* (EEC) in 1958 was the first major step towards the integration of European countries. The EEC subsequently became the European Community (EC). It initiated several measures to bring about a high level of integration in Europe. The first major economic initiative was the establishment of the *European Monetary System* (EMS) in 1979, with the *European Currency Unit* (ECU) as the monetary unit. The EMS was aimed at the integration of the monetary systems of European nations to make Europe as a zone of monetary and exchange rate stability. All the members of EEC except the United Kingdom and Greece joined the EMS. The ECU was an artificial composite monetary unit made up of a basket of specified amounts of currencies of the European Community (EC). In other words, the ECU was a weighted average of each of the EMS currencies, the weights being worked out based on each currency's relative GNP and share in intra-EU trade.

The ECU went through a series of turbulent events. Therefore, its member nations met at Maastricht, the Netherlands, in December 1991 and signed an agreement that came to be known as the Maastricht Treaty. As a follow-up, a new international organization called the European Union was created in 1993, with membership extending to 28 European countries to enhance their political and economic integration. The new organization was required to fix the exchange rates between the currencies of member nations and introduce a common European currency replacing individual currencies. Accordingly, a new currency called the euro was created, which became operational with effect from 1 January 1999. The countries that initially signed the agreement were Germany, Belgium, Spain, France, Ireland, Italy, Luxembourg, the Netherlands, Austria, Portugal, and Finland. Greece was admitted into the treaty after two years, but the United Kingdom, Denmark, and Sweden deferred their joining.

Each national currency of the euro countries was irrevocably fixed to the euro at a certain conversion rate. The conversion rate between a pair of currencies was obtained by using the euro conversion rates of the two currencies. On 4 January 1999, the euro started trading at USD 1.18. Originally, the euro was an electronic currency, but on 1 January 2002, euro notes and coins were introduced into circulation. The euro was in circulation side-by-side with the national currencies of the member countries till 2001. From the year 2002, the euro substituted the national currencies of member nations. As per the treaty, all euro zone countries have to follow strict fiscal discipline.

As far as structural framework is concerned, the European Central Bank (ECB) was established in 1998 to monitor the monetary policy of the European Union and maintain price stability. The national central banks of the euro zone countries, together with the European Central Bank, form the European System of Central Banks, which aims at (i) defining and implementing the common monetary policy of the European Union; (ii) conducting foreign exchange operations; and (iii) holding and managing the official foreign exchange reserves of the euro zone nations. As on 1 November 2014, there were 24 countries using the euro. They are Andorra, Austria, Belgium, Cyprus, Estonia, Finland, France, Germany, Greece, Ireland, Italy, Kosovo, Latvia, Luxembourg, Malta, Monaco, Montenegro, the Netherlands, Portugal, San Marino, Slovakia, Slovenia, Spain, and the Vatican City. Only 18 of the 27 members of the European Union (EU) are part of the euro zone, the name for the collection of EU countries that utilize the euro. The countries such as Andorra, Kosovo, Montenegro, Monaco, San Marino, and the Vatican City are not EU members but do officially use the euro as their currencies.

By using a common currency, the member nations aimed at reducing transaction costs involved in the exchange of national currencies. The common currency would help eliminate uncertainties related to foreign exchange rates, and eliminate the need for hedging transactions within the euro zone. The reduction of transaction costs and elimination of foreign exchange risk would encourage trade and investment across the euro zone. With the common currency, the economies of the euro zone countries would become integrated, which would ultimately enhance the competitive strength of the European economies in the international market. It was also expected that the euro, along with the U.S. dollar, would dominate the world economy, and would also result in the political unionization of Europe. The advantages of the single currency may be summed up as below:

- The international trade of the participating countries would increase with the stability in the exchange rates.
- Travellers do not need to change money when travelling through the countries that constitute the euro zone.
- Transaction costs get reduced when countries use the common currency.
- As there is no exchange rate uncertainty, the firms will not face any currency risk.
- Firms can save hedging costs as there is no currency risk.
- Price comparison becomes easy with the common currency.
- Increased cross-border investments across countries in the euro zone.
- Cost reductions and enhanced efficiency will increase international competitiveness of the businesses in the euro zone.
- Common currency might also increase the depth and liquidity of the capital markets in the euro zone.
- Borrowing costs would decrease with enhanced international credibility of the nations in the euro zone.

- Eliminates the problem of current account deficits.
- Central banks in countries of the euro zone do not need to maintain foreign exchange reserves.
- Single currency may also reduce political risks.
- Increased inward FDI with increased market size.
- Credible commitment to low inflation.

But each of the above advantages comes at a cost. Thus, the disadvantages of having a single currency are as below:

- Countries in the euro zone lose independence in the monetary policy as well as in the exchange rate policy.
- Countries in the monetary union cannot address asymmetric shocks without monetary independence.
- Unless the labour markets are highly flexible to encourage labour mobility, nations in the monetary union may not achieve maximum benefits with the single currency.
- The monetary union involving economies with wide variations in development levels may face severe problems. For example, countries such as Greece, Ireland, Portugal, and Spain faced serious fiscal deficit problems in the early part of this decade. But for the bailout packages worked out by the EU, these countries would have pulled out of the union.

Exchange Rate of the Indian Rupee

The Indian rupee (INR) was historically linked with the British pound (GBP) in view of India's political and economic relations with the Great Britain. The Reserve Bank of India (RBI) was empowered to buy and sell foreign exchange as needed. When the IMF was created and member countries were asked to specify the par value of their currency, the Indian Government expressed the par value of the INR at 4.14514 grains of fine gold, which corresponded to the exchange rate of INR 1 = 1s.6d (in the old system, s. denoted shillings and d. denoted pennies, which were smaller denominations of the British pound). The RBI maintained the par value of the INR within the permitted range of ±1 percent using the pound sterling as the intervention currency. The Indian rupee was devalued in September 1949 to 2.88 grains of fine gold; and again it was devalued in June 1966 to 1.83 grains of fine gold. The rupee–pound exchange rate was revised to INR 100/GBP 4.7619. The U.S. dollar parity of the rupee was also fixed at INR 100/USD 13.3333. The exchange rate of the Indian rupee remained unchanged during the period between 1966 and 1971. As per the Foreign Exchange Regulation Act, 1947, the Reserve Bank of India, and in certain cases, the Government of India controlled and regulated the dealings in foreign exchange.

After the collapse of the Bretton Woods system in 1971, major world currencies were brought under floating exchange rate regimes. In December 1971, the INR was linked with the pound sterling, which itself was fixed in terms of the U.S. dollar under the Smithsonian Agreement of 1971. As major currencies including the pound sterling were floating in the foreign exchange market, the RBI felt the need to peg the INR to a basket of currencies in order to ensure its stability. Accordingly, with effect from 25 September 1975, the INR was pegged to a basket of currencies. Although the currencies included in the basket and their relative weights were kept confidential in order to avoid speculation, it was understood that they were the currencies of India's major trading partners. However, the British pound continued to be the intervention currency of the RBI. While maintaining the Indian rupee's value with respect to the basket of currencies, a band of 2.25 percent on either side of the base value of GBP/INR 18.3084 was adopted.

For the first time, the banks in India were permitted in 1978 to undertake intra-day trading in foreign exchange. The exchange rate regime was characterized by daily announcement by the Reserve Bank of India of its buying and selling rates with a spread of 0.5 percent. The banks as authorized dealers were also permitted to trade in cross currencies. The foreign exchange market was highly regulated with several restrictions on external transactions. The exchange rate was also under strict watch. All such controls had in fact propelled the growth of the *hawala* (unofficial) market as a parallel foreign exchange market.

The period between late 1980s and early 1990s was one of most turbulent periods in the economic history of India. Accentuated by the Gulf crisis, the current account deficit widened to 3.2 percent of GDP in 1990–91, and the capital flows dried up. The Indian rupee was devalued by 9 percent and 11 percent between 1 and 3 July 1991 to counter the massive drawdown in the foreign exchange reserves, to instill confidence among investors and to improve competitiveness in the external sector. This effectively brought to close the regime of the pegged exchange rate. It was against this backdrop that the Indian Government undertook certain economic reforms, following the recommendations of the High level Committee on Balance of Payments (Chairman: Dr C. Rangarajan).

In 1992, the RBI instituted a dual exchange rate under the liberalized exchange rate management system (LERMS), according to which 40 percent of export proceeds and inward remittances were to be purchased at the official exchange rate as determined by the Reserve Bank of India. The remaining 60 percent of the receipts and all payment transactions were to take place at the market exchange rate. However, all capital receipts and capital payments continued to be under the control of the RBI, and these transactions were to be made at the market rate, except in the case of the IMF and other multilateral agencies. Although the LERMS served to impart stability to the external value of the Indian rupee, the spread between the official exchange rate and the market rate widened over time. Further, other distortions including the diversion of remittances took place. Therefore, the Government of India decided to converge the dual rates with effect from 1 March 1993, whereby all foreign exchange receipts could be converted at market-determined exchange rates. The INR was allowed to float, but within the framework of the RBI. With this change, India had a managed float and the RBI could intervene in the market by buying and selling foreign exchange as needed. The restrictions on a number of other current account transactions were also relaxed as per Article VIII of the Articles of Agreement of the IMF, leading to current account convertibility in August 1994. Thus, the Indian rupee is determined by demand and supply forces in the foreign exchange market. However, the Reserve Bank of India closely monitors exchange rate movements and intervenes, if necessary. The exchange rate policy of the RBI is to ensure that the exchange rate of the INR moves in an orderly way, without much volatility.

On 2 August 1993, foreign exchange trading in India switched over from indirect quotes to direct quotes, with the U.S. dollar as the base currency. With the Indian rupee made fully convertible under the current account, foreign exchange trading in India began to be more buoyant. Following the recommendations of the Committee on Fuller Capital Account Convertibility, the capital account has been gradually opened. Although there has also been significant liberalization in capital account outflows, the capital account has been dominated by inflows in the form of portfolio investments including global depository receipt (GDR) issues, foreign direct investments, commercial borrowings, and nonresident deposits.

Following the recommendations of the Expert Group on Foreign Exchange Markets in India (Chairman: O. P. Sodhani) and of the Committee on Capital Account Convertibility

(Chairman: S. S. Tarapore), the Government of India and the Reserve Bank of India have brought about so many reforms for the development of the foreign exchange market. The initiatives mainly aimed at dismantling controls and providing an enabling environment to all participants in the foreign exchange market. The focus has been mainly on developing the institutional framework and increasing the instruments for effective and transparent functioning of the foreign exchange market. The various measures or initiatives of the Government of India and the Reserve Bank of India have had a significant effect on the market structure, depth, liquidity, and efficiency of the foreign exchange market in India. The Indian rupee has shown a strong correlation with many currencies and integrated itself with many currencies, particularly with other Asian currencies.

Depreciation, Appreciation, Devaluation, and Revaluation

In a fixed exchange rate system, governments may change exchange rates to achieve certain objectives. The change may be in either direction, that is, it may be an increase or a decrease. Reduction in the value of a currency relative to another currency is known as **devaluation of currency**, and the opposite phenomenon—an increase in the value of the currency relative to another currency—is referred to **revaluation of currency**. Following the two consecutive wars in 1960s, which resulted in a huge budget deficit, India devalued its rupee against the U.S. dollar from 4.79 to 7.57 in 1966. Again, in 1975 and in 1985 the Indian rupee was devalued to 8.39 and 12, respectively, against the U.S. dollar. In 1991, India faced a serious balance of payment crisis and was forced to devalue the rupee to 17.90 against the U.S. dollar. As an example for revaluation, China announced in July 2005, a revaluation of its currency, marking a 2.1 percent appreciation of the renminbi–U.S. dollar, and a change in its exchange rate arrangement to allow the value of its currency to float, based on market supply and demand with reference to an undisclosed basket of currencies.

In the floating exchange rate system, a currency fluctuates according to the supply and demand in the market. In such a system, exchange rates may move in either direction without direct intervention from the government. Under the floating exchange rate system any increase in a currency value relative to another currency, is called **appreciation of currency**, and a fall in a currency value relative to another currency is called **depreciation of currency**. Let us consider an example to understand these phenomena better. A firm that wants to acquire 1 USD on 15 January 2008 would have to pay INR 39.45. By 20 February 2008, the firm would have had to pay INR 39.68 for the same trade. In this case, the U.S. dollar is said to have appreciated. When the U.S. dollar appreciates, more INR are required to buy the same number of U.S. dollars. The INR is said to have depreciated against the U.S. dollar in such a scenario.

Table 2.2 Movements in Cross-currency Exchange Rates against USD (percent)

Currency	*End-Aug 2013 over end-June 2013*	*End-Dec 2013 over end-Aug 2013*	*Aug 12, 2014 over end-Dec 2013*
Argentine peso	(–) 5.0	(–) 13.1	(–) 21.1
Brazilian real	(–) 7.3	0.2	3.3
Chinese yuan	0.1	1.1	(–) 0.8

(Continued)

Table 2.2 ***(Continued)***

Currency	*End-Aug 2013 over end-June 2013*	*End-Dec 2013 over end-Aug 2013*	*Aug 12, 2014 over end-Dec 2013*
Euro	1.2	4.1	(–) 3.2
Indian rupee	(–) 10.3	7.4	1.3
Indonesian rupiah	(–) 9.1	(–) 10.6	4.5
Malaysian ringgit	(–) 3.7	0.2	3.1
Mexican peso	(–) 2.4	2.1	(–) 0.6
Russian rouble	(–) 1.6	1.6	(–) 9.3
South African rand	(–) 3.1	(–) 1.6	(–) 1.6
South Korean won	3.5	5.2	2.4
Thai baht	(–) 3.0	(–) 2.3	2.3
Turkish lira	(–) 5.3	(–) 4.1	(–) 1.6

Source: Handbook of Statistics on Indian Economy 2013–14, Reserve Bank of India.

Table 2.3 Exchange Rate of Indian Rupee

Month/Year	*SDR*		*USD*		*GBP*		*EUR*		*JPY*	
	High	*Low*	*High*	*Low*	*High*	*Low*	*High*	*Low*	*High*	*Low*
Aug 2010	70.34	71.08	46.02	47.08	72.22	73.69	59.19	61.26	53.34	55.96
Aug 2011	70.65	74.24	44.05	46.13	72.09	75.76	62.87	66.70	55.93	59.98
Aug 2012	83.25	84.81	55.15	56.08	86.00	88.10	68.03	69.92	70.01	71.68
Aug 2013	91.68	103.95	60.74	68.85	91.95	106.03	80.37	91.47	61.04	70.25
Aug 2014	91.78	94.30	60.43	61.56	100.12	103.50	79.65	82.41	58.01	60.64

Source: Reserve Bank of India, *Annual Report 2013–14*.

The percentage of depreciation or appreciation of the U.S. dollar against some select currencies in the world can be seen in Table 2.2. The U.S. dollar appreciated against most currencies. The percentage of depreciation or appreciation has not been uniform across currencies. The major currencies have depreciated against the USD on the fears of tapering of quantitative easing by the U.S. Fed. The INR plummeted to a fresh all-time low of 68.85 against the USD on 28 August 2013, a sharp depreciation of around 13.3 percent between July 23 and August 28, 2013. This was mainly because of the developments in the Indian stock market, following the announcements of commencement of QE tapering by the U.S. Fed, which forced foreign institutional investors to sell their Indian stocks and realize their money in USD. The heavy buying of USD resulted in a sharp depreciation of the INR against the USD. Huge short-term debt redemptions have also put pressure on the INR.

As can be observed from Table 2.3, the Indian rupee touched its historic low of 68.85 against the U.S. dollar in August 2013. But it made a turnaround consequent to the measures taken by the Reserve Bank of India. The measures included relaxation in rebooking of cancelled forward contracts, concessional swap window for attracting FCNR (B) deposits, and

Under the fixed exchange rate regime, any increase in the exchange rate of the domestic currency relative to a foreign currency is known as ***devaluation****, and any decrease is called* ***revaluation****. The same phenomena, under the floating exchange rate regime, are known as* ***depreciation*** *and* ***appreciation****, respectively.*

enhancement in overseas borrowing limits of authorized dealers (Ads). The deferment of QE tapering by the U.S. Fed and also the easing of geopolitical tension over Syria aided the Indian rupee to make a turnaround.

Governments, through their respective central banks, may intervene in foreign exchange operations with certain objectives. For example, a rise in the value of the Indian rupee against the U.S. dollar will translate into a reduction in the INR prices of imports from the United States. This will contribute to the slowing of inflation in India. Therefore, if the Government of India aims at reducing the inflation rate in the country, it may take steps to see that the Indian rupee appreciates, which will translate into a reduction in the inflation rate. Conversely, if the Government of India wants to promote its exports, it may directly intervene in the foreign exchange market, and thereby cause depreciation of the Indian rupee. This will make Indian products cheaper in foreign countries and will result in an increase in the consumption of Indian goods abroad, ultimately leading to an increase in Indian exports. However, the fall or rise in the value of a currency has some distinctly negative consequences for the country's economy. For example, declining INR prices of imports are accompanied by increasing foreign currency prices of Indian goods sold abroad. Indian goods and services become less competitive in the international market as a consequence of the rise in the value of the Indian currency. Similarly, Indian-made import substitutes also become less competitive in the Indian market. The decline in the sales of import substitutes will raise the level of unemployment and its attendant problems. Alternatively, home currency devaluation/depreciation results in higher prices for imported goods and services, and this contributes to spiraling inflation rates in the domestic economy. Imports, which become dearer as a result of devaluation/depreciation of the home currency, also affect the living standards of the people, particularly those who consume foreign goods and services.

Under the fixed exchange rate system, governments may maintain target exchange rates keeping in view different aspects of their respective economies. Whenever the exchange rate becomes untenable, governments may take recourse to currency devaluation or revaluation. Similarly, under the floating exchange rate system, governments may intervene in the foreign exchange market through the buying or selling of currencies. The ultimate aim of the government might be to maintain a rate of exchange at which the home currency is neither overvalued nor undervalued vis-à-vis other currencies.

The governments may effect increase or decrease in the money supply in their respective economies to influence foreign exchange rates. However, an attempt to increase or decrease the money supply in an economy may have implications for the other economy. For example, intervention by the Reserve Bank of India in the foreign exchange market may cause a rise in the supply of money in India, which may have implications even for money supply in the United States. This in turn, will have many other economic implications (changes in interest rates, changes in profit margins and valuation of companies, income redistribution, etc.). For example, the Bank of Japan unexpectedly announced that it would increase holdings of government bonds by JPY 80 trillion and boost exchange-traded fund purchases to JPY 3 trillion. Following the announcement of this monetary stimulus programme, the Japanese yen fell to 112.320 against the USD on 31 October 2014 (weakest since January 2008). The Indian rupee also gained to touch INR 0.54710 against 100 yen on 31 October 2014 on this monetary development of Japan. Following the depreciation of JPY, the stocks of some of the Japanese companies listed in Indian stock markets such as Maruti Suzuki, Hitachi Home Appliances, Sharp India, Ricoh, Honda Siel Power, etc. gained between 1 percent and 7 percent on 31 October 2014. As these companies source raw materials from Japan, the depreciation of yen against the Indian rupee would help them to reduce their raw material cost.

Convertibility of Currency

A currency is considered convertible only if both residents and non-residents have full discretion to use and exchange the currency for any purpose whatsoever. In practice, many currencies in the world are convertible with varied degrees of restrictions and controls. The International Monetary Fund (IMP) stipulates that "no member shall, without the approval of the Fund, impose restrictions on making of payment and transfers for current transactions."

Convertibility of currency may be under current account or capital account. The current account includes all transactions that give rise to or use of the country's income, while the capital account consists of short-term and long-term capital expenditure transactions. According to the Foreign Exchange Management Act, a *capital account transaction* is a transaction that alters the assets or liabilities, including contingent liabilities, outside India of persons resident in India, or assets or liabilities in India of persons resident outside India. Transactions which are not capital account transactions are *current account transactions.*

Current account transactions thus cover the following:

* All imports and exports of merchandise
* Invisible exports and imports
* Inward private remittances (to and fro)
* Pension payments (to and fro)
* Government grants (both ways)

Capital account transactions consist of the following:

* Direct foreign investments (both inward and outward)
* Investment in securities (both ways)
* Other investments (both ways)
* Government loans (both ways)
* Short-term investments on both directions

The Indian rupee is allowed to be convertible under the current account. Accordingly, the INR is fully convertible at market-determined exchange rates on the trade account and on the account of the receipt side of the invisibles. The IMF concept considers convertibility only for current account transactions and leaves it to the discretion of the country to regulate flows on capital account. Although convertibility under capital account is not allowed in India, the Reserve Bank of India follows a constructive and promotional approach and encourages foreign investments in the country. Indian industrialists are also allowed to invest abroad. In other words, exchange control in India is limited to exchange rate monitoring.

In order to move towards fuller capital account convertibility (FCAC), the Reserve Bank of India constituted a committee under the chairmanship of S. S. Tarapore in March 2006. The Committee submitted its report on 31 July 2006. It recommended a broad timeframe of a five-year period in three phases for fuller capital account liberalization: 2006–07 (Phase I), 2007–08 and 2008–09 (Phase II), and 2009–10 and 2010–11 (Phase III). The Committee observed that under an FCAC regime, the banking system might be exposed to greater market volatility.

The Committee also observed that countries intending to move towards FCAC need to ensure that different market segments in their economy are well integrated. If different markets remain segmented, any policy designed to influence market behaviour will not get transmitted to all segments, leading to inefficiency of policy implementation. Therefore, the Committee made certain recommendations for the development and integration of financial markets in the Indian economy. These include specific recommendations for each market—the money market, the government securities market, and the foreign exchange market. The recommendations of the Committee for the foreign exchange (forex) market are:

- The spot and forward markets should be liberalized and extended to all participants, removing the constraint of past performance/underlying exposures.
- Forex business should be separated from lending transactions, and an electronic trading platform on which forex transactions for small and medium customers can take place should be introduced. For very large trades, the Committee proposed a screen-based negotiated dealing system.
- The RBI's intervention in the forex market shall be through the anonymous order matching system.
- There should be an increase in limits for banks on short-term and long-term borrowing/lending overseas to promote more interest parity with international markets.
- FIIs shall be provided with the facility of cancelling and re-booking forward contracts and other derivatives booked to hedge INR exposures.
- Currency futures should be introduced, subject to risks being contained through a proper trading mechanism, structure of contracts, and regulatory environment.
- The existing guaranteed settlement platform of the Clearing Corporation of India Ltd (CCIL) shall be extended to the forward market.
- The banking sector shall be allowed to hedge currency swaps by buying and selling without any monetary limits.

Following the recommendations of the S. S. Tarapore Committee and also of the O. P. Sodhani Committee, several measures have been initiated, some of which are mentioned below:

- The Clearing Corporation of India Limited was set up in 2001.
- The RBI delegated powers to authorized dealers to release foreign exchange for a variety of purposes.
- Technical Advisory Committee (TAC) on Money and Securities Market has been expanded to include the foreign exchange market.
- Hedging instruments such as currency options, interest rate swaps, currency swaps, currency futures, etc. have been introduced.
- Authorized dealers are permitted to initiate trading positions, borrow, and invest in overseas markets subject to certain specifications.
- Authorized dealers are permitted to use derivative products for asset liability management.
- FIIs and NRIs are permitted to trade in exchange-traded derivative products, subject to certain conditions.
- Foreign exchange earners are permitted to maintain foreign currency accounts.
- General permission has been granted to persons resident in India for purchase/acquisition of securities out of funds held in an RFC account, etc. General permission is also available to sell the shares so purchased or acquired.
- A resident Indian can remit up to the limit prescribed by the Reserve Bank from time to time, per financial year under the Liberalised Remittance Scheme (LRS), for permitted

current and capital account transactions including purchase of securities and also setting up/acquisition of JV/WOS overseas with effect from 5, August 2013.

- An Indian party can make an overseas direct investment in any bonafide activity.

International Liquidity and International Reserves

International liquidity refers to those financial resources and facilities that are officially available to a country for settling imbalances in international payments. The various components of international liquidity are gold and foreign currencies held by the monetary authority of a country, borrowing facilities available from the IMF, special drawing rights (SDRs), the borrowing capacity of the country in the international market, and so on. Thus, the term "international liquidity" refers to the country's international reserves as well as its capacity to borrow in the international market. Where gold is held as a reserve asset, its market value is listed, but gold cannot be directly used to settle payments between central banks. In other words, gold is no longer used as a means to settle international payments.

Official reserve holdings may include some foreign currency that is universally acceptable and convertible. Throughout the latter part of the nineteenth century, the British pound served as a universally acceptable currency alongside gold, into which it was convertible. Subsequently, the U.S. dollar has rivalled the GBP as a world currency. Any currency which is to serve satisfactorily as a reserve currency for other countries should satisfy certain conditions. It must be the currency of a great trading nation. The currency should be easily acquired via normal trade. It must have a stable value, or at least, in a world where currencies are losing value, it must lose value no faster than other currencies. It must be a currency that is supported in its home country by a strong banking system. Such a currency must also be free from recurrent scarcity. Any currency which is a candidate for the international reserve must be close to meeting these criteria, and the extent to which it conforms to them is likely to determine its success.

The main purposes of holding foreign exchange reserves are: (i) to maintain public confidence in the capacity of the country to honour its international obligations; and (ii) to increase the capacity of the monetary authority to intervene in the foreign exchange market. In other words, foreign exchange reserves are mainly held for precautionary and transaction motives, and also for achieving a balance between demand and supply of foreign currencies.

India's foreign exchange reserves are shown in Table 2.4. India faced a foreign exchange reserve crisis in the early 1990s, as the reserves were quite inadequate even for the essential needs of the country. At the end of March 1991, India's foreign exchange reserves were meager at just USD 5.8 billion. This was one of the factors behind the country embarking on the liberalization process, and it resulted in the opening up of the economy for foreign investments. Following liberalization, the foreign exchange reserves of the country have

Table 2.4 Foreign Exchange Reserves of India (USD million)

Month/Year	*SDRs*	*Gold*	*Foreign currency assets*	*Reserve tranche position*	*Total*
July 2011	4,609	25,349	286,160	2,972	319,090
July 2012	4,353	25,715	256,573	2,135	288,775
July 2013	4,369	20,747	250,273	2,180	277,568
July 2014	4,423	21,174	292,510	1,702	319,808

Source: Reserve Bank of India, *Annual Report 2013–14*.

increased at a fast pace. Foreign direct investments, ECBs, and portfolio investments have contributed enormously to the foreign exchange reserve kitty of the country. India had foreign exchange reserves of USD 319,808 million at the end of July 2014, as against USD 277,568 million at the end of July 2013. This increase reflects better economic performance on the government's part, and is also a mark of financial strength. The other side of the coin is that a vast build-up of reserves carries costs. Foreign exchange reserves are typically invested in low-yielding securities or deposits. Further, a huge foreign exchange reserves may also fuel inflation in the economy. A distinguishing aspect of foreign exchange reserves of India is that the reserves held by India are not really earned, but rather borrowed in nature. Unlike many other countries, India has not accumulated its reserves by having a surplus under its current account, but rather on account of having capital flows far in excess of the absorptive capacity of the economy.

Let us take a look at some ways to determine how much forex reserve is adequate for a country.

Measures of Adequacy of Foreign Exchange Reserves

There are several indicators of the adequacy of foreign exchange reserves. Some of them are:

- A rule of thumb that has evolved with current account deficit, particularly for developing countries, is that foreign exchange reserves should be equal to at least three months of imports. This measure is more useful in situations where capital flows are strictly controlled. This is called *import adequacy.*
- In the context of a large volume of debt servicing, it is recommended that payment liabilities, in addition to imports, should be taken into account while determining the target level of reserves. This is called *debt adequacy.*
- In the context of volatility of capital flows, reserve adequacy can be measured in terms of a ratio of short-term debt and portfolio stocks to reserves. With such a cushion of reserves, in the event of a reversal of capital flows, the monetary authority would be able to prevent a precipitous depreciation of the exchange rate. This is called *capital adequacy.*
- Another measure of reserve adequacy is the net foreign exchange assets to currency ratio. This would prevent unwarranted expansion of currency and ensure remedial measures are put in place long before a balance of payment deficit reaches crisis levels. This is called *monetary adequacy.*

These alternative indicators of reserve adequacy should provide enough safeguards to countries to arm themselves against any contingency. Though it is very difficult to define the optimum level of reserves in terms of a quantifiable norm, a country may set its own reserve level by keeping in view:

- the structural aspects of its balance of payments;
- the nature of shocks;
- the degree of flexibility in the exchange rate regime; and
- its access to the international capital market.

The more open an economy and the greater the variability of its trade, the greater is the need for reserves. For example, a country that depends heavily on exports may have more volatile export earnings and, therefore, needs a good cushion of foreign exchange reserves. On the other hand, a country that has good access to international capital needs fewer reserves.

However, it has been observed that a country that holds higher reserves usually prospers less than it logically should.

When a country is opened up to international trade and investments, it may face frequent ups and downs in its balance of payments. In other words, a country may be susceptible to a foreign exchange crunch as it becomes more open. The IMF has instituted several schemes to guard against such an eventuality. The scheme of creation and allotment of SDRs to member countries has helped many countries in solving the problem of international liquidity. The other initiatives under which the IMF can help countries increase their international liquidity are the compensatory financial facility, the buffer stock facility, the extended financing facility, and supplementary financing.

The management of international reserves should constantly include assessments of the benefits and costs of holding reserves. The main benefit of holding reserves is that it helps in preventing external crises. The cost is mostly the opportunity cost, which is the forgone return on investment. The reserves may be invested in assets of top quality, but a good proportion of reserves needs to be easily convertible into required resources.

Among various currencies that form the world's foreign exchange reserves, the U.S. dollar is dominant, with more than a 65 percent share, followed by the euro, the Japanese yen, and the British pound. With the decline in relative importance of gold as an international means of payment, the importance of currencies like the U.S. dollar, the British pound, and the euro has grown quite significantly. Although foreign currency assets are maintained as a multicurrency portfolio, they are valued in U.S. dollars.

Intervention and Sterilization

Intervention of central banks or monetary authorities in foreign exchange markets is not a new phenomenon. Until the last decades of the 20th century, most of the currencies had been under the fixed exchange rate regime. It means that direct intervention in the foreign exchange market by the monetary authority was a necessary condition. Because, under the fixed exchange rate regime, the monetary authority must stand ready to defend the exchange rate through direct intervention and monetary policy. That is, the monetary authority should always ready to clear any excess demand or supply of foreign currency to maintain a fixed exchange rate. When soft peg and free floating regimes have come to be adopted by several countries, the intervention of the monetary authorities of most countries has become discretionary. But no monetary authority ever keeps off the foreign exchange market. Intervention by the monetary authority in the foreign exchange market may take different forms, depending on the purpose(s) of intervention.

The monetary authorities intervene in the foreign exchange market for different purposes. Some of them are as below:

- To stabilize the exchange rate by minimizing overshooting in either direction;
- To provide liquidity to the market;
- To reduce exchange rate volatility;
- To avoid disorderly market by leaning-against-the- wind;
- To bring alignment of exchange rates with the fundamentals, thereby bringing exchange rates towards equilibrium;
- To maintain export competitiveness;
- To protect the currency from speculative adventurism;

- To bring change in expectations about future market fundamentals;
- To manage the currency composition of their reserve portfolios;
- To make commercial profit as any other market participant; and
- To conduct market operations on behalf of important customers such as the governments.

A government may use both its monetary policy and exchange rate policy to achieve its macroeconomic goals like price stability or full employment. Under the fixed exchange rate regime, the government has no independent monetary policy. It means that the government must give up its ability to control money supply in its own country to maintain the fixed exchange rate. However, under the floating exchange rate regime, a government can manage its own economy through monetary policy—expanding the money supply to stimulate the demand in the economy, or contract it to rein in inflation.

The central bank of a country buys or sells foreign currency in order to set right the temporary mismatch between the demand and the supply of a foreign currency. Such intervention in the market affects the money supply in the economy. The purchase of foreign currency by the central bank will have an expansionary impact, and the sale of foreign currency will have a squeezing impact on the money supply, which in turn has implications for price stability and financial stability in the economy. For example, the Reserve Bank of India may purchase U.S. dollars from the market in order to create demand for U.S. dollars and thereby prevent the U.S. dollar from depreciating against the INR. When the central bank buys U.S. dollars, it releases fresh INR into the economy. This increases the money supply in the economy. If the Reserve Bank of India does nothing else to offset the transaction of buying the foreign currency by using the domestic currency, then it has engaged in an unsterilized foreign exchange intervention. Rather, the Reserve Bank of India undertakes the purchase or sale of foreign currency, followed by an open market operation of the same size to offset the impact of the purchase or sale of foreign currency on the monetary base. This process is known as the sterilized foreign exchange intervention. For example, the Reserve Bank of India buys USD 10 million worth of U.S. bonds, then without any other action, the rupee money supply would increase by INR 610 million (assuming USD/INR 61). But if the Reserve Bank of India sells INR 610 million worth of treasury securities, then that money is withdrawn from the economy. In other words, the RBI has sterilized the purchase of U.S. bonds by selling the domestic currency termed securities.

Thus, sterilization involves two transactions: (i) sale or purchase of foreign currency and (ii) an open market operation involving the purchase or sale of domestic currency securities in the same size as the first transaction. The purpose of the open market operation is to effectively offset or sterilize the impact of the intervention in the foreign exchange market on the monetary base of the country. Unsterilized intervention refers to sale or purchase of the foreign currency but no open market operations to offset.

The sterilization keeps the base money and the money supply unchanged, and thereby avoids the undesirable expansionary effects of capital inflows. As long as the central bank has enough international reserves, it can sterilize the money supply in the economy. Thus, sterilized intervention provides the central banks with the means of influencing the exchange rates, independent of their domestic monetary policy goals.

The central banks can intervene in the foreign exchange market by participating in the spot market and/or currency derivatives market. The central banks can also influence the exchange rates by some indirect methods such as taxes, restrictions on international transactions, exchange controls, etc.

India has initiated several measures to attract foreign capital into the economy. Consequently, there has been a large increase of capital flows into the Indian economy. During the year 2013–14, India could attract as much as USD 26,385 million through foreign investment inflows (net). But in 2012–13, India got foreign investment inflows of USD 46,711million. It is also observed that capital flows in 'gross' terms affect exchange rates by several times higher than 'net' flows on any day. The capital flows, both inward flow and outward flow, have influenced exchange rates to become significantly more volatile than before. This has forced the Reserve Bank of India to become more active in the foreign exchange market. For example, in June 2014 the Reserve Bank of India made a foreign currency purchase of USD 5,522 million and foreign currency sales of USD 2,880 million. The Reserve Bank of India has also become very active in the currency forward market. At the end of April 2014, the Reserve Bank of India had outstanding net forward sales of USD 32,062 million. In addition to direct intervention in the foreign exchange market, the RBI has initiated a number of steps to manage the excess liquidity in the economy that is caused by foreign exchange inflows. These include a phased liberalization of the policy on the capital account, issuing of Government of India-dated securities/Treasury bills, and increasing the cash reserve ratio. In the process of managing the liquidity in the economy, the Reserve Bank of India has also announced a host of measures to liberalize overseas investments.

***Sterilization** is the process of neutralizing the effects of purchase or sale of foreign currency on the monetary base of the economy.*

Summary

1. The *international monetary system* refers to the laws, rules, monetary standards, instruments, and institutions that facilitate international trade and cross-border investments.
2. Under the *gold standard,* the exchange rate between two currencies was determined by the price of a unit of gold in terms of respective units of the currencies. The *gold exchange rate system* prescribed that only the United States and United Kingdom could hold gold reserves, while other countries could hold gold and U.S. dollars or the British pound as reserves.
3. According to the *Bretton Woods* system, each country had to fix a par value of its currency in relation to the U.S. dollar, which was pegged to gold at USD 35 per ounce. Member countries were expected to maintain their exchange rates within a margin of 1 percent on either side of the par value. The main aim of the Bretton Woods system was to maintain stable exchange rates and, at the same time, economize on gold.
4. Under the *fixed exchange rate system,* governments are committed to maintaining a fixed exchange rate for their currencies against the foreign currency.
5. When countries are under the *floating exchange rate system,* the exchange rate between two currencies is determined by the forces of demand and supply.
6. A country with a *pegged exchange rate* establishes a fixed exchange rate with another currency or a basket of currencies so that the values of the pegged currencies move together over time.
7. The euro has emerged as the common currency for 24 nations.
8. The Indian rupee is allowed to float in the foreign exchange market, but within the framework of the Reserve Bank of India. The central bank may intervene in the foreign exchange market with certain objectives.
9. Devaluation of currency refers to official decrease in the exchange rate and revaluation is the official increase in the exchange rate. When the value of a currency falls in relation with another currency, it is known as depreciation, and when the value of the currency goes up in relation to another currency, it is known as appreciation.
10. Devaluation and revaluation are official changes under the fixed exchange rate system; and depreciation and appreciation are changes that happen under the influence of market forces.
11. *International liquidity* refers to those financial resources and facilities that are available to a country for international financial settlements.
12. *Sterilization* refers to the process of neutralizing the effects of purchase or sale of foreign currency on the money supply in the economy.

Questions and Problems

1. Discuss the evolution of the international monetary system.
2. How is the exchange rate determined under the gold standard? What are the limitations of the gold standard?
3. How can balance of payments disequilibrium be corrected through the flexible exchange rate system?
4. What are the objectives of the Bretton Woods system?
5. What are the advantages and limitations of the floating exchange rate system and the fixed exchange rate system?
6. Explain the concept of managed float.
7. What are the advantages of currency pegging?
8. Describe the Triffin paradox.
9. Define par value of currency.
10. What are the important features of the Smithsonian Agreement?
11. What are the implications of devaluation/depreciation of a currency for trade and investment?
12. Trace the emergence of the euro.
13. What do you mean by sterilization? Why is sterilization required?
14. What is international liquidity? What constitutes international reserves?

Multiple-choice Questions

1. Standard money is _________.

   (a) Monetary unit (b) Gold
   (c) Silver (d) None of these

2. Paper money is known as _________.

   (a) Foreign currency
   (b) Fiat money
   (c) Money created by commercial banks
   (d) None of these

3. Under the gold standard, a deficit in the BOP means that there is _________.

   (a) Excess demand for gold
   (b) Less demand for gold
   (c) Excess demand for US dollar
   (d) None of these

4. Under the gold exchange standard, only _________ were allowed to hold gold reserves.

   (a) USA (b) USA and Brittan
   (c) Brittan (d) None of these

5. Representatives of _________countries participated in the meeting held at Bretton Woods.

   (a) 100 (b) 44
   (c) 144 (d) None of the above

6. A fixed exchange rate system reduces _________-.

   (a) Business risk (b) Currency risk
   (c) Political risk (d) None of these

7. Under a pure floating exchange rate regime, a country may not require _________.

   (a) High foreign exchange reserves
   (b) Current account surplus
   (c) Stable exchange rate
   (d) None of these

8. India is under _________.

   (a) Fixed exchange rate regime
   (b) Independent Floating exchange rate regime
   (c) Managed float
   (d) None of these

9. Currency Union can be categorized under _________.

   (a) Fixed exchange rate regime
   (b) Floating exchange rate regime
   (c) Managed float
   (d) None of these

10. CFA franc is the common currency for _________.

    (a) European Union (b) CEMAC
    (c) USA (d) None of these

11. When a currency value is changed in small quantities, it is known as _________.

    (a) Currency pegging (b) Crawling peg
    (c) Dirty float (d) None of these

12. _________is the most invoicing currency.

    (a) Euro (b) USD
    (c) JPY (d) None of these

13. The par rate of exchange is the ratio between two currencies that would equalize their _________.

    (a) Relative purchasing power
    (b) Inflation rates
    (c) Exchange rates
    (d) None of these

14. The currency of Great Britain is _________.

    (a) Euro (b) Pound sterling
    (c) Yen (d) None of these

15. The main aim of interventional sterilization is to _________.

    (a) Keep the exchange rates unchanged
    (b) Keep the money supply unchanged
    (c) Increase interest rates
    (d) None of these

16. Devaluation is _________.

    (a) Officially reducing the currency value
    (b) Increase in the exchange rate by market forces
    (c) Decrease in the exchange rate by demand and supply
    (d) None of these

Further Reading

1. Richard N. Cooper, *The International Monetary System: Essays in World Economics* (Cambridge: MIT Press, 1987).
2. Robert Triffin, *Gold and the Dollar Crisis* (New Haven: New University Press,1960).
3. G. Bird, ed., *The International Financial Regime* (London: Surrey University Press, 1990).
4. H.G. Grubel, ed., *International Monetary Reforms—Plans and Issues* (Palo Alto: Stanford University Press, 1963).
5. R. McKinnon, *Money in International Exchange* (Oxford: Oxford University Press, 1979).
6. P. De Grauise, *The Economics of Monetary Integration* (Oxford: Oxford University Press, 1992).
7. Robert Solomon, *The International Monetary System,1945–1981* (New York: Harper & Row, 1982).
8. Michael D. Bordo, "The Gold Standard, Bretton Woods, and Other Monetary Regimes: A Historical Appraisal," *Review* (March/April, 1993):123–187.

CHAPTER 3

The Balance of Payments: Implications for Exchange Rates

CHAPTER OBJECTIVES

After studying this chapter, you should be able to:

1. Understand the concept of balance of payments (BOP).
2. Discuss the principles of BOP.
3. Understand the components of the current account, capital account, and reserve account.
4. Analyse the association between national income and international economic transactions.
5. Define BOP identity.
6. Analyse the BOP under alternative exchange rate regimes.
7. Discuss the implications of the BOP for money supply.

Introduction

*The **balance of payments (BOP)** is an accounting statement that summarizes the international economic transactions of a country for a particular period of time.*

However developed a country may be, it has to depend on other countries for something or the other, as no country can produce all that is required for its people. The economies of the world are necessarily interdependent, especially in this era of globalization. Specifically, international trade flows and international capital flows have become the order of the day, making international economic transactions the way of life. It is in this backdrop, a statement of balance of international economic transactions is prepared by every country. Such a statement is called the **balance of payments**, popularly known as **BOP**. In this chapter, we shall discuss the concept and principles of BOP, and analyse its components.

The Balance of Payments Manual

The standards for compiling the BOP are laid out in the International Monetary Fund's (IMF) *Balance of Payments Manual*. The IMF prepares and updates the manual in close consultation with BOP experts in member countries and international organizations including the Organisation for Economic Co-operation and Development (OECD), the United Nations, and the World Bank. The IMF also publishes the *Balance of Payments Compilation Guide* and the *Balance of Payments Textbook*, which are companions to the *Balance of Payments Manual*. So far, the IMF has brought out the Manual in six editions, and the latest edition was released in 2009. As defined in the *Balance of Payments Manual*, the BOP is a statistical statement that systematically summarizes, for a specific time period, the economic transactions of an economy with the rest of the world. The transactions between the residents of a country and the rest of the world involve:

- goods, services, and incomes;
- financial claims on the rest of the world (foreign assets) and liabilities to the rest of the world; and
- transfers.

The BOP is thus an accounting statement that reflects all international economic transactions during a given period, usually a year, between the residents of one country and the residents of other countries. The term *resident* in this context is broad, and includes individuals, governments, government institutions, private non-profit bodies, and enterprises. The IMF's *BOP Manual* has also defined a *transaction* as an economic flow that reflects the creation, transformation, exchange, transfer, or extinction of economic value and involves changes in ownership of goods and/or financial assets, the provision of services, or the provision of labour and capital.

The Manual clearly states that BOP is not concerned with *payments* but with *transactions.* A number of international transactions that are of interest in a BOP context may not involve payment of money, and some are not paid in any sense. These transactions, along with those that involve actual payments, would distinguish between a BOP statement and a record of foreign payments.

Functions of the BOP

The main functions of a country's BOP are:

- The BOP helps understand how various economic transactions are brought into balance in a given period. These transactions can include trade in goods and services; purchase and sale of assets, including securities; and transfer of funds through grants, aids, and repatriations.
- An analysis of the BOP also reveals how a country is paying for its imports and other transactions, the extent of export earnings in the total credits, and the adequacy of foreign exchange reserves.
- The BOP also indicates the extent of external indebtedness of a country, along with its cushion of foreign assets. This enables the government to make appropriate decisions with regard to monetary and fiscal policies, foreign trade, and international payments. In other words, BOP acts as a guide to the monetary, fiscal, trade, and exchange rate policies of a government.
- BOP statistics are also used extensively by business enterprises and others who engage in international economic transactions.

Principles of BOP

The BOP is based on the principles of **double-entry bookkeeping**, according to which two entries—credit and debit—are made for every transaction, so that the total credits exactly match the total debits. All economic transactions which lead to payment, either immediate or prospective, from foreigners to the residents of a country are recorded as *credit entries.* The corresponding debit entries are the payments themselves. Conversely, all transactions which lead to payment by residents to foreigners are recorded as debit entries, and the corresponding payments themselves are recorded as credits. These rules can be better understood with the help of an example. Assume that an Indian firm sells products worth INR 1 million to a firm in the United States, and the US buyer pays for it in Indian currency. The sale of the product is recorded as a credit entry, and the payment made by the foreigner is recorded as a debit entry. Conversely, consider an Indian firm that purchases INR 5 million worth of machinery from a firm in the United States. The import of machinery is recorded as a debit entry to indicate an increase in purchases made, and the corresponding payment is recorded as a credit entry to reflect an increase in liabilities to a foreigner.

*The principles of **double-entry bookkeeping** underlie the preparation of the balance of payments. Accordingly, two entries—credit and debit—are made for every international economic transaction of the country. In an accounting sense, the BOP always balances.*

The following are the rules for credit and debit entries in the BOP:

- An international transaction that leads to a demand for domestic currency in the foreign exchange market or a transaction that is a source of foreign currency is to be recorded as a **credit entry** in the BOP. For example, a US importer who has purchased goods invoiced in Indian currency must purchase Indian currency. This gives rise to a demand for Indian currency. Therefore, such transactions are recorded as credits.
- When India (for example) receives payment from another country, it increases the foreign assets of India. The payment is either credited to the bank account of the resident of India or a claim is created on the non-resident. This increase in foreign assets (or a decrease in foreign liabilities) is recorded as debit entry in the BOP of India.
- A transaction that results in the supply of home currency in the foreign exchange market, or a transaction that uses foreign currency is to be recorded as a **debit entry**. For example, when a firm in India imports machinery from a firm in the United States, the corresponding payment results in a supply of Indian currency, or an increase in the demand for foreign currency. Such transactions are recorded as debits.
- When a payment is made by an Indian resident, for example, to a resident of another country, it reduces the foreign assets of India or increases its liabilities owed to foreigners. This is shown as a credit entry in the BOP of India.
- A transaction that results in a decrease (increase) in the supply (demand) of foreign exchange shall be shown as a debit entry. Conversely, a transaction that results in the decrease (increase) in the demand (supply) for foreign exchange shall be recorded as credit entry in the BOP.

*All **credit entries** in the BOP represent a demand for domestic currency, and all **debit entries** in the BOP represent the supply of domestic currency.*

The IMF has suggested some principles for the valuation of transactions that enter BOP accounting in order to ensure uniformity in the BOP accounts of different countries, which facilitates comparisons across countries and over time. It specifies that all transactions should be valued at market prices. Both imports and exports should be valued on a free-on-board (FOB) basis. The transactions denominated in a foreign currency should be converted into the home currency at the exchange rate prevailing in the market at the time the transaction takes place.

BOP Accounting

The credit and debit items are shown vertically in the BOP of a country by the rules of double-entry bookkeeping. Any economic transaction that gives rise to a payment to foreigners is recorded as a debit with a negative arithmetic sign (–), and any economic transaction that gives rise to a receipt from the rest of the world is recorded as a credit with a positive arithmetic sign (+). Thus, every credit in the account is balanced by a corresponding debit and vice versa. In an accounting sense, the BOP always balances, since every economic transaction recorded in a BOP is represented by two entries with equal values.

The individual items that make up the BOP are shown under five groups of transactions. It may be noted that there are many forms in which a BOP may be presented, and each of these forms has its own merits. A typical BOP format as adopted in India is presented in Table 3.1.

As is evident from Table 3.1, the main entries in the credit side are export of goods and services; unrequited receipts in the form of gifts, donations and grants from foreigners; borrowings from abroad; investments made by foreigners in the country; and receipts on official sales of reserve assets, including gold, to foreign countries and international agencies. The principal items on the debit side of the BOP are imports of goods and services; unilateral payments to foreigners; lending to foreigners; investments abroad; and payments on the purchase of reserve assets or gold from foreign countries and international agencies. Note that exports and imports of gold should be included as ordinary trade items like any other commodity. However, if gold changes hands primarily for

Table 3.1 A Typical BOP Format as Adapted by India

Item/Year	*Credit*	*Debit*	*Net*
A. Current account			
1. Merchandise			
2. Invisibles			
(a) Services			
(b) Transfers			
(c) Income			
Total current account (1+2)			
B. Capital account			
1. Foreign investment			
(a) Foreign direct investment			
(b) Portfolio investment			
2. Loans			
(a) External assistance			
(b) Commercial borrowings			
(c) Short term			
3. Banking capital			
(a) Commercial banks			
(b) Others			
4. Rupee debt service			
5. Other capital			
Total capital account (1 to 5)			
C. Errors and omissions			
D. Overall balance (A+B+C)			
E. Monetary movements			
(i) IMF			
(ii) Foreign exchange reserves			
(Increase – / Decrease +)			
of which SDR allocation			

purposes of adjusting international indebtedness, it is necessary to show these transactions separately.

The BOP broadly consists of current account, capital account, and reserve account. The **current account** records flows of goods, services, and unilateral transfers between residents and non-residents. The **capital account** shows the transactions that involve changes in the foreign financial assets and liabilities of a country. Similarly, the **reserve account** records the transactions pertaining to reserve assets like monetary gold, special drawing rights (SDRs), and assets denominated in foreign currencies. This classification of BOP has been in use for a long time, and almost all textbooks provide the same classification. However, in the recent past, the IMF has switched to a different classification, according to which all transactions are classified into two categories: the current account and the capital and financial account. The BOP capital account is re-designated in the sixth edition of the Manual, as is the capital and financial account. Capital account records credit and debit entries for non-produced non-financial assets and capital transfers between residents and non-residents. The non-produced non-financial assets include assets such as land sold to embassies, sale of leases and licenses, etc. Capital transfers refer to the provision of resources for capital purposes by one party without anything of economic value being supplied as a direct return to that party. Financial account shows net acquisition and disposal of financial assets and liabilities. The sum of the balances on the current and capital accounts represents the net lending (surplus) or net borrowing (deficit) by the economy with the rest of the world. This is equal to the net balance of the financial account. Thus, financial account shows how the net lending to or borrowing from the rest of the world is financed.

*The current account, capital account, and reserve account constitute the BOP of any country. The **current account** records the transactions that involve goods, services, and unilateral transfers. The **capital account** shows the transactions that involve changes in the foreign financial assets and liabilities of a country. The **reserve account** records the transactions pertaining to reserve or liquid assets.*

As many countries, barring the United States and a few others, have been using the conventional classification, the same is used in this text.

The Current Account

The current account records all exports and imports of merchandise and invisibles. *Merchandise* includes agricultural commodities and industrial components and products. *Invisibles* include (a) services, (b) income flows, and (c) unilateral transfers.

Exports of services include spending by foreign tourists in the country and overseas earnings of residents, including firms. This encompasses earnings on various services (like banking, insurance, consulting, and accounting) and earnings of royalties, transportation, and communication. Imports of services include resident tourists' spending abroad, payments made to foreign firms for their services, and royalties on foreign books and movies.

Other items under the current account include profits remitted by foreign branches of Indian firms, interest received on foreign investments, interest paid on foreign borrowing, and funds received from foreign governments for the maintenance of their embassies and consulates. In other words, earnings in the form of interest, dividends, and rent, also known as *factor income,* received by the residents of a country and the income payments (e.g. interest, dividends, rents, etc.) made by the residents of the country to foreigners form part of the current account of the BOP.

Also part of the current account are official transfers like contributions to international institutions, gifts or aid to foreigners, and private transfers like cash remittances by nationals residing abroad (such as non-resident Indians sending money to their relatives in India). As these transfers of funds do not involve any specific services rendered by the residents of the country, they are referred to as *unilateral transfers.* In the case of unilateral transfers, there is a flow of goods, services, or funds in only one direction, as against the merchandise or services trade in which goods or services flow in one direction and payments flow in the opposite direction.

Thus, all commercial transactions (exports and imports of goods and services), private remittances, and transfers of goods and services from the government of the home country to foreign governments (such as the sale of military goods to foreign governments and payment of pensions to persons abroad) constitute the current account of a country.

All exports of goods and services are credited to the current account and all imports of goods and services are debited to the current account. The interests, dividends, and other incomes received on assets held abroad are credited to the current account, while the interests, dividends, and other payments made on foreign assets held in the country are debited to the current account. The remittances received from abroad are credited to the current account, and the remittances made to other countries are debited to the current account. That is, the receipt of funds in the form of gifts and grants under unilateral transfers gives rise to a demand for the home currency, just as the export of goods and services does. Such transactions are recorded as credit entries in the BOP. Similarly, unilateral transfers to foreigners (gifts and aid to foreigners) increase the supply of the home currency in the foreign exchange market, just as the import of goods and services does, so, such transactions are recorded as debit entries in the BOP. Thus, all credit entries represent transactions involving receipts from foreigners and all debit entries represent transactions involving payments to foreigners. In order to satisfy the principle of double-entry bookkeeping, it is necessary to treat unilateral transfers as goodwill being purchased or imported by the donor from the recipient of the grant, gift, or aid.

When the sum of all the debits and the credits is calculated, a country may have a deficit or surplus on the merchandise side of trade. The balance of trade measures whether a country is a net exporter or net importer of goods. A trade surplus indicates that the country's exports are greater than its imports, and a trade deficit indicates that the country's imports are greater than its exports. The invisible items (services and transfers) along with merchandise determine the *actual* current account position, i.e. surplus or deficit. When the country gives away more than it earns or receives from abroad, it is said to have a current account deficit (CAD). On the contrary, when the country earns more than it spends or gives away, it has a current account surplus. A deficit in the BOP on the current account indicates how much the country will have to borrow from abroad by issuing certain financial securities like bonds, stocks, and bills to finance its CAD. The country may also sell its foreign investments (e.g. bonds, stocks, bills, and real assets) to finance its CAD. On the other hand, a current account surplus shows how much the country will have to lend or invest abroad.

The Capital Account

The capital account of BOP reflects the capital inflows and outflows of a country. It measures the purchases and sales transactions of real assets (e.g. land, buildings, and equipment) and financial securities (e.g. stocks and bonds) between residents and non-residents. The difference between such purchases made by the residents of one country (say, India) in all other countries, and such purchases by residents of all other countries in India, is called the balance on capital account.

The capital account includes foreign equity investments, loans, and other foreign investments. Foreign equity investments may take the form of either portfolio investments or direct investments. *Portfolio investments* are cross-border transactions associated with changes in ownership of financial assets and liabilities. *Direct investment* occurs when there are cross-border outflows and inflows of equity capital. Such ownership of a foreign operating business gives a measure of control to the investors. An example of direct investment is an Indian firm promoting a business in a foreign country. When a foreign institutional investor buys the equity stock of an Indian company, it is an instance of portfolio investment.

Note that portfolio investment involves the buying of foreign financial assets (e.g. shares and bonds) without any change in the control of the concerned company, whereas foreign direct investments may result in the transfer of control of the company.

Loans refer to long-term borrowings by the government or corporations, including concessional loans. Short-term borrowings and investments, called short-term financial assets or money market securities, also form part of the capital account. Changes in foreign assets and liabilities of the banking sector are also shown in the capital account. The capital account is thus the net balance of all foreign borrowing, foreign lending, foreign investment, and foreign divestment by the government, corporations, and individuals. Any change in these assets will affect the future income to be received by the country (income exports) and the future income to be paid abroad (income imports).

From the perspective of India, all purchases of domestic assets by foreigners are credited to the capital account, and all purchases of foreign assets made by the residents of India are debited to the capital account. Sales of domestic assets by foreigners are debited to the capital account, while sales of foreign assets by Indians are credited to the capital account. Increases in loans to foreigners by residents are debited to the capital account, while increases in loans to residents by foreigners are credited to the capital account. Conversely, decreases in loans to residents by foreigners are debits and decreases in loans to foreigners by residents are credits to the capital account. As far as holding of currencies is concerned, increases in domestic currency holdings by foreigners are credits to the capital account, and increases in holdings of foreign currency by residents are debits to the capital account. Decreases in domestic currency holdings by foreigners are debits, while decreases in holdings of foreign currency by residents are credits.

The Reserve Account

The official reserve account of the BOP measures a country's official reserves, which are in the form of liquid assets like the gold. The other items shown in the reserve account are foreign exchange in the form of balances with foreign banks and the IMF, and the government's holding of SDRs. While an increase in the holdings of foreign currency reserves by the country's central bank (e.g. Reserve Bank of India, RBI) is debited to the official reserve account, a decrease in the holdings of foreign currency reserves by the country's central bank is credited to the reserve account.

The major functions of foreign exchange reserves are as follows:

- The monetary authority of a country may intervene in the foreign exchange market through the official reserve account by buying or selling the foreign exchange to maintain the exchange value of the domestic currency at a desired level. A country holding reserves will have the power to defend the exchange rate of its home currency in the foreign exchange market. For example, if the Indian government wants to maintain the value of INR against the USD, it can sell USD to buy INR.
- The surplus or deficit on current account and capital account are reflected in changes in official reserves. A drop in reserves occurs when the country sells off its reserve assets like gold to acquire foreign exchange to finance a deficit in its BOP (deficit in current account and capital account put together). A BOP surplus (surplus in current account and capital account put together) may lead to the acquisition of reserve assets from foreign agencies. Such adjustments are made in the official reserve account to maintain BOP equilibrium.
- The transactions using official reserves that give rise to the demand for domestic currency are recorded as credits, and the transactions that give rise to the supply of domestic currency are shown as debits in the official reserve account.

Errors and Omissions

The net credit balance in one of the three accounts (current account, capital account, or official reserve account) of the BOP of a country should have a corresponding net debit balance in one or in a combination of the two other accounts. For example, net capital outflow would result in some combination of capital account deficit and an increase in official reserves, while net capital inflows would result in a capital account surplus and a decrease in official reserves. This combination will be such that the sum of the current account balance, capital account balance, and balance on official reserve account is zero. This always keeps the BOP in *equilibrium* in the accounting sense. It means that there is no possibility of a deficit or surplus in the overall (cumulative) BOP, if all the international transactions are recorded. A deficit or surplus in the BOP would then arise only when some transactions are totally omitted or incorrectly recorded, or when the corresponding entries and payments appearing in the BOP are different. Errors may also arise when the accounting entries carry estimated values. Further, the BOP does not explicitly account for illegal transactions, but such omissions do influence the foreign exchange supply and demand. Omissions may also occur on account of some unreported flows of income and capital. In all such cases, the accounting entry of errors and omissions may be used as a balancing item in the BOP so that the total credits and debits of the three accounts—current, capital, and official reserves—shall equal zero. In other words, a balancing debit or credit is recorded in the BOP as a statistical discrepancy.

As the BOP of every country is prepared on the basis of the principles of double-entry bookkeeping, the world as a whole will have neither a trade deficit nor a surplus. Yet, the world trade data do not show a balance. The implication of this discrepancy is that some of the flow of income, capital, or both are neither reported nor correctly stated.

Examples 3.1 to 3.6 will help us understand how BOP entries on the current account and the capital account are made.

Exports appear as a credit entry in the current account because they are a source of foreign currency. The importer needs to buy the home currency of the exporter to pay for the exports. The payment is recorded as a debit entry in the capital account—a reduction in foreign liabilities.

Example 3.1

An Indian firm exports goods worth INR 50 million to a firm in the United States. The US firm pays from its bank account kept with the State Bank of India in Mumbai. What will the BOP entries for this transaction be?

Solution

The BOP entries for this transaction are shown as below:

	Current account	
	Credit	**Debit**
Export of goods	(+)INR 50 million	
	Capital account	
	Credit	**Debit**
Withdrawal from SBI (decrease in foreign liabilities)		(–)INR 50 million

Example 3.2

A firm in India imports equipment from a firm in the United States by paying INR 60 million. The US firm deposits that amount in the Mumbai branch of American Express Bank. How would this transaction appear in the BOP?

Solution

The import of equipment results in a supply of INR, and the deposit with the bank in India increases India's foreign liabilities. The corresponding entries are shown as below:

	Current account	
	Credit	**Debit**
Import of equipment		(–)INR 60 million
	Capital account	
	Credit	**Debit**
Increase in foreign liabilities	(+)INR 60 million	

Example 3.3

A bank in India subscribes to bonds issued by a British company in London for GBP 5 million by drawing on an account it has with its branch in London. What BOP entries will this cause?

Solution

This creates the BOP entries as shown below:

	Current account	
	Credit	**Debit**
Increase in foreign assets		(–)GBP 5 million
	Capital account	
	Credit	**Debit**
Decrease in foreign bank deposits	(+)GBP 5 million	

Example 3.4

An Indian resident avails himself of medical treatment in the United States and pays USD 2,000 for it. What BOP entries will this cause?

Solution

The BOP entries are shown as below:

	Current account	
	Credit	**Debit**
Purchase of services		(–)USD 2000
	Capital account	
	Credit	**Debit**
Transfer of funds	(+)USD 2,000	

Example 3.5

An Indian resident purchases INR 1 million worth of shares of a US company by borrowing the equivalent USD amount from a US resident. What will the entries in the BOP be?

Solution

The BOP entries are shown as below:

Capital account	*Credit*	*Debit*
Purchase of foreign asset	(+) INR 1 million	(–)INR 1 million
Increase in foreign liabilities		

Example 3.6

An Indian company has transferred INR 3 million from its bank account to the Indian account of a US based charitable organization to service poor people in an African country. What are the entries in BOP of India?

Solution

The BOP entries are shown as below:

	Current account	
	Credit	**Debit**
Gifts		(–)INR 3 million
	Capital account	
	Credit	**Debit**
Increase in foreign liabilities	(+)INR 3 million	

*An **autonomous transaction** is a transaction undertaken to realize a profit or to reduce costs. An **accommodating transaction**, on the other hand, is undertaken to correct the imbalance in the autonomous transaction.*

The transactions that constitute the BOP may also be categorized into autonomous transactions and accommodating transactions. An **autonomous transaction** is a transaction undertaken for its own purpose, that is, to realize a profit or to reduce costs. An **accommodating transaction**, on the other hand, is undertaken to correct the imbalance in the autonomous transaction. Autonomous transactions are known as *above-the-line transactions,* and accommodating transactions are known as *below-the-line transactions.* According to the IMF, all transactions other than those involving reserve assets are to be "above the line." Any imbalance in above-the-line transactions can be set right by drawing down or adding to reserve assets. A deficit/surplus in a country's BOP may thus refer to the deficit/surplus on all autonomous transactions taken together.

Current, Capital, and Reserve Account - A Relationship

The BOP on the current account may result in a deficit or a surplus. If the payments are more than the receipts under the current account, it will result in a deficit, and if the receipts are more than the payments, the current account will show a surplus. A country may adopt different methods to finance its current account deficit (CAD) and to deploy its current account surplus. The country may borrow from abroad by issuing securities like bonds, equity stocks, and/or it may sell some of its operating businesses abroad in order to finance the deficit. Thus, a CAD may result in a reduction in a country's foreign assets (real assets and financial assets) or in an increase in its foreign liabilities.

If a country has a current account surplus, it may buy foreign assets which include financial assets like bonds and shares. It may utilize its current account surplus to redeem or pay off some or all of its foreign liabilities. In other words, a surplus in the BOP on the current account would result in acquiring new foreign assets or reducing foreign liabilities.

A CAD means that the country spends more abroad than it earns abroad, which implies that the country has to borrow from abroad or sell its foreign assets. Conversely, a current account surplus means that the country spends less abroad than it earns abroad, leading to net foreign investment. Thus, any surplus in the current account of a country is exactly offset by a net outflow of capital (or net export of capital), and any deficit in the current account is exactly offset by a net inflow of capital (or net import of capital). In such a situation, the current account balance is equal to the capital account balance so that the country's BOP achieves equilibrium in the absence of the official reserve account. This can be explained with the following example. During a particular year, the exports and imports of India were INR 400 billion and INR 350 billion, respectively. The surplus on the current account was INR 50 billion. During the same period, India's holdings of assets in foreign countries increased by INR 110 billion, and foreign holdings of assets in India increased by INR 60 billion. There was thus a net capital outflow of INR 50 billion. The surplus on the current account was exactly matched by the deficit in the capital account and, therefore, the BOP was in equilibrium. The equilibrium can also be achieved by reversing the same set of numbers.

Assuming no changes in the balance on the capital account, any decrease in the net exports or increase in the net imports from the levels at which the BOP is in equilibrium will result in a BOP deficit. Similarly, any increase in the net exports or decrease in the net imports from the equilibrium levels will result in a BOP surplus. Further, assuming no changes in the balance on current account, any increase in the net capital outflows or decrease in the net capital inflows, from the levels at which the BOP is in equilibrium, will also result in a BOP deficit. And a decrease in the net capital outflows or increase in the net capital inflows from the equilibrium levels will result in a BOP surplus. It may be noted that the disequilibrium in the current account is the cause of, or is caused by, a surplus deficit in the capital account.

When there is a BOP deficit, the monetary authority of the country can finance the deficit by drawing on its official reserves holdings. A country can manage its official reserves account in a way that changes in official reserves is equal and opposite in direction (or sign) to the combined balance on the current and capital accounts. Thus,

$$B_c + B_k = \Delta R,$$

where

B_c = Balance on current account

B_k = Balance on capital account

ΔR = Changes in official reserves

A country that is able to produce more than it consumes may save more than its domestic investment. This will result in a net capital outflow. Conversely, a country that spends more than it produces will invest domestically more than it saves and have a net capital inflow. Net capital outflows (capital account deficit) would result in an increase in official reserves and net capital inflows (capital account surplus) would result in a decrease in official reserves. Hence, the sum of the current account balance, capital account balance, and official reserves account balance is always zero, provided there is no statistical discrepancy (i.e. the items of the BOP are correctly measured).

National Income and International Transactions

From an accounting point of view, it is desirable that BOP should demonstrate accounting principles, while at the same time present accurate and meaningful classifications that can be integrated into the general structure of national income accounting. There is a close association between national income and international economic transactions. The national income is either spent on consumption or saved. In other words,

$$\text{National income} = \text{Aggregate expenditure} + \text{Aggregate savings}$$

The aggregate expenditure, known as the *national expenditure*, is the total amount spent on goods and services plus the total capital expenditure (domestic real investment), which increases the nation's productive capacity. Thus,

$$\text{National income} - \text{Consumption expenditure} = \text{National savings} - \text{Investment}$$

National savings is the sum of domestic investment and net foreign investment. The net borrowings or investments from abroad arise when national savings are not enough to meet investment needs.

Symbolically, the national income of a country can be expressed as

$$Y \equiv C + I + G + (X - M); \text{ (a well-known national income identity)}$$

where

Y = gross domestic product
C = private consumption expenditure
I = private domestic investment expenditure
G = government consumption and investment expenditure (government spending)
X = exports
M = imports

The income of the individuals can be consumed (C), saved (S), paid as taxes (T), or transferred abroad (Tr).

$$Y = C + S + T + \text{Tr}$$

By rearranging the above two equations, we can have the following equation.

$$X - M - \text{Tr} = (S - I) + (T - G)$$

T–G represents the gap between the government revenues and government expenditure. This may be called the government budget balance (surplus/deficit).

The current account balance in the BOP can also be defined as

$$\text{CA} = (S - I) + (T - G)$$

In other words, the current account balance is identically equal to net private saving plus net government saving.

The current account balance can also be expressed as

$$\text{CA} = (\text{Private savings} - \text{Private investment}) + (\text{Taxes} - \text{Government expenditure})$$

$$\text{Private savings} + \text{CAD} = \text{Private investment} + \text{Budget deficit}$$

$$\text{Budget deficit} = \text{Private savings} + \text{CAD} - \text{Private investment}$$

Thus, if the budget deficit of a government goes up, then either savings should go up, CAD must go up, or investment should come down. This is the relationship between the CAD and the government budget deficit.

Domestic saving refer to both private saving and government saving. Private saving includes corporate saving as well. Government saving refers to all revenues of the government as reduced by government expenditure on goods and services. Domestic investment refers to private investment plus the capital expenditure of the government.

$$S = I + \text{FI}$$

$$\text{FI (Foreign investment)} = S - I$$

A country makes a foreign investment when its domestic savings are more than sufficient to finance domestic investment spending. A country becomes a net lender to the rest of the world when it has surplus savings to invest abroad (capital outflow). If a country's savings are not sufficient to finance its own investment needs, it must attract foreign savings (capital inflow). Then the country becomes a net borrower from the rest of the world. Therefore, a current account surplus is matched by an equal net capital outflow, while a CAD is matched by an equal net capital inflow. In case, a country has a CAD, it implies that it purchases (imports) foreign goods and services more than the value of the goods and services it sells (exports). Such a country has to attract foreign investment to finance its CAD. In other words, the current account deficit is the reflection of a low level of national savings relative to investment (or savings rate is lower than the rate of investment).

A further elaboration on CAD can also be made as follows:

$$Y \equiv C + I + G + (X - M)$$

Domestic demand is represented by $(C + I + G)$, known as absorption, while $(X - M)$ represents the external demand.

The above identity can be stated as:

$$X - M = Y - (C + I + G)$$

Current account balance = Income (output) – Spending (absorption)

If exports exceed imports, it means that the national product (Y) is more than the aggregate of consumption, private domestic investment, and government investment, and reverse is the case if imports exceed exports. It may be noted that domestic savings minus domestic investment equals net foreign investment. So, a deficit in a current account means that the domestic savings of the country are less than what the country invests, implying that the country is a capital importer. In order to reduce the CAD, the country should increase its national product as well as its domestic savings. A fall in the rate of investment may also reduce the deficit in the current account. A reduction in foreign capital inflows may result in a fall in the CAD. The reduction in foreign capital inflows may reduce the available supply of capital in the country, leading to a rise in real domestic interest rates. Higher interest rates, in turn, stimulate more savings, particularly private savings. This balances the savings and investment in the economy, reducing the CAD.

A CAD is not always bad. In fact, fast-growing economies import more goods and services and always run CAD. It is also said that a CAD is a reflection of a strong economy. The best example is the United States, which has a large CAD. However, capital ordinarily flows from developed countries to capital-starved developing economies. This implies that developing countries would have CAD. As CAD is financed by capital inflows, countries with CAD are construed to have good investment opportunities. Thus, a country with a

CAD maintains high consumption expenditure and at the same time increases investment in the country. The CAD can be self-correcting in the long run. That is, once the projects set up with foreign capital are completed, the country will have greater availability of goods and services. This will reduce imports if these goods and services are import substitutes. If they are not, the country's exports will increase. Thus, a country with a CAD will have a favourable BOP in the long run. However, domestic investment with foreign capital will have future outflows of income in the form of dividend, interest, rents, and so on.

The current account balance of some select countries can be observed from Table 3.2. Countries such as the US, the UK, South Africa, India, Australia, France, and Mexico persistently maintain a CAD, while countries such as Japan, China, Singapore, Sweden, Russian Federation, Germany and the Republic of Korea maintain current account surplus. According to the *CIA World Fact Book* (2014-04-12), only 59 countries have had current account surplus, while as many as 133 countries have been under CAD as at the end of the year 2013. The top five countries having current account surplus are Germany (USD 2,57,100 million); China (USD 1,76,600 million); Saudi Arabia (USD 1,32,200 million); the Netherlands (USD 82,900 million); and Russia (USD 74,800 million). Japan had a current account surplus of USD 56,600 million. These countries are the top exporters of their savings to other countries. Their savings would have gone abroad looking for more profitable investment opportunities.

Table 3.2 Current Account Balance of Select Countries (Percent of GDP)

Country	*2007*	*2008*	*2009*	*2010*	*2011*	*2012*	*2013*
Australia	−6.8	−5.0	−5.0	−3.6	−3.0	−4.4	−3.3
Brazil	0.1	−1.7	−1.5	−2.2	−2.1	−2.4	−3.6
China	10.1	9.3	4.9	4.0	1.9	2.6	2.0
France	−1.0	−1.8	−1.4	−1.3	−1.8	−1.6	−1.5
Germany	7.2	6.0	6.1	5.9	6.3	7.4	7.0
India	−0.7	−2.4	−2.0	−3.2	−3.2	−4.8	−2.5
Japan	4.9	2.9	2.9	4.0	2.1	1.0	0.7
Korea	1.1	0.3	3.7	2.6	1.6	4.2	6.1
Mexico	−1.4	−1.8	−0.9	−0.4	−1.1	−1.3	−2.1
Russia	5.6	6.2	4.0	4.4	5.1	3.5	1.6
Singapore	26.2	14.6	17.0	24.0	23.0	17.6	18.4
South Africa	−7.0	−7.3	−4.0	−1.9	−2.3	−5.2	−5.8
Sweden	8.9	8.7	5.9	6.0	5.8	5.8	6.0
Switzerland	9.0	1.1	7.1	13.8	6.0	8.5	15.0
UK	−2.5	−5.5	−2.0	−6.2	−9.7	−6.2	−7.9
US	−5.0	−1.5	−1.7	−3.3	−1.3	−3.8	−4.5
Canada	0.8	0.2	−3.0	−3.6	−2.8	−3.4	−3.2

Source: International Financial Statistics, IMF.

The top five countries having CAD are the US (USD 3,60,700 million); the UK (USD 93,600 million); Brazil (USD 77,630 million); India (USD 74,790 million); and Canada (USD 59,500). Australia had a CAD of USD 44,900 million. These countries are the top importers of foreign savings to finance their investments.

China became the world's largest trading nation in 2013 as measured by the sum of exports and imports of goods, overtaking the US. China's annual trade in goods was estimated to be about USD 4 trillion in 2013, while that of the US was about USD 3.82 trillion.

Many of the small but developing nations such as Nepal, Bhutan, Cuba, Greece, Nigeria, Angola, etc. have had current account surplus, while even developed nations such as the US, the UK, Canada, Australia, New Zealand, etc. had a CAD. The developing economies which have more investment opportunities than they can afford to undertake with low levels of domestic savings may attract a large inflow of foreign capital. These countries may grow faster provided they have used the foreign capital efficiently. But, in practice, many of the developing countries have current account surplus. It implies that capital flows from developing economies to developed economies. It might be because of better investment opportunities (in terms of return and risk) available in the developed countries and also of their currencies being hard. Of course, very poor countries also run CAD but they are financed by official grants and loans by international organizations and some developed nations. A country should also have absorption capacity to attract foreign capital flows.

Developed countries like the US, the UK, etc. run a huge CAD and attract foreign capital in a large measure from all levels of economies whether they are developed nations or developing nations. For a long time, Japan was the largest current account surplus economy, while the US was on the opposite side with the largest CAD; and the capital flow from Japan to the US was the largest bilateral capital flow in the world. In the 21st century, Germany, China, and Saudi Arabia have emerged as the top current account surplus countries, overtaking Japan. The US, which provides the international currency, is the largest debtor country, importing massive capital from several countries, notably from Japan, China, Belgium, Brazil, the UK, Taiwan, etc. to cover its huge CAD. China and Japan top the list of foreign investors in the US Treasury bonds. As at the end of March 2014, China held the US Treasury bonds to the value of USD 1,268.4 billion, followed by Japan (USD 1,219.5 billion). India has also emerged as one of the top lenders to the US government. India accounts for about 1.2 percent of total foreign investments in US Treasury bonds of about USD 6 trillion. Despite its huge fiscal deficit, India had parked USD 146.2 billion, out of its foreign exchange reserves, in the US Treasury securities.

The BOP and Exchange Rates

BOP equilibrium is a condition where the sum of debits and credits in the current account as well as the capital account is zero so that the official reserve balance becomes zero. But in many situations, the BOP might be in disequilibrium because of several factors. Some of these factors are:

- Fundamental changes in economies, including technological changes, changes in methods of production, and changes in consumer tastes affect the country's exports and imports, causing disequilibrium in the BOP.
- Changes in national income also influence the position of the BOP. For example, an increase in the national income of a country may lead to an inflationary rise, which will cause disequilibrium in the BOP. During inflationary periods, the prices of exports would rise. As a result, exports may suffer and, at the same time, the imports bill of the country may rise, leading to a CAD.

- The stage of economic development of the country may also influence the BOP equilibrium. A developing country may have to import a large quantity of capital goods, along with raw materials, components, and technology. This may lead to disequilibrium in the BOP of the country.
- The cost at which a country borrows or lends funds also influences the equilibrium position of the BOP. Economic transactions between nationals give rise to supply and demand for a country's currency, which in turn determines the foreign exchange rate. As economic transactions between a country and other nations depend on income and price changes in the country, disequilibrium (deficit or surplus) in the BOP of a country can be adjusted through monetary and fiscal policies.

As discussed earlier, all credit entries in the BOP give rise to a demand for home currency and a supply of foreign currency, whereas all debit entries give rise to a supply of home currency and a demand for foreign currency. When goods and services are sold to overseas buyers, the importers may have to purchase the home currency of the exporter in order to pay for the goods and services. Even if the exports are invoiced in the foreign currency, the exporter will purchase the home currency by selling the foreign currency that he receives. In either case, the exports give rise to a demand for home currency in the foreign exchange market. Conversely, the import of goods and services gives rise to a supply of home currency. Therefore, the importer will have to supply the home currency in order to make payments to the exporter. If the goods and services are invoiced in the foreign currency, the importer has to buy the foreign currency by supplying adequate home currency. Similarly, unilateral transfers like receipt of gifts, grants, and aid also give rise to a demand for the home currency. Also note that the demand for home currency results in the supply of foreign currency, as the supply of home currency is associated with the demand for foreign currency.

The current account balance (deficit or surplus) has implications for exchange rates. A country having CAD may face depreciation of its home currency unless it attracts foreign capital. Any delay in attracting foreign capital may complicate the economic issues facing the country. So the country may increase the interest rates in order to attract the capital flows. This measure may impact the exchange rate of the domestic currency. The current account surplus may also impact the exchange rate but in a converse process. The changes in official foreign exchange reserves of a country may also influence the exchange rate.

BOP Under Floating Exchange Rate Regime

Under the floating exchange rate regime, exchange rates are determined by the forces of demand and supply of currencies. With floating exchange rates, there is no change in the official reserves because the monetary authority of the country does not usually intervene in the foreign exchange market to influence the exchange rate. Accordingly, the deficit or surplus in the current account will be exactly equal to the surplus or deficit in the capital account, provided there are no errors and omissions. Thus,

$$\text{Current account balance} = (-)\ \text{Capital account balance}$$

or

$$\text{Current account balance} + \text{Capital account balance} = 0$$

This implies that current account and capital account are inversely related. A deficit balance in one account is offset by a surplus in the other. For example, a deficit in a current account caused by excess of imports over exports may be financed with foreign borrowing or by selling off foreign assets. So, a negative balance in the current account is offset by a positive balance in the capital account. The CAD may also be the result of a capital account surplus arising from foreign borrowing. As mentioned earlier, the monetary and fiscal policies of the government also influence both the accounts. For example, a government may borrow from abroad to finance its fiscal deficit. The inflow of foreign funds increases the demand for home currency, resulting in the appreciation of the home currency against the foreign currency. This will cause a reduction in exports and an increase in imports, leading to a CAD. Besides, heavy foreign borrowing may cause a large payment of interest, which could again strain the current account. If the foreign investments made earlier are now sold off to finance the CAD, future income receipts will come down. This will further increase the CAD. Thus, foreign borrowing (debt) may result in catastrophic consequences.

To explain further, any disequilibrium in a country's BOP can be corrected through changes in the exchange rates. If a country has a deficit in its BOP, the exchange rate of its currency would depreciate as a consequence. This would make the country's exports cheaper in terms of foreign currency, and it would make the country's imports dearer in terms of its domestic currency. As a result, the country's exports would improve, and imports would be discouraged. This will ultimately adjust the deficit in the country's BOP. Conversely, if a country has a BOP surplus, its exchange rate would appreciate. This would make the country's exports dearer in terms of foreign currency, and make the country's imports cheaper in terms of domestic currency. As a result, exports would get discouraged, and imports get encouraged. Adjustment of a surplus in the BOP is brought about in this way. The floating exchange rate system automatically keeps the BOP of all countries in equilibrium. The floating exchange rate system also would solve the problem of international liquidity by keeping the BOP of all countries in equilibrium. However, time is needed for exchange rate changes to bring about changes in BOP. Such lagged effect is based on the theory of J-curve, which is described in the following paragraphs.

*The phenomenon of deterioration and eventual improvement in a country's balance of trade is known as the **J-curve effect**.*

Depreciation in a country's currency increases the prices of imports in terms of domestic currency. The increase in prices of imports may reduce the quantity of imports. However, if price elasticity of demand is inelastic for imported goods, the higher prices of imports may result in a higher value of imports. In other words, depreciation in the home currency may deteriorate the country's balance of trade. But depreciation in domestic currency makes exports cheaper in terms of foreign currency and this will increase the volume of exports. The value of exports thus increases with the increased quantity of exports. However, if the export demand is price inelastic, then depreciation in the home currency may not cause an increase in the volume of exports. Further, in the short run, exports may not increase even with the decline in export prices. This is because exporters may need more time to increase production to meet increasing demand. It would also be some time before foreign customers switch to imported products, despite their cheaper prices. In other words, a country's balance of trade may deteriorate following depreciation of its currency when the value of exports does not sufficiently increase to compensate for the increase in the value of imports.

The worsening of a country's balance of trade following depreciation of its currency is temporary. In the long run, many import substitutes would be brought into the market and resident customers would adjust their preferences towards import substitutes. Similarly, in the long run, exporters would be able to increase their production, and foreign customers would also switch over to these products. As a result, the country's balance of trade would turn around and eventually improve. The phenomenon of deterioration and eventual improvement in a country's balance of trade is known as the **J-curve effect** (Figure 3.1).

Appreciation of the exchange rate may create a contra picture of the J curve. Following the appreciation of a country's currency, its exports would become dearer, and imports cheaper. But due to inelasticity of exports and imports, the quantity of imports and exports may not change in the short run. Following the appreciation of the home currency and consequent reduction in the prices of imports, the total spending on imports may come down if the quantity imported does not increase due to price inelasticity of demand. However, the value of exports may decline in the short term. If exports do not decline as much as the

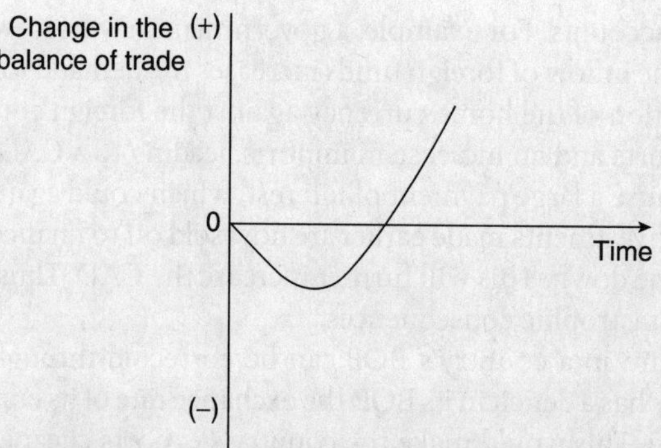

Figure 3.1

J-curve after Depreciation of Currency

decline in the value of imports, the country's balance of trade would show a surplus in the short run. However, in the long run, the quantity of imports would increase following a decline in import prices, and the quantity of exports would decrease following an increase in the foreign currency prices of exports. The net result is a worsening of the country's balance of trade. If this phenomenon is plotted on a graph, it would take the shape of an inverted J curve, as shown in Figure 3.2.

Thus, depreciation or appreciation of a country's currency against a foreign currency would make the exchange rate unstable in the short run due to inelastic imports and exports. However, other factors which also have a bearing on the exchange rate may become dominant and bring stability in the exchange rates.

BOP Under Fixed Exchange Rate Regime

The BOP identity can be stated as

Current account balance + Capital account balance + Changes in official reserve account = 0

or,

$$B_c + B_k + \Delta R \equiv 0$$

$$-\Delta R \equiv (B_c + B_k)$$

This means that the sum of the current account balance, capital account balance, and changes in official reserve account is zero, provided there are no errors and omissions in

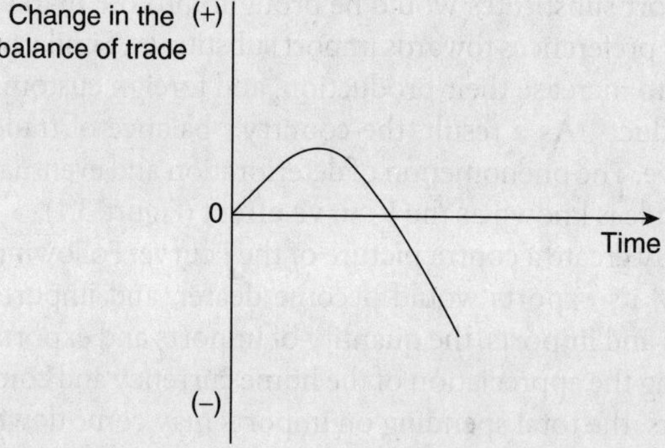

Figure 3.2

J-Curve after Appreciation of Currency

the preparation of the BOP. In other words, an increase or a decrease in the official reserve account equals (but is opposite in sign to) the combined surplus or deficit in the capital account and current account. The negative sign of the changes in official reserves indicates the supply of home currency available to buy official reserve assets (e.g. gold, foreign currency, etc.). It means that the official reserves would increase with a surplus BOP (i.e. combined surplus of current account and capital account). Thus, under the fixed exchange rate system, the disequilibrium in a BOP can be corrected by effecting suitable changes in the official reserves.

If a country has a combined surplus in the current account and capital account, it will result in a rise in the home currency value of the foreign currency. In order to prevent the value of the home currency from rising (appreciating), the government should absorb the excess foreign currency through the official reserve account. This will result in an increase in the supply of home currency. The expansion of money supply in the economy will increase the demand for goods and services, leading to inflation. The inflationary tendencies will in turn reduce the exports and increase the imports. As a result, the combined surplus in the current account and capital account will vanish, bringing the BOP into equilibrium. However, in case of a combined deficit, the process of reaching BOP equilibrium will be the reverse.

The BOP and Money Supply

*A **surplus** in the BOP results in an increase in the money supply in the economy, and a **deficit** in the BOP results in a decrease in the money supply.*

As discussed earlier, the BOP of a country is in equilibrium when the combined balance of current account and capital account is zero. For example, during a particular period, if the total receipts from foreigners for the goods and services they have imported from India, and the real and financial assets they have acquired in India are equal to the total payments made by India during the same period to foreigners for goods and services imported and the real and financial assets acquired abroad by the residents of India (including corporations and the government), the BOP of India will be in equilibrium for that period. The disequilibrium in BOP arises when receipts from abroad exceed payments made abroad (resulting in a surplus in BOP), and when payments made abroad exceed receipts from abroad (resulting in a deficit in BOP). Such imbalance, between receipts from foreigners and payments to foreigners, may cause changes in the money supply in the economy. The public holdings of demand deposits and public holdings of paper money and coins constitute the money supply in the economy. How disequilibrium in the BOP brings about changes in money supply is explained below.

The residents of a country receive bank drafts in foreign currency or claims to foreign currency upon sale of their goods and services to foreigners. In rare cases, they receive actual money. These foreign currency-denominated instruments are sold to banks, whereupon the domestic currency is normally credited to the demand deposit accounts of the sellers. The receipt of foreign currencies, thus, creates domestic currency-denominated demand deposits in the banking system. On the other hand, importers and others who have to pay to foreigners, buy the required foreign currency from banks, in exchange for their domestic currency. It means that payments in foreign currencies would reduce the demand deposit balances of buyers of foreign currency. In case a country has a surplus BOP, there will be an increase in the overall holdings of foreign currencies by the banking system. This will lead to a net increase in the demand deposit holdings of the public. Thus, the surplus in the BOP increases money supply in the economy, if all else remains the same. And, a deficit in BOP will have the opposite effect of the surplus. That is, the combined deficit in current account and capital account will reduce the money supply in the economy, if all else remains the same.

The increase or decrease in money supply has a direct effect on the price levels in the economy, which in turn influences the value of the exports and imports of a country.

Changes in money supply that result from disequilibrium in the BOP, may also bring about changes in interest rates, which in turn influence cross-border investments and capital flows. To elucidate, an increase in the money supply may cause prices to rise. The higher prices in turn cause imports to increase and exports to fall, resulting in a deficit in the balance of trade. The increase in money supply may also increase spending on investment, both domestic and foreign. The increase in demand for domestic financial assets will increase their price and lower the domestic interest rates. The lower interest rates make domestic investment less attractive relative to foreign financial assets. This tends to worsen the BOP on the capital account. The reduction in money supply may also influence both the current account and the capital account of BOP, but in the reverse manner. What is to be understood by the above discussion is that the money supply in the economy affects exchange rates, not directly, but through price levels, investments, and income distribution.

Under the fixed exchange rate system, the monetary authority of a country puts more of its currency into the economy when it has purchased foreign currency, to prevent excess of foreign currency in the market. This would in turn stop the value of domestic currency from rising in foreign exchange market. The same monetary authority has to take the opposite action in light of deficit in the BOP. But under the floating exchange rate system, the exchange rates are determined by the forces of supply and demand for the currencies. In an economy with a deficit or surplus in the BOP, the forces of demand and supply influence the exchange rates to move to the levels at which the disequilibrium in the BOP is eliminated. Therefore, a deficit or surplus in the BOP of a country is a short-lived phenomenon. Further, under the fixed exchange rate system, the increase or decrease in the money supply is automatic depending upon whether BOP is in a surplus or in a deficit. However, under the floating exchange rate system, the money supply in the economy does not automatically increase if there is a surplus in the BOP, or decrease if there is a deficit in the BOP.

Any increase in the net capital outflow or decrease in the net capital inflow will result in a deficit in the BOP on the capital account. Conversely, any decrease in the net capital outflow or increase in the net capital inflow will result in a surplus in the BOP on the capital account. As rational investors buy those assets which give the highest yield, given the risk involved, the net capital outflow is inversely related to the rate of interest in the domestic economy. That is, the lower the rate of interest in the domestic economy, the larger is the net capital outflow (or the smaller is the net capital inflow). It is also observed that the $X - M$ balance varies inversely with the domestic income level. The higher the Y, the smaller the net export balance, or the larger the net import balance. A current account surplus implies that a country is not consuming as much as it is producing. This has long-term implications for the development of a country, particularly a developing country. A developing country would need to consume what it is capable of producing. Also, it needs to build up its productive assets in order to achieve high rates of growth. In other words, a country may run a CAD and finance it by borrowing from outside (i.e. capital account surplus). But this does not mean that running a CAD would automatically result in the development of the country. The way the current account is financed and the purposes for which the external borrowings are used are also very important. To put it differently, if the capital account surplus resulting from the CAD is used to finance productive activities, then the economy will be better off in the long run. Conversely, if the capital account surplus is used to finance immediate consumption needs, the country's long-term economic interests will be in jeopardy.

India's BOP

In this section, we will examine the structure of India's BOP and evaluate it in terms of current account deficit or surplus.

The BOP Structure

The current account, the capital account, and the reserves, which constitute the structure of India's BOP, are presented in a summary form below.

The Current Account The current account records the following:

- *Merchandise trade,* which consists of the merchandise debit representing the import of goods and the merchandise credit relating to the export of goods.
- *Services,* which include travel (expenditure by foreign tourists in India on the receipts side, and expenditure by Indian tourists abroad on the payments side); transportation (receipts and payments on account of goods and natural persons, as well as other distributive services like port charges, bunker fuel, and warehousing); insurance (insurance on exports, premiums on life and non-life policies, and reinsurance premiums from foreign insurance companies); government transactions not included elsewhere (inward remittances towards maintenance of foreign embassies, diplomatic missions, and offices of international/regional institutions in India, and outward remittances on account of maintenance of Indian embassies and diplomatic missions abroad, and remittances by foreign embassies on their account); and miscellaneous items (business services including communication, construction, financial, software, news agency services, royalties, copyright, license fees, and management services).
- *Transfers,* both official and private. These include grants, donations, gifts, migrants' transfers by way of remittances for family maintenance, repatriation of savings, transfer of financial and real resources linked to change in resident status of migrants, and assistance received by the government from bilateral and multilateral institutions.
- *Income,* which includes investment income receipts comprising interest received on loans to non-residents, dividend/profit received by Indians on foreign investment, reinvested earnings of Indian FDI companies abroad, interest received on debentures, floating-rate notes, commercial paper, fixed deposits and funds held abroad by authorized dealers out of foreign currency loans/export proceeds, payment of taxes by non-residents/refunds of taxes by foreign governments, interest/discount earnings on RBI investment, and investment income comprising of payment of interest on non-resident deposits, payment of interest on loans from non-residents, payment of dividend/profit to non-resident shareholders, reinvested earnings of FDI companies, payment of interest on debentures, floating rate notes (FRNs), CPs, fixed deposits, government securities, and charges on SDRs.

The Capital Account The capital account of the country records the following:

- *Foreign investment,* which consists of foreign direct investment and portfolio investment—FIIs' investment, and funds raised through GDRs/ADRs by Indian companies and through offshore funds.
- *External assistance,* which includes aid extended by India to foreign governments under various agreements and repayment of such loans as well as external assistance to India (which includes multilateral and bilateral loans received under the agreements between India and other countries/international institutions and repayments of such loans by India except loan repayment to erstwhile "Rupee Area" countries that are covered under the rupee debt service).
- *Commercial borrowings,* which include loans extended by EXIM bank to various countries and repayment of such loans, withdrawals/repayment of loans including buyers credit, suppliers credit, FRNs, CPs, bonds, and foreign currency convertible bonds (FCCBs) issued abroad by Indian corporations.

- *Short-term loans to India* and repayments with a maturity of less than one year.
- *Banking capital,* which includes foreign assets of commercial banks, such as foreign currency holdings and INR overdrafts to non-resident banks; foreign liabilities of commercial banks—non-resident deposits and other liabilities; and others—movement in balances of foreign central banks and international institutions, and movement in balances held abroad by Indian embassies.
- *Rupee debt service,* or principal repayments on account of civilian and non-civilian debt in respect of Rupee Payment Area and interest payment thereof.
- *Other capital,* such as leads and lags in export receipts, subscriptions to international institutions, quota payments to the IMF, remittances towards recouping the losses of branches/subsidiaries, and residual items of other capital transaction not included elsewhere.

The Official Reserve Account The official reserve account comprises changes in foreign currency assets held by the RBI and SDR balances held by the Government of India.

Effective March 1993, foreign currency transactions are converted by crossing the average spot buying and selling rate for US dollars in the foreign exchange market, and the monthly averages of cross rates of non-US dollar currencies based on the London market.

A Retrospective Evaluation

Before India embarked upon planned development in the early 1950s, it had a very huge deficit in the BOP due to high imports and capital outflows. In the beginning of the planned period, import substitution was recognized as the appropriate strategy. The thrust of the Indian government's policy during the period was not on exports. This was because of the belief that, given a large domestic market, exports need not be an engine of economic growth. Further, because of the traditional nature of the country's exports, growth in external demand for India's products was considered inelastic. At the same time, as the policy of the government was to implement rapid industrialization, imports of heavy machinery and industry equipment surged. As a result, the CAD of the country increased phenomenally.

Until the 1970s, external assistance dominated as a financing instrument in the BOP. Later, the government recognized the importance of self-reliance and found new sources of financing the imports (e.g. remittances from Indian workers). The management of the BOP was thus critically dependent on a sizeable improvement in earnings from exports and invisibles.

The BOP saw a severe crisis in the early 1990s, following the Gulf War and other developments. India's foreign currency assets depleted rapidly from USD 3.1 billion in August 1990 to USD 975 million on 12 July 1991. The CAD rose to 3.1 percent of the GDP in 1990–1991. Around the same time, the credit rating of the country was lowered, which restricted the country's access to commercial borrowing. It was against this backdrop that a high level committee headed by Dr C. Rangarajan was appointed in 1991. The committee recommended, among others, liberalization of current account transactions, leading to current account convertibility, and a compositional shift in capital flows from debt to non-debt creating flows. Accordingly, the government adopted the Liberalized Exchange Rate Management System (LERMS) in March 1992. In August 1994, the government accepted Article VIII of the Articles of Agreement of the IMF and moved towards current account convertibility. Capital account liberalization also started as a part of wide-ranging reforms.

It was also recognized that trade policies, exchange rate policies, and industrial policies should be integrated in order to improve the overall productivity, and competitiveness of the economy. The government initiated measures to increase the competitiveness of exports of both goods and services. In recent years, there has also been significant liberalization of the outflows of funds. This is reflected in the increasing international operations of Indian corporations. At the same time, there have been sustained foreign capital inflows with the opening up of the capital account on inflows. Further, there has been a shift in the commodity composition of India's trade. India's export base, which consists of commodity and country composition, is considered to be far more diversified now than ever before. The preponderance of capital goods in India's import basket also signifies the industrial capacity expansion for domestic consumption as well as exports.

India's BOP on different accounts is shown in Table 3.3. As can be observed from the table, India has been continuously experiencing a trade deficit, which stood at INR 8,848.45 billion in 2013–14 as against INR 10,644.56 billion in 2012–13. Although the CAD has been happening every year, the year 2013–14 witnessed far less a figure as compared to that of the previous year. However, the BOP on the capital account (surplus) has registered

Table 3.3 India's BOP—Key Indicators (INR Billion)

Item/Year	*2011–12*			*2012–13*			*2013–14*		
	Credit	*Debit*	*Net*	*Credit*	*Debit*	*Net*	*Credit*	*Debit*	*Net*
A. Current account									
1. Merchandise	14,825.17	23,946.47	(–) 9,121.29	16,676.90	27,321.46	(–)10,644.56	19,310.74	28,159.18	(–)8,848.45
2. Invisibles	10,534.80	5,173.23	5,361.57	12,188.93	6,340.47	5,848.46	14,117.73	7,146.79	6,970.95
3. Total current account	25,359.97	29,119.70	(–)3,759.73	28,865.83	33,661.93	(–)4,796.10	33,428.47	35,305.97	(–)1,877.50
B. Capital account									
1. Foreign investment	11,212.13	9,324.75	1,887.38	11,698.22	9,151.69	2,546.53	14,906.78	13,310.29	1,596.50
2. Loans	6,764.57	5,867.09	897.48	84,33.53	6,742.79	1,690.73	8,134.42	7,675.41	459.01
3. Banking capital	4,278.27	3,568.29	709.98	45,54.07	3,651.40	902.68	65,44.82	5,028.18	1,516.64
4. Rupee debt service	0.00	3.81	(–) 3.81	0.00	3.13	(–) 3.13	0.00	3.04	(–) 3.04
5. Other capital	641.43	942.16	(–) 300.73	970.73	1250.20	(–) 279.46	1,338.01	2,009.03	(–) 671.02
Total capital account	22,896.39	19,706.10	3,190.29	25,656.56	20,799.22	4,857.34	30,924.03	2,8025.95	2,898.08
C. Errors and omissions	0.00	115.60	(–) 115.60	145.78	0.00	145.78	49.63	109.67	(–) 60.04
D. Overall Balance (A + B + C)	48,256.36	(–) 685.03	54,668.17	207.02	64,402.13	63,441.59	960.54	48,941.40	54,461.15
Forex reserves (Increase –/ Decrease +)	685.03	--	685.03	0.00	207.02	(–) 207.02	0.00	960.54	(–) 960.54

Source: Handbook of Statistics on Indian Economy 2013–14, Reserve Bank of India.

a phenomenal growth over the period. The capital account has shown a surplus in all years because of increasing capital flows that include external commercial borrowings and foreign direct investment flows. As a result, foreign exchange reserves—comprising foreign currency assets, gold, SDRs, and the reserve portion's position with the IMF—have increased in 2012–13 and 2013–14. A negative change in the official reserves means the supply of home currency—to buy foreign currency assets including gold—will lead to an increase in the official reserve account. When a country is running out of reserves, it can supplement its official reserves through foreign borrowing. However, further borrowing will eventually result in paying higher interests and higher future CADs. A country may thus have a difficult BOP situation when the deficit in the combined current and capital accounts persists for a long time.

As can be observed from Table 3.3, the trade balance (deficit) increased greatly over the period due to increases in oil imports and non-oil imports which mainly include capital goods. The current account has shown a deficit balance in all years. Whenever the invisibles (net) are less than the trade deficit, the current account shows a negative balance. It means that the invisibles are inadequate to finance the entire trade deficit. The merchandise trade deficit indicates that exports are also not enough to finance imports. The growth in imports has outperformed the growth in exports, resulting in a huge merchandise trade deficit. In contrast to India, countries like Japan, China, and Russia maintain a trade surplus. In spite of a huge trade deficit, India is in a comfortable position because of increasing exports of services and surging capital inflows.

Diversification of international trade, particularly exports, is essential as a long-term policy for the sustained economic growth of a country. Concentration of exports in a few goods and services creates the risk of deteriorating terms of trade, income volatility, etc. Exports can be diversified by expanding the product-mix of exports. Geographic diversification of international trade is more important than product diversification. India has achieved both product diversification as well as geographical diversification. India's exports have shifted from dependence on primary commodities towards manufacturing exports. Technology-intensive engineering goods and petroleum products have emerged as the drivers of India's exports in place of traditional items such as gems and jewellery, and textiles and textile products. Ores, minerals, metals, and petroleum products have contributed to the high growth of exports. India's major exports have also shifted from developed regions to diversified markets such as Asia, OPEC, and African countries.

There are various measures by which a country can correct a disequilibrium in the BOP, particularly CAD. The measures may be directly aimed at encouraging exports and discouraging imports. Export promotion measures include controlling inflation and improving the production facilities in the country, so as to augment production. Imports can be discouraged by increasing tariffs, fixing import quotas, and encouraging the use of import substitutes.

If a country's gross exports increase, or its gross imports decrease, its output and income may rise. Conversely, a country's output and income may fall when the gross exports of the country fall or its gross imports rise. Therefore, it is important to make efforts to promote exports and/or discourage imports, so that the country's output and income rise. However, export promotion depends on several factors, such as:

- the inflation rate in the domestic economy relative to the inflation rates in other economies,
- the tariff and trade policies of foreign countries, and
- the income levels in other countries.

All these factors are external. Thus, we see that the exports of a country are determined by external factors as well. Conversely, the volume of imports is determined by factors that are mostly internal (i.e. based on the domestic economy).

Summary

1. The *balance of payments* is an accounting statement that shows all international economic transactions during a given period. The main objective of the BOP is to enable all concerned to understand how various international economic transactions, like trade in goods and services, purchase and sale of assets including securities, and transfer of funds are brought into balance in a given period.

2. The balance of payments is based on the principles of double-entry bookkeeping, according to which two entries—credit and debit—are made for every international economic transaction, such that the total credits must exactly match the total debits.

3. The balance of payments broadly consists of the current account, capital account, and reserve account. The *current account* records flows of goods, services, and unilateral transfers. The *capital account* shows the transactions which involve changes in financial assets and liabilities of a country. The *reserve account* records the transactions pertaining to reserve assets like monetary gold and SDRs.

4. In the absence of official reserve transactions, the current account balance shall be equal to the capital account balance, so that the country's BOP will be at equilibrium.

5. A country that is able to produce more than it consumes will save more than its domestic investment and will have a net capital outflow. Conversely, a country that spends more than it can produce will invest more than it saves domestically and will have a net capital inflow.

6. All credit entries in the BOP give rise to the demand for home currency and to the supply of foreign currency, whereas all debit entries give rise to the supply of home currency and to the demand for foreign currency. Thus any disequilibrium in a country's balance of payments can be corrected through changes in the exchange rates.

7. The phenomenon of deterioration and eventual improvement in a country's balance of trade as a result of depreciation of its home currency is known as the *J-curve effect*. Appreciation of the home currency may result in the improvement and subsequent worsening of the balance of trade. Such a phenomenon is known as the *inverted J-curve effect*.

8. Under the fixed exchange rate regime, a country may initiate certain measures like devaluation or revaluation of currency, control of inflation, or fixing of import quotas to correct disequilibrium in the BOP. When a country is under the floating exchange rate regime, any disequilibrium in its BOP will be corrected by market forces.

9. The receipt of foreign currency would increase the money supply in the economy, and payment in foreign currency would reduce the money supply in the economy.

Questions and Problems

1. Explain the concept of balance of payments.
2. Discuss the significance of balance of payments.
3. Explain the major components of BOP.
4. What could be the main causes for a current account deficit or surplus?
5. How can a country manage a continuous current account deficit?
6. Is it desirable to have a continuous current account surplus? Why?
7. Discuss the implications of BOP identity.
8. Explain how a country's BOP data is useful.
9. What is a balance of trade deficit?
10. Describe the J-curve effect.
11. What are the implications of the inverted J-curve effect?
12. Under the floating exchange rate regime, what are the consequences of a current account deficit/surplus?
13. What would happen to the BOP if the home currency is devalued under a fixed exchange rate regime?
14. Why does the central bank of a country intervene in the foreign exchange market?
15. Why should the sum of the balance in the capital account and the balance in the current account be zero? How are discrepancies accounted for?
16. Explain the relationship between the current account balance and a country's savings and investment.
17. Record the following transactions in the BOP of India:
    a. A firm in India has exported goods worth USD 10 million to a firm in the United States and the payment is settled by a 120-days bill.

b. **A merchant in Mumbai has imported machinery from the United Kingdom, billed at GBP 2 million. The payment is made immediately by transfer of funds through a bank in India.**

c. **An Indian citizen has undergone medical treatment in the United States and paid USD 0.50 million by a cheque drawn on a bank in India.**

d. **A firm in India has issued bonds for INR 100 million in Japan.**

e. **A resident in India has received USD 0.25 million as dividend from a company in the United States.**

Case Study

On fears of tapering of the quantitative easing (QE) programme by the Federal Reserve, there had been sudden stops and reversals in the capital inflows to emerging economies. As a result, the currencies of emerging economies have become extremely volatile and many of them experienced significant depreciation pressure. The Indian rupee depreciated sharply by around 19.4 percent against USD, from 55.40 on 22 May 2013 to 68.85 on 28 August 2013 on the back of sharp reversals in capital inflows and unsustainable level of CAD (4.8 of GDP in 2012–13). The problem was accentuated by weak macroeconomic fundamentals in 2012–13 like GDP growth rate (4.5 percent); inflation (7.4 percent); and fiscal deficit (4.9 percent of GDP). The overarching concerns about the early tapering of US QE also triggered large selloffs, leading to heightened volatility in financial markets of emerging economies. At the same time, some of the developed countries like the US increased their attractiveness with better yields.

To stem the volatility in the foreign exchange market, the RBI initiated several measures. Apartment from several administrative as well as monetary measures, the RBI made net sales to the tune of USD 10.8 billion in the foreign exchange market during the period, May–August 2013. The RBI also intervened in the forward market with RBI's outstanding net forward sales of USD 9.1 billion as at end-August 2013. All these measures brought some stability to the Indian rupee. Shrugging off QE tapering fears, the Indian rupee stabilized around the level of 61–62 per USD by the end of September 2013. The FII inflows also resumed and CAD narrowed to 1.7 percent of GDP in 2013–14. The measures taken by the RBI to stabilize the exchange rate of the rupee, also helped in stabilizing the financial markets in the country.

The key macroeconomic variables for the last 4 years are presented in the following table:

Macroeconomic variables	2010–11	2011–12	2012–13	2013–14
GDP growth rate	8.91	6.69	4.47	4.74
Fiscal deficit (centre + states) as % of GDP	6.9	8.1	7.2	6.7
Inflation (CPI)	10.5	8.4	10.2	9.5
Exports (USD bn)	250.5	309.8	306.6	318.6
Imports (USD bn)	381.1	499.5	502.2	466.2
Trade Deficit (USD bn)	130.6	189.8	195.7	147.6
Invisibles (USD bn)	84.6	111.6	107.5	115.2
Current account deficit (USD bn)	45.9	78.2	88.2	32.4
CAD as % of GDP	2.7	4.2	4.7	1.7
Capital account (USD bn)	62.0	67.8	89.3	48.8
Capital account as % of GDP	3.6	3.6	4.8	2.6
Forex assets excluding gold (USD bn)	296.7	296.6	295.7	303.6
Short-term debt (USD bn)	65.0	78.2	96.7	92.7
External debt (USD bn)	317.9	360.8	404.9	426.0
Ratio of external debt to GDP (%)	18.2	20.5	22.0	23.3

You are the CEO of an MNC engaged in the manufacture of equipment used in renewable energy generation. The internal project management team has identified India as one of the most potential business destinations, and submitted a note to you with the above-mentioned data to study the feasibility of locating a manufacturing plant. How would you look at India as your business destination? What factors you would consider as enabling factors? Which of the aspects would you consider as risk generating? What strategies would you work out to counter the risk-generating factors?

Multiple-choice Questions

1. Balance of Payments forms a part of a country's ________
   (a) GDP (b) net national income
   (c) national Accounts (d) none of these
2. BOP indicates the level of ________.
   (a) GDP of a country (b) indebtedness of a country
   (c) exchange rates (d) none of these
3. BOP is based on principles of ________.
   (a) single-entry bookkeeping
   (b) double-entry bookkeeping
   (c) international accounting
   (d) none of these
4. When a country receives a payment from another country, it ________.
   (a) increases foreign assets
   (b) decreases foreign assets
   (c) does not affect the BOP
   (d) none of these
5. An international transaction that increases the demand for domestic currency is recorded as ________ in BOP.
   (a) credit entry (b) debit entry
   (c) error entry (d) none of these
6. A transaction that results in decrease in the supply of foreign exchange shall be shown as a ________ in BOP.
   (a) debit entry (b) credit entry
   (c) capital entry (d) none of these
7. All credit entries in BOP represent the ________ domestic currency.
   (a) demand for (b) supply of
   (c) exchange rate of (d) none of these
8. An NRI sends money in USD to his family members in India. This transaction comes under the ________ of BOP of India.
   (a) trade account (b) capital account
   (c) current account (d) none of these
9. The central bank of a country intervenes in the foreign exchange market through ________.
   (a) capital account
   (b) current account
   (c) official reserve account
   (d) none of these
10. Transactions that give rise to the supply of domestic currency are shown as ________ in the official reserve account.
    (a) debits (b) credits
    (c) errors (d) none of these
11. A current account deficit means that the country spends ________ abroad than it earns abroad.
    (a) more (b) less
    (c) same (d) none of these
12. Current account balance is defined as ________.
    (a) $CA = S - I$ (b) $CA = Y - S$
    (c) $CA = Y - I$ (d) none of these
13. $(C + I + G)$ is known as ________.
    (a) absorption (b) output
    (c) external demand (d) none of these
14. For the year 2013, ________ tops the list of countries having current account surplus.
    (a) Germany (b) China
    (c) Japan (d) none of these
15. Under the floating exchange rate regime, current account balance plus capital account balance equals ________.
    (a) zero (b) one
    (c) hundred (d) none of these
16. A surplus in BOP results in a/an ________ in money supply in the economy.
    (a) increase (b) decrease
    (c) constant (d) none of these
17. The phenomenon of deterioration and eventual improvement in a country's balance of trade is known as the ________.
    (a) Tobin effect (b) J-curve effect
    (c) Keynesian effect (d) none of these

Further Reading

1. Donald Kemp, "Balance of Payments Concepts—What Do they Really Mean?" *Federal Reserve Bank of St. Louis Review*, (July 1975): 14–23.
2. Leland Yeager, *International Monetary Relations*, (New York: Harper & Row, 1965).
3. Joan Salop and Erich Spitaller, "Why does the Current Account Matter?" *IMF Staff Papers* (March 1980): 101–34.
4. K. Alec Chrystal and Geoffrey E. Wood, "Are Trade Deficits a Problem ?" *Review* (Jan/Feb 1988): 3–11.
5. Richard N. Cooper, "The Balance of Payments in Review," *Journal of Political Economy* (August 1966): 379–395.
6. Reserve Bank of India, *Balance of Payments Compilation Manual* (Mumbai: Reserve Bank of India, 1987).
7. Tamim Bayoumi, "Saving-investment Correlations", *IMF Staff Papers*, (June 1990): 37:2.
8. Maurice Obstfeld and Kenneth Rogoff, *Foundations of International Macroeconomics*, (MIT Press, 1996).

CHAPTER 4

International Parity Relationship

CHAPTER OBJECTIVES

After studying this chapter, you should be able to:

1 Explain how exchange rates are determined.
2 Discuss the factors that influence the demand and supply of currency.
3 Understand purchasing power parity and its various forms.
4 Discuss interest rate parity and forward rate parity.
5 Explain the international Fisher effect.
6 Analyse the interrelationships between various parity conditions.
7 Briefly discuss exchange rate forecasting.

Introduction

Exchange rates are important not only for business organizations but also for governments and individuals. Any change in exchange rates in either direction influences their cash flows. So, it is in everyone's interest to know how exchange rates move and what factors influence them.

Broadly speaking, exchange rates are influenced by product prices and interest rates, which, in turn, are determined by several factors. Exchange rates are even one such factor. Changes in exchange rates cause and are caused by changes in product prices and interest rates. Exchange rates (spot as well as forward), product prices, and interest rates have equilibrium relationships, also known as *parity relationships,* governed by the law of one price. Parity relationships are driven by arbitrage. This chapter explains the essence of these parity relationships or conditions.

Exchange Rate Determination

The foreign exchange rate is determined by several forces, which are known as demand forces and supply forces.

The exchange rate is the price of one country's currency in terms of another country's currency. As in the case of commodities, goods, or services, the price of a currency is influenced by the demand for and supply of the currency. So, any change in the exchange rate is the result of a change in the supply and demand forces. The point of intersection of the demand and supply gives the equilibrium exchange rate.

Demand for Currency

A country's currency is in demand when foreigners buy the goods and services exported by that country, or when they buy financial assets denominated in that currency. For example, demand for the US dollar is derived from demand in other countries for US goods, services and USD-denominated financial assets. Any increase in the foreign currency's dollar value is an increase in the foreign currency's price of US goods and services, and USD-denominated assets. This results in a reduced demand for US goods, services, and USD-denominated assets abroad. The converse happens when the foreign currency's US dollar value decreases. With the depreciation of a foreign currency relative to the US dollar, US goods, services, and USD-denominated assets become expensive in the foreign country. Suppose the exchange rate of INR against the US dollar is at INR 60.75. If the exchange rate increases to USD/INR 62, the price of US goods and services in terms of INR increases. As a result, the demand for US goods and services in India decreases, leading to a fall in the demand for US dollars. The opposite happens if the exchange rate decreases to USD/INR 60.00.

Taking another example, assume the exchange rate of the US dollar against the Indian rupee is INR/USD 0.0167. The US dollar price of a colour television set is USD 500. The Indian consumer pays INR 29,940 for the CTV set. If the exchange rate increases to INR/USD 0.0200, then the Indian consumer has to pay only INR 25,000 for the same CTV set. In view of the reduction in the price of the US CTV set in terms of Indian rupees, the demand for US CTVs will increase. This would, in turn, increase the demand for US dollars in order to import more CTVs. Thus, the demand for a currency in the foreign exchange market increases with the depreciation of that currency.

The demand curve is the graphical representation of the demand schedule. It shows various quantities of a currency that participants in the foreign exchange market are willing and able to buy at each exchange rate during a specific period of time. Thus, the demand curve of a currency shows the price of the currency that is demanded at each possible exchange rate. As shown in Figure 4.1, the demand curve slopes downward, which implies that as the exchange rate goes down, other things remaining the same, the demand for the currency goes up, and vice versa. In other words, the exchange rate and the demand for the currency are inversely related. However, the demand for the currency is influenced not only by its exchange rate but also by other factors. Therefore, the relationship between the exchange rate and the quantity demanded is established by assuming other factors remaining constant. When other factors do not remain constant, the law of demand fails to hold, and demand may lose its inverse relationship with the exchange rate.

Taking India as an example, the demand for foreign exchange emanates mainly from the import of goods and services, invisible payments in the current account, repayment of external debt including external commercial borrowings (ECBs) and short-term trade credit,

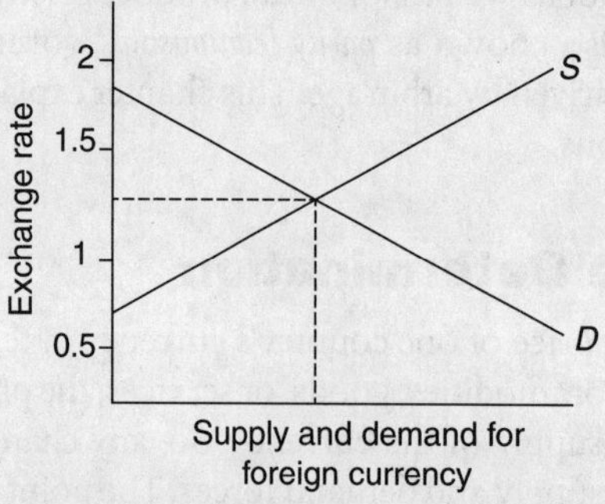

Figure 4.1

Demand and Supply of a Currency

redemption of bank deposits made by foreign residents including NRIs, and outflows on account of direct foreign investments and portfolio investments.

Supply of Currency

A country's currency is supplied in the course of paying for the country's imports. The supply of a currency also takes place when foreign currency-denominated assets are purchased by the residents of the country. Thus, the supply of a currency derives from the demand for imported goods, services, and assets denominated in the foreign currency. In India, for example, the major sources of supply of foreign exchange are:

- receipts in the current account through exports and remittances;
- inflows in the capital account through foreign direct investment, portfolio investment, and ECBs; and
- bank deposits made by foreigners including NRIs.

When a country's imports are priced (invoiced) in a foreign currency, the resident buyers sell their domestic currency for the foreign currency in order to pay for imported goods and services. Even if the imports are invoiced in the domestic currency, the foreign recipients would instantly sell the domestic currency for foreign currency, which again contributes to the supply of the currency in the foreign exchange market. For example, the supply of the US dollar as against the Indian rupee depends upon the demand for Indian goods, services, and INR-denominated financial assets in the United States. If the exchange rate between the USD and INR decreases to, say, 0.0167 from 0.0175, the cost of Indian goods and services in terms of USD comes down. As a result, US demand for Indian goods increases, ultimately leading to an increase in the supply of US dollars. Suppose the exchange rate of the US dollar as against the Indian rupee is INR/USD 0.0175. An Indian car in the United States is priced at INR 5,00,000. So the US customer has to pay USD 8,750 to buy the car. If the exchange rate becomes INR/USD 0.0167, the US customer has to pay only USD 8,350 to get the same car. In other words, the price of the Indian car in terms of US dollars comes down with the appreciation of USD against INR. As a result, there will be an increased supply of Indian cars to meet the increased demand, ultimately leading to an increased supply of US dollars. Therefore, the supply curve of the US dollar slopes upward with its appreciation. The same is true with any other currency in the foreign exchange market. As in the demand for a currency, other factors also influence the supply of a currency. However, the other factors are assumed to be constant in establishing the relationship between the exchange rate and the supply of a currency. The supply curve is also shown in Figure 4.1. The supply curve shows the volume of a currency that would be supplied at various exchange rates.

Note that the elasticity of demand for imports determines the direction of the supply curve of the currency. If the demand for imports is elastic, the supply curve of the currency slopes upward. But, if the demand for imports is inelastic, the supply curve of the currency slopes downward. When the demand for imports is inelastic, depreciation of the home currency raises the prices of imports more than it reduces the quantity of imports. As a result, the value of imports increases, leading to a downward-sloping currency supply curve. This will have implications for exchange rate stability.

The point of intersection of the demand and supply curves in the graph (Figure 4.1) is the equilibrium exchange rate. The **equilibrium exchange rate** is the exchange rate at which the demand for a currency is equivalent to the supply of the same currency.

However, there are several factors other than the exchange rate that also influence the value of exports and imports, and thus the currency demand and supply. As can be seen from Figure 4.2, a shift in currency demand and supply curves creates new equilibrium exchange rates.

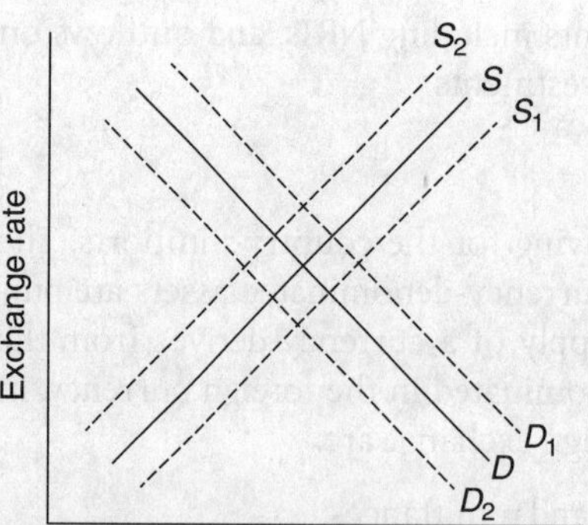

Figure 4.2

Shift in Currency Demand and Supply

The **equilibrium exchange rate** is the exchange rate at which the demand for a currency is equivalent to the supply of the same currency.

Factors Affecting Exchange Rates

There are several factors that influence the exchange rate through their effects on the currency demand and supply, leading to a new equilibrium exchange rate. This section outlines these important factors.

Inflation Rate

The term *inflation* is defined in different ways to indicate its various underlying causes. Inflation was first defined by the new-classical economists as a galloping rise in prices consequent to an excessive increase in the quantity of money. This definition implies that inflation is the result of expansion of the money supply in excess of real output growth in the economy. The traditional approach classifies the theory of inflation into *demand–pull theory* and *supply* or *cost–push theory.* According to the demand–pull theory, the general price level rises because the demand for goods and services exceeds the supply at the existing prices. This is due to changes in government spending, taxes, and money supply. The supply-side inflation may be a wage-push inflation, profit–push inflation, or supply–shock inflation. But other economists including Harry G. Johnson, Edward Shapiro, and J. R. Hicks, who did not subscribe to the argument that money supply alone is the cause of inflation, defined inflation as a persistent and appreciable rise in the general level of prices. According to them, inflation is not always a monetary phenomenon. Apart from money supply, there are other factors that influence general price levels (or cause inflation) in the economy.

Relative inflation rates, interest rates, economic growth rates, political factors, social factors, and government controls are the major factors that influence exchange rates through their effects on currency demand and supply.

Irrespective of the type of inflation or its causes, inflation influences exchange rates by affecting the competitiveness of the country's goods and services in the international market. In view of inflation, a country's exports may become costlier and thus fail to compete in the international market. As a result, the country's exports would decline, leading to a decline in the supply of foreign currency. It is, in fact, the relative rates of inflation in countries that causes changes in currency demand and supply. For example, suppose that the inflation rate in both India and the United Kingdom is 6 percent. As the inflation rates are the same in two countries, the currency demand and supply curves shift in proportion to the rate of inflation, which means the exchange rate will not be affected by inflation.

When the inflation rates are different in different countries, exchange rates are affected. For example, if the inflation rate is 4 percent in the United States and 6 percent in India at a particular time, the US consumers would buy fewer Indian goods and services, leading to a decline in the supply of US dollars at every exchange rate. This will shift the US dollar supply curve upward by the inflation rate. As US goods and services in India become cheaper relative to Indian goods and services, the Indian consumers will switch to US substitutes, leading to increased demand for US dollars. This will shift the demand curve upward by the inflation rate. Thus, a higher rate of inflation in India relative to the inflation rate in the United States will simultaneously increase US exports to India and reduce Indian exports to the United States.

As per the data for September 2014, countries such as Iran, Afghanistan, Zimbabwe, Guinea, Venezuela, and Burma have high inflation rates, at least two-digit figures.The developed countries (e.g. the US, the UK, Germany, Canada, and Japan) along with China maintain a low rate of inflation, less than 3 percent. Countries that have a moderate rate of inflation include India, Brazil, Argentina, Egypt, Russia, Nigeria, and Turkey. Countries such as Sweden, Switzerland, Spain, Portugal, Israel, Greece, and Poland maintain a very low rate of inflation, some of them even have a negative inflation rate. The other factors remaining the same, a country with a consistently lower rate of inflation maintains high currency value relative to the currencies with higher rate of inflation. The countries with a higher rate of inflation typically see depreciation in their currency in relation to the currencies of their trading partners.

Economic Growth Rate

The country's economic growth rate also influences the demand and supply of foreign currency. The higher the economic growth rate, the more economic transactions there are, both within the country and across countries. This will cause outflow and inflow of foreign currency, leading to a new equilibrium exchange rate.

Different countries have different levels of economic growth. It is estimated that the world output would grow by 3.7 percent in 2014. China and India are the world's fastest growing economies with a growth rate of 7.3 percent and 5.4 percent, respectively, in 2014. Countries such as Spain and Italy experienced negative growth rates in 2012 and 2013. All the countries in the Euro Area put together had a negative growth rate in 2012 and also in 2013. The advanced economies are expected to have moderate economic growth rates in 2014. The US is expected to have a higher growth rate of 2.8 percent than U.K (2.4 percent), Germany (1.6 percent), Japan (1.7 percent), and Canada (2.2 percent).

Interest Rate

The interest rate in the economy also influences the exchange rate through supply and demand for foreign exchange. When the interest rate in an economy rises, investors pump in more funds by subscribing to various debt securities issued by the government and the corporates. If foreign investors bring in foreign currency to buy the domestic currency for investment, the supply of foreign currency increases. This causes the domestic currency to appreciate. Similarly, if the interest rate in other countries rise, there will be a shift of investible funds to other countries, leading to an increase in the value of other currencies. Thus, the increase or decrease in interest rate in the economy results in an increase or decrease in the supply and demand for foreign currency. This shifts the demand and supply curves to new positions and, thereby, a new equilibrium exchange rate is determined. However, the increase or decrease in interest rate would be effective only if the relative change in interest rate is more than that in other countries.

The interest rates vary among the countries. As per the World Bank, the real interest rate (lending interest rate adjusted for inflation) in 2013 was 18.4 percent in Brazil, 4.2 percent in China, 3.2 percent in India, 7.0 percent in Indonesia, 1.9 percent in Japan, 2.2 percent in Mexico, 3.4 percent in Russian Federation, 5.2 percent in Singapore, 1.7 percent in the US, and (-) 1.2 percent in the UK. The other factors remaining the same, the countries with a higher interest rate would attract more foreign funds than the countries with low interest rates.

Political Factors

Political factors do influence the demand and supply of foreign currency. Political stability in the country may attract a large amount of investment funding in foreign currencies, as investors may find the country to be less risky and more rewardingto invest. On the other hand, any instability in the political governance of a country may drive away investors from the country and cause the outflow of funds to other economies. It is not only the political stability, but also the political ideology or policies of the government that may influence the exchange rate. For example, a particular political party in power may accelerate the process of liberalization and opening up of the economy, thereby attracting foreign funds. A different political party in power with an opposite political ideology may keep foreign investors at a distance, and thereby discourage the flow of foreign currency into the economy. Some political decisions may also influence the exports and imports of a country, thereby influencing the exchange rate. Thus, the actions and activities of political institutions in a country may influence the foreign exchange rate through the supply and demand for foreign currencies.

Current Account Deficit

Deficit in the current account of a country shows that the country spends more on foreign goods and services than what it receives from other countries on the same. To make up for the deficit, the country has to attract foreign investments, borrow from other countries, reduce its foreign currency assets, or do a combination of them. All such transactions do influence the demand and supply of foreign currencies and thereby the exchange rates.

Social Factors

The demand and supply of foreign currency are also influenced by social factors like literacy, education levels, communal and religious harmony, risk perceptions of people, and other demographic characteristics. For example, communal and religious harmony in a country may attract large foreign investments. Similarly, high literacy and education levels may increase cross-border movement of people and cross-border flow of funds. This will have influence on the demand and supply of currencies on the foreign exchange market.

Government Controls

Governments may impose several controls and barriers on imports, exports, remittances, and investments. All such controls influence the demand and supply of currencies on the foreign exchange market. Governments may also directly intervene in the foreign exchange market and influence exchange rates. Therefore, exchange rates are highly susceptible to government controls, barriers, and interventions.

It is evident from our discussion that the demand and supply of foreign exchange are influenced by several interrelated and interactive factors, ranging from economic factors and government controls to social and political factors. Some of these factors may have a negative effect, while others have a strong positive influence on exchange rates. Further, some of these factors have a long-term impact, while others may have a temporary and short-term effect. For example, speculative and psychological factors may cause short-term fluctuations, while strong economic fundamentals may have a long-lasting impact on the demand and supply of foreign exchange.

The BOP Theory of Exchange Rates

The balance of payments (BOP)—a statement of receipts and payments of foreign exchange based on the concept of double-entry bookkeeping—represents the demand for and supply of foreign currencies. The credit balance shows receipts of foreign exchange, and the debit balance shows payments in foreign exchange. As stated earlier, the exchange rate is the result of a currency's supply and demand in the foreign exchange market. The forces of supply and demand, in turn, are determined by various items in the balance of payments. The demand for a foreign currency against the domestic currency arises from the debit items in the balance of payments, and the supply of foreign currency arises out of credit items in the balance of payments. In other words, the items on the credit side increase the supply of foreign currencies, and the items on the debit side increase the demand for foreign currencies. When a country's BOP is at a deficit, the demand for foreign currencies is more than their supply. This leads to a shift in the supply and demand curves of foreign currencies and a new equilibrium exchange rate. There are several forces that influence the items of balance of payments, particularly exports and imports. All such forces influence the exchange rate. The BOP approach to exchange rate determination assumes a perfect foreign exchange market and a perfect international market for goods and services. The main criticism against this approach is that the BOP itself is a function of the exchange rate and, therefore, it cannot explain the determination of the exchange rate.

The Purchasing Power Parity (PPP) Theory

The **purchasing power parity (PPP) theory**, developed by Gustav Cassell—a Swedish economist—in the early 1900s, describes the relationship between the average price levels in a country and its exchange rates. Having its roots in the *law of one price,* the PPP theory states that the exchange rate between any two currencies is said to be at equilibrium when the purchasing power of the two currencies is the same anywhere in the world. More specifically, the home currency price of a commodity in different countries, when converted into a common currency at the spot exchange rate, is the same in all countries across the world. In other words, a currency should have the same purchasing power (command over goods and services) in all countries. Purchasing power parity theory has many applications. For example, as each country measures its output (GDP) in its own currency, it becomes necessary to convert that data into a common currency in order to compare the value of the output of different countries. One of the several approaches to that conversion uses the PPP rate, which is defined by IMF as "the rate at which the currency of one country would have to be converted into that of another country to buy the same amount of goods and services in each country."

*Having its roots in the law of one price, the **purchasing power parity (PPP) theory** states that the home currency price of a commodity in different countries, when converted into a common currency at the spot exchange rate, is the same in all countries across the world.*

The Law of One Price

The law of one price postulates that identical goods or services must always sell at the same price. That is, if a commodity or product can be sold in two different markets, its price should be the same in both markets. However, equalization of prices is possible only under the following conditions:

- There are no transportation costs.
- There are no transaction costs.

The **law of one price** states that if a commodity or product can be sold in two different markets, its price should be the same in both markets, given that there are no transportation costs, transaction costs, tariffs, or restrictions on the movement of goods, and that there is no product differentiation or obstructions in the free flow of information.

- There are no tariffs.
- There are no restrictions on the movement of products.
- There is free flow of information.
- There is no product differentiation.

The law of one price holds only when the conditions listed here exist. It is obvious that the price of a commodity will vary if there *is product differentiation,* that is, if the products produced in different countries vary in terms of parameters such as quality, quantity, and appearance. *Restrictions on the movement of products,* in the form of bans and quotas on the amount of goods exported from or imported to the country, obstruct free movement of goods (to the extent desired to equalize prices) from one market to another. As a result, the prices in different markets cannot become equalized. The *absence of free flow of information* also makes the price of a product differ from market to market.

Further, the law of one price holds only in the *absence of transportation costs, transaction costs,* and *tariffs* (such as export tax and import duty) that are imposed on the movement of products from one market to another. If such costs exist, the price of the product may differ from market to market to the extent of such costs/tariffs. And if the price difference between the markets is more than the difference between the costs/tariffs involved in the movement of goods, it gives rise to an *arbitrage opportunity* for traders to buy the product in one market and sell in another to make a profit. Such traders, who buy a product in one market and sell in another market for a profit, are known *as product* or *commodity arbitrageurs.* Thus, arbitrage is a process of buying and selling of something of value to make a riskless profit by taking advantage of price differential between the markets. The absence of risk is a distinguishing feature of arbitrage.

Every rational trader seeks to buy a commodity at a low price and to sell the same at a high price. A trader would never miss an opportunity to make a profit, particularly when it is without risk or investment. If, for instance, a silver bar weighing 1 kg is priced at INR 26,025 in Market A, and the same is traded at INR 25,500 in Market B, the trader would buy the silver in Market B and sell it in Market A. This would yield a profit of INR 525 per kg of silver that is traded, and other traders will also be motivated to buy silver in Market B and sell it in Market A. This will cause an increase in the demand for silver in Market B—the market where the price is lower—and an increase in the supply of silver in Market A, where the price is higher. The increasing demand will raise the price in Market B, while the increasing supply will lower the price in Market A. This process will continue till the price for silver equalizes in both the markets. Thus, the traders' arbitrage activities will continue till the opportunity for profit is eliminated. However, arbitrage cannot operate in some cases. For example, arbitrage cannot work in the case of non-traded goods (e.g. personal services, real estate, etc.). It means that the inter-market price differential cannot be eliminated by arbitrage in the case of non-traded goods.

International comparison of prices expressed in different currencies cannot be made unless they are converted into a common denominator. For example, to compare the price of a commodity in Indian market with the price of the identical commodity in the US market, we have to translate Indian rupee price into USD price or vice versa. A typical trader who wants to buy a product manufactured in the US, first, has to buy the US dollars and then use the dollars to buy the product. It means that he exchanges his home currency for foreign currency, then exchanges the foreign currency for the foreign product. Thus, the rupee price of the product can be derived by the following simple arithmetic calculation:

Indian rupee price of a product = Indian rupee price of USD × USD price of a product

Relaxing one of the assumptions of the law of one price, the above equation can be restated as follows:

$$\text{Indian rupee price of a product} = \text{Indian rupee price of USD} \times \text{USD price of a product} + \text{Transaction costs}$$

Forms of PPP

There are two versions of PPP—the absolute version and the relative version. In this section, we shall take a look at both these versions of PPP.

The Absolute Form The law of one price states that if a commodity or product can be sold in two different markets, its price in terms of a common currency should be the same in both the markets. If, instead of a product or an asset, a standard basket of goods and services is involved, its price in different countries should also be the same when measured in a common currency. If the price measured in a common currency is not the same, traders will engage in arbitraging to earn a profit until the price in different countries measured in a common currency equalizes. Note that when prices are different in different countries, it is not only arbitrageurs who can exploit the situation, but also regular traders (genuine buyers) who would buy the basket in the cheaper market and avoid the market where the price is higher. This means that regular traders also have a role in equalizing the prices between markets.

Let us assume that the price of a standard basket of goods and services in India as represented by its price index is P_{INR}. The price of the same basket of goods and services in the United States as represented by its price index is, say, P_{US}. In such a case, the spot exchange rate (S_0) between INR and USD (expressed as the number of units of INR per unit of USD) is expressed as

$$S_0 = \frac{P_{INR}}{P_{US}}$$

The spot exchange rate between INR and USD can also be expressed as S_0(USD/INR). Therefore,

$$P_{INR} = P_{US} S_0(\text{USD/INR}), \quad \text{and}$$

$$P_{US} = \frac{P_{INR}}{S_0(\text{USD/INR})}$$

Thus, the INR price of a commodity or a basket of goods and services in India is the US dollar price of a commodity or a basket of goods and services in the United States, multiplied by the exchange rate of Indian currency per US dollar. This implies that the INR price of a basket of goods and services in India must be the same as the INR price of the basket in the United States. To generalize, the price of a standard basket of goods and services should be the same in all countries when measured in a common currency.

Put differently, the exchange rate between two currencies equals the ratio of the general price indices of the two countries. For example, the general price index in the US is at 530 and the general price index in UK at 435. The equilibrium exchange rate between the USD and GBP is: 530 ÷ 435 = 1.2184. This rule is known as the *absolute version of purchasing power parity.* Thus, the PPP, in its absolute version, states that the exchange rate at any time exactly reflects the ratio of price indices in two countries, or the purchasing powers of two currencies.

Absolute PPP is also known as the *static form of PPP.* The law of one price, which is the basis for absolute form of PPP, states that the prices in different countries tend to be equal if the markets are perfect (i.e. there are no transportation costs, transaction costs, etc.). In other

*The **relative version of PPP**, or the **dynamic form**, states that the percentage change in the exchange rate between the domestic currency and the foreign currency should equal the percentage change in the ratio of price indices in the two countries.*

words, the absolute version of PPP holds only when there are no frictions such as transportation costs, transaction costs, quotas, and tariff barriers. In reality, however, such frictions are bound to exist. In view of such market imperfections, the prices of standard baskets of goods and services in different countries may not be the same when measured in a common currency. Deviations from absolute PPP may also occur in the absence of the same goods and services and in the same proportion in each country's basket of goods and services. All the ills of price indices may also be attributed to the absolute form of PPP.

The Relative Form In view of serious limitations of the absolute version of PPP, an alternative form, known as the **relative version** or **dynamic form of PPP**, is used. The relative form of PPP, stated in terms of rates of inflation, is considered to be a better determinant of exchange rates. It states that the percentage change in the exchange rate between the domestic currency and the foreign currency should equal the percentage change in the ratio of price indices in the two countries. That is, the exchange rate would change to offset the difference in the inflation rates between the two countries. The foreign currency depreciates when the inflation rate in the foreign country is more than the domestic inflation rate, and the foreign currency appreciates when the domestic inflation rate is more than the foreign country's inflation rate. This means that the currency of a country with a high rate of inflation should depreciate relative to the currency of a country with a lower rate of inflation.

A relative change in price indices between two countries over a particular period of time should result in a change in the exchange rate between their currencies over that period. If this happens, the relative purchasing power is the same between the countries. The consuming public will, therefore, have the same purchasing power for foreign goods as well as for domestic goods. Also note that the relative PPP holds even in the presence of market imperfections such as transaction costs, transportation costs, and tariff barriers.

Thus, in the absolute form of PPP, the price levels as represented by price indices are considered in their absolute values, while in the relative form, the rates of change in price levels (or change in inflation rates) are considered. Let $S_0(\mathrm{B/A})$ be the spot exchange rate between the currency of Country X (denoted by "A") and the currency of Country Y (denoted by "B"). Further, let P_x and P_y be the price levels in Country X and Country Y, respectively. According to absolute PPP, the relationship between the exchange rate and price levels at time "0" is

$$S_0(\mathrm{B/A}) = \frac{P_x(0)}{P_y(0)}$$

At time "1", the relationship will be

$$S_1(\mathrm{B/A}) = \frac{P_x(1)}{P_y(1)}$$

To generalize, at time *t*,

$$S_t(\mathrm{B/A}) = \frac{P_x(t)}{P_y(t)}$$

The relative form of PPP is defined as

$$\frac{S_t(\mathrm{B/A})}{S_0(\mathrm{B/A})} = \frac{p_x(t)/p_x(0)}{p_y(t)/p_y(0)} \tag{4.1}$$

The right-hand side of Eq. 4.1 is the ratio of the changes in the price levels in Country X and Country Y. To express the equation in terms of inflation, let i_x and i_y be the rates of inflation in Country X and Country Y, respectively.

Now,

$$\frac{p_x(t)}{p_x(0)} = 1 + i_x$$

and

$$\frac{p_y(t)}{p_y(0)} = 1 + i_y$$

By substituting these values in Eq. 4.1, the relative form of PPP can be expressed as

$$\frac{S_t(B/A)}{S_0(B/A)} = \frac{(1+i_x)^t}{(1+i_y)^t} \tag{4.2}$$

$$S_t(B/A) = S_0(B/A) \times \frac{(1+i_x)^t}{(1+i_y)^t}$$

Eq. 4.2 can be stated in terms of percentage change in the exchange rates for one period (i.e. $t = 1$):

$$\frac{S_t(B/A) - S_0(B/A)}{S_0(B/A)} = \frac{i_x - i_y}{1 + i_y}$$

As mentioned earlier, the currency of a country with a higher rate of inflation should depreciate relative to the currency of another country which has a lower rate of inflation. For example, suppose that the inflation rate is 6 percent in India and 4 percent in the United States. Applying the PPP theory, we would conclude that the INR value of the US dollar must rise by about (1.06/1.04 –1) percent, or 1.92 percent, to equalize the INR price of goods in the two countries. In view of the relatively high inflation in India, the domestic products command higher prices than the imported products (US goods). So, consumers in India will demand more imported goods. At the same time, consumers in the United States will demand lesser quantities of Indian goods because they are highly priced relative to their domestic goods. This puts upward pressure on the value of the US dollar. The increasing demand for US goods in India will continue till the US dollar has appreciated by about 2 percent. At that stage, the prices paid for US products by Indian consumers will be equal to the prices of comparable products made in India. That is, the relative purchasing power between Indian currency and the US currency will become equal. In fact, the increased price of US goods in India is about 6 percent, covering the inflation rate in the United States at 4 percent and appreciation of the US dollar relative to the Indian rupee by 2 percent. The increased price is equal to the 6 percent inflation rate in India. Now, suppose that the US dollar has appreciated by, say, 1 percent instead of 2 percent. In this scenario, the increased price of US products will be less than the 6 percent inflation rate in India. That is, US products will continue to be cheaper than comparable Indian products. In other words, any level of appreciation of the US dollar relative to the Indian rupee below 2 percent will make US products cheaper and more attractive than comparable Indian products. On the other hand, US consumers will reduce imports from India till the US dollar appreciates to the extent that Indian products are no more expensive than US goods. The PPP theory mainly contends that consumers will switch over to domestic goods or services whenever imports are costlier, and will switch over to foreign goods whenever imports are cheaper. This process will influence the exchange rate. Of course, the main limitation in this process is the availability of substitute goods or services. If substitute goods or services are not available, consumers cannot make a shift.

The relationship between the inflation differential and the changes in exchange rates is graphically represented in Figure 4.3. The vertical axis represents the percentage change in the exchange rate. The horizontal axis represents the inflation differential (difference in the inflation rates between the home country and the foreign country). The PPP line represents the equilibrium between the price-level changes and the exchange rates. For example, the 2 percent inflation differential should be offset by the 2 percent depreciation of the home currency relative to the foreign currency. Where the inflation differential is greater or lower than the appreciation or depreciation of home currency, a situation of disequilibrium exists. However, the arbitrage process will ultimately bring the exchange rates in line with the inflation differential.

Example 4.1

The consumer price index in India rose from 200 to 216 over the period 1 January–31 December and the US consumer price index increased from 100 to 105 over the same period. The exchange rate between USD/INR on 1 January was INR 44. What should be the exchange rate between the Indian rupee and the US dollar on 31 December?

Solution

The rate of inflation in India:

$$\frac{216}{200} - 1 = 1.08 - 1 = 0.08 \text{ or } 8\%$$

The rate of inflation in the United States:

$$\frac{105}{100} - 1 = 0.05 \text{ or } 5\%$$

The equilibrium exchange rate between USD/INR on 31 December:

$$S_t(\text{USD/INR}) = S_0(\text{USD/INR}) \times \frac{(1+i_h)}{(1+i_f)}$$

$$= 44 \times \frac{(1+0.08)}{(1+0.04)}$$

$$= 45.2571$$

The percentage change in the exchange rate:

$$\frac{45.271-44}{44} = 0.0286 \text{ or } 2.86\%$$

Note that the same solution can be obtained from the following:

$$(1+0.08)/(1+0.05) - 1 = 0.02857 \text{ or } 2.86\%$$

This implies that the USD should appreciate by 2.86 percent in order for the exchange to be in equilibrium as per PPP.

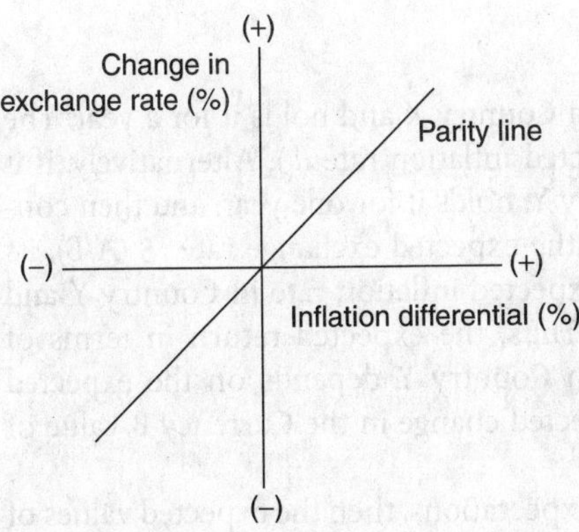

Figure 4.3

Purchasing Power Parity

PPP can also be represented by the following approximation when inflation is low (assuming "A" as home currency and "B" as foreign currency):

$$\frac{S_t\,(B/A) - S_0\,(B/A)}{S_0\,(B/A)} = i_h - i_f$$

This, however, is a poor approximation when the inflation rate is high; it is useful only when the inflation differential is small.

If the home currency depreciates by more than is warranted by the PPP, the competitiveness of the home country increases in the world market. Conversely, if the home currency depreciates by less than the inflation rate differential, the competitiveness of the home country weakens. For example, as a consequence of the increase in the inflation rate in India relative to European countries, the Indian rupee depreciates against the euro. But the rate of depreciation of the Indian rupee is much higher than is warranted by PPP. As a result, companies in eurozone countries that export to India will be adversely affected because the euro becomes more expensive relative to the Indian rupee, reducing the demand for products produced in eurozone countries. At the same time, companies in India that export to eurozone countries will benefit because their products become cheaper to consumers in eurozone countries.

The Expectation Form The **expectation form of PPP** involves the exchange rate and the inflation rates being expressed in expected terms, and it states that the expected percentage change in the exchange rate equals the expected inflation differential in the two countries, provided the market participants are risk-neutral and the markets are perfect. The expectation form of PPP is also known as the *efficient market form* of PPP.

The *expectation form* of PPP implies that the expected percentage change in the exchange rate is equal to the expected inflation differential in the two countries.

The expectation form of PPP can be represented as

$$\hat{i}_x = \hat{i}_y + \hat{S}(A/B)$$

or

$$\hat{S} = (A/B) = \hat{i}_x - \hat{i}_y$$

where

A = currency of Country X
B = currency of Country Y
$\hat{S}$ (A/B) = expected spot exchange rate

$\hat{i}_x$ = expected inflation rate in Country X
$\hat{i}_y$ = expected inflation rate in Country Y

Suppose a firm buys a standard basket of goods in Country X and holds it for a year. The firm can expect to get a return equal to the expected inflation rate (i_x). Alternatively, if it buys the same standard basket of goods in Country Y, holds it for one year, and then converts its return in Currency B into Currency A at the expected exchange rate, $\hat{S}$ (A/B), its expected return will be equal to the sum of the expected inflation rate in Country Y and the expected change in the spot exchange rate. Thus, the expected return in terms of Currency A from holding the basket of goods in Country Y depends on the expected change in inflation rate in Country Y, and the expected change in the Currency B value of Currency A.

If the market participants are rational in their expectations, then the expected values of the exchange rate and the inflation rates will equal the actual rates of change in these variables on the average over a long period of time. In other words, if the expectation form of PPP holds, the relative version of PPP also holds on the average over a long period of time.

The Big Mac Index

The Economist introduced the Big Mac index—a light-hearted guide to how far currencies are from their fair value—in 1986, and since then, it has been publishing the index every year. The index measures the undervaluation or overvaluation of currencies. It also indicates which currencies are correctly valued. The index is based on the absolute version of the theory of PPP, which states that the exchange rate between two currencies should adjust to equalize the price of a standard basket of goods and services between the two countries. The basket of goods in the Big Mac index is the McDonald's Big Mac hamburger. As per PPP, the Big Mac hamburgers would cost the same in all countries where they are available. The Big Mac is chosen because it is available in a common specification in about 120 countries worldwide. Therefore, it is possible to compare the currencies of several countries using the Big Mac index.

Table 4.1 Big Mac Index—Select Countries (24 July 2014)

Country	*Local price*	*USD exchange rate (actual)*	*USD price*	*Implied PPP of USD*	*Under (–)/Over (+) value against USD (%)*
Brazil	13	2.22	4.80	2.71	22.11
UK	2.89	0.59	4.93	0.60	2.71
Canada	5.64	1.07	5.25	1.18	9.51
China	16.9	6.20	2.73	3.52	(–) 43.14
Euro Area	3.679	0.74	4.95	0.77	3.31
India	105	60.09	1.75	21.90	(–)63.56
Japan	370	101.53	3.64	77.16	(–)24.00
Malaysia	7.63	3.17	2.41	1.59	(–)49.76
Mexico	42	12.93	3.25	8.76	(–)32.27
Philippines	160	43.21	3.70	33.37	(–)22.77
Russia	89	34.84	2.55	18.56	(–)46.72

(Continued)

Table 4.1 ***(Continued)***

Country	*Local price*	*USD exchange rate (actual)*	*USD price*	*Implied PPP of USD*	*Under (−)/Over (+) value against USD (%)*
South Africa	24.5	10.51	2.33	5.11	(−)51.41
Sweden	40.7	6.84	5.95	8.49	24.17
Turkey	9.25	2.09	4.42	1.93	(−)7.75

Note: 1. Implied PPP of USD = Price in local currency/Price in USD
2. Increase/decrease = (Implied PPP of USD/Actual exchange rate of USD) −1

On 24 July 2014, the Big Mac is priced at USD 4.795 in the US. According to PPP, the USD 4.795 should buy exactly one Big Mac in any other country on conversion into local currency at the current exchange rate. As it can be observed from Table 4.1, there are some currencies that are overvalued against the USD and there are also currencies which are undervalued against the USD. It may also be noticed that the currencies of the countries like China, India, Japan, Malaysia, Russia, South Africa, etc. are undervalued; and the currencies of the countries such as Sweden, Brazil, UK, Canada, etc. are overvalued against the USD. When the exchange rates deviate from parity line, the currencies face pressure for change. For overvalued currencies, the pressure is to depreciate and for undervalued currencies the pressure is to appreciate. Therefore, in the long run the currency rates tend toward parity.

The Economist publishes periodically the selected undervalued and overvalued currencies, which can be used to forecast currency values. In spite of certain frictions in the form of variations in taxes, production and distribution costs, etc. the Big Max Index gives an idea how the currency rates might move over the long term. Thus, the Big Mac Index is not expected to be a perfect measure of equilibrium exchange rates. It can be taken as a rule of thumb but with certain limitations.

Departures from PPP

In the real world, there may be deviations from parity due to many reasons. Some of these reasons are:

- As the PPP theory has its origin in the law of one price, all assumptions that underlie the law of one price are equally applicable to PPP. The presence of constraints on the movement of products, transaction costs, transportation costs, and tariffs may lead to deviation from PPP. In other words, it is free trade which can equalize prices in a common currency across the countries.
- Non-traded items such as immovable goods (e.g. land and buildings), highly perishable commodities (e.g. milk and vegetables), and hospitality services may cause departures from PPP. This is because they cannot be moved from one country to another to cash in on the price differential between the countries.
- The inherent limitations of price indices as a measure of price-level changes also make PPP an approximate measure. Different countries may use different baskets of goods and services in the construction of the price index. The price indices of different countries may be different in terms of the proportion of commodities used in the construction of the price index.
- There are many factors other than the prices of goods and services which influence exchange rates. Sometimes, other factors may dominate the role of inflation in

influencing exchange rates. In such situations, the PPP theory cannot give a correct estimate of exchange rates.

- The PPP theory holds only in the long run. In other words, long run changes in exchange rates are in line with long run differences in inflation rates.

It should be noted that PPP holds more during periods of hyperinflation, when the money supply is usually out of control. With excess supply of money in the economy and expectations of a continuing rise in price levels, money turns over swiftly. That is, the increasing velocity of money (the average number of times each unit of money changes hands during a given period) will bid up the price level and drive down the exchange value of the home currency in the foreign exchange market. As mentioned earlier, inflation is one of the several determinants of the exchange rate. Whenever the inflation rate is very high and becomes a dominant factor, the exchange rate moves up proportionately with the inflation differential between the two countries. In such situations, the price adjustments become almost continuous, making the exchange rates move towards parity. It is also observed that the exchange rates move towards their parity levels in the long run as the prices adjust fully and completely. In other words, the PPP theory may not have a practical relevance in the short run. In situations of normal price-level changes (i.e. low inflation rate) or in the short run, the determinants of exchange rate other than inflation will have a significant role in exchange rate determination.

In spite of certain limitations, the PPP-based exchange rates are used in many economic analyses. For example, the PPP-based exchange rates are used, instead of market-determined exchange rates, in ranking the countries on their GDP. The PPP-based exchange rates are used as benchmarks in many other situations as well.

The Real Exchange Rate

What we generally talk about in the foreign exchange dealings is the nominal exchange rate. But really speaking, when we buy a currency, we are interested in what can be bought with it. That is where the real exchange rate comes in. For example, a person has purchased USD 100, which can buy him a colour television set with certain specifications. But he deferred his purchase decision to the next year due to some personal reasons. After one year, he finds that the USD 100 was not enough to buy the same colour television set, which he thought of buying a year back. It means that his money value has come down over one year. In the same vein, the concept of real exchange rate may be understood.

Suppose the exchange rate between the USD and the euro is USD 1.30. A standard basket of goods costs EUR 10,000 in the eurozone and the same in the US costs USD 13,000. The real exchange rate can be calculated as (USD 1.30 × EUR 10,000)/USD 13,000 = 1. Further, suppose the exchange rate between the euro and the USD has increased to USD 1.3946, but the price of the standard basket of goods remains the same in both the places. In such an eventuality, the real exchange rate increases to 1.073. This increase in the real exchange rate implies that the purchasing power of the USD over the goods in the eurozone has gone down. To offer further explanation, suppose the exchange rate between the USD and EUR is USD 1.2975 with the price of the standard basket of goods in both the places remaining the same. In this case, the real exchange rate decreases to USD 0.9981. A decrease in the real exchange rate implies that the US dollar price of the standard basket of goods in the eurozone has gone down. It means that the purchasing power of the US dollar has increased over the goods in the eurozone.

To define the real exchange rate, let us consider this example. At the end of March 2014, the exchange rate between Indian currency and the US dollar was USD/INR 61.45, while at the end of March 2008, it was USD/INR 40. This means that the nominal (actual) exchange

*The **real exchange rate** is the nominal exchange rate adjusted for changes in the relative purchasing power of the currency.*

rate between INR and USD has increased by 53.63 percent over 6 years. But what is important and relevant in determining the relative competitiveness of the nations is the change in the **real exchange rate**, which is the nominal exchange rate, adjusted for inflation differential between the two countries. The real exchange rate is a measure of change in the relative purchasing power of the two currencies concerned.

The real exchange rate between two currencies, say, INR and USD, can be defined as

$$R_t(\text{USD}/\text{INR}) = S_t(\text{USD}/\text{INR}) \times \frac{(1+i_f)^t}{(1+i_h)^t} \quad (4.3)$$

where

R_t = real exchange rate between two currencies at time t
S_t = nominal exchange rate at time t
i_f = rate of inflation in the foreign country during the period t
i_h = rate of inflation in the home country during the period t

Thus, the real exchange rate is the product of the nominal exchange rate between two currencies and relative price levels in each country. For example, between 1 January and 31 December, the rate of inflation in India was, say, 5 percent and in the United States it was 3 percent. In view of the relatively higher rate of inflation, the exchange rate between the Indian rupee and the US dollar changed from INR 44 to INR 46 over the same period. Therefore, from Eq. 4.3, the real exchange rate between INR and USD on 31 December was INR 45.1238 [i.e. 46 × 1.03/1.05]. The USD has experienced a 2.55 percent [i.e. (45.1238 – 44)/44] appreciation in purchasing power relative to the INR.

Taking another example, it is assumed that during the period between 1 July 2013 and 30 June 2014, the rate of inflation was 3 percent in the United States and 2 percent in the United Kingdom. In line with the relatively higher rate of inflation in the United States, the exchange rate between the US dollar and the British pound moved from USD 1.6175 to USD 1.7085. Thus, the real value of the British pound on 30 June 2014 relative to 1 July 2013 was USD 1.6919 [i.e. 1.7085 (1.02/1.03]. Hence, the real exchange rate moved from USD 1.6175 to USD 1.6919 over the period, which means that the GBP has appreciated by 4.6 percent in real terms.

If PPP holds (i.e. there is no deviation from PPP), the change in the exchange rate offsets the inflation differential, and so much so the real exchange rate remains unchanged. In other words, the relative competitiveness of the two countries does not get affected by the inflation differential, if PPP holds good. If PPP does not hold, a change in the nominal exchange rate affects the relative competitiveness of the two countries. In such situations, the change in the real exchange rate may be more or less than is warranted by PPP.

In order for the PPP to hold, $(1+i_h)/(1+e)(1+i_f)$ should be unity. In other words,

$$(1+i_h)/(1+e)(1+i_f) = 1 \quad (4.4)$$

where

e = percentage change in nominal exchange rate.

If this value of $(1+i_h)/(1+e)(1+i_f)$ is greater than unity, the domestic currency has depreciated by less than is warranted by PPP, and if it is less than unity, the domestic currency has appreciated by more than is warranted by PPP. For example, the inflation rate between 1 April 2007 and 31 March 2008 was 7 percent in India and 3 percent in the United States. During the same period, the exchange rate (USD/INR) moved from 42 to 43. So, the left-hand side of Eq. 4.4 becomes

$$(1+0.07)/(1+0.0238)(1+0.03) = 1.0147$$

As the obtained value is more than 1, it means the INR has depreciated against the USD by less than is warranted by PPP. In other words, the INR has depreciated by less than the inflation differential. This weakens the competitiveness of Indian industries in the US market.

Changes in the real exchange rate have implications for the competitiveness of a country in international trade. As mentioned earlier, a change in the real exchange rate reflects the change in the purchasing power of one currency relative to another. A real appreciation of a currency makes the country's exports more expensive, leading to reduced sales and profit margins for the businesses. A real appreciation of domestic currency also affects the real profitability of producing import substitutes. Conversely, a real depreciation of home currency relative to foreign currency enables the home country to be competitive in the international market and realize increased exports. Thus, any deviation from relative PPP will result in real exchange rate gains or losses.

The Real Effective Exchange Rate (REER)

The bilateral exchange rates between the domestic currency and other currencies may not be of much use in determining the international competitiveness of a country when it has trade relations with some countries only. The bilateral movements of a currency may not indicate the overall change in the home currency value against the currencies of the country's trading partners. Therefore, an overall measure of the movement of the home currency against the country's major trading partners' currencies is of great significance. It is in this context that the concept of effective exchange rate has come into prominence. The *effective exchange rate,* also called *multilateral exchange rate,* is a weighted average rate that is calculated by weighing the exchange rates between the home currency and other major currencies, using the different countries' shares in the home country's foreign trade as weights. Thus, the effective exchange rate is a measure of the overall value of one currency against a basket of currencies. As trade weights are used in the computation, the effective exchange rate is also called trade-weighted exchange rate.

The effective exchange rate can be a *nominal effective exchange rate* (NEER) or a *real effective exchange rate* (REER). The NEER is obtained by using nominal exchange rates, while the REER is derived by adjusting the NEER for price differences between a country and its trading partners. According to the IMF, the REER is computed as the weighted geometric average of the prices of the domestic country relative to the prices of its trade partners.

The NEER indicates the extent by which the exchange rate of the currency of a country changed relatively to exchange rates of the trading-partner-countries compared to a base year. The change in the NEER, however, does not reflect change in the purchasing power of the currency. It also does not indicate to what extent the competitiveness or export potential of the country has changed over a specific period of time. To address these issues, the REER is computed and used. The REER is an index of a country's real exchange rate.

There are different methods followed in the computation of the REER. The Reserve Bank of India calculates the NEER as geometric-weighted averages of bilateral exchange rates of domestic currency in terms of foreign currency:

$$\text{NEER} = \prod_{i=1}^{n} \left(\frac{e}{e_i}\right)^{w_i}$$

The RBI also defines REER as the weighted average of NEER adjusted by the ratio of domestic prices to foreign prices.

$$\text{REER} = \prod_{i=1}^{n}\left(\frac{e}{e_i}\times\frac{P}{P_i}\right)^{w_i}$$

where

e = exchange rate of INR against SDR in indexed form

e_i = exchange rate of currency *i* against SDR (i.e. SDRs per currency *i*) in indexed form

e/e_i = exchange rate of INR against currency *i* in indexed form

P = India's wholesale price index

P_i = consumer price index of country *i*

w_i = weight attached to country *i* in the index

n = number of countries/currencies in the index other than India

The Special Drawing Right (SDR) is used as the numeraire currency in the construction of CPI-based REER, since the exchange value of the SDR is determined by a weighted average of a basket of major currencies, which would offset fluctuations in individual currencies. The exchange rate of a currency is expressed as the number of units of numaraire (SDRs) per i^{th} currency. A rise in "e" or "e/e_i' thus represents an appreciation of Indian rupee relative to the currency 'i' and vice versa.

Thus, the REER is the weighted average of real exchange rates of the domestic currency to the currencies of the country's trading partners. For example, the Indian rupee depreciates relative to GBP with a higher inflation rate, and appreciates at the same time relative to EUR with a lower inflation rate. The REER will reflect the exchange rate of the Indian rupee as a weighted average of these changes.

To simplify the calculations, let us first consider bilateral exchange rates. For example, the bilateral NEER of Indian rupee relative to USD is stated as

$$B_{\text{NEER}} = [(USA/INR_0)/(USA/INR_t)] \times 100$$

where

USA/INR_t = nominal exchange rate for period, *t*

USA/INR_0 = nominal exchange rate for the base period

The bilateral REER of Indian rupee relative to USD is stated as

$$B_{\text{REER}} = [(USA/INR_0)/(USA/INR_t)] \times 100\ [CPI_{\text{US}}/CPI_{\text{IN}}]$$

where

CPI_{IN} = changes in the consumer price index in India for a period "*t*" relative to base period, "0"

CPI_{US} = changes in the consumer price index in the US for a period "*t*" relative to base period, "0"

The NEEP/REEP is thus calculated as the weighted average of all the relevant bilateral effective exchange rates for the currencies of all trading-partner-countries. The Reserve Bank of India prepares 36-currency and 6-currency indices of the REER of the Indian rupee. It also prepares the indices separately with export-based weights and trade-based weights. The 6-currency countries are China, Hong Kong, Eurozone, Japan, the UK, and the USA. The 36-currency countries include Argentina, Australia, Brazil, Canada, Taiwan, Egypt, Thailand, Japan, the UK, the USA, China, Sweden, Pakistan, Bangladesh, etc.

When the REER increases (decreases), the domestic currency is considered to be depreciating (appreciating) in real terms relative to the currencies of trading-partner-countries. In effect, the competitiveness of domestic goods in the international market increases (decreases). A currency is fairly valued when its REER is at 100. As can be observed from

Table 4.2, the REER of Indian rupee for 6-basket was above the 100 mark in all the years. Further, the REER based on the 6-currency basket is higher than that based on the 36-currency basket. This is mainly due to the CPI-based inflation differential being higher with the six countries (mainly advanced economies) than with the 36-group of economies, which mostly include emerging and developing economies. All these figures indicate that the Indian rupee is overvalued, or stronger. The overvaluation was more pronounced in 2010–11 as well as in 2011–12. It means that the Indian rupee has to depreciate so that the Indian goods would become more competitive in the international market. But, given the fact that India imports much more than it exports, it makes sense for the Indian rupee to remain slightly overvalued.

Thus, the REER keeps adjusting for both inflation rate differentials and movements in the exchange rates of the currencies of all the trading-partner-countries. As the REER reflects the intrinsic value or purchasing power of a currency in the global market, the monetary authority of the country may very closely monitor the movements in the REER and bring about necessary corrections of the REER to avoid sudden volatility in the exchange rate. The monetary authority of a country may also fix an exchange rate band (e.g. ±0.5 percent) around the REER, and intervene when the REER is outside the band.

Interest Rates and Exchange Rates

Movement of funds from one country to another is a common phenomenon. Investors move their funds from one country to another and from one asset to another in order to maximize their wealth. Investors borrow in markets where interest rates are low and then exchange the local currency to invest in markets where interest rates are higher. This situation, known as *carry trade,* gives market participants an opportunity for arbitrage. For example, one-year Swiss franc LIBOR (See Chapter 8 for a discussion on LIBOR) is quoted at 2.22 percent, while the US dollar LIBOR is at 4.68 percent. This offers an opportunity for arbitrage. But investors need to consider the exchange rates as well. They determine the value and return for foreign currency-denominated assets.

Thus, while buying foreign currency-denominated assets, investors need to take into consideration future payments in the foreign currency, as well as any change in the relative

Table 4.2 CPI-based REER (Trade Weighted)

Year	*CPI-36 currency basket*	*CPI-6 currency basket*	*USD/INR*	*CPI-based inflation rate (%)*
2004–05	100.0	100	44.9	4.0
2005–06	102.4	104.4	44.3	3.7
2006–07	100.8	103.8	45.3	6.8
2007–08	109.2	113.4	40.2	5.9
2008–09	99.7	103.9	45.9	9.2
2009–10	103.9	110.7	47.4	10.6
2010–11	112.7	124.5	45.6	9.5
2011–12	110.3	121.2	47.9	9.5
2012–13	105.6	117.1	54.4	10.2
2013–14	103.3	112.4	60.5	9.5

Source: Reserve Bank of India, Annual Report 2013–14.

value of the two currencies. Suppose the risk-free interest rate is 4.5 percent in the United States and 8 percent in India. Would this lead to a diversion of investment funds from the United States to India? Not necessarily. Investors have to consider interest rates, as well as the expected change in the foreign exchange rate over the period during which the investment is held. The return on the investment in India by a US investor is the explicitly stated interest rate/dividend rate as converted into US dollars.

Suppose an investor has a certain amount of funds to invest. He considers several investment opportunities and decides to put some funds initially in a bank deposit for six months. So, each INR of the deposit will become INR $(1 + K_h/2)$ after six months, where K_h is the domestic interest rate per annum. Further, suppose he deposits INR 1 million at 6 percent annual rate of interest for six months. His total wealth after six months will be INR 1 million $(1 + 0.06/2)$ = INR 1.03 million. The same may be stated symbolically as $P(1 + K_h)^t$.

Alternatively, the investor decides to invest in a USD-denominated bank deposit for six months, which offers an interest rate of 8 percent per annum. The spot exchange rate is USD/INR 43.75. So, each INR invested for six months in the US dollar deposit will give USD $[1/43.75\,(1 + 0.08/2)]$ = USD 0.02377. Thus, for an investment of INR 1 million, the investor will receive USD 23,771 after six months. What about the INR equivalent after six months? This figure is less certain, because of possible changes in the exchange rate during the six-month period. Thus, it may be stated as $P(1 + K_f)^t\,(S_t/S_0)$; (where K_f = foreign interest rate; S_0 = current spot exchange rate; S_t = expected spot exchange rate at the end of the period "t").

Thus, an investor has a choice of investing either in their domestic country or in a foreign country. The strategy he adopts depends on his payoffs.

If $P(1+K_h)^t > P(1+K_f)^t\,(S_t/S_0)$; better to invest in one's native country

$P(1+K_h)^t < P(1+K_f)^t\,(S_t/S_0)$: better to invest in a foreign country

$P(1+K_h)^t = P(1+K_f)^t\,(S_t/S_0)$: equilibrium position

In the first two situations above, there will be a flow of investments from the home country to the foreign country, or from the foreign country to the home country. For example, the interest rate in India is 9 percent, and the interest rate in the US is 4 percent. An Indian investor has INR 1 million to deposit in a bank for one year. His options are to either invest in an INR-denominated deposit or to invest in a USD-denominated deposit. The current spot exchange rate is USD/INR 60.00. He expects the spot exchange rate to be USD/INR 62.00 at the end of the year. If he opts for an INR-denominated deposit, his initial investment of INR 1 million will become INR 1.09 million after one year. Alternatively, if he decides on a USD-denominated deposit, he would get USD 0.0167 million on conversion; when deposited at 4 percent it would become USD 0.01733 million after one year. After reconversion at USD/INR 62.00, he would get INR 1.0747 million. Since a INR-denominated deposit yields more money than the USD-denominated deposit, any depositor would prefer an INR-denominated deposit to a USD-denominated deposit. Given the current spot exchange rate and the expected spot exchange rate after one year, the funds will flow from the US to India. It is here that the interest rate arbitrage comes into play, thereby bringing the yields from the two investments to the same level, known as an equilibrium level. In order to have an equilibrium situation (no tendency for funds to move into the domestic country or out of the domestic country), either the interest rate in India should come down or the interest rate in the US should move up such a way that the investor will become indifferent between the two alternative investment opportunities. At the equilibrium level, the interest rate differential between the domestic country and the foreign country will just offset the exchange rate differential between the current spot rate and the expected spot rate at the end of the period "t". Considering two countries, India and the US as an example, this relationship may be expressed as

$$(K_h - K_f) = \{S_t\ (\text{USD/INR}) - S_0(\text{USD/INR})\}/S_0(\text{USD/INR})$$

This is known as the **uncovered interest rate parity**. It is assumed that the markets are perfect (particularly, free mobility of capital across the countries), and the investors are risk neutral.

In the case of investment in foreign currency-denominated assets, the investor has to make a guess or scientific expectation about the future exchange rate. To this extent, the investment in the foreign-currency denominated assets is not the same as the investment in domestic-currency-denominated assets. Therefore, the investor has either to avoid running risk, or to expect risk premium. One way of eliminating risk is to hedge by entering a forward contract, which will provide an assured amount in the home currency to be received after the investment period.

Continuing with the example as discussed above, if the six-month forward exchange rate is USD/INR 45, then the amount of INR received for each Indian rupee invested originally in the USD-denominated deposit will be

$$\frac{F_t(\text{USD/INR})}{S_0(\text{USD/INR})}\left(1+\frac{K_{US}}{2}\right)$$

where

F_t = forward exchange rate for period t
K_{US} = interest rate on USD-denominated investment
S_0 = spot exchange rate

Therefore, the Indian rupee amount to be received after six months for each rupee invested in the USD-denominated deposit will be

$$\text{INR}\frac{45}{43.75}\left(1+\frac{0.08}{2}\right) = \text{INR } 1.0697$$

The rate of return per annum will be

$$\left(\frac{1.0697-1}{1}\right)\times 2 = 0.1394 \text{ or } 13.94\%$$

It is to be noted that the investor has converted the INR amount into US dollars at the spot exchange rate and invested that amount in the USD-denominated deposit. Simultaneously, he has sold the US dollars forward at the six-month forward exchange rate. Thus, the sequence of transactions involved in the investment abroad is:

1. Convert home currency to foreign currency at the current spot rate (S_0).
2. Deposit the foreign currency-denominated amount at the foreign currency interest rate (K_f).
3. Sell forward at F_t, the maturity value of the foreign currency-denominated deposit.

Note that all these operations take place at the time of investment. So, any change in the exchange rate during the investment period does not matter for the investor. In other words, the investment is made completely riskless.

To generalize, let us denote the foreign currency and the domestic currency by A and B, respectively. The spot rate and the forward rate between A and B are expressed as S_0(A/B)and F_t(A/B), respectively. On conversion, for every unit of domestic currency, the investor would get $1/S_0$(A/B) of foreign currency. The proceeds of the investment in foreign currency at the end of period, t will be

$$\frac{1}{S_0(\text{A/B})}\times(1+K_f)^t$$

This, when converted into the domestic currency at the forward rate, will give

$$\frac{F_t(A/B)}{S_0(A/B)} \times (1+K_f)^t$$

Therefore,

$$A_t = \frac{F_t(A/B)}{S_0(A/B)} \times (1+K_f)^t \tag{4.5}$$

where

A_t = amount to be received in home currency at the end of the period t, when the foreign investment is made.

Eq. 4.5 can also be written as

$$\begin{aligned} A_t &= (I_h / S_0)(1+K_f)[S_0(1+P)] \\ &= I_h(1+K_f)(1+P) \end{aligned}$$

where

I_h = initial investment amount in terms of home currency
P = forward premium (discount)

The investor has two options: either invest domestically (investment in domestic currency-denominated securities) or invest abroad (investment in foreign currency-denominated securities). In both options, the amount to be received at maturity, in terms of domestic currency, is a certain, known amount. Between the two options, the investor would prefer domestic investment if and only if

$$(1+K_h)^t > \frac{F_t(A/B)}{S_0(A/B)} \times (1+K_f)^t$$

This is because, in this case, the domestic investment would give a higher return than the foreign investment. Alternatively, the investor will prefer an investment in foreign currency-denominated securities if and only if

$$(1+K_h)^t < \frac{F_t(A/B)}{S_0(A/B)} \times (1+K_f)^t$$

The investor will be indifferent between a home currency-denominated security and a foreign currency-denominated security if and only if

$$(1+K_h)^t = \frac{F_t(A/B)}{S_0(A/B)} \times (1+K_f)^t$$

In this case, the return on both the investments is the same. As the investor is 'covered' or insured against the currency risk, the return on the investment in the foreign-currency denominated assets is the same as that from investment in the domestic-currency denominated assets. This satisfies the law of one price and therefore, this is also known as the **covered interest rate parity.**

From the above discussion, it is clear that an investor may have an option to invest in either home currency-denominated assets or foreign currency-denominated assets. However, the return on foreign currency-denominated investments will depend on two factors: the *interest rate* and the *foreign exchange rate*. Since foreign exchange rates change from time to time due to various factors, the investor is exposed to foreign exchange risk. In order to hedge such a risk, the investor may enter into a forward contract for the relevant period. By having a forward contract on hand, the investor knows the amount of his return upon maturity of the foreign currency-denominated investment.

Borrowing and Lending

A situation may also arise in which the investor has to decide whether to borrow in home currency or in foreign currency. The decision, of course, will depend on the cost of borrowing. For every unit of home currency borrowed, the borrower has to pay $(1 + K_{bh})^t$ units of home currency at the end of period *t*. Borrowing one unit of home currency is equivalent to borrowing $1/S_0(A/B)$ units of foreign currency. Therefore, the units of foreign currency the borrower has to pay at the end of period *t* are

$$\frac{1}{S_0(A/B)} \times (1+K_{bf})^t$$

If these are converted into home currency at the forward rate, this gives the following units of home currency:

$$\frac{F_t(A/B)}{S_0(A/B)} \times (1+K_{bf})^t$$

Therefore, borrowing in home currency is profitable if and only if

$$(1+K_{bh})^t < \frac{F_t(A/B)}{S_0(A/B)} \times (1+K_{bf})^t$$

where

K_{bh} = home currency borrowing rate
K_{bf} = foreign currency borrowing rate

Alternatively, borrowing in foreign currency is profitable if and only if

$$(1+K_{bh})^t > \frac{F_t(A/B)}{S_0(A/B)} \times (1+K_{bf})^t$$

The borrower will be indifferent to borrowing in either currency if and only if

$$(1+K_{bh})^t = \frac{F_t(A/B)}{S_0(A/B)} \times (1+K_{bf})^t$$

Borrowing in one currency and lending in another, or investing in securities denominated in another currency with the currency risk covered (or hedged) in the forward market, is known as *covered interest arbitrage*. For example, let us assume that an investor borrows USD 10 million in the United States for one year at the interest rate of 4 percent per annum. By borrowing in US dollars, he incurs a liability in the USD (short position). He converts that amount to British pounds at an exchange rate of GBP/USD 1.75, and receives GBP 5.72 million. He then invests GBP 5.72 million in the GBP-denominated bank deposit for one year, at an interest rate of 6 percent. Simultaneously, he sells forward the maturity value of the deposit (GBP 6.0571 million) in exchange for the US dollar-amount at the forward rate of GBP/USD 1.80. By depositing the proceeds of the loan, the investor creates an asset (long position). Thus, after one year, the investor receives USD 10.9028 million, repays the loan amount with interest (USD 10.40), and finally makes a profit of USD 0.5028 million.

In this example, the investor creates a portfolio known as arbitrage portfolio which is completely self-financed. Three points are noteworthy in this example. First, the investor does not commit his own funds at any time. In other words, he creates an investment without any of his money being involved. Second, the net cash flows on the date of maturity are known with certainty because all the variables involved—the spot rate, the forward rate, and the interest rate in the United States and in the United Kingdom—are known with certainty. It means that the investor creates a portfolio which is completely risk-free. Third, the forward sale of GBP against USD is equivalent to lending the present value of USD and borrowing the present value of GBP.

In this example, borrowing in US dollars and investing in British pounds has resulted in a profit. This is possible if and only if

$$(1+K_{US})^t < \frac{F_t(\text{GBP/USD})}{S_0(\text{GBP/USD})} \times (1+K_{UK})^t \tag{4.6}$$

where

K_{US} = interest rate on US dollar-denominated deposit/investment

K_{UK} = interest rate on British pound-denominated deposit/investment

However, if inequality 4.6 reverses, then borrowing in British pounds and investing in the US dollar-deposit will be profitable. The investor becomes indifferent between the two deposits if and only if

$$(1+K_{US})^t = \frac{F_t(\text{GBP/USD})}{S_0(\text{GBP/USD})}(1+K_{UK})^t$$

or

$$F_t(\text{GBP/USD}) = S_0(\text{GBP/USD})\left[\frac{(1+K_{US})^t}{(1+K_{UK})^t}\right]$$

or

$$K_{US} = K_{UK} + \frac{F_t(\text{GBP/USD}) - S_0(\text{GBP/USD})}{S_0(\text{GBP/USD})} \times (1+K_{UK})^t$$

Interest Rate Parity

While PPP deals with the law of one price in the market for goods and services, interest rate parity (IRP) concerns with the law of one price in the financial market. According to the law of one price, two financial products that are equal to each other must sell for the same price. The law of one price underlying the IRP describes the relationship between forward rates and interest rates. More specifically, **interest rate parity** states that, in an efficient market with no transaction costs, the currency of a country with a higher (lower) interest rate should be at a forward discount (premium) in terms of the currency of the country with a lower interest rate. What one gains from the interest rate differential is offset by the forward rate differential (difference between the spot rate and forward rate). In other words, the spread between the spot rate and forward rate is influenced by the interest rate differential between the two countries.

*The **interest rate parity theory** states that the difference in the interest rates (risk-free) on two currencies should be equal to the difference between the forward exchange rate and the spot exchange rate if there are to be no arbitrage opportunities.*

For example, the interest rates in the United States and in India are 6 percent and 8 percent, respectively. An investor in the United States has USD 1 million to invest either in the United States or in India. If he invests in the United States, he will receive USD 1.06 million after one year. If he wants to invest in India, he first has to buy the INR equivalent of USD 1 million at the current spot rate, which is at INR 60.8700. So, he gets INR 60.87 million on conversion. When it is invested at 8 percent, the investor will receive INR 65.74 million after one year. But the amount he will receive in US dollar terms after one year depends on the future spot rate. In order to avoid uncertainty with regard to the future spot rate, the investor may choose to enter a one-year forward contract. So, his cash flows in US dollars will depend on the forward rate. Table 4.3 shows the cash flows of the investor at some alternative forward rates.

As evident from Table 4.3, as long as the forward rate is less than 62.00, what the investor will get in US dollar proceeds will be more than what he would get by investing in the United States itself. At the forward rate of 62.00, the US dollar proceeds will be equivalent to the investment proceeds in the United States (USD 1.06 million). Thus, at the forward rate of 62.00, the interest rate differential in favour of India (2 percent) is offset by the forward premium of 2 percent (approximately) on the US dollar in terms of the Indian rupee, with no transaction costs. In other words, the forward rate and the interest rate differential are in parity at this point, and the investor is indifferent to whether he invests in the United States or in India.

A forward rate other than 62.00 leads to disequilibrium between the interest rate differential and the forward rate differential. If the interest rate differential is greater than the forward premium (in percentage points) on the USD, the investor will be better off by investing in India. If the interest rate differential is less than the forward premium (in percent), the Indian investor can be better off by investing in the US.

Suppose an Indian investor has INR 10 million to invest. If he invests in India, the investment will become INR 10.80 million after one year. If he invests in the US, on conversion of INR 10 million, he will get USD 0.1643 at the exchange rate of USD/INR 60.8700. After one year, this investment in the United States at the interest rate of 6 percent will become USD 0.1742 million, and the cash flows in terms of INR at different forward rates are shown in Table 4.4. It shows that the Indian investor will be better off if he invests in the US when the forward premium (in percent) on the USD is more than the interest rate differential between the two countries.

When the spot rate and forward rate of USD/INR are at 60.87 and 62.00, respectively, the forward premium on the USD is 2 percent (approximately). If the US interest rate remains at 6 percent, an investment of USD 1 million becomes USD 1.06 million in one year. If the US

Table 4.3 Cash Flows of an Investor at Alternative Forward Rates

Forward rate (USD/INR)	*Cash flows after one year (USD million)*
61.00	1.078
61.50	1.069
61.7355	1.065
62.00	1.060
63.00	1.044

Table 4.4 Proceeds of Investment at Different Forward Rates

Forward rate (USD/INR)	*Cash flows after one year (INR million)*
61.00	10.626
62.00	10.794
63.00	10.968

investor wishes to invest in India, the cash flows of the investor at varying rates of interest in India are shown in Table 4.5. As evident from Table 4.5, if the interest rate differential in favour of India is less than the forward premium (2%), the US investor will not gain anything extra by investing in India. On the other hand, if the interest rate differential in favour of India is more than the forward premium (2%), the US investor will gain by investing in India.

In the same way, consider an Indian investor who has INR 10 million to invest. If he invests in the United States at a 6 percent rate of interest, given the spot rate of 60.87 and forward rate of 62.00, the investment will become INR 10.80 million after one year. Alternatively, if he invests in India, his cash flows after a year at varying rates of interest are as shown in Table 4.6. As can be observed from Table 4.6, the Indian investor will be better off by investing in the United States when the Indian interest rates are less than 8 percent. If the interest rates in India are greater than 8 percent, he will be better off by investing in India because, in such cases, the interest rate differential is greater than the forward premium.

The relationship between the interest differential and the forward differential is shown graphically in Figure 4.4. The horizontal axis represents the forward discount or premium on the foreign currency (annualized), and the vertical axis represents the interest rate differential (annualized) in favour of the home country.

The interest parity line in Figure 4.4 represents the points where the forward premium (positive) or discount (negative) on the foreign currency is in equilibrium with the interest rate differential. For example, if the interest rate differential is 3 percent in favour of the home country, then the currency of the foreign country must be selling at a 3 percent forward premium for the equilibrium to exist. If they are in disequilibrium, there is an arbitrage incentive to move funds from one country to the other. For example, if the interest rate differential is 4 percent and the forward premium on the foreign currency is 5 percent, then it is profitable to move the funds abroad as this will yield an additional 1 percent with exchange risk covered.

Thus, funds will move from the home country to a foreign country if the interest rate differential (annualized) in favour of the home country is less than the forward premium (annualized). On the other hand, if the interest rate differential in favour of the home country is more than the forward premium, funds will move from the foreign country to the home country.

It should be noted that IRP holds only when there are no covered interest arbitrage opportunities. In other words, $(1 + K_h)/(1 + K_f)$ must be equal to F_t/S_0 so that there is a no-arbitrage situation.

Table 4.5 Cash Flows in USD at Varying Interest Rates

Indian interest rate (%)	*Interest rate differential in favour of India (%)*	*Cash flows after one year (USD million)*
5	(–)1	1.03
6	0	1.04
7	1	1.05
8	2	1.06
9	3	1.07
10	4	1.08

Table 4.6 Cash Flows in INR at Varying Interest Rates in India

Indian interest rate (%)	*Interest rate differential in favour of India (%)*	*Cash flows after one year (INR million)*
5	–1	10.50
6	0	10.60
7	1	10.70
8	2	10.80
9	3	10.90
10	4	11.00

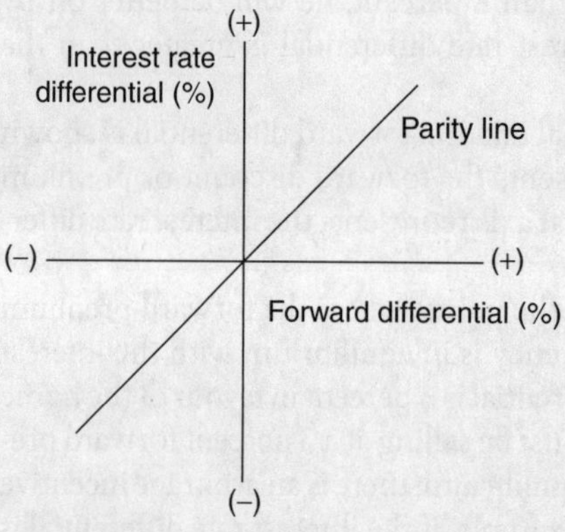

Figure 4.4

Interest Rate Parity

Thus, IRP can be represented by the following equation:

$$\frac{(1+K_h)^t}{(1+K_f)^t} = \frac{F_t}{S_0}$$

The same can be approximated as:

$$t(K_h - K_f) = \frac{F_t - S_0}{S_0}$$

This means that the interest rate differential is approximately equal to the forward rate differential. If interest parity holds, the forward rate is an unbiased predictor of the future spot rate. In such a case, the above equation can be expressed as

$$t(K_h - K_f) = \frac{E(S_t) - S_0}{S_0}$$

where

$E(S_t)$ = expected spot rate at time

t = Time peroid in years coinciding forward contract peroid

Thus, the interest rate differential equals the expected spot rate differential. Such a relationship is called an *uncovered interest parity relationship.* If the interest rate is 9 percent per annum in India and 6 percent per annum in Australia, the uncovered interest parity relationship would imply that the AUD is expected to appreciate against the INR by about 3 percent.

Example 4.2

The interest rates in India and the United States are 8 percent per annum and 6 percent per annum, respectively. The current spot rate is USD/INR 39.4354. If IRP holds, what is the three-month forward rate?

Solution

The three-month forward rate (F_{90}) will be:

$$F_{90} = 39.4354[(1+0.08/4)/(1+0.06/4)]$$
$$= 39.6297$$

The USD has a forward rate (90 days) of INR 39.6297, resulting in an annualized premium of about {[(39.6297 —39.4354)/39.4354] × 4} percent, or 1.97 percent. This forward rate can also be taken as the expected spot rate in three months.

Example 4.3

The spot rate of the Indian rupee against the British pound is 75. The interest rate in the United Kingdom is 8 percent and in India it is 6 percent. What is the forward rate premium (or discount) of the Indian rupee with respect to the British pound if IRP exists? What is the forward rate (one year) of the British pound in terms of the Indian rupee?

Solution

From the perspective of the Indian investor, the forward premium (or discount) of the GBP with respect to the INR will be:

$$P = \frac{1+K_h}{1+K_f} - 1$$
$$= \frac{(1+0.06)}{(1+0.08)} - 1 = -0.0185$$

Thus, the GBP is at a forward discount of 1.85 percent with respect to the INR.

The one-year forward rate of the GBP is:

$$F_t = S_0(1+\text{P})$$
$$F_1 = 75(1-0.0185) = 73.61$$

Example 4.4

The following are the interest rates and spot rates of exchange:
Spot rate: USD/INR 39.45/50
Interest rates in India: 10 percent–10.25 percent p.a.
Interest rates in the US: 7 percent–7.25 percent p.a.
If IRP holds, what are the forward quotes?

Solution

$$F_{\text{bid}} \leq 39.50\frac{(1+0.1025)}{(1+0.07)} \text{ or,}$$

$$F_{\text{bid}} \leq 40.70$$

$$F_{ask} \geq 39.45\frac{(1+0.10)}{(1+0.0725)} \text{ or,}$$

$$F_{\text{ask}} \geq 40.4615$$

The limits for forward quotes are 40.4615–40.70.

In order to avoid arbitrage, the actual forward quotes must overlap the two limits obtained in Example 4.4. For example, a forward quote of 40.4600–40.4645 is acceptable. In other words, a range of forward quotes can satisfy the IRP. It may be noted that there is no exact relationship between spot rates and forward rates when there are transaction costs like the bid–ask spread.

If there is no IRP, arbitrageurs will take advantage of the interest rate differential that is not fully covered by the forward premium or discount. Let us consider an example to understand how this happens. Suppose an Indian firm is required to pay USD 1 million to settle an import bill. The current spot rate is USD/INR 61.8537, and the one-year forward rate is USD/INR 62.4537. So, the firm can acquire USD 1 million at a cost of INR 61.8537 million. Suppose the firm borrows USD 1 million from a bank for one year at an interest rate of 5 percent p.a. and uses that amount to settle the import bill. After one year, the firm has to repay the loan with interest, which comes to USD 1.05 million. In order to avoid the currency risk, the firm purchases this amount (USD 1.05) one-year forward at a cost of INR 65.5763 million. To have this amount of INR 65.5763 million after one year, the firm now makes a deposit of INR 60.72 million with a bank at a rate of interest of 8 percent p.a. The firm can thus save INR 1.135 million by not purchasing the US dollars spot.

Suppose the above example is modified so that the firm is required to settle the import bill after one year. The current spot rate is USD/INR 61.8537 and the one-year forward rate is USD/INR 62.4537. The annual interest rate on the USD-denominated deposits is 6 percent. The firm can have INR-denominated loans at 5 percent p.a. So, if the firm buys USD 1 million forward, it has to pay INR 62.4537 million one year hence. Alternatively, the firm now purchases USD 0.9434 million in the spot market by paying INR 58.35 million and deposits the USD proceeds with a bank at an interest rate of 6 percent p.a. This becomes USD 1 million after one year. The firm borrows INR 58.35 million at an interest rate of 5 percent p.a. So, the loan commitment for the firm after one year is INR 61.27 million, which is less than the amount of payment on the forward contract.

In the two situations we just discussed, a firm could save some money or make arbitrage profit because there is deviation from IRP. In other words, the interest rate differential and forward rate differential do not match, creating scope for arbitrage transactions.

The covered interest rate arbitrage provides a linkage (a) between the interest rates in two different currencies; (b) between the forward rate and the spot rate; and (c) between the money market and the foreign exchange market. For example, an arbitrageur borrows

USD 1 million in the United States at 5 percent for one year and converts it to Indian rupees at the spot rate of USD/INR 61.50. This amount is invested in deposits with a commercial bank in India at an interest rate of 8.5 percent for one year. Simultaneously, the arbitrageur sells INR 66.73 million (the amount which he will get after one year) for US dollars at the one-year forward exchange rate of USD/INR 62.00. At the end of the year, he will receive USD 1.076 million. The arbitrageur will then use USD 1.05 million to repay the loan with interest and finally make a profit of USD 0.0263 million. In this transaction, there is no investment on the part of the arbitrageur, as investment in the transaction is made with borrowed funds. However, the profit of USD 0.0263 is guaranteed.

As US dollars are sold in the spot market for Indian rupees, and Indian rupees are sold forward for US dollars, there will be changes in the demand and supply of these two currencies in the market. As a result, the Indian rupee may appreciate in the spot market and depreciate in the forward market. Simultaneously, the interest rates in India as well as in the United States may also be affected because of the flow of funds from one country to another. This process of transferring funds in one currency to another currency will continue until IRP is achieved. In this example, the arbitrage process will specifically influence the interest rates and foreign exchange rates in the following ways:

- The interest rates in the United States will rise.
- The interest rates in India will fall.
- The INR will appreciate in the spot market.
- The INR will depreciate in the forward market.

Note that the foreign exchange market (both spot and forward) is more sensitive than the money market. Therefore, foreign exchange rates react quickly to a change in their determinants, and a disequilibrium in foreign exchange rates can be set right faster than a disequilibrium in interest rates.

In the real world, some factors may prevent or affect the movement of funds across countries, causing deviations from IRP. Let us discuss a few examples of such situations. If risk-averse investors wish to diversify their investments even at the cost of sacrificing some returns in order to reduce risk, the IRP does not hold. Further, all along the discussion of the IRP, it is assumed that the investors are risk neutral. If that not being the case, any risk premium in favour of one currency or the other may lead to deviations from the IRP as well. Controls that are imposed by governments on the movement of capital across countries may not encourage the arbitrage process. The difference in the taxes between two countries may also affect the free movement of funds from one country to another. Liquidity needs and other considerations may force investors to hold domestic securities even though the expected return on foreign currency-denominated assets is higher. This prevents investment shifts between currencies. While defining the IRP, it is assumed that the markets are efficient. By being efficient, the markets fully reflect all the available information and there are no unexploited opportunities for profit.

Although deviations from interest parity may provide the opportunity to make a riskless profit, there may be no arbitraging because of transaction costs, controls, and taxes.

A situation in which a deviation from the IRP may not result in arbitrage profit is when the borrowing rate of interest is different from the lending rate of interest, reflecting the bid–ask spread in interest rates. The bid rate is different from the ask rate in the foreign exchange market as well. The difference between the bid and ask rates, both in the money market and the foreign exchange market, is the major transaction cost. In this situation, arbitrage profits

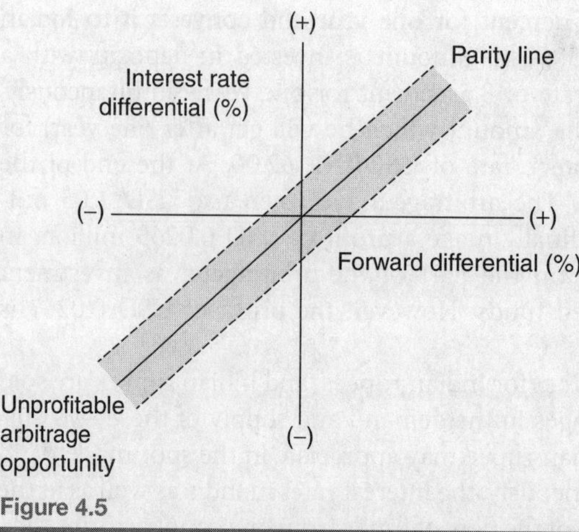

Figure 4.5

IRP with Unprofitable Arbitrage Opportunity

may not be sufficient to compensate for the transaction costs. Thus, the IRP line may have a band around it, as shown in Figure 4.5, and the deviations within the band will not represent arbitrage opportunities with profit. It is only the deviations from the band that will result in arbitrage profits. The width of the band around the parity line depends on the extent of transaction costs.

Forward Rate Parity

*The **forward parity theory** states that forward rates are unbiased predictors of future spot exchange rates.*

The **forward rate parity theory** states that forward rates are unbiased predictors of future spot exchange rates. In other words, the **forward rate** of a currency relative to another currency reflects the future spot rate of exchange. The relationship between the forward exchange rate and the expected future spot rate between two currencies can be stated as

$$F_t(X/Y) = ES_t(X/Y)$$

where

$F_t(X/Y)$ = forward rate of one unit of Currency X in terms of Currency Y for delivery in *t* days/months

$ES_t(X/Y)$ = expected spot rate of one unit of Currency X in terms of Currency Y on the maturity date of the forward contract

For example, the market expects that the US dollar will trade at INR 62.00 in six months, and the forward rate for the six-month period is INR 62.645. Market participants, particularly speculators, would sell US dollars forward at INR 62.645 and expect to buy the same at INR 62.00 when they are required to deliver the dollars. The speculators expect to make a profit of INR 0.645 on each US dollar traded. When many participants do the same, the forward rate will go down until it is no longer greater than the expected future spot rate. The forward selling of the US dollar will continue until the forward rate is no longer greater than the expected spot rate. Conversely, if the expected spot rate in the six-month period is INR 62.00 and the forward rate for the six-month period is INR 61.545, speculators would buy USD forward at INR 61.545 and expect to sell the same at INR 62.00 to make a profit of INR 0.455 on each US dollar traded. In the course of buying the USD forward, participants will drive up the forward rate until it is no longer lower than the expected future spot rate.

The buying and selling of foreign currency in the forward market will also have implications for future spot rates. The squaring of forward contracts at maturity will put pressure on the future spot market. In other words, pressure from the forward market is transmitted to the spot market, and thus influences the spot rates. Similarly, pressure from the future spot market is also transmitted to the forward market and thereby influences the forward rates.

When the forward rate is no longer greater or lower than the expected future spot rate, the forward rate and the expected future spot rate are in equilibrium. In other words, $F_t = E(S_t)$. There is no incentive to buy or sell the currency forward in this scenario. A graphical representation of this relationship is shown in Figure 4.6. The vertical axis measures the expected future spot rate, and the horizontal axis measures the forward rate differential. The parity line joins the points where the forward premium or forward discount on foreign currency is in equilibrium with the expected percentage change in the home currency value of the foreign currency. That is, the forward rate differential should equal the expected rate of change of the spot exchange rate:

$$\frac{F_t - S_0}{S_0} = \frac{E(S_t) - S_0}{S_0}$$

For example, an expected 3 percent depreciation (appreciation) of foreign currency should be matched by the 3 percent forward discount (premium) on the foreign currency. Further, consider a situation where the market expects 4 percent depreciation of foreign currency, but speculators are selling the foreign currency at 3 percent forward discount. In this situation, the forward differential and the expected future spot rate will be in disequilibrium. This will ultimately be set right in the course of buying and selling of foreign currency.

When the forward rate and the expected future spot rate are in equilibrium, the interest rate differential between two currencies is equal to the expected rate of change in the spot rate. This relationship is known as *uncovered interest rate parity.* For example, the interest rate is 4 percent in the United States and 6 percent in India. In this situation, the Indian rupee would be expected to depreciate against the US dollar by about 2 percent. However, in reality, the forward rate may not exactly reflect the expectation of the future spot rate because of the risk premium on the forward contract. In other words, forward market participants would demand a risk premium for bearing the risk of the forward contract. This would make the forward rate different from the expected future spot rate, resulting in deviation from the parity line.

The forward rate and the future spot rate are influenced by current expectations of future events. As people get new information, they update their expectations about future events, leading to changes in exchange rates. Therefore, the FRP is also known as *forward expectation parity* (FEP).

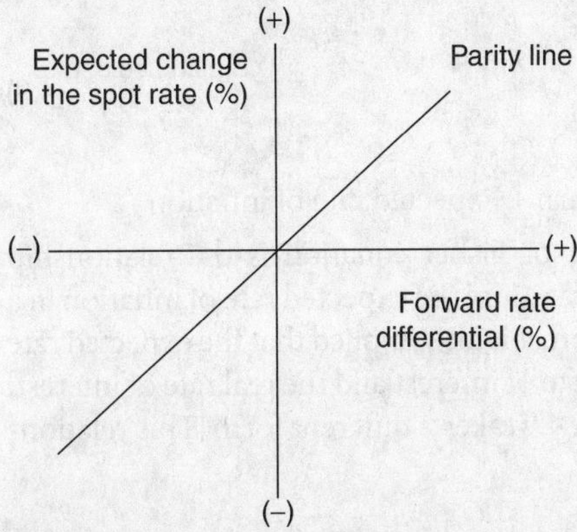

Figure 4.6

Forward Rate Parity

The Fisher Effect

Interest rates can be classified as nominal interest rates and real interest rates. The *nominal interest rate* is the rate of exchange between current money and future money. For example, a deposit of INR 100 today will be worth INR 110 after one year. The deposit carries a 10 percent nominal interest rate per annum. But in the days of rising prices, the nominal rate of interest is different from the real rate of interest. The *real rate of interest* is measured in terms of the purchasing power of money. If the value of money is measured in terms of its purchasing power over goods and services, the value of money changes when prices change. During the period of inflation, money loses value because fewer goods and services can be purchased with the same amount of money. Thus, what is important is not the quantity of money that one has but rather what and how many goods and services the money will buy. In other words, it is the real interest rate and not the nominal interest rate which is important and relevant to the investor.

*The **Fisher effect**, or the **Fisher equation**, represents the relationship between the nominal interest rate, the real interest rate, and the expected rate of inflation in a country.*

It is in this context that the **Fisher equation**, or the **Fisher effect**, assumes importance. According to Irving Fisher, the nominal rate of interest consists of two components: the real rate of return and the expected rate of inflation. This relationship can be represented as:

$$1 + \text{Nominal rate of interest} = (1 + \text{Real rate of return})(1 + \text{Expected rate of inflation})$$

Let K be the nominal rate of interest, r be the real rate of interest, and i be the expected rate of inflation. Now,

$$(1+K) = (1+r)(1+i)$$

$$(1+r)^t = \frac{(1+k)^t}{(1+i)^t} \tag{4.7}$$

By solving Eq. 4.7 for K, we have

$$K = r + i + ri \tag{4.8}$$

In other words,

$$\text{Nominal rate of return} = \text{Real rate of return} + \text{Expected rate of inflation} + (\text{Real rate of return} \times \text{Expected rate of inflation})$$

Assume that an investor expects a 5 percent real return on his investment when the economy is experiencing a 10 percent inflation rate. The Fisher equation indicates that the investor should get a nominal interest rate of 15.5 percent.

If r and i are small, then ri also becomes small. So, from Eq. 4.8, the nominal interest rate can be approximated as

$$K = r + i \tag{4.9}$$

Thus, in this situation,

$$\text{Nominal rate of return} = \text{Real rate of return} + \text{Expected rate of inflation}$$

As evident from our discussion, the Fisher effect or Fisher equation is the relationship between the nominal interest rate, the real interest rate, and the expected rate of inflation in a country. This relation is also called the Fisher relation. It is also implied that the expected rate of inflation is the difference between the nominal rate of interest and the real rate of interest.

When more than one currency is involved, Eq. 4.9 takes a different form. This relationship is explained here:

According to IRP,

$$\frac{F_t}{S_0} = \frac{(1+K_h)^t}{(1+K_f)^t} \tag{4.10}$$

where

K_h = nominal rate of interest in a home country
K_f = nominal rate of interest in a foreign country

Substituting the Fisher equation (Eq. 4.7) in both sides of Eq. 4.10,

$$\frac{(1+K_h)^t}{(1+K_f)^t} = \frac{(1+r_h)^t(1+i_h)^t}{(1+r_f)^t(1+i_f)^t} \tag{4.11}$$

If the law of one price holds for real rates of return in different countries, then $r_h = r_f$. If the real rates of interest are different in different countries, arbitrage activities would cause capital to flow from the country with the lower real return to the country with the higher real return. For example, if the real interest rate is 4 percent in the United States and 5 percent in India, capital would flow from the United States to India. But arbitrage would bring the expected real returns in different countries to be equal instantaneously. When r_h equals r_f, r_h and r_f cancel from the right-hand side of Eq. 4.11.

Thus,

$$\frac{(1+K_h)^t}{(1+K_f)^t} = \frac{(1+i_h)^t}{(1+i_f)^t} \tag{4.12}$$

where

K_h = nominal home currency interest rate
K_f = nominal foreign currency interest rate
i_h = expected inflation rate in a home country
i_f = expected inflation rate in a foreign country

When K_f and i_f are relatively small, Eq. 4.12 can be approximated as

$$K_h - K_f = i_h - i_f$$

This means that the interest rate differential equals the inflation differential. Thus, the investments denominated in the currency of the country having a higher expected rate of inflation should bear higher rates of return than the investments denominated in the currency of the country with a lower expected rate of inflation. In other words, a rise (fall) in the inflation rate in a country will result in a proportionate increase (decrease) in the interest rate in that country. This is also graphically represented in Figure 4.7, where the horizontal axis

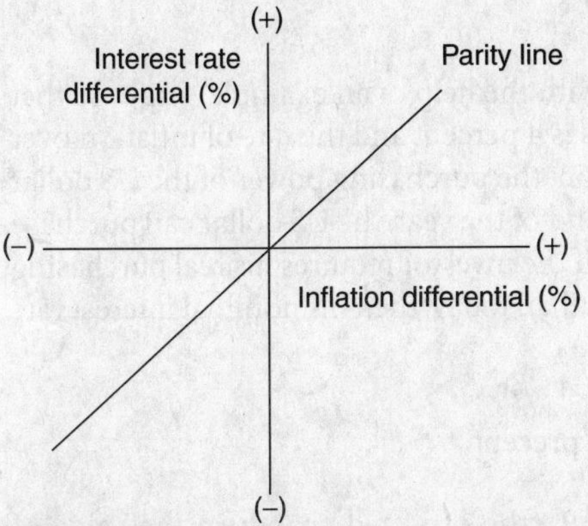

Figure 4.7

Parity between Interest Rate and Inflation Rate

measures the difference in the expected rates of inflation between the home country and the foreign country. The vertical axis measures the interest rate differential between the countries for the same time period.

The parity line joins all points for which

$$K_h - K_f = i_h - i_f$$

or,

$$K_h - i_h = K_f - i_f$$

The International Fisher Relation

The PPP theory implies that the real interest rate is the same across the world, and it is only the nominal interest rate which varies from country to country, depending on the expected inflation rate. So, any difference in the actual interest rates between two countries is because of a difference in the inflation rates of the two countries. Furthermore, the exchange rate between two currencies changes depending on the inflation rate differential between the two countries. The combination of these two effects of inflation is the *international Fisher relation* or *effect*. The international Fisher effect or relation is also known as the *Fisher open condition*. "Open" here refers to an open economy.

The international Fisher effect suggests that the nominal interest rate differential reflects the expected change in the spot rate. A rise in the inflation rate in a country will be associated with a rise in the interest rate in the country and a fall in the country's currency value. This implies that the expected return on domestic investment should be equal to the expected return on foreign investment.

By assuming that markets are perfect and investors are risk-neutral, the international Fisher effect can be expressed as

$$\frac{(1+K_h)^t}{(1+K_f)^t} = \frac{(1+i_h)^t}{(1+i_f)^t}$$

or,

$$\frac{(1+K_h)^t}{(1+K_f)^t} = \frac{E(S_t)}{(S_0)} \tag{4.13}$$

This explains the expected spot rate in terms of relative nominal interest rates.

By subtracting 1 from both sides of Eq. 4.13, we have

$$\frac{t(K_h - K_f)}{(1+K_f)^t} = \frac{E(S_t) - S_0}{S_0}$$

Let us understand the international Fisher effect with the help of an example. Suppose that the real required rate of return in the United States is 4 percent and the rate of inflation over the year is expected to be 3 percent. In this situation, the purchasing power of the US dollar will become USD (1/1.03), or USD 0.9708. At the end of the year, the US dollar can purchase only 97.08 percent of what it can purchase today. If the investor requires his real purchasing power to be 4 percent higher at the end of the year than today, then his nominal interest rate should be:

$$0.9708(1+K) = 1.04 \quad \text{or,}$$

$$K = 0.0713 = 7.13 \text{ precent}$$

According to the international Fisher relation (IFR), the expected change in the value of foreign currency will be positive when the domestic interest rate (nominal) is greater than the foreign interest rate (nominal). In other words, the foreign currency appreciates

Example 4.5

The annual interest rate is 4 percent in the United States and 6 percent in India. The current spot rate is USD/INR 45. If a change in the Indian inflation rate causes the expected future spot rate to rise to USD/INR 47, what should the Indian interest rate be?

Solution

$$\frac{47}{45} = \frac{1+K_h}{(1.0.06)} \text{ or,}$$

$$K_h = 10.7 \text{ percent}$$

So, the interest rate in India should be 10.7 percent per annum.

Example 4.6

The interest rate in India is 12 percent and the interest rate in the United States is 6 percent. What should the percentage change in the value of the USD be according to the international Fisher effect?

Solution

$$\text{Percentage change in the value of USD} = (1 + 0.12)/(1 + 0.06) - 1$$
$$= 0.0566 \text{ or } 5.67 \text{ percent}$$

Thus, the value of the USD should appreciate by 5.67 percent. This would make the return on investment in India equal to the return on investment in the United States.

when the domestic interest rate is greater than the foreign interest rate. Conversely, the expected change in the value of foreign currency will be negative when the domestic interest rate (nominal) is lower than the foreign interest rate (nominal). So, the foreign currency depreciates when the domestic interest rate is lower than the foreign interest rate.

The international Fisher effect in the expectation form of relative PPP can be represented graphically, as shown in Figure 4.8.

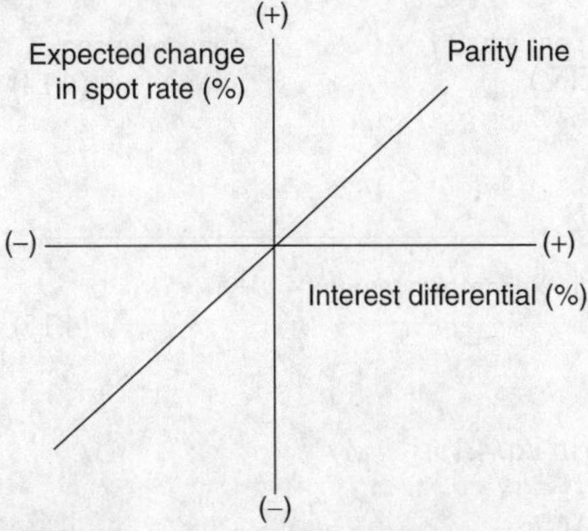

Figure 4.8

The International Fisher Effect

The vertical axis in Figure 4.8 shows the expected change in the exchange rate (in percent), and the horizontal axis measures the interest rate differential (in percent) between two countries for the same period. The parity line is arrived at by joining the points where

$$t(K_h - K_f) = \frac{E(S_t) - S_0}{S_0}$$

This is an approximated form of the IFR. In other words, the interest rate differential between any two nations is an unbiased predictor of the future change in the spot rate of exchange between the two currencies.

The parity line shows that an interest differential of, say, 2 percent in favour of the home country should be offset by the expected 2 percent appreciation in the home currency value of the foreign currency. If they are not in equilibrium, funds would flow from one country to another until real returns are equal in both countries. Investors usually invest in countries where the real returns are the highest. This will tend to reduce the returns in these countries because of greater supply of funds. Simultaneously, this will also tend to increase the returns in the countries from which the funds are withdrawn because of reduced supply of funds.

Interrelationship of Parity Conditions

The parity conditions described in this chapter are interrelated. For example, interest rates cause and are caused by changes in forward rates of foreign exchange, which, in turn, depend on the expected future spot rate of foreign exchange. The inflation differential between the countries influences interest rates, forward rates, and future spot rates as well.
According to IRP,

$$\frac{(1+K_h)^t}{(1+K_f)^t} = \frac{F_t}{S_0}$$

Or

$$\frac{(1+K_h)^t}{(1+K_f)^t} = \frac{E(S_t)}{S_0}$$

According to PPP,

$$\frac{[1+E(i_h)]^t}{(1+E(i_f)]^t} = \frac{E(S_t)}{S_0} \tag{4.14}$$

And according to FRP,

$$\frac{F_t}{S_0} = \frac{E(S_t)}{S_0} \tag{4.15}$$

Replacing the value *of* $E(S_t)/S_0$ obtained in Eq. 14.14 in Eq. 4.15,

$$\frac{F_t}{S_0} = \frac{[1+E(i_h)]^t}{(1+E(i_f)]^t}$$

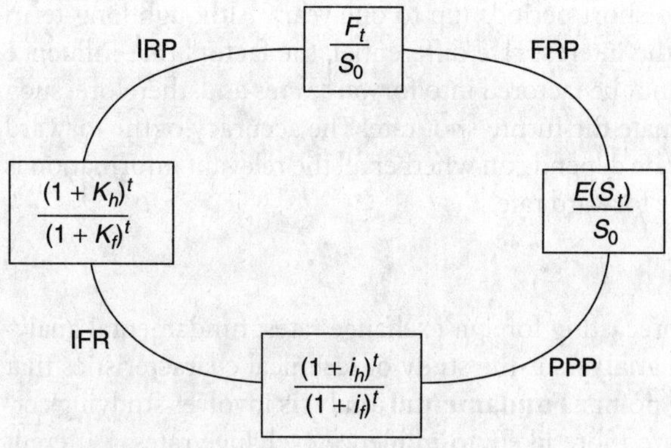

Figure 4.9

Interrelationship of Parity Conditions

Now, according to the IFR,

$$\frac{(1+K_h)^t}{(1+K_f)^t} = \frac{[1+E(i_h)]^t}{(1+E(i_f))^t} \quad \text{or,}$$

$$\frac{E(S_t)-S_0}{S_0} = \frac{t(K_h-K_f)}{(1+K_h)^t} \quad \text{or,}$$

$$\frac{(F_t)-S_0}{S_0} = \frac{t(K_h-K_f)}{(1+K_f)^t}$$

All international parity conditions are interrelated and form a circuit, as shown in Figure 4.9. This implies that any condition can be derived from the others. If any two parity conditions hold precisely, there cannot be any deviations from the other parity conditions. All parity conditions hold only over very long period of time.

All parity conditions, whether PPP, IRP, FRP, or IFR, are far from reality. Several factors lead to deviations from parity. For example, transaction costs, political risks, tax advantages, liquidity differences, tariffs, quotas, differences in the structure of price indices, and the presence of non-tradable goods and services are the major factors that contribute to departures from parity conditions.

Exchange Rate Forecasting

Exchange rate forecasts are used for several purposes. They can be used in making hedging decisions, investment decisions, and financing decisions. Forecasts may also help speculative business in the foreign exchange market.

Foreign exchange rates are influenced by several factors in many ways or directions, often in opposite or conflicting directions. A good number of models have been developed to explain how different factors influence exchange rates.These models are also used to predict or forecast the exchange rates of currencies.

The Forward Rate as an Unbiased Estimate

The forward rate is generally used as an unbiased estimate of the future spot rate. But the forward rate may not accurately reflect the future spot rate where the markets are not perfect or efficient. Moreover, forward rates are available only for short maturities and, therefore, their forecasting horizon is limited to short periods (up to one year). Although long-term forward rates can be deduced from the interest rate differential, the factors that influence the exchange rate in the long run cannot be factored into forward rates and, therefore, such forward rates may not correctly estimate the future spot rate. The accuracy of the forward rate as a predictor of the future spot rate depends on whether all the relevant information is used by the market in determining the forward rate.

Approaches to Forecasting

Fundamental analysis *involves studying certain macroeconomic variables that are more likely to influence exchange rates.* ***Technical analysis,*** *on the other hand, is the study of technical characteristics that are expected at major market turning points.*

There are two basic approaches to forecasting foreign exchange rates: fundamental analysis and technical analysis. **Technical analysis** is the study of technical characteristics that are expected at major market turning points. **Fundamental analysis** involves studying certain macroeconomic variables that are more likely to influence exchange rates. Different models have been developed to analyse how different macroeconomic variables are likely to influence the demand and supply of a currency. Of these, three models, which are popularly referred to, are briefly described in the following lines.

The ***monetary model*** *attempts to predict a proportional relationship between nominal exchange rates and the relative money supply between nations.*

The Monetary Model The **monetary model** is one of the earliest attempts to explain the relationship between the nominal exchange rate and a set of monetary fundamentals. The monetary model attempts to predict a proportional relationship between nominal exchange rates and relative supplies of money between nations. Economies that follow a relatively expansionary monetary policy will observe depreciation of their currencies, while those that follow a relatively restrictive monetary policy will observe appreciation of their currencies.

The monetary model suggests that the exchange rate is determined by three independent variables:

- relative money supply,
- relative interest rates, and
- relative national output.

The basic monetary model describes the long run equilibrium relationship among relative money supplies, relative income levels, relative interest rates, and the nominal exchange rate. The monetary model assumes stable domestic and foreign money demand functions, perfect capital mobility, and uncovered interest parity. The basic monetary model can be expressed as:

$$\log e = \alpha + \beta_1 \log(M_d - M_f) + \beta_2 \log(i_d - i_f) + \beta_3 \log(Y_d - Y_f)$$

where

M_d = money supply in domestic economy
M_f = money supply in foreign economy
i_d = domestic country interest rate
i_f = foreign country interest rate
Y_d = real output in domestic country
Y_f = real output in foreign country
$\log e$ = natural logarithm of exchange rate

Some monetary models also incorporate the difference in inflation and the difference in accumulated trade balances. To forecast the exchange rate one year hence, one has to estimate the values that the independent variables will assume in one year, and then estimate the exchange rate in one year.

There are two versions of the monetary model: *flexible-price monetary model and sticky-price monetary model.* The flexible-price monetary model assumes that PPP always holds.

It further assumes that changes in price levels instantaneously translate into changes in exchange rates. Thus, the real exchange rate is constant over time. The sticky-price monetary model, on the other hand, assumes that prices of goods are sticky in the short run, and PPP holds only in the long run. Therefore, a change in the nominal money supply causes a change in the real money supply, which, in turn, results in interest rate changes and capital flows.

Both versions of the monetary model—the sticky-price monetary model and the flexible-price model—imply that an increase in the real output of a country will lead to the depreciation of its currency because growth in real income increases the demand for money to finance a larger value of transactions. But the two models differ on the implications of changes in the domestic interest rate. According to the sticky-price monetary model, an increase in the domestic interest rate will attract foreign capital inflows, which, in turn, will cause the domestic currency to appreciate. In contrast, according to the flexible-price model, an increase in the domestic interest rate will reduce the demand for domestic money, causing the currency to depreciate. In other words, an increase in interest rate, if it is caused by monetary tightness, will lead to the appreciation of the home currency, or if it is caused by inflation, will result in depreciation of the home currency.

The Asset Market Model According to the **asset market model**, an asset price consists of a fundamental value plus a term that reflects expectations of future changes in the asset price. The foreign exchange is viewed as a financial asset and its price (exchange rate) is determined by the demand and supply for the stock of foreign exchange. Exchange rates, as with other financial asset prices, are determined by expectations of future events. As expectations change, exchange rates would also change. Thus, the current spot rate of a currency is a reflection of expectations of future market events. This model is based on the assumption that asset markets are efficient and fully reflect all available information. In other words, the current spot rate must have incorporated all relevant information and the exchange rate will then change only on the receipt of new information. Since new information comes in randomly, the exchange rate will change randomly with information being instantaneously absorbed into the exchange rate.

*The **asset market model** views foreign exchange as a financial asset and accordingly, its price (exchange rate) is determined by the demand and supply for the stock of foreign exchange.*

The Portfolio Balance Model

The **portfolio balance model** is based on the premise that people divide their total wealth between domestic and foreign money, and domestic and foreign bonds, depending on their expected return and risk. Three assets are involved in the portfolio balance model: money (M), domestic bonds denominated in the home currency (B), and foreign currency bonds (FB). The domestic bonds are the sum of bond holdings of households and the monetary authority. It is assumed that there is a fixed net supply of domestic bonds.

Foreign bond holdings are also held by the public and the monetary authority. These holdings can increase or decrease over time, via the current-account surplus or deficit. The monetary base (money) is the sum of the domestic bond holdings and the foreign bond holdings (in domestic currency terms) of the monetary authority. Foreign currency bond holdings can be converted into the domestic currency by multiplying them with the exchange rate. An increase in financial wealth in a country can be held as money, domestic bonds, or foreign bonds. The change in the demand for the three assets must sum to one. The monetary authority of a country can increase the money supply in the economy (an increase in the monetary base) by buying either domestic bonds (an open market operation) or foreign bonds (a non-sterilized foreign exchange operation). A sterilized foreign exchange operation refers to keeping the money supply in the economy at its original level (the level before the foreign exchange operation). The monetary authority can sell or buy domestic bonds from the public so that the money supply held by the public returns to its initial level. Thus, the

*According to the **portfolio balance model**, investors would adjust their portfolios, consisting of domestic money, foreign money, domestic bonds, and foreign bonds, keeping in view their risk–return characteristics.*

public holds less (more) foreign bonds and more (less) domestic bonds. A sterilized foreign exchange operation can influence the exchange rate without changing the money supply. A detailed discussion on sterilization is presented in Chapter 2.

According to the portfolio balance model, the total financial wealth (TW) in a country is distributed as

$$TW = M + B_h + SF_h$$
$$= B_m + SF_m + B_h + SF_m$$

where

$M = B_m + SF_m$
B_m = domestic bond holdings of the monetary authority
S = spot exchange rate
F = foreign bond holdings of the monetary authority
B_h = domestic bond holdings of households
F_h = foreign bond holdings of households

Money demand is a function of the interest rate, the expected change in the exchange rate, and the output and financial wealth in a country. It is inversely related to the interest rate and the expected change in the exchange rate, and positively related to domestic income and financial wealth. The demand for bonds (domestic and foreign) to be held by households is also a function of the interest rate, the expected change in the exchange rate, and the output and financial wealth of the country. The demand for domestic bonds is inversely related to the expected change in the exchange rate and domestic income, and positively related to the interest rate and financial wealth. However, the demand for foreign bonds is inversely related to the domestic interest rate and domestic income, and positively related to the expected change in the exchange rate and financial wealth.

Risk-averse investors diversify their investments across assets so that risk-adjusted return is the same for all assets. Bonds are not perfect substitutes and, therefore, there is always portfolio diversification in terms of bonds between countries. The proportion of wealth allocated to any bond is positively related to its return. Investors may choose to allocate a larger proportion of their wealth to domestic bonds when domestic interest rates are rising. This implies that the proportion of investment in foreign bonds varies inversely with the domestic interest rate. The wealth in domestic money may not carry any return. Investors are likely to hold a portfolio of currencies to minimize exchange rate risk.

If the demand for money increases (individuals attempt to build up their cash balances), it causes a reduction in spending on goods and assets, including foreign goods and assets. This will result in a surplus BOP and an appreciation of the external value of the home currency. A rise in the incomes of people may also result in a surplus BOP. The increased demand for money raises the domestic interest rate. Foreign bonds are sold in the portfolio adjustment process and there will be foreign capital inflow. As investors acquire the domestic currency to make investments, the demand for the home currency increases and the exchange rate will appreciate. But, according to the monetarist approach, an increase in the domestic interest rate will lead to a fall in the demand for money in the home country. This will cause the home country's money supply to exceed its demand. In an open economy, this will lead to the domestic currency depreciating rather than appreciating.

The monetary authority of a country issues bonds in the open market. This means that it exchanges bonds for money. With the increase in the supply of bonds in the open market, domestic interest rates go up. This leads to the appreciation of the domestic currency because of the increase in capital inflows from abroad. As domestic interest rates are high, investors allocate more wealth to domestic bonds, even by liquidating their foreign bonds. Thus, the rise in interest rates and appreciation of value of the domestic currency will result in portfolio adjustment.

Having discussed the main models under fundamental analysis, let us take a look at what technical analysis involves. Technical analysis is the study of the technical characteristics that are expected at major market turning points. It focuses on studying historical data of exchange rates and the volume of trade. The foreign exchange markets have cyclical movements. An active market participant who is able to identify the turns in the market would be able to buy at bottoms and sell at peaks. Unlike fundamental analysis, where factors like interest rates and inflation rates are studied, technical analysis is based purely on the study of the behaviour of past exchange rates and the volume of currencies traded.

Technical analysts use certain tools to identify past patterns and use these to predict future exchange rates. The main methods of technical analysis are charting (using various types of charts) and trend analysis (using mathematical or statistical models). Technical analysis is based on the assumption that history repeats itself, so market participants use different kinds of charts to find recurring price patterns. They can also use mathematical calculations (e.g., moving averages, momentum, etc.) to identify turning points or trends in the market.

Summary

1. **The exchange rate of a currency is determined by the forces of demand and supply of the currency.**
2. **A country's currency in the foreign exchange market is in demand when foreigners buy the goods and services exported by the country. The demand for a currency also arises when foreigners desire to buy financial assets denominated in that currency.**
3. **A country's currency is supplied in the course of paying for imports of goods and services. The supply of a currency also increases when foreign currency-denominated financial assets are purchased by the residents of that country.**
4. **The graphical representations of the demand schedule and the supply schedule are called the** *demand curve* **and the** *supply curve,* **respectively. The point of intersection of the demand and supply curves gives the equilibrium exchange rate of a currency vis-à-vis another currency. The quantity of a currency supplied equals the quantity demanded at the equilibrium exchange rate.**
5. **The factors other than the exchange rate that influence the currency supply and demand are inflation, economic growth rate, interest rates, political factors, social factors, etc. The equilibrium exchange rate changes whenever the positions of the demand and supply curves change under the influence of these factors.**
6. **The** *purchasing power parity* **(PPP) theory states that the percentage change in the exchange rate between the domestic currency and the foreign currency should equal the percentage change in the ratio of price indices in the two countries. The expectation form of PPP involves all the variables being expressed in expected terms.**
7. *Real exchange rate* **is the** *nominal exchange rate* **between two currencies adjusted for relative price level changes in the two countries.**
8. **According to** *interest rate parity* **(IRP) theory, financial products that are equal to each other must sell for the same price. Thus, the currency of a country with a higher (lower) interest rate should be at a forward discount (premium) in terms of the currency of another country with a lower (higher) interest rate.**
9. **The** *Forward rate parity* **theory states that forward rates are unbiased predictors of future spot rates of foreign exchange. In other words, the forward rate of a foreign exchange should equal the expected future spot rate on the date of the maturity of the forward contract.**
10. **The** *Fisher equation* **defines the relationship between the nominal interest rate, the real interest rate, and the expected rate of inflation in a country.**
11. **There are two basic approaches to forecasting foreign exchange rates:** *fundamental analysis* **and** *technical analysis.* **Fundamental analysis involves studying certain macroeconomic variables that are more likely to influence the exchange rates. Technical analysis is the study of technical characteristics that are expected at major market turning points.**

Questions and Problems

1. How do you derive the demand for a currency?
2. How is the supply curve of a currency derived?
3. What are the factors that influence the demand for a currency?
4. How is the exchange rate determined by the forces of demand and supply?
5. How does inflation shift the supply curve of a currency?
6. How do factors other than the exchange rate influence the currency demand and supply?
7. What is the law of one price?
8. Explain the absolute and relative versions of purchasing power parity.
9. Discuss the implications of deviations from purchasing power parity for exchange rate determination.
10. The inflation rate in the United Kingdom is expected to be 4 percent per annum, and the inflation rate in India is expected to be 7 percent per annum. If the current spot rate is GBP/INR 98.87, what is the expected spot rate in two years?
11. The interest rates in the United States and the United Kingdom are 6 percent and 8 percent per annum, respectively. If the current spot rate for the British pound is USD 1.6183, what is the spot rate implied by these interest rates three years from now?
12. What is interest rate parity? How are interest rates and forward rates related?
13. Establish the relationship between the forward rate and the expected future spot rate.
14. The exchange rate between the Indian rupee and the US dollar moves from INR 61.7865 at the beginning of the year to INR 60.123 by the end of the year. At the same time, the US price index rises from 120 to 130, and the Indian price index moves from 130 to 145. What are your comments on the appreciation of the Indian rupee?
15. The cost of borrowing British pounds is 14 percent per annum. During the year the inflation rate in the United States is 6 percent and the inflation rate in the United Kingdom is 8 percent. At the same time, the exchange rate changes from GBP/USD 1.60 at the beginning of the year to GBP/USD 1.50 at the end of the year. What is the real US dollar cost of borrowing British pounds for one year?
16. If the expected inflation rate is 10 percent and the real required return is 6 percent, what is the nominal interest rate according to the Fisher effect?
17. The spot rate and 90-day forward rate between Japanese yen and the US dollar are USD/JPY 116 and USD/JPY 110, respectively. Based on forward rate parity, by how much is the US dollar expected to appreciate or depreciate over the next 90 days? What is the forecast of the spot rate of exchange in 90 days?
18. The current spot rate between Canadian dollar and British pound is GBP/CAD 2.13 and the one-year forward rate is GBP/CAD 2.10. The real risk-free interest rate is 4 percent in both Canada and the United Kingdom. The Canadian inflation rate is 6 percent. What is the nominal risk-free rate of interest required in the United Kingdom? What is the United Kingdom's inflation rate if the equilibrium relationship holds?
19. What is the international Fisher relation? How are interest rates and inflation differentials related?
20. The current spot exchange rate and one-year forward rate between the Australian dollar and the British pound are GBP/AUD 2.53 and GBP/AUD 2.60 respectively. The prime rate in the United Kingdom is 12 percent. What should the Australian prime rate be? How much should the British pound change in value during the next year as per forward parity?
21. A firm has USD 10 million to invest in any currency. The following quotes are available:

    Spot rate: USD/GBP 0.52
    Six-month forward rate: USD/GBP 0.54
    Interest rate in the United Kingdom: 12 percent per annum
    Interest rate in the United States: 8 percent per annum
    Compute the profit based on the initial investment of USD 10 million.
22. The current spot exchange rate is USD/INR 45 and the three-month forward exchange rate is USD/INR 44.5. The risk-free annual interest rate is 6 percent in the United States and 8 percent in India. An investor can borrow up to INR 45 million or USD 1 million. Determine whether interest rate parity holds. If not, show how to realize the profit through covered interest arbitrage.
23. A firm in India has purchased goods for USD 1 million in the United States, payable in three months. The firm has enough cash at its bank in Mumbai, which pays 5 percent per annum. Currently, the spot exchange rate is USD/INR 45 and the three-month forward exchange rate is USD/INR 44.5. In the United States, the money market interest rate is 6 percent per annum. There are two alternative ways of paying for the goods purchased by the firm:
    a. Keep the funds at its bank in Mumbai and buy USD 1 million forward.

b. Buy a certain US dollar amount today and invest the amount in the United States for three months so that the maturity value becomes equal to USD 1 million.

Which method should the firm prefer? Why?

24. Discuss briefly the methods of forecasting exchange rates.

Multiple-choice Questions

1. In normal situations, the demand curve of a currency slopes ________.

   (a) upward (b) downward
   (c) horizontal (d) none of these

2. Exports and remittances contribute to the ________ of foreign currency.

   (a) demand
   (b) supply
   (c) both demand and supply
   (d) none of these

3. For equilibrium exchange rate, the demand and supply of a currency are ________.

   (a) not equal (b) equal
   (c) at equilibrium (d) none of these

4. The entries in the credit side of BOP represent ________ of foreign currency.

   (a) supply (b) demand
   (c) growth (d) none of these

5. When the purchasing power of two currencies is the same, their exchange rate is ________.

   (a) constant (b) at equilibrium
   (c) depreciating (d) none of these

6. The law of one price assumes ________.

   (a) no transaction costs
   (b) no transportation costs
   (c) no trade barriers
   (d) all the above three

7. Arbitrage results in ________.

   (a) Risk premium (b) Riskless profit
   (c) Capital investment (d) None of these

8. The relative form of PPP uses ________.

   (a) absolute prices (b) inflation rates
   (c) SDRs (d) none of these

9. For overvalued currencies the pressure is to ________.

   (a) depreciate (b) appreciate
   (c) remain constant (d) none of these

10. Real exchange rate is the nominal exchange rate adjusted for ________.

    (a) interest rate differential
    (b) inflation differential
    (c) growth rate differential
    (d) none of these

11. A real appreciation of a currency makes the exports ________.

    (a) more expensive (b) less expensive
    (c) increase (d) none of these

12. When REER is at 100, the home currency is said to be ________.

    (a) overvalued (b) undervalued
    (c) fairly valued (d) none of these

13. The law of one price with reference to interest rates and the risk being hedged is also known as -------.

    (a) covered interest rate parity
    (b) uncovered interest rate parity
    (c) arbitrage
    (d) none of these

14. Interest rate parity assumes that the markets are ________.

    (a) efficient (b) inefficient
    (c) imperfect (d) none of these

15. When interest rate differential is equal to forward rate differential, it is known as ________.

    (a) purchasing power parity
    (b) interest rate parity
    (c) forward rate parity
    (d) none of these

16. Forward rates are ________ predictors of future spot rates.

    (a) biased (b) unbiased
    (c) approximate (d) none of these

17. According to the Fisher equation, the nominal interest rate has the components of ________

    (a) real interest rate and expected inflation rate
    (b) real interest rate and forward rate
    (c) real interest rate and economic growth rate
    (d) none of these

Further Reading

1. Bradford Cornell, "Relative Price Changes and Deviations from Purchasing Power Parity," *Journal of Banking and Finance* 3, no. 3 (1979): 263–279.
2. Alan C. Shapiro, "What does Purchasing Power Parity Mean?" *Journal of International Money and Finance* (December 1983): 295–318.
3. M. Berg and G. Moore, "Foreign Exchange Strategies: Spot, Forward and Options," *Journal of Business Finance and Accounting* 18 (April 1990): 449–457.
4. Frederic S. Mishkin, "Are Real Interest Rates Equal Across Countries? An Empirical Investigation of International Parity Conditions," *Journal of Finance* 39 (December 1984): 1345–1357.
5. Ross Levine, "An Empirical Inquiry into the Nature of the Forward Exchange Rate Bias," *Journal of International Economies* 30 (1991): 359–370.
6. Kevin Clinton, "Transaction Costs and Covered Interest Arbitrage: Theory and Evidence," *Journal of Political Economy* (April 1988): 358–370.
7. I. A. Moosa, *Exchange Rate Forecasting—Techniques and Applications* (London: Macmillan Press Ltd, 2000).

CHAPTER 5

Management of Foreign Exchange Exposure and Risk

CHAPTER OBJECTIVES

After studying this chapter, you should be able to:

1. Discuss the concepts of foreign exchange exposure and foreign exchange risk, and understand how they are measured.
2. Define real exchange rate and nominal exchange rate from the perspective of foreign exchange exposure.
3. Classify foreign exchange exposure into economic and translation exposures, and understand how economic exposure can be further categorized into various types of transaction and operating exposures.
4. Discuss the management of transaction exposure and highlight various hedging techniques.
5. Describe the management of operating exposure.
6. Gain an overview of different currency translation methods.

Introduction

Foreign exchange rates never remain constant. At times, they may change widely and violently. However hard a currency is, its value is subject to change relative to other currencies. As economies in the world become more and more integrated, a significant change in the value of any one currency will affect the businesses world over. For instance, if the Japanese yen substantially appreciates against the U.S. dollar, it will adversely affect the competitive position of Japanese firms in the world market, particularly in the U.S. market. This, in turn, will have implications for world trade and significant economic consequences for many countries in the world.

The economic consequences of changes in foreign exchange rates may be direct or indirect. That is, many entities are affected by changes in foreign exchange rates either directly, indirectly, or both ways. Along with firms or corporations engaged in different kinds of businesses, governments and individuals are also affected by exchange rate changes. Further, changes in foreign exchange rates may affect not only operating cash flows, but also the home currency values of the assets and liabilities of a firm. For example, consider a firm in India that has borrowed USD 1 million from a firm in the United States. The INR value of the loan changes with changes in the exchange rate between the Indian rupee and the

U.S. dollar. An appreciation (depreciation) of a foreign currency would decrease (increase) the domestic currency value of a liability denominated in the foreign currency. Converse is the case for assets denominated in a foreign currency. Similarly, a firm engaged in export or import-oriented business would be exposed to exchange rate movements. Thus, the assets, liabilities, and operating cash flows of enterprises are all subject to foreign exchange changes. It is not out of context to mention that the foreign exchange rates and stock market returns tend to be significantly correlated and, therefore, they move in tandem but may not necessarily be in the same direction. For example, the S&P BSE SENSEX fell down to 17,968.08 on 27 August 2013 from 19,317.19 on 1 August 2013. At the same time, the Indian rupee–U.S. dollar exchange rate moved from 60.4435 on 1 August 2013 to 67.3152 on 27 August 2013. On 28 August 2013, the rupee nosedived by 3.7 percent to an all-time low of 68.85, before closing at 68.80/81, but the S&P BSE SENSEX opened at 17,851.44, touched a high of 18,101.84 and a low of 17,448.71, before closing at 17,996.15.

Changes in foreign exchange rates can affect not only firms engaged in international business but also those engaged in domestic business. Even if domestic firms buy raw materials and other components in the domestic market and sell their products exclusively in the domestic market, they may face competition from imports. Further, any change in exports caused by a change in the exchange rate would influence domestic sales as well. In other words, any change in the foreign exchange rate would influence both exports and imports, which in turn will affect the domestic market as well.

It is everyone's concern to know how changes in foreign exchange rates affect their endeavours. As corporations are the major entities to be affected, directly or/and indirectly, by changes in foreign exchange rates, it is all the more necessary for them to study the changes in exchange rates and adopt appropriate strategies to manage the risk emanating from such changes.

Foreign Exchange Exposure and Risk: A Comparison

In this section, we shall discuss the concepts of foreign exchange exposure and foreign exchange risk, and analyse how these two concepts differ.

Foreign Exchange Exposure

A change in the exchange rate may bring about a change in the value of an asset, liability, or/and operating income either through their direct relationship or through common underlying factors. Michael Adler and Bernard Dumas have defined **foreign exchange exposure** as the measure of "the sensitivity of changes in the real domestic currency value of assets, liabilities or operating incomes to unanticipated changes in exchange rates". The sensitivity can be expressed by the following regression line:

***Foreign exchange exposure** is the measure of the sensitivity of changes in the real domestic currency value of assets, liabilities, or operating incomes to unanticipated changes in exchange rates; **foreign exchange risk** is the variance of the domestic currency value of assets, liabilities, or operating incomes that is attributable to unanticipated changes in foreign exchange rates.*

$$\Delta RV = \alpha + \beta(\Delta S) + \mu \qquad (5.1)$$

Here,

ΔRV = Change in the real domestic value of a particular item (asset, liability, or operating income) or change in the real value of a group of assets, liabilities, or operating incomes

ΔS = Unanticipated changes in exchange rate between domestic currency and foreign currency

β = Slope of the regression line (i.e., regression coefficient) measuring the sensitivity of the value of the item to unanticipated changes in foreign exchange rate

α = Constant

μ = Random error

The regression equation can be statistically estimated by the least square method with historical data on ΔRV and ΔS. The regression line can also be obtained graphically by plotting the values of ΔRV and ΔS, and fitting a line to the scatter of points. The slope of the regression line gives the measure of exposure.

The beta coefficient measures the exposure of the item with respect to the corresponding exchange rate. In other words, the β value represents the value of the item in foreign currency that is at risk due to unanticipated exchange rate fluctuations. Algebraically, the beta coefficient can be defined as

$$b = \text{Cov (DVA}, S)/\text{Var }(S)$$

Here,

Cov (DVA, S) = Covariance between the domestic currency value of foreign-currency-denominated asset/liability/operating item and the exchange rate.

Var (S) = Variance of the exchange rate

The positive value of β is known as a *long exposure,* and the negative value of β is known as a *short exposure.* Note that the β value is always expressed in units of the foreign currency.

In terms of domestic currency, the values of foreign-currency-denominated assets, liabilities, and operating cash flows of firms are exposed to not only the effects of exchange rate changes, but also to effects of changes in the values of other factors. These factors may operate at either the macro level or the micro level, and cause uncertainty in the realized values of various business items. As these factors change, so do the values of various assets, liabilities, or operating incomes of firms. For example, interest rates, inflation rates, foreign exchange rates, technological advances, raw material, and other input supplies have a direct or indirect impact on the business operations and on the values of assets and liabilities of a firm. As these variables by themselves are subject to various uncertainties, the business operations as well as the values of assets and liabilities of firms are always at a risk.

The regression equation (Eq. 5.1) implicitly assumes that the values of the assets, liabilities, or operating incomes are influenced by several factors, including changes in the foreign exchange rate. If it is assumed that the value of receivables, payables, deposits, and loans are influenced by changes in the foreign exchange rate alone, the values of α and μ in the equation become zero. Then, the equation will be reduced to

$$\Delta RV = \beta(\Delta S)$$

$$\beta = \Delta RV/(\Delta S)$$

If β, the regression coefficient, is zero with respect to the domestic currency value of any foreign currency denominated asset, liability, or operating income/expense, such items are said to be unexposed to currency risk. It means that they are insensitive to exchange rate changes. They may be either independent of foreign exchange rate movements, or the change in the exchange rate exactly offsets the change in the foreign currency value of the item. For example, a U.S. firm owns some property in India. Whenever the Indian rupee depreciates (appreciates) against the USD, the Indian rupee price of the property goes up (down) by the same proportion. In this case, the U.S. dollar value of the India-based property is insensitive to the changes in the exchange rate. It means that the change in the exchange rate exactly offsets the change in the foreign currency value of the asset as the local price of the asset is negatively correlated with the exchange rate. Hence, the asset is not exposed to currency risk. Similarly, if a domestic currency is anchored to a foreign currency, then the exchange rate changes between these two currencies may not affect the international business transactions of a local firm.

Consider a firm that had a USD-denominated investment whose value was USD 2 million. At the exchange rate of USD/INR 44, the investment in terms of Indian rupees was

INR 88 million. In view of inflation in the United States at the rate of 3 percent, the investment value subsequently increased to USD 2.06 million. On the other hand, the U.S. dollar depreciated to INR 42.718, at which the investment in terms of Indian rupees was again INR 88 million. It may be observed from this example that though the foreign exchange rate has changed, the investment value in terms of domestic currency has not changed. This is because the domestic currency value of the investment has gone up in the same proportion. Therefore, the foreign exchange exposure on the investment is zero. In other words, the domestic currency value of the asset is insensitive to exchange rate changes. Though zero exposure is an ideal situation, in reality it is difficult to find such assets and liabilities. The values of assets or liabilities and foreign exchange rates may not change in the same proportion or may not move concurrently to give rise to zero exposure.

The values of the monetary items are always subject to foreign exchange exposure. Let us assume that the spot rate of USD/INR was INR 61.75 a month ago, and is INR 62.00 at present. In this scenario, an Indian firm which has 30-day receivables of USD 60 million will find that their value has increased from INR 3705 million to INR 3720 million. For a change of INR 0.25/USD, there is a change of INR 15 million in the value of the receivables. Thus, the β of receivables can be calculated as

$$\text{INR 15 million} = \beta \times \text{INR 0.25/USD}$$

or

$$\beta = \text{USD 60 million}$$

The receivables have a foreign exchange exposure of USD 60 million, and this is the amount that is at risk to unexpected changes in foreign exchange rates.

Conversely, a firm which has 60-day payables of USD 60 million will experience a downward sloping relationship between the INR value of payables and the foreign exchange rate. The unexpected change in the foreign exchange rate from USD/INR 61.75 to USD/INR 62.00 will result in an extra INR amount of payables. The beta value for payables is calculated as

$$\beta = (-)\text{INR 15 millon/INR 0.25}$$

$$= (-)\text{ USD 60 millon}$$

Thus, the exposure on the receivables or payables is USD 60 million. This is the amount that is at risk due to unanticipated changes in the exchange rate between the Indian rupee and the U.S. dollar. Note that the amount of exposure is as much as the value of receivables or payables.

An unexpected appreciation of the Indian rupee will bring down the INR value of receivables denominated in the U.S. dollar. At the same time, the burden of payables in U.S. dollars will be reduced, as the appreciation of INR results in a lower INR amount of the liability. In this situation also, the amount of exposure is as much as the value of receivables or payables.

Consider another example. A firm in India has made an investment in the United States, the market value of which is USD 5 million when the exchange rate is USD/INR 45. The investment subsequently increased to USD 5.5 million, and the exchange rate also changed from USD/INR 45 to USD/INR 46.5. Then,

$$\Delta RV = (\text{INR } 46.5 \times \text{USD 5.5 million}) - (\text{INR } 45 \times \text{USD 5 million})$$

$$= \text{INR 30.75 million}$$

Assuming that the random error (μ) is zero, the exposure (β) can be calculated as follows:

$$\text{INR 30.75 million} = \beta(\text{INR 1.5/USD})$$

$$\beta = \text{USD 20.5 million}$$

Here, the exposure on the investment of USD 5 million is larger than the value of the investment itself.

Suppose the market value of the investment has decreased to USD 4.75 million with the exchange rate changing from USD/INR 45 to USD/INR 44.5. Then,

$$\Delta RV = (\text{INR } 44.5 \times \text{USD } 4.75 \text{ million}) - (\text{INR } 45 \times \text{USD } 5 \text{ million})$$
$$= (-)\text{INR } 13.62 \text{ million}$$

In this case, the exposure is

$$(-)\text{INR } 13.62 \text{ million} = \beta(-\text{INR } 0.5/\text{USD})$$
$$\beta = \text{USD } 27.24 \text{ million}$$

That is, the exposure on the USD 5 million investment is USD 27.24 million.

Further, suppose the investment value increased from USD 5 million to USD 5.05 with change in the exchange rate from USD/INR 45 to USD/INR 43.75. Then,

$$\Delta RV = (\text{INR } 43.75 \text{ USD } 5.05) - (\text{INR } 45 \times \text{USD } 5 \text{ million})$$
$$= (-)\text{INR } 4.06 \text{ million}$$

The exposure (β) would be

$$(-)\text{INR } 4.06 \text{ million} = \beta(-\text{INR } 1.25/\text{USD})$$
$$\beta = \text{USD } 3.25 \text{ million}$$

In this case, the exposure on the investment is less than the market value of the investment.

From the examples we just discussed, it is evident that the amount of exposure of any item may be zero, equal to, less than, or more than the value of the item itself.

By definition, foreign exchange exposure exists only if the change in the exchange rate is unpredictable. That is, foreign exchange exposure arises only if the actual change in the exchange rate is different from the anticipated change. For example, suppose a firm has fixed the price for its product to be exported on a 30-day credit by taking into account the anticipated changes in its home currency value relative to a foreign currency. In this case, the exporter is free from foreign exchange exposure. However, if the foreign exchange rate changes from what had been expected, then the exporter will have to deal with foreign exchange exposure.

The management of a firm would try to deal with unanticipated changes in the exchange rate while assuming that anticipated changes have already been discounted by the market. That is, the markets compensate for changes in exchange rates that are anticipated or expected. For example, assume a firm has a USD 10 million bank deposit. The current spot rate is USD/INR 61.75, and the three-month forward rate is INR 62.00. After three months, the spot rate is INR 62.50. In this case, the unexpected depreciation of the INR is INR 0.50 per U.S. dollar. The gain in the INR value of the deposit is INR 5 million. The exposure is USD 10 million (i.e., INR 5 million/0.50). This is the amount that is subject to unanticipated changes in the exchange rate. As the forward rate is an unbiased estimate of the future spot rate, the forward rate is used to calculate the unexpected change in the exchange rate. That is, the forward rate of a particular duration can be compared to the actual spot rate on the date of the maturity of the forward contract, and the difference, if any, is taken as unexpected change in the exchange rate.

Unanticipated exchange rate changes can also affect domestic assets, liabilities, and operating incomes of firms. For example, a firm's domestic borrowings are affected by domestic interest rate changes, which, in turn, are influenced by unanticipated exchange rate changes. Even though there is no conversion from foreign currency into domestic currency, the domestic liability is exposed to exchange rate movements. The foreign exchange exposure of suppliers may also influence the exposure of a firm even if it does not have any cross-border transactions.

Foreign Exchange Risk

The terms *foreign exchange exposure* and *foreign exchange risk* are used interchangeably although they are conceptually different. Maurice D. Levi defines **foreign exchange risk** as "the variance of the domestic currency value of assets, liabilities, or operating incomes that is attributable to unanticipated changes in foreign exchange rates." By definition, foreign exchange risk depends on the exposure, as well as the variability of the unanticipated changes in the relevant exchange rate. Formally stated,

$$\text{Var}(\Delta RV) = \beta^2\ \text{Var}(\Delta S),$$

where

$\text{Var}(\Delta \text{RV})$ = Variance of the change in value of a business item caused by unanticipated changes in the foreign exchange rate

β = Regression coefficient which describes the systematic relation between (ΔRV) and (ΔS)

$\text{Var}(\Delta S)$ = Variance of unanticipated changes in the foreign exchange rate

This model implies that the foreign exchange rate risk is a function of the exposure and variance of exchange rates. The exposure or the unpredictable nature of exchange rates alone cannot result in a foreign exchange risk. For example, let us assume that a British firm is engaged in the export and import business, and its operations are mostly with Japan. So the operating cash flows of the firm are highly sensitive to the changes in the exchange rate between GBP and JPY. In this case, the firm has a very high foreign exchange exposure. However, it is expected that the exchange rate of JPY/GBP in the next six months would be almost steady. In view of the stability of exchange rates, the cash flows of the firm are not expected to change. Although, the firm has a large foreign exchange exposure, it has no currency risk because there is no variability of the operating cash flows attributable to changes in the exchange rates.

Real and Nominal Exchange Rates

As discussed in Chapter 4, the *real exchange rate* is the actual (nominal) exchange rate adjusted for the inflation differential between the two countries. While assessing the impact of exchange rate changes on the value of the firm, it is necessary to consider the underlying relative rates of inflation associated with each currency. In other words, a distinction should be made between the effects of nominal exchange rate changes and the effects of real exchange rate changes on the cash flows of a firm. Such a distinction has significant implications for foreign exchange risk management. For example, if a change in relative price levels is accompanied by an equal change in the nominal exchange rate, the real cash flows of a firm will not be affected. Alternatively, if the real exchange rate changes, then the real cash flows of the firm will get altered. This is because changes in the real exchange rate affect the relative competitiveness of the firm. The nominal exchange rate, however, affects the assets, liabilities, or cash flows fixed in terms of a foreign currency. The foreign exchange exposure is defined with reference to the real values of the assets, liabilities, or operating cash flows. In other words, the exposure is assessed with reference to the values adjusted for inflation or deflation. But whenever inflation or deflation is difficult to measure, the nominal values of assets, liabilities, or cash flows are considered.

Types of Exposure

As shown in Figure 5.1, foreign exchange exposure may broadly be categorized into economic exposure and translation exposure. **Economic exposure** refers to potential changes in all future cash flows of a firm that result from unanticipated changes in exchange rates.

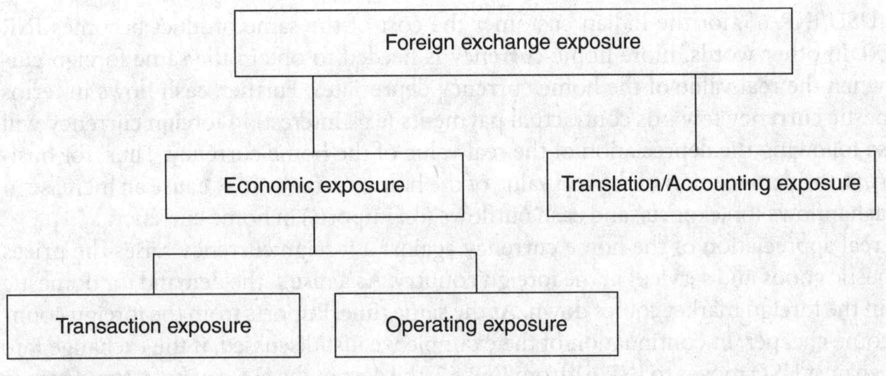

Figure 5.1
Foreign Exchange Exposure

The changes in foreign exchange rates would impact monetary assets and liabilities, as well as future cash flows. Thus, economic exposure may further be classified into transaction exposure and operating exposure. *Transaction exposure* refers to potential changes in the value of contractual future cash flows, or monetary assets and liabilities, resulting from changes in the exchange rate. *Operating exposure,* on the other hand, represents the potential changes in the value of non-monetary or real assets and liabilities due to unanticipated changes in exchange rates.

Foreign exchange exposure may broadly be classified into economic exposure and translation exposure. ***Economic exposure*** *refers to potential changes in all future cash flows of a firm that result from consequent on unanticipated changes in exchange rates. On the other hand,* ***translation exposure*** *results from restatement of values of the items of financial statements of a multinational corporation (MNC).*

Translation exposure is also known as *accounting exposure.* It results from a restatement of the values of the items of financial statements of a multinational corporation (MNC). In other words, translation exposure arises when items of financial statements that are stated in foreign currencies are restated in the home currency of an MNC. Depending on the movements of relevant foreign exchange rates, such a restatement may result in foreign exchange gains or losses.

Economic Exposure

Exchange rate fluctuations influence the future cash flows of a firm. That is, the value of a firm is subject to transaction exposure as well as operating exposure. **Transaction exposure** arises when a firm's contractual obligations, or monetary assets and liabilities, are exposed to unanticipated changes in exchange rates, while **operating exposure** arises when a firm's real assets or operating cash flows are exposed to unanticipated changes in exchange rates. In other words, economic exposure refers to the impact of unexpected fluctuations in exchange rates on future cash flows arising out of foreign-currency–denominated contractual transactions (monetary), as well as on the future cash flows to be generated by the real assets (non-monetary) of a firm.

Economic exposure is classified into transaction exposure and operating exposure. ***Transaction exposure*** *arises when the firm's contractual obligations are exposed to unanticipated changes in exchange rates, while* ***operating exposure*** *arises when the firm's real assets or operating cash flows are exposed to unanticipated changes in exchange rates.*

Although the value of a firm is exposed to both real and nominal changes in exchange rates, it is the changes in the real exchange rate that have significant economic implications for the relative competitiveness of exporters as well as importers. A real depreciation of the home currency against a foreign currency lowers the prices of domestic goods and services in the foreign country. For example, if the INR depreciates against the USD, it will make Indian goods cheaper in the United States and, as a result, the demand for Indian goods in the United States will go up. Exports invoiced in a foreign currency and foreign-currency denominated remittances, including interest and dividend incomes, also increase cash inflows in terms of domestic currency. However, depreciation of the home currency makes imports costlier. For example, assume a motor car is imported to India at USD 10,000. If the exchange rate is USD/INR 62, the product cost to the Indian customers is INR 6,20,000, and if the exchange rate is USD/INR 63, for the Indian customer the cost of the same product becomes INR 6,30,000. In other words, more home currency is needed to obtain the same foreign currency when the real value of the home currency depreciates. Further, cash flows in terms of domestic currency towards contractual payments (e.g., interest) in foreign currency will increase following the depreciation of the real value of the home currency. Thus, for business firms, the depreciation of the real value of the home currency may cause an increase in both cash inflows (on exports) and cash outflows (on imports) in home currency.

A real appreciation of the home currency against a foreign currency raises the prices of domestic goods and services in the foreign country. As a result, the demand for domestic goods in the foreign market comes down. At the same time, imports from the foreign country become cheaper. In continuation of the example we just discussed, if the exchange rate of INR against USD moves to INR 61 from INR 62, the cost of the U.S.-manufactured motor car to the Indian customer comes down to INR 6,10,000 from INR 6,20,000. This may lead to a decline in the demand for domestic goods because residents are able to get foreign substitutes at lower prices in terms of domestic currency. Further, cash flows in terms of domestic currency towards contractual payments (e.g., interest) in foreign currency will decline following the depreciation of the real value of the home currency. Thus, for business firms, the appreciation of the real value of the home currency would cause a reduction in both cash inflows (on exports) and outflows (on imports) in terms of home currency.

In summary, importing firms tend to gain from a real appreciation of their home currency and lose from a real depreciation, whereas exporting firms tend to gain from a real depreciation and lose from a real appreciation of their domestic currency. However, the extent of such gains or losses depends on the firm's production and marketing strategies, which ultimately influence the operating exposure of a firm.

It should be noted that purely domestic firms may also have economic exposure. For example, assume that a toy-making company in India buys all its raw materials and supplies locally and sells all its products (toys) locally. The general contention is that the Indian company is not subject to economic exposure as all its transactions are domestic and in Indian rupees. However, in reality, the company faces competition from foreign firms in its local market. Any change in the exchange rate affects the competitiveness of all firms in the Indian market. Customers of toys shift from foreign firms to Indian firms and vice versa depending on the price difference between the competitive firms. This shift of customers will affect the cash flows of the Indian firm. Thus, the purely Indian company is also subject to economic exposure even though it is not engaged in any international transactions.

Transaction Exposure It is common practice for many a business entity, particularly MNCs, to enter into foreign-currency-denominated transactions. These transactions may involve future cash inflows and outflows in foreign currency. Any change in the exchange rate between the time a transaction is initiated and the time the transaction is settled in home currency thus affects the cash inflows and outflows in home currency terms. *Transaction exposure* refers to potential changes in the value of contractual cash flows that arise due to unexpected changes in the foreign exchange rate. It is a measure of the sensitivity of the home currency value of assets and liabilities in a foreign currency to unanticipated changes in the exchange rate. A firm is subject to transaction exposure when it has monetary items whose values are contractually fixed in foreign currencies and do not change with the exchange rate. The monetary items of a firm, such as receivables and payables, denominated in different foreign currencies, are exposed to changes in the respective foreign exchange rates. For example, let us consider a firm in India that has sold goods worth USD 1 million to a client in the United States on three-month credit terms. When the firm receives USD 1 million after three months, it will have to convert the U.S. dollars into INR at the spot rate prevailing at that time. Since the future spot rate is not known exactly, the INR receipts from this foreign-currency-denominated transaction become uncertain. If the U.S. dollar appreciates (or depreciates) against the INR, the INR receipts will be higher (or lower). Thus, the firm will have gains or losses in INR terms, depending on whether the foreign currency has appreciated or depreciated. Similar gains or losses can be recorded with transactions that involve the firm in contractual foreign-currency-denominated debt obligations like bills payable.

Transaction exposure also arises when a firm borrows or lends in a foreign currency. For instance, consider a firm in India that borrows USD 1 million from a firm in New York for three years. During the period, if the U.S. dollar appreciates against the Indian rupee, the borrower will have a greater burden in terms of INR. Conversely, if the foreign currency depreciates, the borrower will have a lower burden in terms of home currency. In the same way, a lender in India who has lent a certain amount in U.S. dollars to a firm in the United States may experience a gain or loss in terms of home currency as a consequence of appreciation or depreciation of the U.S. dollar against the Indian rupee. Thus, whenever a firm has foreign-currency-denominated contractual cash flows (monetary assets and monetary liabilities), it is subject to transaction exposure. Depending on the *net monetary assets position* (monetary assets less monetary liabilities) and also on the direction of exchange rate changes, the firm may experience a net gain or a net loss on transaction exposure.

*Transaction exposure can be managed by hedging techniques as well as operational techniques. **Hedging techniques** include forwards, money market hedges, futures, options, and swaps. **Operational techniques** include exposure netting, leading and lagging, and currency of invoicing.*

Many firms generally have financial contracts denominated in foreign currencies. The number of such firms has increased phenomenally in recent years as a result of globalization of trade and investments. Therefore, firms should manage their transaction exposure judiciously by adopting appropriate techniques or strategies.

There are many techniques by which the firms can manage their transaction exposure. These techniques can be broadly divided into hedging techniques and operational techniques. Hedging refers to taking an offsetting position in order to lock in the home currency value for the currency exposure, eliminating the risk arising from changes in the exchange rate. The important hedging techniques are forwards/futures, money market hedges, options, and swaps. Operational techniques include exposure netting, leading and lagging, and currency of invoicing. Figure 5.2 illustrates the various techniques that are employed in managing transaction exposure.

Hedging with Forwards and Futures A forward contract is a legally enforceable agreement to buy or sell a certain amount of foreign currency on a specified date at an exchange rate fixed at the time of entering the contract. Firms may hedge their transaction exposure by

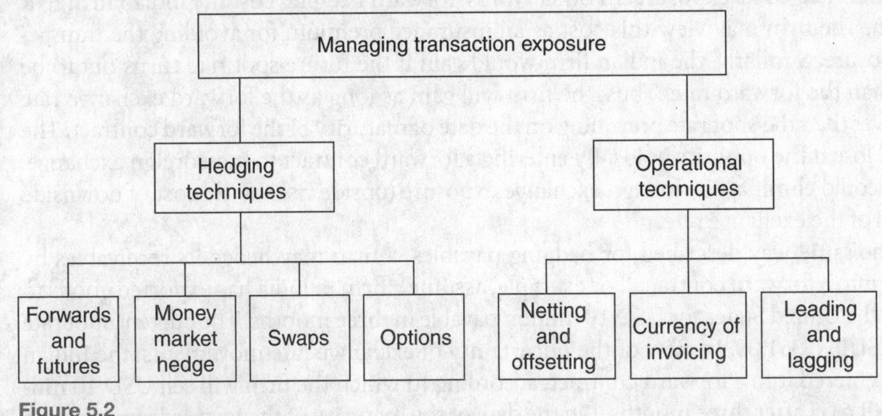

Figure 5.2

Managing Transaction Exposure

Example 5.1

A company in India has exported goods worth USD 10 million to a U.S. firm, payable three months from now. At the same time, it has purchased equipment from the same U.S. firm for USD 5 million, payable in the next three months. The spot rate is USD/INR 42. What is the transaction exposure of the Indian company? Suppose the INR appreciates against the USD and the exchange rate becomes USD/INR 41 in the three-month period. What is the transaction loss to the Indian company?

Solution

$$\text{Net exposure in USD} = \text{Inflows} - \text{Outflows} = \text{USD 10 million} - \text{USD 5 million}$$
$$= \text{USD 5 million}$$
$$\text{Exposure in terms of INR} = \text{INR 210 million}$$
$$\text{Transaction loss} = \text{INR } 210 \times [(42-41)/42] = \text{INR 5 million}$$
$$\text{Or, USD 5 million} \times (42-41) = \text{INR 5 million}$$

entering into forward contracts. That is, a firm may buy or sell the foreign currency forward and thereby avoid fluctuations in the home currency value of the foreign-currency denominated fixed future cash flows. For example, a firm in India has imported goods from a U.S.-based firm for USD 5 million on six-month credit. To hedge this transaction exposure, the firm has entered a forward contract to buy USD 5 million at a forward rate of USD/INR 61.00. On the date of maturity of the forward contract, the firm will deliver INR 305 million to the counter-party and in return receive USD 5 million. This happens regardless of the spot rate on the date of maturity of the forward contract. Thus, the USD payable is exactly offset by the USD receivable, and the Indian firm's transaction exposure is hedged by a forward contract. However, it may also happen that the payables in INR under the forward contract will be lower (or higher) than those under the unhedged position if the future spot rate turns out to be lower (or higher) than the forward rate (USD/INR 61.00). If the future spot rate turns out to be lower than the forward rate, the Indian firm would have lost an opportunity to benefit from a weak U.S. dollar. For example, if the spot rate is USD/INR 60.00 on the date of maturity of the forward contract, the Indian firm would have paid only INR 300 million if it had not hedged its exposure. In other words, forward hedging cost the Indian firm INR 5 million. The firm may view this cost as an insurance premium for avoiding the transaction exposure. Similarly, the Indian firm would gain if the future spot rate turns out to be higher than the forward rate. Thus, the firm will gain as long as the forward exchange rate (F_n) is lower than the spot rate prevailing on the date of maturity of the forward contract. The firm will lose if the opposite holds. By entering a forward contract to buy foreign exchange, the firm could eliminate its foreign exchange exposure (upside risk) at the cost of downside potential of the exchange rate.

In the same way described for hedging payables, a firm may hedge its receivables by entering into a forward contract. For example, assume a firm in India has exported goods to a firm in the United States for USD 10 million payable in three months. The current spot rate is, say, USD/INR 61.00. In view of the uncertainty of exchange rate movements, the Indian firm has entered into a forward contract, according to which the firm will sell USD 10 million at INR 61.5 after three months. On the date of the maturity of the forward contract, the Indian firm sells USD 10 million and receives INR 610.5 million. Suppose that, on the date of maturity of the forward contract, the spot rate is INR USD/INR 60.50. The Indian firm is benefited by INR10 million as the spot rate is lower than the forward rate. If, however, the spot rate is higher than the forward rate, say, INR 62, the Indian firm will lose money as it could have sold the foreign currency at a higher rate by remaining un-hedged. As in buying forward, gains and losses may also arise in selling the foreign currency forward, depending on the future spot rate and the forward rate. Note that the firm could eliminate the foreign exchange exposure (downside risk) at the cost of the upside potential of the exchange rate by entering a forward contract to sell the foreign currency.

A firm's decision on hedging (or not hedging) depends on three considerations: (i) the real cost of hedging; (ii) the anticipated absolute gains and losses that are most likely to arise from hedging; and (iii) the expected transaction costs. We shall discuss each of these factors here:

- *Real cost of hedging*: The preceding analysis suggests that the firm has to decide whether or not to hedge by taking into consideration the difference between the home currency per unit of foreign currency to be received (or paid) with hedging (i.e., forward rate, denoted by F_t), and the home currency per unit of foreign currency to be received (paid) without hedging (i.e., future spot rate, denoted by S_t). So, what is relevant in the analysis is not the current spot rate, but the future spot rate (anticipated spot rate at the time of maturity of the forward contract). In other words, the firm has to take into consideration the *ex-ante* (pre-event) values but not the *ex-post* (after the event) rates of foreign exchange. However, the gain or loss from hedging will be known only ex-post.

  The real cost of hedging in percentage terms can be obtained from Eq. 5.2. This measurement is particularly useful when the firm is comparing the real cost of hedging for various currencies.

  $$\text{Real cost of hedging} = (F_t - S_t)/S_t \tag{5.2}$$

  If it is anticipated that the foreign currency will strengthen during the period of the forward contract, the real cost of hedging receivables will become positive. It means the firm would receive a lower amount of home currency by hedging and, therefore, hedging of receivables is not preferred. At the same time, the real cost of hedging payables will become negative with the anticipated appreciation of foreign currency. The burden of payables in domestic currency may become lower by not hedging if the foreign currency is most likely to appreciate over the maturity period of the forward contract. So, hedging of payables is not worthwhile.
- *Gains/losses*: The hedging decision can also be made by considering the anticipated absolute gains and losses that are most likely to arise from forward hedging. Such gains and losses can be computed as:

  $$\text{Gain/loss} = (F_n - S_t) \times \text{Amount involved in the transaction}$$

  Here,

  F_n = Forward rate for period *n* (contract maturing at time *t*)

  S_t = Future spot rate at time *t*

  If the future spot rate is lower than the forward rate (i.e., the foreign currency is at a forward premium), the firm will gain on the sale of foreign currency forward. Conversely, the firm will gain on buying the foreign currency forward when the future spot rate is higher than the forward rate (i.e., the foreign currency is at a forward discount).

  Furthermore, the risk perception and risk aversion of the firm may also influence the decision of whether or not to hedge a particular transaction exposure. A firm that is more risk averse may hedge every transaction exposure, and a firm that is less risk averse may leave some of its foreign transactions open (unhedged). If the forward rate is an unbiased predictor of the future spot rate, the hedging of transaction exposure may become superfluous.

- *Transaction costs*: In the previous analysis, it is assumed that there are no transaction costs. In reality, however, transaction costs do exist and, therefore, firms should take them into consideration. Further, the bid–ask spread in the forward market is generally wider than in the spot market. The depth of the two markets and also the maturity period of the forward contract generally govern the difference in the spread between the two markets. The larger spread in the forward market as compared to the spot market can be considered the cost of a forward hedge, the benefit of which is the certainty of the home currency value of the foreign-currency-denominated asset or liability.

As forwards and futures have many common characteristics, hedging the foreign exchange exposure with currency futures is similar to hedging exposure with forward contracts. A detailed discussion on forwards and futures is presented in Chapter 6.

Money Market Hedging A firm can lock-in the home currency value of future cash flows in foreign currency through a money market hedge. *Money market hedging* involves simultaneous borrowing and lending or investing in the money market, with an aim to avoid or reduce foreign exchange exposure of receivables or payables. A firm that wants to hedge foreign exchange exposure on receivables (payables) may borrow (lend) foreign currency in the money market, so that its assets and liabilities in the same currency will match. Only firms that have access to the international money market can use this type of hedging effectively. Any restrictions on the borrowing or lending in the foreign currency may limit the use of this technique. Nevertheless, money market hedging is particularly used for cash flows in currencies for which there are no forward markets.

Example 5.2

A U.S.-based MNC has sold its product (invoiced in the U.S. dollar) to a firm in the United Kingdom. The invoice amount is USD 10 million. The payment is due three months from today. The current spot rate is USD/GBP 0.5252. It is expected that the U.S. dollar will depreciate by 5 percent over the three months period. The three-month forward rate as quoted is USD/GBP 0.54. What is the expected loss to the British firm, and how can it be hedged?

Solution

Expected future spot rate = USD/GBP 0.5515
The expected loss without hedging can be calculated as:
Invoice amount = USD 10 million, which is equivalent to GBP 5.252 million at the current spot rate.
After three months, the British firm has to pay USD 10 million × GBP 0.5515 = GBP 5.515 million.
Expected loss = GBP 0.263 million (in view of depreciation of USD by 5%).
The loss under forward cover will be:

Payment after three months with a three-month forward contract is GBP 5.40 million

$$\begin{aligned}\text{Loss} &= \text{GBP } 5.40 \text{ million} - \text{GBP } 5.252 \text{ million} \\ &= \text{GBP } 0.148 \text{ million}\end{aligned}$$

So, by entering into a forward contract, the British firm could reduce its loss by

(GBP 0.263 million – GBP 0.148 million) = GBP 0.115 million.

Example 5.3

An Indian company exports its products to the United States, Japan, and Europe on 90-days credit terms. The cost and sales information is presented in Table 5.1. Table 5.2 presents the exchange rates of the U.S. dollar, the Japanese yen, and the euro. Analyse this data and discuss if the company should have hedged its receivables.

Table 5.1 Cost and Sales Information

	United States	*Japan*	*Europe*
Variable cost per unit (INR)	400	220	520
Selling price per unit	USD 15	JPY 700	EUR 12
Sales	USD 1,00,000	JPY 7,50,000	EUR 9,50,000

Table 5.2 Exchange Rates

	USD/INR	*JPY/INR*	*EUR/INR*
Spot rate	39.29/39.35	0.3611/0.3695	58.0579/58.0900
Three months forward	39.3520/39.3625	0.3720/0.3825	58.2600/58.2695
Spot rate after three months	39.4123/39.4230	0.3745/0.3850	58.3016/58.3175

Note: A quote like: 39.4123/39.4230 means that the bank will give INR 39.4123 to buy one U.S. dollar, and will require INR 39.4230 to sell one U.S. dollar.

Solution

If the receivables are hedged, the contribution is as shown in Table 5.3.

Table 5.3 Receivables are Hedged

Sales	*USD 1,00,500*	*JPY 7,49,000*	*EUR 95,040*
Selling price per unit	USD 15	JPY 700	EUR 12
Units sold	6,700	1,070	7,920
Variable cost per unit (INR)	400	220	520
Variable cost (INR)	26,80,000	2,35,400	41,18,400
Three-month forward rate	39.3520	0.3720	58.2600
INR value of sales	39,54,876	2,78,628	55,37,030
Contribution (INR)	12,74,876	43,228	14,18,630

Total contribution: INR 27,36,734

Table 5.4 shows the outcome of leaving the receivables unhedged.

Table 5.4 Receivables are Not Hedged

Spot rate after three months	39.4123	0.3745	58.3016
INR value of sales	39,60,936	2,80,500	55,40,984
Contribution (INR)	12,80,936	45,100	14,22,584

Total contribution: INR 28,48,620

A glance at Tables 5.3 and 5.4 reveals that the total contribution without the receivables having been hedged is greater than what it would have been had the receivables been hedged. Therefore, the company should not have hedged its receivables.

There is a direct relation between money market hedging and forward contract hedging. In fact, money market hedging creates homemade forward market hedging. Borrowing at the home currency interest rate and investing at the foreign currency interest rate are similar to hedging foreign currency payables by purchase of foreign currency forwards. On the other hand, borrowing at the foreign currency interest rate and investing at the home currency interest rate are akin to the hedging of foreign currency receivables by sale of foreign currency forwards.

Money market hedging involves taking a money market position to hedge exposure on foreign currency receivables or foreign currency payables. An exporter who wants to hedge receivables in a foreign currency may borrow a certain amount in the currency denominating the receivables, get that foreign-currency-denominated amount converted into home currency in the spot market, and then invest it for a period coinciding with the period of receivables. Then the exporter pays off the foreign currency loan with the receivables amount. For example, assume a firm in India has 90-day receivables of USD 10 million. First, the firm may borrow an amount such that the principal and interest after 90 days will be equal to the receivable amount. The annual rate of interest on the U.S.-dollar-denominated loan is 8 percent (or 2 percent for 90 days). The firm initially borrows USD 9.80 million [i.e., USD 10 million/(1 + 0.02)]. Then, the borrowed amount is converted into INR at the spot rate of, say, USD/INR 43. So the firm realizes an amount of INR 421.57 million, and invests that amount at 10 percent per annum. On the day when the firm realizes the receivables amount, it will have its investment matured for INR 432.11 million. By using the receivables amount, the firm will pay off the USD-denominated loan of 10 million.

Suppose the 90-day forward rate is USD/INR 43.25. The cash inflows under forward market hedge are INR 432.50 million. Thus, forward market hedging would yield higher amounts of receivables in home currency than money market hedging. This difference in cash flows arises because there is no parity between the forward rate and the interest rate differential (i.e., no interest rate parity).

The steps involved in money market hedging on receivables can be summed up as follows:

1. Borrow in the foreign currency in which the receivables are denominated at the prevailing interest rate.
2. Convert the borrowed currency to domestic currency at the spot bid rate.
3. Invest that amount at the prevailing interest rate for the period of the receivables.
4. Repay the foreign currency loan with the amount realized through receivables.
5. Realize the maturity value of the investment.

Importers who want to hedge their payables may borrow a certain amount in their home currency, convert that amount at the spot rate into the currency in which the payables are denominated, and then invest that amount for a period matching the payables. For example, consider an Indian importer who has USD 50 million 90-day payables. The interest rate in the United States is 8 percent per annum or 2 percent per 90-day period. This means an amount of USD 49.02 million invested or borrowed today will become USD 50 million at the end of a 90-day period at an interest rate of 8 percent per annum. So the importer borrows an amount of INR 2,108 million at an interest rate of 10 percent per annum or 2.5 percent per 90-day period, and converts this into USD 49.02 million at the current spot rate of USD/INR 43. Then that amount (USD 49.02 million) is invested at 8 percent per annum for 90 days, which will become USD 50 million at the end of the 90-day period. On the day when the importer has to pay off the import bills, he will have an amount of USD 50 million sufficient for clearing the dues. Further, the importer has to pay back the loan of INR 2,160.7 million (principal plus interest).

To draw a comparison between money market hedging and forward market hedging, assume the 90-day forward rate at USD/INR 43.75. The cash outflows using the forward market hedge amount to INR 2,157.50 million (50 million × 43.15) and the cash outflows under the money market hedge are INR 2,160.7 million. Thus, the importer could save INR 3.2 million by using the money market hedge instead of the forward market hedge.

In sum, the steps involved in money market hedging on payables are:

1. Borrow, if necessary, a certain amount in home currency at the prevailing borrowing rate.
2. Buy the foreign currency in which the import bill has to be paid at the ask rate.
3. Invest the proceeds realized above (2) at the prevailing lending rate for the period of payables.
4. Receive the maturity value of the investment.
5. Pay off the payables denominated in foreign currency.
6. Repay the domestic currency debt, if borrowed.\

Significantly, money market hedge and forward market hedge yield the same results if and only if interest rate parity holds. In order for the interest rate parity to hold, the forward premium or discount should reflect the interest rate differential between the two currencies. In such a case, the hedger becomes indifferent between money market and forward market hedging. If the interest rate parity fails to hold, the proceeds from the money market hedge will not be the same as those from the forward market hedge. In other words, imperfections in the money markets may make money market hedging different from forward market hedging. Transaction costs also yield different results for these two types of hedging techniques.

Hedging with Currency Options The main problem with forward contract and money market hedging is that they insulate the exporter or importer from adverse exchange rate movements, but they don't allow the exporter or importer to benefit from favourable exchange rate movements. Currency option hedging is a technique that avoids this problem. A *currency option* is a contract that gives the buyer the right, but not the obligation, to buy or sell a specified currency at a specified exchange rate in the future. Options are basically of two types: put options and call options. A *put option* gives the option holder the right to sell a specified quantity of foreign currency to the option seller at a fixed rate of exchange on or before the expiration date. A *call option* gives the option holder the right to buy a specified quantity of foreign currency from the option seller at a predetermined exchange rate on or before the expiration date. A firm that wants to protect itself against the appreciation of a foreign currency may buy a call option on that currency. Conversely, a firm that wants to protect itself against depreciation of a particular foreign currency may buy a put option on that currency. An important feature of options is that there is no obligation on the part of the holder of the option contract to buy or sell the stated currency at the exercise price. If the spot rate of a currency moves against the interests of the option holder, he will just let that option contract expire.

Options can be used to hedge both receivables and payables in foreign currency. A firm that has an obligation to make payments in foreign currency may hedge its payables or foreign currency outflows by buying a call option on the currency in which the payables are denominated.

By buying a call option, the firm knows the maximum amount that it has to pay in home currency and, at the same time, can benefit if the exchange rate ends up below the strike rate. Similarly, an exporting firm may hedge its receivables or foreign currency inflows by buying a put option. This will ensure that a minimum quantity of domestic currency is received for foreign currency inflows. At the same time, the exporter may also benefit if the domestic currency price of the foreign currency becomes higher than the strike rate. Option contracts thus protect the buyer or holder against adverse exchange rate movements without depriving the firm of the opportunity to benefit from favourable exchange rate movements. It is this feature which distinguishes the option contracts from forward contracts. For example, consider a firm that has sold forward its U.S. dollar receivables for delivery in three months at the exchange rate of USD/INR 60.50. Suppose on the maturity date of the forward contract, the spot exchange rate turns out to be USD 61.75. In this case, the firm has lost an opportunity to benefit from a strong U.S. dollar. In forward contract hedging, the firm may have to forgo an opportunity to benefit from favourable spot exchange rate changes. Alternatively, suppose the firm purchased an American style three-month put option on the U.S. dollar with an exercise price of INR 61.00. By this contract, the firm would have the right, but not the obligation to sell the U.S. dollar at INR 61.00, regardless of the future spot rate. In other words, the firm would exercise its put option on the U.S. dollar whenever the future spot exchange rate falls below the exercise rate of INR 61.00. So, the firm is assured of a minimum rate of INR 61.00. Thus, the option contract protects the firm if the U.S. dollar weakens, and at the same time gives it the opportunity to benefit if the U.S. dollar strengthens. In the same way, to hedge its payables in a foreign currency, a firm can buy a call option, which bestows on the firm the right to buy the foreign currency on or before a specified date at a specified exchange rate, regardless of the future spot rate. By buying a call option, the firm has an opportunity to benefit from favourable exchange rate changes.

Not only exporters and importers but also investors can use currency options to hedge their transaction exposures. Investors may also hedge their future payments or receipts of funds in foreign currency by buying options. Currency options can also be used to hedge contingent foreign currency outflows. For example, in international bidding, a firm has to pay only if its bid is accepted. In such a situation, the firm may buy a call option and lock in a maximum exchange rate at which it has to buy the foreign currency, while limiting its downside risk to the call premium in the event the bid is not accepted. So, currency options can also be effectively used when the amount of a foreign currency outflow is uncertain.

Currency options provide firms a flexible means of hedging against foreign exchange exposure. Option strategies such as spreads, straddles, and strangles, and exotic options like barrier options, knock-in and knock-out options, range forwards, and forward reversing options offer great opportunities to traders to hedge their transaction exposures. Readers may refer to Chapter 7 for a detailed discussion on options strategies. Call options with a low premium but high strike rate, and put options with a low premium and low strike rate are also available. To put it simply, options are highly flexible and versatile hedging tools. The option holder (or buyer) has to pay a *premium* upfront for the benefits of options. As we'll see in Chapter 6, the counter-party of a forward contract does not need to make any upfront payment. There is no premium or fee (with the exception of broking charges, if any) for buying or selling a forward contract. Therefore, while preferring an option contract to a forward contract, the option buyer has to assess whether the advantages with a currency option are worth the price (option premium) paid for the option.

Hedging with Swap Contracts A swap is an agreement between two parties to exchange a cash flow in one currency against a cash flow in another currency according to predetermined terms and conditions. To put it differently, a swap agreement requires periodic payments from one party to the other in order to safeguard against unfavourable exchange rate movements. A firm which expects certain cash flows in a foreign currency in the future may enter into a swap contract in order to hedge those cash flows against foreign exchange rate fluctuations. For example, consider an Indian firm that has a ten-year loan of GBP 5 million at an interest rate of 8 percent per annum. The interest amount has to be paid at the end of each year of the ten-year period. Thus, the Indian firm is faced with foreign

Example 5.4

A firm in Mumbai wants to buy equipment costing USD 5 million from a company in New York. The Indian firm will be permitted to pay the amount in three months.

The current spot rate of the U.S. dollar is USD/INR 45. The firm expects the spot rate of the U.S. dollar to change in three months. The spot rate may be USD/INR 44, 44.5, 46, 46.5, or 47. The three-month forward rate is USD/INR 46. The interest rate is 6 percent per annum in India and 4 percent per annum in the United States.

In the Indian options market, a call option on the U.S. dollar with an expiration date coinciding with the three month period has an exercise rate of INR 46. The option premium is INR 10,000. The put option has also the same values for the same three month period.

Calculate the cash flows under each alternative course of action.

Solution

1. Suppose the payment remains unhedged. The expected cash outflows after three months in INR in this scenario are presented in Table 5.5.

Table 5.5 Expected Spot Rate Versus Cash Outflows

Expected spot rate (INR)	*Cash outflows (INR million)*
44.0	220.0
44.5	222.5
46.0	230.0
46.5	232.5
47.0	235.0

2. If the firm enters a forward contract to buy USD 5 million, after three months, the cash outflow in INR will be:

$$\text{INR } 46 \times \text{USD } 5 \text{ millon} = \text{INR } 230 \text{ millon}$$

3. Now, let's see what the cash flows will be if the firm chooses a money market hedge. The firm borrows a certain amount of money in INR and converts that amount to U.S. dollars, and invests this amount to receive USD 5 million after three months.

   The amount in U.S. dollars to be invested is:

$$\text{USD } 5 \text{ millon}/\ (1+0.01) = \text{USD } 4.951 \text{ millon}$$

   The amount in INR that needs to be borrowed and converted into U.S. dollars for investing is INR 222.77 million.

   The amount to be paid after three months with interest is INR 226.11 million [INR 222.77 million (1 + 0.015)].

4. If the firm hedges the payment with an option (strike rate INR 46 and option premium INR 10,000), then the cash flows will be as shown in Table 5.6.

Table 5.6 Cash Flows if the Payment is Hedged with an Option Contract

Spot rate USD/INR	*Option premium (INR)*	*Total amount to be paid for USD 5 million (INR million)*
44.0	10,000	220.01
44.5	10,000	222.51
46.0	10,000	230.01
46.5	10,000	230.01
47.0	10,000	230.01

exchange exposure. In order to hedge this exposure, the firm enters into a swap contract by which the firm receives an amount in GBP equivalent to the interest amount payable each year for ten years and also GBP 5 million at the end of the ten-year period from the counterparty of the contract. This is against the delivery of a fixed amount of INR each year of the ten-year period. The firm will pay a predetermined amount in INR each year, regardless of future spot rates. In other words, the Indian firm has locked in the amount of INR the GBP payments will convert to, in ten years. Consider another example in which a U.S.-based MNC wants to finance its subsidiary in an emerging market economy by issuing bonds. Instead of issuing bonds in the local currency of its subsidiary, it may issue bonds denominated in U.S. dollars and then use a swap to convert the payment of interest and principle into the relevant local currency. Currency swaps are generally used to hedge long-term transaction exposures.

Netting and Offsetting A firm may have a transaction exposure portfolio with exposures in different currencies. When exchange rates change, there may be gains on some currencies and losses on others. Exposure netting is a portfolio approach to hedging, according to which a firm may manage its trade transactions in such a way that exposures in one currency will be offset by exposures in the same or other currencies. For example, suppose a firm has receivables of USD 1 million and at the same time payables of USD 1 million. So, the USD receivables cancel out the USD payables, leaving no net exposure. In case both the amounts are different, the firm can use the receivables to settle the payables and hedge the residual or net amount of receivables or payables. A firm can hedge the residual exposure (exposure remaining after netting) rather than hedging each currency exposure separately when it has a portfolio of currency exposures. A long position in one currency, say, USD, can be offset by a short position in the same currency. If two currencies are positively correlated, a firm can offset a long position in one currency with a short position in the other currency. Thus, a gain (loss) on the receivables due to appreciation (depreciation) of a currency will be matched by a loss (gain) on the payables due to appreciation (depreciation) of another currency. This, in fact, provides a natural hedge. However, if two currencies are negatively correlated, then a long (short) position in one currency can be offset by a long (short) position in the other currency. A firm can have more stable cash flows if it has currency diversification, which can limit the potential impact of changes in any single currency on the cash flows of a firm.

Currency of Invoicing Importers and exporters can also shift foreign exchange exposure by getting their exports or imports invoiced in their own currency. This method of hedging does not eliminate foreign exchange exposure but shifts it from one party to another.

For example, if a firm invoices its imports in its domestic currency, it need not face foreign exchange exposure on its payables. But the counter-party (i.e., the exporter) will face the foreign exchange exposure. Similarly, a firm can shift its entire exchange risk to the importer by invoicing its exports in its domestic currency. Thus, if the importing firm can get the payables invoiced in its home currency, the exporter will face the foreign exchange exposure, and if the exporting firm can invoice its exports in its home currency, the importer will face the foreign exchange exposure. Exports are often invoiced in the exporter's currency. Since the amounts are received or paid sometime after the invoice is made, the expected exchange rate is a significant consideration. If a currency is more volatile, then invoicing in such a currency can be avoided.

It is also a common practice for both parties—the exporter and the importer—to agree to use a currency other than their respective currencies to invoice their transactions. For example, an Indian exporter and a Japanese importer may agree to use the U.S. dollar as the invoice currency. Further, in the case of some currencies, there may not be a regular market for currency derivatives like options and futures. Therefore, traders may use a third currency, which is less volatile in value or whose country of origin has a developed currency derivative market.

Sometimes, exporters and importers agree to share the foreign exchange exposure by getting a part of the trade invoiced in, say, the importer's home currency, and the rest of the trade invoiced in the exporter's home currency. Such invoicing is known as *mixed currency invoicing.* Trade transactions may also be invoiced in one of the standard currency baskets such as euro or SDR, and thereby the foreign exchange exposure is reduced. Trade transactions may also be expressed in terms of composite currency unit made of different currencies. Such private currency baskets, also known as *cocktails,* are designed to avoid violent fluctuations in individual exchange rates.

A firm may wish to have its exports invoiced in the currency in which it is required to pay for its imports. For example, an Indian firm may like to invoice its exports to the United Kingdom in GBP so that it can use GBP receivables to pay off its future payables in GBP. But it may be difficult to match foreign currency inflows and outflows in terms of amount and time. A firm may not be able to invoice the amount of its exports to match the amount of payables it has in the same currency, and it may also not be able to match the time of its foreign currency inflows with the time of its foreign currency outflows. In such an eventuality, the firm will have some degree of foreign currency exposure, which can be hedged by other methods.

The pattern of invoicing in India's trade is presented in Table 5.7. As can be observed from Table 5.7, most of India's international trade is invoiced in U.S. dollars, followed by euro. It shows that the traders prefer mostly the USD to any other currency. The important factors that govern invoicing are historic relationships between the trading partners and the relative bargaining powers of partners. Currency invoicing is a matter to be decided by the exporter, the importer, or both. Sometimes, however, neither of the parties involved may have any choice, as in the case of crude oil exports, which are conventionally invoiced in the U.S. dollar.

Leading/lagging Strategy Transaction exposure can also be managed by shifting the timing of receipt or payment of foreign currency in accordance with expectations of future exchange rate movements. A firm may lag the receivables and lead the payables in hard currencies. It may also lead the receivables and lag the payables denominated in weak currencies. By doing so, it can avoid the loss from the depreciation of the soft currency and benefit from the appreciation of the hard currency. For example, suppose that an Indian firm has three-month payables denominated in U.S. dollars. As the U.S. dollar is a strong currency and is expected to appreciate against the Indian rupee, any delay in the settlement of the U.S. dollar payables will put additional burden on the Indian firm. Therefore, the firm

Table 5.7 Invoicing of India's Exports and Imports (Percent)

Currency	*Exports*					*Imports*				
	2008–09	*2009–10*	*2010–11*	*2011–12*	*2012–13*	*2008–09*	*2009–10*	*2010–11*	*2011–12*	*2012–13*
GBP	2.77	2.81	2.47	2.31	2.31	0.89	0.66	0.71	0.50	0.42
USD	84.06	84.75	86.41	87.01	88.41	86.06	83.91	85.38	88.67	86.06
JPY	0.48	0.35	0.22	0.26	0.15	2.3	1.98	1.73	1.41	1.47
EUR	10.85	10.13	8.88	8.14	6.97	9.82	12.61	11.13	8.29	9.44
Other currencies	1.84	1.96	2.02	2.28	2.16	0.93	0.84	1.05	1.13	2.61

Source: Reserve Bank of India.

may settle the payment immediately and avail the cash discount, if any. Conversely, if the firm has receivables in a weak currency (e.g., Hungary's currency, the forint), it may lead the receivables. As weak currencies are expected to depreciate, any delay in the settlement of receivables will reduce the amount of receivables in terms of home currency. If a firm has certain debt obligations in weak currencies, it may lag the payment. Conversely, if the debt obligation is in a strong currency, the firm may advance the payment. Neglecting to do so may lead to an increase in the debt burden with the appreciation of the strong currency, which is a likely event.

Borrowing or lending in hard currencies carries lower rates of interest as compared to weak currencies. Further, the firm may avail the cash discount if it leads the payables. On the advance settlement of receivables, the firm may offer a cash discount to its customers. Therefore, any gain arising on leading or lagging needs to be considered along with the interest rate differential and other costs associated with leading or lagging.

To compare a forward hedge with the leading of payables, the following example may be considered. Suppose an Indian company has 90-day payables of USD 1 million. The current spot rate is USD/INR 39 and the 90-day forward rate is USD/INR 39.5. The U.S. trader allows a cash discount of 2 percent for immediate payment. The borrowing rate in India is 8 percent p.a. If the firm opts for forward cover, the outflows would be INR 39.5 million. The company may lead the payables by borrowing an amount of INR 39 million at an interest rate of 8 percent p.a. This involves a repayment of INR 39.78 million after three months. The company would get a 2 percent cash discount on immediate payment of the dues. In other words, the company could save INR 0.78 million on immediate payment, which equals the interest on the borrowing. Thus, there is an overall saving of INR 0.50 million over the forward hedge.

The ***management of operating exposure*** *involves decision making with respect to plant location, sourcing of raw material, production, technology, pricing of products, product development, and selection of markets.*

Operating Exposure A firm that has eliminated transaction exposure may still remain exposed to operating exposure. Operating exposure refers to the sensitivity of future operating cash flows to unexpected changes in the foreign exchange rate. In other words, operating exposure is a measure of the extent to which the value of operating cash flows generated by the firm's real assets would change as a result of unanticipated changes in the foreign exchange rate. As the prices and quantities of inputs and outputs of a firm are influenced by foreign exchange rates, any change in exchange rates is likely to affect the firm's revenues and costs, and thus its operating profits.

Changes in exchange rates would influence the cost of raw materials, wages, and costs of other components, and thereby cause changes in the relative competitive strength of firms. The location of plants, sourcing of raw material, production, and marketing, which includes sales and distribution, are the most important variables in this regard. Changes in exchange rates may also bring about changes in the revenues of a firm through changes in the demand for the product(s) of the firm. In other words, the location of the market(s) also influences the operating exposure of the firm.

Consider the following comprehensive example. A firm in India has a wholly owned subsidiary in Canada which manufactures and sells 50cc motorbikes in Canada. It imports some of its components from the U.S. and the rest is locally sourced. It expects to sell 2,000 motorbikes in Canada for the next quarter of the year at a selling price of CAD 2,630. The cost of components for each motorbike is expected to be CAD 1,000 (imported: CAD 550 which is priced in USD 496.84 at the exchange rate of USD/CAD 1.107). The current exchange rate is CAD/INR 55.19. The other variable costs are CAD 300 per motorbike. The summarized projected cash flows for the next quarter are as follows:

Sales (2,000 units at CAD 2,630 per unit)	CAD 52,60,000
Cost of components	20,00,000
Fixed overhead costs	7,00,000
Other variable costs	6,00,000
Depreciation allowance	1,00,000
Net profit before tax	CAD 18,60,000
Tax @ 30%	5,58,000
Profit after tax	13,02,000
Depreciation (add back)	1,00,000
Operating cash flows in CAD	14,02,000
Operating cash flows in INR	773,76,380

It may be noted that any change in the exchange rates between Indian rupee and Canadian dollar, and the U.S. dollar and Canadian dollar will affect the operating cash flowsof the firm.

Operating exposure cannot be eliminated by using financial hedges. Operating exposure arises from the effects of changes in the exchange rate on the basic operations of a firm and, therefore, any attempt to reduce or avoid operating exposure should involve suitable and effective decisions with regard to the various operations of a firm. The firm should study the effects of changes in exchange rates on the cash flow-generating capacity of each of its real assets and initiate measures to effectively counteract the negative effects and also capitalize on the opportunities. Further, it may view the operating exposure as its long-term concern, and accordingly take steps to manage it. With a long-term perspective, the firm may restructure its entire operations (by, say, shifting its sources of inputs, changing the input mix, or by shifting the plant locations) keeping in view the exchange rate-sensitive costs and revenues.

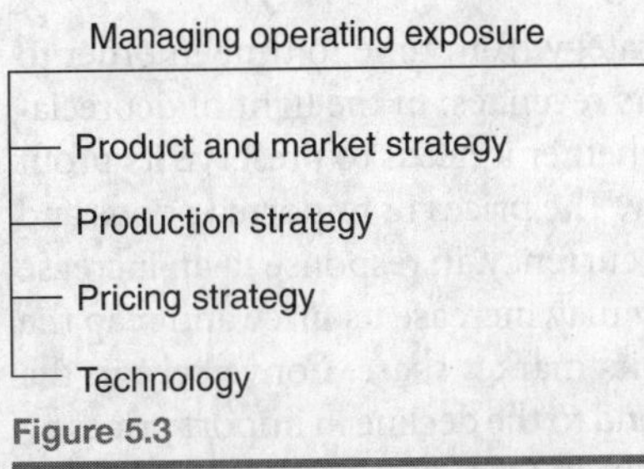

Figure 5.3

Managing Operating Exposure

Thus, the management of operating exposure involves decision making with respect to plant location, sourcing of raw material, production, technology, pricing of products, product development, and selection of markets in order to avoid fluctuations in the future operating cash flows of the firm due to changes in the foreign exchange rates. Figure 5.3 outlines some ways of managing operating exposure.

Product and Market Strategy In the face of exchange rate fluctuations, a firm may change its product strategy, which covers decisions with regard to new product development, product mix, and product line. When the domestic currency appreciates, the firm will have a decline in its international market share and its profits will dwindle. In order to keep up its international market share and profitability, the firm may introduce new products and adopt new market strategies. The new products and new market strategies may fetch new customers and new sales, which will offset the loss of existing customers that resulted from the appreciation of domestic currency against the foreign currency. In other words, a firm may reorient its product line and product mix in order to serve a new target group of customers when the home currency value is appreciating. Conversely, when the home currency value is depreciating, besides consolidating its existing markets, it can penetrate into new markets by expanding its product line or product mix. As depreciation of domestic currency is equivalent to appreciation of foreign currency, a firm can shift its marketing efforts toward countries with overvalued currencies.

Production Strategy A firm can also manage its operating exposure by making appropriate decisions with regard to production facilities, which include sourcing of inputs, plant location, and using alternative plants. It may shift the source of its raw materials and other components to a country whose currency is stable or least affected by global macroeconomic changes. It may also outsource the supply of components to a country whose currency is linked to the currency of a country that is a big export destination for its products. Firms should, however, have flexibility in making substitutions among various sources of inputs.

Another way for a firm to manage its operating exposure is to locate its plant in a country whose currency is stable. Firms, particularly MNCs, may enjoy greater freedom to allocate production among plants located in different countries in line with changing foreign exchange rates so that the cost of production will be the least. Shifting production facilities across countries may also hedge firms against exposure to country-specific political risks. While making a decision to shift production facilities offshore in order to cope with exchange rate fluctuations, firms may have to consider other factors like proximity to suppliers, productivity, and coordination. In other words, they have to consider cross-border variations in input factors including labour costs, productivity, tariffs, and legal and social infrastructure in making plant location decisions. Geographically diversified firms can effectively insulate themselves from operating exposure to individual currencies.

Pricing Strategy A firm may review its pricing strategy from time to time in order to deal with the effects of exchange rate fluctuations on its revenues. In the light of depreciation of its home currency, a firm may have to decide whether it needs to preserve its profit margin or market share by changing its pricing strategy. The prices of imported goods and services may go up following depreciation of the home currency. In response to an increase in import prices, a firm selling within its home country may increase its price and reap the benefits, or may keep its price unchanged to increase its market share. Conversely, in the wake of appreciation of domestic currency, it may respond to the decline in import prices by reducing its domestic price so as to maintain its market share. Of course, any price reduction may lead to a decline in profit margins. The firm may also need to consider factors like the elasticity of demand and economies of scale before implementing any change in its domestic pricing.

A firm selling overseas can gain a competitive advantage when its home currency depreciates. This competitive advantage can be used to either penetrate into new markets or skim the cream of the markets. Of course, it all depends on the elasticity of demand for the product and other factors like economies of scale, the cost structure, and the competitive environment. Conversely, in the wake of appreciation of the home currency, a firm selling overseas may keep its prices in terms of the domestic currency constant and maintain its profit margin. In doing so, it may find its sales volume and market share declining. Alternatively, if the firm's decision is to reduce the price in domestic currency terms, the market share of the firm remains unaffected, but its profit margin declines.

It is evident from our discussion that when the home currency depreciates, firms that manufacture products for export may have to decide whether they should (a) hold the price denominated in the foreign currency constant and try to sell the same or higher quantity, or (b) hold their domestic-currency-denominated price constant and try to increase the sales volume. They need to work out the cash flows and profit margins of the two options and arrive at a decision by considering the price elasticity of demand and other factors. The following example will illustrate how such decisions are made. Assume that a firm in India is exporting its product to the United States at USD 2, equivalent to INR 120. When the exchange rate between INR and USD changes from USD/INR 60 to USD/INR 62, the firm may maintain the product price at INR 120 and sell the product in the United States at USD 1.935. This may result in an increase in the market share of the Indian firm in the US market. As depreciation makes the Indian rupee cheaper to foreigners, the firm can also charge a higher Indian rupee price without altering the price denominated in the foreign currency. Thus the firm may increase the Indian rupee price to INR 124 and maintain the product price in U.S. dollar terms at USD 2. If the prices of competitors from other countries and within the United States remain at their previous level, the Indian firm can sell all it wishes without altering the U.S. dollar price and thereby increase its profit margins in domestic currency terms. Now, suppose that the INR appreciates against the USD. The product cost goes up in U.S. dollar terms in such a scenario. If the Indian firm is faced wih competition from the local manufacturers whose USD costs did not rise, it will not be able to raise the U.S. dollar price of its product without risking a reduction in sales. In other words, the Indian firm cannot let the exchange rate pass through the U.S. dollar price. *Exchange rate pass-through* refers to the extent to which exchange rate changes are absorbed in the price of the product. With full pass-through, the changes in exchange rate will not have an impact on the traders' profit margins.

A firm cannot change its prices whenever there is a change in foreign exchange rates. If it keeps adjusting prices in response to changes in exchange rates, the price of the product becomes unstable, ultimately leading to customer dissatisfaction. So, every firm should have a long-term pricing strategy to avoid frequent changes in its pricing, while at the same time responding to exchange rate changes.

Technology Technological factors also play an important role in operating exposure management. The technology used by a firm should be flexible and capable of adjusting to changes in the sourcing of inputs, composition of inputs, production methods, and levels of production. In order to respond to exchange rate fluctuations, a firm may make efforts to reduce the domestic currency cost of its products. Efforts may be aimed at increasing the productivity of the various factors of production. This may entail changing the technology through modernization or upgrades.

Unlike other types of foreign exchange exposure, operating exposure is a complex phenomenon that cannot be measured or effectively controlled and managed. As exchange rate fluctuations affect all facets of a firm, despite its best efforts, there remains at least some element of operating exposure that cannot be hedged or eliminated. This is why operating exposure is also called the *residual foreign exchange exposure.*

Though exchange rate fluctuations affect the revenues and cost structure of firms that are directly involved in international trade, firms that are not involved in international trade may also be affected by exchange rate fluctuations. For example, a firm which is faced with a decline in its exports following appreciation of its domestic currency may concentrate on the domestic market and become a strong competitor to purely domestic firms. As a result, the competitive environment in the domestic market changes, affecting input costs as well as output prices. Even macroeconomic changes that are brought about by exchange rate fluctuations may influence the costs and revenues of a firm that may not be involved in exporting or importing.

Translation or Accounting Exposure

An MNC may have subsidiaries located in different countries, with each subsidiary preparing its financial statements in its local currency. These financial statements need to be consolidated with that of the parent unit in order to present the overall performance of the company. It is also necessary to bring the financial statements of subsidiaries that are denominated in different currencies into consolidated statements denominated in a common currency for uniformity and inter-unit comparison. The consolidation process begins with the translation of the various items of financial statements into the home currency of the parent unit. The translation of assets, liabilities, expenses, revenues, gains, losses, and cash flows is done according to the principles or standards prescribed by the accounting authority in the country of the parent unit. Nevertheless, the restatement of financial accounts will result in gains or losses with changes in foreign exchange rates since the previous reporting period. For example, consider a U.S.-based MNC that has a subsidiary company in India. At the beginning of the financial year, the subsidiary unit has fixed assets worth INR 1,000 million and current assets worth INR 500 million. By the end of the year, the value of fixed assets increased to INR 1,300 million and current assets to INR 750 million. When translating these assets into U.S. dollars at the current spot rate, which was USD/INR 43 at the beginning of the year and USD/INR 47 at the end of the year, the asset values are as presented in Table 5.8.

It is evident from the table that the MNC has recorded a translation gain of USD 8.73 million on the assets of its Indian subsidiary. It may register a translation loss on certain other balance sheet items of the subsidiary unit. Such changes in the consolidated financial statements of an MNC due to exchange rate movements over time are referred to as *translation exposure.*

The extent of translation gains or losses depends on the volume of business conducted by each subsidiary unit, the location (country) of the subsidiary unit, and the accounting method(s) used by the subsidiary unit as well as the parent unit. In other words, the

Table 5.8 Translating Assets into the Current Spot Rate

	At the beginning of the year (USD million)	*At the end of the year (USD million)*	*Gains/losses (USD million)*
Fixed assets	23.26	27.66	4.40
Current assets	11.63	15.96	4.33

magnitude of translation exposure is determined by the extent of changes in the exchange rates between the home currency of the parent unit and the local currencies in which the accounts are prepared by the subsidiaries. If a subsidiary unit is in a country with an unstable currency, translation of the financial items of that subsidiary may result in a large magnitude of exposure. Further, the methods of translation adopted by the parent unit and the extent of involvement of a subsidiary in the operations of the parent unit may also influence the magnitude of translation exposure. As different accounting standards and rules of different countries treat the various items of financial statements differently, the MNCs may experience gains and losses. Note that the question of translation exposure does not arise if any of the subsidiaries prepares the accounts in the home currency of the parent unit. Thus, translation exposure arises only upon transforming the financial items of subsidiary units measured and stated in different currencies into a common currency—the currency of the parent unit.

Though there are some controversies with regard to the utility and relevance of translation exposure (as mere restatement of financial items does not involve cash flows), the consolidation of financial statements does help management and others concerned in making right and meaningful decisions.

MNCs adopt several methods to translate the financial statements of their subsidiaries. These are shown in Figure 5.4. Different methods attempt to treat the various items of financial statements differently. A company adopts a particular method depending on its policy as well as the dictates of the accounting authority of the country in which the parent company is located.

The principal methods used to translate financial statements are the current/non-current method, the monetary/non-monetary method, the temporal method, and the current rate method.

Current/non-Current Method According to the current/non-current method, the values of all the current assets and liabilities of a foreign subsidiary are translated into the home currency of the parent company at the current spot exchange rate. However, the non-current assets and liabilities are translated at the historical exchange rates, that is, the spot rate at the time a particular asset item was acquired or a liability item incurred. Thus, the translation of the values of the assets according to the current/non-current method may result in a gain or loss, depending upon whether the foreign subsidiary has positive working capital or negative working capital in the local currency, or whether the exchange rate has appreciated or depreciated over the period of reference.

As far as income statements are concerned, all items except those associated with non-current assets/liabilities are translated at the average exchange rate during the reference period. The items of income statement associated with non-current assets or liabilities (e.g., depreciation, amortization, write-off, etc.) are translated at the rate at which the corresponding items in the balance sheet are translated.

Monetary/non-Monetary Method A firm's assets and liabilities may be categorized into monetary and non-monetary items. The monetary assets and liabilities are those that involve contractual cash flows. Further, *monetary assets* represent a claim to receive, whereas

Currency translation methods
- Currency/non-current
- Monetary/non-monetary
- Temporal
- Current rate

Figure 5.4

Currency Translation Methods

monetary liabilities involve an obligation to pay. The firm knows in advance when such claims will get realized and when the obligations have to be discharged. That is, the size and timing of cash flows are known in advance in the case of monetary items of the balance sheet. Items like long-term debt, trade creditors, sundry debtors, deposits, overdrafts, and cash are examples of monetary items of the balance sheet. Non-monetary balance sheet items are also known as real assets and liabilities. They include physical assets, human assets, inventory, etc. Thus, *non-monetary assets and liabilities* are those that do not have contractual payoffs.

Under the monetary/non-monetary method, monetary items are translated at the current spot exchange rate, and non-monetary items are translated at historical exchange rates, as done in the case of non-current items. The average exchange rate during the reference period is applied to translate the items of the income statement, except those items related to non-monetary assets, for which the exchange rate as applicable to their respective non-monetary assets is considered.

Temporal Method Under the two methods we just discussed, the choice of the exchange rate (current spot rate or historical spot rate) depends upon the type or nature of the asset/liability. But in the temporal method, the choice of the exchange rate is based on whether the balance sheet item is originally evaluated at historical cost or market value. If an item is originally stated at historical cost, its translation is carried out at the historical spot rate of exchange. Alternatively, if the item is originally stated at its market value, the translation is carried out at the current spot rate of exchange.

Income statement items are translated at an average exchange rate during the period of reference. But the cost of goods sold, depreciation expense, and amortization charges are translated at the historical rate of exchange, irrespective of whether the corresponding balance sheet items are translated at the historical rate or at the current spot rate of exchange.

Current Rate Method Under the current rate method, all the items of the balance sheet and income statement are translated at the current spot rate of exchange. Since all the items are translated at the current spot rate, the proportion or ratio of different items of accounts will remain the same. However, MNCs will experience a translation gain or loss resulting from the appreciation or depreciation of the home currency of the parent unit. If the value of the foreign-currency denominated assets is more than that of the foreign-currency denominated liabilities, depreciation (appreciation) of the home currency results in a loss (gain).

The following example explains how different currency translation methods would yield translation gains or losses. Assume a U.S.-based subsidiary of an Indian MNC has prepared its balance sheet in the U.S. dollar. The exchange rate between the INR and the U.S. dollar was USD/INR 45 at the beginning of the year, and it changed to USD/INR 42 by the end of the year. The effect of this change in exchange rate on the balance sheet items of an MNC under the four translation methods is depicted in Table 5.9. As can be observed, different methods have yielded different figures as translation gains or losses.

As can also be observed from the table, the Indian MNC gets a maximum translation gain of INR 1,350 million under the monetary/non-monetary method. The current rate method yields a maximum translation loss of INR 2,400 million as a result of the appreciation of the Indian rupee against the U.S. dollar.

Table 5.9 Effect of Appreciation of the Local Currency Under Different Translation Methods

	USD million	*Values in INR at historical rate (USD/INR 45)*	*Values after the appreciation of INR to USD/INR 42 (INR million)*			
			Monetary/ non-monetary method	*Temporal method*	*Current/ non-current method*	*Current rate method*
Assets						
Cash and marketable securities	100	4,500	4,200	4,200	4,200	4,200
Receivables	200	9,000	8,400	8,400	8,400	8,400
Inventory (at market rate)	150	6,750	6,750	6,300	6,300	6,300
Prepaid expenses	50	2,250	2,250	2,250	2,100	2,100
Total current assets	500	22,500	21,600	21,150	21,000	21,000
Net fixed assets	1,000	45,000	45,000	45,000	45,000	42,000
Goodwill	50	2,250	2,250	2,250	2,250	2,100
Total assets	1,550	69,750	68,850	68,400	68,250	65,100
Liabilities						
Payables	250	11,250	10,500	10,500	10,500	10,500
Other current liabilities	150	6,750	6,300	6,300	6,300	6,300
Total current liabilities	400	18,000	16,800	16,800	16,800	16,800
Long-term debt	350	15,750	14,700	14,700	15,750	14,700
Net worth	800	36,000	37,350	36,900	35,700	33,600
Total liabilities and equity	1,550	69,750	68,850	68,400	68,250	65,100
Translation gain (loss)	—	—	1,350	900	(300)	(2,400)

In fine, exchange rates change over time due to several factors. The changes in exchange rates ultimately affect the operational results of firms. No firm or individual can forecast exchange rates with accuracy. So, the firm can at least measure its exposure to exchange rate changes, and manage the exposure by adopting suitable exposure management techniques.

Summary

1. Foreign exchange rates are susceptible to several factors and, therefore, never remain constant. Changes in foreign exchange rates have a significant influence on the economies in the world, more so in these days of globalization of trade and investment.
2. Business firms, especially those engaged in international trade and investment, are exposed to foreign exchange fluctuations. Foreign exchange exposure and foreign exchange risk are conceptually different. Foreign exchange exposure is defined as the sensitivity of changes in the real domestic currency value of assets, liabilities, or operating incomes to unanticipated changes in exchange rates. Foreign exchange risk, on the other hand, is measured by the variance of the domestic currency value of assets, liabilities, or operating incomes that is attributable to unanticipated changes in foreign exchange rates.
3. Foreign exchange exposure is broadly divided into economic exposure and translation exposure.
4. Economic exposure refers to potential changes in all future cash flows of a firm resulting from unanticipated changes in exchange rates. There are two types of economic exposures: transaction exposure and operating exposure.
5. Transaction exposure refers to potential changes in the value of contractual cash flows that arise due to unexpected changes in the foreign exchange rate. Transaction exposure can be managed by hedging techniques or by operational techniques. The principal techniques include currency forwards, currency futures, currency options, currency swaps, currency of invoicing, exposure netting, and leading and lagging.
6. Operating exposure refers to sensitivity of future operating cash flows to unexpected changes in the foreign exchange rate. The management of operating exposure involves decision making with respect to production, product, pricing, etc.
7. Translation exposure arises when the items of financial statements prepared in foreign currencies are restated in the home currency of the MNC. The principal currency translation methods are current/non-current method, monetary/non-monetary method, temporal method, and current rate method.

Questions and Problems

1. Distinguish between foreign exchange exposure and foreign exchange risk.
2. Why do firms need to manage foreign exchange exposure?
3. What is economic exposure? How can firms manage their economic exposure?
4. What is transaction exposure? How is it different from translation exposure and from operating exposure?
5. Explain the need for cross hedging.
6. What initiatives should a firm's management take to cope with operating exposure?
7. Explain the methods by which translation exposure can be measured.
8. Explain the significance of real exchange rate.
9. Explain the implications of PPP for operating exposure.
10. What are the advantages of hedging foreign exchange exposure by a lead/lag strategy?
11. Explain the process of exposure netting.
12. What is hedging by invoice currency?
13. How do product and production strategies help a firm hedge its operating exposure?
14. What are the limitations of pricing as operational hedging?
15. An Indian firm has imported machinery from an MNC in New York for USD 2 million. The firm is permitted to pay the amount six months from now. The interest rate is 10 percent per annum in India and 8 percent per annum in the United States. The current spot rate is USD/INR 61. The six-month forward rate is USD/INR 62. How would the firm hedge its foreign currency exposure?
16. A U.S.-based MNC has purchased goods worth JPY 700 million from a Japanese firm, payable in three months. The current exchange rate is USD/JPY 117 and the three-month forward rate is USD/JPY 120. The interest rate is 8 percent per annum in the United States and 4 percent in Japan. The MNC wants to use a money market hedge to hedge this yen account payable. Explain the process of money market hedging in this case.

17. A firm based in the United Kingdom has a three-month account payable of INR 200 million. The current exchange rate is GBP/INR 92, and the three-month forward rate is GBP/INR 93. The firm can buy the three-month option on INR with an exercise rate of GBP/INR 92.75 for the premium of 0.005 pence per INR. The interest rate is 6 percent per annum in the United Kingdom and 10 percent per annum in India. Calculate the cash flows under different methods of hedging.

Multiple-choice Questions

1. Foreign exchange exposure is a measure of ________.
   (a) sensitivity (b) risk
   (c) variance (d) none of these
2. The positive value of beta is known as ________.
   (a) long exposure (b) short exposure
   (c) no exposure (d) none of these
3. If the beta value is zero, the relevant asset is ________ currency risk.
   (a) not exposed to (b) exposed to
   (c) unaffected by
4. Foreign exchange exposure exists only if the change in the exchange rate is ________.
   (a) unpredictable (b) predictable
   (c) not as expected (d) none of these
5. Foreign exchange risk depends on ________.
   (a) exposure
   (b) exposure and variability of unanticipated changes
   (c) unanticipated changes
   (d) none of these
6. Transaction exposure is a part of ________.
   (a) operating exposure (b) economic exposure
   (c) translation exposure (d) none of these
7. Translation exposure is also known as ________.
   (a) accounting exposure (b) economic exposure
   (c) transaction exposure (d) none of these
8. Purely domestic firm may also have ________.
   (a) economic exposure (b) translation exposure
   (c) accounting exposure (d) none of these
9. Option is an example of ________.
   (a) hedging technique (b) operational technique
   (c) netting (d) none of these
10. The difference between forward rate and future spot rate may be considered as ________.
    (a) cost of hedging (b) return
    (c) spread (d) none of these
11. Most of India's international trade is invoiced in________.
    (a) Australian dollar (b) American dollar
    (c) Canadian dollar (d) none of these
12. Lead the receivables denominated in ________.
    (a) weak currencies (b) hard currencies
    (c) U.S. dollar (d) none of these
13. Operating exposure can be eliminated by ________.
    (a) financial options and futures
    (b) financial hedges
    (c) production and marketing strategies
    (d) none of these
14. Under monetary/non-monetary method, the monetary items are translated at ________.
    (a) historical spot rate (b) current spot rate
    (c) future spot rate (d) none of these
15. Under the current rate method all ________ are translated at current spot rate.
    (a) current assets
    (b) income statement items
    (c) balance sheet items and income statement items
    (d) none of these

Case Study

Table 5.10 presents the exchange rates of the Indian rupee in relation to some widely used hard currencies in the world.

Table 5.10 Year-on-year Exchange Rates of the Indian Rupee in Relation to Hard Currencies (Jan–Dec)

Date	*USD/INR*		*JPY/INR*		*CHF/INR*		*EUR/INR*		*GBP/INR*	
1994	0.03%		11.93%		13.13%		NA		5.48%	
(Jan–Dec)	31.37	31.38	28.08	31.43	21.12	23.90			46.37	48.91
1995	11.95%		8.56%		27.75%		NA		70.74%	
(Jan–Dec)	31.37	35.12	31.46	34.16	23.94	30.44			49.05	54.32
1996	7.90%		–9.77%		–75.05%		NA		7 7.04%	
(Jan–Dec)	35.18	35.85	34.04	30.92	30.49	25.90			54.56	60.59
1997	9.57%		–2.28%		7.76%		NA		5.90%	
(Jan–Dec)	35.87	39.28	30.94	30.23	26.75	27.06			61.46	65.09
1998	8.39%		23.48%		74.77 %		NA		9.39%	
(Jan–Dec)	39.23	42.52	30.05	37.10	26.84	30.79			64.63	70.70
1999	2.42%		73.27%		–7 7.87%		–12.37%		0.70%	
(Jan–Dec)	42.48	43.51	37.53	42.51	30.98	27.30	50.09	43.89	70.20	70.27
2000	7.43%		–4.64%		3.57 %		–7.97%		–7.22%	
(Jan–Dec)	43.49	46.72	42.68	40.70	27.57	28.54	44.25	43.37	70.47	69.61
2001	3.39%		–9.93%		–0.45%		–2.97 %		0.42%	
(Jan–Dec)	46.66	48.24	40.79	36.74	28.97	28.84	43.94	42.66	69.65	69.94
2002	–0.60%		70.54%		79.02%		76.95%		9.68%	
(Jan–Dec)	48.28	47.99	36.62	40.48	29.08	34.61	43.01	50.3	70.14	76.93
2003	–5.70%		5.47%		5.70%		73.73%		4.87%	
(Jan–Dec)	48.02	45.57	40.42	42.64	34.75	36.73	50.38	57.30	77.37	81.13
2004	–4.32%		–0.04%		4.57%		3.4 7 %		2.86%	
(Jan–Dec)	45.61	43.64	42.55	42.53	36.81	38.50	57.43	59.39	81.68	84.02
Average of the last 3 yrs			–2.26%	1.38%	9.04%	9.56%	6.i	06%		
Average of the last 5 yrs			0.54%	2.47%	4.25%	3.26%	3.	53%		
Average of the last 10 yrs			3.25%	4.07%	5.83%	NA	5.	77%		

Source: Mecklai Financial Services Ltd. Reproduced with permission.

Notes: Positive numbers denote depreciation of the INR, and negative numbers denote appreciation of the INR; rates are based on the Indian market opening rates.

Questions

After carefully studying the given data, answer the following questions:

1. What could be the reasons for the appreciation of the **INR** against some currencies and the simultaneous depreciation against others?
2. Against which currency or currencies is the **INR** more volatile? Why?
3. Suppose you are an exporter and are given a choice of invoice currency. Which currency would you prefer for invoicing? Why?
4. As an importer, which currencies would you like to include in the currency cocktails for invoicing? Why?

Further Reading

1. Michael Adler and Bernard Daumas, "Exposure to Currency Risk: Definition and Measurement," Financial Management (Summer 1984): 41–50.
2. Christine R. Hekman, "Measuring Foreign Exchange Exposure: A Practical Theory and its Application," Financial Analysts Journal (Sept/Oct 1983): 59–65.
3. James E. Hodder, "Exposure to Exchange Rate Movements," Journal of International Economics (November 1982): 375–386.
4. Alan C. Shapiro, "Defining Exchange Risk," The Journal of Business (January 1977): 37–39.
5. C. Kent Garner and Alan C. Shapiro, "A Practical Method of Assessing Foreign Exchange Risk," Midland Corporate Finance Journal (Fall 1984): 6–17.
6. Alan C. Shapiro, "Exchange Rate Changes, Inflation, and the Value of the Multinational Corporation," Journal of Finance (May 1975): 485–502.
7. Maurice D. Levi, International Finance (New York: McGraw–Hill Inc., 1996).

CHAPTER 6

Currency Forwards and Futures

CHAPTER OBJECTIVES

After studying this chapter, you should be able to:

1. Discuss the principal characteristics of currency forward contracts and currency futures contracts.
2. Distinguish between currency forwards and currency futures in terms of the cash flows that they generate.
3. Understand the relationship between currency futures prices and spot rates.
4. Discuss the pricing of currency futures.
5. Explain the concepts of hedge ratio and cross hedging.

Introduction

Individuals and firms including government organizations are exposed to risk in situations where their holdings and commitments can change in value due to unexpected changes in business conditions. The more open (in terms of trade and investments) a country, the more exposure to risks. There are different types of risks that individuals and firms are exposed to in their day-to-day operations. One such risk is the *currency risk,* also known as the *foreign exchange risk.* It refers to the risk faced due to changes in exchange rates. A firm has foreign currency exposure when its income flows and/or capital flows are affected by unanticipated changes in foreign exchange rates. For example, an Indian firm has supplied ready-made garments to the U.S., and the payment would be made in three months in U.S. dollars. The firm is faced with the risk of the U.S. dollar depreciating against INR when the payment is made. If the U.S. dollar depreciates, the firm would receive a lesser amount of sale proceeds when the U.S. dollars are exchanged for Indian rupees. Thus, what originally was a profitable transaction might turn out to be a loss due to changes in the exchange rate. The foreign exchange risk is more acute for firms that deal in multiple currencies.

The following are the common income flows and capital flows of a firm that are affected by exchange rate changes. It can also be said that they are the sources of foreign exchange risk.

- Payments for imports in foreign currency
- Export proceeds to be received in foreign currency

- Cash inflows and cash outflows as royalties, dividends, interest, etc., in foreign currency.
- Outstanding expenses in foreign currency
- Accrued incomes in foreign currency
- Outstanding liabilities in foreign currency
- Debt servicing or loan repayments in foreign currency
- Offshore investments and assets that are valued in foreign currency
- Remittances on contractual obligations to be made or to be received in foreign currency
- Accounts receivables and payables in foreign currency

As exchange rate changes may be in either direction, they don't cause adverse effects to a firm always. It all depends on the nature of transactions and capital flows. The following are the effects of a falling exchange rate (depreciation) of home currency against foreign currency. The contrary may occur if domestic currency appreciates against foreign currency.

- Costs of imports may go up.
- Domestically produced products would become more competitive against imported counterparts.
- Capital expenditure in terms of domestic currency may go up if foreign machinery, equipment and technology are involved.
- Cost of servicing the debt denominated in foreign currency may go up in terms of domestic currency.
- Exports may become more competitive in terms of cost.
- Inward investments may increase.
- Outward investments may decrease.
- Accounts payables in foreign currency may become more expensive in terms of domestic currency.
- Accounts receivables in foreign currency may increase the cash flows in terms of domestic currency.
- All inward foreign remittances including dividends and interest may become rosy in terms of domestic currency.
- All outward foreign remittances may become burdensome in terms of domestic currency.
- The value of foreign investment(s) in terms of domestic currency may increase.
- The value of foreign currency liabilities in terms of domestic currency may increase.
- All outstanding expenses to be paid in foreign currency may become more burdensome in terms of domestic currency.
- All accrued incomes in foreign currency may enhance the profitability of the firm in terms of domestic currency.

Thus, changes in the exchange rate can have a significant impact on several business decisions. Foreign exchange risk is mainly faced by exporters and importers when their foreign currency receipts or payments might either become worthless or cost more in terms of the domestic currency between the time the goods are sold or purchased and the time when the payment is received or made. Apart from exporters and importers, others who face the risk of exchange rate fluctuations include international investors, international borrowers and lenders, banks, financial institutions, individuals who maintain foreign currency deposit accounts, and travellers.

Hedging is a method of reducing the risk of loss caused by changes in the exchange rate. The hedger tries to protect himself against loss arising from exchange rate changes by transferring the risk to some other(s). It consists of purchase or sale of an equal amount of the same currency, almost simultaneously in a different market with the hope that a change in the exchange rate in one market will be offset by an opposite change in the other market. There are various hedging devices available to business firms to insulate themselves from currency risk. Originating in agricultural marketing, forwards, futures, and options have been around for quite some time as important risk-management devices. We shall discuss currency forwards and futures in this chapter. Options are discussed in Chapter 7.

Currency Forward Contracts

A forward contract is a contract that protects the holder from adverse changes in the exchange rate by locking-in an agreed exchange rate. More formally stated, a **currency forward contract** is a legally enforceable agreement in which two parties agree to buy and sell a specified amount of one currency against another currency at a fixed time in the future and at a specified exchange rate. By entering a forward contract, the holder can obtain a right and, of course, an obligation as well, to buy or sell a specified quantity of a currency at a specified exchange rate and at a specified date in future, thereby transfer the risk to the counterparty. A long position implies that the holder agrees to buy the underlying currency, while a short position implies that the holder agrees to sell the underlying currency.

*A **currency forward contract** is a legally enforceable agreement in which two parties agree to buy and sell a specified amount of one currency against another currency, at a fixed time in the future and at a specified exchange rate.*

Let us take an example to understand a typical forward contract. Consider an Indian company that has just purchased equipment from a firm in the United States for USD 5 million, payable in six months. The spot rate is USD/INR 61.75. In the next six months it is expected that the INR might depreciate against the USD. To guard against such an exchange rate risk, the Indian firm has entered a six-month forward contract with a local bank, at an exchange rate of USD/INR 62.00. As per the terms of the forward contract, the Indian company will pay the bank INR 310 million for USD 5 million to be paid by the bank to the company. The company will use this USD 5 million to pay for its import of equipment. The Indian company has thus offset a short position in U.S. dollars by a long position in the forward contract, thus eliminating the foreign exchange risk. The net cost of the equipment when covered with a forward contract is INR 310 million, no matter what happens to the spot rate of USD/INR in six months. But the forward contract may result in a gain or loss to the parties, depending on the spot rate of the underlying currency at the time the forward contract matures. Such gain or loss, of course, is not related to the current spot rate.

Apart from hedgers, speculators and arbitrageurs do participate in the forward market. Speculators take positions in the forward market in order to profit from exchange rate fluctuations. Arbitrageurs seek to earn risk-free profit through covered interest rate differential. Active forward markets exist only for a few currencies like USD, EUR, CAD, JPY, GBP, and CHF. Forward markets do not exist for some currencies, particularly those of underdeveloped economies.

The salient features of forward contracts are:

- They are private deals between two parties to exchange future cash flows.
- There is no cash outflow at the initiation of the forward contract.
- They are not standardized contracts, and forward markets are self-regulated.
- They have flexibility with respect to contract sizes and maturity periods or expiration dates.
- The terms and conditions of forwards are all negotiable. Currency forward contracts can be customized to suit the needs of each party.
- As the size and maturity of a forward contract exactly matches that of the underlying cash flow exposure, a forward contract provides a perfect hedge [i.e. the gain (loss) on the underlying position is exactly offset by the loss (gain) on the forward position].
- They are mostly interbank transactions, traded over-the-counter by telephone or telex.
- Though there is no secondary market as such for forward contracts, banks that are involved in forward trading do make two-way forward markets in all major currencies at all times.
- Sometimes forward contracts are transactions between banks and large corporate clients.
- As contracts are private deals, there is no insistence on margins. However, when the deal is between a bank and a corporate client, the bank may insist on margins when the bank's relationship with the customer is not that good. In other words, banks exercise discretion when insisting on whether a margin account is to be established.
- As currency forward contracts are private deals, there is a strong possibility that any one of the parties may back out or fail to honour the terms of the contract. Thus, forward contracts are prone to default risk.

Hedging with a currency forward contract is simple and easy. A trader may visit a bank and enter into a forward contract to buy or sell a foreign currency. By entering a forward contract, the participant knows how much he will have to pay or receive at the end of the forward contract.

Valuation of Forward Contract Forward contracts like other derivative securities have a value. As there are no cash flows at the initiation of a forward contract, the value of a forward contract is zero at the time of the contract. As the time progresses, the forward contract may get a value depending on the spot rate. To understand the concept more clearly, consider the following example. A firm based in India has a surplus amount of INR 10 million which can be invested elsewhere for three months. It has two options: (i) to deposit with a local bank and earn an annual rate of return of 6 percent; and (ii) to convert INR 10 million to U.S. dollars and place a deposit with an American bank and earn an annual rate of return of 4 percent. Since the firm would expect to receive the deposit back in U.S. dollars on maturity of the 3-month deposit, it would cover the foreign exchange exposure by selling U.S. dollars forward. According to interest rate parity, any advantage an investor might get from the higher rate of interest would be offset exactly by a weaker exchange rate when the foreign currency denominated proceedings are converted to home currency. If this were not to be true, the arbitrage would be set in motion. This would push the forward rate in such a way that there would be no profit that can be made by borrowing U.S. dollars, and convert them for investing in Indian currency while at the same time covering the foreign exchange risk by entering into a forward contract. Thus, as per the interest rate parity, the forward rate is a function of the relative interest rates of two currencies, which can be expressed as:

$$\text{Forward Rate} = \text{Spot Rate} \times \frac{1+\left[r_d \times \left(\frac{d}{365}\right)\right]}{1+\left[r_f \times \left(\frac{d}{365}\right)\right]}$$

where

r_d = Domestic currency risk-free interest rate (also known as 'term' currency interest rate)

r_f = Foreign currency risk-free interest rate (also known as 'base' currency interest rate)

d = Number of days until the settlement date

The above formula would give a 'fair value'. If the prevailing forward rate exceeds the fair value, one can sell the base currency forward and buy the same currency at the spot rate, and thereby make an arbitrage profit. If the prevailing forward rate is less than the fair value, the arbitrageur can make a profit by buying the base currency forward and selling it spot.

Forward rates are usually quoted in swap points which represent the difference between the forward rate and the spot rate. The following formula may be used to arrive directly at the swap points:

$$\text{Forward Swap Points} = \text{Spot Rate} \times \left\{ \frac{1+\left[r_d \times \left(\frac{d}{365}\right)\right]}{1+\left[r_f \times \left(\frac{d}{365}\right)\right]} - 1 \right\}$$

or

$$\text{Forward Swap Points} = \text{Spot Rate} \times \frac{\left[r_d \times \left(\frac{d}{365}\right)\right] - \left[r_f \times \left(\frac{d}{365}\right)\right]}{1+\left[r_f \times \left(\frac{d}{365}\right)\right]}$$

For example, the spot rate of USD/INR is 61.735. The interest rate in India is 8 percent per annum and the same in the U.S. is 7.50 percent. The one-year-forward swap points may be calculated as per the above formula, which comes to 2871 points. Thus, the magnitude of swap points is determined by the interest rate differential. The market participants quote swap points as two-way rates in the same way as spot rates. If the domestic interest rate is

Example 6.1

The current spot exchange rate between INR and USD is USD/INR 47. The risk-free interest rates in India and in the United States are 7 percent and 5 percent, respectively. What is the 90-day forward rate? (Use continuously compounding.)

Solution

The 90-day forward rate will be:

$$F_{90} = 47e^{(0.07-0.05)\times(90/365)}$$
$$= \text{INR } 47.2324$$

Example 6.2

A U.S.-based firm has USD 1 million to invest for 182 days. It has two options. One option is to deposit with a local bank at 7 percent rate of interest per annum. The second option is to convert U.S. dollars to British pounds and invest in a London-based British bank at an annual interest rate of 6 percent. The spot exchange rate is GBP/USD 1.6181. What is the 182-day forward rate? Suppose the prevailing forward rate is GBP/USD 1.6545. Is there any arbitrage opportunity? If so, how it can be exploited?

Solution

If the firm invests in the U.S., its wealth would increase to USD 1.035 million after six months.

Alternatively, if it decides to invest in a British bank, then its wealth position would be as follows.

On conversion to British pounds, the USD 1 million would become GBP 0.6180 million. When invested at 6 percent per annum, the amount would become GBP 0.6366 million after six months.

Forward rate = Future value in quote currency/Future value in base currency

1.035/0.6366 = 1.6258

The forward rate can also be computed by using the formula.

$$F_{(GBP/USD)} = 1.6181 \times [(1 + 0.035)/(1 + 0.30)]$$

$$= 1.626 \text{ (same as above)}$$

Since the prevailing forward rate (GBP/USD 1.6545) is more than the fair value of forward contract, the firm can undertake the following arbitrage transactions:

- Borrows USD 1 million at 7 percent interest rate per annum for six months. The loan becomes USD 1.035 million after six months.
- Sells USD 1 million at GBP/USD 1.6181 to get GBP 0.6181 million.
- Deposits GBP 0.6181 for six months at an annual interest rate of 6 percent. This would become GBP 0.6366 million after six months.
- Sells GBP 0.6366 million forward at GBP/USD 1.6545 to get USD 1.0533 million.

Thus, the arbitrageur can make a profit of USD 0.0183 million.

higher (lower) than the foreign interest rate, the forward points will be added (subtracted) to the spot rate to arrive at the implied outright forward.

Basis The spot rate and the forward rate converge upon maturity of a forward contract; otherwise, there will be arbitrage opportunities. But before maturity, they may differ, and the difference is known as the *basis*. Thus, the basis is expressed as:

$$\text{Basis} \equiv S_t - F_{t,T}$$

where

S_t = Spot rate of a currency at time t
T = Maturity period of a forward contract
F_t = Forward rate of a contract initiated at time t

The basis may be positive or negative, depending on the movement of spot rate as well as forward rate. The basis becomes positive when the forward rate falls or the spot rate rises, or both happen at the same time. If the forward rate is falling, a person with a short position in the forward contract will gain. Similarly, a person with a long position in a foreign exchange will benefit from the rising of the spot rate. In other words, if the basis is positive and increasing, or negative and narrowing, a person with a short position in a forward contract will benefit. Conversely, a person with a long position in a forward contract will profit if the basis is negative and widening, or positive and narrowing.

According to interest rate parity,

$$F_{t,T} = E(S_{t,T}) = S_t[(1+R_d)^T / (1+R_f)^T$$

where

$F_{t,T}$ = Forward rate of a contract with a maturity peroid, T
$E(S_{t,T})$ = Expected spot rate upon maturity of a forward contract
R_d = Domestic interest rate
R_f = Foreign currency interest rate

Thus, basis is proportional to the ratio

$$\left(\frac{1+R_d}{1+R_f}\right) - 1 \cong R_d - R_f$$

Thus, *basis* simply refers to the interest rate differential. The basis risk is the uncertainty about the basis, as interest rate differential does not remain constant. Prior to expiration of a forward contract, any change in the nominal interest rate(s) in one or both countries of the currencies involved would change the forward rate through interest rate parity. This brings about a change in the relationship between the forward rate and the spot rate, which would become the source of basis risk.

Currency Futures Contracts

A **currency futures contract** is a standardized agreement to sell or buy a set of amount of a currency for another specified currency at a fixed rate and date. A futures contract is an agreement between two parties: the party that agrees to sell a particular currency (a *short position*) and the party that agrees to buy the currency (a *long position*) at a negotiated exchange rate. The profit or loss on a futures contract depends on the daily movements of its price. Currency futures are always *exchange-traded contracts*. In other words, currency futures contracts are initiated and traded through an organized exchange. The basic function of the futures exchange is to transfer risk from the hedger to someone who is willing to bear the risk for profit. Organized exchanges provide customers protection and grievance procedures, besides other benefits. Every aspect of a futures contract is standardized except its price. In the final agreement between the two parties, everything (the currency, quantity of currency, exchange rate, and the date and method of delivery) is specified. Although forwards and futures serve the same purpose, they are different operationally.

*A **currency futures contract** is a standardized agreement to sell or buy a specified amount of a currency for another specified currency at a fixed rate and date. The basic function of the futures exchange is to transfer risk from the hedger to someone who is willing to bear the risk for profit.*

The implications of a futures contract are briefly explained with the following example. Suppose a U.S. firm has a commitment to pay GBP 10 million to a British firm in December 2015. So, the U.S. firm purchases the required number of December futures contracts at a price of GBP/USD 1.6183. It is the futures contract and not the GBP that is bought and sold. By purchasing the futures contract, the U.S. firm can be sure that its obligation will be USD 16.183 million, no matter what happens to the spot rate of GBP/USD during the period of the futures contract. If the actual spot exchange rate on the date of the maturity of the futures contract, 20 December 2015, is equal to the futures price, then there is no gain or loss on the futures contract, aside from the transaction cost. If the GBP appreciates and the spot exchange rate is GBP/USD 1.6300 on 20 December 2015, then the futures contract requires the U.S. firm to buy GBP 10 million for USD 16.183 million at the futures price of 1.6183. This same purchase in the spot market would cost USD 16.30 million, resulting in a USD 0.117 million gain for the firm over the market rate of exchange. On the contrary, if the spot rate on 20 December falls to GBP/USD 1.600, the U.S. firm still has to pay USD 16.183 million for GBP 10 million, according to the terms of the futures contract. In other words, the purchase of GBP 10 million in the spot market on 20 December would cost only USD 16.00 million. Thus, the opportunity cost for the U.S. firm on the long futures contract would be USD 0.0183 per each GBP. Theoretically, the exchange rates in the spot market and futures market tend to move parallel to one another. When a futures contract expires, the exchange rates merge into one rate.

Futures Payoffs

A payoff is the likely profit or loss that would accrue to the holder of a futures contract with a change in the spot rate of the underlying currency. Futures contracts have linear payoffs. In other words, the profit or loss for the buyer and the seller of a futures contract are unlimited. A market participant who buys a futures contract has a potentially unlimited upside as well as a potentially unlimited downside. For example, an Indian investor has purchased a 3-month currency futures contract when the spot rate is USD/INR 61.7345. When the value of the U.S. dollar moves up (i.e. INR depreciates), the investor starts making profit, and when the U.S. dollar moves down (i.e. INR appreciates), he starts making losses (Fig. 6.1).

The payoff for a market participant who sells a futures contract has a potentially unlimited upside as well as a potentially unlimited downside. Taking an example, a market participant has sold a 3-month futures contract when the spot rate is USD/INR 61.7345. He starts making a profit when the value of the U.S. dollar moves down (i.e. INR appreciates); and when the U.S. dollar appreciates (i.e. INR depreciates), he starts making a loss (Fig. 6.2).

Consider the following example to understand how the market participants can control their payoffs. On 10 March 2015, spot rate of USD/INR: 61.3450; June futures: 61.7345; September futures: 62.0000. It implies that the Indian rupee is set to depreciate against the USD. On the same day, a market participant sells September futures at 62.0000 by holding

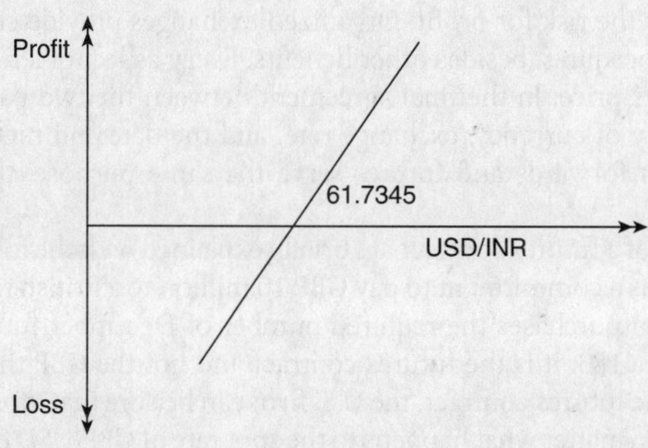

Figure 6.1

Payoff for Buyer of Currency Futures

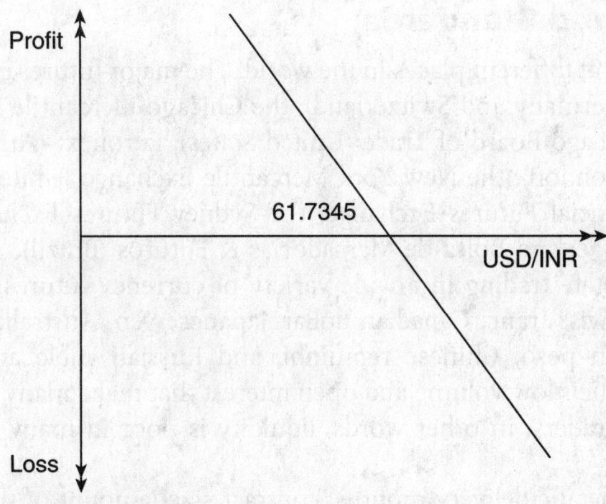

Figure 6.2

Payoff for Seller of Currency Futures

a view that the market is wrong. On 5 September 2015, the spot rate is 61.8546. On realization that he is wrong in his initial expectation, he tries to avoid a loss. Therefore, the market participant closes his futures position by buying September futures at the prevailing price of 61.9000. His quick action not only avoids the loss but yields a small profit of INR 0.1000 per USD. Of course, he would have made a loss had the INR depreciated so fast increasing the price of September futures further.

Consider another example. A firm in India has certain accounts payables, say USD 1 million maturing on 9 September 2015. The spot rate on 10 March 2015 is USD/INR 61.7892. In terms of INR, the firm's commitment is INR 61.7892 million. The firm purchases the September futures at USD/INR 62.2345. By 9 September 2015, the INR has depreciated to 62.5000. The firm closes its futures contract by selling the September futures at 62.5000, thereby realizeing a profit of INR 0.2655 million on its futures contract. By entering a futures contract, the firm could save INR 0.4453 million.

In the above examples, the standard specifications of futures trading (e.g. size of the contract) and transaction costs are ignored to make matters simple.

Long Hedge and Short Hedge

The market participants may use the futures contracts to reduce the risk of adverse exchange rate changes by taking a position in futures, which is the opposite either to a position that they already have in the spot market to a future financial obligation that they have, or they are going to have. A position in futures may be a long position (long hedge) or a short position (short hedge). For example, a firm in the U.S. has imported some goods from Japan on a trade credit payable in 91 days. So, the firm has a currency risk which it wants to hedge. The firm hedges the yen payables by buying JPY December futures. Since the firm has a commitment to deliver a certain amount of foreign currency, it has entered a futures contract. Thus, it is a long hedge, which implies the firm's obligation to take delivery of the currency underlying the futures contract. Conversely, the short hedging involves selling short in the futures market against a long position in the underlying currency in the cash market. For example, a firm in India has accounts receivables in the U.S. dollars realizable in October. It fears changes in the exchange rate and, therefore, decides to hedge its long cash position by selling USD/INR futures with delivery in October.

Futures Exchanges and Standards

Futures exchanges are located at different places in the world. The major futures exchanges in the world are the Eurex (Germany and Switzerland), the Chicago Mercantile Exchange (CME, United States), the Chicago Board of Trade (United States), Euronext (Amsterdam, Brussels, Lisbon, Paris, and London), the New York Mercantile Exchange (United States), the Tokyo International Financial Futures Exchange, the Sydney Futures Exchange, the New Zealand Futures Exchange, and Bolsa de Mercadorias & Futuros (Brazil). Although these futures exchanges facilitate trading in a wide variety of currency futures, the U.S. dollar, euro, British pound, Swiss franc, Canadian dollar, Japanese yen, Australian dollar, New Zealand dollar, Mexican peso, Chinese renminbi, and Russian ruble are largely traded currency futures. It is their low volume and open interest that make many currency futures unsuitable for most traders. In other words, liquidity is poor in many currency futures.

Futures contracts have specific delivery months, contract size (amount of the underlying foreign currency for futures purchase or sale) and maturity date. Each futures exchange has specified its own standards for currency futures trading. Let us take a look at the CME's specifications against the U.S. dollar (Table 6.1). At CME, currency futures are quoted in American terms (i.e. U.S. dollars per unit of foreign currency). The product of the contract size and the current price is the value of a futures contract. For example, suppose the GBP futures traded at CME are worth GBP 62,500. At the price of USD 1.9250, the value of a contract would be USD 120,312.50. The *contract size* is the amount of the underlying currency that has to be delivered under one contract. *Tick* represents the minimum price fluctuation for a particular contract. The minimum tick of the GBP futures contract is 0.0001, and the value of that tick is USD 6.25. In the example, the price moved from 1.9250 to 1.9621, or by 371 ticks. The value of the ticks is 371 × USD 6.25, or USD 2,318.75.

Currency futures trade on a quarterly cycle, with the primary contracts being March, June, September, and December. Besides, a current month contract is also traded. For some currencies, the CME also offers January, April, July, and October as expiration dates. The month during which a contract expires is called the spot month. At CME, the futures mature on the Monday before the third Wednesday of the spot month. The delivery takes place the third Wednesday of the spot month or, if that is not a business day, the next business day. Trading in a contract ends two business days prior to the delivery date.

Table 6.1 CME Specifications Against the U.S. Dollar

Currency	*Contract size*	*Tick value*	*Tick increment*
Australian dollar	AD 100,000	USD 10	.0001
British pound	GBP 100,000	USD 6.25	.0001
Canadian dollar	CD 100,000	USD 10	.0001
Euro FX	Euro 125,000	USD 12.5	.0001
E-mini euro	Euro 62,500	USD 6.25	.0001
Japanese yen	JPY 12,500,000	USD 12.5	.000001
Swiss franc	CHF 125,000	USD 12.5	.0001
Mexican peso	Mex. peso 500,000	USD 12.5	.000025

At CME, open outcry trading is conducted from 7:20 a.m. until 2:00 p.m. Chicago time. But on CME's Globex system, trades are conducted from 5:00 p.m. non-stop until 4:00 p.m. the following day. In other words, currency futures are traded virtually 24 hours a day during the trading week. Therefore, traders can participate any time of the day or night during the trading week to take advantage of the opportunities available. Many factors, such as interest rates, inflation, political stability, and government policies impact exchange rates and thereby create practically continuous trading opportunities.

Futures prices depend on a continuous flow of information. The kind of information and the way market participants absorb it constantly influence the exchange rates. This process is known as *price discovery.* Futures also have a variety of trading time frames: short, medium, or long term.

Margins

In order to cover default risks, futures exchanges prescribe the margins to be kept by both parties in a contract. They require every participant to deposit some amount of money for every contract to help ensure that parties have the financial capacity to meet their obligations should futures prices not go their way. Therefore, every trader who desires to buy or sell futures contracts must open an account with his broker and deposit some amount before a transaction is executed. The amount thus deposited is known as the **initial margin** or **initial performance bond**. The initial margin is a certain percentage of a futures contract value. The initial margin is set large enough to offset any losses arising from day-to-day fluctuations in the price of a futures contract. Unlike a forward contract, which settles only when the contract matures, a futures contract is settled every trading day at the settlement price. This process is known as *marking to market.* The *settlement price* is the price set by the futures exchange after the end of trading on that day. Generally, the settlement price reflects the average of closing prices for the day. Thus, a futures contract is marked to market at the close of each trading day, beginning from the day when the contract is initiated and ending on the day the contract is settled. At the end of each day, a party's gain (loss) is added to (subtracted from) the margin account. Whenever there is a fall in the futures price, the margin account of the party that has a long position will decrease and, conversely, the party that is short will have its margin account increased by the same amount. In other words, as futures trading is a zero-sum game, the seller of a futures contract will have his margin account decreased (increased) by the amount the buyer's margin account is increased (decreased). The concepts of marking to market and settlement price are discussed further in the next section.

The balance in the margin account of the investor should never be negative. In order to ensure that, another kind of margin, known as the **maintenance margin** or *maintenance performance bond,* is prescribed. The maintenance margin (typically about 75 percent of the initial margin) is the lowest amount an account can reach before needing to be replenished. Thus, the counterparty would receive a *margin call,* also known as *a performance bond call,* whenever the balance in its margin account falls below the maintenance margin. For example, assume the initial margin on a futures contract is INR 10,000, and the maintenance margin is INR 7,500. In the process of marking to market, the value of the margin account of the investor has dropped to INR 4,000. So, the investor has to deposit at least an additional INR 6,000 to bring the account back up to the initial margin level of INR 10,000. The additional funds deposited are known as the *variation margin.* Variation margin is insisted upon on a daily basis to keep pace with market movements. Whenever the balance in a margin account falls beneath the maintenance margin, a margin call is made to the concerned party. Then the party has to provide the variation margin immediately or within a very short period of time. Otherwise, the futures exchange may exercise its right to liquidate the position of such an investor in order to make up for any losses.

*The **initial margin** is a certain percentage of the value of a futures contract that is to be deposited by each trader at the time of the contract. The **maintenance margin** is the lowest amount an account can reach before needing to be replenished.*

The trading transactions on a futures exchange are done through the members of the exchange *clearing house*. Brokers who are not members of the clearing house need to do their business through clearing house members. In futures trading, investors maintain their margin accounts with their respective brokers. Much in the same way, the members of a clearing house are required to maintain margin accounts with the clearing house and add funds to their respective margin accounts whenever required. Such margins are known as *clearing margins*. Depending on price fluctuations, the balance in a margin account varies when the futures contracts are marked to market on a daily basis. However, the clearing margins are computed on either a gross or a net basis for a member. If it is computed on a gross basis, the total of all long positions of a member is added to the total of all his short positions. If it is a net basis, the long positions and short positions of a clearing member will be netted. For example, suppose a clearing member has two clients, one with a long position in 100 contracts and another with a short position in 150 contracts. If it uses a gross basis, the clearing margin would be computed on the basis of 250 contracts. If it uses a net basis, the clearing margin would be calculated on the basis of 50 contracts. Net margining is widely used.

The minimum levels for initial and maintenance margins are fixed by futures exchanges, keeping in view the variability of the exchange rate of a currency. So, the margin levels vary from currency to currency and from exchange to exchange. CME uses a computerized risk-management program called Standard Portfolio Analysis of Risk (SPAN) to decide on margin requirements. Individual brokers may fix their own margins to be deposited by their clients, but those margins may not be lower than those specified by the respective exchanges. Depending on the type of traders, whether hedgers or speculators, margin requirements may vary. Day trades may attract lower margin requirements as they are assumed to be at a lower risk of default. When a contract is liquidated, the market participant will be refunded the initial margin plus or minus any gains or losses that occur over the span of the futures contract.

Securities like treasury bills are also accepted for initial margins, but maintenance margins are generally in cash only. The counterparty that fails to deposit additional margin money will have its long/short position liquidated.

***Leverage** refers to having control over a large portion of a contract, with a small amount of investment. It is the inverse of the percentage margin requirement*

It is in this context the concept of leverage comes into effect. **Leverage** refers to having control over a large portion of a contract, with a small amount of investment. Futures contracts are considered to be highly leveraged positions because the initial margins are relatively small. A market participant puts up a mere fraction (10 to 15 percent in most situations) as margin, yet he has full control over the contract. In fact, the money one puts up is not actually to purchase a part of the contract; it is to act as a performance bond.

Leverage is the inverse of the percentage margin requirement. For example, if the notional contract value is USD 100,000 and the required margin is USD 2,000, then a market participant can trade with 50 times leverage or "50:1." The lower the initial margin, the higher is the leverage. Leverage is a double-edged sword as it can produce greater profits or greater losses. It is the possibility of excessive gains that sparks interest in futures contracts. That possibility, however, comes with greater risk.

Marking to Market

The concept of *marking to market* can be better explained with an example. Assume that a firm having a USD 20,000 account balance with the clearing house of CME purchases ten March Canadian dollar futures contracts at a rate of CAD/USD 0.9966, the contract size being CAD 100,000. The total U.S. dollar value of the futures contract is USD 0.9966 × 100,000 × 10, or USD 996,600. The current initial margin is, say, USD 1,800 for one contract. So, the total initial margin required is USD 18,000. Since the account balance is USD 20,000, the initial margin is met with the cash in the account. On the second day of trading, the settlement price declines to USD 0.9916. In other words, the value of one contract has dropped by 0.0050 or 50 ticks, resulting in a loss of USD 500 per contract and USD 5,000 on ten contracts. The value of the futures contracts now is USD 991,600. The total value of the 10 contracts has declined from USD 996,600 to USD 991,600 or a loss in value of USD 5,000. This amount is deducted from the account as profits and losses are continually marked to market throughout each trading day. Now, the total account balance of the firm is USD 20,000–USD 5,000, or USD 15,000. Suppose the maintenance margin on one CAD futures contract is USD 1,200. The total maintenance margin on the ten-contract position is USD 12,000. As the account balance is above the maintenance margin, no action is required on this account.

Further, suppose that on the next day the settlement price is USD 0.9986. The value of the contract increases by 0.0070 or 70 ticks per contract, resulting in a gain of USD 700 per contract or USD 7,000 for the ten contract positions. The value of the contract is now USD 0.9986 × 100,000 × 10, or USD 998,600. The value of the account also increases to USD 15,000 + USD 7,000, or USD 22,000. As the account balance is above the maintenance margin of USD 12,000, no action is required on this account.

On the fourth day, there is a drop in the settlement price to USD 0.9816 from USD 0.9986. The value of the futures contract decreases by USD 0.017 or 170 ticks, resulting in a loss of USD 1,700 per contract and USD 17,000 on the ten contract positions. Now, the value of all ten contract positions is USD 0.9816 × 100,000 × 10, or USD 981,600. The value of the margin account decreases to USD 22,000 – USD 17,000, or USD 5,000. This is lower than the maintenance margin of USD 12,000. Therefore, the firm is required to bring in at least USD 15,000 to meet the initial margin requirement to continue holding the ten futures contracts.

Thus, by marking to market at the end of each trading day, the margin account of each party to the currency futures contract is adjusted to reflect the counterparty's gain or loss. When the margin money according to the marking to market is received from the counterparty with a long position (i.e. the party that has purchased the futures), the clearing house adds to the margin account of the counterparty with a short position (i.e. the party that has sold the futures) by the same amount. In other words, when the long position's account is adjusted up, the short position's account is adjusted down by the same amount and vice versa. Thus, between the buyer and the seller, currency futures trading is a zero-sum game. That is, the sum of the long and short daily settlement is zero.

The **settle price**, also known as the **settlement price**, is a price representative of futures contract prices at the close of daily trading on the exchange. When the futures are marked to market at the end of each trading day, the previous trading day's futures contract is settled, and a new one-day futures contract is formed at the settlement price. Thus the counterparties realize their profits or losses on a day-to-day basis rather than all at once upon the maturity of the contract. The daily settlement as per the marked-to-market procedure reduces the default risk of the futures contract.

*The **settle price**, also known as the **settlement price**, is a price representative of futures contract prices at the close of daily trading on the exchange.*

In the process of marking to market, the daily settlement of the futures contract amounts to entering a forward contract each day and settling the same before entering another one. The previous day's forward contract is replaced by a new one-day forward contract with the delivery price equal to the settlement price of the previous day's contract.

Settlement

Currency futures transactions can be closed out either through delivery of the underlying foreign currency on full settlement or by an *offsetting trade*. A market participant can offset his position by taking an equal but opposite position. That is, a market participant can exit from his futures position before the contract expires by taking an equal but opposite futures position (selling if already bought or buying if already sold). For example, consider a U.S.

trader who goes long on September JPY futures on 10 July. He can close out his position on, say, 16 August by shorting one September JPY futures contract. In this case, the trader's gain or loss depends on the changes in the futures price between 10 July and 16 August. Thus, market participants do not have to wait until the expiration date to complete their trade. Further, market participants need not necessarily take delivery of the currency in the contract upon its maturity. For example, if a trader's long position in U.S. dollar futures is profitable, the trader need not literally take delivery of the U.S. dollar at the time the contract matures. Rather, the trader may sell the futures contract of the same amount in the U.S. dollar just prior to the maturity of the long position. The long position and the short position get cancelled on the books of the futures exchange, and the trader receives the profit in cash. For example, assume that a U.S. firm expects on 18 March that it will have to purchase some input components worth CHF 125,000 from a firm in Switzerland in June. In order to hedge currency risk, the U.S. firm purchases a June CHF futures contract at USD 0.9065. In April, the U.S. firm decides not to buy the input components from the Swiss firm. This means the firm does not require the CHF futures contract. So it sells the futures contract priced at USD 0.8985 on CHF with June settlement. On the date of settlement in June, the firm has offsetting positions in futures contracts. But, as the futures price on the long position is higher than the price on the short position, the U.S. firm incurs a loss. When the transactions are settled by an offsetting trade, a participant's profit or loss comes from the gains or losses that have been posted to their account each day after trading.

When contracts are settled by delivery, the price to be paid is normally the most recent settlement price, which is equal to the closing spot rate of the underlying currency. This will ensure that the futures price converges to the spot rate as the maturity date of the futures contract is approached. In some futures exchanges, the settlement price is the average of the high and low spot rates of the underlying foreign exchange during the day. As the accounts of the parties in the futures contracts are adjusted every day, a participant's profit or loss comes from the gains or losses that have been posted to their account each day after trading. Thus, settlement by delivery is the same as the offsetting trade as far as realization of profit or loss is concerned.

Market participants can also roll over their respective positions from one contract expiration into the next. If a trader holds a long position in an expiration month, he can simultaneously sell that expiration month futures contract and buy the next expiration month futures contract for an agreed-upon price differential. One can also roll a short position just as easily. By transferring or rolling a position forward this way, a market participant is able to hold a futures contract for a longer period of time. For example, if a market participant holds a June futures contract, he can sell the June futures before expiration and buy a December futures contract, and thereby expand the time frame of the trade. Most futures contracts are closed out with an offsetting trade, and only a small proportion of futures contracts are settled by delivery. In other words, offsetting trade is a common phenomenon in the settlement of currency futures contracts.

Limits

Currency futures exchanges may also prescribe daily *price limits* for futures contracts in order to prevent sudden and violent changes in prices. The price limits (upper limit as well as lower limit) for the day are generally fixed on the basis of the previous day's closing price as adjusted to current market trends. The price of futures is allowed to increase or decrease within the price limits set for the day. Only in exceptional circumstances, the price limits are removed. Thus, the price limits act as speed breakers to high volatility in futures prices, thereby prevent speculative trading in futures. But one major problem with the price limits is that the counterparties cannot liquidate their futures positions at will.

The futures exchange may also establish *position limits,* that is, the maximum number of contracts that a party can hold. Position limits are also stated in total value of a currency. The position limits prevent a single seller or buyer from influencing futures prices by selling or buying futures in large quantities. Thus, position limits on par with price limits prevent speculative trading in futures.

The futures exchange may step in and change both price limits and position limits whenever it finds that price limits have become an artificial barrier to normal trading or that the bona fide parties are affected by position limits. Thus, futures exchanges ensure that there are no sudden and violent fluctuations in the futures prices and, at the same time, there is adequate liquidity in the market.

Traders and Trading Operations

This section covers the various types of market participants, spreads, and trading platforms in futures trading.

Types of Traders

As mentioned in Chapter 1, there are different kinds of market participants in currency futures trading. They are broadly classified as hedgers, speculators, and arbitrageurs.

Hedgers Hedgers are those who have exposure to currency risk and are interested in reducing such risk. Hedgers mainly include exporters, importers, borrowers, lenders, and investors. Hedgers go short (long) in futures if they are long (short) in the underlying currency. Futures generate cash flows to offset any decline in the value of the underlying cash flows. For example, consider a trader in India who imports goods from a firm in the United States for USD 1 million, payable in three months. The trader is thus faced with a significant foreign exchange risk. To hedge such a risk, the trader may enter into a futures contract to buy USD 1 million in three months at an exchange rate of USD/INR 61.5679. This strategy enables the trader to insure himself against adverse exchange rate movements. On the other hand, suppose an exporter expects foreign currency receipts in 60 days. To offset adverse exchange rate changes, the exporter may also enter a futures contract. Thus, by holding futures contracts, exporters and importers need not worry about any change in the spot rate of the foreign exchange on the date of settlement of their cash flow transactions. In other words, a futures contract provides a definite exchange rate certainty for both parties of a contract. However, hedgers can reduce or eliminate such currency risks only at the cost of some or all of their potential profits. In general, hedgers take a short position in order to protect against future depreciation of a currency and take a long position to protect against future appreciation of a currency. The aim of the short holders of the contract is to secure as high a value of a currency as possible, and the aim of the holders of the long position is to pay as low a value of a currency as possible.

__Hedgers__ are those who have exposure to currency risk and are interested in reducing such risk. Hedgers mainly include exporters, importers, borrowers, lenders, and investors.

In reality, hedging does not improve profitability or cash flows of the hedger. Nor does it eliminate risk. It merely *transfers* risk to others so that the hedger will not be exposed to unexpected shocks. It may also enable a hedger to lock in a certain profit margin.

Speculators Hedgers always try to transfer or pass on the price risk to someone. The "someone" who is ready to take on such risk by anticipating windfall gains is the **speculator**. The main function of speculators is that they cause transactions in futures markets by holding positions that are opposite to those held by hedgers.

A __speculator__ is one who is ready to take on large risks by anticipating windfall gains. Speculators trade in futures contracts to profit from changes in exchange rates, and in the process they face currency risk, which may ultimately result in a loss.

Based on their analysis of the foreign exchange market, speculators take a definite view of future events in the market and deliberately adopt an uncovered position to benefit from exchange rate changes. They bet on price movements and are not interested in taking physical delivery of the underlying currency. Speculators thus get into futures contracts to profit from changes in exchange rates, and in the process, they face currency risk which may ultimately result in a loss.

Speculators may be day traders who try to cash in on price movements during a single day, or they may be position traders who maintain their futures positions for longer periods of time, for weeks or months. Speculators sell what they think is overpriced and buy what they think is underpriced. Depending on their judgement, speculators take short or long positions in futures, and carry them in order to make profits.

Speculators also get involved in spread trading. *Spread trading* refers to the act of buying one futures contract and selling another futures contract. Spreads are of two kinds—*intra-currency spreads* and *inter-currency spreads*. In the case of intra-currency spreads, speculators can buy and sell futures on the same currency for two different maturity dates. Inter-currency spreads involve the buying and selling of futures contracts with the same maturity date, but with two different underlying currencies.

***Arbitrageurs** are traders who make a risk-less profit by simultaneously entering into buy and sell transactions in two or more markets. By simultaneously entering into buy and sell transactions in different markets, arbitrageurs can make a profit without net investment and risk.*

Arbitrageurs *Arbitrage* is a process in which a trader makes a riskless profit by simultaneously entering into buy and sell transactions in two or more markets. By simultaneously entering into buy and sell transactions in different markets, arbitrageurs can make a profit without net investment and risk. An arbitrage opportunity is, therefore, a "no money down and no risk" opportunity.

Arbitrageurs play a very vital role when futures prices and spot rates are not in accord. Whenever a currency futures contract price gets out of line with the spot rate of the underlying foreign currency, arbitrageurs start buying or selling transactions, and thereby cause the foreign exchange rate and/or futures contract price to rise or fall. This will ultimately bring equilibrium between the futures contract price and the spot rate of the underlying foreign currency, leading to an end of arbitrage opportunities.

Arbitrageurs also keep futures prices in line with forward rates. For example, assume the forward rate for GBP/USD for June is USD 1.9569. At the same time, the GBP futures for delivery in June are priced at USD 1.9500. The arbitrageur would simultaneously buy the June GBP futures at USD 1.9500 and sell an equivalent GBP June forward at USD 1.9569. Thus, the arbitrageur would earn a profit of USD 431.25 on a futures contract size of 62,500. This amount becomes bigger with a greater number of futures contracts. However, this profit will evaporate once other traders start cashing in on the price differential. In other words, the futures price and forward rate will move in such a way that arbitrage opportunity eventually disappears.

Spreads

Market participants may assume short or long positions in order to exploit the opportunities arising on the depreciation or appreciation of a currency against another currency. Traders in futures contracts may also adopt *spread strategies,* which involve taking advantage of the exchange rate difference between two different futures contracts of the same pair of currencies. The spreads may be calendar spreads, inter-market spreads, and inter-exchange spreads. A *calendar spread* refers to simultaneous buying and selling of two futures contracts of the same type, having the same exchange rate but different maturity dates. In the case of *inter-market spread,* a market participant may go long in one market and short in another market with contracts of the same period. The *inter-exchange spread* may be any spread in which each position is created in different futures exchanges. Spread strategies are less risky than naked positions.

Trading Platforms and Participants

Every organized futures exchange provides the needed infrastructure and methods for trading futures. The infrastructure includes trading platforms through which trade is carried out.

Trading platforms are of two types: the physical trading floor and the electronic trading floor. Each of these platforms and methods of trading are briefly described here.

Physical Trading Futures exchanges provide physical floors for trading in futures contracts. Physical floors are also known as *trading pits.* A pit is a physical place earmarked for trading futures in a specific currency, and it has different sections corresponding to different contract expiration months. The trading on the floor takes place through the *open outcry method.* In open outcry, brokers flail and shout in a pit. The *buyer-brokers,* having decided how much they are willing to pay, shout their bids (price and quantity) to other brokers in the pit. The *seller-brokers* do the same with their orders. The quantity and price are indicated through hand signals and a vocal open outcry. The price of a futures contract is determined in the trading pit when the seller's quote and the buyer's quote match. Each action of the broker in a pit is recorded electronically. Though the whole process may look chaotic and confusing to an onlooker, the open outcry method is in fact an accurate and efficient trading system. It is an age-old method of trading in futures contracts but is still in vogue. Nowadays, it is facilitated by modern electronic gadgets like display boards that display price quotes, including quotes in other futures exchanges, and computers to record the transactions that take place through the open outcry method.

The trading floor of an exchange has two principal participants—floor brokers and floor traders. *Floor brokers* act as agents for the investing public and execute trades on their behalf. In other words, floor brokers execute orders for the accounts of clearing members and their customers. *Floor traders,* also known as *locals,* mostly trade for their own accounts, but can act as floor brokers as well. Different-coloured jackets are worn by floor brokers and floor traders who trade in the pits.

Runners are responsible for passing on the customer's order to the floor traders. They communicate all matters relating to market orders to the floor trader. They also bring the filled orders to the brokerage firm's desk for confirmation to the customers. Runners, therefore, are the link between the customers and the floor brokers in the trading pit.

The other professionals who are involved in futures trading are futures commission merchants, scalpers, day traders, and position traders. A *futures commission merchant* (FCM) provides direct services to the public to trade futures. Similar to a broker for stocks, the FCM holds and manages the customer's account, executes the customer's trades, and maintains all records required to do business with the customer, including keeping a record of all open positions in futures and the balance in the account. A *scalper* is a person who holds a position in futures trading for a very short period of time, attempting to make profit off the bid–ask spread. A *day trader* holds positions for a very short time (from minutes to hours) and makes many trades each day. The trades are entered and closed out within the same day. A *position trader* holds a position for the long term with an aim to make a profit from the move in the primary trend. Position trading is the opposite of day trading.

Electronic Trading Futures are also traded on the electronic trading platform. In this system, buy and sell orders are executed through computerized trading systems. On the electronic trading platform, customer orders are routed directly to the appropriate exchange trade-matching engine, where they are executed electronically. The trade-machine engine in electronic trading is like a trading pit in the open outcry method. The major advantage with electronic trading is speed and accuracy. Moreover, electronic trading is relatively cheaper. Despite such merits of electronic platforms, major futures exchanges in the world still retain their trading floors, integrating them with their electronic platforms. Some futures contracts are allowed to be traded on the floor and electronically side-by-side; some use electronic trading during after-hours (after floor hours), and some others are solely electronic.

Types of Orders

There are different types of buy or sell orders. The frequent types of orders are market orders, limit orders, stop-limit orders, stop-loss orders, and market-if-touched orders (MIT). *Market order* refers to an order to buy or sell a futures contract at the best current price. In other words, an investor may ask his broker to buy or sell a certain number of futures contracts at the best available price. In the case of *limit orders,* the investor placing an order specifies the buy or sell price. The investor may also indicate how long the limit order will be valid. A limit order can be outstanding for part of a day, a full day, several days, a week, or a month. The limit order can also be open-ended, or good until cancelled. When and if the futures price reaches the limit order price, the broker will execute the order. An order becomes a market order if a specified price limit is reached. Such orders are known as *MIT orders.* Some investors may ask their brokers to close out their positions if the futures price falls (rises) to or below (above) a specified level below (above) the current price. Such orders are known as *stop-loss orders,* as investors want to limit their losses. If stop orders are combined with limit orders, then they become *stop-limit orders.*

Clearing House

Every futures exchange has a clearing house that guarantees the performance of the parties to each futures contract. The clearing house has its own members, and all futures transactions are carved out through its members. The members of the clearing house may be different from exchange members. In every buying or selling of futures contracts, the clearing house of the exchange is necessarily involved as a party. When two parties, buyer and seller, agree to the price, quantity, expiration month, and the underlying asset, the clearing house then assumes the obligation to buy the seller's contract, and to sell it to the buyer. In other words, the buyer of a futures contract acquires a long position with the clearing house, while the seller acquires a short position with the clearing house. Thus, the clearing house becomes a buyer to every seller and a seller to every buyer of futures contracts, and thereby it assumes the responsibility of discharging the contract as per the terms and conditions. This gives the buyer and the seller a guarantee that their futures contract will be honored. The clearing house also allows each trader to close out his position independently of the other.

Public Quotes

Many newspapers and magazines carry currency futures quotations. The columns of futures quotations show the currency underlying the futures contract, the exchange it is traded on, the contract size, the prices (opening price, the highest price, the lowest price, and the settlement price), the change in settlement price, lifetime highs and lows, open interest, and the volume of trading. All these have obvious meanings except open interest, which gives the number of outstanding contracts at the end of the day. *Open interest* is a measure of how many futures contracts in a given currency exist at a particular time. The number of futures contracts can increase or decrease every day, depending on opening and closing transactions. However, if a trade involves a closing transaction by one participant and an opening transaction by the other, then the open interest will not change, as the number of contracts remains unchanged.

Forwards and Futures: A Comparison

Currency futures contracts and currency forward contracts serve the same purpose of hedging currency risk. Both are derivatives or contingent claims. The prices of both are influenced by expected future spot rates. Futures can be closed before the expiration of the contract. If they were to be closed before expiration, the market value of a futures contract is the settlement price on the day. However, there are certain basic differences between forward and futures contracts.

Broad Differences

Currency forwards are customized contracts, while currency futures are standardized contracts. Forwards are mostly interbank transactions, whereas futures contracts are traded on organized exchanges. To facilitate easy trading, exchanges specify certain standardized features in terms of contract size, transaction amount, maturity period, or expiration date. Being standardized contracts, currency futures provide better liquidity, fewer price fluctuations, and lower transactions costs.

Currency forward contracts, being non-standardized, provide the advantage of flexibility. For example, consider a firm that has a transaction exposure from a foreign exchange inflow of USD 12.622 million. It can match its exposure exactly with a forward contract. This may not be possible with a futures contract, because the size of futures contracts is standardized, and the amount of USD 12.622 million may not fit into the standardized amounts. Similarly, the timing of foreign currency cash flows may not exactly match with the standard expiration dates prescribed by the organized futures exchanges. However, the expiration date of a forward contract can be fixed to coincide with the date on which the foreign currency cash flows are expected. Thus, the forward contract can be a perfect hedge against currency risk, by providing amounts that exactly match with the size and timing of foreign currency cash flows. As futures contracts have standardized amounts of the underlying foreign currency and also specific delivery months with a specific day of the month, the amount or timing of foreign currency cash flows may not match with the standardized futures contracts. There may be a mismatch between the amount of the currency exposure and the contract size of the futures, and also between the maturity of the futures contract and the timing of cash flows of the underlying exposure. However, currency futures provide a perfect hedge when the amount of exposure is an even multiple of a standard futures contract and the timing of cash flows of the exposed currency matches with the delivery date of a standard futures contract.

Another difference between forwards and futures is that forward rates are generally quoted in European terms, whereas futures prices are quoted in American terms. Further, most forward contracts are settled by actual delivery, whereas a very small proportion of futures contracts are settled by delivery.

Like the currency forward contract markets, the currency futures exchanges also have market makers and bid-ask spreads. However, the gap between the bid price and the ask price is narrow in futures contracts as compared to that of forward contracts.

Cash Flows under Forwards and Futures

A trader who buys (sells) a currency forward contract agrees to buy (sell) the underlying foreign currency at a specified future time and at a specified price. When the contract is made, the purchaser (seller) of the forward contract pays (receives) nothing. At the time of maturity, the buyer of the forward contract (long position) receives the specified foreign currency, which is delivered by the seller of the forward contract (short position), while the seller receives the contract amount at the forward rate from the buyer.

The value of a forward contract changes between the time it is negotiated and the time it matures, because the value of the right to buy or sell changes as the spot rate of the underlying foreign exchange changes. When the contract is made, the forward has no value, and at the time of maturity also the forward contract has no value because the forward rate converges with the spot rate. In between these points in time, the value of the forward contract changes depending on the expected or anticipated spot rate of the underlying currency at the time of maturity of the forward contract. If the expectation is something different from the forward rate, then it creates arbitrage opportunities. If the forward rate is greater than the anticipated spot rate, arbitrageurs would sell forward and buy spot, and if the anticipated spot rate is greater than the forward rate, arbitrageurs would buy forward and sell spot. These transactions would thus produce arbitrage profit. However, such arbitrage opportunities are purely temporary and very short-term phenomena. Very soon the anticipated spot rate of the underlying foreign exchange would equal the forward rate, and the arbitrage opportunity would cease to exist. The same mechanism works with currency futures trading as well.

Forward contracts are settled on the date of the maturity of the contract, whereas futures positions are settled on a daily basis. That is, in the case of futures contracts, gains and losses from a day's trading arise on a daily basis, and they are debited or credited to a party's account each day. Thus, cash flows under a forward contract are different from cash flows under a corresponding futures contract.

To illustrate cash flows under a forward contract and a futures contract, the following example is given. A forward contract and a futures contract on the U.S. dollar are entered into on date D1 to buy U.S. dollars at an exchange rate of USD/INR 44 for settlement on date D4. The cash flows of a forward contract and of a futures contract at different spot rates, forward rates, and futures rates are shown in Tables 6.2 and 6.3.

It can be observed from Table 6.2 that there are no cash flows during the period D1 through D3. As the settlement price increases, the forward contract to buy USD at INR 44 becomes much more valuable. But the full value of the forward contract is realized only on the settlement date.

Along the lines of the forward contract, the value of futures contract changes with the settlement price (see Table 6.3). Though the marked-to-market procedure creates cash flows every day of the futures contract period, the sum of the cash flows from futures is the same as that in the forward contract. But there is a difference in the timing of the cash flows. In the case of futures, cash flows occur throughout the contract period, whereas in forwards cash flows occur only on the maturity date, as illustrated above. This causes a difference in the ultimate net gain or loss to be realized by the counterparty to a futures contract and by the counterparty to a corresponding forward contract. This difference arises because of certain operational differences that exist between the futures and the forwards. The changes in the spot rate of the underlying foreign exchange are reflected daily in the futures contract, while they are realized only at maturity of the forward contract. As the day-to-day changes in the futures price are settled daily through the margin account under the marked-to-market procedure, there will be an increase or a decrease in the margin account of the counterparty of a futures contract. Whenever there is an increase in the margin account, the counterparty can withdraw the amount over and above the initial margin, and whenever the margin account drops below the maintenance margin, the counterparty has to replenish it.

A margin call resulting from unfavourable changes in futures prices may force the trader to liquidate some of his or her assets or borrow to post the additional margin. Similarly, any withdrawal from the margin account when it is in excess of the initial margin may be

Table 6.2 Cash Flows of the Forward Contract

Date	*Forward rate (USD/INR)*	*Settlement price (USD/INR)*	*Cash flows from forward (INR)*
D1	44	42	0
D2	44	43	0
D3	44	45	0
D4	44	46	46 – 44 = 2

Table 6.3 Cash Flows of the Futures Contract

Date	*Futures price (USD/INR)*	*Settlement price (USD/INR)*	*Cash flows from futures (INR)*
D1	44	42	(–) 2
D2	42	43	01
D3	43	45	02
D4	45	46	01

reinvested at a prevailing interest rate. As a result of reinvestment or liquidation of existing assets, or as a result of borrowing at an interest rate, the gain or loss on a futures contract and a forward contract shall not be the same. Further, as interest rates are uncertain at the time of entering into contract, the holders of futures also face interest rate risk and reinvestment risk. The differences in transaction costs and default risk also distinguish the futures contract from the forward contract in terms of their cash flows. Thus, the treatment of margins and other factors make a sea of difference between the forwards and the futures.

The long position will benefit market participants if futures prices tend to rise when interest rates are high. This is because if a market participant receives cash flows when the interest rates are high, he would invest those cash flows at a high rate of interest. Conversely, the short position will benefit market participants if futures prices tend to fall when interest rates are low. Whenever the long position benefits, the futures price will exceed the forward rate, and whenever the market favours the short position, the futures price will be below the forward rate. However, forward rates and futures prices tend to be equal in the long run. Whatever profitable difference exists between the forward rate and the futures price at any time is wiped out through the arbitrage process.

Example 6.3

A U.S. company has made sales for which it will receive GBP 10 million in 90 days. The current spot rate is GBP/USD 1.6971. As the company will want to convert GBP 10 million into USD, it is exposed to the risk that GBP will fall below the current spot rate. To protect itself against a declining GBP, the company sells its expected GBP receipts by using futures contracts at a futures rate of GBP/USD 1.6820.

How many futures contracts will the company need to protect its receivables of GBP 10 million? Also calculate the profit and loss on the futures position if the spot rate of GBP/USD at maturity of the futures is 1.6800, 1.6810, 1.6850, or 1.6980. Ignore transaction costs.

Solution

The standard futures contract size is GBP 62,500. So the company has to sell 160 futures contracts to protect its receivables of GBP 10 million.

The profit and loss on the futures position are calculated in Table 6.4.

Table 6.4 Profit and Loss on the Futures

	Expected spot rate (GBP/USD)			
	1.6800	1.6810	1.6850	1.6980
Inflows (USD million)	16.820	16.820	16.820	16.820
Outflows (USD million)	16.800	16.810	16.850	16.980
Profit/loss (USD million)	0.020	0.010	(–)0.030	(–)0.160

Relationship between Spot Rates and Futures Prices

Futures prices reflect the present thinking of traders about future happenings. In other words, futures prices are projections made by traders on the basis of whatever information they have. If that prediction is taken to be valid by a lot of traders, it will affect how people react in the spot market. Thus, as the spot rate of the underlying currency changes, so will the value of its futures contract. If the spot rate of the underlying foreign exchange rises, there will be a greater demand for futures contracts that have locked-in the exchange rate of the currency. As the maturity date of the futures contract comes closer, the futures price and the spot rate tend to converge. That is, on the date of the maturity of the futures contract, the futures price either equals or becomes very close to the spot rate of the underlying foreign currency. Any significant difference between the futures price and the spot rate during the contract period may give rise to an arbitrage opportunity. For example, the spot rate of GBP/USD is quoted at 1.6183 on 20 November 2015, while the December 2015 GBP/USD futures contract is quoted at 1.6190. Thus, the basis (difference between the futures prices and the spot rate) is 3 pips (1.6190 – 1.6187 = 0.0003). This small value of the basis may not give rise to an arbitrage opportunity. The arbitrage opportunities, even if they were to exist, may not last for a long time. As arbitrageurs exploit the opportunity, the futures price and the spot rate would change, and ultimately they tend to be equal. Thus, at the time of the maturity of the futures contract, the difference between the spot rate and the futures price (i.e. basis) tends to become zero.

For example, assume that a firm in the United States has subscribed to British corporate bonds at a par value of GBP 1 million. These bonds will be redeemed at their par value in the month of June, and the amount will most likely have to be converted into USD when received. The current spot rate is GBP/USD 1.9650. This means that the GBP 1 million is currently worth USD 1.965 million. Between now and June, this value can go up or down as the GBP appreciates or depreciates. To avoid this uncertainty, the firm wants to hedge its foreign exchange exposure by using GBP futures. The three-month futures price is GBP/USD 1.9650. So the firm decides to sell GBP futures at GBP/USD 1.9650, expecting receipt of USD 1.9650 million. Suppose on the day of maturity of the futures contract in June, the spot exchange rate is GBP/USD 1.9500. This would mean that the value of GBP 1 million would be USD 1.9500 million. Thus, there is a loss of 0.0150 million in cash position. The firm can now close out its futures position at the new spot rate of GBP/USD 1.9500 by buying the required number of futures contracts. Having bought the futures contracts at GBP/USD 1.9500 that were earlier sold at GBP/USD 1.9650, there is a gain of USD 0.0150 on each GBP 1 million. Thus, the gain in the futures position exactly offsets the loss in the cash position.

As the maturity date of the futures contract comes closer, the futures contract price and the spot rate of the underlying currency tend to converge.

Taking another example, a firm in India has three months duration payables of USD 1 million. They fall due on 15 September. On 10 June, the spot rate is USD/INR 61.7523 and September futures price is USD/INR 62.00. Thus, the basis is 0.2477. Suppose on 15 September, the spot rate is 62.1200 and the futures price is 62.3677. There is a loss in cash position and a gain in futures position. But the loss in cash position is exactly offset by the gain in the futures position. Thus, there is no gain or loss to the firm on the whole. It could be possible because the basis (futures price–spot rate) remains constant. When there is a perfect correlation between changes in spot rate and changes in futures price, the basis would remain constant. Any change in the basis would give rise to a gain or a loss to the market participants.

The need for hedging techniques like futures arises only when the future spot rates of foreign exchange cannot be predicted with certainty. To put it differently, in a world of uncertainty, it is necessary to enter into hedging contracts like futures in order to safeguard against currency risk. While entering into a futures contract, the hedger should predict the future spot rate of a foreign exchange, and, based on such prediction, should negotiate and settle the futures price with the counterparty.

Traditionally, there are three theories that deal with the relationship between futures prices and the expected spot rates. They are the expectation hypothesis, normal backwardation, and normal contango.

The Expectation Hypothesis

The ***expectation hypothesis, normal backwardation,*** *and* ***normal contango*** *theories deal with the relationship between futures prices and expected spot rates.*

According to the **expectation hypothesis**, the futures price is the expected spot rate of the underlying foreign exchange on the maturity date of the futures contract. That is, the futures price is an unbiased estimate of the future spot rate. So the expected profit to either position of a futures contract would be zero. The expectation hypothesis, thus, is based on the assumption of risk neutrality. But in an uncertain world, market participants cannot be risk neutral and, therefore, the expectation hypothesis cannot be a valid proposition.

The Normal Backwardation Theory

John Maynard Keynes and John Hicks, economists of international repute, also felt that the expectation hypothesis fails to correctly explain futures prices. They propounded an alternate theory, known as the **normal backwardation theory** or the normal backwardation hypothesis, according to which hedgers want to be in a short position in a futures contract. Hedgers induce speculators to take the corresponding long positions in futures by making the expected return from a long position greater than the risk-free rate. This makes the futures price less than the expected spot rate, but it continues to rise over time, so that speculators get adequate compensation for the risk they are bearing. In other words, by being less than the spot rate at any time before maturity, the futures price continues to rise as the futures contract nears maturity, and it equals the spot rate at maturity. Figure 6.3 shows the behaviour of the normal backwardation curve. The normal backwardation theory further states that the speculators' expected profit is the hedgers' expected loss, and hedgers are prepared to bear such losses in order to shed the risk of uncertain exchange rates.

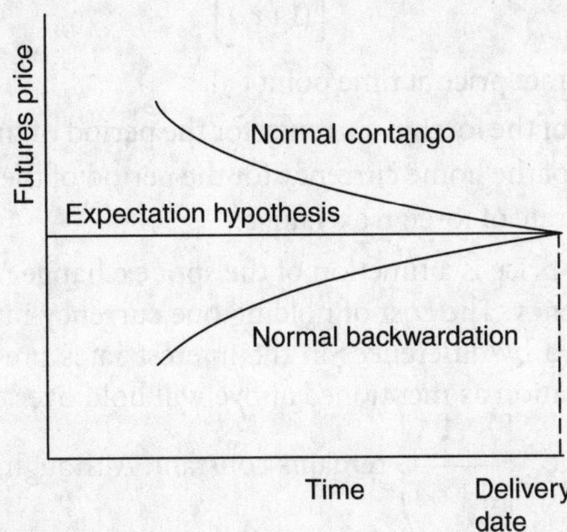

Figure 6.3

The Price of a Futures Contract

The Normal Contango Theory

The **normal contango theory**, or simply, contango, works contrary to normal backwardation. According to Keynes and Hicks, if hedgers want to hold long positions in a futures contract, speculators should hold short positions. Therefore, the futures price must be above the expected spot rate, but must decline over time so that speculators who are short in futures will get adequate returns for the risk they are bearing. Thus, according to the contango theory, the futures price continues to fall, but is greater than the expected spot rate at any time as the futures contract nears maturity. At the maturity of the futures contract, the futures price equals the spot rate, as shown in Figure 6.3.

Pricing of Currency Futures

To explain the issue of pricing of currency futures, let us take an example of an Indian investor who wishes to invest a certain amount for one year. He could invest in a one-year risk-free security issued by the Government of India. Alternatively, he could buy U.S. dollars with home currency and use the U.S. dollars to buy a one-year U.S. risk-free U.S. security. Further, the investor could short sell the requisite number of one-year U.S. dollar futures contracts. With such an arrangement the investor would know exactly how much INR he would receive a year later. In other words, there is no risk associated with the investments, as both the investments are risk-free and the investor knows exactly what amount the investments will yield in home currency after one year.

The strategy of investing INR 1 in a risk-free Indian security that has a return of r_d will provide a cash inflow of INR 1 $(1 + r_d)$ after one year. Similarly, the strategy of investing INR 1 in a risk-free U.S. security has a return of r_f. The current spot rate is S_0 and the futures price is F_t. Thus, the investment of INR 1 in the risk-free U.S. security will provide an INR cash inflow of (INR $1/S_0)(1 + r_f)F_t$ after one year. Since the two strategies cost the same (i.e. INR 1), their payoffs must be equal.

$$\text{INR } 1(1+r_d) = F_t\left\{\frac{INR\,1}{S_0}\times(1+r_f)\right\}$$

Therefore, the futures price of the U.S. dollar can be determined in terms of the interest rate parity equation as:

$$F_t = S_0\left\{\frac{(1+r_d)}{(1+r_f)}\right\}$$

where

F_t = Futures contract price at time point t

r_f = Interest rate of the foreign currency for the period of the futures contract

r_d = Interest rate of the home currency for the period of the futures contract

S_0 = Current spot rate of foreign exchange

Thus, the futures contract price is a function of the spot exchange rate and the cost of carrying the underlying currency. The cost of holding one currency rather than another is an opportunity cost measured by differences in the interest rates prevailing in the two currencies. The fair value equation as mentioned above will hold over the life of the exposure only if the interest rate ratio, $\left\{\frac{(1+r_d)}{(1+r_f)}\right\}$ remains constant. Although, the futures price converges with the spot rate at expiration of the futures contract, prior to expiration there is a possibility that the interest rate may change in one or both currencies. Consequent to the changes in the interest rate(s), the forward premium or discount will be changed by the interest rate parity. The risk of unexpected change in the interest rates and thus in the relationship between the spot rate and the futures price is called the basis risk.

Consider the following example to understand the deviations of the futures price from its fair value. A market participant has purchased a June 2015 EUR/USD futures contract (EUR 125,000). The spot exchange rate is 1.2926. The prevailing interest rate in the U.S. is 4 percent per annum. The euro currency interest rate is 6 percent per annum.

Given these figures, the fair value of the futures contract is calculated as EUR/USD 1.2888 by interest rate parity. Since the domestic currency interest is less than the foreign currency interest rate, the futures should trade at a discount to the spot rate. Thus, there is no arbitrage profit as detailed below:

Borrow USD 161,575 at 4 percent per annum	
Sell U.S. dollars to get 1,25,000 euros at a spot rate of EUR/USD 1.2926	
Borrowing cost for 60 days at an annual rate of interest of 4% (0.007 × 1,61,575)	(–)USD 1,131
Return on investment of 1,25,000 euros at 6% p.a. for 60 days	EUR 1,250
Sell EUR 1,25,000 to get USD at the futures price after two months (1,25,000 × 1.2888)	USD 1,61,100
Convert EUR 1,250 to USD (1,250 × 1.2888)	USD 1,611
Total amount to be received	USD 1,62,711
Loan amount to be repaid	USD 1,62,706

There is no arbitrage profit as both the amounts are approximately the same.

Let us assume that the futures price is USD/EUR 1.3000, a deviation from the fair value of 1.2888. Since the futures price is greater than the fair value, there is an arbitrage opportunity. In this situation, the arbitrageur may act in the following way to make a risk-less profit.

Borrow USD 1,61,575 at 4 percent per annum	
Sell U.S. dollars to get 1,25,000 euros at a spot rate of EUR/USD1.2926	
Borrowing cost for 60 days at an annual rate of interest of 4% (0.007 × 161,575)	(–)USD 1,131
Interest on investment of 1,25,000 euros at 6% p.a. for 60 days	EUR 1,250
Sell EUR 125,000 to get U.S. dollars at the futures price of 1.3000 after two months	USD 1,62,500
Convert EUR 1250 to USD (1,250 × 1.3000)	USD 1,625
Total amount to be received	USD 1,64,125
Loan amount to be repaid	USD 1,62,706
Arbitrage profit	USD 1,419

Conversely, if the futures price is below the fair value, the arbitrageur buys futures and sells an equivalent amount of the currency in the spot market, thereby making an arbitrage profit as above. By buying (selling) euros at the spot rate and selling (buying) EUR/USD futures, the arbitrageurs would push up (push down) the spot rate and/or push down (push up) the futures price to establish equilibrium pricing levels. Thus, arbitrageurs monitor and promptly act upon situations where the futures price and spot rate are misaligned, and eventually bring fair value pricing to the market. If transaction costs (e.g. commissions, fees, etc.) were to be factored into the model, futures tend to trade within a band around its theoretical fair value, and the width of the band reflects the amount of the transaction costs. In such a case, the reference rate for buying and selling of futures is not the theoretical fair value but the band.

Consider another example. If the current spot rate is USD/INR 46 and the Indian and U.S. one-year risk-free rates are 6 percent and 4 percent, respectively, then the one-year futures price of the U.S. dollar will be

$$\text{INR } 46 \times \left(\frac{1.06}{1.04}\right) = \text{INR } 46.88$$

The futures price is also defined as

$$F_t = S_0 + I - B$$

where

I = Absolute amount of interest in home currency on the spot rate for the futures contract period

B = Value of benefits of ownership

The term $(I - B)$, also known as the cost of carry, is stated as

$$\text{Cost of Carry} = S_0 \left\{ \frac{(r_d - r_f)}{(1 + r_f)} \right\}$$

Further,

$$I = S_0 \frac{r_d}{(1 - r_f)}$$

$$B = S_0 \frac{r_f}{(1 + r_f)}$$

By using the data in the example given above, the cost of carry is

$$\text{INR } 46\left(\frac{0.06 - 0.04}{1 + 0.04}\right) = \text{INR } 0.88$$

$$I = \text{INR } 46\left(\frac{0.06}{1 + 0.04}\right) = \text{INR } 2.65$$

This is the amount of interest foregone by the investor by selling the U.S. dollars in the futures market instead of the spot market.

$$B = \text{INR } 46\left(\frac{0.04}{1 + 0.04}\right) = \text{INR } 1.77$$

This is the benefit of owning U.S. dollars instead of selling them.

The futures price is greater than the current spot rate (i.e. futures trade at a premium to the spot rate) when the risk-free interest rate in the home currency is greater than the foreign risk-free interest rate. In market parlance, this is known as 'negative carry' for the reason that costs are incurred to buy and carry foreign currency. Conversely, the futures price is less than the current spot rate (i.e. futures trade at a discount to the spot rate) when the domestic risk-free interest rate is less than the foreign risk-free rate. This situation is known as 'positive carry' because earnings accrue from buying and carrying foreign currency. It is in this context that the concept of 'carry trade' is used, which involves buying a high-yielding currency and funding it with a low-yielding currency, similar to the adage 'buy low, sell high'. Thus, the difference between the futures price and spot rate exists because of the difference in the risk-free interest rates between the two currencies.

However, the futures pricing model as discussed in the above paragraphs is more relevant to forward pricing because, in the forward contract, the proceeds are realized only upon maturity of the contract. In the case of futures contract, cash flows occur periodically during the course of the contract because of marking to market. Therefore, the actual timing and quantum of such cash flows as well as interest rates in the economy need to be factored into the model to make it more relevant.

The Hedge Ratio

Hedging, in general, refers to making an investment to reduce the risk of adverse price movements. It involves taking an offsetting position in a related security of an existing position. In a **perfect hedge**, an investor undertakes a position that would eliminate the risk of an existing position. For example, assume that a U.S.-based MNC expects to receive GBP 5 million in a month's time from a British company. To protect its receipts against a drop in value, the MNC has sold eighty 30-day British pound futures, each of size GBP 62,500. This is an example of a perfect hedge. In order to be a perfect hedge, a position should necessarily have a 100 percent inverse correlation with the underlying position. The opposite of perfect hedge is the **naked position**, which is a position not hedged from market risk. A naked position faces both potential gain and potential loss.

__Hedging__ refers to making an investment to reduce the risk of adverse price movements. A __perfect hedge__ is a position that necessarily has a 100 percent inverse correlation with the underlying position. The opposite of perfect hedge is the __naked position__, which is a position not hedged from market risk.

The hedge ratio is the ratio of the value of a futures contract to the value of the underlying exposure. The hedge ratio (HR) of a futures contract is given by the following formula:

$$HR = \frac{\text{Amount (value) in futures contract}}{\text{Amount (value) exposed to currency risk}}$$

Measured in the same currency, the hedge ratio should be unity or close to unity for a perfect hedge. So, a perfect hedge in the futures contract is the same as the underlying currency exposure. But perfect hedges are rarely found in practice. For example, futures traded on the CME Globex call for settlement during the months of March, June, September, and December (the March quarterly cycle). A U.S.-based firm has 3-month accounts receivables of EUR 2,50,000 maturing on 10 June. But there is no EUR/USD futures maturing on that date as exchange-traded contracts mature on the third Wednesday of the March quarterly cycle. On 2 April, the spot rate of EUR/USD is 1.2926 and June, September, and December futures are traded at 1.3254, 1.3679, and 1.41234, respectively. As the futures price converges with the spot rate on the day the futures contract matures, the June futures contract is more appropriate. Because June futures have less time period from maturity to the present day as compared to September and December futures, it is, therefore, more likely that its price will have moved closer to its spot rate. Even with a sell of near contract, i.e. June, the firm is not able to get a perfect hedge of the currency risk involved in the transaction. Thus, there is a maturity mismatch.

A hedge cannot be perfect in the following situations:

- Futures are not available on the currency in which the hedger has exposure. In other words, there is a currency mismatch.
- It is uncertain when exactly the expected cash flows would materialize. In such cases, it may become necessary to liquidate the hedging contract (e.g. futures contract) before its maturity date. Even otherwise, the maturity dates of futures contracts may not correspond perfectly with the cash flows to be hedged, leading to a maturity mismatch.
- The futures contracts are available in fixed or standard sizes and, therefore, the size of the futures contracts may not match with the size of the cash flows to be hedged.

So it is only accidental if futures provide perfect hedges by matching the currency, size, and timing of the underlying transaction. A mismatch between the maturity of the underlying cash flows and that of the futures contract leads to **delta hedging**; a mismatch between the currencies leads to **cross hedging**; and a combination of mismatches in both underlying assets and maturity leads to **delta cross hedging.**

A mismatch between the maturity of the underlying cash flows and that of the futures contract leads to __delta hedging__; a mismatch between the currencies leads to __cross hedging__; and a combination of mismatches in both underlying assets and maturity leads to __delta cross hedging__.

The spot rate of a currency fluctuates randomly over the life of the futures contract and converges with the futures price upon expiration of the futures contract. The relationship between the sport rate and the futures contract price can be established by the following regression equation:

$$\Delta S_t = \alpha + \beta \Delta F_t + e_t$$

Here

ΔS_t = Percentage change in the spot rate, $[(S_t - S_{t-1})/S_{t-1}]$

ΔF_t = Percentage change in the futures price, $[(F_t - F_{t-1})/F_{t-1}]$
α = Intercept
β = Regression coefficient, which measures changes in futures price relative to changes in spot rate
e_t = Error term (changes in spot rate that are not caused by changes in futures price)

The regression equation is estimated by using historical data. It is assumed that the historical relation between the spot rates and futures prices is an approximation of the future relation. The sensitivity of the change in the spot rate to the change in the price of the futures contract is called **delta**. Delta is measured by the slope (β) of the regression line. β, also known as the required **hedge ratio**, is

$$\beta = \rho\left(\frac{\sigma_s}{\sigma_f}\right)$$

where

ρ = Coefficient of correlation between ΔS_t and ΔF_t
σ_s = Standard deviation of ΔS_t
e_F = Standard deviation of ΔF_t

If $\rho = 1$ and $e_s = \sigma_F$, the hedge ratio, β becomes unity. Such a hedge is called a perfect hedge.

In view of the fact that currency futures contracts are standardized with a limited number of maturities, there may be a mismatch between the maturity of a futures contract and the underlying currency exposure. When there is a maturity mismatch, the basis risk makes a futures hedge riskier. In such cases, a delta hedge is used to find the optimal number of futures contracts to be bought or sold. For example, on 15 January a U.S. firm expects to receive GBP 3.125 million on 15 April 2015. The futures contracts available in CME are March, June, September, and December. The March futures could hedge against the currency risk through the third Wednesday of March and, therefore, cash flows would remain unhedged after that. The June futures can hedge the currency risk through April. So the U.S. firm can sell June futures. Now, the question is how many futures contracts should the firm sell, given that the contract size is GBP 62,500 and σ= 1.25? As there is a maturity mismatch, a delta hedge is used. Accordingly, the optimal number of futures contracts (N) is

*The sensitivity of the change in the spot rate to a change in the price of the futures contract is called **delta**. Delta is measured by the slope (b) of the regression line. b is also known as the **required hedge ratio**. The minus sign of b indicates that the futures position is opposite to the underlying exposure*

$$N = \beta \times \frac{\text{Amount of cash flows exposed}}{\text{Size of the futures contract}}$$

$$N = 1.25 \times \frac{3.125\text{ million}}{62{,}500}$$

$$= 62.50$$

Thus, the firm should sell 63 futures contracts. This is more than the number of futures contracts (50) with a perfect hedge. The amount involved in the futures contract is GBP 3.9375 million. In other words, the delta hedge provides a number of contracts or amount of futures contracts that is different from what it would be with the perfect hedge.

What the U.S. firm actually does in this example is that it receives GBP 3.125 million on the date of settlement in April, and converts it into U.S. dollars at the current spot rate. Simultaneously, it liquidates the June futures contracts by taking an equal but opposite futures position. When it sells the GBP for USD, it may gain or lose depending on the spot rate on the date of conversion (15 April). At the same time, the firm may gain or lose on the futures transaction depending on the price of June futures on 15 April. Thus, the firm may have a net gain or loss depending on the movements of interest rates that determine spot rates as well as futures contract prices. If interest rate differentials are more volatile, the basis risk will be larger. This makes the futures hedge position more risky. The delta hedge minimizes the risk of the hedged position by giving the optimal number of futures contracts to be bought or sold, as opposed to the optimal number of futures contracts for the perfect riskless hedge.

Cross Hedging and Delta Cross Hedging

Cross hedging involves using a financial contract in one currency to hedge the exposure in another currency. If futures are not available in a desired currency, the hedger may enter into a futures contract on a currency that is closely related to the desired currency. Such types of futures contracts are known as cross hedges. Though a cross hedge may not be a perfect hedge against exposure, it can at least partially cover the exposure. When futures are not available in a desired currency, the hedger should carefully identify another currency that is highly correlated with the desired currency. For example, the U.S. dollar and the Canadian dollar are highly correlated. So, a currency exposure in the U.S. dollar can be hedged with a futures contract in the Canadian dollar.

*If futures are not available in a desired currency, a hedger may enter into a futures contract on a currency that is closely related to the desired currency. These types of futures contracts are known as **cross hedges.***

Hedgers generally do not find problems with the exchange risk of major currencies, as different kinds of derivatives are always available to use. However, they may find it difficult or impossible to use derivatives to hedge the risk in trading the currencies of small and developing countries where financial markets are not developed. In such situations, hedgers may consider using cross hedging to manage their currency exposures. Sometimes other futures, like commodity futures, may be used effectively to cross hedge the exposure in minor currencies. Thus, cross hedging can be done with different kinds of futures. But the effectiveness of such cross hedging depends on the strength of the relationship between the underlying currency exposure and the selected futures contract.

Thus, a cross hedge is required when there is a currency mismatch, but not a maturity mismatch. The regression equation for a cross hedge can be stated as

$$\Delta S_{1t} = \alpha + \beta \Delta S_{2t} + e_t$$

Here

ΔS_{1t} = Percentage change in the spot rate of Currency 1 (as against the domestic currency) in which the underlying cash flows are exposed

ΔS_{2t} = Percentage change in the spot rate of Currency 2 (as against the domestic currency) in terms of which the cash flows are hedged

α = Intercept

β = Regression coefficient

e_t = Error term

When there is a maturity mismatch and currency mismatch, a delta cross hedge is used. The optimal hedge ratio in this regard is estimated from the following regression equation:

$$\Delta S_{1t} = \alpha + \beta \Delta F_{2t} + e_t$$

Here

ΔS_{1t} = Percentage change in the spot rate of Currency 1 (as against the domestic currency) in which the underlying cash flows are exposed

ΔF_{2t} = Percentage change in the futures price of Currency 2 (as against the domestic currency) in terms of which the cash flows are hedged

α = Intercept

β = Regression coefficient

e_t = Error term

If the maturity and currency of the underlying exposure match, there will be a perfect hedge, leading to complete elimination of currency risk. In such a situation, the futures contracts will be as good as the forward contracts.

The U.S. Dollar Index (USDX) Futures

The U.S. Dollar Index (USDX) was created by the U.S. Federal Reserve in 1973 to provide an external bilateral trade-weighted average of the U.S. dollar as it freely floated against global currencies. The index is computed with six highly traded currencies such as the euro, Japanese yen, British pound, Canadian dollar, Swedish krona, and Swish franc. Before the euro came into existence, the original USDX contained ten currencies. On inclusion of the euro into the index, currencies such as the West German mark, the French franc, the Italian lira, the Dutch guilder, and the Belgium franc got displaced.

The USDX is calculated as a geometric weighted average of the change in six foreign currency exchange rates against the U.S. dollar relative to March 1973. When the U.S. dollar declines in value against this average, the index rises, and vice versa. The USDX measures the U.S. dollar's general value relative to a base of 100.00. A quote of 105.50 means that the U.S. dollar's value has risen 5.50 percent since this base period. March 1973 was chosen as the base period because it represents a significant milestone in foreign exchange history, when the world's major trading nations allowed their currencies to float freely against each other. The index, which is continuously updated, measures the average value of the USD against six major world currencies. The six currencies included in the U.S. Dollar Index represent 17 countries (12 euro zone countries and five others), which have a large stake in the international trade of the United States. The six currencies with their weights in the index are listed in Table 6.5.

The formula used for calculating USDX is as below:

$$USDX = 50.14348112 \times EUR/USD^{(-)0.576} \times USD/JPY^{0.136} \times GBP/USD^{(-)0.119} \times USD/CAD^{0.091} \times USD/SEK^{0.042} \times USD/CHF^{0.036}$$

As can be observed, when the USD is the base currency, the value is positive. It means that the USDX and the exchange rate of the currency pair should move in the same direction. When the USD is the quote currency, the value is negative. It implies that the USDX and the exchange rate of the currency pair should move in the opposite direction. The USDX gives an idea of the relative strength of the USD around the world. It measures the U.S. dollar general value relative to a base 100. For example, if the index is 87, the U.S. dollar has fallen 13 percent since the start of the index.

The futures contracts on the USDX are traded on different platforms including the Inter Continental Exchange (ICE) electronic trading platform. The size (value) of a futures contract is specified at USD 1,000 times the index value. For example, if the index value is 87.2345, the value of the contract is USD 8.2345. It means that each full index point is worth USD 1,000 (1.000 = USD 1,000). The smallest price increment for trading in the USDX futures contract is 0.005, which is worth USD 5. The contracts are settled quarterly (March, June, September, and December). The quarterly settlement at the expiration of the contract is on the third Wednesday of the contract month.

Unlike many index futures, the USDX futures contract is a physically delivered contract. That is, the contract settles by physical delivery of the index's six component currencies in the percentages indicated in the composition of the index. If a futures contract is held

Table 6.5 USDX Currencies and Their Weights

Currency	*Weight*
Euro (EUR)	0.576
Japanese yen (JPY)	0.136
British pound (GBP)	0.119
Canadian dollar (CAD)	0.091
Swedish krona (SEK)	0.042
Swiss franc (CHF)	0.036

through final settlement, the holder of a long position is required to deliver the basket of currencies in the index in the weights specified and in turn receives U.S. dollars. On the other side, the holder of the short position in a futures contract receives the basket of currencies and pays U.S. dollars. The U.S. dollar amount for physical delivery in the final settlement is determined by multiplying the settlement price of the USDX futures contract on the final trading day with USD 1,000.

Currency Futures in India

Following the foreign currency crisis, particularly the crisis of inadequate foreign exchange reserves during the early 1990s, India embarked on a series of structural reforms with regard to the foreign exchange market. More importantly, the country has shifted from a pegged exchange rate regime to a floating exchange rate, of course, with a provision that the RBI can intervene in the foreign exchange market, if and when necessary, only to smoothen any undue volatilities or disorderly market behaviour. Alongside, the Indian rupee has been made fully convertible under the current account as per Article VIII of the Articles of Agreement of the International Monetary Fund. Further, to advance the Indian foreign exchange market to international standards, a well-developed derivatives market has become essential, and towards this end several initiatives have been taken. One such initiative has been the introduction of currency futures. The National Stock Exchange was the first exchange to launch currency futures on 29 August 2008, followed by the BSE on 1 October 2008, MCX-SX on 7 October 2008, and the United Stock Exchange on 20 September 2010. Initially, trading in USD–INR futures contracts was permitted. Subsequently, futures contracts between rupee and euro, rupee and pound, and rupee and yen have also been introduced on these exchanges.

The Reserve Bank of India has issued a set of directions and guidelines for trading in currency futures. The major aspects of these are highlighted as follows:

- Minimum contract size of the currency futures contract would be USD 1,000 for USD/INR; EUR 1,000 for EUR/INR; GBP 1,000 for GBP/INR; and JPY 1,00,000 for JPY/INR.
- Currency futures contract would be quoted in rupee terms. However, the outstanding positions would be in USD, EUR, GBP, and JPY for USD/INR, EUR/INR, GBP/INR, and JPY/INR futures contracts, respectively.
- Currency futures contracts shall have a maximum maturity of 12 months.
- All monthly maturities from 1 to 12 months would be made available.
- Currency futures contracts shall be settled in cash in INR.
- Settlement price would be the Reserve Bank of India Reference Rate on the date of expiry.
- Last date for trading of the contract shall be two working days prior to the final settlement day. They would expire on the last working day (excluding Saturdays) of the month.
- Any bank, included in the Second Schedule to the RBI Act, 1934, and specifically authorized by the RBI for this purpose, is eligible to become a participant in currency futures trading.
- Clearing Corporation acts as a central counterparty to all trades and performs full novation.
- Initial margin requirement shall be based on a worst-case loss of a portfolio of an individual client across various scenarios of price changes. The various scenarios of price changes would be so computed so as to cover a 99% VaR over a one-day horizon.

- A portfolio-based margining approach shall be adopted to take an integrated view of the risk involved in the portfolio of each individual client comprising his positions in futures contracts across different maturities.
- A currency futures position at one maturity which is hedged by an offsetting position at a different maturity would be treated as a calendar spread. The calendar spread margin shall be at a value of ₹400 for a spread of one month, ₹500 for a spread of two months, ₹800 for a spread of three months, and ₹1,000 for a spread of four months or more for a USD/INR contract; the calendar spread margin shall be at a value of ₹700 for a spread of one month, ₹1,000 for a spread of two months, and ₹1,500 for a spread of three months or more for an EUR/INR contract; the calendar spread margin shall be at a value of ₹1,500 for a spread of one month, ₹1,800 for a spread of two months, and ₹2,000 for a spread of three months or more for a GBP/INR contract; the calendar spread margin shall be at a value of ₹600 for a period of one month; ₹1,000 for a spread of two months and ₹1,500 for a spread of three months or more for a JPY/INR contract. For a calendar spread position, the extreme loss margin shall be charged one–third the mark to market value of the far month contract.
- Extreme loss margin of 1% for a USD/INR contract; 0.3% for an EUR/INR contract; 0.5% for a GBP/INR contract; and 0.7% for a JPY/INR contract on the mark to market value of the gross open positions shall be deducted from the liquid assets of the clearing member on an online, real-time basis
- Initial margin and extreme loss margin shall be deducted from the liquid assets of the clearing member.
- Liquid assets for trading in currency futures would be maintained separately in the currency futures segment of the Clearing Corporation.
- Mark to market gains and losses shall be settled in cash before the start of trading on $T + 1$ day.
- Client margins have to be compulsorily collected and reported to the exchange by the members.
- Clearing Corporation shall segregate the margins deposited by the clearing members for trades on their own account from the margins deposited with it on the client account.
- Clearing Corporation, shall on an ongoing basis and at least once in every six months, conduct back testing of the margins collected via-à-vis the actual price changes.
- Surveillance system of the exchanges shall be designed keeping in view all the relevant aspects.
- Reporting to the media shall have the following details in a uniform format on a daily basis.

  a. Contracts description;
  b. Number of contracts traded;
  c. Notional value;
  d. Open
  e. High
  f. Low
  g. Close
  h. Open interest (in number of contracts)

- Position limits:

Currency pair	*Client level*	*Trading member level*	*Clearing member level*
USD/INR	Gross open positions of the client across all contracts shall not exceed 6% of the total open interest or USD 10 million, whichever is higher.	Gross open positions of the trading member across all contracts shall not exceed 15% of the total open interest or USD 50 million, whichever is higher. Gross open position of a trading member, which is a bank, across all contracts, shall not exceed 15% of the total open interest or USD 100 million, whichever is higher.	No separate position limit is prescribed at the level of the clearing member. However, the clearing member shall ensure that his or her own trading position and the positions of each trading member clearing through him are within the limits specified for trading members.
EUR/INR	Gross open positions of the client across all contracts shall not exceed 6% of the total open interest or EUR 5 million, whichever is higher.	Gross open positions of the trading member across all contracts shall not exceed 15% of the total open interest or EUR 25 million, whichever is higher. Gross open position of a trading member, which is a bank, across all contracts, shall not exceed 15% of the total open interest or EUR 50 million, whichever is higher.	No separate position limit is prescribed at the level of clearing member. However, the clearing member shall ensure that his or her own trading position and the positions of each trading member clearing through him or her are within the limits specified for trading members.
GBP/INR	Gross open positions of the client across all contracts shall not exceed 6% of the total open interest or GBP 5 million whichever is higher.	Gross open positions of the trading member across all contracts shall not exceed 15% of the total open interest or GBP 25 million, whichever is higher. Gross open position of a trading member, which is a bank, across all contracts, shall not exceed 15% of the total open interest or GBP 50 million, whichever is higher.	No separate position limit is prescribed at the level of clearing member. However, the clearing member shall ensure that his or her own trading position and the positions of each trading member clearing through him is within the limits specified for trading members.
JPY/INR	Gross open positions of the client across all contracts shall not exceed 6% of the total open interest or JPY 200 million, whichever is higher.	Gross open positions of the trading member across all contracts shall not exceed 15% of the total open interest or JPY 1,000 million, whichever is higher. Gross open position of a trading member, which is a bank, across all contracts, shall not exceed 15% of the total open interest or JPY 2,000 million, whichever is higher.	No separate position limit is prescribed at the level of clearing member. However, the clearing member shall ensure that his or her own trading position and the positions of each trading member clearing through him is within the limits specified for trading members.

The Reserve Bank of India, in its circular dated 20 June 2014, has permitted the foreign portfolio investors (FPIs) to deal in currency futures contracts or exchange-traded currency options subject to the following conditions:

- FPIs shall be allowed access to the currency futures or exchange-traded currency options for the purpose of hedging the currency risk arising out of the market value of their exposure to Indian debt and equity securities.
- Such investors can participate in the currency futures/exchange-traded currency options through any registered or recognized trading member of the exchange concerned.
- FPIs can take positions—both long (bought) as well as short (sold)—in foreign currency up to USD 10 million or equivalent per exchange without having to establish existence of any underlying exposure. The limit will be both day-end as well as intra-day.
- An FPI cannot take a short position beyond USD 10 million at any time and to take a long position beyond USD 10 million in any exchange without having an underlying exposure.

The popularity of forwards and futures has increased over the past few decades. Forwards and futures, along with other derivative securities like options, have become indispensable hedging tools for every investment manager. As forwards and futures have close linkages with the underlying currency positions, the development of forwards and futures markets has a significant bearing on the foreign exchange market. Though forwards and futures can be viewed as insurance policies against adverse exchange rate movements, they can also be combined with positions in the underlying currencies to create a payoff structure that is otherwise unavailable. In other words, forwards and futures enable investors to create portfolios synthetically and maximize their returns without an increase in the risk profile.

A Glimpse of Two Major Futures Exchanges

Among various derivative contracts, currency futures are of recent origin. The first currency futures exchange was set up by the CME in 1972 in the United States. Later, many countries, including some emerging market economies such as Brazil, Korea, and Mexico, set up currency futures exchanges. South Africa introduced currency futures exchange on 18 June 2007.

A brief profile of the world's leading futures exchanges is presented in the following sections.

Eurex

Eurex Group is a world leader in trading and clearing, technology and risk management. It comprises of six companies, viz., Eurex Exchange, International Securities Exchange, European Energy Exchange, Eurex Clearing, Eurex Bonds, and Eurex Repo. Eurex Exchange, popularly known as Eurex is the European Electronic Exchange (Futures Exchange) based in Frankfurt, Germany. Eurex is the successor to the Deutsche Terminborse (DTB), Germany's first fully computerized exchange, and the first German exchange for trading financial futures. The DTB merged with Deutsche Borse AG and in 1998 it merged with the Swiss Options and Financial Futures Exchange to form Eurex. The Eurex Group has partner relationships with Irish Stock Exchange, Helsinki Exchange Group Ltd, Tel Aviv Stock Exchange, Bombay Stock Exchange, Korea Exchange, Singapore Exchange, and Taiwan Futures Exchange. Eurex has funded Eurex U.S. to compete with the U.S. derivative exchanges.

Eurex is one of the largest global derivatives exchanges, with a product suite comprising the most actively traded and liquid market in EUR-denominated equity index derivatives. It also trades the most liquid fixed incomes markets in the world. Eurex is the world's first electronic cross-border exchange, now offering more than 1,900 products across a growing range of asset classes.

Since June 2013, Eurex runs completely on Deutsche Borse's global trading architecture T7. This advanced technology enables the Eurex to further expand its leading position in the global derivatives trading industry. In terms of volume, it is the world's largest derivatives exchange. It has created a decentralized and standardized access system with 432 participants in 17 countries. Members are linked to the Eurex system through a dedicated wide-area communications network. Access points have been installed in Amsterdam, Chicago, New York, Helsinki, London, Madrid, Paris, Hong Kong, Tokyo, and Sydney. Eurex operates in three trading phases: pre-trading from 7:30 a.m. to 9:00 a.m.; trading from 9:00 a.m. to 8:00 p.m.; and post-trading from 8:00 p.m. to 8:30 p.m.

***Eurex** is the European Electronic Exchange (Futures Exchange) based in Frankfurt, Germany. In terms of volume, it is the world's largest derivatives exchange.*

The Chicago Mercantile Exchange (CME)

The **CME** is the world's largest exchange for futures and options. It was the world's first financial exchange to introduce currency futures in May 1972. It initially introduced futures in seven foreign currencies such as the U.S. dollar, British pound, Deutsche mark, French franc, Japanese yen, Mexican peso, and Swiss franc. It was also the first futures exchange to introduce standardization of futures contracts.

*The **Chicago Mercantile Exchange (CME)** is the largest and most diverse financial exchange in the United States. It has the largest options and futures contracts open interest (number of contracts outstanding) of any futures exchange in the world, reflecting high liquidity.*

CME is the largest and most diverse financial exchange in the United States. It has the largest options and futures contracts open interest (number of contracts outstanding) of any futures exchange in the world, reflecting high liquidity. It trades in several asset classes, which include futures on interest rates, currency, equities, and stock indices. It also offers trading in exotic classes such as weather and real estate derivatives.

CME was founded in 1898 as the Chicago Butter and Egg Board and evolved into the CME in 1919. Originally, the exchange was a not-for-profit organization. It became a shareholder-owned corporation in November 2000. It is the first U.S. financial exchange to demutualize. It went public in December 2002, and became the first U.S. exchange to do so. The CME expanded its international presence through strategic alliances with exchanges and clearing organizations. It has a mutual offset system with Singapore Exchange Derivatives Trading Ltd and has entered into memoranda of understanding with the Shanghai Stock Exchange, the Shanghai Futures Exchange, and the China Foreign Exchange Trading System. It is also a partner in One Chicago LLC, a joint venture created to trade single-stock futures and narrow-based stock indices. It has an agreement with Reuters to bring direct foreign exchange futures trading to the international foreign exchange market. The International Monetary Market (IMM) was formed in May 1972, as a division of the CME, to trade futures in U.S. treasury bills, foreign currency, certificates of deposit, and eurodollar deposits. The CME acquired the Chicago Board of Trade (CBOT) in July 2007, and the New York Mercantile Exchange (NYMEX) in August 2008. These three entities now form the CME Group, which currently deals in almost every aspect of commerce.

CME Group offers the widest range of global benchmark products across all major asset classes, based on interest rates, equity indexes, foreign exchange, energy, agricultural commodities, metals, weather and real estate. The products include both exchange-traded and over-the-counter derivatives. The CME Direct Technology offers side-by-side trading of exchange-listed and over-the-counter markets. CME offers trading in a wide variety of futures on currencies such as the U.S. dollar, euro, British pound, Swiss franc, Canadian dollar, Japanese yen, Australian dollar, New Zealand dollar, Mexican peso, Russian ruble, etc.

Trading in CME is conducted in two methods: open outcry and Globex. The CME Globex trading system was introduced in 1992, and it became the first global electronic trading platform for futures contracts. It allows market participants to trade from booths at the exchange or while sitting at their homes or offices. CME currency futures trade virtually 24 hours a day, day or night, during the trading week.

Summary

1. A firm has exposure to currency risk when its income flows and/or capital flows are affected by unanticipated changes in exchange rates.
2. The prominent hedging devices available to a firm to insulate itself from exposure to currency risk are currency forwards, currency futures, and currency options.
3. A *currency forward contract* is a legally enforceable agreement in which two parties agree to buy and sell in the future, a specified amount of one currency for another currency, at a fixed exchange rate.
4. A *currency futures contract* is a standardized agreement to deliver or receive a specified amount of a specified currency at a fixed rate and date.
5. Clearing house services, margins, and marking to market are the important features of the futures exchange.
6. *Hedgers, speculators,* and *arbitrageurs* are the participants in the futures market.
7. Though currency forwards and currency futures serve the same purpose, they differ on certain aspects. Forwards are mostly interbank transactions, whereas futures are traded on organized exchanges. The marking-to-market procedure that underlies the margin requirement makes the profit/loss in a futures contract different from that in a corresponding forward contract.
8. The mismatch between the maturity of the underlying cash flows and the futures contract leads to *delta hedging;* the mismatch between the currencies leads to *cross hedging;* and the combination of mismatches in both underlying asset and maturity leads to *delta cross hedging.*
9. Traditionally, there are three theories that deal with the relationship between currency futures prices and expected spot rates. They are the *expectation hypothesis, normal backwardation,* and *normal contango.*
10. The price of a currency futures contract is a function of the spot exchange rate and the cost of carrying the underlying currency.

Questions and Problems

1. How are currency forward contracts different from currency futures contracts?
2. Why are margins maintained with respect to a currency futures contract but not with currency forward contracts?
3. What is marking to market? What are its advantages and disadvantages?
4. Describe the relationship between spot rate and future rate.
5. Explain the concept of basis with suitable examples.
6. What is cross hedging? How it is different from *delta cross* hedging?
7. Define hedge ratio. What purpose(s) does it serve?
8. Discuss the theories that explain the relationship between the prices of currency futures and the expected spot rates of foreign exchange.
9. Explain the basic model of futures price in terms of interest rate parity.
10. On 20 December, a trader takes a short position in a British pound futures contract that matures on 24 December. The agreed-upon rate of exchange is GBP/INR 82. The contract size is GBP 1 million. At the close of trading on 20 December, the settlement rate of the futures contract is GBP/INR 81.5, and on the next day it falls to GBP/INR 80.75. However, on 22 December, the settlement rate rises to GBP/INR 83, and on 23 December, it again falls to GBP/INR 82. Upon maturity of the futures contract, the British pounds are delivered, and on that date the spot rate is GBP/INR 83.75. Explain the daily settlement process and calculate the profit or loss to the trader.
11. The forward-ask price on U.S. dollars for 10 January is USD/INR 45 and, at the same time, the price of U.S. dollar futures for delivery on 10 January is USD/INR 45.75. How could an arbitrageur profit from such an opportunity?
12. A trader buys a Canadian dollar futures contract at a price of INR 40. The contract size is CAD 1 million. If the spot rate for the CAD at the date of settlement is CAD/INR 41, what is the gain or loss on this contract to the trader?
13. The settlement price on an Australian dollar futures contract is AUD/INR 34. A trader has a short position in one contract, the size of which is AUD 0.5 million. The margin account of the trader currently has a balance of INR 10,000. The next three days' settlement prices are INR 33.75, INR 33.90, and INR 33.25. Calculate the changes in the margin account from daily marking to market and the balance of the margin account after the third day.

14. A firm in India expects to receive USD 12 million from its customers in the United States on 20 December. On this day, i.e. 20 September, the current spot exchange rate is USD/INR 45. The current U.S. dollar futures price for December delivery is USD/INR 46. The size of the futures contract is USD 1.20 million. How many futures contracts should the Indian firm buy or sell in order to hedge this forward exposure? What is the firm's net profit or loss on 20 December if the spot rate on that date is USD/INR 44.75?
15. If the spot rate of the British pound is USD 1.92, the annual interest rate is 4 percent in the United States and 6 percent in the United Kingdom. What is the price of a 90-day futures contract?

Multiple-choice Questions

1. Source of foreign exchange risk is _________.

   (a) Imports (b) Exports
   (c) Investment abroad (d) All the above

2. If a domestic currency appreciates against a foreign currency, the cost of servicing a debt denominated in the foreign currency _________.

   (a) Goes up (b) Goes down
   (c) Remains the same (d) None of these

3. A long position in a forward contract implies that the holder agrees to _________ the underlying currency.

   (a) Sell (b) Buy
   (c) Surrender (d) None of these

4. Forward markets are _________.

   (a) Standardized (b) Self-regulated
   (c) Government owned (d) None of these

5. Forward rate is a function of relative _________ of two currencies.

   (a) Inflation rates (b) Interest rates
   (c) Spot rates (d) None of these

6. If the domestic interest is higher than the foreign interest rate, the swap points are _________ to the spot rate to arrive at the implied outright forward rate.

   (a) Added (b) Subtracted
   (c) None of these

7. Basis is the difference between _________.

   (a) Forward rate and spot rate
   (b) Spot rates of two currencies
   (c) Forward rates of two currencies
   (d) None of these

8. Futures contracts are _________

   (a) Standardized (b) Customized
   (c) Self-regulated (d) None of these

9. Tick represents _________ change in the price.

   (a) Maximum (b) Minimum
   (c) No (d) None of these

10. A futures contract is settled every day at _________.

    (a) Settlement price (b) Forward rate
    (c) Spot rate (d) None of these

11. Margins are fixed by keeping in view the _________.

    (a) Spot rate
    (b) Futures price
    (c) Variability in exchange rate
    (d) None of these

12. Day traders may attract _________ margin requirements.

    (a) Higher (b) Lower
    (c) No (d) None of these

13. Futures contracts are highly _________.

    (a) Profitable (b) Leveraged
    (c) Volatile (d) None of these

14. Hedgers go short in futures if they are _________ in the underlying position.

    (a) Long (b) Short
    (c) Non-committal (d) None of these

15. Speculators always expect _________.

    (a) Normal gains (b) Windfall gains
    (c) Riskless trade (d) None of these

16. Arbitrageurs make _________.

    (a) Riskless profit
    (b) Profit with moderate risk
    (c) Profit with small capital
    (d) None of these

17. _________ can be a perfect hedge against currency risk.

    (a) Forward contract
    (b) Futures contract
    (c) Both forward and futures
    (d) None of these

18. Most _________ contracts are settled by actual delivery.

    (a) Forward (b) Futures
    (c) Forward and futures (d) None of these

19. Gap between bid and ask price is ________ in the case of the futures contract.

(a) Wide (b) Narrow
(c) Zero (d) None of these

20. As the maturity date nears, the futures price and spot rate tend to become ________.

(a) Closer (b) Different
(c) Apart (d) None of these

21. Basis remains constant when there is ________ between changes in spot rate and changes in futures price.

(a) Positive correlation (b) Negative correlation
(c) No correlation (d) None of these

22. Mismatch between currencies leads to ________.

(a) Delta hedging (b) Cross hedging
(c) Delta cross hedging (d) None of these

Further Reading

1. B. Cornell and M. Reinganum, "Forwards and Futures Prices: Evidence from Foreign Exchange Markets," *Journal of Finance* 36 (December 1981): 1035–1045.

2. M. D. Fitzgerald, *Financial Futures* (London: Euromoney Publications, 1983).

3. Daniel Siegal and Diane Siegal, *Futures Markets* (Chicago: Dryden, 1990).

4. John C. Hull, *Options, Futures, and Other Derivatives* (New Jersey: Prentice Hall, 1997).

5. Robert A. Strong, *Derivatives* (Cincinnati, Ohio: Thomson Learning, 2002).

CHAPTER

7

Currency Options

CHAPTER OBJECTIVES

After studying this chapter, you should be able to:

1 Describe currency options and understand their relevance.

2 Identify different forms of options.

3 Explain the payoff profiles of standard options.

4 Understand the concept of option value.

5 Discuss the determinants of currency option price.

6 Analyse options trading strategies.

7 Explain the applications of options pricing models.

8 Discuss option Greeks.

9 Define options on futures.

10 Distinguish between forwards and options, and analyse when each of these is appropriate.

11 Discuss options trading in India.

Introduction

Options are versatile and flexible hedging tools widely used by traders, investors, and speculators. There are different kinds of options, such as stock options, commodity options, and currency options. Although options as financial instruments have a very long history, trading in currency options first began in the1980s. Volatile foreign exchange markets, capital account liberalization, and financial innovations have all contributed to the growth and development of options markets across the world. And despite their relatively short history, currency options have been growing in popularity over time. According to the BIS Triennial Central Bank Survey (2013), the global foreign exchange market turnover (daily average) in options increased from USD 87 billion in 1988 to USD 207 billion in 2010 and to USD 337 billion in 2013. The U.S. dollar is the most widely used currency in options, accounting for more than 87 percent of the global daily average turnover in options.

Currency options are used in a variety of situations in which foreign exchange exposure and risk are involved. Traders, corporations, and investors use options to hedge the price risk they face in their operations. In addition, currency options are used by those with small amounts of capital to speculate on exchange rate changes and take advantage of market movements.

The flexible character of options enables market participants to create tailor-made risk management strategies.

Like currency forwards and futures, currency options are *derivative securities,* in the sense that their value is derived from the value of the underlying position. As exchange rates change, so do option values. A feature of options that distinguishes them from forwards and futures is that with options only one party (the seller of the option) has an obligation to execute the contract (either to buy or sell), whereas in forwards and futures both parties are obligated to execute the contract. The buyer of an option is under no obligation to buy/sell at the strike price, and may walk away from the contract at maturity and transact in the spot market, if the spot rate has moved in his favour. Thus, an option combines the protection provided by a forward contract with the flexibility to deal in the spot market. The main objective of hedging with currency options is to get the best protection at the least possible cost.

*An **option** is a contract that entitles the buyer or holder of the option to a right to buy or sell the underlying asset, security, or currency. The seller (also called writer) of the option grants this right at a price, which is known as the option premium.*

An **option** is a derivative contract in which the writer of the option grants the buyer the right, but not the obligation, to purchase from or sell to the writer the underlying foreign currency or another contract at a specified rate, within a specified period of time or at a fixed date.

Some important features of options are as follows:

- The writer of an option, also called the seller, grants the right to buy in return for a certain amount of money, which is known as the *option premium* or *option price.* The option premium is therefore a fee to be paid by the buyer for receiving the right to buy or sell the underlying currency or another financial contract. The option premium is paid upfront.
- The price at which the buyer of a call option has the right to purchase the underlying foreign currency, or at which the buyer of a put option has the right to sell the underlying foreign currency, is called the *exercise price* or *strike price.*
- The date on which the contract matures, or after which the contract becomes void, is called the *expiration date.*
- In colloquial terms, buying an option is *going long* and writing an option is *going short.* In other words, the buyer or holder of an option takes the *long position,* and the writer or seller of an option takes the *short position.*
- A currency option is like a stock option or commodity option, except that the underlying asset is foreign exchange.
- The downside risk of an option for the buyer is limited to the premium he pays to the writer of the option. Although the premium is small, the probability of losing it is very high. As far as the writer of an option is concerned, he receives a premium, but is exposed to unlimited loss, if the market moves against his position.
- Options enable the buyer of an option to exercise his right only if it is in his interest. The option holder may let the option contract expire, if the rate stated in the option is not to his advantage. This is known as the *throwaway feature* of options. Here, "exercising" refers to the action taken by the holder of the option to buy or sell the underlying foreign currency at the option strike price.

Currency options can be categorized into call options *and* put options. *They can also be classified as* American options *and* European options. Exchange-traded options *and* over-the-counter (OTC) options *form a different kind of classification of options.*

Forms of Options

Options may take different forms, like call options, put options, European options, American options, exchange-traded options, and over-the-counter (OTC) options. A brief description of each of these is given in the following paragraphs.

Call Options and Put Options

An option that grants the buyer the right to *purchase* the underlying currency from the seller (writer) is called a **call option**. In contrast, if the buyer is granted the right to *sell* the underlying currency to the writer, such an option is called a **put option**. The call option buyer expects the underlying foreign currency to strengthen against the home currency during the life of the option. For put options, on the other hand, the buyer's forecast would be that the foreign currency will weaken against the home currency during the life of the option. Call and put options are simple but standard options. They are also known as *vanilla options.*

*A **call option** gives the option buyer the right to buy the underlying currency from the writer, while a **put option** gives the buyer the right to sell the underlying currency to the option seller.*

Call and Put Options as Insurance Contracts Buying a call option is like buying an insurance contract against the risk of high foreign exchange rates. For example, consider an Indian firm that faces a future outflow of USD 100,000. So, it may buy a call option on the U.S. dollar at a strike price of, say, INR 60.4356. This gives it the right to buy USD 100,000 at INR 60.4356. In other words, the firm will pay no more than INR 60.4356 per USD. Much in the same way, buying a put option is like buying an insurance contract against the risk of low foreign exchange rates. For example, consider an Indian firm that expects a future inflow of USD 200,000. So, it might buy a put option on USD at a strike price of INR 61.7890 This means that the firm cannot get less than INR 61.7890 per USD. Thus, the call option sets a maximum price for the holder of the option to buy the underlying foreign currency, and the put option sets the minimum price for the holder of the option to sell the underlying foreign currency.

As every foreign exchange transaction involves buying one currency and selling another, every currency option is both a call and a put. For example, a call option to buy USD is equivalent to a put option to sell INR. Thus, a put option on the foreign currency is nothing but a call option on the domestic currency, and a call option on the foreign currency is equivalent to a put option on the domestic currency.

As in any insurance contract, the premium is paid to the seller (writer) of the option by the buyer for receiving a privilege (the right to buy or sell). The premium is also the maximum amount the option buyer will lose in case of adversity. The seller of the option is obligated to take the opposite underlying exchange rate spot position if the buyer of the option exercises his right. Thus, the seller of the option is likely to face exchange rate risk, and the premium paid by the buyer is supposed to cover such risk. As option writers face unbounded risk, they seek to protect themselves by hedging or offsetting transactions. An example of such transactions is given in the following paragraphs.

Alternative Scenarios Assume that an Indian firm has an obligation in three months' time to pay USD 10 million for importing merchandise. The firm has the following alternatives:

(a) *Remain unhedged.* This would involve purchasing the USD 10 million at the prevailing spot rate on the date of payment in three months.

(b) *Hedge by buying USD forward.*

(c) *Hedge by using options.*

If the firm decides to take the third choice, then it will buy a USD call option. The effect of buying the call option is to place a ceiling on the cost of imports without limiting the potential benefit, if the spot rate of the USD/INR falls.

The Indian firm purchases a three-month call option at a strike price of USD/IND 61.3489 and pays an option premium. On the date of expiry of the option, the firm might face the following scenarios:

- **Scenario I:** The spot rate of USD/INR is 61.1234. As the spot rate is lower than the strike price, the firm lets the option expire and buys USD 10 million in the spot market at INR 61.1234.

- **Scenario II:** The spot rate of USD/INR is 61.8967. In this scenario, as the spot rate is higher than the strike price, the firm exercises the option and buys USD 10 million at the strike price of INR 61.3489.

Now, consider an example of put option. The same Indian firm, for example, exported goods to the United States for USD 5 million. The amount is payable in six months. So, the firm has purchased a six-month put option with a strike price of USD/IND 61.3489. The firm has also paid an option premium. On the day of maturity, the firm might face the following scenarios:

- **Scenario I:** The spot rate of USD/INR is 61.9789. As the spot rate is higher than the strike price, the firm lets the put option expire and sells USD 5 million in the spot market at INR 61.9789.
- **Scenario II:** The spot rate of USD/INR is 61.2312. In this situation, the firm exercises the put option and sells USD 5 million at the strike price of INR 61.3489.

It may be noted that a long position in the foreign currency can be hedged by being long in foreign currency puts, and a short position in the foreign currency can be hedged by being long in foreign currency calls.

Exotic Options

The main objective of the buyer of exotic options is to reduce or totally avoid the upfront option premium payable for standard options like calls and puts.

In recent times, many kinds of options based on more complex conditions have been designed in order to meet a wide variety of requirements of market participants. *Exotic options* are options that have features of two or more different kinds of options. They include *knock-in options, knock-out options, reverse knock-in options, reverse knock-out options,* and *average rate options.* The main objective of the buyer of exotic options is to reduce or totally avoid the upfront option premium payable for standard options like calls and puts. Here, it is important to note that, for reducing or totally avoiding the premium, the option buyer may give up a part of the protection or benefit.

Knock-in options are similar to vanilla options except that they come into effect only, if the spot rate of the underlying currency reaches a particular level during the life time of the option. If the *knock-in level* is not reached before the expiration date of the option, the option does not get a life. For example, a put option with a strike of USD/INR 60.7345 may incorporate an additional feature or condition that the option would come into effect only if the spot rate of USD/INR moves above INR 61.1245 at any time during the life time of the option. Much in the same way, a call option may have an additional condition that the option would come into effect only, if the spot rate of the underlying currency moves below a particular level, say USD/INR 61.00. By any chance, if the spot rate never moves above/below that level before the expiry date, the option would not come into effect. Once the options are knocked-in, they become the standard put/call options. Generally, the value of a knock-in option is lower than that of a standard option (vanilla), because a knock-in option may not come into effect at all during the lifetime of the option. Thus, in the case of knock-in options, the buyer risks not having any cover or benefit at all, if the spot rate of the underlying currency fails to reach a specified trigger level.

Knock-out options are also similar to vanilla options, except that they cease to exist, if the spot rate of the underlying currency reaches a particular level during the life of the option. If the *knock-out level is* reached before the expiration date of the option, the option becomes void. For example, a put option with a strike of USD/INR 61.000 may incorporate an additional feature or condition that if the spot rate of USD/INR moves above INR 61.5678 at any time during the life of the option, the option gets knocked out. In the same way, a call option with a strike price of, say, USD/INR 61.5678 may have an additional condition that the option would cease to exist, if the spot rate moves below a particular level, say,

USD/INR 61.1234. Until the spot rate reaches the pre-specified rate, the option is like a standard option.

Knock-out levels are usually set such that the option lapses when it is out-of-the-money. It all depends on the forecast of the future spot rate of the underlying currency. Knock-out levels are also related to the relative premium cost of the option. Generally, the closer the knock-out rate is to the spot rate, the cheaper is the option. Once the knock-out position is reached, the buyer may have to remain uncovered, deal in the spot market, deal in the forward market, or select a new option. Options that get knocked out when the spot rate of the underlying currency touches a higher trigger level are also known as *up-and-out options,* while those that get knocked out when the spot rate hits a lower trigger level are called *down-and-in options.*

A knock-in option in which the barrier is in-the-money (i.e. above the spot rate for a call, or up and in, and below the spot rate for a put, or down and in) is called a *reverse knock-in option.* A knock-out option in which the barrier is in-the-money (above the spot rate for a call, and below the spot rate for a put) is called a *reverse knock-out option.*

Knock-in and knock-out options are also known as *barrier options,* as they incorporate a barrier level (trigger level) of spot rate of the underlying currency to come into effect or to cease to exist. As can be observed from our discussion, option have additional conditions locking in the direction of the movement of the spot rates opposite to the direction desired for the options to be in-the-money. The barrier levels depend upon the forecast of the future spot rates of the underlying currency as well as the relative premium cost of the option. Traders buy barrier options when they have a specific view about the movement of spot rates and want to reduce the cost of options. The closer the knock-out level is to the spot rate, the less expensive is that option, because the probability that the barrier will be reached is increased. On the other hand, the closer the knock-in level is to the spot rate, the more expensive is the option, because of the higher probability that the barrier will be reached. Knock-in and knock-out options are used to design cost-effective hedging strategies as they carry lower premiums.

Barrier options are also of two types: *single-barrier options* and *double-barrier options.* If an option has barriers on either side of the strike price (i.e. one trigger price above the strike price and the other trigger price below the strike price), it is known as a double-barrier option. An option that has one barrier, which may be either greater than or less than the strike price, is known as a *single-barrier option.*

Another category of exotic options is *basket options.* Basket options are a cost-effective solution to managing multi-currency exposures on a consolidated basis. A basket option is an option with a strike price based on the weighted value of the component currencies in a portfolio of currencies. If the total value of the component currencies according to their spot rates is less favourable than the strike price, the basket option will be allowed to lapse. Alternatively, if it is more favourable, the holder of the option exercises the option. Basket options are more useful for fund managers who want to protect the total value of a basket of currencies against unfavourable movements of spot rates. The cost of basket options is generally lower than multiple single-currency options. The lower the correlation between the currencies that constitute the basket, the greater the cost savings.

Average-rate options are another category of exotic options. The strike prices of these options are determined through an averaging process at certain time intervals. The averaging dates can be as frequent as required, and need not be at regular intervals. The averaging amounts do not have to be equal. The option specifies the currency pair, the contract amount, the expiry date, the strike price, and the averaging dates. On the date of maturity of the option, the holder of the option will receive the difference between the weighted-average spot rate over the given period and the agreed strike price, if the option is in-the-money.

For example, assume an Indian firm exports goods to the United States and receives USD 5 million every month in the following year. In order to protect against currency risk, the firm buys a one-year average-rate put option at a strike rate of USD/INR 61.1234. The firm receives USD 5 million every month and sells the U.S. dollars in the spot market. At expiration, the strike price of INR 61.1234 is compared with the average rate over the year, based on the rate fixed on a particular day in a month. If the average of the 12 monthly exchange rates on the prescribed days is higher than the strike price, the writer of the option will, at expiration, compensate the firm with cash payment equal to the difference between the strike price and the average rate over the period on the contracted amount. If, on the other hand, the average of the 12 monthly exchange rates is lower than the strike price, the firm will conclude that it would have been able to benefit from favourable currency rates over the year by dealing in the spot market. Thus, the option is allowed to expire.

In the case of a call option (average-rate option), if the average of the 12 monthly rates is lower than the strike price, the writer of the option will, at expiration, pay to the firm an amount equal to the difference between the strike price and the average rate over the period on the contracted amount. If, on the other hand, the average of the 12 monthly fixings is higher than the strike rate, then by dealing in the spot market, the firm would have been able to benefit from favourable currency rates over the year. In this situation, the option is allowed to lapse.

A *range forward* is an option that requires the hedger to simultaneously buy a put option and sell a call option. The amounts and maturity dates for both options are usually the same and the strike prices are set to be out-of-the-money. The strike price of the call is greater than the forward rate, and the strike price of the put is less than the forward rate. The strike prices are set in such a way that their midpoint is at or near the forward rate. In range forwards, the hedger has the flexibility to determine the range between the strikes of the two options. A wide range offers more opportunity to gain from favourable spot rate movements, but simultaneously increases exposure to losses. Conversely, a tighter range reduces the potential for both profits and losses. Further, the strike prices are chosen such that the premium of the call and the put are equal. For example, consider a firm that has a USD 0.50 million liability one month from now. The current spot rate is USD/INR 61.5634, and the one-month forward rate is USD/INR 61.9867. The firm buys an out-of-the-money call option with a strike of INR 62.0000, and sells an out-of-the-money put option with a strike of INR 61.6453. The premium received on the put option exactly offsets the premium paid on the call option. If the spot rate on the expiry date of the option is above INR 62.0000, the firm exercises the call at INR 62.0000. Alternatively, if the spot rate is less than INR 61.6453, the put option is exercised. Finally, if the spot rate on the expiry date is between INR 61.6453 and INR 62.0000, the firm pays the prevailing spot rate to buy USD 0.50 million. Thus, range forwards provide the flexibility to benefit from favourable exchange rate movements, while limiting risk to an acceptable level at a small or no cost.

Participating forwards protect traders against unfavourable changes in the spot rates of foreign exchange, while letting them participate in favourable changes in spot rates. For example, consider a company that has purchased an out-of-the-money U.S. dollar three-month call at a strike price of USD/INR 61.9678, underlying USD 1 million. This gives the company the right to buy U.S. dollars at the rate of INR 61.9678 in three months' time. At the same time, the company sells an in-the-money U.S. dollar three-month put at the same strike price, underlying USD 0.50 million. This obliges the company to buy U.S. dollars at INR 61.9678, if the option is exercised. These two contracts create a participating forward that guarantees INR 61.9678 as the lowest selling price and let the company participate in favourable exchange rate movements, if the spot rate moves above INR 61.9678. There are no upfront costs. If, at expiry, the USD dollar strengthens to INR 62.0000, the company will exercise its call option and buy U.S. dollars. In this scenario, the put option will expire. However, if the U.S. dollar weakens to a spot rate below INR 61.9678, the buyer of the put option will exercise the put option at INR 61.9678, and the call option will expire. So, the company is committed to paying INR 61.9678 for 50 percent of the call option amount, and in return the company has a free call option for the remaining 50 percent of the exposure that has been hedged. The company has anticipated the depreciation of USD. But to hedge itself against the possible appreciation of the U.S. dollar, it has purchased the USD call option. To finance the purchase of this call, the company has sold a put option for a smaller amount. Depending on the type of exposure, the underlying put amount may be less than or greater than the underlying call amount. For example, in the case of exporters, the underlying put amount will be less than the underlying call amount, and in the case of importers, the underlying call amount will be less than the underlying put amount. Further, the amount of downward exposure or upward exposure one is prepared to bear, will determine the extent of participation in favourable movements of spot rates.

In addition to the type of options described here, there are options like look-back options, compound options, and contingent options. Many innovative option products are continuously being developed, particularly by banks, to satisfy the requirements of their clients. Speculators also take part in these innovations.

American-style Options and European-style Options

*American options can be exercised at any time up to and including the expiration date of the contract, whereas **European options** can be exercised by the option holder only on the expiration date of the option contract.*

American-style options are options that can be exercised at any time up to and including the expiration date. Options that can be exercised only on the expiration date are referred to as European options or **European-style options**. From these definitions, it is obvious that American options offer more flexibility in terms of the period when they can be exercised. Thus, an American option is at least as valuable as the equivalent European option as it provides the buyer with more opportunities. However, American options are analytically more complex. In view of this, the bulk of trading in the options market, particularly in the interbank market, consists of European options.

Exchange-traded Options and OTC Options

Options, like other derivatives, are traded either in an organized exchange or in the over-the-counter (OTC) market.

Exchange-traded options offer the advantage of a standardized exercise price and expiration date. Transaction costs are lower for exchange-traded options than for OTC options. The clearing house associated with exchange-traded options may perform the functions as it does in the futures market. It positions itself between every buyer and seller of an option, and acts as a guarantor of an option trade. In other words, the clearing house becomes a buyer to every seller and a seller to every buyer, and thereby guarantees performance on the part of every participant. Since the option buyer pays the premium at the time the contract is initiated, he may not be required to post any security margin. However, the option writer is required to provide collateral to ensure performance on his part when the option is exercised. The main disadvantage of the exchange-traded options is that the options cannot be tailored to meet the special needs of the end users, because the market offers standardized contracts and amounts for a limited number of currency pairs and for selected maturity dates.

Currency options are traded on a number of organized exchanges worldwide. For example, the Philadelphia Stock Exchange (PHLX) offers USD-settled options on the Australian dollar, British pound, Canadian dollar, euro, Japanese yen, and the Swiss franc. The underlying contract size is 10,000 units of foreign currency (1,000,000 for the Japanese yen). Since the options are USD settled, no delivery or receipt of foreign currency occurs. The exercise style of PHLX currency options is European. This means that the options can be exercised only on the last trading day prior to expiration (usually a Friday). However, they can be bought or sold prior to expiration. The clearing house of the PHLX is known as the Options Clearing Corporation (OCC).

Over-the-counter options are private option arrangements between brokerage firms and other institutional dealers. The parties enter into private options when they need a contract with characteristics that are not available with exchange-traded options. The specifications of OTC options, such as the amount, exercise price, and expiration, are generally negotiable. So, these options can be tailor-made according to the requirements of the parties. In other words, OTC options can be customized like forward contracts. The OTC options market is a 24-hour market and it has its own conventions and practices. It also offers a large number of currency pairs and maturities (from same day to some years in the future). Commercial banks and investment banks are the principal players in the OTC options market, and they are generally the principal writers of currency options. The major clients or buyers of currency options are commercial enterprises, corporations, and financial institutions that are exposed to currency risks. The OTC options market consists of the retail market segment as well as the wholesale market segment. The retail segment is mostly composed of traders, corporations, and financial institutions; whereas the wholesale market consists of commercial banks, investment banks, and specialized trading firms. Typically, OTC options are negotiated for much larger amounts than exchange-traded options. The volume of trading in OTC options is much larger than that of exchange-traded options.

The main limitation of OTC options is that they are risk-prone, because the counterparty may sometimes be unable to perform in accordance with the terms of the contract. That is, default risk is a major concern in the OTC market, as OTC options are not generally collateralized. The default risk, however, is one sided. The seller of an option does not face such risk because he receives the option premium upfront. But the buyer may be worried about the seller's ability and integrity to honour the terms and conditions of the option. Further, OTC options are less liquid as they cannot be sold or purchased quickly at a reasonable price.

It may be noted that the OTC options market is not a market in the traditional sense, because there is no central trading location. Most of the trading is conducted by telephone or through electronic trading networks. The two markets—the exchange-traded options market and the OTC options market—are competitors, but they also complement each other. Market participants use both markets to determine option prices, and they also cash in on arbitrage opportunities whenever they exist between the two markets.

In-the-Money, Out-of-the-Money, and At-the-Money

The strike rate of an option may be higher or lower than the spot rate during the period of the option. It is also possible that the strike rate equals the spot rate. Depending on the movement of the spot rate, the options may be termed as in-the-money, out-of-the-money, or at-the-money.

*A call option is said to be **in-the-money** if the strike rate is below the spot rate of the underlying currency. On the contrary, a put option is in-the-money if the exercise rate is above the spot rate.*

In-the-Money

A call option, which gives the holder the right to buy a foreign currency, is said to be **in-the-money** when its strike rate is below the spot rate. This is because the option holder can buy the underlying foreign currency at a rate that is below the spot rate. The reverse is true for put options. A put option, which gives the buyer the right to sell the underlying foreign currency, is said to be in-the-money when the exercise rate is above the current spot rate. The option holder will be better-off whenever the underlying foreign currency can be sold at a strike price that is above the current spot rate. To be substantially profitable (covering even the option premium), the option must be deep enough in-the-money. An option has intrinsic value when it is in-the-money.

Out-of-the-Money

A call option is **out-of-the-money** when it is not profitable to exercise the option at the current spot rate. When the strike price is above the spot rate, it is better to buy the underlying foreign currency at the spot rate than to exercise the option. A put option is out-of-the-money when the strike price is lower than the spot rate. The option holder will be worse-off, if the underlying foreign currency is sold at the strike price when it is below the current spot rate. Thus, out-of-the-money options expire and become worthless.

An option is ***out-of-the-money*** *if it is not profitable to exercise the option at the current spot rate. An option whose strike price exactly equals the spot rate is said to be* ***at-the-money****.*

An American-style option can be exercised at any time prior to its maturity. If an option is out-of-the-money at any time before maturity, it does not imply that it has no value. As long as there are chances that an option would become profitable, if exercised at a spot rate any time during the life of the option, that option has a value.

At-the-Money (ATM)

An option whose strike price exactly equals the spot rate is said to be **at-the-money**. In this case, the option has no intrinsic value. The probability of an out-of-the-money option actually moving into the exercise range before expiration is significantly less than that of an option that is already at-the-money.

Disposing of Options

The buyer or holder of an option may ultimately do one of the following with their options: exercise the option, sell the option at the market rate, or let the option expire. If the spot rate of the underlying foreign currency is favourable such that exercising the option becomes profitable, the option holder naturally *exercises the option* and makes a profit. If it is an American option, the option holder exercises the option at an appropriate time when he can maximize the profit before the option expires. To reach a decision, the option holder assesses whether the total proceeds at the expiration date would be greater if he were to hold the option, or if he were to exercise it prior to expiration and reinvest the cash proceeds until the expiration date.

Before the expiration date, another alternative for the option holder is to *sell the option itself at the market rate* to book the profit or to minimize the loss of the option premium. As long as an option has time remaining before expiration, it has time value. If the option holder wishes to sell it for its value, the next buyer can capture the remaining time value.

The third alternative is to *let the option expire*. If the spot rate movements are not favourable and thus not profitable to the option holder, he will allow the option to expire. This will restrict the option holder's loss to the option premium.

The Chemistry of Options

Options create different kinds of cash flows when purchased/sold or disposed of. The cash flows that arise from the perspective of the buyer and the writer are described in this section.

The Payoff Profile for the Call Option Buyer

A call option gives the holder the right to purchase a currency against another currency at a stated price, on or before a stated time. The writer of the option must deliver the underlying currency if the buyer chooses to exercise the option. Depending on the spot rate of the underlying currency, the option buyer makes a profit or loss. Suppose a market participant has entered into a 90-day call option by paying an option premium of INR 1 per USD for the right to buy USD 10 million at a strike rate of USD/INR 45. The net profit or loss on this call option at expiration at several possible spot rates is shown in Table 7.1.

At a spot rate of INR 45 or below, the option will not be exercised, resulting in a loss of INR 10 million, which is the option premium. At a spot rate above INR 45 but below INR 46, the option will be exercised, but the gain will not be sufficient to cover the option premium. At a spot rate of INR 46, the gain on the option just equals the option premium. This price is known as the *break-even rate.* Above a spot rate of INR 46, the option will be in-the-money to cover the option premium and yield a net profit. Beyond the break-even rate, the numerous possible spot rates yield unlimited profit. Thus, it is evident that a call option holder may not choose to exercise his right when the strike price is greater than the spot rate of the underlying currency, because it would be better to buy the underlying currency in the spot market than acquiring it by exercising his right to buy from the option writer.

The profit for the call option holder can be calculated as follows:

Profit = (Spot rate of the underlying currency) – (Strike price + Option premium)

The Payoff Profile for the Call Option Writer

An option is a zero-sum game, and a gain (loss) for a buyer of an option is a loss (gain) for the writer of the option. Therefore, the payoff profile for the writer of a call option can be obtained by reversing the signs on the values in the payoff profile for the buyer of a call option. The payoff profile in the example of the call option buyer (Table 7.1) shows that the writer earns INR 10 million for the option when the spot rate is USD/INR 45 and below. In such situations, the option is not exercised. At a spot rate above INR 45, the option will be exercised, and the writer will lose what the buyer gains. Thus, the writer of a call option hopes for the spot rate to be lower than the exercise rate, and accordingly expects the gain of the option premium.

When a market participant writes call options based on his underlying positions, he is said to be writing *covered calls.* The main purpose of this option strategy is to generate

Table 7.1 Payoff Profile for the Call Option Buyer

	Alternative spot rates(USD/INR) at expiration							
	40	42	44	45	46	48	50	52
Receipts on spot sale of USD (INR million)	–	–	–	–	460	480	500	520
Payment of premium (INR million)	10	10	10	10	10	10	10	10
Payment on exercise of option (INR million)	–	–	–	–	450	450	450	450
Net profit/loss (INR million)	(–)10	(–)10	(–)10	(–)10	0	20	40	60

additional income for a foreign currency holding that is not expected to change significantly in value in the near future. However, speculators write calls without owning the underlying foreign exchange. Such calls are known as *naked calls* or *uncovered calls*. The main idea behind writing naked calls is to speculate on changes in the foreign exchange rate and earn a profit. However, such speculative strategy involves a high degree of risk.

The profit for the call option writer can be calculated as follows:

Profit = Premium – (Spot rate of the underlying currency – Strike price)

The Payoff Profile for the Put Option Buyer

A put option gives the option holder the right to sell a currency against another currency at a specified price on or before a specified time. When the option holder chooses to exercise his right, the seller of the option must take delivery of the underlying currency and pay for the same as per the terms of the option. To describe the payoff profile of a put option buyer, consider an example in which a trader has purchased a 90-day put option at a strike rate of USD/INR 45 by paying an option premium of INR 1 per USD. The contract size is USD 10 million. The profit/loss at the expiration of a put option at several possible spot rates is shown in Table 7.2.

If the spot rate falls to INR 40, the holder of the put option will deliver USD 10 million (worth INR 400 million), and receive INR 450 million. Thus, the option holder will make a profit of INR 40 million, after factoring in the option premium of INR 10 million. As the spot rate falls further, the net profit to the option holder rises. Below a spot rate of INR 44, the gain on the put option will be more than the option premium. At a spot rate of INR 44, the gain on the put option equals the option premium, resulting in no profit and no loss to the option holder. At a spot rate above INR 44 but below INR 45, the holder would exercise the option. But the gain will be less than the option premium. At a spot rate of INR 45 and above, the option holder would not exercise the option and, therefore, would incur a loss of INR 10 million (the option premium). Thus, the holder of the put option will not exercise his right when the strike price is less than the spot rate of the underlying currency, because it would be better to sell the underlying currency at the spot rate than to exercise his right to sell the underlying currency to the option writer.

The profit for the buyer of the put option is defined as follows:

Profit = Strike price – (Spot rate of the underlying currency + Option premium)

Table 7.2 Payoff Profile for the Put Option Buyer

	Alternative spot rates (USD/INR) at expiration							
	38	40	42	44	45	46	48	50
Receipts on exercise of option (INR million)	450	450	450	450	–	–	–	–
Payment of premium (INR million)	10	10	10	10	10	10	10	10
Payment on spot purchase of USD (INR million)	380	400	420	440	–	–	–	–
Net profit/loss (INR million)	60	40	20	0	(–)10	(–)10	(–)10	(–)10

The Payoff Profile for the Put Option Writer

In the case of put options, the put option holder can exercise the option any time before the option expires, or at expiration. If the holder chooses to do so, the writer must pay the strike rate for each unit of the foreign currency contracted.

The buyer of a put option always wants the foreign exchange rate to go down as this enables him to make a profit. The writer of the put option, on the other hand, wants the foreign exchange rate to go up, or at least to remain above the exercise rate. If that happens, the put option will expire worthless, and the writer will not have to buy the underlying currency.

The payoffs for the writer of a put option are the values in Table 7.2, with signs reversed. The put option writer will make a profit of INR 10 million (paid for the option) when the spot rate is INR 45 and above, as at such levels of spot rate the option is not exercised. At a spot rate below USD/INR 45, the option will be exercised, and the writer will lose what the buyer gains. The writer of a put option always hopes for the spot rates to be higher than the strike rate, and accordingly expects a gain equal to the option premium. Thus, the payoff profile of the writer of an option is the mirror image of the option buyer's payoff profile.

The profit for the writer of the put option is calculated as follows:

$$\text{Profit} = \text{Premium} - (\text{Strike price} - \text{Spot rate of the underlying currency})$$

Graphical Representation of Payoff Profiles

The payoff profiles of option buyers and sellers are graphically represented in Figures 7.1 and 7.2. Figure 7.1 shows the payoff profile for buying and writing a call option. The strike rate of the option is denoted by *K*, and the option premium is denoted by *p*. As long as the spot rate is less than or equivalent to the strike rate, the buyer incurs a loss, which is equivalent to the option premium paid by the option holder. As can be observed in Figure 7.1, the buyer can make a profit only when the spot rate exceeds the sum of the strike rate and the option premium ($K + p$). The spot rate over and above ($K + p$) will yield an unlimited net profit to the buyer of the option. Since the option is a zero-sum game, the payoff profile of the writer of the option is a mirror image of the buyer's.

Figure 7.2 shows the payoff profile for the buyer as well as the writer of a put option. As can be observed, the put option buyer incurs a loss as long as the spot rate is equivalent to or greater than the strike rate. The maximum loss is the option premium paid by the buyer.

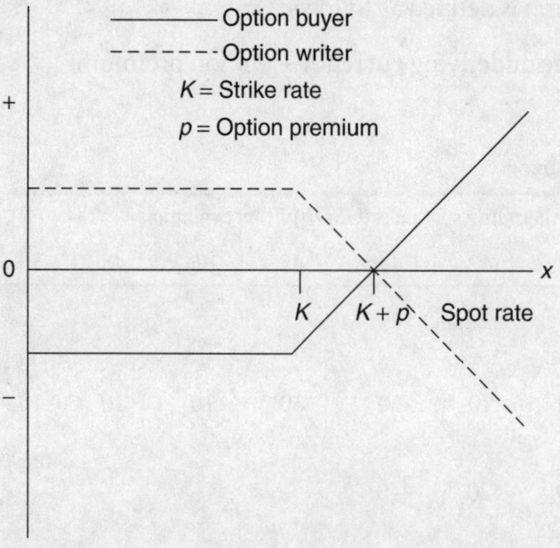

Figure 7.1

The Payoff Profile of a Call Option

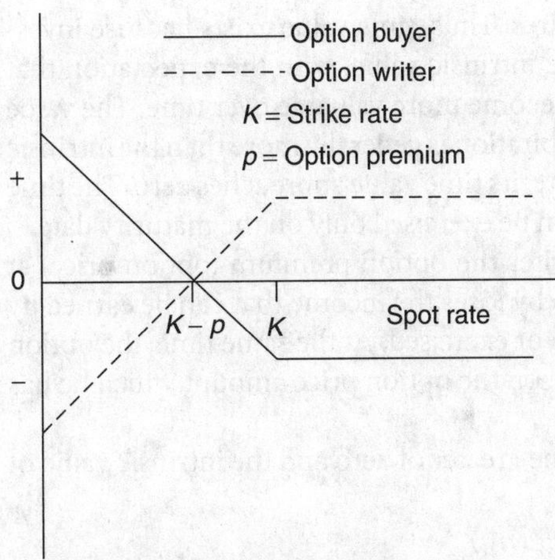

Figure 7.2

The Payoff Profile of a Put Option

As the spot rate falls and becomes lower than the strike rate minus the premium ($K - p$), the option yields a profit to the buyer of the put option. At the extreme, if the spot rate falls to 0, the buyer's profit will reach its maximum possible value. As in the call option, the payoff to the writer of a put option is equal in magnitude, but opposite in sign, to that of the option holder.

As can be observed from Tables 7.1 and 7.2, the options are at-the-money (ATM) when the spot rate is INR 45 and, therefore, the option buyer will lose the option premium of INR 10 million. The call option is in-the-money, if the spot rate is above INR 45, and the put option is in-the-money when the spot rate is below INR 45. The put option is out-of-the-money, if the spot rate is above INR 45, and the call option is out-of-the-money when the spot rate is below INR 45. The option premium of INR 10 million can be equated with an insurance premium for covering unfavourable events. If no unfavourable event takes place, the insurance contract simply expires.

Option Value

The value of an option comprises two components: time value and intrinsic value.

$$\text{Option value} = \text{Intrinsic value} + \text{Time value}$$

The **intrinsic value** of an option is the financial gain made by the holder of the option, if it is exercised immediately. In other words, the intrinsic value is the amount by which the option is in-the-money; it is the difference between the current spot rate of the underlying foreign exchange and the strike price. For example, the intrinsic value of a call option on the U.S. dollar with a strike price of INR 45 and a spot rate of INR 46 would be INR 1/USD. The intrinsic value of a call option for a spot rate below the exercise rate is zero. For a put option, the intrinsic value equals the amount by which the spot rate is below the exercise rate.

*The value of an option comprises two components: time value and intrinsic value. The **intrinsic value** of an option is the amount by which it is in-the-money. The **time value** of an option is the difference between the market value of the option and its intrinsic value. Note that an option can have time value only if it has time remaining before expiration.*

European options can be exercised only on their expiry date. However, they have intrinsic value if the corresponding forward rate exceeds the strike price. Out-of-the-money options and ATM options have no intrinsic value and can have only time value.

The **time value** of an option, also referred to as the *extrinsic value,* is the excess of the option value over its intrinsic value. In other words, the time value of an option is the difference between the market value of an option and its intrinsic value. When the option premium is the market value, the difference between the option premium and the option's intrinsic value (non-negative) is referred to as the option's time value. An option can have time value only if it has some time remaining before it expires. Thus, time value exists because investors are willing to pay more than the immediate intrinsic value, with the expectation that the option may move more in-the-money and become more valuable over time. The value of an American-style option any time prior to expiration is generally more than the intrinsic value. As the option approaches its expiration date, its time value approaches zero. The time value of a European option is always zero as it can be exercised only on the maturity date.

The buyer of an option pays the option writer the option premium (option price) at the time the option is purchased. The buyer thereby loses the income that can be earned by investing the option price until the option is sold or exercised. At the same time, the option writer (seller) has an opportunity to earn income on the option price amount which he has received upfront.

At expiration, the option value must equal the greater of zero and the intrinsic value of the option. Therefore,

$$C_T = \text{Max}\,(S_T - K, 0)$$
$$P_T = \text{Max}\,(K - S_T, 0),$$

where

C_T = Value of a call option at expiration
P_T = Value of a put option at expiration
K = Strike price
S_T = Spot rate of the underlying foreign exchange at expiration of option

At expiration, a European-style option and the corresponding American option will have the same terminal value. At any time prior to maturity, the American-style option must have a value that is at least as large as the maximum of its intrinsic value and zero. Thus,

$$C_t \geq \text{Max}\,(0, S_t - K) \quad \text{and}$$
$$P_t \geq \text{Max}\,(0, K - S_T)$$

where

C_t = Value of a call option at time t
P = Value of a put option at time t
S_t = Spot rate of underlying foreign exchange at time t

Option values can never be negative. A call option is in-the-money if $S_t > K$, ATM if $S_t = K$, and out-of-the-money if $S_t < K$. Similarly, a put option is in-the-money if $K > S_t$ ATM if $K = S_t$, and out-of-the-money if $K < S_t$.

Bounds for Option Prices

Every option contract has upper and lower bounds for its price. If the actual option price is above the upper bound or below the lower bound, there will be profitable opportunities for arbitrageurs.

A call option contract, whether American or European, gives the holder the right to buy the underlying foreign currency at a specified rate. The option can never be worth more than the spot exchange rate of the underlying foreign currency. Thus, the spot rate of the underlying foreign currency is the upper bound of the option price. This relationship can be expressed as follows:

$$C_t \leq S_t$$

A put option, whether American or European, gives the holder the right to sell the underlying foreign currency at a specified rate. In other words, the put option can never be worth more than the strike rate. Symbolically,

$$P_t \leq K$$

If these relationships do not hold, arbitrageurs can easily make a riskless profit by buying and selling the underlying foreign currency as well as the options.

A European-style put option will not be worth more than the strike price at expiration. At any time before expiration, it must not be worth more than the present value of the strike price. Therefore,

$$P_e \leq Ke^{-r(T)}$$

where

P_e = Value of a European put option
T = Time until option expiration
r = Risk-free interest rate

The lower bound for the value of a European call option is

$$c_e \geq \text{Max}\left[\frac{S_T}{(1+r_f)} - \frac{K}{(1+r_h)}, 0\right]$$

where

S_T = Spot rate at the time of maturity of the option contract
r_f = Foreign country interest rate corresponding to the length of option period
r_h = Home country interest rate corresponding to the length of option period
K = Strike price
C_e = European call option

To illustrate these relationships, let us consider two portfolios.

Portfolio I

- Buying one European call option; and
- Lending or investing an amount equivalent to the present value of the exercise rate of the call option at rate, r_h for the option period.

Portfolio II

- Lending an amount equivalent to the present value of one unit of a foreign currency at rate, r_f, corresponding to the period of the option.

The outflow for Portfolio I is

$$C_e + \frac{K}{(1+r_h)}$$

On expiration, if the spot rate of the underlying foreign exchange is less than or equal to the strike rate, the call option holder will let his option expire. However, if the spot rate is greater than the strike rate, the option holder will exercise the option. The value of the option will thus be the difference between the spot rate at the time of expiration and the strike rate. However, regardless of what happens to the spot rate of the foreign currency, the option holder will get back the amount lent with interest, which is equivalent to the strike rate of the call option. Since the worst that can happen to a call option is that it expires worthless, its value must be non-negative.

As far as the second portfolio is concerned, the outflow is

$$\frac{S_T}{(1+r_f)}$$

On the date of maturity, the investor will get back his amount, along with an interest amount at the foreign rate of interest. In home-currency terms, he will receive an amount of the underlying foreign currency at the spot rate prevailing at the time of expiration of the option.

If the spot rate at expiration is greater than the strike rate, Portfolios I and II would pay off the same amount—the spot rate of the foreign currency. If the spot rate is less than or equal to the strike rate, Portfolio I has a larger payoff than Portfolio II. To prevent arbitrage, Portfolio I will be priced to sell for at least as much as Portfolio II. This leads to the following lower bound on the value of the European call option:

$$c_e \geq \text{Max}\left[\frac{S_T}{(1+r_f)} - \frac{K}{(1+r_h)}, 0\right]$$

Similarly, for a European put option, the lower bound on the values is

$$P_e \geq \text{Max}\left[\frac{K}{(1+r_h)} - \frac{S_T}{(1+r_f)}, 0\right]$$

As in the case of a call option, two portfolios can be considered for a put option. Portfolio I consists of buying a put option and of lending a certain amount to get a strike rate at the end of the option contract. Portfolio II involves lending the present value of the strike rate at the foreign interest rate for the option period.

According to interest rate parity, the forward rate is given by the following equation:

$$F_T = \frac{S_t(1+r_h)}{(1+r_f)} \quad \text{or}$$

$$\frac{F_T}{(1+r_h)} = \frac{S_t}{(1+r_f)}$$

where

F_T = Forward rate for the time until option expiration

Thus, the lower bound of European options is restated as

$$C_e \geq \text{Max}\left[\frac{F_T - K}{(1+r_h)}, 0\right]$$

and

$$P_e \geq \text{Max}\left[\frac{K - F_T}{(1+r_h)}, 0\right]$$

Example 7.1

The current spot rate of the U.S. dollar is USD/INR 45. The 90-day interest rates (annualized) in India and the United States are 10 percent and 8 percent, respectively. The 90-day call on one U.S. dollar has a strike rate of INR 43. What is the lower bound on this European call option if the spot rate at the expiration date of the option contract is USD/INR 42 or USD/INR 45?

Solution

The two portfolios to be considered are as follows:

Portfolio I

Purchasing a European call option with a strike rate of INR 43 with premium C, and lending at the present value of INR 43, or [43 ÷ (1 + 0.10/4)], or INR 41.95. So, the total outlay is INR (C + 41.95).

Portfolio II

Lending an amount equivalent to the present value of one unit of foreign currency, or USD [1 ÷ (1 + 0.08/4)], or USD 0.9804. So, the total outlay in domestic currency is INR (45 × 0.9804) = INR 44.12.

Suppose that the spot rate at expiration is USD/INR 42. In this scenario, the call option is worthless and Portfolio I is worth INR 43. Portfolio II is worth USD 1, which is INR 42. Now, consider a second scenario, where the spot rate is USD/INR 45. Now, Portfolio I is worth INR 45 [that is, (INR 45 – INR 43) + INR 43], whereas Portfolio II is also worth USD 1, or INR 45. It is evident that if the spot rate is greater than the strike rate, Portfolios I and II have the same payoff. If, however, the spot rate is less than the strike rate, Portfolio I has a larger payoff than Portfolio II. Hence,

$$C_e + \text{INR } 41.95 \geq \text{INR } 44.12,$$

or

$$C_e \geq \text{INR } 2.17$$

This is the lower bound on the European call option value.

Determinants of Option Price

The major determinants of option price are the intrinsic value of the option, volatility of the underlying exchange rate, time to expiration of the option contract, the inflation differential, the interest rate differential, and the exercise price of the option.

There are several factors that influence the price of an option. Changes in any of these factors will bring about changes in option prices. Therefore, to be able to use currency options effectively, one needs to know how an option value reacts to changes in these variables or factors. The most important factors are briefly discussed in this section.

Intrinsic Value

Intrinsic value is what the option would be worth, if it is exercised immediately. Other things being equal, the higher the intrinsic value of an option, the higher is the option price. The intrinsic value, in turn, is determined by the currency spot rate and the strike rate. An option lets the option holder buy the underlying currency at a predetermined exercise price. So, the lesser the strike rate, the greater should be the worth of a call option. Further, as the spot rate of the underlying currency increases, the intrinsic value of the call option increases; this ultimately leads to an increase in the option price.

The intrinsic value of a put option changes in a direction opposite to that of a call option. Thus, the extent of the option in-the-money determines the price of the option. An option that is out-of-the-money has no intrinsic value and, therefore, no value. The value of an option can never be negative, as the option holder can always throw away the option. Thus, the value of an option must be either zero or the intrinsic value of the option, whichever is higher.

Volatility of the Spot Rate

As mentioned earlier, the holder of a call option benefits from an increase in the spot rate, but has limited downside risk in the event of spot rate decreases. Similarly, the holder of a put option benefits from a decrease in the spot rate, but has limited downside risk in the event of spot rate hikes. *Volatility* refers to the movements of the spot rate of the underlying currency pair around the trend. There are two kinds of volatility: historical volatility and implied volatility. *Historical volatility* refers to past movements of the exchange rate. When measured (usually by standard deviation), it gives a reasonable idea of how the exchange rate is likely to move in the future. *Implied volatility* reflects how the market itself expects the spot rate of the underlying currency to move. It is the volatility implied in the actual option premium of the traded option. Thus, implied volatility, which is the market's current estimate of the future spot rate behaviour of the underlying currency, is a critical factor in option pricing. With an increase in the volatility of the spot rate, the probability that the currency will do well or very poorly, increases. The higher the volatility, the greater is the probability that the option will expire in-the-money. In such cases, the option writer will face more risk and, therefore, he expects more risk premium. Consequently, the price of options will be high when the spot rate volatility is high.

As an example, consider two possible exchange rate situations: a high-volatility situation and a low-volatility situation. In a high-volatility situation, the exchange rate for USD/INR ranges from, say, INR 45 to INR 48. In a low-volatility situation, the exchange rate ranges from, say, INR 46 to INR 47. In both situations, the average exchange rate is INR 46.5. The exercise rate on a call option is also INR 46.5. The option payoffs in these two situations will be as shown in Table 7.3.

It is evident from Table 7.3 that the average option payoff is greater in the high-volatility situation than in the low-volatility situation. In other words, the option value increases as the volatility of the underlying exchange rate increases. The buyer will therefore pay more, and the seller will also demand a higher price for an option, if the volatility of the underlying exchange rate is higher.

Time to Expiration

An American-style option becomes more valuable as its time to expiration increases. If the maturity period is longer, there will be a greater chance that, at some time, the spot rate of the underlying currency will move in such a way as to benefit the option holder. For example, a currency option expiring in three months will have more value than the same option expiring in one month, because the spot rate of the underlying currency has more time left to eventually move in a favourable direction. For this extra life of the contract, the seller of the option demands an extra option premium (price). Thus, the longer the time to expiration, the higher the option price.

As explained earlier, American-style options have greater flexibility (they can be exercised at any time before the expiry date) as compared to European-style options and, therefore, American-style options are more valuable than European-style options. An American-style option can have a value that is at least as great as the maximum of its intrinsic value and the value of the corresponding European-style option, because the American-style option can also be held till maturity and its value cannot fall short of the corresponding European-style option. Further, a shorter-maturity European-style option can have more value than a similar European-style option with a longer maturity. This is because the longer the period, the more is the uncertainty with regard to the realizable value of the option.

Table 7.3 Option Payoffs in High and Low-volatility Situations

High-volatility situation							
USD/INR Exchange rate	45	45.5	46.0	46.5	47.0	47.5	48.0
Option payoff	0	0	0	0	0.5	1.0	1.5
Low-volatility situation							
USD/INR Exchange rate	46.0	46.25	46.5	46.75	47.0	—	—
Option payoff	0	0	0	0.25	0.5	—	—

The Inflation Rate Differential

A country with a high inflation rate relative to other countries will experience a decline in the value of its currency. An expected decline in the foreign exchange value of a currency increases the value of the put option on the currency. On the other hand, a country with low inflation rate will experience an increase in the value of its currency, which makes the call option on that currency worth more. Thus, the inflation rate differential between the home country and the foreign country also influences the value of the option.

The Interest Rate Differential

The foreign exchange value of the currency of a country with higher rates of interest tends to decline vis-à-vis those with lower rates of interest. All other things being equal, the greater the expected decline in the foreign exchange value of a currency, the higher is the value of a put option, and the lower is the value of a call option on the currency. Conversely, the greater the expected increase in the foreign exchange value of a currency (as a consequence of the decline in interest rates), the higher is the value of a call option, and the lower is the value of a put option on the currency. The value of a call option on a foreign currency increases, if the domestic interest rate rises or the foreign interest rate falls. The converse is true for put options.

The Strike Price

Strike price is also one of the variables that influence the value of an option. An in-the-money option is more valuable than an out-of-the-money option. The more an option is in-the-money, the higher is its intrinsic value, but the lower is its time value. An option that is ATM has the maximum time value. An option can be in-the-money, at-the-money, or out-of-the-money as determined by the strike price. Other things being equal, the higher the strike price, the lower is the price for a call option, but the greater is the price for a put option.

Trading Strategies

Call options and put options are the basic types of options. More complex and tailored structures are designed and engineered from these basic categories to meet the variety of requirements of end users. Market participants can make different trading strategies to create different payoff functions by combining basic options in different forms. The most popular of such option strategies are briefly described in this section.

Straddles

A market operator may expect the spot rate to make a big move, either up or down, but he may not have a precise idea of the *direction* in which the exchange rate will move. It is in this context that straddles come in handy. A **straddle** is an option combination that involves the simultaneous buying or selling of a call and a put with the same underlying foreign exchange, exercise price, and expiration date. A *long straddle* involves buying a call option and a put option, while a *short straddle* requires the sale of a call and a put. An at-the-money (ATM) call gives the buyer the upside potential, but it does not give any benefit in case of a large decline in the exchange rate. If an ATM put is added to the call, the buyer can profit from large movements in the exchange rate in either direction.

*A **straddle** is a type of option combination that involves simultaneous buying or selling of a call and a put with the same underlying foreign exchange, exercise price, and expiration date.*

Traders—both buyers and sellers—try to cash in on the volatility of foreign exchange rates. A straddle strategy is used by buyers during highly volatile market conditions, while sellers use this option strategy in stable market conditions. Sellers expect neither sharp rises nor sharp falls in the exchange rate of the underlying currency, while buyers expect a sharp swing in the exchange rate but are not able to anticipate the direction of change.

A long straddle becomes profitable if exchange rates rise or fall subsequent to the buying or selling of options. If the spot rate moves close to the strike rate of the option at expiration, the straddle leads to a loss. In other words, if the market remains stable without much volatility, the buyer loses the premium he paid for the option. But, if there is a large move in either direction, the straddle will result in a substantial profit. If the spot rate rises above the strike price, the buyer will exercise his right to the call option. The sharper the rise, the greater is the chance of making huge profits. If, however, the spot rate falls below the strike price, the buyer will exercise his right to the put option. The sharper the decline in the spot rate, the greater is the chance of earning a good profit.

Consider, for example, an investor who creates a straddle by buying both a put and a call with a strike rate of USD/INR 45 and an expiration date in three months. The call option premium is INR 1.25 per U.S. dollar, and the put option premium is INR 1 per U.S. dollar. Suppose the spot rate on expiration is INR 44. The call expires worthless, but the put is worth INR 1. If the exchange rate moves to INR 45, a loss of INR 2.25 is experienced. This is the maximum loss that can happen. If the exchange rate moves up to INR 55, a profit of INR 7.75 is made for each U.S. dollar of the contract amount, and if the exchange rate moves down to INR 30, a profit of INR 12.75 is made for each U.S. dollar of the contract amount.

When there is a likelihood that the foreign exchange rate will move towards the strike rate as expiration approaches, market participants may create a *top straddle* by selling a call and a put with the same exercise price and expiration date on the same underlying foreign currency. If the spot rate of the underlying currency remains very close to the strike price, the options will expire worthless and the writer will have both premiums to his advantage. This represents the maximum profit to the seller of the straddle. However, the seller of the straddle will incur losses, if there is a sudden swing in the spot rate in either direction, and such loss is unlimited. This is the reason why writing a straddle is considered to be a high-risk strategy.

Consider the following example to assess the profitability of a long/short straddle (purchasing both a call and put option/selling both a call option and a put option) at different spot rates.

An investor has the following rates available in Indian foreign exchange market.
Put option premium on USD: INR 0.030 per USD
Call option premium on USD: INR 0.035 per USD
Strike price for both call option and put option: 61.5678

The profitability of a long straddle is tabulated below:

	Spot rate (USD/INR) at the expiration of option				
	61.5000	*61.5028*	*61.5678*	*61.6328*	*62.0000*
Cash flows on call option	(0.0350)	(0.0350)	(0.0350)	0.0300	0.3972
Cash flows on put option	0.0378	0.0350	(0.0300)	(0.0300)	(0.0300)
Net cash flows	0.0028	0.0000	(0.0650)	0.0000	0.3672

It can be observed from the above table that there are two break-even points for a long straddle at the spot price of 61.5028 and 61.6328. One of them is below the strike price and the other is above the strike price. Maximum loss occurs when the spot rate is equal to the strike price. In other words, the straddle buyer would lose both option premiums when the spot rate is just equal to the strike price.

The profitability of a short straddle is tabulated below:

	Spot rate (USD/INR) at the expiration of option				
	61.5000	61.5028	61.5678	61.6328	62.0000
Cash flows on call option	0.0350	0.0350	0.0350	(0.0300)	(0.3972)
Cash flows on put option	(0.0378)	(0.0350)	0.0300	0.0300	0.0300
Net cash flows	(0.0028)	0.0000	0.0650	0.0000	(0.3672)

As can be observed from the above table, there are two break-even points for a long straddle at the spot price of 61.5028 and 61.6328. It is the same as in the long straddle. The maximum loss occurs when the spot rate is equal to the strike price. In other words, the straddle buyer would lose both option premiums when the spot rate is just equal to the strike price. The cash flows of a short straddle are exactly opposite to the cash flows of a long straddle.

Strangles

A strangle is similar to a straddle except that the call and the put have different strike rates. In other words, the put and call options on the same currency will have different strike rates but the same expiration date. A typical strangle involves buying a call with a strike price above the current spot rate and a put with a strike price below the current spot rate of the underlying foreign exchange. Like the straddle-buying strategy, the strangle-buying strategy involves expectations about market movements. Buyers expect a sharp swing in the spot rate of the underlying currency in either direction. Strangles, like straddles, yield net gain on drastic movements in spot rates, but a loss on moderate movements. The profit to be obtained with a strangle depends on how far apart the strike rates are. That is, the value of a strangle option increases along with the volatility of the spot rate of the underlying currency. The seller of strangle option will earn maximum profit, if the spot rate remains between both the strike prices, but his loss will be substantial if the spot rate moves far from the strike price. Thus, a short strangle strategy is a risky strategy, as the writer's potential loss is unlimited. However, the writer earns maximum profit, if both the put and the call options expire worthless.

Consider the following example to understand currency strangles:
Put option premium on USD: INR 0.030 per USD
Call option premium on USD: INR 0.035 per USD
Strike price for call option: 61.6328
Strike price for put option: 61.5678

The profitability of a long strangle is tabulated below:

	Spot rate (USD/INR) at the expiration of option				
	61.5000	61.5028	61.5678	61.6328	62.0000
Cash flows on call option	(0.0350)	(0.0350)	(0.0350)	(0.0350)	0.3322
Cash flows on put option	0.0378	0.0350	(0.0300)	(0.0300)	(0.0300)
Net cash flows	0.0028	0.0000	(0.0650)	(0.0650)	0.3022

As can be observed from the above table, the call option is in the money at the spot rate above 61.6328, and the put option is in the money at the spot rate below the strike price. At the spot rate of 61.5028, the strangle buyer would break even.

The profitability of a short strangle is tabulated below:

	Spot rate (USD/INR) at the expiration of option				
	61.5000	*61.5028*	*61.5678*	*61.6328*	*62.0000*
Cash flows on call option	0.0350	0.0350	0.0350	0.0350	(0.3322)
Cash flows on put option	(0.0378)	(0.0350)	0.0300	0.0300	0.0300
Net cash flows	(0.0028)	0.0000	0.0650	0.0650	(0.3022)

*A **strangle** involves buying a call option with a strike price above the current spot rate and a put option with a strike price below the current spot rate of the underlying foreign exchange.*

As can be seen from the above table, the strangle seller has a break-even point at the spot rate of 61.5028. The strangle seller gets the maximum gain at a spot rate between the two strike prices.

Strips, straps, and condors are some other speculative strategies that combine call options with put options. A *strip* involves a long position in one call and two puts with the same strike rates, same expiration dates and the same underlying foreign currency. A strap consists of a long position in two calls and one put with the same strike rates, expiration dates, and the same underlying foreign exchange. A *condor* involves four different strike rates: two for writing a condor and two for buying a condor.

Spreads

__Option spreads__ are speculative strategies in which a market participant simultaneously buys and sells options of the same type—two or more calls, or two or more puts—but with different strike rates and/or expiration dates.

Option spreads are speculative strategies in which a trader is simultaneously long and short in options of the same type, i.e. two or more calls, or two or more puts, but with different strike rates and/or expiration dates. The main purpose of option spreads is to realize a profit, if the underlying foreign exchange rate moves in a certain direction, while at the same time limiting the loss, if it does not.

The popular types of spreads are bull spreads, bear spreads, butterfly spreads, calendar spreads, and diagonal spreads. Let us take a look at each of these spreads.

Bull Spreads A trader, sometimes, believes that the spot rate of a currency is likely to rise, but he may not believe it will rise very much. In such cases, the trader wishes to sell off the extreme upside potential. Therefore, he buys a call option on a currency and, at the same time, writes a call against the same currency, but at a higher strike price.

A bull spread can be created by buying a call option on a foreign currency with a lower strike rate, and selling a call option on the same foreign currency with a higher strike rate. Both option contracts have the same expiration date. For example, consider a firm that buys a call option on the U.S. dollar at a strike rate of INR 45. Simultaneously, it sells a similar call option at a strike rate of INR 47. If the spot rate is, say, INR 46, the firm exercises the call option. But the option that the firm sold will not be exercised. However, if the spot rate of the underlying foreign exchange is INR 48 instead of INR 46, both the calls will be exercised. In this situation, the firm will make a profit on its long call position, but it will lose in the short call.

Bull put spreads can be created by buying a put with a lower strike rate and selling a put with higher strike rate. With such spreads, if a foreign currency appreciates significantly, neither put will be exercised, and the net gain will be the difference in the premiums. If a foreign currency depreciates significantly, the maximum gain will be the difference in strike rates minus the difference in premiums. In bull spreads, the initial net investment is the difference in the two premiums. Thus, bull spread strategies yield a limited profit, if the foreign currency appreciates and a limited loss, if it depreciates. They limit the trader's profit potential as well as his potential loss. Here, the term *bull* refers to rising exchange rates.

Bear Spreads Suppose a trader believes that a currency value is likely to fall, but he does not think it will fall very much. In this situation, he can sell off the extreme downside by creating a bear spread. A bear spread is created by buying the higher-strike call and selling the lower-strike call. Bear spreads can also be created by using puts instead of calls. A trader can create a bear put spread by buying a put with a higher strike rate and selling a put with a lower strike rate.

Bearish call/put spreads are the reverse of bullish call/put spreads. A market participant, while entering into a bear spread contract, expects the foreign currency to depreciate. Like bull spreads, bear spreads limit both the profit potential and the downside risk to the option holder. Bull spreads and bear spreads are also known as *vertical spreads.*

Butterfly Spreads Consider a situation where an investor believes that the foreign exchange rate will end up very close to the current spot rate. To get a payoff in such situations, the trader may expose himself to a small constant loss, if the spot rate ends up anywhere outside a particular range. A butterfly spread can be created by buying a call option with a lower strike rate, say X_1; buying a call option with a relatively higher strike rate, say X_2; and selling two call options with a strike rate that is halfway between X_1 and X_2. The halfway strike is generally close to the current spot rate of the underlying foreign exchange. Buying a butterfly spread yields a limited profit when there is a significant change in the exchange rate in either direction. However, for moderate changes, it results in a loss. Similarly, selling a butterfly spread involves selling two calls at an intermediate rate, and buying one call on either side. This strategy yields a little profit for moderate changes and limited loss for significant changes in either direction.

Butterfly spreads can also be created by using put options. This can be done by buying a put with a lower strike rate, buying a put with a higher strike rate, and selling two puts with an intermediate strike rate. A butterfly spread can also be sold by following the reverse of the buying strategy.

Calendar Spreads Calendar spreads involve simultaneous buying and selling of two options identical in all respects except their expiration dates. Calendar spreads can be created with put options as well as call options. They can be created by selling a call option with a specified strike rate, and buying a longer-maturity call option with the same strike rate. A trader can also buy a short-maturity option and sell a long-maturity option.

Calendar spreads are also known as *horizontal spreads,* as the options are selected horizontally from the columns of the financial pages that report option prices. A bull (an investor who believes that the market will rise) buys a call option with a distant expiration, and writes one that is near expiration. A bear (someone who believes that the market will decline) does the opposite. Short-maturity options are less valuable than long-maturity options because of time value.

Diagonal Spreads Diagonal spreads involve options with different expiration dates and different strike rates. Diagonal spreads are created by selecting options diagonally from the option listings in the financial press. Diagonal spreads can be bullish or bearish, and depending on the speculative strategies, different types of diagonal spreads are created.

Vertical, horizontal, and diagonal spreads get their name from the layout of the option listings in the financial press in the early days.

The Binomial Option Pricing Model

Though options are basically risk-reduction tools, they are used by investors to anticipate future levels of the underlying foreign exchange rates. In other words, option values are also used as parameters for estimating the future spot rate of foreign exchange. In fact, option value and future spot rate of the underlying foreign exchange have a cause and effect relationship, but it is difficult to discern which one is the cause and which one is the effect. Nevertheless, the forecast spot rate of underlying currency is used to determine the theoretical value of a currency option.

The binomial option pricing model is a popular technique used in determining the prices of different forms of options. The model is based on the assumption that there are only two possible states (rise or fall) of the spot rate of the underlying foreign exchange. The other main assumptions underlying this model are:

- There are no arbitrage opportunities.
- All riskless investments are priced to earn the risk-free rate.
- The interest rates, both foreign and domestic, are constant.
- There are no transaction costs, taxes, and margin requirements.
- Short selling is allowed without any restrictions.

The model primarily involves constructing a tree, known as a *binomial tree,* to represent possible states that might be assumed by the underlying foreign exchange rate over the life of the option. For example, consider the following example: The current spot rate of USD/INR is 45. It is expected that in one year, the INR price of the U.S. dollar will rise to INR 55 or fall to INR 40. This can be illustrated through the binomial tree in Figure 7.3. In the figure, uS_1 represents the spot rate of the foreign currency after one year with upward movement, and dS_1 represents the spot rate of the foreign currency after one year with downward movement.

Further, suppose Mr X can either buy or sell a call option on the U.S. dollar with an exercise rate of INR 47. The option is a European-style option that expires in exactly one year. So, on expiration, the call will have the values shown in Figure 7.4.

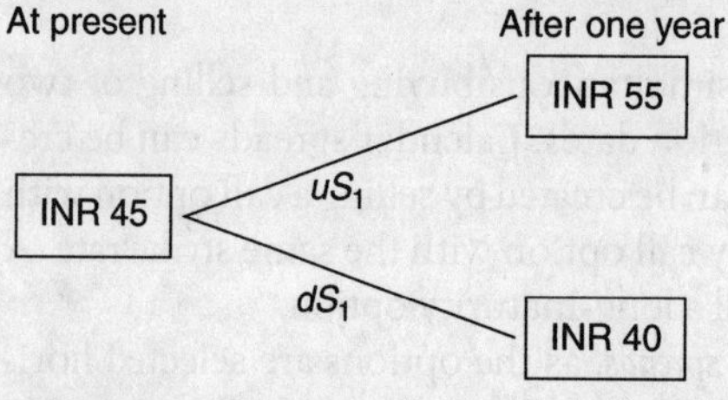

Figure 7.3

INR Price of the USD

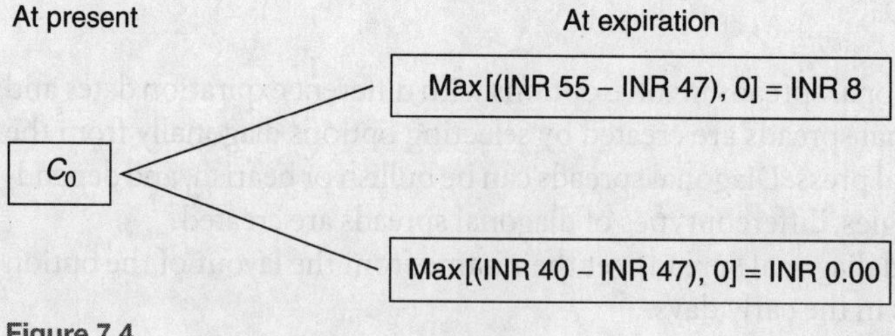

Figure 7.4

Value of the Call Option on Expiration

Though Mr X does not know what the call option is worth today, he knows what it is worth at expiration, given the forecast of the INR price of the U.S. dollar. If, for example, the expected value of the U.S. dollar is INR 47, what should be the price of the corresponding option contract today (C_0)?

The option values can be expressed as

$$C_{1u}=\text{Max}[(uS_1-K),0]$$
$$C_{1d}=\text{Max}[(dS_1-K),0]$$

where

C_0 = Current option value

C_{1u} = Option value after one year (at expiry) when upward movement takes place in the exchange rate

C_{1d} = Option value after one year (at expiry) when downward movement takes place in the exchange rate

uS_1 = Spot rate of foreign currency at expiry of call option, with upward movement

dS_1 = Spot rate of foreign currency at expiry of call option, with downward movement

K = Strike rate of the option

Thus, the domestic currency value of a foreign currency can either move up from the current spot rate (S_0) to a new level (uS_1) or down from current spot rate (S_0) to a new level (dS_1). Thus, at option expiry, the spot rate of foreign exchange will be either uS_1 or dS_1.

To derive a one-period binomial option pricing model for a call option, a synthetic risk-free portfolio, the payoff from which is identical to the payoff from the call option at option expiry, is designed. It is a risk-free portfolio because there is no uncertainty about the value of the portfolio at the end of the year (upon expiry of the option). Since the portfolio has no risk, the return earned on it must equal the risk-free interest rate.

The basic idea in designing a portfolio is that if the payoff from owning a call option can be replicated by purchasing the underlying foreign currency and borrowing funds, the price of the option is then, at most, the cost of creating the replication strategy.

Thus, to construct a replicating portfolio, N_d units of domestic currency are invested in a domestic risk-free security, and N_f units of foreign currency are invested in a foreign risk-free security, such that at option expiry, the value of the portfolio will be exactly equal to the value of the call option under every possible value of the spot rate of exchange.

Using the payoff matrix, we arrive at the following equations:

$$N_d e^{r_d} + uS_1 N_f e^{r_f} = C_{1u} \tag{7.1}$$

$$N_d e^{r_d} + dS_1 N_f e^{r_f} = C_{1d} \tag{7.2}$$

where

e^{r_d} = Continuously compounded domestic risk-free interest rate for the given period

e^{r_f} = Continuously compounded foreign risk-free interest rate for the given period

N_d = Number of units of domestic currency invested in domestic risk-free security

N_f = Number of units of foreign currency invested in foreign risk-free security

The left-hand expressions in Eqs. 7.1 and 7.2 represent the payoff from the portfolio with upward and downward movements, respectively, in the spot exchange rate.

Since Eqs. 7.1 and 7.2 are linear equations with two unknowns, the values of the two variables can be obtained by substitution.

So

$$N_d = \frac{uC_{1d} - dc_{1u}}{(u-d)e^{r_d}} \tag{7.3}$$

$$N_f = \frac{C_{1u} - C_{1d}}{(u-d)S_1 e^{r_f}} \tag{7.4}$$

As stated earlier, the portfolio and the call option should have identical payoffs at the end of the period. So, it is implied that they have identical values at the beginning of the period as well. Therefore,

$$C_0 = N_d + S_0 N_f$$

Substituting Eqs. 7.3 and 7.4 for N_d and N_f in Eqs. 7.1 and 7.2, the current value of the call option is

$$C_0 = \frac{[pC_{1u} + (1+p)c_{1d}]}{e^{r_d}}$$

where

$$P = \frac{e^{r_d - r_f} - d}{(u-d)}$$

u = One plus the percentage change in the foreign currency value if the domestic price of foreign currency goes up (i.e. the foreign currency appreciates)

d = One plus the percentage change in the foreign currency value if the domestic price of foreign currency goes down (i.e. the foreign currency depreciates)

If p is the probability of an upward movement in the spot rate, then $(1 - p)$ is the probability of a downward movement. Although p is not an explicit forecast, it is generated by the model. In other words, p is an implied probability of an upward spot rate movement. In order to avoid arbitrage opportunities, the model requires that:

$$d < \frac{(1+r_d)}{(1+r_f)} < u$$

If r_d and r_f are continuously compounded, then

$$d < e^{r_d - r_f} < u$$

where

r_d = Domestic risk-free interest rate for the given period

r_f = Foreign risk free interest rate for the given period

Thus, $N_d < 0$ and $N_f > 0$, implying that a portfolio consisting of domestic currency borrowing and a foreign currency deposit equals a long position in a call on one unit of the foreign currency.

For the data in the example illustrated by Figure 7.3, the values for u and d are calculated as

$$u = \frac{55}{45} \text{ or } 1+\frac{(55-45)}{45} = 1.2222$$

$$d = \frac{40}{45} \text{ or } 1+\frac{(40-45)}{45} = 0.8889$$

$$C_{1u} = \text{Max } \{0, (\text{INR } 55 - \text{INR } 45)\} = \text{INR } 10$$

$$C_{1d} = \text{Max } \{0, (\text{INR } 40 - \text{INR } 45)\} = \text{INR } 0.0$$

Thus, the option value will be either INR 10 or INR 0.0 at the end of the year. Having got the option value, the equivalent portfolio can be computed as

$$N_d = \frac{[1.2222(0.0) - 0.8889(10)]}{(1.2222 - 0.8889)e^{0.10}} = -\text{INR } 24.13$$

$$N_f = \frac{(10.0 - 0.0)}{[1.2222 - 0.8889(45)]e^{0.07}} = \text{USD } 0.6217$$

At maturity, the INR repayment is

$$24.13 \times e^{0.10} = \text{INR } 26.67$$

If the spot exchange rate has moved up, the value of foreign investment is:

$$1.2222(\text{INR } 45)\ (\text{USD } 0.6217)e^{0.07} = \text{INR } 36.67$$

In other words, the value of the investment is (INR 36.67 – INR 26.67), or INR 10, which is the same as the payoff from the call option C_{1u}. If the exchange rate has moved down, the investment value is INR 26.67. This will be enough to repay the borrowing. The value of the portfolio equals C_{1d}, which is zero. Therefore, the current value of the option (C_0) on one U.S. dollar is the outlay involved in acquiring the portfolio, which comes to (USD 0.6217 × INR 45) – INR 24.13 = INR 3.85.

The approach to the pricing option as described here is oversimplified, given that only two possible future states for the underlying foreign currency are assumed. In fact, it is unrealistic to assume only two possible outcomes for the future spot rate of a foreign exchange. To improve the accuracy of the process, the expiration date forecast of spot rates can be expanded to allow for numerous possibilities. The consequences of this expansion can be assessed by considering a simple revised forecast that includes only one additional potential spot rate, as given in Figure 7.5. Futher, the procedure can be extended by making the periods smaller and smaller, so that a fair value for the option can be calculated. Therefore, the time to expiration may be divided into as many sub-intervals as possible so that, at any point in time, the subsequent spot rate can only move up or down.

Although the basic approach to calculating C_0 is still conceptually valid, the exact methodology must be modified to account for more possibilities. In the example we are discussing, when only one additional sub-interval is introduced (sub-period S_1), the price tree takes the shape shown in Figure 7.6.

This tree diagram indicates that before the current spot rate can reach INR 55, it must first move up to INR 46 in sub-period S_1 before moving up a second time to its final value of INR 55. Similarly, the lower extreme of INR 40 can only be reached by two consecutive downward price changes. However, there are two different paths to the terminal outcome in the middle, INR 46.75, one up followed by one down, both reaching INR 46.75.

The next step in the process is to calculate the call option value by working backwards on each pair of possible spot rates with a strike rate of INR 47.

The two time-period foreign exchange binomial tree can be generalized as shown in Figure 7.7.

The corresponding option value of the binomial tree is shown in Figure 7.8.

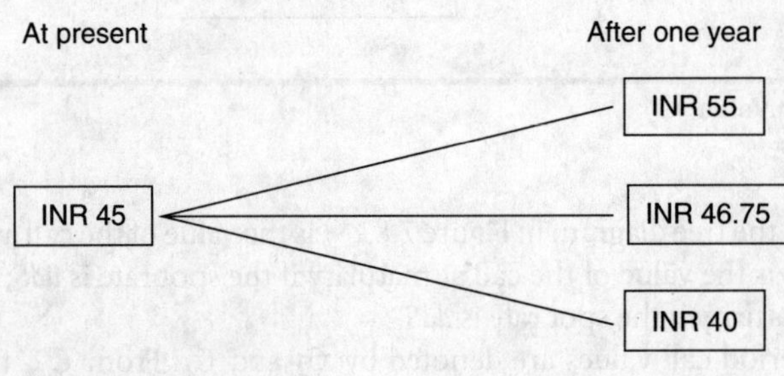

Figure 7.5

A Revised Forecast of Spot Rates

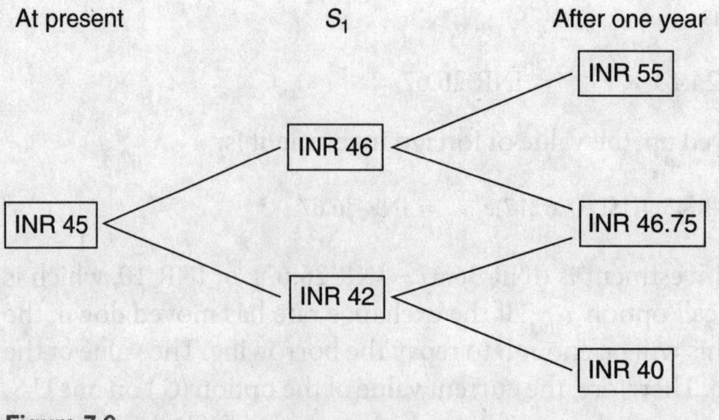

Figure 7.6

Spot Rates with Additional Interval

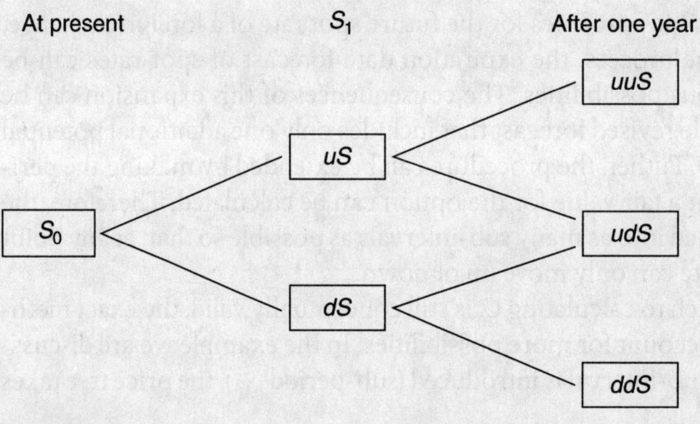

Figure 7.7

The Two-time-period Foreign Exchange Binomial Tree

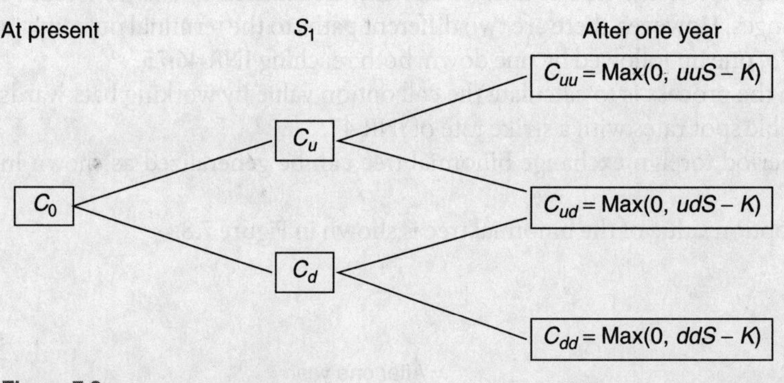

Figure 7.8

The Corresponding Option Value

As can be observed from the tree diagram in Figure 7.8, C_{uu} is the value of the call at maturity if the spot rate is *uuS;* C_{ud} is the value of the call at maturity if the spot rate is *udS*; and, C_{dd} is the value of the call at maturity if the spot rate is *ddS*.

The intermediate period call values are denoted by C_u and C_d. From C_u, the option value can go to C_{uu} or C_{ud}. So, to find C_u, a portfolio that will pay C_{uu} needs to be designed if the spot rate of foreign exchange moves up, or C_{ud} if it moves down:

$$C_u \frac{PC_{uu} + (1-P)C_{ud}}{e^{r_d/n}}$$

and

$$C_d \frac{PC_{ud} + (1-P)C_{dd}}{e^{r_d/n}}$$

Note that n denotes the number of sub-periods to maturity. If the sub-period is say, six months, then the annual interest rate (r_d), needs to be changed to $r_d/2$.

Accordingly, p is defined as

$$p = \frac{e^{(r_d - r_f)/n} - d}{(u-d)}$$

Having obtained the C_u and C_d, the C_0 (the current value of the call option) can be worked out as follows:

$$C_0 = \frac{p^2 C_{uu} + 2p(1-p)c_{ud} + (1-p)^2 c_{dd}}{e^{r_d/n}} \tag{7.5}$$

Thus, the current value of a call option is the present value of its expected value at expiry. The expected value at expiry is given as the sum of possible call values at expiry, each weighted by the probability of its occurrence. For example, p is the probability of C_{uu} as the spot rate goes up in each of the two sub-periods. Similarly, $(1-p)$ is the probability for C_{dd}.

Thus, options are evaluated by starting at the expiry of the option and working backwards to find its current value. The value at each sub-period can be calculated as the present value of the expected value at expiry. Denoting T as the period of the option contract and t as the sub-period, the value of the option at $(T-t)$ can be calculated as the present value of the expected value at time T for a time period t. Similarly, the value at each sub-period at $(T-2t)$ can be calculated as the expected value at time $(T-t)$ discounted for a time period t, and so on. By working back through all the sub-periods, the value of the option at time zero is obtained. In the case of an American option, it is necessary to check at each sub-period to know whether early exercise of the option is preferable to holding the option for a further time period t.

Eq. 7.5 can be extended to any number of sub-periods by recognizing that the value for C_j is one of the inputs for valuing the option in the preceding sub-period. Thus, the general binomial option valuation model is stated as

$$C_0 = \frac{1}{e^{r_d}} \sum_{j=0}^{n} \frac{n!}{j!(n-j!)} p^j (1-p)^{n-j} \text{Max}\{0, (u^j d^{n-j})S_0 - K\}$$

where

n = Number of sub-periods to maturity
r_d = Domestic interest rate through expiration
j = Up movements in the spot rate of the foreign exchange
$n-j$ = Down movements in the spot rate of the foreign exchange

The ratio gives $n!/j!(n-j!)$ the number of distinct paths that lead to a particular terminal value, $p^j(1-p)^{n-j}$ is the probability of getting to that value; and Max $\{0, (u^j d^{n-j})S_0 - K\}$ is the payoff associated with that value. The value of p is

$$p = \frac{e^{(r_d - r_f)T/n} - d}{(u-d)}$$

where

$u = e^{\sigma\sqrt{T/n}}$

$d = 1/u$

σ = Volatility (annual basis) of spot exchange rate as measured by standard deviation.

T = Time to expiration of option contract

r_d = Domestic risk-free interest rate for the whole period of the option contract

T/n = Length of each of n sub-periods of the life of the option

r_f = Foreign risk-free interest for the life of the option

To understand how T/n is calculated, assume that the life of the option is nine months. The sub-period duration is, say, three months. This means the life of the option has three sub-periods. Then, T= 0.75 (in terms of a year); and T/n = 0.25.

Let us understand the calculation of p with an example. Assume that the spot exchange rate between the British pound and U.S. dollar is GBP/USD 1.6972. The risk-free interest rate per annum is 4 percent in United States and 5 percent in the United Kingdom. The volatility of the exchange rate is 10 percent per annum. The life of the call option on British pounds is one year, which is divided into four sub-periods. Thus we have the following values:

$$r_d = 0.04;\ r_f = 0.05;\ \sigma = 0.10;\ \text{and } T/n = 0.25$$

$$u = e^{0.10 \times \sqrt{0.25}} = 1.0513$$

$$d = 1/1.0513 = 0.9512$$

$$P = \frac{e^{(0.04-0.05)0.25} - 0.92512}{1.0513 - 0.9512} = 0.4625$$

In a risk-neutral world, every investor is risk neutral in the sense that the investors require no compensation for risk. Accordingly, the expected return on all securities is the risk-free interest rate. This has implications for the option pricing model, which relies on the risk-neutral probabilities of the underlying foreign exchange increasing and decreasing in value. To illustrate the principle of risk-neutral valuation, suppose an investor knows that funds can be invested risk-free over one year at a continuously compounded rate of 10 percent. After one year, one unit of a currency will be worth $1 \times e^{0.10} = 1.1052$ for an effective annual return of 10.52 percent. The risk-neutral investor would be indifferent between investing in the risk-free rate of 10.52 percent and investing in the foreign currency, if it also has an expected return of 10.52 percent.

The Black–Scholes Valuation Model

The binomial option pricing model expects the spot rate of foreign exchange to change in distinct upward or downward movements. It is, therefore, is a discrete model. In reality, however, the spot rate of foreign exchange changes continuously over time. The Black–Scholes model has been developed to deal with such movements.

The Black–Scholes pricing model applicable to European-style currency options, as applied by Nahum Biger and John C. Hull, can be stated either in terms of spot exchange rates or in terms of forward exchange rates:

$$C_e = [F_T N(d_1) - KN(d_2)]e^{-r_d T} \quad \text{or,} \tag{7.6}$$

$$C_e = e^{r_f T}[S_0 N(d_1)] - e^{-r_d T}[KN(d_2)]$$

$$P_e = Ke^{-r_d T} N(-d_2) - S_0 e^{-r_f T} (N(-d_1) \quad \text{or,}$$

$$P_e = e^{-r_d T}[KN(-d_2) - F_T N(-d_1) \qquad (7.7)$$

The value of a put option can also be derived from put–call parity (see Section 7.13) in the following way:

$$P_e = C_e + (K - F_T)e^{-r_d T}$$
$$P_e = C_e - e^{-r_f T} S_0 + e^{-r_d T} K$$

In each of these equations,

C = Value of European call option on one unit of foreign currency
P = Value of European put option on one unit of foreign currency
S_0 = Current spot rate of foreign exchange rate
F_T = Current forward exchange rate for delivery at time T
K = Exercise price on one unit of foreign currency
r_d = Risk-free domestic interest rate in continuously compounded return
r_f = Risk-free foreign interest rate in continuously compounded return
T = Time to expiration of the option expressed as a fraction of one period
$N(.)$ = Standard normal cumulative distribution function

$$d_1 = \frac{\left\{ In\left(\frac{S_0}{K}\right) + \left[rd - rf + \left(\frac{\sigma^2}{2}\right)\right] T \right\}}{(\sigma\sqrt{T})} \quad \text{or}$$

$$d_1 = \frac{\left[In\left(\frac{F_T}{K}\right) + \left(\frac{\sigma^2}{2}\right) T \right]}{(\sigma\sqrt{T})}$$

Here,

$$d_2 = d_1 - \sigma\sqrt{T}$$

σ = Instantaneous standard deviation of the change in the spot exchange rate

P_e = Value of European put option on one unit of foreign currency

ln = Natural logarithm

$N(d_1)$ can also be interpreted as the probability of a call option expiring in-the-money. Since a put option with the same exercise rate is in-the-money whenever a call is out-of-the-money and vice versa, the probability of a put option expiring in-the-money is $[1–N(d_1)]$. Here, $N(d_1)$ is also called the *Black–Scholes Delta*. It measures the sensitivity of the option value to the changes in the spot rate.

The Black–Scholes option model is based on certain assumptions. Some of the key assumptions are:

(i) The risk-free interest rates are known and constant over the life of the option.
(ii) The probability distribution of foreign exchange rates is lognormal.
(iii) The option is to be exercised only at maturity, if at all.
(iv) There are no transaction costs.

Note that generally, the Black–Scholes model is valid only for European options. But the binomial model is valid for both European-style and American-style options.

Eqs. 7.6 and 7.7 are related through interest rate parity, which states in continuously compounded returns that

$$F_T = S_0 e^{(r_d - r_f)^T}$$

Thus, there is a direct relationship between interest rates (both domestic and foreign) and option values. In other words, interest rates affect the value of an option. For example, consider an American put option. If there is a significant decline in the spot rate of the underlying foreign exchange, the put option goes deep in-the-money. In such a situation, the holder of an American put option can exercise it immediately and invest the intrinsic value gained at an interest rate. In other words, a long position in a put can be hedged by borrowing in domestic currency and investing in foreign currency. Similarly, a long call is hedged by borrowing in foreign currency and investing in domestic currency. All things being equal, the higher the domestic interest rate relative to the foreign interest rate, the higher is the probability of early exercise of an American put option. Conversely, the higher the foreign interest rate relative to the domestic interest rate, the higher is the probability of early exercise of an American call option.

In the options market, traders use the Black–Scholes model-based computation of implied volatility to express their quotes. In other words, implied volatility is used as the metric or standard of measurement. Option prices are quoted in units of Black–Scholes implied volatility rather than in units of a currency. The price of an option as determined according to the Black–Scholes model is taken as a given, and the volatility that is implied by that price is calculated and quoted. This facilitates easy comparison of relative values of different options. It is also useful for studying changes in the market price of an option over time. *Bid volatility* is the Black–Scholes implied volatility at which the market maker is prepared to *buy* the option, whereas *offer volatility* refers to the Black–Scholes implied volatility at which the

Example 7.2

The current spot rate between the INR and the U.S. dollar is INR 45. The strike rate of a 90-day European call on the U.S. dollar is INR 46. The interest rate is 8 percent per annum in India and 6 percent per annum in the United States. The estimated volatility (σ^2) of the exchange rate is 10 percent. What is the current value of the option?

Solution

$$d_1 \frac{\left(\frac{45}{46}\right) + \left[0.08 - 0.06 + \left(\frac{0.10}{2}\right)0.25\right]}{0.10\sqrt{0.25}}$$

$$= (-)0.0896$$

$$d_2 = d_1 - 0.10\sqrt{0.25}$$

$$= (-)0.1396$$

$$N(d_1) = 0.4641$$

$$N(d_2) = 0.4443$$

$$C_e = 45e^{-0.06(0.25)}0.4641 - 46e^{-0.08(0.25)}0.4443$$

$$= \text{INR } 0.54 \text{ per U.S. dollar}$$

market maker is prepared to *sell* the option. The options market is, therefore, aptly described as the market for volatility.

Put–Call Parity

Hedging through an option long position is an appropriate strategy in times of high volatility of exchange rates of the underlying currency. Hedging through an option short position, on the other hand, is advantageous in times of low volatility of exchange rates. Sometimes, it is advantageous to adopt a combined strategy. To understand when a combined strategy may be used, let us consider the case of an Indian importer who has a bill of USD 1 million to pay in three months. The importer can hedge this transaction by a forward contract or by buying a call option and selling a put option (the purchase of a call is financed by the sale of a put). As the strike prices of both options are the same, the payoffs from the portfolio of options (combination of call and put options) will be the same as that obtained with a forward purchase of the underlying currency. In other words, the forward payoff can be replicated by a combination of a long ATM call and a short ATM put. Thus, the payoffs from a forward contract are identical to the payoffs from buying a put option and selling a call option when the forward rate equals the strike price of the option portfolio.

Consider a trader who has the following option portfolio:

1. Sell a put at the strike price of USD/INR 40 for maturity on 30 June for notional USD 1 million.
2. Purchase a call at the strike price of USD/INR 40 for maturity on 30 June for notional USD 1 million.

If these two positions are combined, the payoffs will be similar to the payoffs created from a forward long position in USD at INR 40 for the same maturity, as shown in Table 7.4. As the payoffs are obtained on the expiration date, the options involved in this example are European options. If the payoffs are not the same, it would create arbitrage opportunity.

Taking another example, assume the USD is quoted at INR 40 spot and at INR 39.85 three months forward. A three-month European call on USD with a strike price of INR 39 is quoted at INR 0.50, and a three-month European put with the same strike price is quoted at INR 0.25. At these rates, a trader has purchased a call option and sold a put option. Simultaneously, he has sold USD three months forward. On the date of maturity, if the spot rate is above INR 39, the put option expires and the trader exercises the right to buy USD at INR 39. So, his total cash outflow in the options will be INR 39 plus the difference in the call premium, that is, INR 0.25. He then delivers USD on his forward contract and receives INR 39.85. Thus, the trader makes a profit of INR 0.60 per USD. Suppose the spot rate moves below INR 39 on the date of maturity. The trader allows his call option to expire. But, the put option is exercised by the holder. The total cost to the trader will be INR 39 (strike price of put option) plus INR 0.25 (difference in the premiums). He then delivers the USD in compliance with the forward

Table 7.4 Spot Rate and Payoffs at Maturity

Spot rate at maturity	*Payoff at maturity*	
	Buy call and sell put	*Forward position*
39.75	(–)0.25	(–)0.25
40.00	0.00	0.00
40.25	0.25	0.25

contract and receives INR 39.85. Thus, he makes a profit of INR 0.60 per USD. Further, in the situation of the strike price being equal to the spot rate on the date of maturity, the trader makes the same profit. However, this arbitrage opportunity ceases to exist sooner than later, finally resulting in the following equation:

$$P_e - C_e = K - S_T = F_{0,T} - S_T \quad \text{or}$$

$$P_e - C_e + K = F_{0,T}$$

where

P_e = Value of put option
C_e = Value of call option
K = Strike price
$F_{0,T}$ = Forward rate for period 0,T
S_T = Spot rate at the maturity of the forward/option

Put–call parity states that the option premium (upfront) differential should be equal to the difference between the present value of the strike price discounted at the domestic interest rate and the present value of the future spot rate or forward rate (in terms of interest rate parity) discounted at the foreign interest rate.

Consider the following portfolio as an example:

- A British investor invests in the United States a certain amount $[1/(1 + r_f)]$ in U.S. dollars to get one USD after one year, at the U.S. interest rate of r_f. This will be equivalent to S_1, the spot rate of USD/GBP at the end of the year.
- The same investor buys a put option on USD with an exercise price of K in terms of GBP.
- He also borrows an amount equivalent to $K/(1 + r_h)$ in Britain, r_d being the British interest rate. So, the loan will become an amount of K in terms of GBP at the end of the year.
- In addition, the investor buys a call option on USD with an exercise price of K.

The payoffs of this portfolio are shown in Table 7.5.

The payoffs vary, depending on the spot rate of the USD on the expiration date (at the end of the year). The payoffs on the call option will be the same as that of the portfolio shown in Table 7.5. Since the portfolio and the call option have identical payoffs, they must have the same price. Thus,

$$C_e = p_e + \frac{S_1}{(1+r_f)} - \frac{K}{(1+r_h)} \tag{7.8}$$

Substituting the interest-parity equation in Eq. 7.8,

$$C_e - P_e = \frac{F_1 - K}{(1+r_h)}$$

Table 7.5 Payoffs of the Portfolio

	If $S_1 > K$	*If* $S_1 < K$
Investment	S_1	S_1
Put option	0	$K - S$
Borrowing	(–) K	(–) K
Total	$S_1 - K$	0

The term $[(F_1 - K)/(1 + r_h)]$ is the present value of the difference between the one-year forward rate and the strike price.

As far as American options are concerned, the put–call parity relationship does not lead to equality as there is a possibility of early exercise. Therefore, only an upper and a lower bound on the value of an American put option can be derived:

$$C_t + K - S_t e^{-r_f T} \geq P_t \geq C_t + Ke^{-r_d T} - S_t$$

where

t = At present

T = Number of days for expiry of the option from t

If the inequality is not satisfied, arbitrage opportunities will arise. However, the arbitrage process will ultimately lead to satisfying the inequality.

Put–call parity establishes a relationship between forward and option contracts. It also illustrates how puts, calls, interest rates, and forward rates are related. Put and call premiums can also be set relative to one another by this parity relationship. For example, if calls for a particular currency are traded, but there are no market quotes for the corresponding puts, the market rate for the put option can be deduced from the quotes of the call option.

The Greeks

Both option writers (sellers) and option buyers are exposed to risk when they enter into options, especially OTC options. Commercial banks and financial institutions maintain a large portfolio of option positions with resultant exposures. The risk for option traders increases phenomenally when the options are structured to satisfy the individual needs of the clients and do not correspond to the standardized options traded on the exchanges. So, it is difficult to hedge such exposures. For effective hedging of positions arising from the buying and writing of options, one needs to analyse the risks faced by an option trader.

Option Greeks measure the sensitivity of an option's price to quantifiable factors. *Delta, gamma, vega, theta, rho,* and *phi* are the type of option Greeks. A brief description of each of these is given in this section. An understanding of the Greeks helps in effective hedging of exposures.

Delta

The currency option **delta** refers to the rate of change of the option price relative to change in the underlying foreign exchange rate. The option delta is also called the *hedge ratio.* It is the amount of the long (short) position the hedger must have in the underlying currency per option that he writes (buys) to have a risk-free offsetting investment. This will result in the hedger receiving the same terminal value at maturity irrespective of whether the underlying foreign exchange rate increases or decreases. To put it differently, the option *delta* measures the sensitivity of the option value to very small change in the spot rate of the underlying currency. If the option premium is plotted on the Y-axis against the value of the underlying currency on the X-axis, a convex curve is obtained. The slope of this convex curve is the option delta. The delta of an option changes with changes in the spot rate of the underlying currency. Therefore, delta has to be rebalanced periodically in order to remain completely covered or hedged.

*The option **delta** measures the sensitivity of the option value to very small changes in the spot rate of the underlying currency.*

Mathematically, delta is the partial derivative of the option price with respect to the spot rate of the underlying currency:

$$\Delta = \frac{\partial C}{\partial S}$$

where

C = Value of the option
S = Spot rate of the underlying currency
The delta of a European call option on a currency, in terms of the Black–Scholes model, is

$$\Delta = e^{-r_f T} N(d_1)$$

For a European put option on a currency, the delta is

$$\Delta = e^{-r_f T}[N(d_1)-1]$$

The Black–Scholes model implies a riskless portfolio that is created by taking a position in the underlying currency for a position in the option.

The same can also be expressed as follows:

$$h = \frac{C_u - C_d}{S_0(u-d)} \text{ (or)}$$

$$h = \frac{S_0(u-d)}{C_u - C_d}$$

This indicates the number of call options needed to create a risk-free hedge portfolio. Suppose that a hedge ratio is (–) 2.00. The hedger can create a risk-free hedge portfolio by purchasing one unit of the underlying foreign currency and selling two call options.

For example, assume that the exchange rate between INR and USD is INR 46. The exchange rate at the end of the next three months has two possibilities: either INR 48 or INR 45. A firm can create a portfolio of a certain amount of U.S. dollars (call it delta, or Δ) and one call option at a strike rate of, say, INR 47, in such a way that there is no uncertainty of the value of the portfolio at the end of three months. That is, the firm can combine a long position (buying) in the U.S. dollar and a short position (selling) in the call option. Suppose the exchange rate goes up to INR 48. The buyer of the option will exercise his option and the firm will lose INR 1. If the exchange rate turns out to be INR 45, the option buyer will not exercise the option, and the firm will neither gain nor lose.

The portfolio will be risk free if the value of the portfolio is the same, whether the exchange rate moves up to INR 48 or falls to INR 45. That is

$$\text{INR } 48\Delta - \text{INR } 45 = \text{INR } 1\Delta - 0$$

$$\Delta = \frac{(1.0-00)}{(48-45)} = 0.333$$

This can also be stated as

$$\text{Option delta } (\Delta) = \frac{\text{Difference in option values}}{\text{Difference in exchange rates}}$$

In this example, the firm will have a risk-free portfolio if it combines a long position in USD 0.333 with a short position in one call option. If the exchange rate increases to INR 48, the value of the portfolio will be

$$(\text{USD } 0.333 \times \text{INR } 48) - \text{INR } 1 = \text{INR } 14.98$$

And if the exchange rate falls to INR 45, the value of the portfolio will be

$$(\text{USD } 0.333 \times \text{INR } 45) = \text{INR } 14.98$$

Thus, the value of the portfolio at the end of three months remains INR 14.98, irrespective of the increase or decrease in the exchange rate of the underlying currency, i.e. USD.

If the risk-free interest rate is 8 percent per annum, the present value of the portfolio will be

$$\frac{\text{INR } 14.98}{\left(1+\frac{0.08}{4}\right)} = ₹14.69$$

Since the current exchange rate is INR 46, the value of the call option can be obtained as follows:

$$\text{INR } 46 - \text{Value of call opation} = \text{INR } 14.69$$
$$(\text{INR } 46 \times \text{USD } 0.333) - \text{Valus of call opation} = \text{INR } 14.69$$
$$\text{Value of call option} = \text{INR } 15.32 - \text{INR } 14.69 = \text{INR } 0.63$$

Example 7.3

Suppose the U.S. dollar now sells at INR 46 (S_0), and the exchange rate will either increase by INR 4(u) or fall by INR 1(d) by year-end. A call option on the U.S. dollar has an exercise rate of INR 47, and the time to expiration is one year. The risk-free interest rate is 6 percent. What is a fair value for the call at time 0?

Solution

The possible payoffs to the option holder at the end of the year are shown in Figures 7.9 and 7.10.

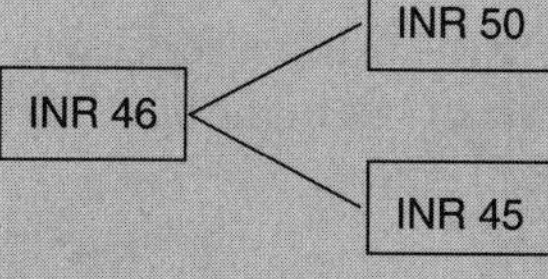

Figure 7.9

Exchange Rate

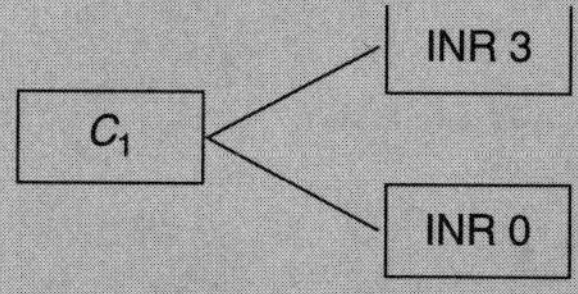

Figure 7.10

Call Option Value

It is assumed that the investor can borrow an amount equivalent to the current spot rate of the USD by issuing a 6 percent risk-free bond. Table 7.6 presents the payoffs to the call option holder.

Table 7.6 Payoffs in Up State and Down State

	Payoff in upstate (at year end)	*Payoff in down state (at year end)*	*Current spot rate*
U.S. dollar	INR 50	INR 45	INR 46
Risk-free bond	INR 48.75	INR 48.75	INR 46
Call	INR 3.00	INR 0.0	?

The call option can be replicated with an appropriate combination of the U.S. dollar and risk-free bonds. In other words, the composition of a portfolio that will precisely replicate the payoffs of the call option needs to be determined.

Consider a portfolio with X_1 U.S. dollars and X_2 risk-free bonds. In the up state, such a portfolio will have a payoff of INR $50X_1$ plus INR $48.75X_2$, whereas in the down state it will have a payoff of INR $45X_1$ plus INR $48.75X_2$. Thus, two linear equations can be formulated:

$$50X_1 + 48.75X_2 = 3 \tag{7.9}$$

$$45X_1 + 48.75X_2 = 0 \tag{7.10}$$

Subtracting Eq. 7.10 from Eq. 7.9,

$$50X_1 \ + 45X_1 = 3 \quad \text{or,}$$

$$X_1 = 0.60$$

Substituting the value of X_1 in Eq. 7.9, we have

$$50(0.06) + 48.75X_2 = 3$$

Therefore, $X_2 = (-)\,0.5539$

This means that the investor can replicate the payoff from the call by short-selling the risk-free bond or borrowing at the risk-free rate and purchasing U.S. dollars. In other words, the replicating portfolio provides the same payoffs as the call. Table 7.7 shows the payoffs in upstate and down state.

To obtain the portfolio, the investor has spent INR 27.6 and purchased USD 0.6 (at USD/INR 46). However, of the amount spent, INR 25.48 (INR 46 × 0.5539 = INR 25.48) is provided by the proceeds from the short sale of the bond. In other words, only INR 2.12 of the investor's own funds is spent, which is the fair value of the call option.

Generally, the value of the call option can be obtained from the following equation:

$$C_0 = X_1 S_0 + X_2 B$$

where B = Price of the bond.

Table 7.7 Replication of Payoffs to Call Option Holder

	Payoff in up state	*Payoff in down state*
Purchasing U.S. dollars	INR 30 (i.e. 50 × 0.60)	INR 27 (i.e. 48.75 × 0.5539)
Loan repayment	INR 27	INR 27
Net payoff	INR 3	INR 0

By using the data given in Example 7.3, the call value can be obtained as follows:

$$C_0 = (0.60)(\text{INR } 46) - 0.5539\ (\text{INR } 46)$$
$$= \text{INR } 2.12$$

For the same data, the hedge ratio (*h*) is

$$h = \frac{3-0}{50-45} = 0.60$$

The hedge ratio represents the number of units of foreign currency to be purchased.

Simultaneously, an amount should be borrowed (risk-free) by short selling the bonds. This amount is:

$$B = PV(hdS_1 - C_{1d});\ PV = \text{Present Value}$$
$$B = PV(0.6 \times 45 - 0)$$
$$= \text{INR } 25.48$$

It may be noted that the figure in parentheses is the value of the bond at the end of the period. Therefore, the value of the call option can also be computed as

$$C_0 = hS_o - B$$
$$= 0.6\ (\text{INR } 46) - \text{INR } 25.48$$
$$= \text{INR } 2.12$$

At the fair value, the call option attains its equilibrium position. If the call is selling for either more or less than this amount, there would be an arbitrage opportunity in which an investor could buy the cheaper of the two alternatives (call and underlying foreign currency) and sell the more expensive one, thereby achieving a guaranteed profit.

To understand how an arbitrage opportunity is created, let us assume that the call option discussed in Example 7.3 is selling for INR 4 as against the fair value of INR 2.12. That is, the call is *overpriced*. In this case, the investor would consider writing one call, buying 0.6 U.S. dollars at INR 46, and borrowing INR 25.48. When this is done, the net cash flows at $t = 0$ (at present) would be as shown in Table 7.8.

This indicates that the investor has a net cash inflow.

At the end of the year, the investor's net cash flows will be as shown in Table 7.9. It is evident from Table 7.9 that the aggregate payoffs in both the situations is zero, implying that

Table 7.8 Present Net Cash Flows for the Overpriced Call

Call premium received	INR 4.00
Buying USD 0.6	INR 27.60
Borrowing at risk-free rate	INR 25.48
Net cash flows	INR 6.12

Table 7.9 End-of-year Net Cash Flows for the Overpriced Call

	Payoff in up state (INR)	*Payoff in down state (INR)*
Writing call	(–)3	0.0
U.S. dollars	30	27.0
Loan repayment	(–)27	(–)27.0
Net cash flows	0.0	0.0

the investor has no risk of loss, or the investor is not required to pay any money later on. In fact, the investor could generate a free net cash inflow of INR 6.12.

Now, assume that the call is selling for INR 1.50. That is, the call is *underpriced*. In such a situation, the investor would consider buying one call, short selling 0.6 U.S. dollars, and investing INR 25.48 at the risk-free rate. The net cash flows in this situation would be as shown in Table 7.10.

At the end of the year, the investor's net cash flow will be as shown in Table 7.11. Once again, the net aggregate value is zero in both the situations, indicating that the investor has no risk of loss in the future. On the other hand, the investor could generate free net cash of INR 0.62. Such arbitrage opportunities, however, will go away when many investors start doing the same. This will lead to the call price ultimately settling down at the fair value.

A call option has a positive hedge ratio and a put option has a negative hedge ratio. Under the Black–Scholes model, the hedge ratio for a call option is $N(d_1)$, and the hedge ratio for a put option is $[N(d_1) - 1]$. For a call option, $0 < \text{delta} < 1$, because $N(d_1)$, the area under standard normal curve, ranges from 0 to 100 percent. For a put option, $-1 < \text{delta} < 0$. As stated earlier, delta is a measure of option sensitivity. So, if $N(d_1)$ is 0.252, this means that for a very small unit change in the exchange rate of the underlying foreign currency, the option would change by about 25 percent.

The option delta is used in pricing of options as well as in hedging of positions. For example, a firm can hedge a forward U.S. dollar obligation of USD 1 million with a long call option on USD. For a long call with a hedge ratio of + 0.50, the firm should take a USD 2 million option position to offset the underlying USD 1 million obligation. The same USD 1

Table 7.10 Present Net Cash Flows for the Underpriced Call

Buying one call	(–)INR 1.50
Short selling 0.6 U.S. dollars	INR 27.60
Risk-free investment	(–)INR 25.48
Net cash flows	INR 0.62

Table 7.11 End-of-year Net Cash Flows for the Underpriced Call

	Payoff in up state (INR)	*Payoff in down state (INR)*
Investment in a call option	3.00	0.0
Buying 0.60 USD (to offset short selling)	(–)30.00	(–)27.0
Realising risk-free investment	27.00	27.0
Net cash flows	0.0	0.0

million obligation can also be offset by writing a USD 4 million put option if the hedge ratio is (–)0.25. Conversely, a future cash inflow of USD 1 million can be hedged with a short position of USD 1.43 million on a USD call option if the hedge ratio is (+)0.70. If the hedge ratio is (–)0.40, the USD 1 million future cash inflow can be hedged with a long position of USD 2.5 million on a U.S. dollar put option.

The delta of an option is a function of variables like interest rates and exchange rates. As these variables change, the delta of an option changes. Therefore, there is a need for

Example 7.4

An Indian firm has written a six-month European option to sell USD 1 million at an exchange rate of USD/INR 44. The current spot rate is USD/INR 44.5. The risk-free interest rate is 7 percent per annum in India and 5 percent per annum in the United States. The volatility of the U.S. dollar is 20 percent. Calculate the delta of the option. How can the short position in the option be hedged by short selling currency and using currency futures?

Solution

The delta of a put option is

$$[N(d_1)-1]e^{-r_f(T-t)}$$

$$d_1 = \frac{In\left(\frac{S}{E}\right)+\left(\frac{\sigma^2}{2}\right)(T-t)}{\sigma\sqrt{T-t}}$$

$$= \frac{In\left(\frac{44.5}{44}\right)+\left(\frac{0.20}{2}\right)(0.5)}{0.20\times\sqrt{0.5}}$$

$$=0.15$$

Therefore, $N(d_1)=0.5596$ (from tables of cumulative normal distribution)

$$\text{Delta of the call opation} =(0.5596-1)e^{-0.05\times 0.5}$$

$$=(-)0.4295$$

This is the long position in one put option. The delta of the firm's total short position equals USD 429,500 (USD 1 million × 0.4295). Therefore, short selling of USD 429,500 is required to neutralize the delta of the option position.

If, for example, the firm decides to hedge by using six-month currency futures, then

$$e^{-(r_h-r_f)0.5}$$

$$e^{-(0.02)0.5}$$

$$=0.99005$$

So, the short position in currency futures for delta hedging is:

0.99005 × USD 429,500

= USD 425,226

Depending on the standard size of the currency futures, the firm should decide the number of currency futures contracts to be shorted.

Delta can also be calculated for a portfolio of options and other derivatives where there is a single underlying currency. The delta of the portfolio is a weighted sum of the deltas of the individual derivatives in the portfolio. Thus, the delta of a portfolio is given by

$$\Delta P = \sum w_i \Delta_i$$

where

Δ_i = Delta of ith derivative
w_i = Amount of ith derivative in the portfolio

periodical reviewing and adjustment of the hedge. This is known as *rebalancing.* However, continuous adjustment of the hedge may not be feasible in view of transaction costs. This is the reason why the hedge remains less than perfect. Though an option can be hedged by taking an opposite position in the underlying currency, in most cases option positions are hedged by opposite positions in currency futures.

Gamma

Gamma refers to the sensitivity of the delta or rate of change of the delta with respect to the underlying exchange rate.

Gamma is the second partial derivative of the option's price with respect to the underlying exchange rate. It is the sensitivity of the delta or rate of change of the delta with respect to the underlying exchange rate. It is the second partial derivative of the portfolio with respect to the exchange rate:

$$\Gamma = \frac{\partial^2 C}{\partial^2 S}$$

Gamma measures the risk inherent in a delta hedge. If gamma is large in absolute terms, the delta is highly sensitive to the underlying foreign exchange rate. In such cases, the frequency of adjustment to delta is relatively higher. On the other hand, a small value for gamma indicates that the options delta changes slowly. Therefore, the adjustments needed to keep a portfolio delta neutral are relatively infrequent. Options have a positive gamma for long positions and a negative gamma for short positions. Like the delta, the gamma also varies with certain variables. For example, the gamma of an option increases as the time to maturity decreases, but it decreases with volatility. Gamma takes maximum value for options ATM and declines and approaches zero as the option moves deep into-the-money or out-of-money A negative gamma means that the rate of losses increases as losses are sustained, and the rate of profit falls as profits are experienced.

Theta

*The **theta** of derivative of an option price is the rate of change of the value of the derivative with respect to time to expiration, assuming all else remains the same.*

The **theta** of derivative of an option price is the rate of change of the value of the derivative with respect to time to expiration, assuming all else remaining the same. Formally stated,

$$\text{Theta} = \frac{\Delta\text{Option premium}}{\Delta\text{Time to expiration}}$$

Thus, theta is the expected change in the option premium for a small change in the time to expiration. Theta is also referred to as the *time decay* of the option. All other things remaining constant, as the expiry date comes closer, the value of the option falls. In other words, option premium decreases at an increasing rate as the expiry date comes closer, because there is less time in which a change in the spot rate could occur. Generally, the theta of an option is negative for long positions and positive for short positions. An option with a positive theta will gain in value as time passes, whereas an option with a negative theta will decay over time. Thus, a negative theta will work in favour of short positions in options and against long positions (whether calls or puts). Further, theta is greater for an option that is near-the -money than for an option which is deep in- or out-of-the-money.

Vega

The value of an option also depends on the volatility of the underlying foreign exchange rate. The derivative of the option price with respect to volatility is called **vega** (also known as lambda). In other words, vega measures the sensitivity of the option value to changes in the volatility (measured by standard deviation) of the underlying foreign exchange rate. Mathematically expressed,

*The derivative of the option price with respect to volatility is called **vega** (also known as lambda).*

$$\nu = \frac{\partial C}{\partial \sigma}$$

If vega is high in absolute terms, the derivative's value is very sensitive to small changes in volatility. A positive *vega* results in profits from an increase in volatility. That is, as the volatility of the spot rate increases, the option value would also increase. Thus, options with high volatility carry more value. All else remaining the same, vega is greater for long-term options.

Rho and Phi

Interest rates have direct influences on option prices. Interest rate changes in either currency affect the option's premium or value. The expected change in the option premium for a small change in the domestic interest rate is termed as *rho.* Similarly, the expected change in the premium for a small change in the foreign interest rate is *termed as phi.* Expectations about the interest rates help in determining the option price. For example, if the domestic interest rate is likely to be higher than the foreign interest rate, it can be forecast that the foreign currency will appreciate. This lowers the call option price but increases the put option price.

Forwards/Futures and Options: A Comparison

Forwards and options are used to hedge foreign exchange exposure. Speculators also use these tools to take on risk, and make windfall gains. In other words, these tools may be used for different purposes. As hedging devices or as speculative tools, forwards and options are different and, therefore, their appropriateness in a situation is determined on the basis of their expected payoffs. The major differences between the forwards/futures and options are: The buyer of a currency option takes advantage of both spot markets and forward markets. When a market participant buys a currency option, he buys insurance against currency risk in the form of a forward contract (i.e. the right to buy or sell the underlying currency on maturity at the specified rate). At the same time, the holder or buyer of the option can also take advantage of favourable exchange rates in the spot market on or before the expiry date of the option. Options have extraordinary potential profits for buyers. But such advantage is missing in the case of forwards/futures, though they do provide insurance to traders against currency risk.

With forwards/futures, buyers and sellers have an equal chance of gaining and losing. But this is not the case with options. The writer (seller) of the option will have a payoff profile that is the mirror image of the buyer's. When the holder of the option can have unlimited profits, it means that the seller of the same contract is exposed to potentially unlimited losses. This happens because options allow the option holder to benefit from spot rate movements in one direction and not to lose from spot rate movements in the other direction. Thus, there is no symmetry of payoff profiles in the case of options. That is, the buyer and the seller of an option contract do not have an equal chance of gaining and losing. On the other hand, forwards provide a linear payoff profile for both the buyer and the seller.

Options can be combined in a number of ways, and their specifications can be changed to create a variety of exotic options. In other words, options are more complex products vis-à-vis forwards/futures. This makes options more difficult to price.

The cash flow effects of forwards and options are analysed with the following example.

Suppose an Indian firm in Mumbai has accounts receivables of USD 1 million in three months. The receivables amount in terms of INR will depend on the realized spot exchange rate at the time of actual settlement of accounts receivables. The receivables amount in terms of INR using forwards and options is shown in Table 7.12.

The expected receivables amounts in INR resulting from remaining unhedged are shown in the top row of Table 7.12. If the receivables in U.S. dollars are sold forward at INR 47, the amount to be received will be INR 47 million, irrespective of what happens to the spot rate by the time of settlement. If the firm buys put options on the U.S. dollar at a strike rate of INR 47, the option will be exercised, if the spot rate is below INR 47. If the spot rate ends up above INR 47, the company will get more by selling USD at the spot rate than by exercising the option. The payoffs on put options with different strike rates and option premiums are also shown in Table 7.12. If the spot rate is INR 48, then the put option at a strike rate of INR 47 will not be exercised, and the U.S. dollars will be sold spot for INR 48 million. But INR 1.5 million has been paid for the option, so the net receipts to the firm are INR 46.5 million. Similarly, if the spot rate ends up at INR 50, the net receipts will be INR 48.5 million. If the spot rate is at the exercise price, INR 47, the net receipts in terms of INR will be the same, whether the U.S. dollars are sold at the spot rate or the option is exercised. In either case, the net receipts will be INR 45.5 million. If the spot rate is below INR 47, the put option will be exercised and the net receipts will be INR 45.5 million.

Instead of buying a put option at a strike rate of INR 47, the firm may buy one at a strike rate of INR 48 with an option premium of INR 2/USD. Alternatively, it may buy a put option at a strike rate of INR 46 with an option premium of INR 1/USD. The net INR receipts associated with these option strategies are also shown in Table 7.12.

A comparison of the net INR receipts under forwards and options reveals that options are better than forwards if the spot rate ends up very high, but they are worse than forwards if the spot rate ends up very low. To generalize, the hedger should assess the benefits that accrue with hedging of uncertain cash flows and, at the same time, foresee the unhedged situation. The overall assessment of both alternatives may sometimes lead to a point where unhedging may be a better strategy. Thus, the market participant should assess the cash flows not only under different hedging strategies like options, forwards, and futures, but also without the hedging of uncertain cash flows. By comparing the expected net cash flows under different alternative strategies, the market participant can adopt the best possible strategy.

Table 7.12 The Effects of Hedging

	Receivables (INR million) at different future spot exchange rates (USD/INR)					
Hedging tools used	44	45	46	47	48	50
Unhedged	44	45	46	47	48	50
Forward USD sale at INR 47	47	47	47	47	47	47
INR 47 put option at INR 1.5/USD	45.5	45.5	45.5	45.5	46.5	48.5
INR 48 put option at INR 2/USD	46	46	46	46	46	48
INR 46 put option at INR 1/USD	45	45	45	46	47	49

Futures Options

Futures options are also known as options on futures. As the name indicates, these options have futures as the underlying asset. That is, trading in a futures option calls for delivery of certain futures contracts in a particular currency rather than the currency itself. For example, assume a U.S.-based firm has entered a call futures option on British pounds. On exercise of such a contract, the firm receives a long position in the futures on British pounds, plus cash equivalent to the excess of the current futures price over the strike price. Suppose, the same firm has entered a put futures option on euros. On exercise of the option, the firm receives a short position in the futures on euros, plus an amount of cash equivalent to the excess of the strike price over the current futures price. It may be noted that the holder of the futures option will not exercise the option, if there is a loss on the futures contract. When the option on futures is exercised and the futures contract delivered, the holder may sell the futures contract at a price that provides him exactly the same profit that he would have got with a straight option on the currency. As in basic options, the payoff profile of the seller of futures options must be the mirror image of that of the buyer.

More specifically, suppose the U.S.-based firm is holding a British pound call futures option (contract size of GBP 62,500) for December delivery at a strike price of USD 1.6972. The current price of December futures on GBP is USD 1.7000. Since the spot price of the futures is greater than the strike price, the holder exercises the option. So the firm will receive a long position in December futures on GBP at a price of USD 1.6972. This means that the option writer will have a short position in the same futures. The U.S. firm also receives cash of USD 175 (i.e. difference between USD 1.7000 and 1.6972, multiplied by 62,500). When the option on futures is exercised and the futures contract delivered, the holder may sell the futures contract at a price that provides him exactly the same profit that he would have made with a straight option on the currency.

The major advantage with futures options is that the holder can allow the option to expire, if the spot market for the future contract is more profitable. Also, the holder is protected against adverse changes in exchange rates. These advantages are absent in basic futures contracts.

Currency Options Trading in India

As part of economic liberalization initiatives, authorized dealers in India were permitted to have access to a wide range of derivative products available in established international exchanges and offer cross-currency options to their corporate customers and other interbank counterparties to hedge their foreign currency exposure. These currency options can be used as a hedge for foreign currency loans, provided that the option does not involve Indian rupees, the face value does not exceed the outstanding amount of the loan, and the maturity of the contract does not exceed the unexpired maturity of the underlying loan. Banks can also purchase options to hedge their cross-currency proprietary trading positions. Authorized dealers can offer such cross-currency options on a fully-covered and back-to-back basis only. If a hedge becomes naked in part or full, it should be marked to market at regular intervals.

To develop the derivatives market in India and add to the spectrum of hedge products for hedging currency exposures, the Reserve Bank of India appointed a Technical Committee in 2002 to study and prepare a roadmap for the introduction of currency options in India. The Technical Committee observed the following advantages with the introduction of currency options in Indian derivatives market:

- Hedge for currency exposures to protect the downside while retaining the upside by paying a premium upfront. This would be a big advantage for importers, exporters as well as businesses with exposures to international prices. Currency options would enable the Indian industry and businesses to compete better in international markets by hedging currency risk.

- Non-linear payoff of the product enables its use as hedge for various special cases and possible exposures. For example, if an Indian company is bidding for an international assignment where the bid quote would be in dollars but the costs would be in rupees, then the company runs a risk till the contract is awarded. Using currency swaps or forwards would create reverse positions if the company is not allotted the contract, but the use of an option contract in this would freeze the liability only to the option premium paid upfront.
- The nature of the instrument again makes its use possible as a hedge against uncertainty of the cash flows. Option structures can be used to hedge the volatility along with the non-linear nature of payoffs.
- Attract further foreign exchange investment due to the availability of another mechanism for hedging foreign exchange risk.

In view of these advantages, the Committee felt that a rupee options market would complement the spot and forward foreign exchange market to provide the complete universe of hedging instruments for corporate customers. Currency options that are based on a unique parameter, the volatility of the underlying, help to complete the derivatives market in India.

Based on the recommendations of the Technical Committee, the RBI introduced foreign currency rupee options effective from 7 July 2003 under certain terms and conditions. The important terms and conditions are:

- Under the foreign currency INR options facility, authorized dealers can offer currency options designated in a currency pair, where the Indian rupee is one currency.
- All authorized dealers having a minimum CRAR of 9 percent are permitted to offer foreign currency INR options on a back-to-back basis. To begin with, they are permitted to offer only vanilla European options.
- Authorized dealers that have adequate internal control, risk monitoring/management systems, and mark-to-market mechanism, and fulfill the following criteria are allowed to run an option book (open position) after obtaining a one-time approval from the RBI:
    - Continuous profitability for at least three years.
    - Net NPAs at reasonable levels (not more than 3 percent of net advances).
    - Minimum CRAR of 10 percent.
    - Minimum net worth not less than INR 300 crore.
- Customers can purchase call or put options.
- Options cannot be used to hedge contingent exposures (except for exposures arising out of submission of tender bids in foreign exchange.
- Importers and exporters having underlying unhedged foreign currency exposures in respect of trade transactions, evidenced by documents (firm order, letter of credit, or actual shipment) may write plain vanilla standalone covered call and put options in foreign currency-rupees and receive premiums subject to AD Category I banks satisfying that the customers have sound risk management systems and have adopted AS 30 and AS 32. The pricing of the premium may be done in a transparent manner. These options may not be combined with any other derivative products.
- Customers can enter into packaged products involving cost reduction structures provided that the structure reduces the risk and does not involve customers receiving a premium.
- Authorized dealers may quote the option premium in INR or as a percentage of the INR notional on an annualized basis.

- Option contracts may be settled either by a delivery on a spot basis or by net cash settlement in Indian rupees on a spot basis, as specified in the contract.
- Only one hedge transaction may be booked against a particular exposure for a given time period.
- Customers who have genuine foreign currency exposures are eligible to enter option contracts.
- Authorized dealers can use the foreign currency INR options for the purpose of hedging trading books and balance sheet exposures.
- Market makers would be allowed to hedge the delta of their option portfolio by accessing spot markets. Other Greeks may be hedged by entering into option transactions in the interbank market.
- Banks should put in place systems necessary for marking to market the portfolio on a daily basis.
- The Reserve Bank of India has also allowed Indian corporations need-based access to international exchanges like LME, Simex, LIFFE, and CBOT for a wide range of derivative products including cross-currency options.
- Cross-currency options should be written by AD Category I banks on a fully covered back-to-back basis. The cover transaction may be undertaken with a bank outside India, an off-shore banking unit situated in a Special Economic Zone or an internationally recognized option exchange or another AD Category I bank in India.

Summary

1. An *option* is a derivative contract in which the writer of the option grants the buyer of the option the right, but not the obligation, to purchase from or sell to the writer the underlying currency or another contract at a specified rate, within a specified period of time or at a fixed date.
2. Options may take different forms like call options, put options, European-style options, American-style options, exchange-traded options, and OTC options.
3. An option which grants the buyer the right to purchase the underlying currency from the seller (writer) is called a *call option.* In the case *of put options,* the buyer is given the right to sell the underlying currency to the writer of the option.
4. Options that can be exercised at any time up to and including the expiration date are known as *American-style options.* Options that can be exercised only at the expiration date are called *European-style options.*
5. Depending on the spot exchange rate of the underlying currency, an option may be *in-the-money, at-the-money,* or *out-of-the-money.*
6. An option is a zero-sum game, and a gain or loss for a buyer of an option contract is a loss or gain to the writer of the option. Therefore, the payoff profile of the writer of an option can be obtained by reversing the signs on the values in the payoff profile for the buyer of the option.
7. The value of an option comprises two components: time value and intrinsic value. The *intrinsic value* of an option is the economic value of the option if it is exercised immediately. The *time value* of an option is the excess of the option value over its intrinsic value.
8. The important factors that influence the option value are intrinsic value, volatility of spot rate, time to expiration, inflation differential, and interest rate differential.
9. Straddles, strangles, and spreads (bull spreads, bear spreads, butterfly spreads, calendar spreads, and diagonal spreads) are various option strategies.
10. The two important option pricing models are the *binomial model* and the *Black–Scholes model.* The binomial pricing model is a discrete model, whereas the Black–Scholes model is a continuous model.
11. Option *delta* measures the sensitivity of the option value to changes in the spot rate of the underlying currency.
12. Options are better hedging strategies, especially when the spot rate of foreign exchange is likely to end up very high.

Questions and Problems

1. What is a currency option? Distinguish between a call option and a put option.
2. Discuss the determinants of a currency option value.
3. What determines the intrinsic value and the time value of an option?
4. Explain an option that is in-, at-, or out-of-the-money.
5. What is the hedge ratio? How it is useful in the pricing of option contracts?
6. How are the cash flows different under options, futures, and forwards of the same structure?
7. Between an American-style call option and a European-style call option, which one is more valuable and why?
8. Mr X purchased a U.S. dollar put option at a premium of INR 0.50 per USD. The contract amount is USD 1 million. If the exercise rate is USD/INR 45 and the spot rate of the U.S. dollar on the date of expiration is USD/INR 45.75, what is Mr X's profit or loss on the put option?
9. Mr Y sells a call option on British pounds at a premium of INR 1 per GBP. The contract amount is GBP 1 million. If the exercise rate is GBP/INR 80, and the spot rate on the date of expiration is GBP/INR 82, what is Mr Y's profit or loss on the call option?
10. The premium on 15 September on a 15 December British pound put option is 5 cents per GBP at a strike rate of GBP/USD 1.90. The forward rate for 15 December is GBP/USD 1.92, and the quarterly U.S. interest rate is 2.5 percent. If put–call parity holds, what is the current price of a 15 December British pound call option with an exercise price of GBP/USD 1.90?
11. On 20 December, the call premium on a 20 June option contract is 6 cents per British pound at a strike rate of GBP/USD 1.92. The 180-day interest rate is 6 percent in London and 5 percent in the United States. If the current spot rate is GBP/USD 1.95 and put–call parity holds, what is the put premium on a 20 June British pound contract with an exercise rate of GBP/USD 1.92?
12. The exchange rate between the Indian rupee and the British pound is INR 82. The exchange rate at the end of next three months has two possibilities: either INR 83 or INR 80. The three-month call option contract has a strike rate of INR 81. If the risk-free interest rate in both countries is 6 percent per annum, what is the value of the call option?
13. The current spot rate is GBP/USD 1.90, and the 90-day forward is GBP/USD 1.92. There is an offer to sell a put on GBP 1 million with a strike rate of GBP/USD 1.88 in return for selling a call on the same amount and for the same conditions. Would you accept the ffer?
14. A European call option on the U.S. dollar has an exercise rate of INR 46 with a maturity date six months from now. The current spot rate of exchange is INR 45 and the risk-free rate in both India and the United States is 6 percent. The estimated instantaneous standard deviation of the USD/INR exchange rate is 8 percent per year. What is the value of the option?

Multiple-choice Questions

1. The buyer of ________ has no obligation to buy or sell and may walk away from the contract.

   (a) Futures contract (b) Forward contract
   (c) Option (d) None of these

2. Option premium is paid by the buyer for receiving ________.

   (a) Underlying currency
   (b) Right to buy/sell
   (c) Contracted amount
   (d) None of these

3. In colloquial terms writing option is ________.

   (a) Going long (b) Going short
   (c) Entering contract (d) None of these

4. An option which grants the buyer the right to buy the underlying currency is called ________.

   (a) Put option (b) Call option
   (c) Exotic option (d) None of these

5. The main objective of buying exotic option is to reduce ________.

   (a) Risk (b) Option premium
   (c) Extra costs (d) None of these

6. Knock-in and knock-out options are also known as ________.

   (a) Put options (b) Call options
   (c) Barrier options (d) None of these

7. The options that can be exercised at any time before their expiration are known as ________.

   (a) European options (b) American options
   (c) Exotic options (d) None of these

8. Exchange-traded options are ________.
   (a) Customized
   (b) Standardized
   (c) Tailored to specific requirements
   (d) None of these
9. ________ may not be required to post any margin.
   (a) Option writer (b) Option buyer
   (c) Option broker (d) None of these
10. A________option is in-the-money when the strike rate is below the spot rate.
   (a) Put (b) C(a)ll
   (c) Exotic (d) None of these
11. A________option is out-of-the-money when the strike rate is below the spot rate.
   (a) Call (b) Put
   (c) Knock-out (d) None of these
12. Break-even rate is the spot rate at which the gain on the option is ________the option premium.
   (a) Above (b) Below
   (c) Equal to (d) None of these
13. Time value of an option is the difference between ________ and ________.
   (a) Market value, intrinsic value
   (b) Market value, option premium
   (c) Option premium and market value
   (d) None of these
14. A call option can never be worth more than the________.
   (a) Option premium
   (b) Spot exchange rate of the underlying currency
   (c) Futures price
   (d) None of these
15. Higher the strike price, the lower is the price of the ________.
   (a) Call option (b) Put option
   (c) Exotic option (d) None of these
16. If a market participant is simultaneously long and short in options of the same type, it is called ________.
   (a) Option spread (b) Straddle
   (c) Strangle (d) None of these
17. Buying the higher strike call and selling the lower strike call is known as ________.
   (a) Bull spread (b) Bear Spread
   (c) Straddle (d) None of these
18. In times of high volatility of the exchange rate of the underlying currency, option ________ is an appropriate strategy.
   (a) Long position (b) Short position
   (c) Straddle (d) None of these
19. Rate of change of option price relative to change in the underlying foreign exchange rate is known as________.
   (a) Delta (b) Gamma
   (c) Vega (d) None of these
20. ________ provide linear payoff for both buyer and seller.
   (a) Forwards (b) Options
   (c) Exotic options (d) None of these

Case Study

Foreign currency rupee options have been introduced recently in India. A U.S.-based consultancy firm would like to know whether option quotations in India are based on a scientific method or done on a hunch. The firm has asked you to examine and submit a report on this issue. An extract of option price quotations is supplied in Table 7.13, along with the following information:

The risk-free interest rate is 8 percent per annum in India and 4 percent per annum in the United States. The variability of the Indian rupee against the U.S. dollar is assumed to be 12 percent. Other particulars, if any, required for logical computations can be assumed.

You may use the Black–Scholes model to calculate the option prices and implied volatility. Note that, in Table 7.13, ATM (at-the-money forward rate) strike refers to the option sold with a strike price equivalent to the prevailing forward price for the maturity of the option.

Table 7.13 Option Price Quotations

USD/INR spot: 45.1325				
Expiry	*1 month*	*3 months*	*6 months*	*12 months*
Strike	44.75	44.75	44.75	45.00

(Continued)

Table 7.13 **(*Continued*)**

	USD/INR spot: 45.1325			
Expiry	*1 month*	*3 months*	*6 months*	*12 months*
Call	0.48	0.60	0.74	0.80
Put	0.06	0.14	0.22	0.41
Strike	*45.00*	*45.00*	*45.00*	*45.25*
Call	0.30	0.44	0.58	0.66
Put	0.13	0.22	0.31	0.51
ATM strike	*45.15*	*45.18*	*45.22*	*45.31*
Call	0.21	0.34	0.46	0.63
Put	0.19	0.30	0.41	0.54
Strike	*45.25*	*45.25*	*45.25*	*45.50*
Call	0.17	0.31	0.45	0.54
Put	0.24	0.34	0.42	0.63
Strike	*45.50*	*45.50*	*45.50*	*45.75*
Call	0.08	0.20	0.34	0.44
Put	0.41	0.48	0.55	0.76

Source: Mecklai Financial Services Ltd.

Further Reading

1. Nahum Biger and John C. Hull, "The Valuation of Currency Options," Financial Management (Spring 1983): 24–28.
2. Mark Garman and Steve W. Kohlhagen, "Foreign Currency Option Values," Journal of International Money and Finance (1983): 231–237.
3. Ian Giddy, "The Foreign Exchange Option as a Hedging Tool," Midland Corporate Finance Journal (Fall 1983): 32–42.
4. John C. Hull, Options, Futures, and Other Derivatives (New Delhi: Prentice Hall of India Pvt. Ltd, 2001).
5. Robert A. Strong, Derivatives (Singapore: Thomson Asia Pvt. Ltd, 2002).
6. David DeRosa, Currency Derivatives—Pricing Theory, Exotic Options and Hedging Applications (New York: John Wiley and Sons, 1998).
7. J. Hull and A. White, "Hedging the Risks from Writing Foreign Currency," Journal of International Money and Finance (June 1987): 131–152.
8. Hans Stoll, "The Relationship between Put and Call Option Prices," Journal of Finance (December 1969): 801–824.

CHAPTER

8 Financial Swaps

CHAPTER OBJECTIVES

After studying this chapter, you should be able to:

1 Review the importance of financial swaps as risk management tools as well as profit-generating strategies.

2 Explain the concept of financial swaps and trace their evolution.

3 Understand various types of interest rate swaps and highlight the role of the intermediary in interest rate swap deals.

4 Explain the concept of forward rate agreement.

5 Highlight the importance of other derivative products like swaptions, caps, floors, and collars.

6 Explain the nature and importance of currency swaps.

7 Understand the nature of foreign exchange swaps.

8 Illustrate the determination of swap values.

9 Gain insight into credit default swaps.

Introduction

With the integration of global financial markets, a wide variety of innovative financial products have come into use. Financial swaps are one of these products. By virtue of being more flexible in nature as well as in operations, financial swaps enable market participants to structure swap deals according to their requirements. Strictly speaking, financial swaps are not financial instruments that can be issued by organizations to raise funds. Rather, they are techniques used by firms to manage their asset–liability mismatch in terms of interest rates and currencies. Swaps are also used to overcome constraints, like the non-availability of some maturities in certain markets and the lack of desired liquidity for certain financial products. Further, they are used to hedge certain financial risks like interest rate risk and exchange rate risk. Swaps also provide lucrative business for swap dealers, particularly commercial banks and financial institutions. Thus, all the parties (counterparties as well as the swap dealer) can benefit from swap transactions.

A **financial swap** is an agreement between two parties to exchange cash flows (a series of periodic payments) according to a formula. Financial swaps, like currency options, currency forwards, and currency futures are derivative securities that play an important role in financial risk management. However, they differ from other derivatives in terms of the period of risk coverage. While forwards, futures, and options cover short-term financial risks, swaps cover long-term exposure to financial risks, including currency risk. For cash flows in some currencies, hedging techniques like forwards and futures may not be available. In such cases, swaps—currency swaps in particular—can be used to hedge the cash flows to be received or paid in the foreign currency so that their currency risk is avoided. Currency swaps and interest rate swaps are the popular varieties of financial swaps. *Currency swaps* are mainly used for debt financing in the required currency at a reduced cost due to comparative advantages. *Interest rate swaps* have become important instruments to match maturities of assets and liabilities and also to obtain cost savings.

*A **financial swap** is an agreement between two parties to exchange cash flows according to a formula.*

Financial swaps are of recent origin. The first major swap contract in the history of financial swaps was the contract between the World Bank and IBM arranged by Salmon Brothers in the early 1980s. But the financial arrangements, like parallel loans and back-to-back loans, out of which financial swaps evolved, have a long history. So, any discussion on financial swaps warrants a mention of parallel loans and back-to-back loans.

Parallel Loans

Branching out by businesses is not a new phenomenon. It is a common practice in business circles to diversify business operations into new locations outside the country of origin. When a company has established a subsidiary unit in a foreign country, an issue to be addressed by the parent company is how to finance the subsidiary unit. One method of funding the subsidiary unit by the parent company is to raise funds in its domestic market and lend these funds to the subsidiary unit abroad. This has its own implications for both the parent firm and the subsidiary unit. With such an arrangement, both the parent unit and the subsidiary unit have the problem of currency risk, besides having to face restrictions on cross-border currency transactions. An alternative method is to raise funds directly in the country in which the subsidiary unit is located. This arrangement of raising funds in a foreign country to finance foreign operations is a natural hedge against currency risk. But this may cause an increase in the cost of funds. If a company wants to raise funds in a foreign market, it has to offer a higher rate of interest than what the domestic company is required to pay. In other words, the foreign company has a relative advantage of borrowing in its domestic market than in the foreign market. Another alternative method is a **parallel loan**, an arrangement in which a company borrows in the country where it has a relative advantage in terms of cost of funds, and then loans these funds to a foreign affiliate located in its home country at a rate lower than what the subsidiary unit would have had to pay. Conceptually, a **parallel loan** involves two parties providing loans simultaneously to each other on the condition that the loans will be paid back on a specified date in future.

*A **parallel loan** refers to an arrangement in which a foreign company borrows in the country where it has a relative advantage in terms of cost of funds, and then loans those funds to a foreign affiliate located in its own country at a rate lower than what the subsidiary unit would have had to pay in the domestic market.*

The concept of parallel loans can be effectively explained with an example. Consider a Japan-based company with a subsidiary in the United States, and a U.S.-based company with an affiliate in Japan. Suppose the interest rates in the United States are 5 percent for U.S. companies and 7 percent for foreign companies. Further, the interest rates in Japan are 4 percent for Japanese companies and 6 percent for foreign firms. In a parallel loan, the U.S.-based company borrows a certain amount at 5 percent in the U.S. market and lends the funds to the Japanese subsidiary in the United States at 5 percent, saving the Japanese subsidiary 2 percent. Similarly, the Japanese parent company raises a loan at 4 percent and lends that amount to the U.S. subsidiary in Japan at 6 percent, saving the U.S. subsidiary 2 percent. The timing of the cash flows and the principal amounts are set to satisfy both parties. Moreover, the Japanese subsidiary can use its USD-denominated revenues to repay the loan provided by the U.S.-based company, and the U.S. subsidiary can use its Yen-denominated revenues to repay the loan given by the Japanese company. Thus, each company has given a loan in its

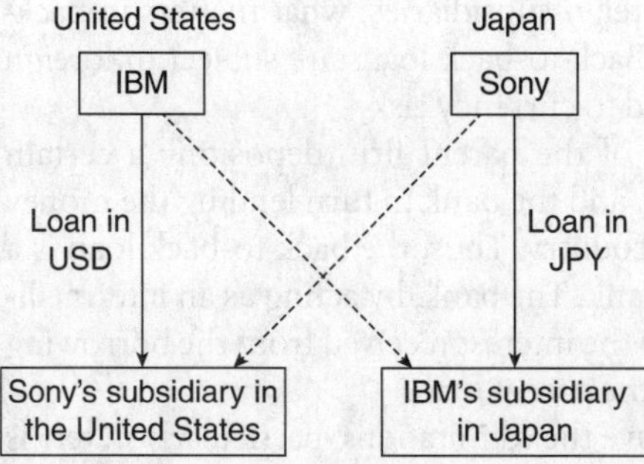

Figure 8.1

A Parallel Loan Arrangement

domestic currency to the other company in exchange for a loan in the foreign currency. The same amount will be paid back by both companies at the end of the loan period. There are two swaps, one swap at the initiation of the loan contract and another swap at the specified future date.

In some cases, the interest rates that the subsidiaries have to pay on their respective borrowings are the same rates that they would have paid had they borrowed directly in the markets of the countries in which they are located. In such cases, the parent companies would earn some margin, which is the difference between the rate at which they have borrowed and the rate at which they have lent. A typical parallel loan arrangement is illustrated in Figure 8.1.

By engaging in parallel loan arrangement, firms can avoid restrictions and taxes on cross-border currency transactions. There is no currency risk for either firm in such a transaction, because each is borrowing and repaying in the same currency. Further, each firm can pay interest according to the prevailing market rates in the country where funds are lent. Parallel loans are particularly useful when a company is engaged in a foreign project and expected to receive the cash flows in the foreign currency. Without parallel loan arrangement, if a company is engaged in a foreign project, the project may have a negative net present value consequent on depreciation of the foreign currency. Parallel loan is also a better method for effectively utilizing the blocked funds.

A serious limitation of parallel loans is that they are prone to default risk. If any party to the parallel loan agreement defaults, it does not release the other party from its obligation. Moreover, as there is no intermediary in parallel loan deals, it is difficult to identify counterparties with similar needs.

Back-to-Back Loans

Back-to-back loans are used by multinational corporations to finance their subsidiary units located in different countries. Four parties are involved in a parallel loan arrangement, but in a back-to-back loan arrangement, only two parties are involved. Consider the following example to understand how back-to-back loans are used. A Japanese company has a subsidiary in the United States, and a U.S. firm has a subsidiary in Japan. The Japanese company would like to fund its subsidiary in the United States, and the U.S. firm also wants to fund the capital expenditure of its subsidiary in Japan. The Japanese parent firm borrows yen in the Japanese capital market and lends the principal amount to the U.S. parent. Similarly, the U.S. parent firm borrows in the U.S. capital market, and lends the U.S. dollar amount to the Japanese parent company. At maturity, the principal amounts are re-exchanged so that the two parent firms can redeem their respective debts. Each parent firm can also pay to the other the periodical debt service. Though the parent companies in turn re-lend the foreign currency proceeds to their foreign subsidiaries, what matters in back-to-back loans is the original principal exchange. Back-to-back loans are subject to foreign exchange controls, and the parties are also exposed to currency risk.

***Back-to-back loans** may take the form of the parent firm depositing a certain amount of funds with a bank in its home country, and the bank in turn lending the money to the firm's subsidiary unit located in a foreign country.*

Back-to-back loans may also take the form of the parent firm depositing a certain amount of funds with a bank in its home country, and the bank in turn lending the money to the firm's subsidiary unit located in a foreign country. Thus, the back-to-back loan is a type of intercompany loan channeled through a bank. The bank, by acting as an intermediary, gets a margin, which is the difference between the interest received from the borrowing unit and the interest paid on the deposit made by the parent firm.

Both parallel loans and back-to-back loans have their limitations, particularly in terms of default risk and foreign exchange controls and regulations. The loans are carried on the accounting books of both firms. This limits additional borrowing and limits the leverage of these firms. Financial swaps were developed to address the problems associated with parallel loans and back-to-back loans. Financial swaps, therefore, are a natural extension of parallel loans and back-to-back loans, but without the drawbacks of these modes of financing.

Types of Swaps

***Interest rate swaps**, currency swaps, foreign exchange swaps, and non-deliverable currency swaps are the major types of financial swaps that are popular these days.*

A variety of swaps are traded in financial markets. The most important and widely used of these are interest rate swaps, currency swaps, foreign exchange swaps, and non-deliverable currency swaps.

Interest Rate Swaps

An **interest rate swap** is an agreement between two parties to exchange interest payments on a specific notional principal amount for a specific maturity. Since the principal amount is notional (theoretical), there is no exchange of the principal amount between the parties. The principal amount is simply taken as a reference amount for computing the interest amount. An interest rate swap thus involves the exchange of one set of cash flows for another. Each set of cash flows is determined by the reference index, the notional principal, and the dates of exchange.

*An **interest rate swap** is an agreement between two parties to exchange interest payments on a specific notional principal amount for a specific maturity.*

Interest rate swaps are widely used by commercial banks, investment banks, insurance companies, government agencies, and trusts. They are used as effective vehicles to hedge interest rate exposure; to reduce the cost of funding; to obtain higher yielding investment assets; and to take speculative positions. Interest rate risk is the main factor that prompts firms to engage in interest rate swaps. Interest rate risk arises due to fluctuating interest rates that affect the earnings or value of a portfolio. It may also be referred to as term-structure risk or basis risk. *Term-structure risk* arises on changes in the fixed interest rate term structure. For example, term-structure risk arises if interest rates are fixed on a liability for a period that differs from that on the offsetting asset (maturity mismatch). If fixed-/floating-rate assets are financed with floating-/fixed-rate liabilities, then again term-structure risk arises. *Basis risk* arises due to changes in spreads, that is, changes in the relationship between interest rates on lending and borrowing.

Basically, there are two types of interest rate swaps: *coupon swaps* and *basis swaps*. The following sections will provide a holistic sketch of each of these two varieties of swaps.

Coupon Swaps A coupon swap is the most common form of interest rate swap. Also known as a *plain vanilla interest rate swap*, a **coupon swap** is an agreement between two parties in which one party agrees to pay to the other party cash flows equal to the interest at a predetermined fixed rate on a notional principal amount for a certain number of years, and the other party is obliged to pay the counterparty cash flows equal to the interest amount at a floating rate, on the same notional principal amount for the same period of time. Thus, under a coupon swap, a series of payments calculated by applying a fixed rate of interest to a notional principal amount is exchanged for a stream of payments similarly calculated using a floating rate of interest. This kind of swap is also known as a *fixed-to-floating interest swap.*

*A **coupon swap** is an agreement between two parties in which one party agrees to pay to the other party cash flows equal to the interest at a predetermined fixed rate on a notional principal amount for a certain number of years, and the other party pays the counterparty cash flows equal to the interest amount at a floating rate, on the same notional principal amount for the same period of time.*

To understand the concept of coupon swaps, let us consider an example. A company with a relatively poor credit rating may be compelled by market conditions to borrow funds with a short maturity (floating rate) to finance its long-term assets, even though it prefers to borrow at a long-term fixed interest rate. The company believes that long-term interest rates are going to rise and, therefore, it seeks protection against the impact of higher interest rates on its profitability. One way out for the company is to enter into an interest rate swap to pay a fixed-rate index in exchange for receiving payments tied to the floating-rate index. By entering a swap contract, the company can close out its exposure to changes in short-term interest rates, but take on an exposure to long-term interest rates that may correspond to the company's long-term assets.

To further understand how coupon swaps work, consider a swap in which Firm X agrees to pay Firm Y an interest amount at the rate of 6 percent per annum with semi-annual compounding on a notional principal amount of USD 1 million. At the same time, Firm Y agrees to pay in return to Firm X the six-month LIBOR on the same notional principal amount. The swap is a five-year swap initiated, say, on 1 June 2014. But the interest payments are exchanged every six months. Firm X may use the swap to transform its five-year bond, paying a semiannual coupon of 7 percent. The firm expects the interest rates to rise in the near future. As Firm X does not wish to sell its holding, it can convert its investment into a synthetic floating rate with reference to LIBOR. Similarly, the counterparty—Firm Y—may use the swap contract to transform its floating-rate loan (investment) into a fixed-rate investment. The floating rate is LIBOR plus 50 basis points (one basis point equals 0.01 percent, and basis point is usually denoted by "bp"). This swap is illustrated in Figure 8.2.

After entering into a swap, Firm X has the following set of cash flows:

(i) It receives 7 percent interest rate on the five-year bond;
(ii) It receives LIBOR as per the terms of the swap; and
(iii) It pays a 6 percent interest rate to the counterparty as per the terms of the swap.

Thus, Firm X will have a net interest inflow of LIBOR + 1 percent. In other words, Firm X transforms an investment (five-year bond) with a fixed rate of interest at 7 percent into an asset earning LIBOR + 100 basis points.

Similarly, Firm Y has the following cash flows:

(i) It receives LIBOR + 50 bp on its investment (loan);
(ii) It receives a 6 percent fixed interest rate from Firm X as per the terms of the swap; and
(iii) It pays LIBOR to Firm X in return for the 6 percent received under the swap.

These cash flows will net out to an interest inflow of 6 percent + 50 bp. Thus, Firm Y transforms a loan, yielding LIBOR + 50 bp into an investment earning a fixed rate of 6.5 percent.

In our example, the first exchange of payments takes place on 1 December 2014, six months after the initiation of the agreement. Firm X pays to Firm Y, USD 0.03 million, which

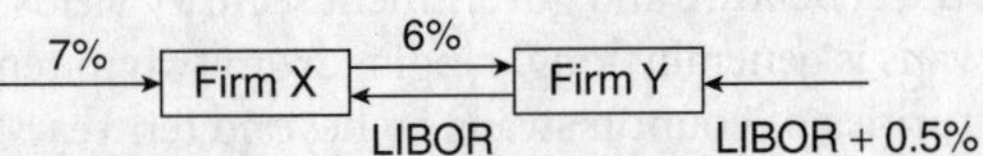

Figure 8.2

The Coupon Swap

is the interest on the principal of USD 1 million for six months at 6 percent per annum. Firm Y pays to Firm X interest on the principal of USD 1 million at the six-month LIBOR prevailing six months prior to 1 December 2014 (i.e. on 1 June 2014). If the six-month LIBOR on 1 June 2014 is 5 percent per annum, then Firm Y pays to Firm X USD 0.025 million (i.e. USD 1 million × 0.05/2). As far as the first payment of interest is concerned, there is no uncertainty, since the interest rate is determined by the LIBOR at the time the contract is signed.

The next exchange of payments takes place on 1 June 2015, one year after initiation of the contract. Firm X pays USD 0.03 million to Firm Y, and Firm Y pays interest on the principal of USD 1 million to Firm X at the six-month LIBOR prevailing six months prior to 1 June 2015, i.e. on 1 December 2014. Suppose that the six-month LIBOR on 1 December 2014 is 5.5 percent per annum. Then, Firm Y pays USD 0.0275 million to Firm X.

Since the swap is a five-year swap, in total there are ten exchanges of payment. Conventionally, interest rate swaps are structured so that one party remits the difference between the two payments to the other party.

As evident from this analysis of cash flows, firms may use swap contracts to transform their investments earning a fixed rate into investments earning a floating rate, or vice versa.

Likewise, investors can use swaps to transform a liability with a fixed rate of interest into a floating rate, or to transform a liability with a floating rate into a fixed rate of interest. For example, assume that Company B has a floating-rate loan of USD 10 million at LIBOR + 100 bp. Similarly, Company A has a fixed-rate loan of USD 10 million, on which it pays interest at 7 percent per annum. Both the companies can enter into a swap, according to which the cash flows will be:

- Company B pays LIBOR + 100 bp to its outside lenders.
- Company B receives LIBOR + 50 bp under the terms of the swap.
- Company B pays interest at 6.5 percent to Company A as per the terms of the swap.
- Company A pays interest at 7 percent to its outside lenders.
- Company A pays LIBOR + 50 bp under the terms of the swap.
- Company A receives interest at 6.5 percent under the terms of the swap.

Thus, for Company B, the swap can have the effect of transforming a liability at a floating rate of LIBOR + 100 bp into a liability with a fixed rate of 6.5 percent. Similarly, for Company A, the swap can have the effect of transforming a liability at a fixed rate of 7 percent into a liability at a floating rate of LIBOR + 50 bp.

Basis Swaps A **basis swap** is a floating-to-floating interest rate swap. With the exception of reference rates, basis swaps are the same as coupon swaps. In a basis swap, two parties agree to exchange floating interest payments, but based on different reference indices. A swap between a three-month LIBOR and a six-month LIBOR, or a swap between the prime rate and LIBOR are examples of basis swaps. A bank that lends at the prime interest rate but finances itself at the T-bill rate may use a prime-to-treasury bill rate swap. Firms may use basis swaps in order to eliminate basis risk, also known as *spread risk*. For example, a bank that lends at the prime interest rate and finances itself at LIBOR may face basis risk due to the possibility that the gap between the prime interest rate and LIBOR might become narrow. That would negatively affect the profitability of the bank. Another example is a firm that might hedge a long position in debentures by shorting government securities. Here, the firm is exposed to changes in the spread between the debenture and government security yields.

*A **basis swap** refers to two parties agreeing to exchange floating interest payments based on different reference indices.*

The period of both coupon and basis swaps is generally long, ranging from two to ten years. There are also cases in which the maturities of coupon swaps go beyond ten years. The two sets of interest cash flows are denominated in the same currency. The counterparty which offers fixed payments in a swap contract is also known as *a fixed-rate payer.* The counterparty which makes payments that depend on the movement in a specified interest rate index (e.g. LIBOR) is known as the *floating-rate payer.*

In both coupon swaps and basis swaps, interest cash flows are exchanged between the parties, and the actual amounts of cash flows are calculated on the agreed-upon notional principal amount at a fixed or a floating rate of interest. *Fixed-rate payments* are made periodically: quarterly, semiannually, or annually. *Floating-rate payments* are set in advance, but paid in arrears. For example, a 10-year loan carries an interest rate at three-month LIBOR + 100 bp per annum. The life of the loan is divided into three-month periods. For each period, the rate of interest is set at 1 percent per annum above the three-month LIBOR at the beginning of the period. However, interest is paid at the end of the period. Each floating-rate payment has three dates: Date 1 is the setting date, on which the floating rate applicable for the next payment is set; Date 2 is the date from which the next floating payments start to accrue; and Date 3 is the date on which the payment is due. The swaps have different settlement dates, with a specified period market index (e.g. six-month LIBOR) as the floating rate. The London Interbank Offer Rate, popularly known as LIBOR, is the most commonly used floating-rate index. Prime rates and T-bill rates are also used as reference rates for floating interest. The exact reference rate is specified in each case at the beginning of a given settlement period.

LIBOR is the interest rate offered by banks on deposits from other banks in Eurocurrency markets. LIBOR is also an important benchmark rate in international financial markets. It is determined by the British Bankers Association by taking into account the rates quoted by the leading multinational banks. LIBOR is available on one-month deposits, two-month deposits, three-month deposits, and so on. But LIBOR changes daily depending on time period as well as supply and demand for funds in the Eurocurrency market.

Other Types of Interest Rate Swaps Coupon swaps and basis swaps are not the only kinds of interest rate swaps one can construct. A swap can be constructed with two different kinds of floating indices or with two different kinds of fixed indices. There are also exotic swaps, like delayed-start swaps, collapsible swaps, indexed principal swaps, forward swaps, callable swaps, puttable swaps, and zero-coupon swaps. The *delayed-start swap* is a regular plain vanilla swap with the additional feature that the start date of the swap is not immediate. The *collapsible swap* is a combination of a plain vanilla swap with a swaption (discussed later in this chapter) on that swap. The *indexed principal swap* is a swap in which the principal is not fixed for the life of the option, but is tied to the levels of interest rates. The size of the principal increases as interest rates decline. In a *forward swap*, payments under the swap start at a specific future date. A *callable swap* gives the fixed-rate payer the right to terminate the swap before the maturity date, and on the other hand, a *puttable swap* gives the floating-rate payer the right to terminate the swap before the maturity date. A *zero-coupon swap* involves all fixed interest payments to be postponed until the maturity date of the swap. This means all fixed interest payments are made in a lump sum at the maturity of the swap. But floating-rate payments are made periodically according to the terms of the swap.

Comparative Advantages in Interest Rate Swaps Interest rate swaps are popular mainly because of comparative advantages enjoyed by the counterparties. Some firms have a comparative advantage in borrowing in certain markets, say, floating-rate markets, while other firms have a comparative advantage in fixed-rate markets. A firm will benefit if it goes to a market where it has a comparative advantage. This leads to situations where a firm borrows at a fixed rate when it really wants to opt for a floating-rate loan, or borrows at a floating rate when it wants a loan at a fixed rate. In such situations, swaps help firms to transform fixed-rate loans into a floating-rate loans, or vice versa.

Consider the following scenario, for example: Company X and Company Y face the interest rates as shown in Table 8.1.

The table shows that Company Y pays a higher rate of interest than Company X in both fixed and floating rate markets. This may be due to the lower credit rating of Company Y. An overall glance at each one's interest rates reveals that Company Y has a comparative

Table 8.1 Interest Rates for Company X and Company Y

	Fixed rate	*Floating rate*
Company X	8%	Six-month LIBOR + 50 bp
Company Y	9%	Six-month LIBOR + 75 bp

advantage in the floating-rate market, as the extra rate that it pays in the floating-rate market over the rate paid by Company X is relatively low. Therefore, Company X borrows in the fixed-rate market at 8 percent per annum, and Company Y borrows in the floating-rate market at LIBOR + 75 bp. They then enter into a swap, such that Company X ends up borrowing at a floating rate, and Company Y ends up borrowing at a fixed rate. The swap can thus be negotiated in such a way that both companies would be benefited.

Lenders may have the option of increasing the spread over LIBOR, if the borrower's credit rating declines. In extreme circumstances, the lender may even refuse to roll over the loan at all. However, lenders at a fixed rate do not have the option of changing the terms of the loan in this way. In some cases, the spread over LIBOR is guaranteed in advance regardless of changes in the credit rating of the parties.

Intermediation in Interest Rate Swap Deals In the early days of financial swaps, the parties to the swap had to find each other and settle the deal without any intermediary, and it was very difficult for a party to find another party with parallel funding needs. Often, it was a sheer coincidence that the required pattern of cash flows of the counterparties matched with each other. This gave rise to the need for an intermediary institution that could satisfy both counterparties in terms of their cash flow requirements. Accordingly, banks and other financial institutions have emerged as intermediaries in swaps. In the process of intermediation, a bank or a financial institution enters into two separate offsetting contracts—one with the first counterparty and the other with the second counterparty. The intermediary bank assumes full responsibility of discharging the contract and, therefore, is exposed to default risk. As compensation, the intermediary enjoys the benefit of a spread, that is, the difference in the interest received and the interest paid. In other words, the spread earned by the intermediary partly compensates it for the default risk. Since the intermediary takes the role of counterparty to both the parties, and thereby bears the risk of default by either party, the liability holders do not need to investigate the creditworthiness of the other party. This facilitates swapping by debtors of relatively low credit worthiness.

In reality, it is unlikely that the counterparties will approach an intermediary bank at exactly the same time and want to take opposite positions exactly in the same swap. Therefore, the intermediary banks may warehouse the swaps in order to meet the demand for swaps without requiring simultaneous availability of a matching counterparty. A bank may maintain a large portfolio of swaps, many of which offset one another. The net exposure, if any, is hedged, generally by the use of financial futures. If interest rates fall, the price of futures contracts will increase, providing the bank with a gain that compensates for a fall in interest rate.

To assess the role of the intermediary in a swap deal, consider an example. Firm A borrows USD 1 million for three years at a fixed interest rate of 7 percent, and uses these funds to extend medium-term advances to its customers who would pay LIBOR + 50 bp. The profitability of Firm A's transactions depends on LIBOR, which is a floating-rate index. Whenever LIBOR is less than 6.5 percent (7% −0.50%), Firm A will incur a loss; and if LIBOR is greater than 6.5 percent, the firm will gain.

Firm B invests USD 1 million in three-year bonds at a coupon rate of 9 percent, but its funding is through a floating-rate loan at LIBOR + 25 bp. If LIBOR is higher than 8.75 percent, Firm B will lose money, and if LIBOR is less than 8.75 percent, the firm will actually gain. Thus, the profitability of Firm B depends on the actual level of LIBOR.

The two firms in this example may seek to enter into a swap through an intermediary bank in order to reduce the risk that may threaten their profitability. The details of the swap are as follows: Firm A enters into a contract with an intermediary bank, according to which it pays six-month LIBOR to the bank over three years, on a notional principal amount of USD 1 million. In return, the bank agrees to pay an interest amount, calculated at the rate of 7.5 percent, on a notional principal amount of USD 1 million for three years.

Thus, the cash flows of Firm-A are:

Receives from customers on advances: LIBOR + 50 bp
Pays to the bank: (LIBOR)
Receives from bank: 7.5%
Pays on borrowing: (7%)
Cost of funds: (LIBOR – 0.5%)
Margin: 1%

Similarly, Firm B enters into a swap with the same bank and, accordingly, pays the interest amount calculated at 8 percent on a notional principal amount of USD 1 million for three years. In return, the bank pays six-month LIBOR over three years. Thus, the cash flows of Firm B are:

Receives interest on USD 1 million investment in bonds: 9%
Pays to the bank: (8%)
Receives from the bank: LIBOR
Pays on a loan: (LIBOR + 25 bp)
Cost of funds: (8.25%)
Margin: 0.75%

The bank, which acts as an intermediary, will have the following cash flows:

Receives from Firm A: LIBOR
Pays to Firm A: (7.5%)
Receives from Firm B: 8.0%
Pays to Firm B: (LIBOR)
Net margin: 0.5%

It is evident that the three parties can get a certain percentage of margins, by entering into swaps. Firm A can reduce volatility in its earnings by entering into a swap. It can transfer the risk of loss due to fluctuations in LIBOR to the intermediary bank. It can also reduce the cost of funds to (LIBOR – 50 bp). Finally, it has a locked-in spread of 100 bp on its portfolio. Similarly, Firm B can reduce volatility in its interest payments on its loan. It can do so by transferring to the bank the risk of higher interest payments on its loan due to fluctuations in LIBOR. Finally, Firm B can earn a lock-in spread of 75 bp. The bank as an intermediary can also earn 50 bp.

As is evident from this analysis, the intermediary bank enters into two offsetting swaps with the counterparties. If neither of the counterparties defaults, the bank is certain to make a profit of USD 5,000 (USD 1,000,000 × 0.005). But, there is no guarantee that neither party defaults. Therefore, the net profit is the price for the services of the bank to the counterparties and also compensation for the risk of default.

The swap can be represented by the diagram shown in Figure 8.3.

Market making in Interest Rate Swaps The intermediaries in swaps are also known as **swap dealers**. They make markets in swaps by quoting a fixed interest rate they are willing to pay for a specified floating interest rate, and a fixed interest rate they are ready to receive in exchange for a specified floating interest rate. Thus, swap dealers, as market makers in swap contracts, quote two rates in the *bid–ask swap rates.* The *bid rate* is the fixed interest rate the swap dealer is willing to pay, and the *ask rate* is the fixed interest rate that the dealer is ready to receive for a certain floating interest rate. Sometimes, the counterparty may wish to receive or pay at a rate other than the rates quoted by the swap dealer. In such a case, the swap dealer

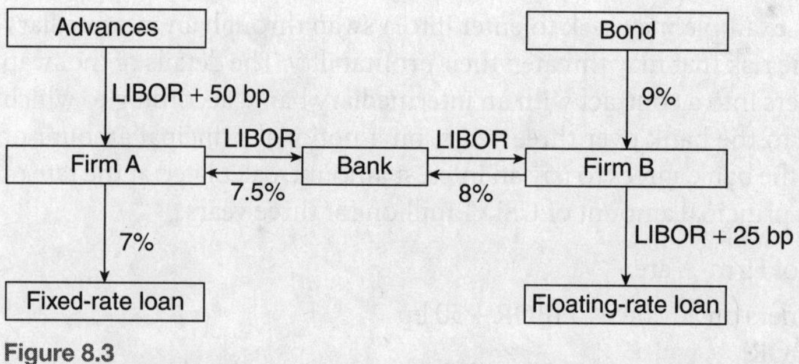

Figure 8.3

Intermediation in Swap Deal

The intermediaries in swaps are also known as ***swap dealers****. They make markets in swaps by quoting the fixed rate they are willing to pay for a specified floating interest rate and the fixed rate they are ready to receive in exchange for the specified floating interest rate.*

may adjust the floating interest rate by adding or subtracting a margin over the reference rate. Such types of transactions are known as *off-market swaps.* As bid–ask rates are close to the long-term interest rates on high-quality bonds, swap dealers may also adjust these rates, depending on the interest rates in the market.

Swap spreads are determined by supply and demand at any given time. If many parties want to receive a fixed interest rate rather than a floating interest rate, swap spreads tend to fall. If the reverse happens, swap spreads tend to rise.

Although bid–ask terms are commonly used in swap transactions, the counterparties do not really buy or sell anything. Instead, they enter into a contract to exchange future cash flows based on two different interest rates—one is tied to a yield on a comparable security (fixed rate), and the other is determined at a later date (floating rate). However, going by the same terminology of bid–ask, LIBOR is interpreted as the real thing involved in the deal, and the fixed interest rate is then the price paid or received in exchange for LIBOR. Therefore, the fixed-rate payer is said to be buying LIBOR, and the fixed-rate receiver is said to be selling LIBOR.

Swaptions: Options on Interest Rate Swaps Swaptions are another category of popular derivative instruments. A *swaption* is an agreement between the buyer and the seller that gives the buyer the right, but not the obligation, to enter into an interest rate swap on predetermined terms with regard to the rate of interest, notional principal, floating-rate index, maturity, and so on.

There are two kinds of swaptions: a *call swaption,* also known as *a payer swaption,* and *a put swaption,* also known as a *receiver swaption.* The call swaption gives the buyer the right, but not the obligation, to enter into a swap contract, according to which he will receive a predetermined floating interest rate and pay a certain fixed rate of interest. On the other hand, the put swaption gives the buyer the right to enter into a swap contract with the terms that he will receive a certain fixed rate of interest and pay a predetermined floating rate of interest.

For example, consider a firm that will have to finance an investment in the next six months with ten-year floating-rate bonds, but wishes to swap into fixed interest rate payments. In order to have certainty with regard to fixed interest rate payments, the firm has entered into a swaption, according to which it gets the right to receive six-month LIBOR for a fixed rate of 6 percent for 10 years starting in six months. If the fixed rate on a regular ten-year interest rate swap in six months turns out to be higher than 6 percent, the firm will exercise the option and get the swap for 6 percent. In other words, the swaption will entitle the firm to pay a below-market fixed interest while receiving LIBOR. If, by any chance, the fixed interest rate is lower, the firm will allow the swaption to expire and enter into the swap contract on the current terms.

On the other side, another firm has entered into a swaption that gives it the right to receive a fixed rate of interest of, say, 7 percent in return for a floating rate, say, a six-month LIBOR for a five-year period, starting from a certain date six months from now. Suppose that, at the maturity of the option, the market swap rate is less than 7 percent. The firm will then exercise the option and accordingly enter into a swap. The firm, therefore, will be able to enter into a swap at more favourable terms because of swaption.

Thus, the holder of a swaption can benefit from favourable interest rate movements and, at the same time, protect itself from unfavourable interest rate movements, of course at a cost. The seller of a swaption has an obligation to discharge the agreement according to the stated terms, in return for the upfront premium paid by the buyer. Swaptions are also different from forward swaps or deferred swaps in which both the parties are obligated to enter into a swap agreement.

Benefits of Interest Rate Swaps There are two major benefits of interest rate swaps. First, these swaps can be used to hedge interest rate risk. Firms that have borrowed at a floating rate of interest are exposed to the risk of increase in interest rates. A firm can avoid such risk by borrowing at a fixed rate of interest. It may not, however, be able to raise fixed-rate loans due to unfavourable market conditions, including high rates of interest. A low credit rating may also be a disadvantage, if a firm wants to borrow at a fixed rate of interest. If a firm with a low credit rating wants to raise a fixed-rate loan, it can do so only at a higher rate of interest. However, firms can comfortably raise a floating-rate loan and swap that loan for a fixed-rate loan, thereby obtaining fixed-rate funds. For example, a bank raises USD 10 million by issuing five-year bonds at a fixed interest rate of 10 percent, payable six monthly for the purpose of providing mortgages on a floating-rate basis. The bank is exposed to the risk that interest rates might fall. If the interest rates fall, the interest receipts from the mortgages will not be sufficient to meet the interest payments on the bonds. To avoid such interest rate risk, the bank enters a swap and exchanges its fixed-rate liability for one on a floating-rate basis. The gains/losses on the swap offset losses/gains on the original positions being hedged. More specifically, the gain from the higher mortgage receipts arising from higher interest rates is offset by a loss on the swap. On the contrary, if interest rates fall, the mortgage interest receipts will decrease, but that is offset by the gain from the swap.

The second advantage is that interest rate swaps can be used to reduce interest costs. A company with a relatively higher credit rating pays less for funds it raises than a company with a lower rating. The incremental borrowing premium known as *credit quality spread* paid by a company with a lower rating is greater in relation to fixed interest rate borrowings than for floating-rate borrowings. In other words, borrowers of relatively low credit worthiness may face a higher interest rate differential in the fixed-rate market than in the floating-rate market. Such borrowers would gain by borrowing on a floating-rate basis. However, if they are interested in having fixed-rate funds, they could first borrow in the floating-rate market in which they have a comparative advantage, and then swap into a fixed-rate basis. Thus, by borrowing in a market in which they have comparative advantage, they can reduce interest costs. According to the theory of comparative advantage, each of the counterparties has a comparative advantage in a different credit market, and that advantage in one market can be used to obtain an equivalent advantage in a different market to which access is otherwise denied. Let us consider an example of two firms to gain insight into how the theory of comparative advantage works in the case of swaps. Firm X and Firm Y face the interest rates shown in Table 8.2. Firm Y, which has relatively low credit worthiness, faces higher interest rates, but the interest rate differential is higher for a fixed rate than for a floating rate. In other words, Firm Y has a comparative advantage in the floating-rate market. If Firm Y wants fixed-rate funds, it would first raise funds in the floating-rate market in which it has a comparative advantage and then swap into a fixed-rate basis. A possible swap arrangement is shown in Figure 8.4.

Table 8.2 Interest Rates for Firm X and Firm Y

	Floating rate	*Fixed rate*
Firm X	LIBOR + 50 bp	9%
Firm Y	LIBOR + 100 bp	11%

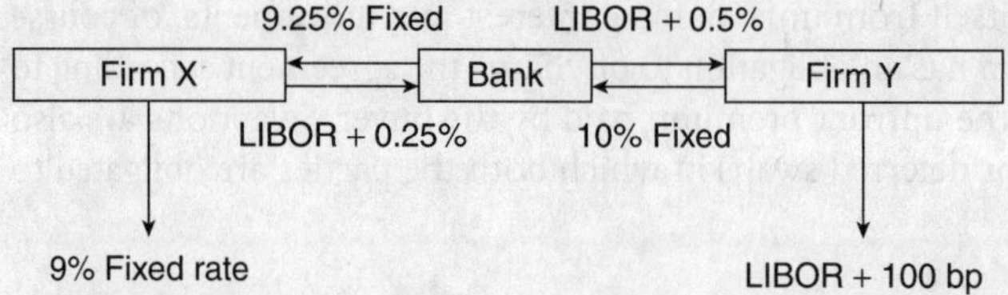

Figure 8.4

Interest Rate Swap for Firm X and Firm Y

The difference between the two interest differentials is 1.5 percent, and this is shared between the three participants in the swap transaction. Firm X receives 9.25 percent fixed, while paying a 9 percent fixed rate to its creditors, and LIBOR + 25 bp to the intermediating bank. So, the net benefit for Firm X is 0.5 percent (a saving of 0.25 percent relative to borrowing directly at LIBOR + 0.50 percent and a saving of 0.25 percent relative to the fixed rate). Firm Y receives LIBOR + 0.50 percent, while paying LIBOR + 100 bp, and 10 percent per annum fixed interest rate to the bank. The net benefit to Firm Y is 0.50 percent (a saving of 1 percent in fixed-rate interest relative to borrowing directly at 11 percent minus an extra burden of 0.50 percent in the floating rate). The intermediary bank receives LIBOR + 0.25 percent from Firm X, plus 10 percent per annum fixed interest rate from Firm Y, and pays 9.25 percent fixed interest to Firm X and LIBOR + 0.50 percent to Firm Y. So, the net benefit to the bank is 0.50 percent for arranging the swap.

There are a number of alternative swap arrangements that can be used according to one's own comparative advantage. As far as risks are concerned, the counterparty that is obliged to pay a floating rate will be at risk from a rising LIBOR, whereas the counterparty that receives the floating rate will be at risk from an opportunity loss in the event of a fall in LIBOR. Both counterparties are also at risk from default by the other.

Value of Interest Rate Swaps An interest rate swap can be viewed as a pair of bond transactions, as a series of forward rate transactions, or as a pair of options, and can be valued accordingly.

If an interest rate swap is considered to be a pair of bond transactions, the swap value is the difference in the values between two bonds. If a bond is purchased, the holder of the bond receives interest, and if a bond is issued, the issuer pays interest. Much in the same way, in an interest rate swap of the plain vanilla variety, the counterparty pays a fixed rate of interest and receives a floating rate of interest. In other words, an interest rate swap involves the exchanging of cash flows associated with a fixed-rate interest bond for cash flows associated with a floating-rate interest bond. For example, assume that Firm A has lent Firm B, USD 1 million at a three-month LIBOR rate, and Firm B has lent Firm A USD 1 million at a fixed interest rate of 6 percent per annum. To put it differently, Firm B has sold a USD 1 million floating-rate bond to Firm A, and purchased a USD 1 million fixed-rate bond from Firm A. So, the value of the swap to Firm B is the difference in the values of the two bonds. The value of the swap can be derived using the following formula:

$$V_s = V_f - V_{fl}$$

where

V_s = Value of interest rate swap

V_f = Value of fixed-rate bond underlying the swap

V_{fl} = Value of floating-rate bond underlying the swap

The initial value of a swap is zero because the counterparties negotiate the terms of the swap in such a way that the present value of the payments must be equal to the present value of the cash flows that will be received. In other words, the present value of the payments made by a party will be equal to the present value of the payments received by the same party. This creates a situation that does not allow arbitrage. However, as time passes, this will cease to be the case. The shape of the forward yield curve used to price the swap initially will change over time, giving the swap a positive net present value for either the fixed-rate payer or the floating-rate payer, notwithstanding that a periodic exchange of payments is made. A firm that has borrowed on a fixed-rate basis will benefit if interest rates rise, because it has locked-in a lower interest rate. But a floating-rate payer benefits, if interest rates fall. Put differently, when interest rates increase, the fixed-rate payer benefits, because the value of the swap increases. In contrast, the fixed-rate receiver will be adversely affected by a rise in interest rates, because this results in a decline in the value of a swap. As a result of changes in interest rates, the cash flows associated with the fixed-rate side and the floating-rate side do not have equal value and, therefore, the swap does have value to one of the counter parties.

Since the cash flows associated with the two kinds of bonds will occur in future, the present value of these cash flows needs to be determined in order to have comparability.

Thus,

$$V_f = \frac{K_1}{(1+r)^1} + \frac{K_2}{(1+r)^2} + \cdots + \frac{K_n P}{(1+r)^n}$$

where

$K_1, K_2, \ldots, K_n$ = Amounts paid by the fixed-rate bond at time 1, 2, …, n

r = Discount rate for the period until the next payment date

P = Par value of the bond

The interest rates of floating-rate bonds are reassessed at certain points in time in the light of the reference rate. Once determined, the interest rate would be fixed for a certain time period (e.g. six months). Thus, floating-rate bonds have variable coupons and each coupon is aligned with market interest rates at predetermined points in time (e.g. every six months). Since, at each coupon adjustment date, the rates of interest are set equal to the required rates of return, which are also the relevant discount rates, the floating-rate bond will equal its par value on that date. As the value of a floating-rate bond is equal to par value on the coupon adjustment date, the valuation of a floating-rate bond can be carried out as if there were only two future cash flows: the next coupon payment and the par value on the coupon adjustment date. Further, as floating-rate bonds tend to revert to their par values on the interest reassessment dates, only the next interest reassessment date is relevant for discounting purposes. Thus, the value of the floating-rate bond is given by the following formula:

$$V_{ft} = \frac{K_f}{(1+r_t)} + \frac{P}{(1+r_t)}$$

where

V_{ft} = Value of the floating-rate bond

t = Period to the next coupon payment (and adjustment date)

K_f = Floating-rate payment (next coupon)

Example 8.1

A bank has a fixed-to-floating interest rate swap, according to which it receives a 10 percent fixed rate of interest semi-annually and pays 6-months LIBOR. The swap, negotiated a year back, has a five-year maturity. The notional principal amount is INR 1 million. The last interest payment was made six months back, when the LIBOR for the current semester was set at 9 percent. The current six-month LIBOR is 8 percent per annum, and the fixed interest rate for a four-year loan is 9 percent. What is the value of the swap?

Solution

The value of the floating-rate loan of INR 1 million will be

$$1{,}000{,}000(1+0.045)/(1+0.04) = \text{INR } 1{,}004{,}808$$

This amount is the present value of the principal amount and the interest to be received six months from now.

The cash flows of the fixed-rate bond (INR 1 million) will be as given in Table 8.3.

Table 8.3 Cash Flows of the Fixed-Rate Bond

At the end of the	*Cash flows (INR)*	*Discount factor at 9%*
6th month:	50,000	0.9569
12th month:	50,000	0.9174
18th month:	50,000	0.8811
24th month:	50,000	0.8475
30th month:	50,000	0.8163
36th month:	50,000	0.7874
42nd month:	50,000	0.7605
48th month:	1,050,000	0.7353

The present value of the above cash flows at 9 percent discount rate is INR 1,070,420. Thus, the value of the swap is (INR 1,070,420 – INR 1,004,808), or INR 65,612. If the bank is in the opposite position of paying fixed rates and receiving floating rates, the value of the swap would be (–)INR 65,612.

Since the period (t) is short, normally six months or less, the value of a flexible rate bond is not significantly sensitive to changes in interest rates. Fixed-rate bonds, which have a long duration for the payment of the interest and the principal amount, are much more sensitive to interest rate movements.

Caps, Floors, and Collars Caps, floors, and collars are popular options-based derivative products in financial markets. **Caps** are derivative instruments used by participants to hedge against a rise in the interest rate or the exchange rate above a certain level. A cap is an agreement in which the seller is obliged to pay the difference between a particular floating-rate index, say, LIBOR, and the cap strike rate whenever that difference is positive. In financial swap transactions, the floating rate is reset periodically according to a pre-specified formula. The time between resets, known as the *tenor,* could be a month (monthly), three months (quarterly), six months (semiannual or biannual), and so on.

__Caps__ are derivatives that provide insurance against a rise in the interest rate or the exchange rate above a certain level.

To understand how a cap works, let us take an example of a firm in India that has raised a floating-rate loan whose interest payments are based on three-month T-bill rates.

Instead of entering into a swap contract to hedge against a rise in the T-bill rate, the firm can buy a cap with the same reset conditions. On each reset date, the firm would compare the T-bill rate with the exercise rate, also known as the cap rate. If it is higher than the cap rate, the firm would exercise the option and receive the difference between the two rates, adjusted for the three-month duration and multiplied by the principal amount (which is notional sometimes). The payment will be made after the three-month period and not on the reset date. If it is lower than the cap rate, the firm will allow the option to lapse, and the interest rate on the loan will be reset as per the current T-bill rate. A cap is thus a contract involving a series of call options. Each individual option is called a caplet.

Let us now consider another example of caps to understand how the amount payable is calculated. A firm has sold a one-year semiannual (or biannual) settlement, a 6 percent cap on six-month LIBOR in return for an upfront option premium. The notional principal amount is USD 10 million. Suppose the settlement date is 1 July, and the LIBOR on that date is 8 percent. The buyer of the cap will receive a settlement of the following amount in arrears:

$$(8\% - 6\%) \times \text{USD}\,10\text{ million} \times \frac{180}{360} = \text{USD}\,0.10\text{ million}$$

A **floor** is an agreement in which the seller is obliged to pay the difference between a particular rate index (e.g. LIBOR) and the floor exercise rate whenever the floating-rate index is below the floor exercise rate. Thus, a floor is akin to a cap, except that a floor provides a hedge against the rate falling below a certain level, known as the **floor rate**. It is a contract composed of a series of put options. Each individual option is called *a floorlet*.

*A **floor** provides a hedge against the interest rate or exchange rate falling below a certain level, known as the **floor rate**.*

For example, consider that a firm has invested INR 10 million in a five-year floating-rate bond. According to the terms of the bond, the firm will get an amount of (six-month LIBOR + 25 bp), the rate being reset every six months. In order to hedge against falling interest rates, the firm has purchased an interest rate floor with a strike rate of 6 percent. The firm has paid 1 percent of the investment as upfront premium to the seller of the floor. As the rate is being reset every six months, the floor contract will have nine reset dates. In other words, the floor contract can be viewed as a portfolio of nine put options on six-month LIBOR with maturities 6, 12, 18, …, 54 months. Thus, the effective return for the firm on its investment depends on the value of LIBOR at all future reset dates. The firm receives payment from the seller when the LIBOR falls below the strike rate (6 percent).

In the case of caps as well as floors, no payment needs to be made by a seller if the floating-rate index is above the floor rate or below the cap rate. The seller of a cap or a floor in return gets an option premium upfront.

A collar is a combination of a cap and a floor. A firm that finds the premium on a cap too high may buy a cap and simultaneously sell a floor. The premium received on the sale of the floor would partly or completely offset the premium paid on the cap. If the premium received is equal to the premium paid, it is called a *zero-cost collar.* In a zero-cost collar, the premiums cancel out. The firm can reduce its burden of premium only by sacrificing some of the potential gains from favourable interest rate changes.

*A **collar** is a combination of a cap and a floor.*

A collar is also designed to guarantee that an interest rate always lies between two given levels. It involves a short position in the cap and a long position in the floor when hedging against a fall in the interest rate. Similarly, a collar is composed of a long position in the cap and a short position in the floor when hedging against a rise in the interest rate.

Currency Swaps

A **currency swap** is a contract between two parties to exchange cash flows denominated in two different currencies. More specifically, a currency swap is a contract between two parties to exchange streams of interest payments in different currencies for a certain period of time and to exchange principal amounts in different currencies at a previously agreed-upon

A **currency swap** is a contract between two parties to exchange streams of interest payments in different currencies for a certain period of time and to exchange principal amounts in different currencies at an agreed-upon exchange rate.

exchange rate at the time of maturity of the contract. Thus, in a currency swap, there are two principal amounts—one for each currency. The exchange of the principal amount at maturity is essential, but the exchange of the principal amount at the beginning is optional. The interest rates involved in the currency swap are expressed on either a fixed or a floating-rate basis in either or both currencies. Currency swaps are also known as cross-currency swaps. Currency swaps and interest rate swaps can be combined to form different types of currency swaps, such as fixed-to-fixed currency swaps, fixed-to-floating currency swaps, or floating-to-floating currency swaps.

In a *fixed-to-fixed currency swap,* one party borrows a certain amount in one currency, say, U.S. dollars, at a fixed rate of interest, and another party raises a loan in another currency, say, Japanese yen, at a fixed rate of interest. Now both the counterparties agree to exchange the loan amounts. Subsequently, they make periodic interest payments in the same currency. At maturity, the principal amounts are re-exchanged. In *a floating-to-floating currency swap,* both parties pay a floating rate, but with different benchmark indices such as LIBOR and T-bill rate. And in *a fixed-to-floating currency swap,* the exchange is between interest payments at a fixed rate in one currency and interest payments at a floating rate in another currency. The swap leg the counterparty agrees to pay is a liability in one currency, and the swap leg the counterparty agrees to receive is an asset in the other currency. Currency swaps based on floating-rate cash flows in a currency other than USD against floating-rate payments in USD are much in use.

Uses of Currency Swaps Currency swaps are mainly used to take advantage of favourable credit markets. In other words, they are used to lower the cost of funds. They can also be used to diversify currency risk. Thus, currency swaps are typically used when one wants to:

- invest in foreign assets without foreign currency exposure;
- issue debt securities in foreign currency at more favourable rates;
- create synthetic foreign currency liability;
- match the assets with liabilities in the same currency; or
- take interest rate advantage.

The following examples can illustrate the use of currency swaps:

1. **Creation of synthetic asset:** A Singapore-based firm wishes to purchase a five-year SGD bond with a minimum credit rating of AA and a yield of not less than (LIBOR + 50 bp). Finding that no such bond is available, the firm purchases a five-year GBP bond with a credit rating of AA at a yield of (LIBOR + 75 bp). The total amount invested in the bond is GBP 10 million. Simultaneously, the firm enters into a cross-currency swap according to which it pays GBP (LIBOR + 75 bp) and receives SGD (LIBOR + 50 bp) over the life of the bond. The spot rate is set at GBP/SGD 2.8070. It is also agreed to exchange principals at the beginning of the swap. Thus, by using the cross-currency swap, the firm creates a synthetic SGD floating-rate bond (asset). The firm does not have any currency exposure in GBP as the currency exposure created by GBP liability is offset by the currency exposure created by the GBP asset. In other words, the firm has a net position only in the base currency of SGD. However, it faces the full credit risk of the GBP bond. If there is a default on the bond, the firm is still obliged to make all remaining payments under the swap or reverse the swap at its future book value.
2. **Creation of synthetic liability:** An Indian firm wants to raise INR 100 million by issuing five-year bonds. The firm can raise the required funds by offering a yield of at least LIBOR + 100 bp. Alternatively, it can issue the bonds in Australia at a yield of 6 percent. It can then enter into a five-year currency swap for a notional amount of INR 100 million, agreeing to receive AUD 6 percent and pay INR (LIBOR + 50 bp). The current spot rate is INR/AUD 0.02879. The swap agreement gives a net position in INR (the base currency). Over the five-year term of the bond, the firm receives the

AUD coupons from the counterparty that it owes to the bond investors and pays INR (LIBOR + 50 bp). At maturity, the firm will receive from the counterparty the AUD bond principal amount that it owes to the bond investors, and in return it will pay INR 100 million irrespective of the then spot rate of INR/AUD. Thus, the firm has created a synthetic INR liability by using the currency swap.

3. **Matching of assets with liabilities in the same currency**: An U.S.-based MNC has a sizeable portion of its assets denominated in SGD with no corresponding SGD liabilities. The firm feels that any fluctuations in the exchange rate will lead to volatility in its earnings. The firm is considering raising SGD in the Singapore market and repaying USD debt as a way to hedge this exposure. The firm is required to pay SGD (LIBOR + 60 bp) in order to do so. Alternatively, the firm can enter a currency swap, according to which the firm will pay SGD (LIBOR + 10 bp), and in return it will receive USD LIBOR. The principal amounts involved are SGD 1.5 billion and USD 1.0 billion. The period of the swap is seven years. In effect, the firm has transferred some of its USD liabilities into SGD liabilities to offset the SGD assets it owns and has thereby reduced its currency exposure. Any currency loss on the asset will be offset by a corresponding currency gain on the currency swap.
4. **Interest rate advantage:** An Indian MNC needs USD 20 million to finance a five-year project of its U.S. subsidiary. At the current exchange rate of USD/INR 45, the Indian MNC could raise a loan of INR 900 million by issuing five-year 10 percent bonds. The MNC would then convert the Indian currency to U.S. dollars to finance the U.S. project. An alternative for the MNC is to raise USD 20 million in the U.S. capital market by issuing five-year 8 percent bonds as against the current normal borrowing rate of 7 percent for a U.S. firm of equivalent creditworthiness. On the other hand, a U.S. MNC has a subsidiary in India, which needs INR 950 million to finance its new five-year project. The U.S. parent can raise USD 21 million in the U.S. capital market by issuing five-year bonds at a fixed interest rate of 7 percent, and convert these funds to INR to finance the project. Alternatively, the U.S. firm can issue bonds in the Indian capital market to raise the needed funds for its subsidiary in India, but it has to offer a 12 percent rate of interest since it is a foreign company in India.

Raising the funds in the local currency of the parent companies and converting them to the currency of the country in which the subsidiaries are located will create transaction exposure due to exchange rate fluctuations. So, the two MNCs are confronted with either transaction exposure or borrowing at a higher rate of interest. A currency swap can be organized to resolve this issue. Though there are many possible ways in which the swaps can be structured, one simple swap structure for the given scenario is as follows:

Each MNC raises the needed funds in the currency of the country in which it has a comparative advantage. Then, the two MNCs enter into a swap which requires that:

- the two MNCs exchange the proceeds received from the sale of bonds;
- the two MNCs make interest payments to service the debt of the other party; and
- at the termination date of the swap, which generally coincides with the maturity of the bonds, both parties re-exchange the principal amounts of their respective bond issues.

Thus, a loan in Indian currency at the interest rate of 10 percent is transformed into a U.S. dollar loan at the interest rate of 7 percent. This makes the Indian MNC better-off than it would be, had it gone directly to the U.S. capital market (with a 1 percent interest rate advantage). Similarly, the U.S. MNC is also better-off, with a 2 percent interest rate advantage, than it would be, if it had gone directly to the Indian capital market. It may seem that the swap is not advantageous to the U.S. MNC as it has to pay the interest at 10 percent as against the Indian MNC paying only 7 percent. But the spot and long-term forward exchange rates will adjust to compensate for the interest rate differential in accordance with the interest rate parity principle. The forward rate is a direct function of the interest rate differential for the two currencies. As a result, a currency with a higher interest rate must have a corresponding lower forward rate. In other words, the exchange of currencies in the future at the current spot rate would offset the present difference in interest rates. Nevertheless, both the companies are exposed to foreign exchange risk when they re-exchange the principal amounts.

The swap between the U.S. MNC and the Indian MNC is illustrated Figure 8.5. Initially, the principal amounts flow in the same direction as the arrows in the Figure 8.5. But the interest payments during the five-year period of the loan and the final principal payment flow opposite to the arrows.

In practice, it is not possible for a company to find another company with mirror-image financing needs. So, a *swap dealer* comes into the picture to meet the individual requirements of the firms. The swap dealer not only acts as an intermediary between the counterparties, but also warehouses the currency swaps. In other words, the swap dealer also takes positions by directly entering into swap agreements with the firms. The dealer gets a margin for his services as well as for foreign exchange risk.

In our example of the U.S. MNC and the Indian MNC, it is assumed that both the companies have made fixed payments. Instead, suppose the Indian MNC seeks a floating rate rather than a fixed rate. In this case, the U.S. MNC would issue floating-rate bonds in the U.S. capital market at a rate of, say, LIBOR + 100 bp. As the currency swap would call for the Indian MNC to service the payments of the U.S. MNC, the Indian MNC would make payments at LIBOR + 100 bp, while the U.S. MNC would still make fixed-rate payments to service the debt obligations of the Indian MNC. So, it becomes a case of a floating-to-fixed currency swap, in which one of the parties pays a fixed rate, and the counterparty pays a floating rate.

Hedging Bond Payments Currency swaps can also be used to hedge bond payments. For example, consider a U.S. firm that wants to issue bonds denominated in Japanese yen, because it can make payments with yen inflows to be generated from its ongoing operations. However, it cannot issue yen-denominated bonds on favourable terms. At the same time, a Japanese firm wants to issue USD-denominated bonds as its cash flows are mostly in U.S. dollars, but it can issue the USD-denominated bonds only at an interest rate much higher than the normal borrowing rate for a firm of equivalent creditworthiness. In this case, both firms can take advantage of currency swaps. The U.S. firm can issue USD-denominated bonds, while the Japanese firm can issue yen-denominated bonds. Then, as per the currency swap, the U.S. firm can exchange yen for USD to make its bond payments, and the Japanese firm will receive yen in exchange for USD to make its bond payments. This currency swap is illustrated in Figure 8.6.

With the U.S. dollar receipts from the Japanese firm, the U.S. firm can make payments to the subscribers of its bond issue. Similarly, the Japanese firm can meet its yen-denominated

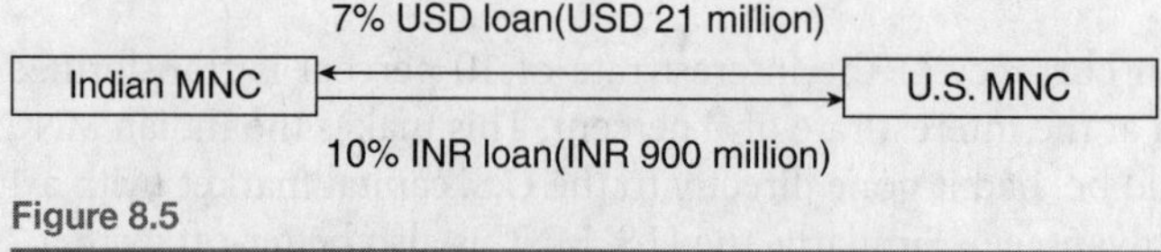

Figure 8.5

Currency Swap Between U.S.MNC and Indian MNC

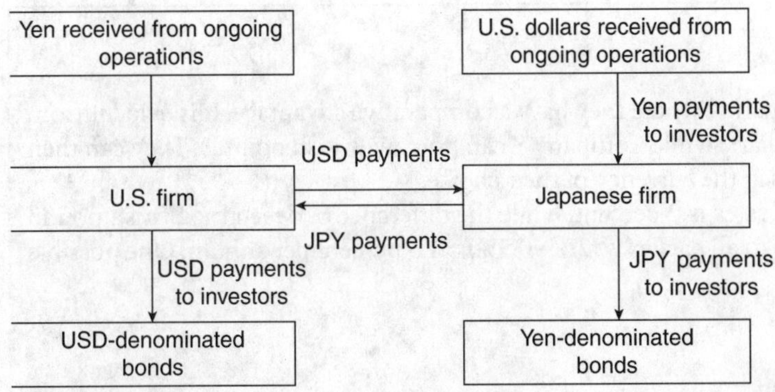

Figure 8.6

Hedging of Bond Payments with a Currency Swap

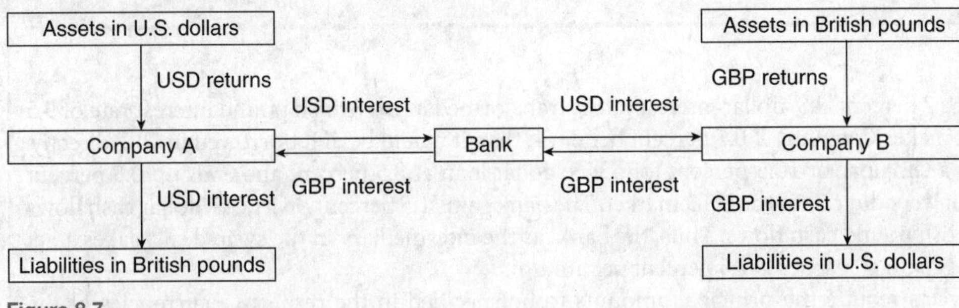

Figure 8.7

Currency Swap Through an Intermediary

obligations through the yen receipts from the U.S. firm. Thus, the two firms can hedge the bond payments by swapping cash flows.

Currency swaps can be carried out through direct negotiation between the counterparties or through a bank acting as an intermediary. For an example of the latter case, consider the following scenario. Company A has a British pound liability against USD-denominated assets. Company B has borrowed funds in U.S. dollars, and purchased assets denominated in British pounds. Both companies have exchange rate exposure, having assets in one currency and liabilities in another. Therefore, they have entered a swap as depicted in Figure 8.7.

The intermediary effectively becomes the counterparty to each participant. The participants need not know the other's identity. The bank, by becoming counterparty to each swap, runs the risk of losses arising from default by one of the parties.

Example 8.2

Company X and Company Y face the interest rates as shown in Table 8.4.

Table 8.4 **Interest rates faced by Company X and Company Y**

	Interest rates for U.S. dollar loan	*Interest rates for British pound loan*
CompanyX	7.0%	10.0%
Company Y	9.0%	10.5%

Company X wishes to have a loan in British pounds, and Company Y desires to have a loan in U.S. dollars. Design an appropriate swap structure.

Solution

Company X and Company Y, each borrows in the market where they have a comparative advantage. It is evident from the given data that Company X can borrow U.S. dollars, while Company Y can borrow British pounds. They can then swap their respective loans in order to get the funds in the currency of their choice.

The difference between the U.S. dollar interest rates is 2 percent, while the difference between the British pound interest rates is 0.5 percent. Therefore, the total gain to all parties is (2% – 0.5%) = 1.5 percent per annum. One possible swap arrangement is shown in Figure 8.8.

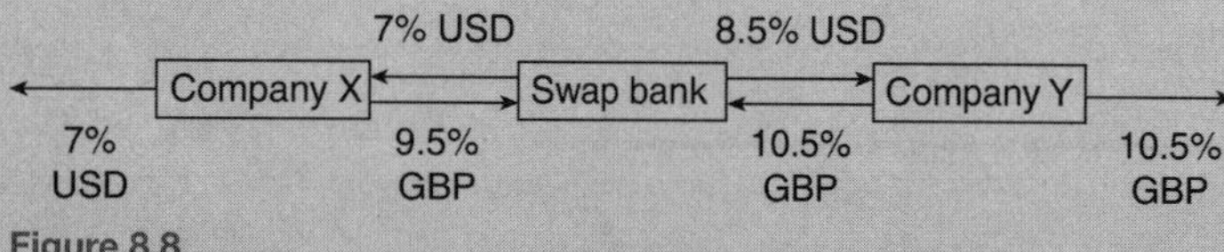

Figure 8.8

A Possible Swap Structure

As evident from the figure, the 7 percent U.S. dollar interest rate is transformed into a British pound interest rate of 9.5 percent for Company X. This makes Company X 0.5 percent better off than it would be, if it borrowed in GBP directly. Similarly, Company Y swaps a GBP loan at 10.5 percent for a U.S. dollar loan at 8.5 percent and ends up 0.5 percent better-off than it would be, if it went directly to the USD market. The bank gains 1.5 percent on its U.S. dollar cash flows and loses 1 percent on its British pound cash flows. Thus, the bank, as the intermediary in the swap deal, makes a net gain of 0.5 percent. The total gain to all parties is 1.5 percent per annum.

All currency swap contracts require the principal amounts to be specified in the respective currencies of the counterparties, and they are generally equal at the beginning of the swap contract period. The principal amounts are usually exchanged at the beginning as well as the end of the contract period. Suppose Company X pays USD 10 million and receives GBP 5.25 million. In each year of the contract period, Company X receives USD 0.70 million (7 percent of USD 10 million) and pays GBP 0.50 million (9.5 percent of GBP 5.25 million). At the end of the swap period, Company X pays the principal amount of GBP 5.25 million and receives the principal amount of USD 10 million.

Swaps allow participants to borrow in markets in which they have comparative advantages. It is mutually advantageous for each party to borrow in the more favourable market and then exchange the currencies borrowed.

$$\text{Value of a currency swap (INR)} = \begin{bmatrix}\text{PV of cash flows} \\ \text{associated with} \\ \text{borrowing in domestic} \\ \text{currency, or value of} \\ \text{the INR bond}\end{bmatrix} - \begin{bmatrix}\text{PV of cash flows associated} \\ \text{with borrowing in foreign} \\ \text{currency, or value of a} \\ \text{foreign currency -} \\ \text{denominated bond}\end{bmatrix} \times \text{Spot exchange rate}$$

Value of Currency Swaps A currency swap involves future cash inflows and future cash outflows. If a currency swap is viewed as a pair of bond transactions, the value of a currency swap is the difference between the present value of cash inflows and the present value of cash outflows.

Let us consider an example to understand how currency swaps are valued. Suppose the interest rate is 8 percent per annum in India and 6 percent per annum in the United States. A swap bank has entered into a three-year currency swap, according to which it receives 9 percent per annum in INR and pays 6 percent per annum in U.S. dollars once a year. The principal amounts are INR 900 million and USD 20 million. The current exchange rate is USD/INR 45. In this case, the present value of cash flows associated with borrowing in the domestic currency is

$$\text{INR}\ [81/(1+08) + 81/(1+08)^2 + 981/(1+0.08)^3] = \text{INR}\ 923.337\ \text{million}$$

Similarly, the present value of cash flows associated with borrowing in the foreign currency is

$$\text{USD}\ [1.2/(1+0.06) + 1.2/(1+0.06)^2 + 21.2/(1+0.06)^3] = \text{USD}\ 20.008\ \text{million}$$

In terms of domestic currency, the present value of cash flows denominated in the U.S. dollar is

$$\text{USD}\ 20.008\ \text{million} \times \text{INR}\ 45 = \text{INR}\ 900.342\ \text{million}$$

So, the value of the swap from the perspective of the swap dealer who has taken a long position in INR-denominated borrowing and a short position in USD-denominated borrowing is

$$\text{INR}\ 923.337\ \text{million} - \text{INR}\ 900.342\ \text{million} = \text{INR}\ 22.995\ \text{million}$$

This amount also represents a liability to the counterparty as swapping is a zero-sum game. If the swap dealer were to pay INR and receive USD, the value of the swap would have been (–)INR 22.995 million.

Non-deliverable Currency Swaps

*A **non-deliverable currency swap** is a swap that involves a hard currency and a restricted currency (e.g. INR), but the settlement of the swap transaction is done through the hard currency.*

Currency swaps can also be quoted on a non-deliverable basis so that all payments are net settled in a hard currency. Thus, a **non-deliverable currency swap** is a swap that involves a hard currency and a restricted currency (e.g. INR), but the settlement of the swap transaction is done through the hard currency. For example, consider a scenario where two firms enter into a currency swap, and one of them is located in a country with a non-convertible or a restricted currency. With a non-deliverable currency swap, the payment due to the firm in the restricted currency is converted into a major currency at the prevailing spot rate on each interest payment date and at maturity. Suppose two firms, an Indian firm and a U.S. firm, have entered into a swap deal. Accordingly, the Indian firm is expected to pay INR 10 million to the U.S. firm, and the U.S. firm is due to pay USD 0.2326 million to the Indian firm at maturity. On the date of maturity of the swap, the exchange rate is USD/INR 45. So, the U.S. firm would pay USD 0.0104 million [i.e. USD 0.2326 million – (INR 10 million/45)] to the Indian firm. Thus, non-deliverable currency swaps allow firms with minor currencies to manage their payment flows.

Foreign Exchange Swaps

*A **foreign exchange swap** is a contract that involves the actual exchange of two currencies (principal amount only) on a specified date, at a rate agreed on at the time of conclusion of the contract, and a reverse exchange of the same currencies at a date in the future, at a rate agreed on at the time of signing the contract.*

A **foreign exchange swap** is a contract that involves the actual exchange of two currencies (principal amount only) on a specified date, at a rate agreed on at the time of conclusion of the contract (the short leg), and a reverse exchange of the same two currencies at a date in the future and at a rate (generally different from the rate applied to the short leg) agreed on at the time of signing the contract (the long leg). Foreign exchange swaps cover both spot/forward and forward/forward swaps. They also include short-term swaps such as "tomorrow/next day" transactions. Thus, a foreign exchange swap consists of two legs: *a spot foreign exchange transaction* and *a forward foreign exchange transaction*.

For example, a firm has GBP 2 million deposited with a bank at a short-term interest rate. It has a funding requirement of USD 0.9747 million in three months. The firm would like to utilize the GBP funds to meet this requirement. At the same time, it does not wish to take any foreign exchange risk on this transaction. So, the firm wants to enter into a foreign exchange swap. Accordingly, it sells the GBP to a bank at the spot rate of USD/GBP 0.4875. In return, the bank delivers USD 0.9747 million to the firm. At the same time, the firm agrees to buy back the GBP 2 million and pay back the USD 0.9698 million after three months' time.

The prevailing interest rates are 6 percent in the United Kingdom and 4 percent in the United States. By entering into a foreign exchange swap with the bank, the firm gives the bank the use of a currency which it could invest at 6 percent, and in return the bank gives the firm the use of USD, the interest on which is 4 percent.

In the three-month period, the bank could earn interest of GBP 0.03 million at 6 percent per annum on the GBP 2 million. At the same time, the firm could earn an interest of USD 0.009747 million on USD 0.9747 million at the interest rate of 4 percent per annum. At the end of three months, the bank and the firm would have accumulated GBP 2.03 million and USD 0.9844 million respectively. So, the forward exchange rate is 0.9844/2.03 = 0.4849.

The bank returns the firm GBP 2 million, and it pays the bank USD 0.9698 million (i.e., USD 0.4849 × 2 million). The gain of USD 0.0049 million (i.e. USD 0.9747 – USD 0.9698) made by the firm is the monetized difference between the interest rates in the two countries or currencies. The 2 percent extra interest on GBP 2 million for three months, translates back to USD 0.0049 million. Thus, the firm is compensated for giving up the higher interest bearing currency. The difference in the spot rate and forward rate (annualized) equalizes the interest rate differential (annualized).

Further, suppose that the firm has surplus funds in a currency with a low interest rate and its funding is in a currency with a higher interest rate. In this case, the gain in the above example will be reversed. The forward rate will be adjusted accordingly.

Foreign exchange swaps are thus used to hedge foreign exchange exposures by swapping temporary surplus funds in one currency into another currency for better use of liquidity. By doing so, a firm can protect against adverse movements in foreign exchange rates, but favourable changes are renounced. Foreign exchange swaps are typically used by organizations, particularly banks, when they want to temporarily reallocate their portfolio into or out of a currency without facing any currency risk.

A Swap as a Series of Forward Contracts

In an interest rate swap, one party pays the fixed interest rate and receives the current floating interest rate on the reset dates, which are evenly spaced throughout the period of the swap. The payment made on each of the reset dates (e.g. every six months) is like an ordinary forward contract for that period. In other words, a swap contract can be considered as a prepackaged series of forward contracts to buy or sell a market index (e.g. LIBOR) at a fixed rate. A forward contract involves the exchange of cash flows at a particular date in the future. An interest rate swap with a single payment date is no different from a forward contract. Accordingly, the value of a swap can also be computed by breaking down the currency swap into a series of forward contracts. Let us take the data given in Example 8.3 to see how the value of a swap can be computed when it is viewed as a series of forward contracts.

The forward exchange rate is given by the following formula:

$$F = Se^{(r_h - r_f)(T-t)}$$

where

F = Forward exchange rate

S = Current spot rate of one unit of foreign currency in terms of home currency

r_h = Risk-free home currency interest rate

r_f = Risk-free foreign currency interest rate

T = Time when the forward contract matures (years)

t = Current time (years)

Since the current spot rate is GBP/USD 1.9231, the one-year, two-year, and three-year forward exchange rates can be calculated as follows:

$$\text{One-year forward exchange rate} = 1.9231e^{003\times 1} = 1.9818$$
$$\text{Two-year forward exchange rate} = 1.9231e^{003\times 2} = 2.041$$
$$\text{Three-year forward exchange rate} = 1.9231\, e^{003\times 3} = 2.1043$$

The exchange of interest amounts involves receiving GBP 0.37 million and paying USD 0.80 million every year. The risk-free interest rate in U.S. dollars is 9 percent per annum. Thus, the values of the forward contracts corresponding to the exchange of interest amounts are

$$(0.37\times 1.9818 - 0.80)e^{009\times 1} = (-)\text{USD } 0.0610 \text{ million}$$
$$(0.37\times 2.0419 - 0.80)e^{009\times 2} = (-)\text{USD } 0.0372 \text{ million}$$
$$(0.37\times 2.1043 - 0.80)e^{0.09\times 3} = (-)\text{USD } 0.0163 \text{ million}$$

The final exchange of principal amounts involves receiving GBP 5.25 million and paying USD 10 million. Therefore, the value of the forward contract corresponding to this is

$$\text{USD } [(5.25 \text{ million}\times 2.1043 - 10)e^{009\times 3}] = \text{USD } 0.7997 \text{ million}$$

The total value of the swap is USD (0.7997 – 0.061 – 0.0372 – 0.0163) = USD 0.685 million. This value is the same as that obtained in Example 8.3.

The value of a swap depends on three fundamental factors: domestic interest rates, foreign interest rates, and foreign exchange rates. Therefore, any change in the value of these factors will bring about a change in the value of the swap. Even though a swap is originally negotiated to have no value to either counterparty, it will become an asset to one and a liability to the other as a result of changes in market interest rates and/or the foreign exchange rate.

The major risk involved in swapping is *credit risk,* which refers to the probability that the counterparty will default. As an intermediary between the two principal counterparties, the swap bank assumes the credit risk. But the swap dealers set the swap spread to compensate

Example 8.3

The risk-free interest rate in UK is 6 percent per annum and the U.S. risk-free interest rate is 9 percent per annum. A bank has arranged a currency swap in which it receives 7 percent per annum in British pounds and pays 8 percent per annum in U.S. dollars once in a year. The principal amounts in the two currencies are GBP 5.25 million and USD 10 million. The swap contract will have another three years' term. The current exchange rate is USD/GBP 0.52 or GBP/USD 1.9231. What is the swap value?

Solution

The present value of cash flows in U.S. dollars is

$$\text{USD } [0.80e^{-0.09\times 1} + 0.80e^{-0.09\times 2} + 0.80e^{-0.09\times 3}] = \text{USD } 9.6438$$

The present value of cash flows in British pounds is

$$\text{GBP } [0.37e^{-0.06\times 1} + 0.37e^{-0.06\times 2} + 5.62e^{-0.06\times 3}] = \text{GBP } 5.3709, \text{ or USD } 10.3288$$

Thus, the value of the swap is (USD 10.3288 – USD 9.6438) = USD 0.685 million.

even such risks. In other words, the swap spread compensates the swap dealer for its services in arranging the swap and for assuming counterparty risk. The swap dealer can also hedge credit risk by using an appropriate futures contract.

Market Quotations for Swaps

Swap dealers, particularly banks, quote a fixed-rate bid–ask spread (either semiannual or annual) against a local standard reference in the same currency. For example, the bid–ask swap quotation for U.S. dollars is, say, 5.00–5.10 percent. This means that the swap bank will pay semiannual fixed-rate USD payments at 5 percent against receiving a six-month dollar LIBOR in an interest rate swap, or it will receive semiannual fixed-rate USD payments at 5.10 percent against paying six-month dollar LIBOR in an interest rate swap.

If the bank quotes, say, 4.50–4.60 percent in USD and 6.50–6.60 percent in JPY against a six-month USD LIBOR, it means that the bank would make semiannual fixed-rate dollar payments of 4.50 percent in return for receiving semiannual fixed-rate yen payments at 6.60 percent in a currency swap, or it will receive semiannual fixed-rate USD payments at 4.60 percent against paying semiannual fixed-rate yen payments at 6.50 percent in a currency swap.

The difference between the bid and ask rates is known as the swap spread, which compensates the swap dealer for providing the swap and for assuming some counterparty risk. Further, the longer the tenor of the swap, the larger is the swap spread because of uncertainty of future events.

Credit Default Swaps

Credit default swaps (CDS) have emerged as a derivative financial instrument in trading of credit risk. The market for CDS is really global, with contracts linked to the credit risk of several MNCs and a number of sovereigns world over. They are also considered to be one of the major culprits in the collapse of financial giants like Lehman Brothers. Upon purchasing a bond or any fixed income-bearing security, the investor faces the risk of financial loss, if the debt issuer defaults on the obligation to pay interest or repay the principal of the loan. A credit default swap is a derivative contract that provides insurance against the risk of default by a debt issuer. A debt issuer, also known as an obligor or a reference entity, is an entity that issues debts in the form of bonds on which it may default. It is a contract between two parties—the protection buyer and the protection seller—with reference to a particular credit event. The protection buyer makes regular premium payments, known as the premium leg, to the protection seller, until a credit event occurs or until expiry of the CDS contract, whichever occurs earlier. The CDS may also be understood as a credit derivative that transfers the credit risk of a reference entity from one party to another. Let us consider an example to understand how credit default swaps work.

Firm A issues a bond with a par value of INR 1 million to Firm B. In CDS terminology, Firm A is the reference entity. To avoid the credit risk, Firm B (protection buyer) enters into a contract known as a CDS with Firm C (protection seller). The amount of protection, INR 1 million is called the notional amount. The protection buyer has an option to have protection against the entire loan amount or a portion of the principal amount of the INR 1 million. The CDS market is a dealer market and, therefore, the transactions take place through dealers. Accordingly, Firm C is a dealer in the CDS which agrees to pay INR 1 million (or whatever notional amount the parties negotiate) to Firm B in case Firm A defaults, and Firm B agrees to make a regular premium payment (annually, half-yearly, quarterly, or monthly) to Firm C. The premium amount depends on the quantum of risk that Firm C perceives in protecting Firm B against the default by Firm A. If Firm C perceives higher credit

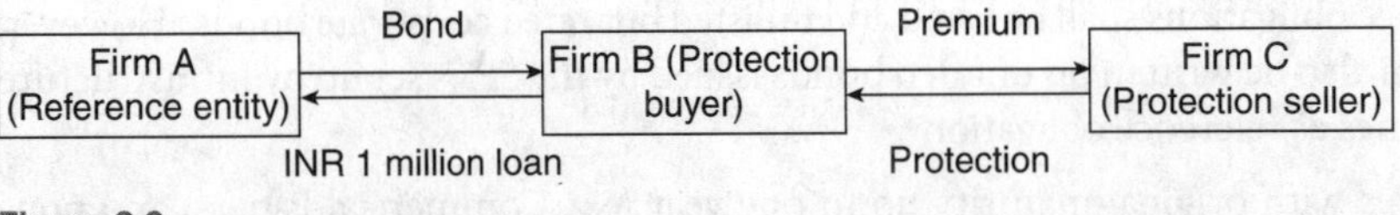

Figure 8.9

A Typical CDS

risk in the transaction, the premium would be larger. The protection buyer can also insist on collateral from protection seller to ensure that the obligation is discharged.

As a dealer, Firm C may acquire an offsetting hedge by entering into a CDS with another party (say, Firm D). Thus, the credit risk is transferred from Firm B to Firm C and then to Firm D. This transfer may extend further to any number of parties, making it a chain of obligations. It may be noted that each transaction between counterparties is a separate contract. If Firm A defaults, Firm B can look only to Firm C, Firm C looks to Firm D, and so on. The premium at each level of transaction is negotiated based on current perception of the risk of default by Firm A. The new protection premium for subsequent contract may be costlier than the original premium negotiated between Firm B and Firm C, if the risk of default by Firm A has increased. No matter how many parties are involved in the chain of obligations, the absolute amount of risk of loss is the same, that is, INR 1 million. The only question is who ultimately pays it. A glance at Figure 8.9 gives a better idea of CDS.

To understand the concept clearly, let us consider another example. Firm B purchases 5-year protection on a bond with a face value of INR 10 million from Firm C at a default swap spread of 400 bp. Firm B, thus, makes a quarterly premium payment of INR 0.1 million (i.e. INR 10 m × 0.04 × 0.25) to Firm C. After one year, the reference entity becomes bankrupt and the bond has a recovery price of INR 75 per INR 100 face value. So, the protection seller (Firm C) compensates the protection buyer for the loss on the face value of the bond which is equal to INR 2.5 million (INR 10 million × (100% – 75%)).

Guidelines of Reserve Bank of India In order to further deepen and widen the debt market in the country, the Reserve Bank of India has introduced a new financial product by issuing guidelines on CDS for corporate bonds. The salient features of these guidelines are highlighted as below:

- Two categories of participants, viz. users and market makers.
- Users of CDS include commercial banks, PDs, NBFCs, mutual funds, insurance companies, listed companies, FIIs, all-India financial institutions, etc.
- Market makers comprise commercial banks, PDS, NBFCs having sound finances and good track record in providing credit facilities and any other institution specifically permitted by the RBI.
- Users are permitted to buy CDS only to hedge their underlying credit risk on corporate bonds. Users are permitted to exit their bought CDS positions by unwinding them with the original counterparty or by assigning them in favour of the buyer of the underlying bond.
- Market makers are permitted to quote both buy and/or sell CDS spreads. They are permitted to buy protection without having the underlying bond. They are required to fulfill the other eligibility norms in terms of CRAR, net NPA, net-owned funds, etc.
- All CDS trades shall have an RBI-regulated entity at least on one side of the transaction.
- The reference entity in a CDS shall be a single legal resident entity and the direct obligor for the reference asset/obligation.

- Reference obligations shall be listed and unlisted but rated corporate bonds. However, CDS can also be written on unrated bonds issued by the SPVs set up by infrastructure companies as reference obligation.
- Securities with original maturity up to one year (e.g. Commercial Papers) and non-convertible debentures shall also be permitted as reference obligations.
- Users cannot buy CDS for amounts higher than the face value of corporate bonds held by them and for periods longer than the tenor of corporate bonds held by them.
- Users cannot exit their bought positions by entering into an offsetting sale contract. They can exit their bought position by either unwinding the contract with the original counterparty or, in the event of sale of the underlying bond, by assigning (novating) the CDS protection, to the purchaser of the underlying bond subject to consent of the original protection seller.
- CDS shall be denominated and settled in INR.
- Obligations such as asset-backed securities, convertible bonds and bonds with call/put options shall not be permitted as reference obligations.
- CDS cannot be written on interest receivables.
- CDS must represent a direct claim on the protection seller.
- CDS must be irrevocable.
- The protection seller shall have no recourse to the protection buyer for credit-event losses.
- Credit event specified in the CDS may cover bankruptcy, failure to pay, repudiation/moratorium, obligation acceleration, obligation default, restructuring, etc.
- For transactions involving users, physical settlement is mandatory. For other transactions, market makers can opt for any of the three settlement methods (physical, cash, and auction), provided the CDS documentation envisages such settlement.

In fine, financial swaps and the financial swap markets have developed by leaps and bounds in many countries over the years. Today, the swap market has become an important organ of international financial markets. In earlier days, swaps used to be customized in terms of the amount and timing of cash inflows and outflows, but swaps now-a-days are standardized according to the conventions set forth by the International Swap and Derivative Association (ISDA). Earlier, banks used to act as brokers to match the requirements of counterparties, but over time commercial banks and investment banks have become active participants in swap deals. With the greater involvement of commercial banks and investment banks in swap deals as market makers, the volume of swaps as well as liquidity have increased phenomenally. In other words, the swap market has evolved into a high-volume and low-margin business. Though standardized, swap contracts have enough flexibility to facilitate designing of several innovative financial products to suit the requirements of the participants.

Summary

1. The importance of financial swaps has increased tremendously over time, particularly with the integration of global financial markets. That is, with fewer barriers to capital flows across countries, the use of financial swaps has increased greatly in recent times.
2. A *financial swap* is an agreement between two parties to exchange cash flows according to an agreed formula. Financial swaps have evolved out of parallel loans and back-to-back loans.

3. Interest rate swaps and currency swaps are the major financial swaps. An *interest rate swap* is an agreement between two parties to exchange interest payments on a certain notional principal amount for a specific maturity. Interest rate swaps are of two types: coupon swaps and basis swaps.

4. Banks and other financial institutions have emerged as intermediaries in swaps. The *intermediaries* also known as swap dealers, make market in swaps by quoting the fixed rate they are willing to pay for a specified floating interest rate, and the fixed rate they are ready to receive in exchange for the specified floating interest rate.

5. A swap can be considered as a series of forward contracts. For example, a one-year swap with a semiannual payment can be considered as a package of two forward contracts, one with a six-month maturity and another with a twelve-month maturity.

6. A *swaption* is an agreement between the buyer and the seller, which gives the buyer the right, but not the obligation to enter into a swap contract on predetermined terms with regard to the rate of interest, notional principal, floating-rate index, and so on. Swaptions may be call swaptions or put swaptions.

7. *Caps, floors,* and *collars are* popular option-based derivative products in the financial markets.

8. A *currency swap* is an agreement between two counterparties to exchange cash flows denominated in two different currencies. Currency swaps may be fixed-to-fixed currency swaps, fixed-to-floating currency swaps, or floating-to-floating currency swaps.

9. Currency swaps can also be used to hedge bond payments.

10. The price of a swap is the rate to be quoted for one stream of cash flows of a swap. Interest rate swaps can be valued by considering a swap as a pair of bond transactions. The value of a currency swap is the difference between the present value of cash inflows and the present value of cash outflows.

11. The major risk involved in financial swaps is the *credit risk*. The swap spread compensates the swap dealer for its services in arranging the swap and for assuming counterparty risk.

12. A *non-deliverable currency swap* is a swap that involves a hard currency and a restricted currency (e.g. INR), but the settlement of the swap transaction is done through a hard currency.

13. A *foreign exchange swap* is a contract that involves the actual exchange of two currencies (principal amount only) on a specified date, at a rate agreed on at the time of conclusion of the contract, as well as a reverse exchange of the same two currencies at a date in the future and at a rate agreed on at the signing of the contract.

14. *Credit default swap* is a kind of derivative security to cover the credit risk.

Questions and Problems

1. Distinguish between parallel loans and back-to-back loans.

2. What is a financial swap? What are the economic benefits of interest rate swaps?

3. Company X in India wishes to have a fixed-rate long-term loan. However, it has access to funds with a floating-rate interest at a margin of 100 bp over LIBOR. The company can also tap the fixed-rate bond market at 12 percent. On the other side, Company Y has access to fixed-rate funds at 10 percent and floating-rate funds at LIBOR plus 50 bp. Company Y would prefer a floating-rate loan.

   (a) How can Company X and Company Y structure their swap?

   (b) How much would Company X pay for its fixed-rate funds?

   (c) How much would Company Y pay for its floating-rate funds?

4. What is market making in swaps?

5. How can swaps be regarded as a series of forward contracts?

6. Explain the mechanism of credit default swaps.

7. What are the economic benefits of swaptions?

8. How are swaps valued?

9. What are the risks associated with financial swaps? How can such risks be managed?

10. Company A desires to borrow British pounds at a fixed rate of interest, while Company B wishes to borrow U.S. dollars at a fixed rate of interest. The interest rates quoted for the two companies are shown in Table 8.5.

Table 8.5 Interest Rates Quoted

	British pounds	*U.S. dollars*
Company A	7.5%	8.0%
Company B	6.0%	10.0%

Design a swap that will be equally attractive to the two companies. It should also net a swap dealer 100 bp per annum.

11. Company P wishes to borrow U.S. dollars at a floating rate of interest and Company R wants to borrow British pounds at a fixed rate of interest. A bank is ready to arrange a swap and requires 50 bp spread. The interest rate quotations are shown in Table 8.6.

Table 8.6 The Interest Rate Quotations

	Company P	*Company R*
U.S. dollars (floating rate)	LIBOR+100 bp	LIBOR+150bp
British pounds (fixed rate)	7.0%	8.5%

Design a swap that is attractive to both the companies.

12. A bank is ready to pay 9 percent per annum and to receive three-month LIBOR in return on a notional principal of USD 20 million with payments being exchanged every three months. The swap has a remaining life of 12 months. The average of the bid and ask fixed rate currently being swapped for three-month LIBOR is 11 percent per annum for all maturities. The three-month LIBOR one month ago was 10.5 percent per annum. All rates are compounded quarterly. Determine the value of the swap.

Multiple-choice Questions

1. ________ covers long-term financial risk.
   (a) Currency option (b) Currency futures
   (c) Financial swap (d) None of these
2. Parallel loan is particularly useful when a firm expects to receive cash flows in ________.
   (a) Foreign currency (b) Domestic currency
   (c) euro (d) None of these
3. Basis risk arises due to changes in ________.
   (a) Inflation rate (b) Spread
   (c) Repo rate (d) None of these
4. Coupon swap is also known as ________.
   (a) Currency swap
   (b) Fixed-to-floating interest rate swap
   (c) Floating-to-floating interest rate swap
   (d) None of these
5. A basis swap is a ________.
   (a) Currency swap
   (b) Floating-to-floating interest swap
   (c) Fixed-to-floating interest swap
   (d) None of these
6. Callable swap gives the ________ the right to terminate the swap before maturity.
   (a) Fixed-rate payer (b) Floating-rate payer
   (c) Swap dealer (d) None of these
7. Bid rate is the ________ the swap dealer is willing to pay.
   (a) Fixed interest rate (b) Floating interest rate
   (c) Spread (d) None of these
8. Call swaption is also known as ________.
   (a) Payer swaption (b) Receiver swaption
   (c) Interest rate swap (d) None of these
9. The initial value of a swap is normally ________.
   (a) Negative (b) Positive
   (c) Zero (d) None of these
10. ________ is used to hedge against rising interest rates.
   (a) Cap (b) Floor
   (c) Floorlet (d) None of these
11. A collar is a combination of ________.
   (a) Coupon swaps (b) Cap and floor
   (c) Basis swaps (d) None of these
12. An example of a credit derivative is ________.
   (a) Credit default swap (b) Currency swap
   (c) Interest rate swap (d) None of these
13. In a credit default swap, the protection premium is paid by ________.
   (a) Reference entity (b) Lender
   (c) Protection seller (d) None of these
14. A foreign exchange swap consists of ________.
   (a) A spot transaction and a forward transaction
   (b) Spot transaction
   (c) Forward transaction
   (d) None of these
15. Non-deliverable currency swap is settled through ________.
   (a) Hard currency (b) Restricted currency
   (c) INR (d) None of these
16. Currency swaps are mainly used ________.
   (a) To reduce currency risk
   (b) To reduce cost of funds
   (c) To invest in foreign currency
   (d) None of these

Case Study

Sri Krishna Industries Limited is an Indian manufacturer of cement-based construction items including sanitary ware. It has a proposal to set up a wholly owned manufacturing facility in Singapore to cater to the needs of the South East Asian market. A Singapore-based management consultancy firm has prepared the project report, according to which the project is estimated to cost USD 100 million. All the civil works and installation of the machinery can be completed in 12 months. The economic life of the project is estimated at 10 years.

The consultancy firm has suggested that the company opt for foreign debt by issuing Eurobonds of USD 40 million. The remaining cost of the project will be equity financed.

Sri Krishna Industries is a South Indian company and is not well known even in other parts of India, let alone in the foreign markets. Therefore, the company has to offer a premium of at least 2 percent over the coupon rate of 7 percent, which is the borrowing rate for well-known companies of equivalent risk.

At the same time, a Korean MNC has worked out proposals to set up a car manufacturing plant in Southern India. The project cost is estimated at INR 4,500 million with an economic life of 10 years. It finds that it must raise INR 1,800 million by issuing 10 percent debentures in India, whereas it can borrow U.S. dollars by issuing Eurobonds at 7 percent in the European Union market.

The spot rate between INR and U.S. dollar is INR 62.5675. The risk-free interest rate is 8 percent in India and 6 percent in the United States.

Questions

1. Set up a currency swap that will benefit each counterparty. How can a bank also be involved in the swapping transaction?
2. Suppose that, after one year of entering the swap, the risk-free interest rate in the United States has increased by 50 bp, while there is no change in the risk-free interest rate in India. Determine the market value of the swap.

Further Reading

1. Cliffort W. Smith, Jr., Charles W. Smithson, and Lee M. Wakeman, "The Evolving Market for Swaps", *Midland Corporate Finance Journal* (Winter 1986): 20–32.
2. Robert H. Litzenberger, "Swaps: Plain and Fanciful," *Journal of Finance* (July 1992): 831–850.
3. Stuart M. Turnbull, "Swaps: A Zero-Sum Game," *Financial Management* (Spring 1987): 15–21.
4. Tong-Sheng Sun, Suresh Sundaresan, and Ching Wang, "Interest Rate Swaps—An Empirical Investigation," *Journal of Financial Economics* (1993): 77–99.
5. R. Dattatreya, R. E. Venkatesh, and V. E. Venkatesh, *Interest Rate and Currency Swaps* (Chicago: Probus Publishing Company, 1994).

CHAPTER

9 Interest Rate Futures

CHAPTER OBJECTIVES

After studying this chapter, you should be able to:

1 Review the basic concepts of interest rates.
2 Distinguish clearly between the spot interest rate and forward interest rate.
3 Explain the concept of yield curve.
4 Discuss the interest rate risk.
5 Explain different forms of interest rate futures.
6 Discuss the Forward Rate Agreement.
7 Understand the RBI Directives on interest rate futures.
8 Gain insight into interest rate futures trading in India.

Interest Rates: Basic Concepts

This section is a prelude to interest rate futures, another important topic in this chapter. As any discussion on interest rate futures presupposes the familiarity of the reader with key concepts like yield to maturity (YTM), yield curve, holding period return, and interest rate risk, a brief description of each of these concepts is presented here.

People generally prefer present consumption to future consumption. However, people defer their consumption to a later date, if they are assured or at least given a hope that they can have more consumption in future than what they can have now. Savings arise from out of these hopes. To motivate the people to defer their consumption and thereby make savings, a reward in the form of interest is paid such that they can have more consumption in future. Thus, *interest rate* is the rate at which the investor can give up his present money for future money. The interest is paid by the other people (dis-savers) who wish to use these savings productively to increase their own consumption in future more than what they have at present. In other words, the dissevers are expected to earn more than what they pay as interest to the savers by productively utilizing the savings. It is in this back-drop the concept of time value of money is introduced. It states that a unit of money received today is worth more than the same money received at some future date. Algebraically, it is stated as follows:

$$PV = \frac{FV_t}{(1+r)^t}$$

The concept of time value of money states that a unit of money received today is worth more than the same money received at some future date.

where

PV = Present value of a unit of money

FV = Future value of a unit of money

r = Rate of interest

t = Period

It can be understood by the above equation that a unit of money to be received in the future is worth less than what it is today. Further, the present value decreases as interest rate increases.

Spot Interest Rate and Forward Interest Rate

There are different interest rates (e.g. nominal interest rate, real interest rate, spot interest rate, and forward interest rate) and different ways of computing interest rates (e.g. yield to maturity). The interest rate that is normally mentioned in investments or money trading is the *nominal interest rate,* and the nominal interest rate adjusted for inflation is the *real interest rate.* The *spot interest rate* (or spot rate to be simple) is the interest rate associated with spot transactions of lending and borrowing. For example, consider that a bank lends INR 100,000 at an interest rate of 12 percent per annum to a customer, to be paid back in two years. The interest rate of 12 percent is the spot rate. Alternatively, an investor deposits INR 89,286 with a bank to receive INR 100,000 one year later. The rate of interest implied in the transaction is 12 percent, which is also known as *yield to maturity.* The YTM is the discount rate that makes the present value of the future money (INR 100,000 in the example) equal to the money invested or deposited today (INR 89,286 in the example). The spot rate may be for different periods (e.g. one-year spot rate, two-year spot rate, etc.). An n-year spot rate is the interest rate on an n-year investment (pure) without intermediate payments. In other words, the interest payment and the principal repayment will be made at the end of period n. The spot rate is also known as the *zero-coupon yield.*

Spot interest rate is associated with spot transactions of lending and borrowing.

Interest rates vary over time because of several factors influencing the interest rates. The longer the time to maturity of the debt security, the higher is the interest rate. For example, one-year debt security carries interest rate (r_1), which is normally lower than the interest rate of the two-year debt security (r_2). In other words, the interest rates increase with longer maturities (i.e. $r_n > r_{n-1} > \ldots > r_3 > r_2 > r_1$). Suppose a one-year bond (X_1) carries a 9 percent rate of interest, and a two-year bond (X_2) carries a 10 percent rate of interest. Both the bonds have a face value of INR 10,000. The present value (PV) of each of them is given as follows:

$$PV(X_1) = 10{,}000/(1 + 0.09) = \text{INR } 9{,}174.31$$

$$PV(X_2) = 10{,}000/(1 + 0.10)^2 = \text{INR } 8{,}264.46$$

The spot rate of each of them is calculated as

$$\text{INR } 9{,}174.31 = 10{,}000/(1 + r_1)$$

$$\text{INR } 8{,}264.46 = 10{,}000/(1 + r_2)^2$$

On solving the above equations, r_1 = 9 percent and r_2 = 10 percent. Given these rates, if one wants to calculate the price of a bond, say a two-year 6% bond having a face value of INR 10,000, he can use the following equation:

$$PV = \frac{600}{(1+0.09)} + \frac{10{,}600}{(1+0.10)^2}$$

$$= \text{INR } 9{,}310.80$$

In the above example, the interest rate for a one-year bond is 9 percent and for a two-year bond is 10 percent. To make the issue simple, let us assume that an investor invests INR 100 in a two-year bond. After two years, he would get INR 121 [i.e. $100 \times (1 + 0.10)^2$]. This can also be stated as the investor receiving the proceeds at 9 percent over the first year and receiving at 11 percent {i.e. $[(1 + 0.10)^2/(1 + 0.09)] - 1$} over the second year. This rate of 11 percent over the second year is known as the forward rate. Thus, the forward rate (F_2) over the second year can be stated as follows:

The yield to maturity is the discount rate that makes the present value of the future money equal to the money invested or deposited today

$$F_2 = \frac{(1+r_2)^2}{(1+r_1)} - 1$$

To generalize,

$$F_n = \frac{(1+r_n)^n}{(1+r_{n-1})^{n-1}} - 1$$

where

F_n = Forward rate over the nth year

r_n = 'n' year spot rate

r_{n-1} = spot rate for $n-1$ years

In brief, the spot interest rate is the interest rate on an investment made for a period of time, say *n*-years starting today. The *n*-year spot rate is also known as the *n*-year zero-coupon yield. The *forward interest rate* is the rate of interest implied by the spot rate for a period of time in the future. A forward interest rate can also be understood as the interest rate (decided now) on the amount to be lent or borrowed at some specific time point in the future, the repayment of which may be at an even more distant time (specified) in the future.

Yield Curve

Yield is the return on an investment, which depends on the rate of interest and price of the security. The yield on an investment may refer to the current yield or the YTM. The current yield is the annual return earned on the price paid for a security. Continuing the example as discussed earlier,

Example 9.1

The following are the spot rates for a zero-coupon bond:

Period			
	1	....	6 percent
	2	....	7 percent
	3	....	8 percent
	4	....	9 percent

Calculate the forward rates over each of the four periods.

Solution

The forward rate over the first period (or year) is the one-period spot rate. The forward rate over the second period, third year and fourth period are given below:

$$F_2 = \frac{(1+0.07)^2}{(1+0.06)} - 1$$

$$= 0.08 \text{ or } 8\%$$

It means that an investor who invests INR 100 in the two-period zero-coupon bond receives INR 114.49 [i.e. INR 100 × $(1.07)^2$] at the end of the second period. In other words, he receives the proceeds at the one-period spot rate of 6 percent over the first period and at the forward rate of 8 percent over the second period:

$$F_3 = \frac{(1+0.08)^3}{(1+0.07)^2} - 1$$
$$= 0.10 \text{ or } 10\%$$

It implies that an investor who invests INR 100 in the three-period zero-coupon bond receives INR 125.97 [i.e. INR 100 × $(1.08)^3$] at the end of the third period. In other words, he receives the proceeds at the two-period spot rate of 7 percent over the first two periods and at the forward rate of 10 percent over the third period:

$$F_4 = \frac{(1+0.09)^4}{(1+0.08)^3} - 1$$
$$= 0.12 \text{ or } 12\%$$

It means that an investor who invests INR 100 in the two-period zero-coupon bond receives INR 131.08 [i.e. INR 100 × $(1.07)^4$] at the end of the fourth period. In other words, he receives the proceeds at the three-period spot rate of 8 percent over the first three periods and at the forward rate of 12 percent over the fourth period.

A forward interest rate is the interest rate (decided now) on the amount to be lent or borrowed at some specific time point in the future.

$$\text{INR } 9{,}310.80 = \frac{600}{(1+\text{YTM})} + \frac{10{,}600}{(1+\text{YTM})^2}$$

By solving the above equation for YTM, we can get a value which is known as the yield to maturity on the bond. The YTM on the bond varies if the coupon rate changes. To make it further simple, let us take an example that an investor has purchased a 9% bond with a face value of INR 10,000. If the bond is purchased at its face value, the current yield is the same as the coupon rate (i.e. 9 percent). If the same bond is purchased at a discount price of INR 9,500, the current yield would be higher at9.47 percent (900/9,500). The YTM is the total return an investor gets by holding a security until its maturity date.

Term structure describes the relationship of spot interest rates with different maturities.

The yield curve is a line graph that plots the relationship between yields to maturity and time to maturity for securities of the same asset class and credit quality. The yield curve starts with the spot interest rate for the shortest maturity, and extends out in time. Thus, the yield curve reflects yield differences, or yield spreads that are due solely to differences in maturity. The relationship between yields or spot rates and maturities is known as the term structure of interest rates.

The slope of the yield curve is normally upward, from left to right, which means that the yields rise as the maturity extends. There are theories such as the Pure Expectation Theory, the Liquidity Preference Theory and the Preferred Habitat Theory, which explain the factors that affect the slope of the yield curve. The essence of these theories is that the long-term bond yields tend to be higher than short-term yields. That is, all other factors remaining the same, the investors expect higher yields for securities with long-term maturities. The farther into the future a security's maturity, the more the uncertainty the security holder faces with regard to the payments (principal and interest) on the security. Therefore, the investors normally expect higher yields for securities of longer maturities. Yield curves also reflect the investors' expectations of interest rates in the future. An upward sloping curve is an indication that interest rates will rise significantly in the future. The yield curve may also take a flat shape when short-term yields rise, while long-term yields fall. This kind of situation may arise when the investors expect economic slowdown. The other situation is when yields on short-term securities are higher than those on long-term securities, giving rise to an inverted yield curve. The inverted yield curve indicates that the interest rates will decline in the future.

The investors use yield curves to identify the interest-bearing securities that are cheap or expensive at any given time. The price of a security is based on the present value of its expected cash flows, or the value of its future interest and principal payments discounted to the present at a specified interest rate(s). Different interest rate forecasts produce different values for a given security.

Holding Period Return

There are different kinds of debt securities like commercial paper (a short-term security), notes (a security with a maturity in excess of one year but less than 10 years), and bonds (a long-term security with a maturity in excess of 10 years). The holding period return (HPR) on investment in a security is the income earned over the holding period as a percentage of investment made at the beginning of the period. Suppose a one-year debt security (face value of INR 1,000) paying an annual interest of INR 120 is purchased for INR 1,000. If the debt security price increases to INR 1,200 by year end, its holding period return for the year is

$$\text{HPR} = \frac{120 + (1200 - 1000)}{1000}$$

$$= 32\%$$

Credit Spread

Credit spread refers to the additional yield an investor gets for acquiring a corporate bond instead of a risk-free security.

The credit spread refers to the additional yield an investor gets for acquiring a corporate bond instead of a risk-free security. As corporate securities have more risk of default than the securities issued by the government, the prices of corporate securities are usually lower, yielding more return to the investors. Credit spread depends on many factors. For example, when inflation rates rise, the credit spread widens. This is because investors must be offered additional compensation in the form of a higher coupon rate for bearing the higher risk associated with corporate securities. When interest rates in the economy are declining, the credit spread generally narrows. When interest rates are declining, the economy is expected to expand in the long run. So, the risk associated with investing in a long-term corporate security may be lower.

Interest Rate Risk

Even as the interest payments are fixed for a security, the price of the security may change depending on the interest rates in the economy. The weak/strong economic conditions in a country may put pressure on interest rates to change. As the interest rates in the economy increase (decrease), the prices of outstanding securities decrease (increase) because potential investors can buy new securities that carry higher rates of interest. An increase in interest rates in the economy results in a higher required rate of return on outstanding securities and thus causes the prices of outstanding securities to decrease. In other words, investors holding outstanding securities that carry lower rates of interest would find a decline in the price of their securities. Conversely, a decline in market interest rates tends to increase prices of outstanding debt securities.

As the debt security prices vary, the investor will experience unexpected gains or losses on his investment. Since the coupon payments and the maturity value of a coupon security are fixed, the riskiness of the security depends only on its price volatility. Among many factors (e.g. creditworthiness of the issuer, liquidity of the debt security, etc.), the interest rate volatility is considered to be the primary cause of volatility in the price of a debt security.

Thus, the debt holder faces a risk called the interest rate risk, which refers to uncertainty over the price of a debt security. For example, when interest rates fall, the price of a debt security rises; when interest rates rise, the price of a debt security falls. Different debt securities respond differently to the changes in the interest rates. The sensitivity of the price of a debt security to interest rates depends largely on the maturity of the debt security. The longer to maturity of the debt security, the higher is the sensitivity of its price to interest rates.

All the investors, whether they are individuals or firms, are exposed to interest rate risk. For example, interest rate volatility increases the risk exposure of insurance companies, commercial banks, mortgage banks and investment banks. When interest rates rise, the market value of their net worth (difference between the market values of assets and liabilities) falls; when interest rates fall, the market value of their net worth rises. There are many methods by which the investors can manage their interest rate risk. For example, the institutional investors can restructure their business to reduce the mismatch between the maturities of their assets and liabilities, and thereby reduce their interest rate risk. Individual investors can also swap their long-term debt securities for short-term debt securities to reduce their interest rate risk. Apart from these, the investors can use interest rate futures to manage their interest rate risk at a relatively low cost. That is, the investors can hedge the interest rate risk of a debt security by buying or selling interest rate futures whose value changes in the opposite direction to the price of the debt security.

Interest Rate Futures

Interest rate futures have emerged as one of the most successful financial derivatives. The first interest rate futures contract was the Eurodollar futures, created in 1975 by the Chicago Mercantile Exchange. Since then, interest rate futures on different debt securities, both short-term and long-term, have been introduced in all major derivative markets in the world.

An *interest rate futures contract* is a standardized contract traded on an exchange to buy or sell a debt security at a certain date in the future at a specified price determined today. Interest rate futures may be on treasury bills, notes, bonds, and so on. For example, an investor buys a March 91-day Treasury bill futures contract. It means that he agrees to buy a 91-day Treasury bill in March. The price of the futures contract is the price the buyer agrees to pay the seller for the security when it is delivered in March. Thus, the interest rate futures contract allows the buyer of a contract to lock-in a future interest rate. The value of an interest rate futures contract changes as interest rates in the economy change. Those who trade in interest rate futures do not usually take possession of the financial instrument. They take an offsetting position in the same futures contract before delivery occurs. For example, the seller of the March 91-day Treasury bill futures contract can settle his position by buying the March 91-Treasury bill futures contract of the same quantity. Operationally, at the expiration of a futures contract, if interest rates are higher than the rate specified in the futures contract, the buyer of the futures contract will pay the seller the difference between the market interest rate and the interest rate specified in the contract. Conversely, if interest rates move lower, the seller of a futures contract will compensate the buyer for the lower interest rate. Thus, a fall in interest rates benefits the buyer (long position), while a rise in interest rates benefits the seller (short position) of a futures contract. Putting it differently, traders in a futures contract make a profit when they buy a futures contract at a price lower than they sell, and suffer a loss when they buy the futures contract at a price higher than they sell. The profit or loss depends on whether the price of the futures contract rises or falls between the time the trader enters the contract and the time he takes an offsetting position. Interest rate futures prices move in the opposite direction of interest rates.

An interest rate futures contract is a standardized contract traded on an exchange to buy or sell a debt security at a certain date in the future at a specified price determined today.

Interest rate futures may be of short-term or long-term. An interest rate futures contract on a 91-day Government of India Treasury bill or Eurodollar futures contract is an example of short-term interest rate futures, while the futures contract on a 10-year Government of India security is an example of long-term interest rate futures. Eurodollar is a dollar deposited in a U.S. or foreign bank outside the U.S. The Eurodollar interest rate is the rate of interest earned on Eurodollars deposited by one bank with another bank. The interest rate underlying the Eurodollar futures contract is a 90-day rate.

The price of interest rate futures is stated on an index basis. The index is calculated by subtracting a futures interest rate from 100. Suppose a market participant buys an interest rate futures contract on three-month Eurodollars at 96.5. It means that the buyer of the contract will get a Eurodollar deposit in a bank at an effective interest rate of 3.5 percent per annum. As the interest rate fluctuates, so does the price index. As the interest rate increases (decreases), the index moves lower (higher). Typically, an interest rate futures contract has a tick (minimum price movement) of 0.01 (1 basis point), which corresponds to a change in the contract value of a security. For example, 1 tick is worth USD 25 for interest rate futures on Eurodollars. However, some contracts have a tick value of 0.005, or half of 1 basis point.

As far as interest rate futures on long-term securities are concerned, the prices are stated in the form of, say, 94-20. This is the percentage of the par value of the underlying security, with the digits after the hyphen denoting 32nds of 1 percent. For example, 94-20 means that the buyer of the futures contract has to pay an amount of 94(20/32) percent (i.e. 94.625 percent) of the face value of the underlying security. If the price of a futures contract is stated as, say, 105-12, it means that the buyer has to pay 105.375 percent of the par value of the underlying security. In addition, the buyer has to pay the interest accrued on the security since the last coupon date. The quoted price of the futures contract plus the accrued interest becomes the cash price of the interest rate futures.

The exchanges also prescribe contract sizes, contract listings, and minimum step sizes of price movement for interest rate futures. For example, the Chicago Mercantile Exchange prescribes USD 1,000,000 as the contract size for U.S. Treasury bills. The contracts are listed in March, June, September, and December. The tick size is 0.005, which is equivalent to USD 12.50. Most futures exchanges trade futures on short-term securities (maturity up to one year) as well as on long-term securities (maturity of 10 years or more). Futures contracts are either physically settled or cash settled. For example, the futures on bonds are generally physically settled. On the other hand, the reference rate futures, which are the futures on reference rates like LIBOR, are cash settled.

The Conversion Factor There are a large number of securities of the same type (e.g. Treasury bond) with different coupons and different time periods remaining for maturity. The seller of the futures contract is allowed to deliver any security at the time of the maturity of the futures contract. Given no conditions, the seller would obviously choose to deliver the least expensive security. But that may impoverish the buyer of the futures contract. To avoid such a situation, futures exchanges have suggested a conversion factor that accounts for varying coupon rates and maturity dates of securities. For example, the Chicago Mercantile Exchange has prescribed that the seller of the futures contract can choose to deliver any bond with a maturity over 15 years and not callable within 15 years, and the conversion factor for any deliverable bond is the present value of all the associated cash flows (discounted at 6 percent), divided by the face value of the bond. The amount to be paid by the buyer of the futures contract to the seller is calculated as follows:

$$\text{Cash paid by the party with long position} = \text{Quoted futures price} \times \text{Conversion factor} + \text{Accrued interest}$$

In other words, the actual price of the security delivered is the quoted futures price times the conversion factor plus accrued interest, if any. If the buyer of the futures contract is required to pay more than the quoted futures price, it means that the seller has delivered more valuable security. For example, a bond with a face value of INR 1,000 is quoted on a futures exchange at INR 950. Its conversion factor is 1.450. The accrued interest on this bond at the time of delivery is INR 120. The cash to be received by the seller of bond (short position) when he delivers the bond or the cash to be paid by the buyer (long position) when he takes delivery of the bond is

$$(950 \times 1.450) + 120 = \text{INR}\, 1,497.50$$

Thus, the delivery price of the bond is INR 1,497.50.

Using Interest Rate Futures for Hedging Interest rate futures contracts are used either to hedge or to speculate on future interest rates and security prices. For example, an investor who expects to suffer losses on his investment portfolio due to rise in interest rates, may hedge interest rate risk by selling interest rate futures. When interest rates rise, the investor loses money on his portfolio. The price of interest rate futures also falls as interest rates rise. As sellers of futures make a gain when futures prices fall, the gain on his futures contract offsets the loss on his original investment portfolio. Suppose the interest rates fall. The investor loses on the futures contract but gains on the original investment portfolio.

Interest rate futures are used either to hedge or to speculate on future interest rates and security prices.

Consider the following example. An investor purchased 2000 units of a Government of India (GOI) Security at a price of INR 97.3456 on 17 January 2015. Subsequently, he has anticipated that the interest rates would rise in the near future. To protect himself against a rise in interest rates and a consequent fall in the value of his investment, he has taken a short position in March interest rate futures at the current price of INR 95.0345. As anticipated by him, the interest rates have risen in the month of March. Consequently, the price of the GOI Security has fallen to INR 96.2345 on 25 March 2015 (the day of settlement of futures contract), and the futures price on the same day was INR 94.9678. Thus, the investor has incurred a loss of INR 2,222 {i.e. (96.2345 – 97.3456) × 2000} on GOI Security. But he has made a profit of INR 133.40{i.e. (95.0345 – 94.9678) × 2000}. In other words, the gain on interest rate futures partially recoups the shortfall on GOI security.

Financial institutions, banks, and corporations as borrowers or lenders/investors generally use interest rate futures to hedge their interest rate risk. These organizations mainly use interest rate futures for planned investment and planned borrowing. A fall in interest rates will affect the profitability of a firm that wants to invest in debt securities (e.g. Treasury bills) sometime in the future. Similarly, a rise in interest rates will make future borrowing costly. Interest rate futures can also be used to avoid any loss on existing investments resulting from changes in interest rates. For example, consider a company that invests USD 10 million in Treasury bills at 5 percent per annum and expects that the interest rate would rise from 5 percent per annum to 6 percent per annum between 1 January 2015 and 30 June 2015. So, on 1 January 2015, the company sells 100 futures contracts at a price of USD 100 for a total of USD 10 million. As expected, the interest rate rises to 6 percent. Therefore, the USD 10 million worth of Treasury bills falls to USD 9.68 million (market value of the bond plus six months interest). The interest rate futures price for the June delivery is 96.80. At the end of June 2015, the company purchases 100 futures at 96.80. So, the net gain for the company is 3.20 percent or 320 basis points. The total value of the portfolio on 30 June 2015 is

Value of treasury bills: USD 9.68 million
Gain on futures contract: USD 0.32 million
Total: USD 10.00 million

Thus, the loss on the value of the Treasury bills resulting from a rise in interest rates is offset by the gain from the short position in the futures contract. The value of the portfolio remains the same even if the interest rate falls instead of rising. A fall in the interest rate would result in a loss on the futures contract. But, that loss is offset by the gain in the value of the Treasury bills. The company locks-in its profit on the investment at the rate of return of 5 percent by selling the futures contracts. But in reality, the price of the underlying security may fluctuate more or less than the futures contract.

Banks also use interest rate futures to hedge the risk arising from fluctuations in interest rates. For example, assume a bank has assets (loans) with rates of interest that adjust every six months. The profitability of this bank will be adversely affected by a decline in interest rates. To hedge against such risk, the bank could purchase interest rate futures on short-term securities to lock-in the price of the short-term securities at a specified future date. If interest rates fall, the gain on the long position in the futures contract could partially, if not fully, offset any reduction in the income of the bank due to the decline in interest rates. Banks can also hedge their net exposure, which reflects the difference between their assets and liabilities, by using interest rate futures. For example, a bank that has USD 1,000 million in long-term assets and USD 900 million worth of long-term liabilities can hedge its net exposure of USD 100 million by creating a short hedge.

Example 9.2

A U.S.-based company has a short-term cash balance of USD 10 million. The company intends to invest in government securities for 120 days. The current spot rate and futures exchange rate (December futures) of USD against GBP are 1.6971 and 1.6950, respectively. The U.S. Treasury bill rate is 5 percent per annum. The British 120-day gilt rate is 5.60 percent per annum.

Compute the implied rate, and advise the company on its short-term investment strategy.

Solution

The implied rate will be

$$\text{Implied rate} = \{(\text{spot rate}/\text{futures rate})[1+(\text{domestic interest rate})\times(120/365)]-1\}(365/120)$$

$$= \{(1.6971/1.6950)[1.(0.05)\times(120/365)]-1\}(365/120)$$

$$= 5.38 \text{ per cent}$$

Since the British gilt rate is greater than the implied rate, the company can do the following:

i. Convert USD 10 million to GBP at the spot rate of GBP/USD 1.6971 to get GBP 5.8924 million.

ii. Invest GBP 5.8924 million in British gilts at 5.60 for 120 days to get GBP 6 million.

iii. Convert the GBP 6 million after 120 days using the futures rate of GBP/USD 1.6950 to get USD 10.17 million.

Thus, the company will be better off by investing in Britain than investing in the United States.

Example 9.3

An investor has sold 200 March interest rate futures on 8.83% GOI 2023 at a price of INR 94.25. The details of the contract are given below. One contract denotes 2000 units.

Expiry date : 26 March 2015
Trade date : 20 March 2015

Daily settlement prices:

19 March	INR 95.00
20 March	INR 94.00
23 March	INR 95.35
24 March	INR 93.25
25 March	INR 93.50

Futures market price on 26 March 2015: INR 92.75
Calculate total gain/loss to the investor.

Solution

Date	*Settlement price (INR)*	*Mark to market (MTM) (INR)*
19 March 2015	95.00	200 × 2000 (94.25 – 95.00) = (3,00,000)
20 March	94.00	200 × 2000 (95.00 – 94.00) = 4,00,000
23 March	95.35	200 × 2000 (94.00 – 95.35) = (5,40,000)
24 March	93.25	200 × 2000 (95.35 – 93.25) = 8,40,000
25 March	93.50	200 × 2000 (93.25 – 93.50) = (1,00,000)

On 26 March 2015, the investor closes out his position by buying 200 contracts at INR 92.85.

Profit on close out: 200 × 2000 (93.50 – 92.85) = INR 2,60,000

Total profit on the trade: INR 3,00,000 + INR 2,60,000 = INR 5,60,000

There are many kinds of interest rate futures strategies that the market participants can consider. For example, an investor can adopt a calendar spread strategy to make short-term gains. A calendar spread is an inter-delivery spread involving simultaneous purchase of one delivery month futures contract and sale of another delivery month futures contract on the same underlying. It is called a calendar spread because it is based on different calendar months. For example, an investor may buy a March 2015 futures contract and simultaneously sell a September 2015 futures contract on a 7.16% GOI Security maturing on 20 May 2023.

A calendar spread is an inter-delivery spread involving simultaneous purchase of one delivery month futures contract and sale of another delivery month futures contract on the same underlying.

Forward Rate Agreements (FRA)

The forward rate is the implied rate from, say year 1 to year 2 such that if the one-year deposit were reinvested at the forward rate from year 1 to year 2, the final yield on this roll over of one-year deposit equals the yield on the two-year deposit. For example, an investor wishes to deposit a certain amount for two years. The interest rates prevailing in the banking system are 8 percent for one-year deposit and 10 percent for two-year deposit. He has two options: deposit for two years or deposit for one year and then reinvest that deposit amount once it matures for a further period of one year. The forward interest rate in this example is calculated as follows:

$$F_{1,2} = \frac{(1+0.10)^2}{(1+0.08)} - 1$$

$$= 0.1204 \text{ or } 12.04\%$$

The forward interest rate, will leave an investor indifferent to whether he invests for a further one year at the one-year forward interest rate or whether he invests for a two-year period at today's two-year deposit rate. In other words, the forward interest rate eliminates any arbitrage profit arising out of the difference between spot interest rates and forward interest rates. Thus,

$$(1 + {}_0K_1)^1 (1 + {}_1K_2)^1 = (1 + {}_0K_2)^2$$

$$(1+0.08)(1+0.1204) = (1+0.10)^2$$

To generalize,

$$(1 + {}_0K_t)^t (1 + {}_tK_T)^{T-1} = (1 + {}_0K_T)^T$$

where

K = Interest rate
t = Time period ($t < T$)

A *Forward Rate Agreement* (FRA) is a contract for locking-in future short-term interest rates. To elaborate, FRA is a contract between two parties to the effect that the seller pays the buyer, at a specified time point in the future, the increased interest cost on a notional sum of money, if the reference interest rate (e.g. LIBOR) at that time has risen above the agreed-upon interest rate, and the buyer pays the seller the increased interest cost, if the reference interest rate at that time has fallen below the agreed upon rate.

A Forward Rate Agreement (FRA) is a contract for locking in future short-term interest rates.

A typical FRA is illustrated in Figure 9.1. It is structured to start at $t = 0$ (trade date on which the FRA is concluded), applicable for the period between $t = S$ (settlement date on which the notional amount of deposit/loan comes into effect) and $t = T$ (date on which the notional deposit/loan expires or matures). In other words, the period between $t = S$ and $t = T$ is the contract period. For example, consider an FRA that is on a three-month interest rate for a six-month period beginning three months from now, $t = 0$. It can be expressed as 3 × 6 FRA, which means there is a locked-in three-month interest rate for three months forward (i.e. starting at the end of the third month from now and ending at the end of the sixth month from now). Similarly, a 12 × 18 FRA locks in a six-month interest rate for one year forward.

The difference between the FRA rate and a reference rate as a percentage of the notional amount is known as the settlement value. It is the amount to be paid by one party to the other on the settlement date. The settlement value is paid at the beginning of the contract period (at the beginning but not at the end of the underlying loan/deposit). The settlement value is calculated as follows:

$$\text{Settlement value} = \frac{(R_{ref} - R_{FRA}) \times N \times \dfrac{n}{365}}{1 + (R_{ref} \times \dfrac{n}{365})}$$

where

R_{ref} = Reference rate

R_{FRA} = FRA rate

N = Notional amount
n = Number of days of contract

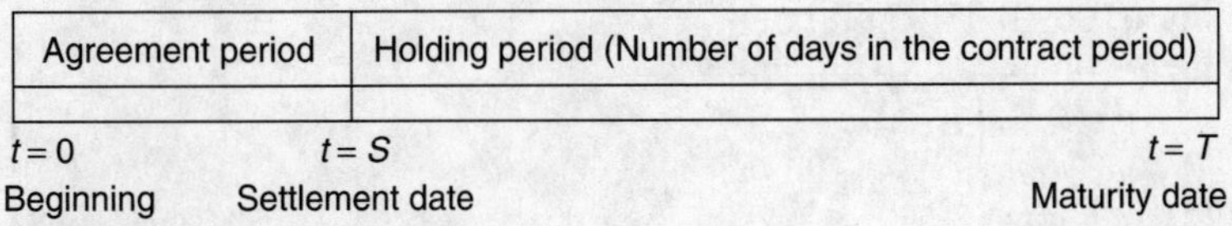

Agreement period	Holding period (Number of days in the contract period)

$t = 0$ Beginning — $t = S$ Settlement date — $t = T$ Maturity date

Figure 9.1

Forward Rate Agreement

As the equation indicates, the settlement value is discounted because it is payable at the start of the period and not, as it generally happens in the cash market, at the end of the period. The seller of an FRA pays the buyer the difference between the floating interest rate and the strike or agreement rate on a notional principal, if the floating-rate index exceeds the strike rate, and receives the difference if the strike rate exceeds the index.

Consider the following example. A U.S. bank has made a three-month loan of USD 10 million at LIBOR against an offsetting six-month deposit that carries a fixed rate of interest. The bank expects a fall in interest rates in the three-month period. When the loan is to be rolled over for the next three months, it has to be done at the new lower base rate. In such a situation, the bank will face erosion in its interest income, while its interest expenditure on deposits will remain unchanged. This will ultimately affect its profits. To hedge against such a risk, the bank sells USD 10 million 3 × 6 FRA at a 6 percent rate of interest. After three months, assume that LIBOR is 5.50 percent. Thus, the agreement rate (6 percent) is the expected rate at the beginning of the holding period or contract period, and the LIBOR on the date of settlement is greater than the settlement rate (5.5 percent). The bank will thus receive USD 0.01247 million [i.e. (0.06 – 0.055) × USD 10 million × (91/365)] on the date of settlement ($t = S$). The present value of the amount at the beginning of the three-month FRA period is USD 0.01229 million {i.e. USD 0.01247 million ÷ [1 + 0.055 (91/365)]}. This is the sum that the buyer of the FRA pays to the bank upfront. This will compensate for the shortfall on the expected income on the USD 10 million loan due to fall of interest rates. This is also the difference in the interest earned on USD 10 million for 91 days at the actual LIBOR and the agreement rate, discounted at the prorated level of the realized LIBOR. The settlement can be made at the end of the six-month period from now, or in advance at the end of the three-month period from now. If the settlement is made in advance, the amount to be paid either by the seller or buyer of the FRA is the present value of the difference between the two interest rates (prorated to the length of the contract period) multiplied by the principal amount. The discount rate in this regard is the prorated settlement rate (e.g. LIBOR). If the settlement is in arrears, there is no need to discount the payment. In other words, the bank invests the amount of USD 0.01229 million along with USD 10 million at 5.5 percent. At the end of the third month, the total return would be USD 149,582, which is the 6 percent annual return contracted in the FRA. If the LIBOR on the date of settlement is greater than the agreement rate, the bank has to pay the present value of the amount of interest that exceeds what is expected from rolling over the loan.

Example 9.4

A bank sells a 3 × 12 FRA for INR 1 million at an annualized rate of 5 percent. Three months after the sale, interest rates have risen to 6 percent. How much cash does the bank pay to, or receive from, the FRA buyer?

Solution

Since the reference rate is more than the FRA rate, the bank has to pay the interest rate differential to the FRA buyer. The amount to be paid by the bank to the FRA buyer is computed as follows:

$$\text{Settlement value} = \frac{(0.06-0.05)\times \text{INR } 1\text{ m}\times \dfrac{272}{365}}{1+\left(0.06\times \dfrac{272}{365}\right)}$$

$$= \text{INR } 9{,}521$$

Banks quote bid–offer rates for different FRAs. For example, a bank may quote 3 × 6 FRA at 5.75% – 5.80%. This means that, on a 3 × 6 FRA, the bank is prepared to pay a fixed rate of 5.75 percent for receipt of a three-month floating-rate index, say, LIBOR, and to receive a fixed rate of 5.80 percent for payment of a three-month LIBOR. The actual payment will be made on the date of settlement, $t = S$, depending on LIBOR on that date.

Business firms can hedge their interest rate risk by entering notional agreements to lend or borrow in the future at the rate of interest determined in the present. For example, consider a company that has a floating-rate loan of USD 10 million and would like to be certain what rate of interest it will be charged on the loan for the three-month period commencing three months from the present. The company may attempt to guarantee what its interest rates will be by entering an FRA with a bank, thereby notionally committing itself to borrowing USD 10 million at, say, 6.50percent (bid–offer spread of 6.50% – 6.45% for U.S. dollars for a three-month period commencing three months from the present) in three months. Settlement interest is used to calculate the compensation payment to pass between the counterparties in an FRA. Suppose the bid–offer spread for this is 6.60%–6.65% when the contract period is reached. The 0.15 percent per annum increase in rates would require the bank to pay the company a sum equivalent to 0.15percent per annum for three months on a USD 10 million loan. The money received would compensate the company for a rise in the rate of interest on its floating-rate loan over the three-month period. If interest rates fall, the compensation payment would be made in the opposite direction so that the company would lose on its FRA but gain from the lower rate on its floating-rate loan. In either case, an interest rate variation on the loan will be offset by a gain or loss on the FRA. Thus, by entering an FRA, the company can remove uncertainty about the interest payable. The rate locked- in the FRA reflects the forward interest rate, and it is not necessarily the current rate at the time of enteringthe FRA.

Example 9.5

A company would like to use an FRA to guarantee the interest payable on a USD 10 million three-month loan to be taken on 1 July 2015. On 1 January 2015, the rate for three-month LIBOR six-month forward is 7 percent p.a. The bank providing the FRA compensates for the deviation of LIBOR on 1 July from 7 percent. Anticipating a borrowing at LIBOR + 50 bp, the company thus locks in an interest rate of 7.5 percent. On 1 July 2015, LIBOR stands at 8 percent. Work out the amount payable.

Solution

$$\text{Amount payable} = \frac{(0.08-0.07)\times\left(\dfrac{91}{365}\right)\times \text{USD}10{,}000{,}000}{1+0.08\times\left(\dfrac{91}{365}\right)}$$

$$= \text{USD } 24{,}445$$

Thus, the actual payment is 1 percent p.a. for three months on USD 10 million, discounted at LIBOR to reflect the fact that the compensation is paid at the beginning of the period, whereas interest is payable at the end of the period. The sum paid by the bank to the company on 1 July is USD 24,445. The company thus borrows USD 9,975,555 instead of USD 10 million. At 8.5 percent p.a., the sum to be paid on 1 October is USD [9,975,555 × 8.5% × (91/365) + 9,975,555], or USD 10,186,954. This is equivalent to paying 7.5 percent on USD 10 million for the three-month period. By using the FRA, the company has locked-in an interest rate of 7.5 percent p.a. and has thus avoided the 1 percent rise in interest rates.

The FRA can also be used by a borrower to lock-in the cost of a loan. For example, a firm wishes to borrow USD 10 million for six months, 12 months from now, but it finds itself exposed to rising interest rates over the next twelve months. To solve this problem, the firm enters into an FRA, whereby it pays a fixed rate of 6 percent to a bank (market maker) in exchange for receiving a six-month LIBOR at the settlement date (12 months from now). Suppose that the six-month LIBOR is 6.5 percent on the rate determination date in 12 months. The amount to be received by the firm in arrears, assuming there are 182 days between months 12 and 18, is USD 25,000 [i.e. (6.5%–6.0%) × USD 10 million × 182/365]. If settled in advance, the firm would receive USD 24,215 {i.e. 25,000/[1 + (0.065 × 182/365)]}. The discounting is necessary because the firm will have to pay interest on its loan at the end of 182 days from the settlement date, while the dealer pays the difference in the interest amounts on the settlement date.

The cost of the loan is calculated as follows: Interest on USD 10 million at 6.5%o for 182 days = (0.065) × USD 10 million × 182/365 = USD 3,25,000 (approximately). The compounded value of the interest difference received from the dealer at 6.5 percent for 182 days is USD 25,000 {i.e. (USD 24,215) × [1 + (0.065 ×182/365)]}. So, the net cost of the loan is USD 300,000 (i.e. USD 3,25,000 — 25,000), which works out to an annual rate of 6 percent. This is the rate locked-in by the firm. Thus, the firm has effectively used the FRA to transfer its interest rate exposure to the market maker.

Both lenders and borrowers can effectively use FRA to hedge themselves against falling or rising interest rates in the economy. Speculators can also use FRA. When they expect a fall in the interest rates, they sell FRA. And when they believe that the interest rates will rise, they purchase FRA.

Interest Rate Futures (Reserve Bank) Directions, 2013

Interest rate futures were introduced in India in June 2003 on the National Stock Exchange through launch of three contracts. All the contracts are valued using the zero-coupon yield curve.

Interest rate futures were introduced in India in June 2003 on the National Stock Exchange through launch of three contracts—a contract based on a notional 10-year coupon-bearing bond, a contract based on a notional 10-year zero-coupon bond, and a contract based on a 91-day Treasury Bill. All the contracts are valued using the zero-coupon yield curve.

The Reserve Bank of India issued comprehensive directions in the name of Interest Rate Futures (Reserve bank) Directions, 2013, on 5 December 2013. The salient features of these directions are mentioned as below:

- Interest rate futures means a standardized interest rate derivative contract traded on a recognized stock exchange to buy or sell a notional security or any other interest-bearing instrument or an index of such instruments or interest rates at a specified future date, at a price determined at the time of the contract.
- The interest rate futures deriving value from the following underlying are permitted on the recognized stock exchanges:
    a. 91-day Treasury Bills;
    b. 2-year, 5-year, and 10-year coupon-bearing notional GOI Security; and
    c. Coupon-bearing GOI Security.
- Persons resident in India are permitted to purchase or sell interest rate futures both for hedging an exposure to interest rate risk or otherwise.
- FIIs registered with SEBI are permitted to purchase or sell interest rate futures subject to the conditions that the total gross long (bought) position in the spot Government securities market and interest rate futures markets taken together does not exceed the

aggregate permissible limit for investment in Government securities, and the total gross short (sold) position of each FII in interest rate futures does not exceed their long position in the Government securities and in interest rate futures at any point in time.

- Other organizations like commercial banks can participate with the permission of their respective regulators.
- The 10-year interest rate futures contract shall satisfy the following requirements:
  a. The contract shall be on coupon-bearing notional 10-year GOI Security.
  b. The coupon for the notional 10-year GOI Security shall be 7% per annum with semi-annual compounding.
  c. The contract shall be settled by physical delivery of deliverable grade securities using the electronic book entry system of the existing depositories.
  d. Deliverable grade securities shall comprise GOI Securities maturing at least 7.5 years but not more than 15 years from the first day of the delivery month with a minimum total outstanding stock of ₹10,000 crore.
- The 91-day Treasury Bill futures shall satisfy the following requirements:
  a. The contract shall be on 91-day Treasury Bills issued by the GOI.
  b. The contract shall be cash settled in Indian rupees.
  c. The final settlement price of the contract shall be based on the weighted average price/yield obtained in the weekly auction of the 91-day Treasury Bills on the date of expiry of the contract.
- The 2-year and 5-year interest rate futures contract shall satisfy the following requirements:
  a. The 2-year and 5-year interest rate futures contract shall be on coupon-bearing notional 2-year and 5-year GOI Security, respectively.
  b. The coupon for the notional 2-year GOI Security shall be 7% per annum, and that of the notional 5-year GOI Security shall be 7% per annum with semi-annual compounding.
  c. The contracts shall be cash settled in Indian rupees.
  d. The final settlement price of the 2-year and 5-year interest rate futures contracts shall be based on the yields on basket of securities for each interest rate futures contract specified by the respective stock exchange in accordance with guidelines issued by the SEBI from time to time.
- The 10-year interest rate futures with coupon-bearing GOI Security as underlying shall satisfy the following requirements:
  a. The underlying shall be a coupon-bearing GOI Security of face value ₹100 and residual maturity between 9 and 10 years on the expiry of futures contract. The underlying security within these parameters shall be as decided by stock exchanges in consultation with the Fixed Income Money Market and Derivatives Association (FIMMDA).
  b. The contract shall be cash settled in Indian rupees.
  c. The final settlement price shall be arrived at by calculating the weighted average price of the underlying security based on prices during the last two hours of the trading on the Negotiated Dealing System-Order Matching (NDS-OM) system. If less than 5 trades are executed in the underlying security during the last two hours of trading, then the FIMMDA price shall be used for the final settlement.
- The 10-year interest rate futures with coupon-bearing notional 10-year GOI Security as underlying and settlement price based on basket of securities shall satisfy the following requirements:

a. The underlying shall be coupon-bearing notional 10-year GOI Security with face value of ₹100. For each contract, there shall be a basket of Government GOI Securities, with residual maturity between 9 and 11 years on the day of expiry futures contract, with appropriate weight assigned to each security in the basket. Exchanges shall determine criteria for including securities in the basket and determining their weights.
b. The underlying security shall have coupons with semi-annual compounding.
c. The contract shall be cash settled in Indian rupees.
d. The final settlement price shall be based on the average settlement yield, which shall be the weighted average of the yields of securities in the underlying basket. For each security in the basket, the yield shall be calculated by determining the weighted average yield of the security based on the last two hours of the trading in the NDS-OM system. If less than 5 trades are executed in the security during the last two hours of the trading, then the FIMMDA price shall be used for determining the yields of individual securities in the market.

Trading in Interest Rate Futures on National Stock Exchange

Currently, the Interest Rate Futures Segment of the NSE offers two instruments, i.e. Futures on 10-year GOI Security (NBF II) and 91-day GOI Treasury Bill (91 DTB). Based on the Directions of the RBI and the guidelines issued thereon by SEBI, the NSE has prescribed product specifications for trading in interest rate futures. The main features of these specifications are mentioned in the following lines:

Futures on 10-year GOI Security

Unit of trading: ₹2 lakh face value of GOI securities (2000 units).
Unit of trading: ₹2 lakh face value of GOI securities (2000 units).
Contract value: Quoted price * 2000.
Tick size: ₹0.0025.
Contract trading cycle: Three serial monthly contracts.
Spread contract: Near–Mid, Near–Far, and Mid–Far.
Expiry day: Last Thursday of the month.
Base price: Theoretical price of the 1st day of the contract and on all other days, daily settlement price of the contract.
Price operating range: +/– 3% of the base price.
Daily settlement: Daily MTM settlement on T+1 in cash based on daily settlement price.
Final settlement: Final settlement on T+1 in cash based on final settlement price.
Daily settlement price: Volume weighted average futures price of last half an hour or theoretical price.
Final settlement price: Weighted average price of the underlying bond based on the prices during the last two hours of the trading on NDS-OM. If less than 5 trades are executed in the underlying bond during the last two hours of trading, then the FIMMDA price shall be used for the final settlement.
Minimum initial margin: 1.5% of the value of the contract subject to minimum of 2.8% on the first day of trading and 0.05% of the notional value of the futures contract thereafter.
Calendar spread margin: ₹800 for spread of one month and ₹1,200 for spread of two months.
Extreme loss margin: 0.50% of the value of the gross open positions of the futures contract. In case of calendar spread positions, extreme loss margin shall be 0.01% of the value of the far month contract.

Mark-to-mark settlement: Positions in the futures contracts for each member are marked to market to the daily settlement price of the futures contracts at the end of each trade day.

Position limits: Client level: 3% of total open interest or ₹200 crore, whichever is higher.
Trading member level: 10% of the total open interest or ₹600 crore, whichever is higher.
FIIs : 10% of the total open interest or ₹600 crore, whichever is higher.
Exchange level: ₹25,000 crore or 25% of the outstanding of underlying whichever is higher for each underlying.

Futures on 91-day GOI Treasury Bill

Unit of trading: ₹2 lakh face value (2000 units).
Contract value: Quoted price * 2000.
Tick size: ₹0.0025.
Contract trading cycle: Three serial monthly contracts followed by one quarterly contract of the cycle March/June/September/December.
Expiry day: Last Wednesday of the expiry month.
Base price: Theoretical price of the 1st day of the contract and on all other days, daily settlement price of the contract.
Price operating range: +/– 1% of the base price.
Daily settlement: Daily MTM settlement on T+1 in cash based on daily settlement price.
Final settlement: Final settlement on T+1 in cash based on final settlement price.
Daily settlement price: ₹(100 – 0.25 * *yw*), where *yw* is the weighted average futures yield of trades during the time limit
Final settlement price: ₹2000 * (100 – 0.25* *yf*) where *yf* is the weighted average discount yield obtained from weekly auction of a 91-day T-Bill conducted by the RBI on the day of expiry.
Mode of settlement: Settled in cash in Indian rupees.
Minimum initial margin: 0.1% of the notional value of the contract on the first day and 0.05% of the notional value of the futures contract thereafter.
Calendar spread margin: ₹100 for spread of one month, ₹150 for spread of two months, ₹200 for spread of three months and ₹250 for spread of four months and beyond.
Extreme loss margin: 0.03% of the value of the gross open positions of the futures contract.
Mark-to-mark settlement: Positions in the futures contracts for each member is marked to market to the daily settlement price of the futures contracts at the end of eachtrade day.
Position limits: Client level: 6% of total open interest or ₹300 crore, whichever is higher.
Trading member level: 15% of the total open interest or ₹1,000 crore,whichever is higher.

Summary

1. **The yield to maturity is the discount rate that makes the present value of the future money equal to the money invested or deposited today.**
2. **Forward interest rate is the rate of interest implied by the spot rate for a period of time in the future.**
3. **The relationship between spot rates and maturities is known as the term structure of interest rates.**
4. **The investors use yield curves to identify the interest-bearing securities that are cheap or expensive at any given time.**

5. The slope of the yield curve is normally upward, from left to right, which means that the yields rise as maturity extends.

6. The credit spread refers to the additional yield an investor gets for acquiring a corporate bond instead of a risk-free security.

7. As the interest rates in the economy increase (decrease), the prices of outstanding securities decrease (increase) because potential investors can buy new securities that carry higher rates of interest.

8. All the investors, whether they are individuals or firms, are exposed to interest rate risk. When interest rates rise, the market value of the net worth of the investors falls; when interest rates fall, the market value of their net worth rises.

9. An interest rate futures contract is a standardized contract traded on an exchange to buy or sell a debt security at a certain date in the future at a specified price determined today.

10. Interest rate futures contracts are used either to hedge or to speculate on future interest rates and security prices.

11. Financial institutions, banks, and corporations as borrowers or lenders/investors generally use interest rate futures to hedge their interest rate risk. They mainly use interest rate futures for planned investment and planned borrowing.

12. A calendar spread is an inter-delivery spread involving simultaneous purchase of one delivery month futures contract and sale of another delivery month futures contract on the same underlying.

13. Forward Rate Agreement (FRA) is a contract between two parties to the effect that the seller pays the buyer, at a specified time point in the future, the increased interest cost on a notional sum of money if the reference interest rate (e.g. LIBOR) at that time has risen above the agreed-upon interest rate and the buyer pays the seller the increased interest cost if the reference interest rate at that time has fallen below the agreed upon rate.

14. Both lenders and borrowers can effectively use the FRA to hedge themselves against falling or rising interest rates in the economy. Speculators can also use the FRA.

15. Interest rate futures were introduced in India in June 2003 on the NSE through launch of three contracts. All the contracts are valued using the zero-coupon yield curve.

Questions and Problems

1. How do you distinguish between the spot rate of interest and the forward rate of interest?

2. The spot rates are as follows:.

Year	Spot rate (%)
1	6
2	7
3	9
4	10

What are the forward rates over each of the four years?

3. Explain yield curve with examples. When would the yield curve become upward sloping?

4. What is interest rate risk? How is interest rate risk associated with the price of the security?

5. How can the banks use interest rate futures to keep up their net worth? Illustrate your answer.

6. An investor has sold 200 September interest rate futures on 8.83% GOI 2023 at a price of INR 95.25. The details of the contract are given below. One contract denotes 2000 units.

   Expiry date : 26 September 2015
   Trade date : 20 September 2015

   Daily settlement prices:

19 Sept.	INR 95.00
20 Sept.	INR 94.00
23 Sept.	INR 95.35
24 Sept	INR 93.25
25 Sept	INR 93.50

   Futures market price on 26 Sept. 2015: INR 92.75

   Calculate the total gain/loss to the investor.

7. What is a Forward Rate Agreement? Explain the mechanism of an FRA.

8. A bank sells a 6 × 12 FRA for INR 1 million at an annualized rate of 6 percent. Six months after the sale, interest rates have risen to 7 percent. How much cash does the bank pay to, or receive from, the FRA buyer?

9. Discuss the salient features of Interest Rate Futures (RBI) Directions, 2013.

10. Do the specifications of NSE discourage the real investors to trade in interest rate futures?

Multiple-choice Questions

1. A unit of money received today is worth ________ the same unit of money to be received tomorrow.

   (a) Less than (b) More than
   (c) Equal to (d) None of these

2. The interest rate mentioned on the face of a corporate bond is the ________.

   (a) Real interest rate (b) Nominal interest rate
   (c) Repo rate (d) None of these

3. Forward interest rate is the rate implied by ________.

   (a) Spot interest rate (b) Real interest rate
   (c) Bank rate (d) None of these

4. Yield on a bond depends on ________.

   (a) Interest rate
   (b) Price of the bond
   (c) Interest rate and price of the bond
   (d) None of these

5. The relationship between spot interest rates and maturities is known as ________.

   (a) Term structure (b) Linear relationship
   (c) Forward relationship (d) None of these

6. The slope of the yield curve is normally ________.

   (a) Upward (b) Downward
   (c) Flat (d) None of these

7. Inverted yield curve indicates that the interest rates will ________.

   (a) Increase (b) Decline
   (c) Remain constant (d) None of these

8. As the security prices vary, the investors experience unexpected ________.

   (a) Gains (b) Losses
   (c) Gains or losses (d) None of these

9. As the interest rates in the economy rise, the net worth of commercial banks will ________.

   (a) Decline (b) Increase
   (c) Remain unaffected (d) None of these

10. Interest rate futures are ________.

    (a) Customized (b) Standardized
    (c) OTC (d) None of these

11. An investor who expects to suffer losses on his or her investment portfolio due to rise in interest rates may hedge interest rate risk by ________.

    (a) Selling interest rate futures.
    (b) Buying interest rate futures
    (c) Entering currency futures contract
    (d) None of these

12. Forward Rate Agreement is a contract for locking-in ________.

    (a) Short-term interest rates
    (b) Long term interest rates
    (c) Lending rates only
    (d) None of these

13. In a FRA, the reference rate is usually the ________.

    (a) LIBOR (b) Repo rate
    (c) Bank rate (d) None of these

Further Reading

1. R. Jarrow and G. Oldfield, "Forward Contracts and Futures Contracts", *Journal of Financial Economics* (December 1981), pp. 373–382.
2. J. C. Cox, J. E. Ingersoll, and S. A. Ross, "A Theory of the Term Structure of Interest Rates", *Econometrica* (1985), pp. 385–407
3. Galen Burghardt, *The Eurodollar Futures and Options Handbook* (New York: McGraw-Hill), 2003.
4. B. Malkiel, "Expectations, Bond Prices and Term Structure of Interest Rates", *Quarterly Journal of Economics* (May 1962), pp. 197–218.
5. J. Hull, *Options, Futures and Other Derivatives* (New Delhi: Prentice-Hall of India), 2005.

CHAPTER 10

Cross-border Investment Decisions

CHAPTER OBJECTIVES

After studying this chapter, you should be able to:

1 Discuss the importance of cross-border investment.

2 Understand the concept of capital budgeting.

3 Estimate the cash flows associated with a project.

4 Distinguish between foreign projects and domestic projects in terms of cash flows.

5 Discuss the approaches to project evaluation.

6 Gain insight into the risks involved in cross-border investments.

7 Define various risk-handling techniques.

8 Understand the concept of real options.

Introduction

Business firms can enter foreign markets through exports, license agreements, investments, strategic alliances, or a combination of these routes. In the case of exports, the exporting firm transfers the final goods or services from the home country to the foreign country. The goods produced in one country are sold in another country through sales agents, distributors, or foreign sales branches or subsidiaries. In the case of a *license agreement,* a domestic firm enters into a contract with a foreign company to market the firm's products in the foreign country. The other party (the licensee) assumes the responsibility of marketing or distributing the goods or services in the foreign country in return for fees or compensation. The licensee may also assume the responsibility of producing as well as marketing the products of the licensor. Such international agreements may take different forms, such as the franchise agreement and the reciprocal marketing agreement.

Firms can also enter foreign markets through investments, which may be foreign direct investment, cross-border mergers and acquisitions, or joint ventures. Foreign direct investment (FDI) refers to the establishment of new production facilities on foreign soil. FDI entails a substantial investment of corporate resources, including managerial resources, in a foreign country. In a *cross-border merger,* two firms—a domestic firm and a foreign firm— pool their resources to form a new venture, and in a *cross-border acquisition,* a domestic firm acquires the use of the productive facilities in a foreign country. Cross-border acquisition may involve the acquisition of assets or equity stock. In cross-border acquisition of assets, a domestic firm acquires the productive capacity (e.g. the manufacturing plant) of a foreign firm, without the liabilities supporting those assets, while in cross-border acquisition of equity stock, a domestic firm buys the equity shares of a foreign company either through a friendly offer or a hostile deal.

A firm can also enter into a foreign country through a strategic alliance, which refers to a collaborative agreement between a domestic firm and a foreign firm. Strategic alliances are mostly in the form of joint ventures, in which two or more firms agree to pool their productive resources to achieve a well-defined goal.

Globalization of business has influenced not only sales, but also manufacturing the world over. It is in this context that international investment decisions have assumed greater importance, particularly in recent years. A firm may invest overseas in order to get returns in excess of that required. Domestic firms may also take up foreign projects in order to diversify their investments. Through international diversification, a firm may be able to reduce risk in relation to expected return. However, foreign projects also involve some risks. For example, they are exposed to country risk (or political risk). Governments may discriminate against foreign projects and impose several taxes. They may also impose restrictions on the remittance of profits arising out of a foreign project to the parent unit. In extreme cases, the foreign government may confiscate the assets of the project without compensation. Country risk can range from mild interference to complete confiscation of assets by the foreign government.

Another risk associated with foreign projects is currency risk (or foreign exchange risk). As foreign exchange rates fluctuate over time, usually in an unpredictable way, it is difficult to predict the cash flows of the foreign project in the domestic currency. All these risks pose serious problems for project evaluation. Although project appraisal and project evaluation are conceptually different, they are used interchangeably here.

Capital Budgeting

Capital budgeting, also known as *investment appraisal*, is a process of analysing and selecting capital projects. The process starts with the estimation of cash flows associated with a project. In capital budgeting, *cash flows* rather than *accounting profits* are taken into consideration, because a firm invests cash in the present, in anticipation of receiving more cash in the future. It is cash that matters in real-life situations such as making payments to workers and creditors. The availability of cash also determines how much dividend a company can pay to its shareholders, notwithstanding huge profits made by the company. Only cash can be reinvested. Accounting profit has many limitations in the context of investment appraisal. A company may have earned a good amount of profit, but may be bogged down with cash shortages. Increasing profits may not lead to increasing cash flows. Thus, cash flows are central to all investment decisions.

***Capital budgeting**, also known as investment appraisal, is a process of analysing and selecting capital or investment projects.*

Cash flows may occur at different stages of a project. Typically, a project requires an initial cash outflow, which is known as the *initial cash outlay*. That is, the project starts with a certain amount of expenditure. After commencement, the project would generate a stream of *net cash flows* (cash inflows minus capital outflows) over its life. At the end of the project, the firm may realize certain cash flows which are known as *terminal cash flows*.

Basic Principles for Cash-flow Estimation

During the estimation of cash flows of a project, the following basic principles are observed:

- *Incremental cash flows* are considered.
- Any resource that is used in the project is valued at the *opportunity cost*.
- *Sunk costs* are ignored in the present investment analysis.

- Changes in *net working capital* are considered.
- Investment and financing decisions are treated separately.
- Added cash flows from *replacement decisions* are considered.
- *Non-cash elements* are not considered.
- *After-tax cash flows* are taken into account.

In this section, we shall look at each of these briefly.

Incremental Cash Flows The principles of investment dictate that only incremental, and not absolute, cash flows be taken into account. **Incremental cash flows** refer to cash flows arising as a consequence of an investment decision. They represent the change in the firm's cash flows that occurs as a result of accepting a project. Incremental cash flows are the difference between the cash flows of a firm with and without the project. Thus, all changes in the firm's revenues and costs that would result from the acceptance of the project are considered in the project appraisal, and the cash flows that would not be changed by the project are disregarded.

Incremental cash flows are cash flows that arise as a consequence of an investment decision.

By taking into consideration the incremental cash flows of a firm, the project evaluation process can take care of *cannibalization,* which is the phenomenon of a new project affecting the sales of the existing project(s) of the same firm. For example, if an MNC undertakes a project that produces a substitute product for its own subsidiary's exports, then sales of the new product may replace the other sales of the MNC. The new product of the MNC may take away sales from its existing products. Let us consider another example to understand how cannibalization may affect investment decisions. Suppose a U.S. company has been exporting a product to India from its home base for a long time. This year, the company has established its own manufacturing facility in India. As a result, the earlier export sales of the company are lost. Therefore, while evaluating the investment in India, the company should consider such lost sales too. Further, it is also possible that a new project creates additional sales for the existing products of an MNC. This is an opposite phenomenon to cannibalization. Any effects (positive or negative) on other parts of the business of a firm resulting from the decision to make a further or new investment should be included in the investment analysis. In reality, however, it is often difficult to estimate the actual magnitude of cannibalization or sales creation.

Opportunity Costs Another fundamental element in investment appraisal is the opportunity cost of the inputs or assets used for the project. The **opportunity cost** of an input or asset refers to the cash flows that the input or asset could generate, if used for a purpose other than the project under consideration. For example, consider a firm that has owned a piece of land for some time. Now, it is considering using that land for a project. The original cost of the land is INR 1 million, but it could be sold for INR 1.5 million. Because the firm must forego the receipt of INR 1.5 million from the sale of the land if it is used for the project, the appropriate cost of this piece of land is INR 1.5 million, and not its original cost. This is the opportunity cost of the land. Taking another example, a firm has certain patent rights. If these rights are sold to others, the firm can get INR 10 million. Instead, the firm decides to use these patent rights to produce a product. The sale value of the patents, i.e. INR 10 million, is an opportunity cost, and it should be added to the project's cash outlay. The opportunity costs of other inputs and assets can be computed in the same way. Thus, any resource that is used in the project is valued at the opportunity cost, regardless of how much cash is paid or involved in acquiring that particular resource.

***The opportunity cost** of an input or asset refers to the cash flows that the input or asset could generate if used for a purpose other than the project under consideration.*

Sunk Costs Sunk costs refer to expenditure already incurred or committed. They are the costs incurred as a result of earlier decisions that cannot be changed or reversed now with the investment decision under consideration. As they are irrevocable, they should be

***Sunk costs** are costs that are incurred as a result of earlier decisions that cannot be changed or reversed now with the investment decision under consideration.*

ignored in the present investment analysis. In other words, historical costs that cannot be recovered, should not be considered in the decision to accept or not to accept a project. For example, a firm had spent INR 0.50 million on a market survey to launch a product. After five years, the firm has revived the idea of launching the same product following a new market survey. Because the old survey cost of INR 0.50 million cannot be recovered whether the new product is launched or not, it should not be considered now.

Changes in Net Working Capital A new project, if undertaken, may give rise to changes in the levels of inventory, debtors, and other liquid assets resulting from changes in the sales of a firm. The current liabilities may also change as a result of the implementation of a new project. New projects will not necessarily give rise to an increase in working capital every time; they may result in a reduction in working capital too. For example, a new technology associated with the proposed project may reduce inventory requirements and thus the working capital requirement. The payables and accruals may also change on the implementation of a new project. So, what is relevant is the change in the *net working capital* (current assets minus current liabilities); the same should be considered in the project appraisal analysis. At the end of the project, a firm may recover partially or completely the investment in working capital. Such working capital recovery should also be treated as cash inflow in the final year of the project.

Separation of Investment and Financing Decisions A project may be financed with both equity and debt capital. Debt involves payment of interest, which is a cash outflow. But such cash outflows (interest expenses) should not be added to the other cash outflows of the project because interest charges relate to financing rather than the investment decision. If the interest payments are charged against the cash inflows of the project, it would amount to double-counting since the discounting process incorporates the interest charges (cost of debt) in the cost of capital of the firm, which is used as a discount rate.

Replacement Decisions Replacement of an existing asset by a new one is also an investment decision. The firm may replace its old asset(s) to reduce the cost of asset maintenance or reduce the cost of other inputs, or to improve the quality of the product produced by the asset. The replacement of the old asset by a new asset would lead to additional cash flows. Thus, appraisal of investment for replacement of an existing machine or equipment before it completes its effective life involves recognition of additional cash flows (costs and benefits) arising from the replacement, rather than the costs and benefits of the new machine in isolation.

Non-cash Elements Non-cash items as such do not have any place in project appraisal. For example, depreciation is a non-cash charge as it does not involve any cash outflow. Therefore, depreciation should not be treated as cash outflow. However, any depreciation tax-shield (tax savings due to depreciation) is taken into account in appraisal of the project.

Tax Effects Taxes have a major impact on the economic viability of a project. Therefore, after-tax cash flows need to be considered in project appraisal. In view of the fact that tax effects will make or break a project, firms seriously consider taxes and their effect on the cash flows of a project.

Appraisal of Foreign and Domestic Projects: Distinguishing Factors

The fundamental principles of investment underlying foreign projects or domestic projects are the same. However, there are certain differences in the evaluation process for foreign and domestic projects. These differences mainly exist in the cash flows and in the discount rate.

Cash Flows As explained earlier, the estimation of cash inflows and outflows associated with a project is the first step in the project appraisal process. In the case of MNCs, the parent unit is in one country and the affiliates are located in other countries. If a subsidiary unit located in a foreign country wants to undertake a project, that project can be evaluated either from the parent firm's perspective or from the perspective of the subsidiary firm itself. Therefore, before attempting to identify the cash flows associated with a project, it is necessary to decide whether the project is to be evaluated from the *parent firm's perspective* or from the *subsidiary unit's perspective*. The subsidiary unit's perspective is also known as the project's perspective, and the parent company's perspective is also known as MNCs perspective. There are arguments for and against evaluating the project from either of the perspectives. Notwithstanding such arguments, it is a common practice to appraise the project from the parent company's perspective when the foreign subsidiary is wholly owned by the parent. When a project is appraised from the parent company's perspective, what matters is not the cash flows that are generated by the project, but the cash flows that are ultimately received by the parent unit.

The viability of a project varies with the perspective because of differences in cash flows. Parent firm's perspective generates a set of cash flows that are usually different from the cash flows generated by subsidiary firm's perspective. This difference arises because of certain factors such as taxes, blocked funds, and transfer pricing. These factors are briefly discussed in the following lines.

- *Tax factors*: The cash flows associated with a project are subject to different kinds of taxes and different tax rates prevailing in different countries. Since only after-tax cash flows are relevant for project evaluation, it is necessary to ascertain when and what taxes are paid in connection with a project. Different countries have different tax laws and tax provisions. A business's profits, with different treatment of the items of profit and loss accounting, are subject to tax at varying rates in different countries. Dividends, remittances, and so on are also treated differently in different countries for tax purposes. In many countries, domestic companies are subject to lower rates of tax than foreign companies. Sometimes, the profits arising from a project may be subject to double taxation. If the parent unit has to pay tax on the funds remitted by the subsidiary unit, the cash flows of the project vary with the perspective. Thus, because of differences in tax treatment, the cash flows of a project differ, depending on the perspective.
- *Blocked funds*: The incomes that are remittable to the parent firm by its subsidiary located abroad may be subject to several restrictions apart from additional taxes. For example, a country that is facing a shortage of foreign exchange reserves, or is not in a position to mobilize foreign funds, may impose restrictions on the remittance of profits by the subsidiary firm to its parent firm. This may result in the blockage of funds at the level of the subsidiary unit. In such a situation, the profits generated by a foreign project cannot be immediately repatriated to the parent company. Such accumulated funds are known as **blocked funds**.

  The blockage of funds may be for a short period or for a long period. The blockage of funds for a long period may strain the financial position of the MNC. Therefore, the MNC may use certain strategies or methods to manage the blocked funds to its advantage. For example, it may adopt methods like transfer pricing, export creation, or direct negotiation with the host government to move blocked funds to the desired destination. If an MNC has prior knowledge about the potential blockage of funds in different countries, it takes certain investment and financing decisions with regard to a foreign project. The MNC would consider the factor of blocked funds in its investment analysis and accordingly, compute the net present value (NPV) or internal rate of return (IRR) of the project. Only those cash flows that are remittable to the parent unit of the MNC are relevant when the project is appraised from the parent firm's perspective. Further, the MNC may consider the likely blocked funds in arranging finances for the project. For example, an MNC may decide to finance a project by mobilizing a certain proportion of needed funds in the host country itself, so that the funds do not need to be repatriated to the parent firm.

*The profits generated by a foreign project that cannot be immediately repatriated to the parent company are accumulated at the subsidiary unit level. Such accumulated funds are known as **blocked funds**.*

Blocked funds can also be effectively deployed in the host country itself. For example, such funds can be reinvested in the subsidiary firm to increase its production facilities, provided such opportunities exist. An MNC may also think of other local opportunities that will give a good return on the investment. Blocked funds may have a zero or a low opportunity cost. The next best thing that can be done is to keep such funds idle in the foreign country or invest in the host country at a rate that may be lower than what the MNC would have got by investing elsewhere. In the absence of restrictions on the repatriation of cash flows, the MNC is free to invest the net cash flows from the project anywhere and get the maximum return for the given risk.

- *Transfer pricing*: Goods and services are often transferred from the parent unit to subsidiary units and vice versa, or from one affiliate to another affiliate of an MNC, to achieve different objectives. **Transfer pricing** involves fixing the price for such transactions of goods and services. One of the objectives of transfer pricing is to increase the profitability of the MNC by reducing its overall tax liability. An MNC can reduce its overall tax liability by siphoning profits away from high-tax unit(s) to low-tax unit(s). For example, an MNC headquartered in New York has an affiliate in India. The parent unit supplies certain components to its subsidiary in India. The tax rate in the U.S. is low, while that in India is high. The MNC, by fixing a high transfer price for the components supplied to the subsidiary, can reduce the taxable profits of its subsidiary in India, and at the same time increase the taxable profits of the parent unit. Since the profits of the subsidiary unit are subject to high tax rates and, at the same time, the profits of the parent unit are subject to low tax rates, the overall effective rate of tax for the MNC may become lower, resulting in higher amounts of after-tax profits.

__Transfer pricing__ involves fixing the price for transactions that involve the transfer of goods and services from the parent unit to an affiliate, or from one affiliate to another affiliate of an MNC.

Corporations may also set up tax-haven affiliates in countries that have low tax rates or no taxes. Such affiliates, known as *offshore financial affiliates,* are used by MNCs to channel funds from the parent unit or other subsidiary units. Some of the affiliates may also be used as reinvoicing centres for transferring goods from one unit to another unit. Such subsidiary units take title to goods sold by the other subsidiary unit(s) and resell those goods to some other affiliate(s) of the MNC or others by reinvoicing. Generally, it is mere paperwork without actual flow of goods through the reinvoicing centre. MNCs may also take to transfer pricing routes in order to reduce foreign exchange exposure and circumvent foreign exchange controls. Restrictions on the movement of goods and services across countries, restrictions on income repatriation, increased tariffs on international trade, and so on, can also be circumvented through transfer pricing.

Transfer-pricing abuse has become a common feature, particularly in intra-corporate transfer of services. MNCs generally fix royalties and consultancy fees at a very high level for services for which there is no market price, and thereby shift expenses towards the affiliates with high tax rates. In recent years, however, governments have taken serious note of the misuse of transfer pricing, and introduced certain measures including tax codes to establish normal prices for intra-corporate transactions in line with arm's length prices. Corporations that resort to abusing transfer pricing are also penalized.

Transfer pricing has a direct effect on the viability of a project. For example, a parent company may set the price for goods and services to be sold to the subsidiary unit (project) at an artificially high level. The subsidiary unit may also be asked to set the price for goods and services to be sold to the parent firm at an artificially low level.

By setting the prices for goods and services sold to subsidiary unit artificially high and that for goods and services bought from the subsidiary unit artificially low, an MNC can move the profits of the project out of the host country and into the country where the parent company is located. But such a policy may distort the viability of the project that is being appraised.

- *Other factors*: Foreign projects may also be offered subsidized financing, which helps an MNC get funds at a below-market rate. This adds additional value to the project. On the other hand, an MNC may also be asked by the foreign government to take on additional negative NPV infrastructure projects in order to gain access to positive-NPV projects in the country. Such projects are known as negative-NPV tie-in projects. MNCs may also enjoy tax holidays offered by some foreign governments to promote foreign direct investment in their countries. The financial implications of all such aspects need to be identified and valued separately in the evaluation of projects.

The Discount Rate People always prefer a certain amount of money now to the same amount of money at some time in the future. A rupee in hand today is worth more than a rupee to be received some time in the future. This is because if one has the rupee now, it can be invested or loaned, and can earn some interest or return. So, one can end up with more than one rupee in the future. This implies that money has *time value*. This time value of money plays a crucial role in project appraisal. Projects generate cash flows at different points in time. The cash flows that occur at different times are not logically comparable as money has time value. Therefore, such cash flows need to be adjusted for their differences in timing. One such adjustment process is discounting. Discounting is a process by which differences in the timing of cash flows are eliminated and cash flows are made comparable. It is the reverse or reciprocal of compounding. *Compounding* is the process of determining the future value of a certain amount today, whereas *discounting* is the process of finding the present value of a certain amount in the future (i.e. a future cash flow). The compound interest rate that is used to discount future cash flows is known as the *discount rate*. For example, given the interest rate of, say, 10 percent, the present value of one Indian rupee to be received after one year can be expressed as $1/(1 + 0.10)^1$. Here, the factor 0.10 is the discount rate. It may be noted that the higher the discount rate, the smaller is the present value of the future money. Further, the longer the time period (i.e. the distance between today and future time), the lower is the present value of the future money.

Discount rate plays a very crucial role in project appraisal. Other things remaining the same, the discount rate determines the selection or rejection of a project. The cost of capital is used as the discount rate in the project appraisal. The cost of capital is defined as the minimum required rate of return on the funds invested in a project (see Chapter 11). The cost of capital and, thus, the discount rate is determined by several factors. For example, the risk involved in a project determines the cost of capital, other things being equal. As foreign projects involve more risk, the cost of capital (discount rate) used in appraising such projects will obviously be higher as compared to that for domestic projects.

Approaches to Project Evaluation

Capital budgeting is a continuous process in every corporate organization. It involves the selection and implementation of projects that maximize the value of the firm. The selection process involves a set of rules and criteria that enable the firm to decide whether to accept or reject a particular project. The rules and decision criteria are formed into different methods of capital budgeting. The commonly used capital budgeting methods *are payback period, net present value, internal rate of return, and profitability index* (*PI*). Of these methods, the NPV method is widely used, because it is simple, yet scientific and sophisticated.

The Net Present Value (NPV) Model

The typical NPV model is given by the following formula:

$$NPV = \sum_{t=1}^{n} \frac{CFAT_t}{(1+K)^t} - I_0 \tag{10.1}$$

If the terminal cash flows of the project are shown separately, then NPV can be stated as

$$NPV = \sum_{t=1}^{n} \frac{CFAT_t}{(1+K)^t} + \frac{TV_n}{(1+K)^n} - I_0 \tag{10.2}$$

where

$CFAT_t$ = Expected net cash flows after taxes in period t
K = Expected cost of capital
I_0 = Initial investment in the project
n = Expected economic life (in years) of the project
TV = Terminal value of the project

The after-tax cash flows associated with a project can be defined as

$$CFAT_t = (R_t - OC_t - D_t - I_t)(1-T) + D_t + I_t(1-T)$$

Eq. 10.1 can also be rewritten as

$$CFAT_t = NI_t - D_t + I_t(1-T) \tag{10.3}$$

In terms of net operating income (NOI) and ignoring the interest expense, Eq. 10.3 can be stated as

$$CFAT_t = (R_t - OC_t)(1-T) + TD_t$$

In these equations,

R_t = Expected sales revenue in period t
OC_t = Expected operating costs in period t
D = Depreciation in period t
I_t = Interest expense in period t
T = Tax rate
NI_t = Net income for period t
TD = Depreciation tax shield (tax saving due to depreciation) for period t

Eq. 10.2 can also be stated as

$$NPV = \sum_{t=1}^{n} \frac{(R_t - OC_t)(1-T)}{(1+K)^t} + \sum_{t=1}^{n} \frac{TD_t}{(1+K)^t} + \frac{TV_n}{(1+K)^n} - I_0$$

K, the cost of capital, is defined as

$$\begin{aligned} K &= K_e(\alpha) + K_d(1-\alpha) \\ &= K_e[E/(E+D)] + K_d[D/(E+D)] \end{aligned}$$

where K_e = Cost of equity
K_d = After-tax cost of debt
E = Amount of equity in the capital structure of the firm
D = Amount of debt in the capital structure of the firm

When an MNC invests in a foreign project, it generates a stream of net cash flows in the foreign currency. To evaluate these cash flows, the MNC may adopt two approaches. Using an example of a U.S.-based MNC investing in India, the two approaches are described here.

Appraisal from the Project's Perspective In the first approach, the project's INR cash flows are discounted at the INR discount rate to generate NPV in Indian rupees. The steps involved in this are:

- Estimate the cash flows of a project in the foreign currency;
- Identify the foreign currency discount rate; and
- Find the NPV in the foreign currency.

These steps can be expressed in the form of the following equation:

$$NPV^f = \sum_{t=0}^{n}\left[E(CF_t^f)/(1+i^f)^t\right]$$

Here,

NPV^f = NPV in the foreign currency
$E(CF_t^f)$ = Expected cash flows in foreign currency at time t
i^f = Foreign currency discount rate

Appraisal from the Parent Company's Perspective In the second approach, the project's INR cash flows (as and when they occur) are converted to U.S. dollar cash flows, and these cash flows are then discounted at the U.S. dollar discount rate to generate a U.S. dollar NPV.

The steps involved in this will be:

- Estimate the cash flows of a project in the foreign currency;
- Estimate the expected future spot rate of exchange;
- Convert foreign currency cash flows to domestic currency at the expected future spot rate; and
- Identify the domestic discount rate and find NPV in the domestic currency.

Thus,

$$NPV^d = \sum_{t=0}^{n}\left[E(CF_t^d)/(1+i^d)^t\right]$$

where

NPV^d = NPV in domestic currency
$E(CF_t^d) = [E(CF_t^f)][E(S_t)]$
$E(S_t)$ = Expected spot rate at time t
$E(CF_t^d)$ = Expected cash flows in domestic currency at time t
$E(CF_t^f)$ = Expected cash flows in foreign currency at time t
i^d = Domestic currency discount rate

The first approach is used for appraisal from the project's perspective, and the second approach is used for appraisal from the parent company's perspective. When a project is appraised from the parent's perspective, the relevant cash flows are those cash flows (converted to functional/domestic currency of the parent unit) that are actually received by the parent unit with regard to the foreign project. When NPV^f is transformed into NPV^d (i.e. $NPV^f \times S_0$), both approaches generally provide exactly the same result. However, if international parity conditions are not in equilibrium, the NPV of a project may not be the same under both these approaches. Further, in certain specific circumstances, the two approaches may not give the same result. For example, the foreign government may impose restrictions on repatriation of net cash flows of a project back to the parent firm. This will change the value of the foreign project from the parent firm's perspective. Thus, given the same tax rates in both the countries (parent's country and subsidiary's country), if all the cash flows of a foreign project are repatriated to the parent firm, and international parity conditions hold, the project appraisal from the perspective of the parent firm would give the same result as the appraisal from the foreign subsidiary's perspective.

As far as the decision to accept or reject the project goes, the project can be accepted, if both the NPVs are positive (greater than zero), and rejected, if both are negative. But in cases where one NPV is positive and the other is negative, it becomes rather complex to decide whether the project should be accepted or rejected. Several other factors need to be considered before the decision.

The following example shows a model of capital budgeting. Here, the MNC is a U.S.-based firm, which is considering the development of a project in India. The project involves manufacturing and selling a product. The initial investment by the parent firm to be made in the year 2015 is USD 100 million. The cost of capital is 12 percent. The expected annual costs and revenues are given in Table 10.1.

$$NPV = (-)100 + \frac{35.45}{(1+0.12)^1} + \frac{34.95}{(1+0.12)^2} + \frac{39.20}{(1+0.12)^3} + \frac{44.67}{(1+0.12)^4} + \frac{40.39}{(1+0.12)^5}$$

$$NPV = \text{USD } 138.72 \text{ million} - \text{USD } 100 \text{ million} = \text{USD } 38.72 \text{ million}$$

Since the project gives a positive NPV, the MNC can consider the launching of the project in India. A few points may be noted in this example. The MNC is faced with multiple risks in launching and operating a foreign project. More importantly, the currency risk and the

Table 10.1 Expected Annual Costs and Revenues (in Million INR)

Items/Year	*2016*	*2017*	*2018*	*2019*	*2020*
Total Revenue	16,000	16,000	16,500	18,000	16,000
Total variable cost	10,000	10,000	10,000	11,000	10,000
Fixed annual expenses	2,800	2,800	2,800	2,800	2,800
Depreciation	1,200	1,200	1,200	1,200	1,200
Earnings before tax	2,000	2,000	2,500	3,000	2,000
Tax @ 30%	600	600	750	900	600
Earnings after tax	1,400	1,400	1,750	2,100	1,400
Net cash flows	2,600	2,600	2,950	3,300	2,600
Amount to be remitted to parent firm	2,600	2,600	2,950	3,300	2,600
Withholding tax (@15%)	390	390	442.50	495	390
Amount remitted to parent firm after withholding tax	2210	2210	2507.50	2805	2210
Salvage value	–	–	–	–	300
Expected exchange rate (USD/INR)	62.3456	63.2400	63.9678	62.7896	62.1523
Net cash flows received by parent firm in USD	35.45	34.95	39.20	44.67	40.39

business risk, which the company has to account for in capital budgeting. The MNC has to forecast a certain exchange rate every year and accordingly arrive at the NPV for the project. But the exchange rates are subject to fluctuations, sometimes so violently to vitiate the entire estimation process. The discount rate is supposed to cover the entire risk factor, and leave a solid return for the investors.

Example 10.1

An Indian firm wishes to invest in a U.S. project. It is estimated that the project will initially cost USD 100 million. The firm expects to have a debt ratio of 52 percent in the project funding. The expected free cash flows (net cash flows after tax) for the next five years are shown in Table 10.2.

Table 10.2 Expected free Cash Flows for the Next Five Years

Year	*1*	*2*	*3*	*4*	*5*
Net cash flows (USD million)	20	35	40	40	50

The risk-free interest rate is 6 percent in India and 4 percent in the United States. The inflation rate is 5 percent in India and 3 percent in the United States. The tax rate is 35 percent in India and 30 percent in the United States. The risk premium is 10 percent in India and 8 percent in the United States. The estimated equity beta for investment in the U.S. is 0.90. The general interest rate is 12 percent in India and 9 percent in the United States. The current spot exchange rate is USD/INR 46.

Evaluate the project.

Solution

The cash flows and discount rates can be expressed in two alternative ways. The INR cost of capital can be used to discount free cash flows in INR, or the U.S. cost of capital can be used to discount free cash flows in the U.S. dollars.

A. To evaluate the project in INR, the following steps can be observed:

1. Convert the initial cost of the project (USD 100 million) into INR at the current spot rate of INR 46, which comes to INR 4,600 million.
2. Forecast the forward exchange rate by using interest rate parity or inflation rate parity.

$$E(\text{USD/INR}) = S_0 \times \frac{(1+i_h)}{(1+i_f)}$$

where

$E(USD/INR)$ = Expected exchange rate between the Indian rupee and the U.S. dollar

S_0 = Current spot rate of exchange

i_h = Inflation rate in home country (India)

i_f = Inflation rate in foreign country (United States)

Accordingly, the expected spot rate after one year is

$$\text{INR } 46 \times (1+0.05)/(1+0.03) = \text{INR } 46.89$$

Similarly, the expected spot rate after two years is

$$\text{INR } 46 \times (1+0.05)^2/(1+0.03)^2 = \text{INR } 47.76$$

Much in the same way, the expected spot rates for other years can also be found.

3. Convert annual net cash flows into INR at the expected spot rates.

4. Discount all cash flows at the INR cost of capital, which is computed in the following way:

After-tax cost of debt: 0.12(1 – 0.35) = 0.078

The cost of equity is

$$K_e = \text{Nominal risk} - \text{free interest rate} + \text{Risk premium} \times \beta$$
$$= 0.06 + 0.10(0.090)$$
$$= 0.15$$

Weighted average cost of capital (WACC) = (0.078 × 0.52) + (0.15 × 0.48) = 0.11

Table 10.3 shows the NPV of the project.

Table 10.3 The NPV of the Project (INR)

Year	*Net cash flows (USD million)*	*Estimated spot rate (USD/INR)*	*Net cash flows (INR million)*	*PV factor at 11%*	*Present values (INR million)*
0	(–)100	46	(–)4,600	1.00	(–)4,600
1	20	46.89	937.80	0.901	855
2	35	47.76	1,671.60	0.812	1,357
3	40	48.67	1,946.80	0.731	1,423
4	40	49.6	1,984.00	0.659	1,307
5	50	50.54	2,527.00	0.593	1,499
					NPV = INR 1,841

B. To evaluate the project in U.S. dollars, the following calculations can be made:

U.S. dollar cost of capital is

$$(1 + \text{U.S. cost of capital}) = (1 + \text{INR cost of capital}) \times \frac{(1+r_f)}{(1+r_h)}$$

$$\text{U.S. cost of capital} = 1 + 0.11 \times (1 + 0.009)/(1 + 0.12) - 1$$
$$= 0.08$$

Table 10.4 shows the NPV of the project in U.S. dollars.

Converting NPV in U.S. dollars into NPV in INR at the current spot rate, the NPV comes to INR 2,011.58 million. Since the NPV is positive, the project can be taken up by the Indian firm. However, the two alternative approaches do not give the same NPV because $(1 + i_h)/(1 + i_f) \neq (1 + r_h)/(1 + r_f)$.

Table 10.4 The NPV of the Project (USD)

Year	*Net cash flows (USD million)*	*PV factor at 8%*	*Present values (USD million)*
0	(–)100	1.00	(–)100.00
1	20	0.926	18.52
2	35	0.857	30.00
3	40	0.794	31.76
4	40	0.735	29.40

(Continued)

Table 10.4 **(Continued)**

Year	Net cash flows (USD million)	PV factor at 8%	Present values (USD million)
5	50	0.681	34.05
			NPV = USD 43.73 million

In other words, the NPV is different under two alternative approaches because the international Fisher relation is not satisfied in this case.

The Adjusted Present Value (APV) Model

The NPV model involves discounting all cash flows at the cost of capital, which measures the risk as well as the opportunity cost of the money invested. The conventional NPV model also implies that the project has the same business risk (both financial risk and operating risk) as that of the MNC as a whole. Further, it is assumed that the debt–equity ratio remains unchanged over the life of the project. But in reality, financial structures and business risks cannot be the same for all projects, and individual projects do not necessarily have the same risk and capital structure as that of the MNC or the firm. Therefore, the conventional NPV model needs to be adjusted to take care of different financial as well as operating risks of the projects. Such an adjusted model is known as the *adjusted present value (APV) model.* The APV model considers that a project will have different discount rates in its evaluation process, depending on the type and quantum of risks involved in the project. In the conventional NPV calculation, only one discount rate is used for all the cash flows of a project, whereas the APV method identifies the cash flows of a project by different components and discounts each one at the appropriate risk-adjusted discount rate.

In the APV model, which is based on the Modigliani–Miller (MM) valuation model, the value of the levered firm is given by the following equation:

Value of the levered firm = Value of the unlevered firm + Value of financing effects

As evident from the equation, the value of the levered firm is the sum of the value of the unlevered firm (all-equity financed firm) and the value of the financing effects. In other words, the NPV of a project has two components: all-equity NPV, and the value of financing effects, which includes interest tax shield.

The *all-equity NPV,* also known as *base-case NPV,* assumes that the project is entirely financed by equity alone. In other words, there are no financing effects on the cash flows of the project. After-tax cash flows, also known *as free cash flows,* are discounted by the project's "all-equity cost of capital."

Financing effects include interest tax shield resulting from the use of debt financing, and other benefits like special tax benefits and subsidies. The interest paid on the borrowed capital is a tax-deductible expense. Therefore, the firm will have a tax shield on the interest amounts. Further, the host government may offer several concessions and incentives to entrepreneurs to encourage industrialization in their respective countries. For example, the government of a country may provide loans at subsidized rates, offer a tax holiday, or reduced tax rates for a certain period to promote foreign direct investment. The value of such concessions and incentives is also included in project evaluation. Issue costs also need to be taken into consideration in project evaluation. Issue costs are the expenses incurred in connection with issuing securities like equity shares and debentures. These costs may tend to reduce the project's APV.

While calculating the value of financing side effects of a project, the cash flows are discounted by their respective risk-adjusted rates. For example, the interest tax shield is discounted by the market cost of debt. Sometimes, a higher discount rate is used to determine the value of the interest tax shield where the interest tax shield is more risky. Thus, the general APV model has the following formula:

$$APV = \sum_{t=1}^{n} \frac{(R_t - OC_t)(1-T)}{(1+K_u)^t} + \sum_{t=1}^{n} \frac{TD_t}{(1+i)^t} + \sum_{t=1}^{n} \frac{TI_t}{(1+i)^t} + \frac{TV_n}{(1+K_u)^n} - I_0$$

The tax savings due to depreciation (*TD*) and tax savings due to interest (*TI*) are discounted at the rate of *i* (the after-tax cost of debt) by assuming that these cash flows are relatively less risky. The all-equity cost of capital is the required rate of return on the project, which includes the risk-free rate of return and the risk premium. In other words, *K* varies according to the risk involved in the project. Each project has its own required rate of return without regard to the firm's other investments.

As discussed earlier, an MNC can appraise a project either from the perspective of its subsidiary unit or from the perspective of the parent firm. But appraising the project from the perspective of the parent firm has many merits, particularly when domestic shareholders own the parent firm, and the MNC owns the subsidiary firm. The shareholders of the parent firm may expect the MNC to maximize their wealth in their domestic currency. Therefore, the cash flows of a project should be converted into the domestic currency of the parent firm, and accordingly it has to be appraised. It is in line with this objective, Donald Lessard has presented a modified APV model:

$$\begin{aligned} APV = &\sum_{t=1}^{n} \frac{S_t(R_t - OC_t)(1-T)}{(1+K_u)^t} + \sum_{t=1}^{n} \frac{S_t TD_t}{(1+i_a)^t} + \sum_{t=1}^{n} \frac{S_t TI_t}{(1+i_b)^t} + \frac{S_n TV_n}{(1+K_u)^n} \\ &+ S_0 BF_0 + S_0 \left[CL_0 - \sum_{t=1}^{n} \frac{LP_t}{(1+i_c)^t} \right] + \sum_{t=1}^{n} \frac{TDR_t}{(1+i_d)^t} - S_0 C_0 \end{aligned} \tag{10.4}$$

The cash flows denominated in foreign currency need to be converted into the home currency or functional currency. Such conversion is done at the expected spot exchange rate (S_t), applicable for the period *t*. In Eq. 10.4, R_t represents only those operating cash flows that can be legally remitted to the parent firm. Blocked funds are not included in the model as they are not allowed to be repatriated to the parent firm. Further, only the incremental costs and revenues are taken into consideration. The parent firm may be given tax credit for foreign taxes paid up to the amount of the tax liability in the home country. For example, consider a U.S. firm that has a subsidiary in Japan. The firm has paid 10 percent as withholding tax on the profits it received from its subsidiary unit in Japan. The firm is in the 25 percent tax bracket in the United States. However, the tax payable in the United States will be reduced to 15 percent of the income, after the credit for the 10 percent is given.

S_0C_0 is the initial outlay or the cost of the project incurred in Year 0, denominated in foreign currency but converted to the home currency of the parent firm at S_0. Further, $\Sigma[(S_tTD_t)/(1+i_a)t]$ denotes the present value of the depreciation tax shield, converted into home currency at the expected spot rate of exchange (S_t) for the respective period. Similarly, $\Sigma[(S_tTD_t)/(1+i_b)^t]$ represents the present value of the tax savings on the amount that could be borrowed, which equals the interest payments (at the market borrowing rate in the domestic economy) that are saved from the reduction in the tax burden.

The tax savings on interest expense depend upon the borrowing capacity of the firm. When the project is undertaken, the asset base of the firm increases, which in turn enables the firm to borrow more. In other words, the borrowing capacity of the firm increases with the project being undertaken, subject to the firm's target debt–equity ratio. For example, if the gross present value (GPV) of the cash flows of the project is, say, INR 100 million, and the target debt–equity ratio (TDE) is, say, 60 percent, then the additional borrowing capacity (ΔB) created by the project is INR 60 million (60% × INR 100 million).

In general, the additional borrowing capacity (ΔB) is given by the following equation:

$$\Delta B = TDE \times GPV$$

and the annual interest tax shield is given by the following formula:

$$(K_d \times T)\Delta B = (K_d \times T)(TDE \times GPV)$$

For example, if the pre-tax cost of debt (K_d) is 10 percent, the tax rate (T) is 35 percent, and ΔB is INR 60 million, then the interest tax shield per annum is:

$$(0.10 \times 0.35)(\text{INR 60 million}) = \text{INR 2.1 million}$$

Thus, the additional borrowing capacity is the target debt–equity ratio times the gross present value of the project, and the tax savings due to interest expense in each year is the tax rate times the pre-tax cost of debt as multiplied by the additional borrowing capacity.

The MNCs may move funds from countries with high taxes to countries with low taxes, thereby reducing their effective tax rates. The MNCs may also shift cash flows by adjusting transfer prices, overheads, and so on. They may also defer the payment of taxes by reinvesting the funds in low tax countries. Therefore, the term $\Sigma[(TDR_t)/(1+i_a)^t]$, which denotes the present value (in home currency) of the expected tax savings from deferrals, inter-subsidiary transfer pricing, and so on, is incorporated in the model.

When an MNC invests in a foreign project, the host government may block funds that the subsidiary firm intends to send to the parent firm. The host government may require the subsidiary to reinvest its earnings locally for at least some period before they can be remitted to the parent firm. The term S_0BF_0 represents the value of the blocked funds that are freed up by the project, and converted into home currency at the spot rate of exchange (S_0). The initial project cost is reduced by this amount (S_0BF_0).

The term $S_0\{CL_0 - \Sigma[LP_t/(1 + i_c)^t]\}$ has two components. The CL_0 represents present value of the concessionary loans (below-market-rate borrowing), if any, converted into home currency of the parent firm at S_0.

The second term $\Sigma[(LP_t)/(1 + i_c)^t]$, is the present value of the repayment on the loan, discounted at the rate of interest that would have been paid in the absence of concessionary financing. These amounts in foreign currency are converted into the home currency of the parent firm at S_0.

Each of these cash flows may have different risks and, therefore, they are discounted at different rates, such as i_a, i_b, i_c and i_d. Thus, the discount rate to be used in project evaluation depends on the cash flows. The cash flows in a particular currency are discounted in that currency. Similarly, the cash flows to equity are discounted at an equity discount rate, and the cash flows to debt are discounted at the cost of the debt. For the cash flows attributed to both equity and debt, the discount rate is the rate appropriate for both debt and equity. Any violation of these rules leads to faulty evaluation of the projects.

As stated earlier, the APV model is better than the conventional NPV method, as it deals separately with the financing effects and the operating cash flows of the project. However, there are certain practical difficulties with the APV model. For example, it is difficult to calculate precisely the interest tax shield when the shareholders and creditors are subject to diverse tax rates and regulations.

Whether it is conventional NPV or APV, the decision is to accept the project, if the NPV or APV is greater than zero. If NPV or APV is less than zero, the project should be rejected. The NPV or APV thus indicates whether a project should be accepted or rejected. A firm may sometimes accept a project by considering other factors of business, even if the NPV or APV is zero.

The step-by-step procedure in calculating APV is summed up as below.

- Identify the operating cash flows of a project, and discount them at the all-equity required rate of return.
- Identify the financing side effects of a project, and discount them separately at the appropriate rate adjusted for their respective systematic risk.
- Combine (1) and (2) to obtain the APV.

Example 10.2

An Indian firm proposes to make a capital investment in the United States. The expected net cash flows of the project are presented in Table 10.5.

Table 10.5 Expected Cash Flows of the Project

Year	*Cash flow (USD million)*
0	(–)23
1	5
2	10
3	10
4	10
5	15

The firm wants to finance the project with its retained earnings. It expects a rate of return of 25 percent on the investment.

U.S. laws permit foreign projects to remit to their parents the maximum annual net cash flows that equal 25 percent of the project cost. However, the firm decides to repatriate not more than USD 5 million to the parent unit, out of the annual net cash flows. The firm can invest the surplus cash flows (blocked funds) in U.S. government securities at an interest rate of 4 percent. The U.S. government permits foreign projects to remit the blocked funds to the parent unit at the end of the project's life.

Assuming the spot exchange rate at USD/INR 45, calculate the NPV from the project's perspective as well as the parent firm's perspective.

Solution

The present values of the net cash flows from the project's point of view are presented in Table 10.6.

Table 10.6 Present Values of the Net Cash Flows from the Project's Perspective

Year	*Cash flows (USD million)*	*PV factor at 25%*	*PV of cash flows (USD million)*
0	–23	1.00	(–)23.00
1	5	0.80	4.00
2	10	0.64	6.4
3	10	0.512	5.12
4	10	0.4091	4.09
5	15	0.3277	4.92
		NPV = USD 1.53 million	

Therefore, the NPV from the project's point of view is USD 1.53 million, which is equivalent to INR 68.85 million at the current spot exchange rate.

The net cash flows and the NPV from the point of view of the parent firm are presented in Tables 10.7 and 10.8, respectively.

Thus, it may be observed that the project is viable (i.e. NPV > 0) from the standpoint of the project itself. However, from the perspective of the parent firm, the project is not viable (NPV < 0). This difference arises because of host country restrictions on the repatriation of project net cash flows.

Table 10.7 Net Cash Flows from the Parent Firm's Perspective

Year	*1*	*2*	*3*	*4*	*5*
Project net cash flows	5	10	10	10	15
Blocked funds	—	—	5	10.20	15.61
Interest on blocked funds	—	—	0.20	0.41	0.63
Total cash flows	5	10	15.20	20.61	31.24
Cash flows Repatriated	5	5	5.00	5.00	31.24
Blocked funds	0	5	10.20	15.61	—

Table 10.8 NPV from Parent Firm's Perspective

Year	*Cash flows (USD million)*	*PV factor at 25%*	*PV of cash flows (USD million)*
0	(–)23	1.00	(–)23
1	5	0.800	4
2	5	0.640	3.2
3	5	0.512	2.56
4	5	0.409	2.05
5	31.24	0.328	10.25
			NPV = (–) USD 0.94 million

It may be noted that the net cash flows can also be converted into domestic currency at the expected spot exchange rate to evaluate the project from the parent firm's perspective.

Example 10.3

The Indian firm proposes to finance the foreign project discussed in Example 10.2 through investors in the United States, who will buy USD 10 million of equity. The firm will finance the rest of the project cost (USD 13 million) with its retained earnings. The firm pays out each year's entire net cash flows as dividend. Calculate the NPV.

Solution

From the project point of view, the NPV remains at USD 1.53 million, or INR 68.85 million. But from the parent firm's point of view, the NPV changes with the revised financing plans. Tables 10.9 and 10.10 present the cash flows and NPV of the project.

Table 10.9 Cash Flows of the Project and Blocked Funds

Year	*1*	*2*	*3*	*4*	*5*
Project net cash flows	5	10	10	10	15
Dividend paid to U.S. investors	2.15	4.30	4.30	4.30	6.45
Blocked funds	—	—	0.70	1.43	2.19
Interest on blocked funds	—	—	0.03	0.06	0.09
Total cash flows	2.85	5.70	6.43	7.19	10.83
Cash flows Repatriated	2.85	5.00	5.00	5.00	10.83
Blocked funds	—	0.70	1.43	2.19	—

Table 10.10 The NPV of the Project

Year	*Cash flows (USD million)*	*PV factor at 25%*	*PV of cash flows (USD million)*
0	(–)13.0	1.00	(–)13
1	2.85	0.80	2.28
2	5.00	0.640	3.20
3	5.00	0.512	2.56
4	5.00	0.409	2.05
5	10.83	0.328	3.55
			NPV=USD 0.64 million

Thus, the foreign project that was earlier not viable (NPV < 0) has now become viable, and shows a positive NPV. Because of a change in the source of finance, the cash flows available to the parent firm have changed, which have made the project worthwhile.

Example 10.4

A U.S. multinational company wants to make a capital investment in India. The estimated project cost is INR 650 million, with a scrap value of INR 50 million after five years. The pre-tax operating cash flows are expected to be INR 300 million per year.

The company wishes to finance the project with the following sources of funds:

- Retained earnings: USD 5 million
- Five-year term loan in India at 15%: INR 200 million
- Five-year term loan in U.S. dollars at 10%: USD 5 million

The corporate tax rate in India is 35 percent, while that in the United States is 30 percent. The Indian government permits overseas companies to remit 50 percent of each year's pre-tax, but after-interest, accounting profit back to the parent firm. The company can invest blocked funds in India at 6 percent (tax free) in government securities. Such funds can be repatriated at the end of the project's life. The remittances from the project are not expected to attract any tax in the United States.

The current spot exchange rate is USD/INR 45. The INR is expected to depreciate against the U.S. dollar by 5 percent per year.

The project has an asset beta of 1.50. The beta of debt is 1.2. In the United States, the risk-free rate of return is 4 percent, and the return on the market index is 14 percent.

Assess the viability of the project.

Solution

The remittances from the project are calculated in Table 10.11.

Table 10.12 shows the cash flows received by the parent firm.

The base-case cash flows are shown in Table 10.13.

Table 10.11 Computation of Annual Remittance

Items	*INR (million)*
Operating cash flows	300
Less depreciation (Straight Line Method)	120
Less interest	30
Accounting profit	150
Tax at 35%	52.5
Profit after tax	97.5
Remittance (150 × 50%)	75.0

Table 10.12 Computation of Blocked Funds

Year	*1*	*2*	*3*	*4*	*5*
Operating cash flows	300	300	300	300	300
Less tax	52.5	52.5	52.5	52.5	52.5
Less interest payments	30	30	30	30	30
Less loan repayment	–	–	–	–	200
Scrap value	–	–	–	–	50
Less tax on scrap value	–	–	–	–	17.5
Blocked funds	–	142.5	293.55	453.66	623.38
Interest at 6%	–	8.55	17.61	27.22	37.40
Net cash flows	217.5	368.55	528.66	698.38	710.78
Cash flows remitted	75	75	75	75	710.78
Blocked funds	142.5	293.55	453.66	623.38	–

Table 10.13 Base-Case Cash Flows

Year	*Cash flows (INR million)*
0	(–)650
1	75
2	75
3	75
4	75
5	710.78

The base-case discount rate is calculated with equity beta. The formula for equity beta (β_e) is

$$\beta_e = \beta_a\left[1+\frac{D}{E}(1-T)\right]-\beta_d\,\frac{D}{E}$$

In this example,

$$\beta_{assets} \text{ or } (\beta_a) = 1.5; \text{ and } \beta_{debt} \text{ or } (\beta_d) = 1.2$$

Value of equity (E) = Retained earnings + U.S. dollar loan
= USD 5 million + USD 5 million

Value of debt (D) = Indian currency loan, converted to U.S. dollars at USD/INR 45
= USD 4.4 million

Tax rate in India (T) = 0.35

Thus, beta of equity (β_e) is

$$\beta_e = 1.5\left[1 + \frac{4.4}{10}(1 - 0.35)\right] - 1.2\left(\frac{4.4}{10}\right)$$
$$= 1.40$$

By using the CAPM, the U.S. dollar discount rate can be calculated as

$$4\% + (14\% - 4\%) \times 1.40 = 18\%$$

And the INR discount rate can be calculated by using the interest rate parity theory in the following way:

$$\frac{\text{Home currency interest rate} - \text{Foreign currency interest rate}}{1 + \text{Foreign currency interest rate}} = \text{Percentage change in home currency value}$$

$$\frac{\text{Indian currency interest rate} - 0.18}{1 + 0.18} = 0.05$$

Therefore, the Indian currency interest (discount) rate = $(0.05 \times 1.18) + 0.18 = 23.90\%$, or 24%. It is the discount rate for cash flows in Indian currency that reflects the combined business and financial risk of cash flows. Therefore, the base-case present values will be as shown in Table 10.14.

The present value of the financing side effects of the project (USD loan tax shield) is:

Interest per year: USD 5 million × 0.10 = USD 0.5 million

Tax shield per year: USD 0.5 million × 0.30 = USD 0.15 million

Table 10.14 The NPV of the Project (Base-case)

Year	*Cash flows (INR million)*	*PV factor at 24%*	*PV of cash flows (INR million)*
0	(–)650	1.00	(–)650.00
1	75	0.806	60.45
2	75	0.650	48.75
3	75	0.524	39.30
4	75	0.423	31.73
5	710.78	0.341	242.38
	NPV = (–)INR 227.39 million = USD 5.05 million		

Assuming that the tax shield amount is reinvested at 6 percent per annum for 4 years starting from the second year, it will become USD 0.6563 million. The present value of the tax shield amount at 10% discount rate is USD 0.4075 million [i.e. $0.6563/(1 + 0.10)^5$].

The adjusted present value can be calculated as:

Base-case present value:	(−)USD 5.0500 million
Present value of interest tax shield:	USD 0.4075 million
	(−)USD 4.6425 million

Thus, the project is expected to have a negative APV of USD 4.6425 million.

Risks in Cross-border Investment Decisions

There are several kinds of risks associated with cross-border investments. These risks may broadly be classified as political risk, currency risk, and inflation risk. It may be noted that these different risks may have overlapping influences on investment projects. An outline of each of these risk factors is presented below.

Political Risk

Political risk arises from the political environment in the host country, that is, the country in which the foreign project is established. The political set-up in the country may influence the residents to purchase or prefer products produced by domestic companies. Such an attitude on the part of local residents may affect the prospects of foreign projects to be set up by MNCs. The actions of the host government may also have significant impact on the success of foreign projects. Thus, investment in foreign countries is sensitive to potential political risks.

The extent of political risk depends on the host country's political system, its economic conditions, and the government's policy towards foreign investment. Underdeveloped countries generally have a high degree of political risk because of their poor economic conditions and volatile political systems. In view of their economic and political conditions, governments of less-developed countries may impose restrictions on foreign investments and the flow of funds across countries. They may restrict repatriation of dividends and interest income, impose additional corporate taxes on the incomes of foreign firms, impose withholding taxes, or control the prices of the products of foreign firms. Political events in the host country may escalate to such a level that they may force the MNC to liquidate the project abruptly or earlier than planned. The extreme form of political risk is the risk of expropriation, in which the host government seizes the assets of the MNC without adequately compensating it. Government bureaucracy and corruption in the host country and its relationship with the MNC's home country government are some other factors that may affect the viability of foreign projects.

Currency Risk

Investment in foreign projects is also subject to exchange rate risk. The earnings of the project, as and when they occur, are generally remitted to the parent company. Such remittances are converted from the subsidiary's local currency to the parent's functional currency. Therefore, the amount to be received by the parent company is also determined by the exchange rate. **Foreign exchange risk** is the risk that the home currency value of foreign currency-denominated cash flows may change as a consequence of fluctuations in exchange rates. Changes in exchange rates affect not only cash inflows, but also cash

Foreign exchange risk *refers to the variability of the home currency value of foreign currency-denominated cash flows caused by fluctuations in exchange rates.*

outflows of the project. Further, if a project is required to serve the markets of many countries, the viability of the project depends upon several exchange rates. Though there are many techniques of hedging foreign exchange risk, it is very difficult to forecast exchange rates, especially when cash flows occur in different currencies. Hence, an MNC may not know what amounts it should hedge.

Firms may handle political risk and foreign exchange risk by raising the required rate of return on the project and/or by adjusting cash flows to reflect the impact of such risks. To raise the required rate of return, it is necessary to adjust the discount rate to higher levels. But using a higher discount rate uniformly for all the cash flows of a project may distort the evaluation of the project. In other words, as different cash flows associated with a project have different risks, there is a need to use different discount rates reflecting the nature and magnitude of risks involved. This entails careful risk evaluation. In practice, firms adopt a rather arbitrary procedure and use their all-equity required rate of return plus an arbitrary risk premium, which is supposed to take care of different kinds of risks. But such an arbitrary procedure distorts the project appraisal. Another method for incorporating risks into foreign investment analysis is adjusting expected cash flows. Cash flows can be adjusted to reflect expected changes caused by a particular risk. It is, of course, relatively easy to make adjustments to cash flows to take care of each kind of risk. If a particular kind of risk is high, the respective cash flows are conservatively estimated. The cutoff payback period of the project may also be shortened in order to cope with various kinds of risks. In other words, firms may seek projects with faster paybacks.

Inflation Risk

Inflation also causes variability in cash flows of a project and influences its financial viability. Although cash inflows as well as outflows are influenced by inflation, the degrees of responsiveness to inflation in both cases are not the same. Revenues may increase differently from costs during a particular period of inflation. Some costs are more sensitive to inflation, but there are also costs (e.g. depreciation) which remain constant irrespective of a rise in the general level of prices. When some costs do not change with inflation, such cash savings may be subject to taxation. The working capital requirement may also increase during the inflationary period. In other words, more funds may have to be tied up in working capital components, especially in inventory and receivables. The salvage value of the project may also be influenced by inflation.

In an inflationary period, the net cash flows of a project are expected to increase at the inflation rate. Such cash flows are known as nominal cash flows. *Real cash flows* are the nominal cash flows adjusted for inflation. Similarly, the *real interest rate* is the nominal interest rate minus the expected inflation rate. Generally, the market cost of capital includes the inflation premium as well. When the nominal cash flows are discounted by the nominal rate of return (assuming that the cash flows and cost of capital rise at the same inflation rate), and the real cash flows are discounted by the real rate of return, the nominal NPV is identical to the real NPV of a project. If the cost of capital, which incorporates the inflation premium, is used to discount the constant (unadjusted) cash flows, then the resulting NPV will be downward biased. Therefore, in order to deal effectively with inflation in project appraisal, it is necessary to build inflation estimates into each cash flow element of the project.

As far as foreign projects are concerned, their expected nominal cash flows can be converted into nominal home currency terms, and discounted at the expected nominal domestic discount rate. If the analysis involves cash flows in foreign currency, the foreign currency discount rate needs to be used. However, if one wants to assess the project in real terms, either in terms of foreign currency or domestic currency, it is necessary to discount the real cash flows at the real discount rate in the same currency. As discussed in Chapter 4, inflation and exchange rates are closely related. The exchange rate of a country with a higher rate inflation tends to depreciate over time. If the inflation of the country in which the project is established increases over time, the cash flows of the project will also increase. But, when converted into the functional currency of the parent firm, such cash flows will be deflated because of the strong exchange rate of the domestic currency.

Incorporating Risk in Investment Decisions

Risk is associated with almost every investment, and more so with foreign investments. Only investments in government securities are relatively risk-free. Risk is understood as variability in the return from an investment. The greater the variability of the expected returns, the greater is the risk of the project.

Estimating Cash Flows

Risk is usually measured by standard deviation or variance of expected cash flows. While estimating different cash flows at different points in time, it is necessary to estimate their respective probabilities. *Probability* is a measure of the likelihood that a particular cash flow will occur. Therefore, in the process of appraisal of a project, the investor should primarily identify or estimate the cash flows along with the likelihood of occurrence of each of these cash flows. For example, consider the forecast of cash flows of a project over its three-year life period, given in Table 10.15

The expected cash flows and standard deviations are calculated as

$$ECF_t = \sum_{j=1}^{k} CF_{jt} \times P_{jt}$$

$$\sigma_t = \sqrt{\sum_{j=1}^{k} (CF_{jt} - ECF_t) P_{jt}}$$

where

ECF_t = Expected cash flows in year t
CF_{jt} = Cash flows of item j in year t
P_{jt} = Probability of cash flows of item j in year t
σ_t = Standard deviation of cash flows in year t

The expected cash flows in Years 1, 2, and 3 can also be calculated.

Table 10.15 Forecast of the Cash Flows for a Project with a Three-year Life

Year 1		*Year 2*		*Year 3*	
Cash flows (INR million)	*Probability*	*Cash flows (INR million)*	*Probability*	*Cash flows (INR million)*	*Probability*
500	0.10	700	0.20	1000	0.10
700	0.30	650	0.10	750	0.20
900	0.40	500	0.40	1500	0.40
1000	0.20	1000	0.30	1200	0.30

Expected cash flows (ECF_1) and standard deviation (σ_1) in Year 1:

$$\text{INR } 500 \times 0.10 = \text{INR } 50$$
$$700 \times 0.30 = 210$$
$$900 \times 0.40 = 360$$
$$1000 \times 0.20 = 200$$

$$ECF_1 = \textbf{INR 820}$$

$$\sigma_1 = \sqrt{[(50-820)^2 \times 0.1 + (210-820)^2 \times 0.3 + (360-820)^2 \times 0.4 + (200-820)^2 \times 0.2]}$$
$$= \sqrt{[59290 + 111630 + 84640 + 76880]}$$
$$= \sqrt{332440}$$
$$= \text{INR } 576.58$$

Expected cash flows (ECF_2) and standard deviation in (σ_2)Year 2:

$$\text{INR } 700 \times 0.20 = \text{INR } 140$$
$$650 \times 0.10 = 650$$
$$500 \times 0.40 = 200$$
$$1{,}000 \times 0.30 = 300$$

$$ECF_2 = \text{INR } 1{,}290$$

$$\sigma_2 = \sqrt{[(140-1290)^2 \times 0.2 + (650-1290)^2 \times 0.1 + (200-1290)^2 \times 0.4 + (300-1290)^2 \times 0.3]}$$
$$= \sqrt{[264500 + 40960 + 475240 + 294030]}$$
$$= \sqrt{1074730}$$
$$= \text{INR } 1{,}036.69$$

Expected cash flows (ECF_3) and standard deviation (σ_3)in Year 3:

$$\text{INR } 1{,}000 \times 0.10 = \text{INR } 100$$
$$750 \times 0.20 = 150$$
$$1{,}500 \times 0.40 = 600$$
$$1{,}200 \times 0.30 = 360$$

$$ECF_3 = \text{INR } 1{,}210$$

$$\sigma_3 = \sqrt{[(100-1210)^2 \times 0.1 + (150-1210)^2 \times 0.2 + (600-1210)^2 \times 0.4 + (360-1210)^2 \times 0.3]}$$
$$= \sqrt{[123210 + 224720 + 148840 + 216750]}$$
$$= \sqrt{713520}$$
$$= \text{INR } 844.70$$

Incorporating the probabilities, the expected NPV of the project can be stated as

$$NPV = \sum_{t=1}^{n} \frac{ECF_t}{(1+R_f)^t} - I_0$$

where

R_f = Risk-free interest rate

I_0 = Initial outlay

The standard deviation of the project (σ), if the cash flows are independent, is given by

$$\sigma = \sqrt{\sum_{t=1}^{n} \frac{\sigma_t^{\,2}}{(1+R_f)^{2t}}}$$

where

σ^2_t = Variance of the expected cash flows in year t

If the cash flows are perfectly correlated, then the standard deviation is:

$$\sigma = \sum_{t=1}^{n} \frac{\sigma_t}{(1+R_f)^t}$$

If the cash flows are neither independent nor perfectly correlated, then the conditional probability distribution approach is followed. Accordingly, the expected NPV and standard deviation of the project are computed.

The expected NPV and the standard deviation can be used to compute the probability that the project will have a negative NPV, a positive NPV, or that it will fall in a range of values, by assuming that the probability distribution is normal or approximately normal.

Risk-handling Techniques

There are different techniques to handle risk in investment decisions. The important techniques include the *risk-adjusted discount rate approach, the certainty equivalent approach, sensitivity analysis, scenario analysis, and the decision-tree approach.*

The Risk-Adjusted Discount Rate Approach According to the **risk-adjusted discount rate approach**, different discount rates are used for different projects, depending on the risk involved in the project. The cash flows of higher-risk projects are discounted at a higher cost of capital, and the cash flows of lower-risk projects are discounted at a rate below the company's average cost of capital. The company's average cost of capital is used for projects that involve average risk, but there is no particular method of specifying exactly how much higher or lower discount rates should be. In other words, the cash flows of a project are risk-adjusted arbitrarily. Further, the same risk-adjusted rate is used throughout the life of the project. If the cash flows are different in the degree of uncertainty from one period to another, such a uniform discount rate does not incorporate the actual risk involved in the project. In other words, the risk-adjusted discount rate should vary, reflecting different degrees of uncertainty associated with the cash flows in different periods. Despite some operational limitations, the risk-adjusted discount rate method is found to be useful, particularly in cases where increasing risk is a function of time.

*A **risk-adjusted discount rate approach** involves using different discount rates on different projects, depending on the risk involved.*

The Certainty Equivalent Approach Under the **certainty equivalent approach**, the investor first evaluates the risk associated with a cash flow and then specifies how much money with certainty would make him indifferent between risk-free and risky cash flows. A certainty equivalent coefficient, which is the ratio of the amount of money someone would require with certainty in order to make him indifferent between that certain amount and an amount expected to be received with risk, is computed. The certainty equivalent coefficient, having an inverse relation with risk, takes a value between 0 and 1. Different investors may have different certainty equivalent coefficients, depending on each one's relative risk aversion. The coefficient is then used to scale down the risky cash flows of a project. In other words, each cash flow of a project is adjusted for risk by multiplying the cash flow with the certainty equivalent coefficient. The riskier the cash flows, the lower are their certainty equivalent values.

*A **certainty equivalent coefficient** is the ratio of the amount of money someone would require with certainty in order to make him or her indifferent between that certain amount and an amount expected to be received with risk.*

The major difference between the risk-adjusted discount rate method and the certainty equivalent approach is that the former makes adjustments to the denominator of the NPV equation, and the latter adjusts the net cash flows in the numerator of the NPV equation. Further, the risk-adjusted method includes the time value of money as represented by the risk-free rate and the risk premium, whereas the certainty equivalent approach keeps them separate.

Sensitivity Analysis The cash flows of a project are influenced by several factors. For example, the sales revenue of a project is influenced by the demand for the product or service produced by the project. Similarly, the profit margins are influenced by input costs. The number of units sold, selling price, operating costs, amount of working capital, capacity utilization rate, foreign exchange rate, and salvage value are the major variables that influence cash flows, and thus the NPV or IRR of a project. **Sensitivity analysis** is a technique that indicates a change in NPV or IRR for a given change in a variable, assuming other variables constant. Sensitivity analysis can also be called *what-if analysis* as it provides answers to a series of "what if" questions. For example, what if the sales of the product increase by 15 percent? What if operating costs decrease by 20 percent? In the international context, what if the host country imposes controls on the payment of dividend? What if the host country increases tax rates? In sensitivity analysis, each variable is changed by some points, keeping other variables unchanged, and a new NPV is found. For example, the price of a product may be increased by, say, 10 percent, and the NPV is found using this input together with the estimates of all other variables. The procedure is repeated by increasing the price by, say, 20 percent. Thus, the NPV is computed for each of the changes in one or more of the variables. Then, a set of NPVs is plotted on the graph against the variable that is changed. For each variable there is a line, the slope of which indicates how sensitive the NPV is to changes in the variable. A steep slope indicates that the NPV is very sensitive to changes in the variable. In contrast, a relatively flat line indicates that the NPV is not very sensitive to changes in the respective variable. Computer models (using program such as Excel) can be used to develop a profile of how sensitive the NPV of the project is to changes in the variables that produce cash flows. This enables the investor to concentrate on the variables that are critical to the project's success.

***Sensitivity analysis** is a technique that indicates a change in the net present value or the internal rate of return for a given change in a variable, assuming that other variables are constant.*

Monte Carlo simulation can also be used in this context. A computer model can be used to choose at random a value for each of the variables that influence the NPV of a project. The value selected for each variable with its probability distribution is used along with the fixed values of other variables to determine the project's NPV. This procedure is repeated to get as many NPVs as possible, which are then used to form a probability distribution of the NPV, with its own expected value (mean) and standard deviation. By using the mean and standard deviation, one can compute the probability that the project will have a negative NPV, a positive NPV, or that it will fall in a range of values.

Scenario Analysis Sensitivity analysis indicates the effect of changes in key variables (one at a time) on the NPV of a project. The effect of simultaneous changes in key variables on the NPV is considered by another technique, known as **scenario analysis**. In scenario analysis, three scenarios—pessimistic, optimistic, and average—are defined with certain probabilities. For example, for a certain project, the probability of a pessimistic scenario is 0.40; the probability of optimistic scenario is 0.35; and the probability of average scenario is 0.25. In each scenario, the values of the key variables are estimated, and then the respective NPV is computed. There is thus an NPV under each scenario with a probability. With these values, the expected value (mean) of the NPV and standard deviation of a project are computed. Given the expected value of the NPV and the standard deviation, one can compute the probability that the project will have a negative NPV or a positive NPV, or that it will fall in a range of values.

The Decision-tree Approach When investment decisions become sequential decisions or multistage decisions, the **decision-tree approach** can be followed. Sequential decisions are a sequence of decisions over time. For example, to introduce a product, first a market survey is conducted to know the market potential. If a good market potential does exist, a prototype of the product is designed. After evaluation of the prototype, it is decided the project should be taken up. If the prototype is found to be good, the firm may go ahead with the manufacturing of the product. At each stage, certain decisions are involved, and each decision has certain consequences. The outcome of each decision is governed by certain probability. The sequence of decisions is mapped out over time in a format similar to the branches of a tree. A decision tree is a graphic representation of the relationship between present decisions and future decisions, along with their consequences. In decision-tree analysis, the expected NPV is computed for each alternative decision. The alternative that yields the maximum expected NPV is the best decision.

*A **decision tree** is a graphic representation of the relationship between present decisions and future decisions, along with their consequences.*

Real Options

All investment decisions are strategic management decisions. Accordingly, investment decisions may not always be based on the profitability analysis provided by techniques like NPV, IRR, and so on. For instance, a firm may not divest even unprofitable division(s), or it may even sell some of its profitable non-priority division(s) for strategic reasons. In the same way, a firm may not undertake an investment project immediately, even if its NPV is positive.

While making an investment decision, a firm may consider two alternatives: (a) to invest today; or (b) to wait for some time, say, one or two years, and think about the investment then. If the decision is to invest immediately, it means that the firm is exercising its option to invest, and it incurs the sunk costs of investment. Generally, now-or-never projects are undertaken immediately, if they are financially feasible. So, the value of such projects is the discounted value of the expected future cash flows net of initial investment. If the project is not a now-or-never opportunity, the firm has the option to delay the project for some time.

Notwithstanding the availability of the option of postponing the investment decision, if the firm exercises its option to invest in the project immediately, it means that it is foregoing investment in the same or similar projects at a future date. Failure to recognize the availability of the option to postpone the investment decision will result in a firm's investing prematurely and failing to capture the maximum potential value of real assets. Alternatively, if the firm exercises the option to postpone the investment and consider investment at a future date, it will be able to get more information about the project (e.g. future demand for the product, future prices, costs, etc). With the arrival of new information about future investment outcomes, the firm can make more informed investment decisions that will fit the circumstances. This provides the firm with flexibility in the timing and scale of investment. Such managerial flexibility is known as **real options**.

*A **real option** exists if a firm has managerial flexibility in the timing and scale of investments. A real option gives a firm the right to make an investment decision (to invest or not to invest, or to abandon or not to abandon) at one or more points in time.*

Managerial flexibility adds value in two ways. First, the firm can defer the initial investment outlay, which is a value addition because of time value of money. Second, the value of the project can change before the option expires. If the change in the value of the project is positive, the firm can exercise the option and be better-off. If the change in the value of the project is negative, the firm will not be worse-off as it does not have to invest in the project. The flexibility of investment decisions is highly valuable and, therefore, must be identified while appraising the projects. Projects with managerial flexibility are more valuable than projects without such strategic elements.

A real option exists if a firm has the right to make an investment decision (to invest or not to invest, or to abandon or not to abandon) at one or more points in time. Between now and the time of the decision, many changes would have taken place, making one or another of the available decisions better for the firm. So the firm will have the right to make whatever decision will suit it best at that time.

Conventional project appraisal techniques like NPV and IRR assume that projects are now-or-never propositions, and the firm has no flexibility to make changes in an investment. They also assume that the future is known with certainty, implying a passive approach to investment analysis. Such assumptions may not have relevance in a dynamic environment. In view of such limitations of traditional methods, a new approach to capital budgeting, known as the *real options approach,* has been developed for appraising projects or developing strategic investment plans under uncertainty. In fact, the real options approach applies financial options theory to real investments (e.g. product-line extensions).

Like financial options, real options give the firm an option, but not an obligation, to pursue an investment opportunity. The value of the real option is the intrinsic value of the option, if exercised today plus the time value of the option. So, the intrinsic value of such an option is the present value of the project minus the cost of investment (also called the *exercise price*). The time value of the option is the additional value of investment arising from waiting for some time in future.

The option to invest, divest, abandon, expand, or contract, and to suspend operations— are all real options in investment decisions. When they are cross-border investment decisions, they involve greater uncertainty due to various complex environmental factors. Greater uncertainty over the future performance of the project will result in a higher value for the real option, which would be a greater incentive for the firm to postpone investment.

Using conventional methods of capital budgeting without considering real options may result in a biased estimate of the true value of a project's NPV. For example, an option to expand may increase the project's upside potential, while an option to abandon may reduce a project's downside risk. Therefore, companies need to incorporate real-option analysis in project appraisal.

Cross-border investments have become common, but they involve complex procedures. It has become almost a necessity for corporations to have international diversification of their investments in order to achieve their desired growth. In appraising foreign projects, the major considerations are exchange rate risk, political risk, and international taxation. In view of the uncertainty surrounding the factors that influence the cash flows of foreign projects, international project appraisal has become a more difficult and complex process. Sophisticated risk-handling techniques backed by computer software have come in handy for the firms to handle complex foreign projects.

Summary

1. **Firms can enter foreign markets through exports, license agreements, investments, or strategic alliances. Any combination of these can also facilitate entry into foreign markets.**

2. **Firms may opt for overseas investment in order to get a return in excess of the required return and to have international diversification of their investments.**

3. **Capital budgeting is a process that involves selection and implementation of projects that maximize the value of the firm.**

4. **Though the fundamental investment principle underlying a foreign and a domestic project is the same, in reality there are certain differences between foreign and domestic projects in their evaluation. These differences are caused by tax factors, foreign exchange regulations, and other factors.**

5. **An MNC can evaluate a foreign project by identifying cash flows in home currency and discounting them at the home currency discount rate. Alternatively, it can evaluate the foreign project by identifying cash flows in foreign currency and discounting them at the foreign currency discount rate.**

6. **In the conventional net present value (NPV) calculation, only one discount rate is used for all the cash flows of a project, but in adjusted present value (APV), the cash flows of a project are identified by different components and then discounted at appropriate discount rates.**

7. **Risk is the variability of the future returns of a project. The greater the variability of the expected returns, the greater is the risk of the project. In appraising a foreign project, political risk, currency risk, and risk arising due to inflation are also taken into account.**

8. **Risk handling techniques include the risk-adjusted discount rate approach, the certainty equivalent approach, sensitivity analysis, scenario analysis, and the decision-tree approach.**

9. **A real option exists if a firm has managerial flexibility in the timing and scale of investments.**

Questions and Problems

1. How is the NPV of a project different from its APV?
2. Why does the NPV differ from the project's perspective to the parent firm's perspective? What factors contribute to such differences?
3. Explain the concept of blocked funds. How are blocked funds treated in project appraisal?
4. Explain the two basic approaches to project appraisal. When will the NPV of a project not be the same under both the approaches?
5. What are the purposes of transfer pricing?
6. What is the value of an unlevered firm?
7. What do you understand by the value of financing effects?
8. How are political risks and currency risks taken care of in project appraisal?
9. How can inflation influence project appraisal? What remedies are available to neutralize the effects of inflation on project appraisal?
10. A U.S.-based MNC is considering undertaking a capital investment in India to manufacture agricultural pesticides. It is estimated that the project will require immediate capital expenditure of INR 1,500 million and INR 50 million of working capital. The life of the project is estimated at five years. The working capital investment will be recovered at the end of the project's life. The project is estimated to generate sales revenue of INR 750 million every year against the annual operating costs of INR 250 million.

    It will have zero salvage value. The corporate tax rate is 35 percent in India and 30 percent in the United States. The risk-free return in the United States is 6 percent and the market return is 14 percent. In the United States, the agricultural pesticides industry has an equity beta of 1.20. The MNC wants to finance the project with debt and retained earnings in equal proportion. The cost of debt is estimated to be 14 percent. The issue costs of debt will be 2 percent and are tax deductible. The current spot rate is USD/INR 46 and the Indian rupee is expected to depreciate against the U.S. dollar at an annual rate of 5 percent.

    Advise the management of the MNC on the project's desirability. You may assume any other data, if required, to use the APV technique.
11. An Indian MNC wants to undertake a project in the United States. The details of the project are as follows:
    - The initial investment of the project is USD 10 million, which will be depreciated over five years by the straight line method. The project has no salvage value.
    - The selling price of the product to be produced by the project is USD 100, and the operating costs are estimated as follows:
        - Materials: USD 40/unit
        - Labour: USD 10/unit
        - Other expenses: USD 5/unit
    - The subsidiary firm in the United States is expected to sell 50,000 units of the product per annum.
    - The corporate tax in India is 35 percent, while in the United States it is 30 percent. The U.S. government imposes 5 percent withholding tax on dividends remitted to the parent firm by the subsidiary. The discount rate on similar projects in the United States is 8 percent. The subsidiary firm is permitted to utilize the blocked funds.

    There is a technology licensing agreement between the parent firm and the subsidiary firm under which the subsidiary firm has to pay royalty to the parent firm at 2 percent of sales. The MNC thinks that it can raise USD 2 million of additional borrowing at an interest rate of 6 percent. The U.S. government may also offer a five-year concessional loan of USD 1 million at an interest rate of 4 percent per annum. The current spot rate is INR/USD 0.0222. It is expected that the U.S. dollar will depreciate on an average of 5 percent per annum. Evaluate the project from the parent firm's perspective.
12. What is risk in investment? How is risk handled in investment decisions?

Multiple-choice Questions

1. Business firms enter foreign markets through __________.
    (a) Franchise (b) Exports
    (c) Both the above (d) None of these
2. Capital budgeting is a process of __________capital projects.
    (a) Analyzing
    (b) Selecting
    (c) Analyzing and selecting
    (d) None of these
3. In capital budgeting __________ are considered.
    (a) Incremental cash flows
    (b) Opportunity costs
    (c) Both the above
    (d) None of these

4. Sunk costs are costs that are incurred as a result of ________.
   (a) Current decisions (b) Past decisions
   (c) Future decisions (d) None of these
5. A special feature of foreign projects is ________.
   (a) Taxes (b) Depreciation
   (c) Blocked funds (d) None of these
6. One of the objectives of transfer pricing is________.
   (a) To reduce overall tax liability
   (b) To reduce costs
   (c) To siphon off funds
   (d) None of these
7. Discounting underlies ________.
   (a) Compounding
   (b) Time value of money
   (c) Expected rate of return
   (d) None of these
8. Foreign projects involve ________discount rate.
   (a) Lower discount rate
   (b) Higher discount rate
   (c) Moderate discount rate
   (d) None of these
9. The widely used capital budgeting method is________.
   (a) NPV (b) IRR
   (c) PI (d) None of these
10. Political risk arises from the political environment in the ________.
    (a) Domestic country (b) Host country
    (c) Developed nations (d) None of these
11. Political risks and other risks can be managed by ________the required rate of return.
    (a) Lowering (b) Raising
    (c) Keeping constant (d) None of these
12. Cost of capital incorporates ________.
    (a) Inflation premium
    (b) Increase in demand for products
    (c) Increase in supply of products
    (d) None of these
13. Certainty equivalent coefficient takes a value between ________.
    (a) 0 and 1 (b) 1 and 5
    (c) 1 and 10 (d) None of these
14. Sensitivity analysis is also known as ________.
    (a) Discounted cash flow analysis
    (b) What if analysis
    (c) Scenario analysis
    (d) None of these
15. A real option gives a firm the right to make________ at one or more points in time.
    (a) Investment decision (b) Abandon decision
    (c) Both the above (d) None of these

Case Study

Indian Breweries Limited is considering undertaking a capital investment in Singapore to manufacture alcoholic drinks. It is estimated that the project will cost SGD 500 million (SGD 400 million of immediate capital expenditure and SGD 100 million of working capital). The economic life of the project is estimated at 10 years. It is also estimated that the project will generate annual revenue of SGD 300 million with annual operating costs of SGD 100 million. The company policy is to follow straight-line depreciation. The project will have zero scrap value.

The company plans to finance the project with the following sources of funds:

- 10% Eurobonds: SGD 200 million
- Retained earnings: SGD 300 million

The issue costs will be 2 percent and are tax deductible.

The breweries industry in Singapore has an equity beta of 1.20. The risk-free return in Singapore is 5 percent and the market return is 15 percent. The corporate tax rate in Singapore is 30 percent. There is no double taxation agreement between India and Singapore. The overseas investors in Singapore are allowed only to remit 50 percent of each year's pre-tax, but after-interest amount, back to the parent. All the blocked funds earn tax-free interest at 5 percent and can only be repatriated at the end of the project life. The project is not expected to attract any tax on the remitted cash flows.

The current spot rate (SGD/INR) is INR 28.5525, and the Singapore dollar is expected to depreciate against INR at an annual rate of 2 percent.

Alternatively, the company has drawn plans for a wholly-owned manufacturing facility in Hong Kong. A major attraction of locating the manufacturing facility in Hong Kong is that the Hong Kong government has promised to arrange for a large portion of the construction cost of the production facility to be financed at a very attractive interest rate if the plant is built there.

The cost of constructing the manufacturing plant is estimated at HKD 100 million. The borrowing capacity created by this investment is HKD 40 million. The rest of the cost of the project can be met by the company through its retained earnings.

The marginal corporate tax rate in Hong Kong is 30 percent. The subsidiary unit in Hong Kong is allowed to repatriate the profits to the parent as and when it wants by paying an additional tax at 10 percent on the amount to be remitted.

The project life is estimated at 10 years. The company may follow the straight-line method of depreciation. The market value of the plant at the end of the project life is difficult to estimate.

One of the most attractive features of the proposal is the special financing the Hong Kong government is willing to arrange. If the plant is built in Hong Kong, the company will be eligible to borrow HKD 40 million at an interest rate of 5 percent per annum. The normal borrowing rate for the company in Hong Kong could be 9 percent. The loan schedule calls for the principal to be repaid in 10 equal installments. The company uses 14 percent as its all-equity cost of capital.

With the commissioning of the Hong Kong plant, the company expects annual sales revenue of HKD 150 million as against the annual operating costs of HKD 75 million.

The current spot rate (HKD/INR) is 5.5950, and it is expected that the INR will appreciate against the HKD by 2 percent per annum on an average over the next ten years. The risk-free interest rate is 7 percent in India and 5 percent in Hong Kong.

Questions

1. Advise the management of the company on the desirability and location of the project. Also comment on the intended financing plans.
2. What types of risk would the company face if it takes up the overseas project? How would such risks be managed?

Further Reading

1. Lawrence D. Booth, "Capital Budgeting Framework for the Multinational Corporation," *Journal of International Business Studies* (Fall 1982): pp. 113–23.
2. John Holland, "Capital Budgeting for International Business: A Framework for Analysis", *Managerial Finance* 16 (1990): pp. 1–6.
3. Donald R. Lessard, "Evaluating International Projects: An Adjusted Present Value Approach" in Donald R. Lessard, (ed.), *International Financial Management: Theory and Applications* (New York: Wiley, 1985): pp. 570–84.
4. Alan C. Shapiro, "Capital Budgeting for the Multinational Corporation", *Financial Management* (Spring 1978): pp. 7–16.
5. Timothy A. Luchrman, "Investment Opportunities as Real Options: Getting Started on the Numbers", *Harvard Business Review* (July–August 1998): 51–67.
6. James S. Ang and Tsong-Yue Lai, "A Simple Rule for Multinational Capital Budgeting," *The Global Finance Journal* 1, (1989): 71–75.
7. Alan C. Shapiro, "International Capital Budgeting", *Midland Journal of Corporate Finance* (Spring 1983): 26–45.

CHAPTER 11

Financing Decisions of MNCs

CHAPTER OBJECTIVES

After studying this chapter, you should be able to:

1 Highlight the importance of financing decisions of MNCs.
2 Understand the concept of cost of capital.
3 Appreciate the importance of cost of capital in project selection.
4 Define capital structure.
5 Identify the factors that influence the capital structure.
6 Discuss various methods of financing foreign subsidiaries or projects.
7 Outline the methods used by MNCs to raise capital.

Introduction

As discussed in Chapter 10, discount rate plays a crucial role in determining the viability or acceptability of a project. The discount rate is the minimum acceptable rate of return on a project. This minimum acceptable rate is known as the *required rate of return (RRR)* for the project. Let us consider an example to understand the concept of the required rate of return. Suppose a firm is considering two projects—Project X and Project Y. These projects require an outlay now, but generate a cash return in the future. Assume that, due to certain constraints, the firm can take up only one of the projects. If it undertakes Project X, it has to forego the opportunity to undertake Project Y and vice versa. Therefore, by taking up Project X, the firm incurs an opportunity cost in terms of what it could have earned on an alternative investment. Suppose that Project Y yields a return of 15%. By undertaking Project X, the firm forgoes the 15% return on Project Y. Hence, the firm should get at least a 15% return on Project X. This is known as the required rate of return on Project X. Thus, the **required rate of return** is defined as the rate of return foregone on the next best alternative investment opportunity.

The higher the risk involved in a project, the more is the required rate of return. In other words, a higher return is required to compensate for a greater risk. However, the required rate of return on the investment in a project with zero risk is not zero. This is because the investor still requires compensation for the passage of time. Such return is known as risk-free return. Thus, the required rate of return on the investment in a project is composed of *risk-free return* and *risk premium*.

The Cost of Capital

Cost of capital is another name for the required rate of return. It is the minimum rate of return required by a firm on its investment in order to provide the rate of return required by the suppliers of capital. The suppliers of capital are broadly divided into equity shareholders and debt holders. That is, the total capital of a firm consists *of equity* (equity share capital plus retained earnings) and *debt* (all borrowed funds). Of course, there are many variants of these two components. These different variants command different required rates of return, depending on the various risks embedded in each component of capital and also the prevailing risk-free rate of return in the economy. The required rate of return on each component of capital is the cost of the particular capital component. Thus, a firm may have *cost of equity, cost of retained earnings,* and *cost of debt*. The cost of capital of a firm is the combined cost of all the sources of capital. It is also known as the overall or *average cost of capital*. As the component costs are usually combined according to the weight of each component in the firm's capital structure, the overall cost of capital is also known as the *weighted average cost of capital (WACC)*. The overall cost of capital represents the rate of return required to compensate the passage of time, as well as to compensate the firm's overall or average level of risk.

*The **cost of capital** is the minimum rate of return required by a firm on its investment in order to provide the rate of return required by the suppliers of capital.*

The cost of capital may also be classified as the explicit cost of capital and the implicit cost of capital. The *implicit cost of capital* is the opportunity cost, or the rate of return on the best alternative investment. The *explicit cost of capital* is the discount rate that equates the present value of expected payments to the sources of funds with the net funds received from those sources of funds.

Components

The cost of capital of a firm can be broken down into cost of debt, cost of retained earnings, and cost of equity.

The Cost of Debt The cost of debt is the rate of return required by the suppliers of debt capital. This rate of return is generally designated as k_d. Consider a company that has issued debentures that have a par value of INR 5,000 at a coupon rate of 10 percent. In this case, k_d is equal to 10 percent. As the interest on debt is tax deductible for the company, it is the interest rate on debt less the tax saving that is actually the cost of debt. Thus, the cost of debt is defined as $k_d(1 - T)$, where T is the company's marginal tax rate. Suppose the marginal tax rate is 30 percent. The cost of debt in the above example is 7 percent. Thus, the cost of debt to the company is less than the rate of return required by lenders (debt holders). The explicit cost of debt (before tax) is the discount rate that equates the net proceeds of the debt issue with the present value of interest payments plus redemption value of the debt. Since the debt can be issued at par, discount, or premium, the net proceeds of the debt issue are relevant here.

When foreign debt is used to finance a foreign project, the cost of debt in the home currency of the parent firm should incorporate the interest on the debt, currency gains or losses, and taxes. Let us look at an example to understand these concepts further.

Example 11.1

An Indian multinational corporation (MNC) has a subsidiary in the United Kingdom. To meet its investment needs, the subsidiary firm wants to raise GBP 10 million by issuing five-year bonds in the British market at a coupon rate of 10 percent per annum, payable annually. The flotation cost is expected to be 2 percent. The corporate tax rate in the

United Kingdom is 25 percent. The current spot rate is GBP/INR 82. The INR is expected to depreciate at 1 percent each year, for the next five years. What is the effective cost of debt to the Indian MNC?

Solution

Sale proceeds of the bond: GBP 10 million

Less floatation cost at 2 percent: GBP 0.2 million

Tax shield on floatation cost: GBP 0.05 million

Net amount to be received: GBP 10 million – GBP 0.20 million

= GBP 9.80 million, or INR 803.6 million

Table 11.1 shows the year-wise net cash outflows.

$$803.6 = \frac{57.98}{(1+k_d)^1} + \frac{62.75}{(1+k_d)^2} + \frac{63.38}{(1+k_d)^3} + \frac{64.02}{(1+k_d)^4} + \frac{926.93}{(1+k_d)^5}$$

$k_d = 0.09$ or 9 percent (approximately)

$k_d = 0.09$ or 9 percent (approximately)

Table 11.1 Annual Net Cash Outflows

Year	*Cash outflows (GBP million)*	*Interest Tax-shield (GBP million)*	*Net cash outflows (GBP million)*	*Exchange Rate (GBP/INR)*	*Net cash outflows (INR million)*
1	1	0.25 + 0.05*	0.70	82.8282**	57.98
2	1	0.25	0.75	83.6649	62.75
3	1	0.25	0.75	84.5100	63.38
4	1	0.25	0.75	85.3637	64.02
5	11	0.25	10.75	86.2259	926.93

Note: *Tax shield on flotation costs to be realized at the end of the first year.
**82/0.99 = 82.8282.

The Cost of Retained Earnings The retained earnings are obviously the funds of the equity shareholders of the company. If the company does not retain the earnings and the entire net profit is paid out to equity shareholders as dividend, the shareholders can reinvest such money and earn some return. So, the cost of retained earnings is the opportunity cost. The minimum required rate of return on the retained earnings is the return that the shareholders could earn on alternative investments of equivalent risk. The return in this context is composed of dividend and capital gain. Thus, the cost of retained earnings (k_p) equals the cost of equity (k_e) as the shareholders could earn that return by simply buying the shares of the company or making equivalent-risk investments.

In the case of a foreign project, the cost of retained earnings should also account for dividend withholding taxes. A *withholding tax* is a tax levied on dividends, interest income, and income from royalties, patents, and copyrights, earned by a firm of one country within the tax jurisdiction of another country. Though the payee (parent firm) is supposed to pay the withholding tax, the amount is collected from the subsidiary (payer). That is, the subsidiary firm is required to withhold a certain percentage of the dividend to be paid to the parent firm and pay it to the tax authorities of the host country. If a subsidiary firm has to pay withholding tax (T)on the dividends repatriated to the parent firm, then the cost of retained earnings is stated as $k_p = k_e(1 - T)$.

The Cost of Equity Cost of equity, designated as k_e, is the rate of discount that equates the present value of expected payments to equity shareholders with the net funds received from the equity issue. There are different models for the cost of equity. One of them is the *dividend growth model* which is given as:

$$k_e = \frac{D_1}{P_0} + g$$

where

D_1 = Dividend per share in the next year

g = Dividend growth rate

P_0 = Present market price of the share

Note that the growth rate will be zero if the company does not retain any of its earnings. In such a case, the cost of equity can be stated as

$$K_e = \frac{D_1}{P_0} = \frac{EPS_1}{P_0}$$

where EPS_1 is the earnings per share in next year.

Another model is the *capital asset pricing model (CAPM)*. CAPM is also used to determine the cost of equity, particularly the cost of capital of an all-equity firm. According to CAPM, the cost of equity is given by the following equation:

$$k_e = R_f + (R_m - R_f)\beta$$

The term R_f is the risk-free rate. The rate of return on the government securities (for example, Treasury bills) is taken as the risk-free return, because there is almost zero possibility of the government defaulting in the payment of interest as well as the principal amount to the securities holder.

The term $(R_m - R_f)$ is the market risk premium measured by the difference between the expected return on the market portfolio and the risk-free return. The term β(beta) measures the amount of risk associated with the equity share in relation to the market. Beta measures the relative systematic risk or non-diversifiable risk of equity share. Thus,

$$\beta = Cov(R_i, R_m) / \sigma^2 R_m$$

where

$Cov(R_i, R_m)$ = Covariance between return on the security and the market portfolio

$\sigma^2 R_m$ = Variance of returns on the market portfolio

The βin the present context is the all-equity beta, or the beta of the unleveraged cash flows. The market portfolio is generally approximated by a well-diversified share price index like the Sensex of the Bombay Stock Exchange (BSE), the Nifty of the National Stock Exchange (NSE), the NYSE Composite Index of the New York Stock Exchange (NYSE), or the S&P 500 Index of the NYSE/ NASDAQ.

While calculating the cost of capital for a foreign project (instead of calculating the cost of capital for the MNC as a whole), it is necessary to use the beta of a comparable firm in the country in which the project is located. The beta of a comparable firm can be taken as the proxy for the beta of the project. The project beta is then multiplied by the risk premium prevailing in the home country of the MNC. This risk premium plus the risk-free rate in the home country is the cost of equity in the home currency of the MNC. The beta of the MNC can also be used for estimating the cost of capital for the project, provided the financial characteristics of the project are typical to the MNC.

Weighted Average Cost of Capital (WACC)

The explicit cost of capital or the cost of capital (*K*) of a firm is the weighted average cost of capital, the weights being in proportion to the individual components of the firm's capital structure. Suppose a firm has a debt capital of INR 500 million and equity capital of INR 800 million. The cost of debt (after tax) is 4 percent, and the cost of equity is 11 percent. So, the weighted average cost of capital is calculated as

$$\frac{500}{800+500}\times(0.04)+\frac{800}{800+500}\times(0.11)=0.0829 \text{ or } 8.29 \text{ percent}$$

Thus, the weighted average cost of capital, simply known as the cost of capital, can be presented as

$$K=\alpha k_e+(1-\alpha)k_d,$$

where

K = Cost of capital
α = Proportion of equity capital
k_d = After-tax cost of debt
k_e = Cost of equity

When the other sources of finance, such as preference capital and retained earnings, are also employed in financing a firm/project, this formula has to be modified to incorporate the individual costs of these sources along with their respective contribution to the capital structure. The weights of the components may correspond to market values or the book values of the various forms of financing. However, the market value weights are more appropriate in the context of maximizing the value of the firm. Further, the weights must be marginal weights that reflect the firm's target capital structure.

Factors Influencing the Cost of Capital

The cost of capital of a firm is influenced by several factors, such as the interest rates prevailing in the economy, the government's tax policies, and the policies of the firm itself. It is, however, important to note that some of these factors are beyond the control of the firm. For example, the interest rates in the economy greatly influence the cost of capital. As the interest rates in the economy rise, the cost of capital of the firm increases. However, no firm has control over the market interest rates. Similarly, the tax policy of the government also influences the cost of capital, as the tax rates are directly used in the calculation of cost of debt. But tax rates are also beyond the control of firms.

Certain policies of a firm also influence its cost of capital. The capital structure policy, the dividend policy, and the investment policy are among the main policies that influence the cost of capital. *Capital structure* refers to the financing mix (mix of debt capital and equity capital) used by a firm. It may also be understood as the proportionate relationship between the debt capital and the equity capital of a firm. Capital structure decisions have implications for project selection via the cost of capital. Firms using debt capital can enjoy a substantial advantage as the interest on debt is tax deductible. In other words, the interest tax shield decreases the cost of debt. However, with the increasing use of debt capital the financial risk (or the risk arising on the use of debt capital) of the firm increases. Though the probability that a firm will go bankrupt is not a linear function of the debt–equity ratio, it goes up at an increasing rate as debt is added after a certain limit. In other words, as debt is added after a particular threshold, the financial risk rises, leading to a higher required rate of return or cost of capital.

A firm has the discretion to change its capital structure by varying the debt and equity proportions. But any decision to change the capital structure will have implications for the overall cost of capital of the firm. For example, if the firm decides to use more debt (because debt capital is cheaper than equity capital) and less equity capital, the proportions of debt and equity capital of the firm will change. This will tend to lower the overall cost of capital of the firm. But the increase in the use of debt beyond some threshold will increase the risk of both the debt and the equity, leading to an increase in component costs and thus, the overall cost of capital. In other words, the disadvantage with the increase in proportion of debt will tend to more than offset the advantage (interest tax shield) of the debt. Thus, the firm has to make a tradeoff between the advantage of debt and the potential risk arising from higher financial leverage, and accordingly determine the optimal capital structure at which the cost of capital is minimum. Keeping in view several factors including debt-servicing capacity, most firms set target proportions for debt and equity in the future, which is known as the *target capital structure*.

The dividend policy of the firm also influences the cost of capital. For example, if a firm decides to pay a higher dividend (higher payout ratio) to the equity shareholders, it has to acquire fresh capital by issuing new securities to fund its increasing business. As the new issue of securities involves floatation costs, the cost of capital will rise. In view of flotation costs, the cost of equity is generally more than the cost of retained earnings. The investment policy of the firm also determines the cost of capital. For example, if a firm decides to take up a project that involves a higher amount of risk, the marginal cost of capital will rise, reflecting the risk associated with the project.

Differences in Cost of Capital across Countries

The cost of capital is not uniform throughout the world. There are some countries (for example, Japan and Germany) where the cost of capital is relatively low compared to countries like India, Argentina, Brazil, and Russia. In fact, all less-developed economies command a very high cost of capital.

Country-wise differences exist with regard to both the cost of debt and the cost of equity. As discussed earlier, the interest rate in any economy is composed of the risk-free rate and the risk premium. Interest rates are generally high in less developed economies because of inflation and high demand for funds. These economies are also capital scarce because of low savings. Moreover, the risk premium (a part of cost of funds) is also very high in less developed countries because of their fragile economies. As far as cost of equity is concerned, the price–earnings (P/E) multiple is higher in less developed economies than in developed economies. The reciprocal of the P/E multiple is the cost of equity for no-growth firms. When the P/E multiple is high, it means that the cost of equity is high. High interest rates and high-risk factors also contribute to the cost of equity in such countries. It is noteworthy that if the financial markets in the world are highly integrated, there may not be much difference in the cost of funds across countries. Moreover, the cost of capital is lower if the financial markets are fully integrated because, in integrated markets, there is a scope for diversifying investments internationally. This, in turn, reduces the financial risk.

Cost of Capital for MNCs and Domestic Firms

The cost of capital for MNCs and domestic corporations varies due to several factors. Some of these factors are described here.

- *Access to global markets*: Although economies are becoming increasingly globalized, financial markets are yet to become integrated. As long as financial markets are not fully integrated, the cost of capital will differ across countries. The best example is Japan, where the cost of capital (both the cost of debt and the cost of equity) is much lower than that of many other countries, including the United States. MNCs have access to financial markets at a global level. So, they can raise funds in market(s) where the funds are cheaper. Although domestic firms may also be allowed access to international financial markets, they may not enjoy the same advantages as the MNCs. Domestic firms may be treated as aliens in international markets, whereas MNCs may not be considered so, due to their international presence. Thus, MNCs can obtain funds at a lower cost because international investors are favourably disposed towards MNCs.

- *Size of the organization*: MNCs are generally very large organizations in terms of business as well as assets. This is an advantage in terms of getting funds at a lower cost, because the suppliers of funds may perceive a lower risk with large organizations. Thus, the size of the organization also plays a role in helping it obtain funds at a lower cost.
- *Stability of cash flow*: MNCs are internationally diversified organizations as they have subsidiaries located in many countries, and have different product lines and product mixes. So, an MNC may have relatively stable cash flows resulting in lower business risk and thus a reduced cost of capital. However, if an MNC is engaged in the production and marketing of a product that has an international market, the cash flows of the MNC are systematically related to the state of the world economy. In other words, the risk associated with the cash flows of an MNC is larger than that of the cash flows of a company whose product has an exclusively domestic market. In such cases, the cost of capital for MNCs may be higher than that of domestic firms.
- *Exchange rate fluctuations*: MNCs are exposed to foreign exchange rate fluctuations to a greater extent. Besides, they also face country risk. Domestic firms, on the other hand, may not be exposed to foreign exchange rate fluctuations as much as the MNCs, and they are also not subject to country risk. In other words, the probability that an MNC will go bankrupt will increase with the MNC being increasingly exposed to several kinds of risk. In such cases, investors (creditors and equity shareholders) may require a higher return, which increases the cost of capital for MNCs.

Cost of Capital: Project versus MNC

The cost of capital for a project is different from the cost of capital for an MNC. The project's cost of capital is the minimum required rate of return on the investment in the project, whereas the cost of capital of an MNC is the overall or the average required rate of return on the investment made in all the projects undertaken by the MNC. The cost of capital is influenced by the risk associated with the cash flows of the investment. As the risk involved in a project may not be the same as the risk of the MNC, the project's cost of capital may not be the same as the MNC's cost of capital.

An MNC's risk is the aggregate of the risks of all its projects. The projects undertaken by an MNC may differ in risk and, therefore, each project will have its own cost of capital. Thus, a project's cost of capital may be equal to the MNCs cost of capital plus or minus the risk adjustment factor, which depends on whether the project's risk is higher or lower than the MNCs risk.

As stated earlier, the cost of capital plays a crucial role in the appraisal and selection of projects. A project's cash flows are discounted by the appropriate cost of capital to determine its net present value (NPV). A project with a positive NPV will provide a rate of return greater than the cost of capital (that is, the minimum required rate of return). It can thus contribute to the value of the firm, and may be considered for selection. When the project is appraised from the parent firm's perspective, the project cash flows in a foreign currency are converted into the functional currency of the parent firm and discounted at the parent firm's cost of capital. If the risk level of the foreign project is the same as that of the parent firm, this approach provides an accurate capital budgeting analysis. If the risk levels are different, the parent firm may arbitrarily adjust (increase or reduce) its cost of capital to derive the required rate of return on the project.

Capital Structure

Financial structure refers to all items on the liabilities side of the balance sheet, including the equity capital of a firm. The financial structure of a firm can thus be taken to represent the various means of financing the firm. **Capital structure**, on the other hand, refers to the proportionate relationship between long-term debt and equity. Equity includes paid-up share capital and reserves and surpluses. Capital structure is also defined as the proportion of the long-term debt and equity used by a firm to meet its investment needs. The return and risk of a firm are greatly influenced by how the assets of the firm are financed (i.e. means of financing), which means that the firm's value is influenced by its financial or capital structure. Financing decisions have a profound effect on the value of a firm. A firm can vary its financing mix or capital structure to get an optimal financing mix so that the overall value of the firm is maximized. The optimal capital structure is the mix of debt and equity that minimizes the cost of capital. The optimal capital structure is, therefore, the minimum-cost capital structure. When the cost of capital is minimized, the overall value of the firm is maximized.

***Capital structure** refers to the proportionate relationship between the long-term debt and the equity capital.*

As discussed earlier, in calculating the weighted average cost of capital, which is the cost of capital for the firm, the proportions of debt and equity in the capital structure of the firm are used. The means of financing the assets of the firm play an important role in determining the cost of capital of the firm. Any change in the mix of debt and equity financing would affect the cost of capital of the firm, which, in turn, influences the viability of the project.

For a domestic firm, the calculation of its capital structure is simple. But for an MNC, it is a complex issue because of its many foreign affiliates. The MNC has to determine not only its overall capital structure, but also the capital structure for each of its subsidiaries operating in different market environments. As the overall capital structure of an MNC is the consolidation of the capital structures of subsidiaries, any change in the capital structure of a foreign affiliate will definitely affect the overall capital structure of the MNC.

Foreign subsidiaries may have two options as far as capital structure is concerned–to follow the capital structure of the parent firm, or to have an independent capital structure. In the first option, the MNC determines its overall capital structure and requires the foreign affiliates to fall in line. But it may not be feasible for the subsidiaries to always follow the capital structure norms of the parent firm. For example, a subsidiary unit may be offered certain financial privileges by the host country in the form of concession loans and other financial subsidies. But the debt–equity norms of the parent unit may not permit the subsidiaries to avail such facilities.

The second option enables the foreign affiliates to take advantage of opportunities available in their local countries to minimize the overall cost of capital of the MNC. In this case, the capital structure for each subsidiary unit is determined, keeping in view the opportunities available locally and also the capital structure norms in the country in which the subsidiary operates. Thus, subsidiaries with access to low-cost funds will have a higher target debt–equity ratio, and subsidiaries that are in higher capital-cost economies will have a lower target debt–equity ratio. The withholding taxes and corporate taxes in the host country as well as in the parent firm's country may also influence the capital structure of the subsidiary firm. The firm will benefit, if it borrows more in the country where the tax rate is higher because of the tax deductibility of interest. But a higher tax rate is applicable to profits and dividends as well. So, the firm should look at the tax from an overall perspective. Generally, the parent firm determines the mix of debt and equity financing of each subsidiary unit in such a way that the MNC's overall cost of capital is low.

Determining the Capital Structure

The ultimate objective of an MNC is to maximize shareholder wealth. Therefore, any financing decision should be consistent with this objective. While determining the appropriate capital structure for itself and for its foreign subsidiaries, the MNC considers various factors that influence the cash flows and earnings per share (EPS). The important factors are:

- *Cash-flow stability*: The cash-flow stability of the firm to service the debt is an important factor to be considered in determining the capital structure. The MNC should analyse the expected future cash flows for servicing the debt–the payment of interest and repayment of principal. The more the stability of future cash flows, the greater the debt capacity of the firm. The *debt capacity* refers to the amount of debt a firm can comfortably service. The MNCs with revenue-generating facilities across several countries are supposed to have more stable cash flows, because the adverse conditions in some country may be offset by the favourable conditions in other countries. Therefore, the MNCs can have a higher proportion of debt in their capital structure as compared to domestic firms. It may be noted that an inability to service the debt may result in financial insolvency.
- *Financing flexibility*: This is another factor considered in determining capital structure. A firm has to maintain some unused debt capacity for future needs. MNCs generally use less debt under normal conditions and preserve their debt capacity to issue debt securities on favourable terms in the future. For example, an MNC can issue long-term debt securities when interest rates are low, and thereby lock-in low interest rates for many years. To get such an advantage, the MNC should maintain financing flexibility.
- *Corporate taxes*: Taxes may make the debt attractive. The higher the corporate tax rate, the greater the advantage of using debt capital. So, MNCs design their capital structure in such a way as to allow their subsidiaries in countries where the corporate taxes are higher, to rely on local debt financing instead of relying on funds from the parent firm. If the subsidiaries borrow locally, they have to pay interest on the local debt. This will reduce the withholding tax, since the earnings remitted to the parent firm will become less. At the same time, the subsidiary would get a tax advantage on interest to be paid on the local debt. Of course, if the subsidiary has poor profitability and pays no tax, the higher tax rates advantage cannot be availed.
- *Flotation costs*: Internal financing is always preferred, since there are no flotation costs associated with the use of retained earnings. Flotation costs are higher in the case of external equity financing as compared to the other methods of financing. Generally, firms prefer slow growth to be financed with retained earnings. Fast-growing or growth-oriented MNCs tend to use more debt financing.
- *Operating leverage*: Firms with high operating leverage (business risk) cannot afford to have more debt in their capital structure. When debt financing is used, there will be an additional risk (financial risk) for the MNC. In other words, a combination of higher business risk and higher financial risk may lead to a higher credit risk (risk of default on loan payments).
- *Cost of funds*: Due to imperfections in global financial markets, countries differ on cost of funds. These imperfections exist mainly in the form of barriers on the flow of funds across countries, or on investments in foreign companies. In view of these barriers, the cost of equity or the cost of debt differs from country to country. In some countries they are relatively lower because of excess supply of funds vis-à-vis demand. So, the MNCs have to change their financing strategies according to the specific conditions prevailing in the countries where their subsidiaries operate.

- *Exchange rates*: Changes in exchange rates also need to be considered in determining the capital structure of MNCs. For example, if the currency of a country in which the subsidiary of an MNC operates is weak against the functional currency of the parent firm, the parent firm allows the subsidiary to borrow in the local currency instead of relying on the funds from the parent firm. This reduces the foreign exchange exposure of the parent unit. On the contrary, if the currency of the country in which the subsidiary operates is anticipated to appreciate, the parent firm may finance the subsidiary by supplying funds raised in the home country, or by transferring internal funds to the subsidiary.
- *Managerial conservatism, lenders' attitude, and credit ratings*: These are also other factors that determine the capital structure of a firm. Companies with a low rating find it difficult to raise debt funds and, therefore, are forced to opt for equity financing.

Financing Foreign Subsidiaries or Projects

MNCs need to take financing decisions with regard to: (a) the proportions of debt and equity to be used by the firm; and (b) where and how the required funds can be acquired to finance the investment needs of the firm.

We have already discussed how decisions regarding the proportions of debt and equity are taken. Here, let us take a look at how the funds required to fund foreign subsidiaries or projects can be acquired by an MNC.

A foreign subsidiary/project may be funded partially or fully by the parent firm. The following approaches may be adopted by the parent firm to finance its foreign affiliates.

(a) The parent company may raise the required funds in the home country and provide equity finance to its foreign subsidiary.

(b) The parent unit provides a small proportion of equity finance to its foreign subsidiaries, and allows the subsidiary firms to borrow the rest of the required funds on their own. The subsidiary firm is allowed to be financially independent after initial financial support from the parent firm. The subsidiary may also be allowed to issue equity shares in the foreign country where it does its business. Such stocks denominated in local currency may also be listed on the local stock exchange. The principle underlying this approach is that the assets that generate cash flows in a foreign currency are financed with the funds raised in the same foreign currency.

(c) The parent entity may raise debt funds on its own and re-lend to its subsidiaries as intra-corporate loans.

The way foreign projects are financed also influences the NPV of the project. Consider the following example. A U.S.-based MNC has identified a project in India. It is estimated that the project will cost USD 100 million, equivalent to INR 4,500 million. The project, which has a life of one year, can generate revenues of INR 10,000 million with operating expenses of INR 2,000 million. The MNC would like to have a debt–equity ratio of 1:1 for the project. This means that the MNC has to raise a loan of USD 50 million, equivalent to INR 2,500 million. The company can raise the INR debt at 12 percent but it costs less (7 percent) if it is raised in USD. The marginal cost of equity for the U.S. firm is 10 percent. The current spot rate of USD/INR is 45 and the expected spot rate after a year is 46. The corporate tax rate in India 33 percent and that in the United States is 30 percent. The company evaluates the project based on two options–either raising the entire debt in INR or raising it in USD.

The NPV of the project under the two alternative financing options is as follows:

NPV for Partial Financing of the Project with INR Debt

Revenues: INR 10,000 million

Operating expenses: INR 2,000 million

Interest on loans: INR 300 million
Earning before tax: INR 7,700 million
Tax at 33 percent: INR 2,541 million
Earnings after tax: INR 5,159 million
Principal repayment of loan: INR 2,500 million
Amount to be remitted to parent firm: INR 2,659 million
Amount received by the parent firm: USD 57.80 million
PV of cash flows at 10 percent: USD 52.55 million
NPV: USD 2.55 million

NPV for Partial Financing of the Project with USD Debt

Revenues: INR 10,000 million
Operating expenses: INR 2,000 million
Earning before tax: INR 8,000 million
Tax at 33 percent: INR 2,640 million
Earnings after tax: INR 5,360 million
Amount to be remitted to parent firm: INR 5,360 million
Amount received by the parent firm: USD 116.52 million
Interest on loan: USD 3.5 million
Interest tax shield: USD 1.05 million
Principal repayment of loan: USD 50 million
Cash flows (116.52 –52.45): USD 64.07 million
PV of cash flows at 10 percent: USD 58.25 million
NPV: USD 8.25 million

The analysis shows that the project generates a higher NPV, if it is partially financed with USD-denominated debt. In the first option the foreign project is partlyfinanced with debt funds raised in the same country. The advantage with this option is that the parent firm's exposure to foreign exchange rate risk gets reduced with debt payments being made in the foreign currency.

Matching Cash Inflows and Cash Outflows An MNC with subsidiaries located in different countries may issue securities denominated in the currency of the host country. So, the subsidiaries can use their inflows in the local currency to pay off their debt in the same currency. For example, a subsidiary in Japan can use JPY inflows to pay off its yen-denominated debt. By using different financial markets, an MNC can match its cash inflows and outflows in a particular currency. When an MNC borrows in a currency and also receives cash inflows in the same currency, it is in a way reducing its exposure to currency risk. Instead, if an MNC uses its functional currency to finance all its subsidiaries, the subsidiaries will have to convert their cash inflows in the local currency to the functional currency of the MNC to repay the debt. This creates a problem of currency risk. To avoid such a risk, the MNC may make financing decisions that might reduce its exposure to exchange rate risk.

Credit Sponsorship An issue related to financing decisions is whether to raise a loan or issue the debt securities in the name of the MNC or the foreign affiliate. If the funds are raised in the name of the MNC, it becomes an added obligation for the parent firm. On the contrary, if the funds are raised locally as a liability of the subsidiary firm, it tends to reduce the country risk. However, the interest rates may be higher for the subsidiary firm than for the MNC, because an MNC is usually considered to be more creditworthy than the subsidiary firm. Thus, the MNC has to make a choice by keeping in view all such tradeoff issues. Generally, the foreign subsidiaries prefer to have an independent financial status after receiving initial support from the parent firm. The MNCs may even encourage their foreign affiliates to borrow in the countries of their operation to avoid certain risks including the risk of expropriation by foreign governments.

The parent firm closely monitors the financial operations of each subsidiary unit to ensure that the overall financial position of the MNC is not affected by the subsidiary firms' decisions and operations. Any default on the part of the subsidiary unit in servicing its debt may adversely affect the overall image of the MNC. This may result in a high cost of capital to the MNC, as investors perceive a higher risk. This may also make it difficult for the MNC to raise funds subsequently for new projects or for expanding its existing operations. To avoid such situations, the parent firm may take on the responsibility of arranging finances for its subsidiary units and assume the legal and moral obligation to honour financial commitments of the subsidiary units, including debt servicing. Thus, the parent firm decides the financial structure of its foreign affiliates not only to minimize the overall cost of capital, but also to uphold the image and financial reputation of itself.

Internal Financing Besides equity and external debt, an MNC may also use funds that are generated internally, to finance its subsidiaries. Subsidiaries can borrow from the parent firm and pay the interest periodically. The principal amounts are also repaid at the end of the loan period. The interest on such debt is also tax deductible. In other words, the subsidiary firm can enjoy the tax shield on interest cost. However, the parent firm has to pay tax on the interest that it receives from the subsidiary. Thus, the MNC will ultimately benefit if the subsidiary's tax rate is higher than that of the parent firm.

Subsidiaries may also be encouraged to plough back their profits by not declaring and remitting dividends to the parent firm. This will have advantages for both the parent firm and the subsidiary. The immediate advantage for the MNC is that it can postpone the payment of tax on dividends from the subsidiary. The advantage for the subsidiary firm is that it can have self-generated low-cost funds for financing its operations and projects.

Parallel Loans and Credit Swaps The other methods of financing subsidiaries are parallel loans and credit swaps. A *parallel loan* is a loan that involves an exchange of funds between firms in different countries. For example, a Japanese company's subsidiary in the United States needs funds in U.S. dollars, while a U.S. company's subsidiary in Japan needs a loan in Japanese yen. The Japanese company may extend a loan to the U.S. subsidiary in Japan, while its subsidiary in the United States may borrow an equivalent amount of U.S. dollars from the U.S. company. The borrowed funds will be repaid on the maturity dates.

Credit swap is also an important method of financing foreign subsidiaries. In a credit swap, the parent firm may deposit a certain amount of funds with a bank in its home country. The bank, in turn, instructs its foreign branch to sanction a foreign currency loan to a subsidiary of the parent that made the deposit. For example, consider an Indian MNC that deposits INR 100 million with the State Bank of India. The State Bank of India, in turn, can instruct its branch in Singapore to give a loan in Singapore dollars to a subsidiary of the Indian firm operating in Singapore.

Methods of Raising Capital

Once an MNC has decided on the capital structure, it has to identify various sources of funds. These sources may be broadly classified as sources for equity capital and debt capital. The various financial instruments that can be issued by an MNC to tap these sources of funds are briefly discussed in this section.

Equity Shares

An **equity share** represents a share of ownership in a company. Being units of ownership, equity shares typically carry voting rights that can be exercised in corporate decisions. Preference shares (preferred stock) differ from equity shares, which are known as common stock or equity stock, in that they typically do not carry voting rights, but they are legally entitled to receive a certain level of dividend payments before any dividends can be issued to equity shareholders.

*An **equity share** represents a share of ownership in a company with voting rights that can be exercised in corporate decisions.*

An MNC can issue equity shares either in the domestic country or in other countries, including the countries in which its subsidiaries are located, depending on where the best prices can be received. It is a normal practice that the MNCs issue equity shares in the country in which the cost of equity, i.e., the required rate of return is the lowest. If capital markets around the world are fully integrated, the cost of equity may be the same in all the countries. But, in reality, most of the capital markets in the world remain segmented and, therefore, the cost of equity cannot be uniform throughout the world. In other words, the required rate of return on equity (cost of equity) is different in different countries, depending on the risk perceptions of the investors as well as a host of other factors. For example, in the countries where capital markets are well developed and the savings rate is high, the cost of equity is lower.

The savings rate in the country also influences the cost of equity. The higher the savings rate, the lower is the cost of equity. Capital markets may also differ in issue costs and transaction costs. When the issuing costs are lower, the proceeds of the issue (after factoring in issuing costs) will be greater. This will reduce the cost of equity in terms of the required rate of return. Similarly, equity shares will have larger marketability, if the transaction costs are lower. This will bring down the required rate of return and thus the cost of equity. In view of differences among countries in terms of the cost of equity, the MNCs may issue equity shares in countries where they can get funds at the minimum cost.

When MNCs issue equity shares outside their home country, such issues are known as *euro equity issues* or *international equity issues.* Euro equity issues are offered simultaneously in more than one country through an international syndicate. Though international equity issues, also known as cross-border equity issues, are a recent phenomenon, they have registered a remarkable growth in volume as well as in value over time. Many leading MNCs have successfully raised huge amounts of funds through euro equity issues.

The concept of *euro equity* came into prominence in the 1980s. Euro equity issues were dormant for a long time, mainly due to restrictions on cross-border equity investments imposed by many countries. As these issues are exposed to many regulations and controls including stringent listing requirements and foreign exchange risks, international investors perceive a greater amount of risk in euro equity issues. However, with the opening up of financial markets due to globalization, the situation has significantly changed. The restrictions on the flow of funds across countries have been eased to a greater extent in recent years. This has helped investors opt for equity issues that diversify their investments internationally. Further, the breadth and depth of international derivative markets have increased over time, which has facilitated the hedging of the risks involved in euro equity issues by investors. One more attractive feature of euro equity issues is that they have a larger profit potential than domestic equity issues or other kinds of capital issues. Added to these, international financial markets have developed in terms of infrastructure and sophistication. This also enhances the marketability and liquidity of euro equity issues. All these developments have made cross-border equity issues more popular as a chief source of financing.

In recent years, a kind of financial instrument, known as *global shares,* has come into the limelight. Global shares are the listed equity shares, which are traded in the same form on any stock market in the world. They are traded in the functional currency of the stock exchange on which they are listed. The clearing and settlement of trades occurs at the global level electronically. Global shares made a beginning in 1998, but are yet to pick up momentum. Depository receipts, discussed in the next section, need the ordinary shares to be converted into depository receipts for cross-border transactions. But in the case of global shares, no such conversion is required. So, trading of global shares is generally less expensive.

Depository Receipts

To circumvent the conditions for listing of equity shares on foreign stock markets and for other benefits, euro-equity issues are structured into depository receipts. **Depository receipts** (**DRs**) are issued in foreign markets against the equity shares of a domestic company. Thus, they are issued as evidence of ownership of the underlying stock of a foreign company. Each depository receipt may represent the ownership of one or more equity shares of a company, depending on the value of a share. The procedure is that a company issues its shares to an international bank, which acts as a depository. The international bank, that is the depository, in turn, bundles a specified number of shares as a depository receipt, and issues them to investors in foreign countries. The dividends on the underlying equity shares are first distributed to the depository. The depository, in turn, pays those dividends to the holders of depository receipts. Thus, depository receipts are not direct holdings in the company, but derivative securities created by the depository that holds the underlying shares. Investors who have subscribed to depository receipts can, therefore, have all the advantages associated with the euro-equity issues without possessing the equity shares of a foreign company.

*A **depository receipt (DR)** is a type of negotiable financial security that gives evidence of ownership in a foreign publicly listed company, but is traded on a local stock exchange.*

Although depository receipts are usually denominated in U.S. dollars, they can be denominated in any currency other than the domestic currency of the issuing company. They are traded freely in international financial markets like any other foreign currency-denominated securities, either through stock exchanges or through OTC.

Depository receipts denominated in U.S. dollars and issued in the United States are known as American depository receipts (ADRs). Therefore, ADRs are the USD-denominated securities representing shares of a foreign company. They are held on deposit by a custodian bank in the home country of the company. ADRs are listed and traded on the stock markets in the United States. So, the U.S. investors can trade in ADRs as they trade in the shares of a local company. The initial success of ADRs resulted in the rise of GDRs throughout the world. Since GDRs are normally listed and traded on many stock exchanges in the world, investors' base of the company would increase with issue of GDRs.

Eurobonds

A **bond** is defined as the contractual obligation of the borrower to make payments of interest at an agreed-upon rate on borrowed funds and repayments of the principal at certain fixed times. Indebtedness evidenced by a bond is documented in the form of a security.

*A **bond** is the contractual obligation of the borrower to make payments of interest at an agreed-upon rate on borrowed funds and repayments of the principal at certain fixed times.*

Bond financing is one of the oldest methods used by corporations, governments, and other bodies to raise capital. The issuance of bonds in domestic and international financial markets became significant when corporations and international development bodies like the World Bank issued bonds to finance postwar reconstruction.

In the international bond market, there are two types of bonds—foreign bonds and Eurobonds. A *foreign bond* is a bond floated in a foreign country and denominated in the currency of the country where they are issued. An example is a Japanese firm issuing USD-denominated bonds in the U.S. market. Yankee bonds denominated in U.S. dollars, and sold in the United States, and Samurai bonds denominated in yen, and sold in Japan are also examples of foreign bonds.

Eurobonds are bonds that are denominated in a currency that is not that of the country in which the bonds are floated. Examples of Eurobonds are: USD-denominated bonds issued outside the United States and GBP-denominated bonds issued outside the United Kingdom. In recent years, there has been substantial growth in the Eurobond market. This is mainly because many high-rated MNCs and international institutions have issued Eurobonds in large amounts. Swap transactions have also added to the growth of the Eurobond market. Financial swaps facilitate corporations in raising funds in one market and swapping one interest rate structure for another. They can also swap one currency proceed for another.

Foreign bonds are usually sold by investment brokers located in the country in which the bonds are floated, whereas Eurobonds are issued simultaneously in many countries through international syndicates of brokers. Though, historically, the U.S. dollar used to be the most preferred currency in which the Eurobonds were denominated, in recent years many currencies like the British pound, the Japanese yen, and the euro have become popular currencies in which the Eurobonds are denominated.

There are different kinds of Eurobonds to satisfy the varied needs of the investors. In recent years, many exotic varieties of Eurobonds have entered international financial markets. Some Eurobonds are convertible into equity shares of the issuing company or some other company. Bonds with equity warrants are also common in financial markets. The warrants entitle the bondholders to purchase a certain number of equity shares at a prespecified price over a predetermined period of time.

A distinction may be made between a debenture and a bond. A debenture is also a long-term debt instrument issued by corporations to obtain funds for their business needs. They are similar to bonds except for their securitization conditions. Debentures are usually unsecured in the sense that they do not carry any lien or pledge on specific assets of the company. They are, however, secured by all properties of the company not otherwise pledged. In case of bankruptcy, debenture holders are considered general creditors.

Fixed-rate Bonds

Fixed-rate bonds are the standard and traditional variety of bonds with medium- and long-term maturities offered in global and domestic financial markets for a very long time. These bonds have a specific maturity date, and the principal value of the bond is repaid on the maturity date. They are straight fixed-rate bonds as the interest in the form of fixed-coupon payments is typically paid annually to the bondholders throughout the life of the bond. These bonds are usually bearer bonds. Because of their simple and straight structure, they are widely accepted in international financial markets.

Fixed-rate bonds are of different types, such as callable bonds, puttable bonds, zero-coupon bonds and convertible bonds. A *callable bond* is a bond that can be redeemed by the issuer at any time prior to its maturity. The major advantage of a callable bond is that it gives an option to the issuer of the bond to redeem the bond to his advantage. The issuer can exercise the option when interest rates are falling. A *puttable bond* is the opposite of a callable bond. It allows the bondholder to sell the bond back to the issuer prior to maturity. As the name indicates, the *zero-coupon bond* does not carry any coupon at all, but the issue price is fixed at a discount in order to give the expected yield to the investor. Some zero-coupon bonds are originally sold at face value, and they are redeemed at an amount in excess of the face value. Thus, the holders of zero-coupon bonds do not receive any interest. The tax implication is that there is no interest income that can be taxable on a year-to-year basis. Instead, the difference between the maturity value of the bond and the issue price is treated as the capital gain and taxed accordingly.

Fixed-rate bond prices are inversely related to the interest rate changes in the economy. For example, if the interest rates increase, the price of the fixed-rate bond declines. As the coupon rates of such bonds are fixed, fixed-rate bonds become unattractive whenever interest rates increase. The opposite situation is observed whenever the interest rates in the market decline. To sum up, fixed-rate bond prices change significantly, if interest rates are extremely volatile.

Financial markets have also witnessed the issuance of dual-currency bonds and multi-currency bonds. A *dual currency bond* involves payment of interest in one currency and repayment of the principal in another. For example, the coupon interest payments may be made in Japanese yen, while the principal may be repaid in U.S. dollars. In the case of *multicurrency bonds,* the investor will have the right to have repayment of the principal amount in one, two, or more currencies.

Floating-rate Notes (FRNs)

Floating-rate notes (FRNs), also known as floaters are bonds with coupon payments indexed to some standard or reference rate. That is, the interest rates in the case of floating-rate notes are variable and determined periodically as a discount or premium to a reference rate. Thus,

$$\text{Coupon rate} = \text{Reference rate} \pm \text{Spread}$$

Though LIBOR is usually used as a reference rate for such purposes, the other reference rates that are used as benchmarks include the interest rate on U.S. Treasury bills (T-bills), Prime rate, or some other short-term interest rates. Once the benchmark is chosen, the issuer of the FRN decides on the 'spread', which is the margin that an issuer adjusts to the reference rate. The level of the spread generally depends upon the issuer's credit rating. The spread is generally expressed in basis points. A basis point is one-hundredth of one percent or 0.01%. The spread is added to the reference rate to determine the coupon rate. The interest rates are quoted as one-month LIBOR + 500 bp, three-month LIBOR + 100 bp, six-month LIBOR + 75 bp, or any other periodicity of the reference rate and the discount/premium. For example, if LIBOR is 3 percent on the day the FRN is issued, the initial coupon will be 3% + 0.5% (in case the spread is 500 bp). The changes in the reference rate affect the rate at which interest accrues on the floater, but does not affect the spread.

The periodicity of the reference rate gives the reference period for the FRN. The interest rate on a floater can be reset as often as daily or as infrequently as once in a year. It is general practice that the interest rate is reset each time an interest payment is made on the floater, which remains constant until the next coupon payment date. For example, in the case of the three-month LIBOR, the interest rate on an FRN is revised quarterly; in the case of a one-month LIBOR, the interest rate is revised monthly; and so on. The shorter the reset period, the smaller is the potential price fluctuation of the FRN. Sometimes, the interest rate may be an average reference rate observed over a certain period like three months or six months. It may be mentioned that the spread (for example, 100 bp, or 50 bp) can be fixed for the whole period of the FRN or can vary over time. For example, it might be 50 bp for the first year and 150 bp for the rest of the period of the FRN. Thus, the yield on floating-rate notes varies with interest rates in international financial markets. As the floater's coupon rate changes with the change in the market interest rates, the price of the floater fluctuates far less than the price of the fixed-rate bond of same maturity. In other words, the FRNs do not experience significant changes in their price due to changes in interest rates as their coupon rates are indexed to a reference rate.

FRNs as medium-to-long-term bonds were introduced in 1970 and became popular in subsequent periods, particularly in the 1980s. In accordance with the shifts in investor preferences, many variations in FRNs like perpetual FRNs, convertible FRNs, etc. have been introduced in recent years. In the case of perpetual FRNs, the principal amount of an FRN is never repaid and, therefore, they are known as quasi-equity instruments. They are conventionally relied upon by financial institutions, such as banks, as a source of primary capital. Some FRNs are issued with a provision that gives the investor the right or the obligation to convert the FRN into a long-term fixed-rate bond. Floaters are also issued with a 'cap', a 'floor', or both. A 'cap' is the maximum interest rate that the issuer will pay regardless of how high the reference may increase. It thus protects the issuer from abnormal increase in interest costs. Conversely, a 'floor' resets the minimum rate that will be paid even if the coupon determined by the reference rate is lower. The 'floor' provision protects the investor from a declining reference rate. Floaters do not accrue interest at a negative rate and, therefore, they have an effective floor of zero. A floater may also be issued as either non-callable or callable. If issued as callable, the floater can be called by the issuer prior to its maturity. It is a disadvantage to the investor as he may be unable to reinvest funds in another security with comparable terms.

Investors who expect that the market interest rates would rise in the future, may consider a floating-rate investment. Although the price of the floater is relatively insensitive to changes in market interest rates, the interest received is dependent on the level of reference rate over the life of the investment. The investor may receive lower amounts of interest, if the reference rate does not move in the future as expected. The investor, of course, has the option to sell the floater in the secondary market at the prevailing price. As with any other debt security, there is a credit risk to the investor of FRN that the issuer will be unable to meet its payment obligations.

Syndicated Eurocurrency Credit

As the name indicates, the syndicated credit is a loan in which a group of financial institutions makes funds available on common terms and conditions to a borrower. In a normal business setting, a firm may have a banking relationship with a number of institutions in its domestic market. If the firm needs more funds than a single bank can or will provide, the borrower draws down its credit lines at other banks, sometimes at less favourable terms. In the Eurocurrency market, if the firm needs a large amount of funds, a syndicate is usually formed and all the institutions in the syndicate will participate in the loan on the same terms and conditions. Syndicated Eurocurrency credit is a relatively new market development dating from the late 1960s. Initially, the syndicated Eurocurrency credit was developed as a sovereign business to provide funds to the governments that have little or no access to the international capital market. Later, it has progressively become an important corporate finance market. Syndicated Eurocurrency credits form more than 50 percent of the medium and long-term borrowings in the international capital market. These credits are primarily meant for trade financing or internationally related business loans.

As an important vehicle of international lending, the syndicated Eurocurrency credit has advantages from the point of view of both lenders and borrowers. For the lenders, it is a means for financial institutions to diversify their risks that arise in international lending. For the borrowers, it allows for efficient arrangement of a large amount of funds than any single lender can effectively provide. Lack of alternative financing in the international market may also create a demand on the part of borrowers for syndicated credit. Thus, syndicated Eurocurrency credit is considered as the most viable of several financing options available to the corporations.

In a typical syndicated Eurocurrency credit, there are three levels of financial institutions, i.e. lead banks, managing banks, and participating banks. The syndicate is led by one or more major banks, known as lead banks. The lead banks are generally the borrower's relationship banks, which play an active role in determining the syndicate composition, negotiating the terms of the loan and administering the facility. They primarily retain a portion of the loan and look for other participants. The other participants may be titled as managing banks and participating banks. The managing banks may underwrite the loan along with the lead banks. The participating banks may simply lend their share of the loan.

The syndicated credit usually takes a form of a term loan in which the funds can be drawn down by the borrower within a specified period of time after the loan is firmly in place. The loan is usually repaid according to an amortization schedule, which varies from loan to loan. The syndicated credit may also take a form of revolving credit in which the borrower is given a line of credit that can be drawn down and repaid with more flexibility than the term loan.

The syndicated Eurocurrency credit is mostly denominated in the U.S. dollar. But the loans in other major currencies such as euro, Great Britain pound, Japanese yen, etc. are also available. A typical syndicated credit may have a maturity between 5 and 10 years, amortization in semi-annual installments, and the interest rate reset every three or six months with reference to LIBOR. The syndicated Eurocurrency credit is usually priced at a margin (spread over LIBOR). The spread over the reference rate depends upon the borrower's credit rating, size and term of the loan, competition in the loan market, etc. The banks may have the option to shift from LIBOR to any other reference rate (e.g. Prime rate). The cost of the credit consists of interest and a number of fees which include arrangement fee, legal fee, underwriting fee, participation fee, utilization fee, commitment fee, prepayment fee, etc. The various fees are received by the members of the syndicate depending upon their role or level of participation in the credit syndication. Some participating banks only earn the spread over the reference rate as their role is minimal.

Syndicate Eurocurrency credits are also traded on secondary markets. The standardization of documentation for loan trading contributes to improved liquidity. More particularly, the transferability clause allows the transfer of the claim to another creditor. The participants in the secondary market may be categorized as market makers, active traders, and occasional investors. Large commercial banks and investment banks act as market makers, giving two-way quotes and taking outright positions.

Note Issuance Facility (NIF)

A new credit instrument called the *Note Issuance Facility (NIF)* or the *Euronote facility* has been in place as a low-cost substitute for syndicated credit. Many borrowers have felt that the credit would become cheaper, if intermediation in syndicated credit is bypassed. In other words, credit would become cheaper, if the funds are accessed directly from the lenders through the issuance of Euronotes under the NIF. An NIF is a medium-term legally binding commitment under which a borrower firm can issue a short-term paper in its own name, and the underwriters of the issue are committed either to purchase any notes that the borrower is unable to sell or to provide standing credit. Although the borrower firm can issue notes, called Euronotes, with one-month, three-month, six-month, or 12-month maturities, the underwriter of the NIF has a legal commitment to provide funding support for five to seven years. The borrower can also obtain medium-term funding by repeatedly rolling over its short-term notes. If the borrower fails at any rollover to place the entire issue with the market, the underwriter either takes up the reminder or provides a loan. When the underwriter provides credit to make up the shortfall, it is known as a revolving underwriting facility. The revolving underwriting facility provides the borrower a medium-term continuous access to short-term credit at a fixed margin.

Under NIF, the role of the banks has shifted from one of a direct lender to one that primarily involves underwriting loans and only sporadically involves direct lending. The banks act as underwriters to buy the borrower's Euronotes or make the borrower a loan to the extent that the borrower cannot place the Euronotes in the market at an interest rate below the 'cap' rate. The 'cap' rate is the interest rate at which the banks will finance the borrower. The banks as underwriters may also voluntarily acquire the Euronotes at the time of the issue so as to resell them at a higher price in the market. In recent years, a growing number of NIFs have been arranged partly or entirely without underwriting commitments. The non-underwritten NIFs are similar to Euro-commercial paper. The borrowers under such facilities are of the highest credit rating. The investors in NIF are international commercial banks, insurance companies, money-market funds, high-net-worth individuals, etc.

The main advantage of NIFs is the draw-down facility. The borrower firm can opt to draw down all or part of its total credit whenever the need arises. It can also roll over a portion of the credit at will and issue notes with different maturities. Thus, NIFs are more flexible and cheaper than syndicated credit. It is observed that the cost of NIF is cheaper on average between 10 and 40 basis points than the syndicated credit. The cost is lower because the lowest interest spread usually more than offsets the other fees, which include underwriting fees, facility fees, etc.

Summary

1. The cost of capital is the minimum rate of return required by the firm on its investment. The explicit cost of capital is the weighted average cost of capital, the weights being the proportions of the individual components of the firm's capital structure.
2. The cost of capital is highly influenced by the capital structure of the firm. A firm that has a high proportion of low-cost funds in its capital structure will have a low cost of capital. The firm's value is maximized when the cost of capital is minimized.
3. The cost of capital is influenced by the financing decision, the dividend decision, and the investment decision of the firm.
4. Capital structure is defined as the proportions of long-term debt and the equity used by the firm to meet its investment needs. The capital structure of a foreign subsidiary may conform to the parent firm's norms, or to the norms of the local companies in the host country.
5. Financing decisions are the decisions taken with regard to: (i) proportions of debt and equity to be used by the firm; and (ii) where and how the required funds can be acquired to finance the investment needs of the firm.
6. A firm can vary its financing mix to get an optimal financing mix. At the optimal financing mix, the value of the firm is maximized.
7. Foreign projects can be financed by different sources of funds. An MNC can raise funds by issuing equity shares and bonds. Bonds may be Eurobonds, fixed-rate bonds, or floating-rate notes. MNCs can also raise funds through euro syndicated credit.
8. To circumvent the conditions for the listing of equity shares on the foreign stock markets and for other reasons, euro equity issues are structured into depository receipts. Depository receipts are issued as evidence of ownership of the underlying stock of a foreign company.
9. Subsidiary firms can also be financed by parallel loans and credit swaps.

Questions and Problems

1. How can its financing decision influence the value of a firm?
2. What are the factors that influence the capital structure of MNCs?
3. Define cost of capital. Why is debt cheaper than equity?
4. What is the significance of the cost of capital in the valuation of a firm?
5. How can foreign projects be financed?
6. Why are Eurobonds more popular than other types of debt securities?
7. What are the special features of a syndicated Eurocurrency credit?
8. What are the general considerations in determining the capital structure of an MNC?
9. Distinguish between ADRs and GDRs.

10. A U.S.-based MNC has a subsidiary in India. The subsidiary is planning to raise INR 500 million to finance a project by issuing five-year 10 percent debentures. The interest is to be paid annually. The debentures will be redeemed at par at the end of the five-year period. The floatation cost is expected to be 2 percent. The corporate tax rate in India is 35 percent. The current spot exchange rate is INR/USD 0.022. The INR is expected to appreciate at the rate of 1 percent each year, for the next five years. What is the effective cost of debt to the U.S. based MNC?

11. A U.S. project has a beta of 1.35. The required rate of return on the market is 15 percent, given the risk-free rate of 6 percent. What is the cost of capital of the U.S. project?

12. A British company has a debt–equity ratio of 0.80. Its cost of debt is 8 percent and cost of equity is 14 percent. The company is considering launching a project in India. The required rate of return is 20 percent. The after-tax cost of debt would be 12 percent. What is the weighted average cost of capital of the Indian project?

Multiple-choice Questions

1. Discount rate is the ________.

(a) Required rate of return
(b) Cost of equity
(c) Cost of debt
(d) None of these

2. Required rate of return on a project with zero risk is ________.

(a) Zero (b) Risk-free rate
(c) Cost of equity (d) None of these

3. Required rate of return is composed of ________.

(a) Risk-free rate and risk premium
(b) Cost of retained earnings
(c) Risk premium
(d) None of these

4. Cost of capital is defined as ________ on a project.

(a) Minimum rate of return
(b) Risk-free return
(c) Maximum return
(d) None of these

5. Weighted average cost of capital is known as ________.

(a) Overall cost of capital (b) Discount rate
(c) Both of the above (d) None of these

6. Implicit cost of capital is the ________.

(a) Overall cost of capital
(b) Opportunity cost
(c) Weighted average cost of capital
(d) None of the above

7. ________ tax deductible.

(a) Cost of equity
(b) Cost of retained earnings
(c) Interest on debt
(d) None of the above

8. Cost of debt is ________ cost of equity.

(a) More expensive than (b) Cheaper than
(c) Equal to (d) None of these

9. Withholding tax is a tax levied on ________.

(a) Cost of capital
(b) Dividend
(c) Dividend, interest, etc
(d) None of these

10. ________ can also be used to estimate the cost of capital of a project.

(a) Beta (b) Flotation costs
(c) Risk premium (d) None of these

11. Cost of equity is more than the cost of retained earnings because of ________.

(a) Tax
(b) Flotation costs
(c) More investment opportunities
(d) None of these

12. Capital structure refers to ________.

(a) Equity capital
(b) Debt capital
(c) Mix of equity and debt capital
(d) None of these

13. Cost of capital in LDC is high because of ________.

(a) Low savings rate (b) High savings rate
(c) Low investment rate (d) None of these

14. Cost of capital in the case of MNCs is generally low because ________.

(a) They are bigger in size
(b) They can negotiate
(c) They can raise the capital wherever the cost of funds is cheaper
(d) None of these

15. A project with a positive NPV can provide return ________the cost of capital.
    (a) Less than (b) More than
    (c) Equal to (d) None of these
16. Firms with ________business risk cannot have higher financial leverage.
    (a) High (b) Low
    (c) Moderate (d) None of these
17. MNC is considered to be ________creditworthy than its subsidiary unit.
    (a) Less (b) More
    (c) Moderate (d) None of these
18. Securities underlying the GDRs are ________.
    (a) Equity shares (b) Debt securities
    (c) ADRs (d) None of these
19. A callable bond can be redeemed by the ________before maturity.
    (a) Investor (b) Issuer
    (c) Bank (d) None of these
20. Spread is also known as ________.
    (a) Margin (b) Discount
    (c) Premium (d) None of these

Further Reading

1. Michael Adles, "The Cost of Capital and Valuation of a two-country Firm," *Journal of Finance* (1974): 119–132.
2. Arthur Stonehill and Thomas Stitzel, "Financial Structure and Multinational Corporations," *California Management Review* (1969): 91–96.
3. Marti Subrahmanyam, "On the Optimality of International Capital Market Integration," *Journal of Financial Economics* 2 (1975): 3–28.
4. Congsheng Wu and Chuck C. Y. Kwok, "Why do US firms choose Global Equity Offerings?" *Financial Management* 31 (2002): 47–65.
5. Alan C. Shapiro, "Financial Structure and the Cost of Capital in the Multinational Corporation," *Journal of Financial and Quantitative Analysis* (June 1988): 211–226.
6. Rene M. Stulz, "Globalization of Capital Markets and the Cost of Capital: The Case of Nestle," *Journal of Applied Corporate Finance* (Fall 1995): 30–38.

CHAPTER 12

Management of Working Capital: An International Perspective

CHAPTER OBJECTIVES

After studying this chapter, you should be able to:

1. Highlight the importance of working capital.
2. Discuss the issues involved in cash management in the international context.
3. Understand the importance of international receivables management and the role of factoring.
4. Explain the importance of inventory management in the international context.
5. Discuss various methods of financing current assets.

Introduction

The management of working capital involves the management of various current assets and current liabilities of a firm, individually as well as in a combination with each other. As the current assets and current liabilities of a firm are affected by factors such as foreign exchange controls, multiple tax jurisdictions, and exchange rate fluctuations, the management of working capital in multinational corporations assumes a special significance. Exchange rate fluctuations affect both the cash inflows and outflows of MNCs, and thereby make working capital management more complex and challenging. Further, the MNCs also have many options with regard to working capital financing. They have access to numerous sources of short-term funds in various currencies. A firm can be managed with a minimum working capital, if it has potential access to many sources of short-term funds.

There are two concepts of working capital—the *gross* concept and the *net* concept. The gross concept, also known as **gross working capital**, refers to all the current assets in the business, while the *net* concept, also known as **net working capital**, is the difference between current assets and current liabilities in the business. *Current assets* include cash, receivables, marketable securities, and inventory. They are the major components of working capital. As they have varying degrees of liquidity, some of them are considered as the most liquid assets and others are less liquid assets. Cash is the most liquid asset in any business. *Liquidity* refers to the ability to meet the cash obligations of the firm when they are to be met. The *current liabilities* are all the short-term liabilities of a firm, and include bills payables (trade credit), bank overdrafts and accruals. These are the firm's liabilities that will mature for payment within one year. In most situations, the value of current assets is more than the value of current liabilities, which results in a positive working capital. However, at times,

***Working capital**, also referred to as **gross working capital**, refers to all current assets of a firm. **Net working capital** is the difference between the current assets and the current liabilities of a firm.*

the value of current assets may be less than the value of current liabilities. This is known as negative working capital. Both positive working capital and negative working capital have implications for the profitability and liquidity of the firm. A high positive working capital impairs the profitability of the firm but provides high liquidity. A negative working capital severely affects the liquidity of the firm. Therefore, no firm wantonly maintains negative working capital. As liquidity is the prime concern in working capital management, it is said that the management of working capital is the management of liquidity of the firm.

Working capital management in any company—domestic or multinational—revolves around three aspects: (i) level of current assets, (ii) level of investment in each type of current asset, and (iii) specific sources of working capital financing. Working capital management is thus concerned with the level of working capital investment and its financing.

The composition and size of working capital largely determines the firm's liquidity. The decision regarding the appropriate level of working capital involves a tradeoff between expected profitability and liquidity. A large investment in current assets would ensure uninterrupted production and sales. Besides, the firm would have no difficulty in meeting the claims of its creditors as and when payments are due. In other words, the firm can avoid cash shortage and a stock-out situation, if it has a sound liquidity position. But a high liquidity position is associated with costs. When a firm maintains higher levels of current assets to maintain high liquidity, a considerable amount of the firm's funds are tied up in current assets, which will ultimately result in lower profitability, as most current assets are either idle assets or lower-profit-earning assets. In other words, the higher the investment in current assets, the lower is the return on investment. Therefore, if a firm wants to have higher profitability, it should maintain lower levels of current assets. But this would expose the firm to greater risk of cash shortage and stock-outs. Therefore, a firm should maintain an optimum level of current assets by balancing its profitability and liquidity. Note that the firm has to decide an optimum level for each of the components of working capital as well. In conditions of certainty, a firm can afford to hold just the minimum required levels of current assets to deal with variations in expected payments, expected sales, and expected lead times. Uncertain situations, however, warrant the holding of safety levels of current assets in excess of normal levels.

In today's world of intense global competition, working capital management receives increasing attention. The goal of many MNCs is to maintain the least level of working capital. Developments in technology have changed the perspective of working capital management. New technology has made it possible for a firm to maintain a minimum or zero level of each of the components of working capital. For example, information technology enables the firm to maintain a minimum or zero inventory without causing any dislocation to the production schedule. Similarly, information systems facilitate efficient and effective cash management and receivables management. It is in this context that the concept of *zero working capital* has come into prominence. Zero working capital refers to the inventories and receivables being completely financed with accounts payable. Developments in computing and communication technologies have now made it possible to maintain working capital at a zero level. Firms with zero working capital are considered to be working more efficiently than others.

As mentioned earlier, *cash* (including marketable securities), *receivables*, and *inventory* are the major current assets of a firm and they constitute its gross working capital. Managing these components is the prime concern of any firm. So, the remainder of this chapter focuses on managing each of these components.

Cash Management

Cash management is primarily the management of cash flows of a firm including its bank account balances. Cash flow management is the process of monitoring, reviewing, and regulating a firm's cash flows. Cash flow management largely determines the survival and prosperity of the business. Cash is the most liquid form of an asset. It includes demand deposits and currency. Cash is also known as an idle or non-earning asset. So, the goal of cash management is to minimize the amount of cash in the business. But this minimum balance of cash should be enough to conduct normal business activities and also meet the unexpected cash needs of the MNC. An MNC generally holds cash to take care of its transaction needs, contingency needs, and opportunity needs. It requires cash to carry out its day-to-day business transactions. As the volume of business increases, the need for cash also increases. In a world of uncertainty, an MNC also needs cash to meet unexpected occurrences or contingencies that may require cash. A firm may be able to meet unexpected events or accidents, if it has sufficient cash balance. Further, an MNC needs cash to profit from certain opportunities that may arise any time. For example, an MNC may find an opportunity to buy a large quantity of raw material before the onset of inflation in a country. It may realize substantial savings on its cash purchases or avail special offers on certain instantaneous cash payments. It may also get a chance to acquire another firm on very favourable terms, if it has adequate holdings of cash and cash-equivalent assets.

Cash management involves cash planning and management of cash flows in the business. By cash planning, an MNC can anticipate its future cash flows as well as its cash needs. It may also enable the management of a firm to reduce the possibility of idle cash and cash deficits. Cash planning involves the preparation of a cash budget based on cash forecasts. A cash budget is a statement that is prepared on the basis of the budgeted activities of the firm. It shows the expected cash inflows and cash outflows of a firm over a certain period, say three months, six months, or one year. Daily or weekly cash budgets with many details are also prepared by MNCs for actual cash control. Cash budgets also show the cumulative cash deficit or surplus during the budgeted period. This helps the firm in making cash-management decisions such as determining the amount of marketable securities to be purchased or sold and the amount of short-term loan to be made by the firm. Thus, the cash budget indicates the expected cash deficit or cash surplus ahead of time. With advance knowledge of cash deficits, a firm can plan for alternative sources of financing. Similarly, with advance knowledge of surplus cash, the firm can plan for appropriate short-term investments. The management of an MNC also seeks to maintain proper control over its cash collection and disbursement. As the collection and disbursement of cash are two sides of the same coin, they will have a joint effect on the overall efficiency of cash management. By monitoring, reviewing, and regulating the cash budget, the organization can reduce the difference between projected cash flows and actual cash flows.

The principles of cash management in domestic firms as well as in MNCs are the same. However, the management of cash in MNCs is a very complex and challenging task in view of the movement of funds across national borders. An MNC collects cash from many sources across countries and makes payments to subsidiaries operating in different countries. In transferring funds between the subsidiaries or from the parent firm to the subsidiary and vice versa, the MNC may face foreign exchange restrictions and controls imposed by governments. The MNCs also feel the impact of exchange rate fluctuations. Further, differences in the tax laws of different countries make the job of cash management very tough. But tax differentials between countries also provide opportunities for MNCs to raise or invest funds to their advantage. The MNCs also take advantage of the treaties (e.g. Avoidance of Double Taxation Treaty) that the governments might have entered into. The other advantages include that the funds of various subsidiaries operating in different countries can be virtually pooled and managed by a centralized authority of the MNC, usually the parent firm. The central authority can also keep a constant watch over the cash balances with the subsidiary units, and move funds from a subsidiary that has excess liquidity to a subsidiary that can absorb excess liquidity. This would facilitate the MNC to operate with smaller balances of cash, thereby deriving the advantages of having minimum cash balance.

Efficiency of Cash Management

Cash collection and disbursement are two sides of the same coin, and the management of a firm always aims at expediting cash collections and decelerating cash disbursements to maximize the value of the firm. The efficiency of cash management, whether in a domestic company or in an MNC, is reflected in the collection and disbursement of cash. It is in these two areas that cash holdings can be economized. For example, assume that the average credit sales of a company per day are INR 75 million. If the company can speed up the payment of its receivables by one day, the cash balance will increase by INR 75 million. If this additional cash is invested to yield a 4 percent return, the company will generate an additional income of INR 3 million per annum. In the same way, a delay in the disbursement of cash will result in substantial savings or additional income to the company. As expediting collections and decelerating disbursements would result in an increase in cash balances that can be profitably utilized by the company, the management of firms always strive to speed up collections and slow down payments without causing inconvenience to their customers and suppliers. Firms design their collection and disbursement policies and programmes by taking into consideration the competitive environment as well as the nature and type of customers and suppliers. Efficient cash management also leads to investment of surplus cash at the maximum return, and borrowing at the lowest cost when there is a cash shortage.

Float

An MNC operating globally may have to maintain hundreds of bank accounts. These accounts may not show the balances that are shown by the corresponding books of an MNC. In other words, an MNC's cash book balance may differ from that of the bank passbook. This difference is known as a float. A **float** is the money arising from the delay in payment of cheques issued by the firm and/or the delay in the collection of cheques issued by others in favour of the firm. For example, the bank account and the cash book of a firm on 1 October show cash balance of INR 5 million. On 3 October, the firm has issued a cheque for INR 1 million to its supplier. The net cash balance as per the cash book of the firm is INR 4 million, but the bank book still shows a balance of INR 5 million. This is because the cheque issued by the firm will take some time to clear. The difference of INR 1 million is called a *disbursement (positive) float*. Further, assume that the firm receives a cheque from one of its customers for INR 50,000. This cheque would also take some time to clear, causing a difference in the cash balance in the bank account and the firm's cash book. This difference is called a *collection (negative) float*. The *net float* is the difference between the disbursement float and the collection float. Thus, a float arises from the delay between the time the drawer writes a cheque and the time the payee actually receives the proceeds of the cheque. There are different sources of delay or float. First, a cheque issued by a firm may take some time to reach the payee. This delay is called *mail float*. Second, the payee of the cheque may take some time to process the cheque internally and deposit it in the bank. Such delay is known *as processing float*. Third, some amount of time is also consumed in clearing the cheque through the banking system. In other words, some delay takes place between the time a cheque is deposited and the time the cash is available to be spent. This delay is known as a *clearing float*. Therefore, delays in the transit, processing, or clearing of cheques would cause a float. The firm should identify the various sources of float, and accordingly plan and make efforts to take advantage of each source so that the availability of its usable funds will increase.

***A float** is the net effect (in terms of money) of the delay in the payment of cheques issued by a firm and/or the delay in the collection of cheques issued by others in favour of the firm.*

Cash Collection

Acceleration of cash collection is an important aspect of cash management. It aims at maximizing the availability of cash for productive use. There are different methods for accelerating cash collection or reducing the collection float. These include lockbox arrangements, concentration banking, and automatic debit or payment by wire. The lockbox system is one of the oldest and most widely used systems of cash collection. An MNC may establish lock-boxes in different places around the world, or rent a postbox and authorize its local bank to pick up the contents in the box. Customers are requested to mail their remittances to the lockbox. The local bank opens the lockbox one or more times daily, collects the cheques, and processes them for clearance. The daily record of receipts is communicated to the MNC through an electronic data transmission system. As lockboxes are established at different geographical locations close to the customers and the bank itself collects the cheques from the lockboxes, the lockbox system reduces mail float as well as processing float. Thus, lock-boxes allow an MNC to increase the availability of funds by a few days over the usual system. The lock-box system is more useful when a firm expects to receive cheques in large denominations, but it needs to check the bank charges for the services provided. The bank normally charges some fee, or it may require the firm to maintain compensating balances (cash balances to be held by the firm to compensate the bank for its services) for the lock-box service. The firm needs to assess the advantages of the lock-box system and its costs before deciding whether to use it.

Another method of accelerating cash collection is concentration banking. The cash-collection arrangement can be either centralized or decentralized. In the centralized arrangement, the payers, particularly customers, are instructed to make remittances directly to a centrally located collection centre. In the decentralized collection system, the firm opens a number of collection centres. They are geographically spread for the convenience of customers. Customers are asked to send their payments to a collection centre close to them. The collection centre receives the cheques from the customers and deposits them in a local bank. The funds are then transferred to the firm's disbursement bank account(s) or concentration bank.

Firms can also accelerate cash collection by asking customers to remit the payments by wire or through automatic electronic debits. In the electronic debit system, the funds are automatically debited from one account and credited to another account. Developments in communication technology have played an important role in advancing such systems.

Cash Disbursement

Effective management of cash disbursements can also increase the availability of cash to the MNC. As explained earlier, cash management always strives to accelerate cash collections and slow down cash disbursements. The combination of fast collections and slow disbursements will result in maximum availability of cash to the organization. But this should be done without affecting its relations with customers and suppliers. For this, the firm needs to study its customers and suppliers spread across countries.

The disbursement float represents a negative balance in the records of the company as against a positive balance at the bank. That is, the disbursement float arises when the cheques issued by the MNC have not been debited to the bank account on which they are drawn. This can be utilized by the MNC to its advantage. Through proper estimation of the disbursement float, the MNC can minimize cash balances with the bank, which ultimately results in effective utilization of cash.

Disbursement control can yield substantial results for an MNC. There are different ways of controlling disbursements, such as zero-balance accounts and electronic fund transfers. A *zero-balance account* (ZBA) is an arrangement with a bank that allows the firm to write cheques against a bank account containing zero balance. This facility works well for MNCs that maintain a master disbursing account to service subsidiaries. As the master disbursing account of the MNC will service all the subsidiary firms' accounts, the subsidiaries can have a zero balance in their accounts. This means that the affiliates of an MNC need not hold cash balances in their bank accounts to issue cheques against their accounts. At the end of the day, just enough funds are transferred automatically from the master disbursing account to the subsidiary accounts to cover the cheques presented for collection. The subsidiary accounts will have a zero balance at the end of the day. Therefore, the zero-balance account eliminates the need to estimate and maintain the cash balance of each disbursement account. This will ultimately lead to increased efficiency in cash disbursements.

With developments in information technology, MNCs have been able to use the electronic fund transfer system, under which all the cash transactions of an MNC are recorded on magnetic tape and cleared directly through an automated clearing house. The need for paper cheques, with their associated mail and processing float, is eliminated with electronic fund transfer. Electronic fund transfers through automatic tellers, special credit cards, or debit cards supported by automated clearing house systems have assumed a lot of importance in these days of fast-changing technology. The Society for Worldwide Interbank Financial Telecommunications (SWIFT) provides a dedicated computer network to support electronic fund transfers. MNCs also use the automatic debiting system, under which funds are electronically deducted from one account and added to another account without any loss of time. With the electronic fund transfer system has been around, the total float in the fund transfer system is reduced to zero. With a perfect electronic fund transfer system, the financial system can become more efficient.

Netting

An MNC that has affiliates spread over many countries may find that some of its subsidiaries have surplus amounts of a currency, while other subsidiaries may need to borrow amounts in the same currency. Similarly, one subsidiary may be hedging a long position in one currency, while another subsidiary may be hedging a short position in the same currency and with the same maturity. There are a large number of inter-firm transactions between subsidiary units, and between subsidiary units and the parent firm. If such transactions are to be settled on a bilateral basis, a large number of currency conversions would take place with substantial transaction costs. By minimizing such inter-affiliate fund-flow transactions, the MNC can substantially reduce transaction costs. The method of payments netting is handy in this regard.

Consider an MNC with its headquarters in India and three subsidiaries located in the U.S., U.K., and Japan. In the course of their business, each affiliate has to pay and receive amounts from the other. Table 12.1 presents the inter-affiliate cash-flow matrix. The transactions are in different currencies, but their equivalence in the functional currency of the MNC is calculated at the spot exchange rate. As can be seen in Figure 12.1, there are 12 foreign exchange transactions involving an equivalent of INR 410 million. In general, there will be a

Table 12.1 Inter-affiliate Cash-flow Matrix (in equivalents of INR million)

Receipts	*Disbursements*					
	India	*U.S.*	*U.K.*	*Japan*	*Total receipts*	*Net*
India	—	20	30	40	90	(10)
U.S.	30	—	40	20	90	5
U.K.	40	30	—	45	115	(5)
Japan	30	35	50	—	115	10
Total disbursements	100	85	120	105	410	0

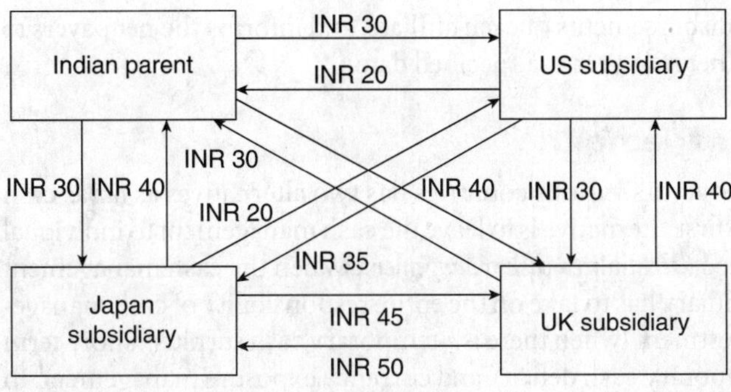

Figure 12.1

Inter-affiliate Transactions without Netting

maximum of $N(N-1)$ transactions among N affiliates of an MNC. As the number of transactions increases, the cost of transferring funds (i.e. transaction costs) increases. To reduce the number of transactions and, thus, the transaction costs, the MNC can take recourse to the netting system.

***Netting** is the process of reducing inter-affiliate fund-flow transactions to minimize transaction costs.*

Netting is the process of reducing the number of cash transactions among the affiliates, and between the affiliates and the parent firm. Netting may be bilateral or multilateral. In *bilateral netting,* the net amount due between each pair of affiliates (between the parent unit and a subsidiary, or between two subsidiaries) is determined at the end of each period, and only that net amount is transferred. In the above example, the parent firm has to pay the equivalent of INR 30 million to its U.S. affiliate and receive the equivalent of INR 20 million from the same subsidiary. Through bilateral netting, the Indian parent firm pays the U.S. affiliate an amount of INR 10 million. Thus, bilateral netting can reduce the number of transactions among the affiliates to $N(N-1)/2$, or even less. As a result, there will be substantial savings in transaction or administrative costs. However, netting is effective only when the affiliates have bilateral transactions.

In the case of *multilateral netting,* each affiliate nets all its receipts against all its payments and then transfers or receives the balance, depending on whether it is a net payer or receiver at the end of each period. Net funds to be received by all the affiliates will equal net funds to be paid by all the affiliates. It can be observed from Table 12.1 that the U.S. affiliate and the Japanese affiliate receive INR 5 million and INR 10 million, respectively, from the parent firm, whereas the U.K. affiliate pays INR 5 million to the parent firm. Thus, multilateral netting will result in a radical reduction in the number of inter-affiliate transfers and will minimize the transaction or administrative costs. As multilateral netting reduces the number and amount of currency conversions required to settle the transactions among the affiliates, the amount of exposure to be hedged gets reduced. Therefore, the MNC is required to hedge only its overall position (currency exposure) in each currency. Another advantage with multilateral netting is that the management of the MNC can have tight control over the movement of funds between the affiliates. Multilateral netting also enables the MNC to shift funds to a country or countries where it can take advantage of interest rate differentials and tax differentials. Multilateral netting is more effective when inter-affiliate transactions have a highly complex structure, providing greater scope for reducing cross-border fund transfer transactions. Multilateral netting cannot be effective, if even a few countries impose foreign exchange controls that may prohibit the subsidiaries joining the multilateral netting system. Multilateral netting presupposes the existence of a centralized cash depository or at least a netting centre manager. The netting centre manager or the centralized cash depository nets out the receivables against the disbursements of each affiliate, and informs the net payers to pay designated amounts to the net receivers at a specified date.

Centralized Cash Management

An MNC with multiple affiliates across various countries has two alternatives as far as cash management is concerned. The first alternative is to leave the cash management to individual subsidiaries, which may be called *decentralized cash management.* When the cash management is left to the affiliates, each subsidiary has to take on the entire responsibility of cash management, including short-term investment (when there is a temporary cash surplus), short-term borrowing (when there is a temporary cash deficit), and currency exposure management. In other words, the entire cash management is from the point of view of the subsidiary. Thus, there is a need to monitor and manage cash flows between the affiliates and between the affiliate and the parent unit to ensure overall success of the MNC's cash management system.

Under the *centralized cash management system,* the cash management of the entire MNC is vested in a centralized cash depository, which may be a special corporate entity. It acts as a netting centre as well as the repository of all surplus funds of subsidiary units. The depository thus pools the excess cash from each subsidiary and pays it to the units as and when they need cash. As different subsidiaries may have excess cash in different currencies, the centralized cash management may maintain a separate pool for each currency. Then the pool in a particular currency can be used to pay for the affiliate that is in need of that currency. The centralized cash management system also undertakes investment of surplus funds or undertakes market borrowing on behalf of the entire MNC. The system takes on the responsibility of exchange risk management for the entire MNC. Thus, the centralized cash management system reduces the burden of cash management at the subsidiary level, allowing the affiliates to concentrate on their main operations.

Some of the advantages of a centralized cash management system are that the cash balances of all the affiliates can be pooled and the system-wide excess cash can be invested at the most advantageous rates. Further, cash deficits can also be taken care of effectively by undertaking market borrowing at the most favourable rates. The centralized cash management system can also ensure adequate liquidity in the system with smaller cash holdings as compared to a decentralized cash management system. The funds are also kept in currencies in which they are highly needed. Centralized cash management may have an investment policy to invest surplus funds in marketable securities denominated in international currencies so that it will not be difficult to meet any payables in future. Under centralized cash management, it is also possible to diversify foreign exchange risk by holding cash or marketable securities in different currencies.

There may, however, be unpredictable delays in moving funds to affiliates with centralized cash management. It may become a serious problem when an affiliate wants to meet some unforeseen expenditure immediately. To meet such unexpected local payment needs, an affiliate may have to keep excess cash balances, but this may go against the principle of centralized cash management. Therefore, the MNC should decide the appropriate degree of centralization of cash management. It may also decide which aspects of cash management can be centralized and which should be decentralized. While deciding the currencies in which the cash balances are to be held and also the quantum of such balances, the MNC should keep in view political risks, taxes, and liquidity preferences along with transaction costs. Besides, it should take into consideration the nature of operations of the subsidiaries and their locations. Information technology facilitates the centralized cash management to get timely information from subsidiaries regarding each subsidiary's cash position. This continual flow of information enables the centralized cash management to take right and timely decisions with regard to investment, borrowing, and exposure coverage.

Example 12.1

A U.S.-based MNC has three subsidiaries located in the United Kingdom, Japan, and India. The following are the cash flow transactions between the units during a particular year:

(a) The parent unit in New York pays USD 10 million to the subsidiary in Japan.
(b) The Indian subsidiary pays INR 7 million to the parent firm and receives INR 5 million from the parent firm.
(c) The subsidiary in the United Kingdom pays GBP 1 million to the parent unit and JPY 10 million to the Japanese subsidiary.
(d) The Japanese subsidiary pays JPY 20 million to the parent firm and INR 10 million to the Indian subsidiary.

The spot exchange rates are: USD/INR 45; USD/JPY 117; GBP/JPY 224; INR/JPY 2.63; GBP/USD 1.90.

Work out the centralized cash management.

Solution

To determine each unit's net position, all the receipts and payments are converted into U.S. dollars.

The parent firm

Receives	INR 7 million	or USD 0.16 million
Pays	(–)INR 5 million	or (–)USD 0.11million
Receives	GBP 1 million	or USD 1.90 million
Pays	(–)USD 10 million	or (–)USD 10.00 million
Receives	JPY 20 million	or USD 0.1818 million
		(–)USD 7.8682 million

The subsidiary in the United Kingdom

Pays	(–)CBP 1 million	or (–)USD 1.90 million
Pays	(–)JPY 10 million	or (–)USD 0.091 million
		(–)USD 1.991 million

The subsidiary in Japan

Pays	(–)JPY 20 million	or (–)USD 0.1818 million
Pays	(–)INR 10 million	or (–)USD 0.222 million
Receives	JPY 10 million	or USD 0.091 million
Receives	USD 10 million	or USD 10.00 million
		USD 9.6872 million

The subsidiary in India

Receives	INR 10 million	or USD 0.222 million
Pays	(–)INR 7 million	or (–)USD 0.16 million
Receives	INR 5 million	or USD 0.11 million
		USD 0.172 million

It is clear that the parent firm pays USD 7.8682 million to the netting centre, the Indian subsidiary receives USD 0.172 million from the netting centre, the Japanese subsidiary receives USD 9.6872 million from the netting centre, and the subsidiary in the United Kingdom pays USD 1.991 million to the netting centre.

Impact of Information Technology on Cash Management

The MNCs usually maintain cash balances in different bank accounts, at different banks, in different currencies, and in different time zones. In view of their geographical spread and multicurrency operations, the MNCs have more complex liquidity requirements and systemic problems as well. Consequently, conventional cash management techniques have become ineffective in serving this purpose. It is in this backdrop that information technology plays a big role in cash management. Banking technology has made a big headway towards improving the efficiency of corporate cash management. Electronic fund transfer (EFT) facilitates the transfer of funds from one account to another in a single bank or across multiple banks. Real-Time Gross Settlement (RTGS) systems provide real-time and irrevocable settlement or transfer of funds across bank accounts. Clearing House Interbank Payment System (CHIPS) and Society for Worldwide Interbank Financial Telecommunications (SWIFT) are computerized systems of international wire transfers. Advances in banking technology have indeed improved the efficiency in processing the transactions. But the success of liquidity management is also dependent on the provision of data. In other words, access to real-time information is crucial for accurate cash-flow forecasting and making informed decisions on funding, liquidity, and counterparty risk. In recognition of this, the MNCs have begun to employ integrated cash-flow and liquidity management solutions. Integrated solutions, apart from other functions, can also make it easier to interpret and manage data to gain greater control over the cash flows in the organization.

Marketable Securities

When a firm has some excess cash, it may park its excess cash in marketable securities. *Marketable securities* are short-term investments, and their maturity is less than one year. They are (especially those that have a maturity of three months or less) cash equivalents as they can be converted to cash at short notice. The term marketability refers to the ability of the firm to convert a security into cash in a very short period of time without a significant price concession. Money market instruments (e.g. Treasury bills, commercial papers, certificates of deposit, and money market mutual funds) are marketable securities.

Firms hold marketable securities for the same motives as they hold cash. However, marketable securities yield some return, which may vary depending on the credit risk and maturity period of the security. This encourages firms to hold marketable securities in lieu of larger cash balances. When a firm needs to increase its cash balances, it can liquidate some marketable securities. While choosing marketable securities for investment, the firm considers a number of factors, which include rate of return, default risk, maturity period, and marketability.

Cash in hand, cash at bank, and marketable securities constitute the most liquid assets of the firm. The firm should always have optimal investment in these assets, keeping in view their respective returns and risks. Among these assets, it is only marketable securities that earn some return. As such, the liquid assets can earn a relatively low rate of return. Therefore, a firm always tries to minimize the investment in liquid assets. But low investment in liquid assets exposes the firm to the risk of bankruptcy. Therefore, a tradeoff between return and risk is required. The management of the firm should always balance the return and risk aspects of liquid assets. Another ancillary issue is the proportion of liquid assets that should be invested in marketable securities. This is a major problem for international cash management, as many currencies and many affiliates are involved. The MNC has to maintain cash balances in different currencies simultaneously to satisfy the needs of subsidiaries located in different countries. There are also several rewarding opportunities (marketable securities denominated in different currencies) available worldwide.

There are some cash management models (e.g. the Baumol model and the Miller–Orr model) that determine the optimal level of investment in marketable securities. Some of these models are deterministic, and others are stochastic. These models give useful insights into cost tradeoffs (cost of holding cash and transaction cost) in effective cash management by considering variables such as the average rate of return on investment in marketable securities, transaction costs for buying and selling of marketable securities, and, most importantly, the variability of cash flows (seasonal/cyclical or stable) of the firm. The MNCs stand on a different footing on all of these parameters as compared to domestic firms.

Management of Receivables

Receivables are another important component of a firm's working capital. They are current assets representing amounts owed to the firm as a result of the sale of goods or services in the ordinary course of business. Receivables arise on the sale of goods or services on credit to customers. The customers may be industrial consumers or ultimate consumers. When credit sales are made to industrial consumers, the receivables take the form of *trade credit,* and when credit sales are made to the ultimate consumers, the receivables take the form of *consumer credit*. Receivables are also known as accounts receivables, trade receivables, or customer receivables.

The effectiveness of receivables management can affect the overall performance of a firm. For example, a reduction of just one day in the average collection period for a firm's receivables may increase its cash flows and improve its pre-tax profits substantially.

The amount locked up in receivables is an investment. So, the credit policy of a firm is governed by its investment decisions. As with other investments, investment in receivables has the primary goal of maximizing the firm's value. Accordingly, when the firm is not able to realize higher profits, net of additional costs associated with administrating the credit policy, it should consider all-cash sales. A firm can remain profitable by investing in accounts receivables if the expected marginal return obtained on each additional unit of receivables investment exceeds the corresponding expected marginal cost of the investment.

A firm can decide to make credit sales to stimulate its revenues. Against this increased revenues there are four major costs that are associated with credit sales. They are: (i) the cost for the use of the funds to carry accounts receivables (financing cost); (ii) administrative expenses (costs for credit investigation and supervision); (iii) credit collection costs; and (iv) bad-debt losses. The management of a firm should evaluate all costs associated with credit sales and adopt a credit policy that can ultimately yield the maximum net return.

A firm may decide on its credit policy by taking into consideration several factors. The credit policy may be liberal at one extreme and stringent at the other extreme. A liberal credit policy may stimulate sales and lead to increased profits, but it may also result in increased bad-debt expenses, in addition to the opportunity cost of funds used. A stringent credit policy results in selling on credit on a highly selective basis. Only highly creditworthy customers are favoured with credit sales. Firms normally follow policies that lie within these two extremes. A firm may also change its credit policy as and when needed. Changing the credit policy means varying the elements of the policy, such as credit standards, credit terms, and collection efforts. *Credit standards* are the criteria a firm follows to determine which of its customers should be extended credit sales and how much. *Credit terms* include the length of the credit period and cash discount. *Collection efforts* include the methods a firm employs to collect the amounts from past due accounts.

A firm establishes its own credit standards to select customers to whom credit sales are affected. It may establish its credit standards by keeping in view the characteristics of its customers as well as its competitors. A high credit standard means that the firm extends credit only to select customers of high reputation and integrity. A tight credit policy with high credit standards may result in a very few bad-debt losses and a low cost of credit administration. But the firm may not be able to expand its sales with such a credit policy. On the contrary, if the firm follows a liberal credit policy with relaxed credit standards, it may be able to expand its sales. But the firm has to carry larger receivables, accompanied by more potential bad-debt losses as well as an increase in the costs of credit administration. Thus, to assess the profitability of a particular credit policy, say, more liberal credit standards, the firm should estimate the additional sales arising from the relaxed credit standards, the increased average collection period, the profitability of additional sales, and the required return on the investment. The standards of the firm will also influence the level of inventories to be maintained in the firm. For example, liberal credit standards may lead to more sales and also more inventories.

While determining its credit standards, the MNC has to examine the credit standards that are followed abroad. In some countries, the credit standards are more relaxed than in the home country. So, to remain competitive, an MNC has to relax its own credit standards. Sometimes, an MNC may follow a liberal credit policy during periods of credit restraint in a country, thereby gaining a competitive advantage over its competitors. An MNC may have the advantage of easy access to funds in the home country or abroad, which enables the firm to carry higher accounts receivables at a lower financing cost. The inflation rate in host countries where the subsidiaries are located, and also in the domestic country, and the foreign exchange rate fluctuations may also influence the credit policy of an MNC.

Credit terms involve both the credit period and the discounts to be given. The credit terms also influence the sales and profitability of the firm. A liberal credit period results in increased sales accompanied by additional investment in receivables. Cash discounts speed up the payment of receivables. The cash discount terms indicate the rate of discount and the period for which it is available. For example, the term "3/15, net 45" means that a 3 percent discount is given, if the payment is made before the fifteenth day after the date of the invoice, and the payment is due by the forty-fifth day. In allowing the cash discount, the firm considers the increased sales resulting from the cash discount as well as acceleration of collections from customers. The cost involved is the amount of discount given to the customers. The firm can also realize opportunity savings from accelerated collections. For example, the average receivables may be reduced from INR 50 million to INR 20 million with the cash discount to be offered. Thus, the firm realizes INR 30 million from accelerated collections by offering cash discount. If the rate of return is 20 percent, the opportunity savings will be INR 6 million. The opportunity savings should offset the cost of discount so that the firm will have a net advantage from the cash discount.

A firm may also determine its collection policy, which, in turn, lays down a clear-cut collection procedure. The collection procedure may involve making telephone calls, mailing letters, and paying personal visits to customers. The firm may also initiate legal action against customers who deliberately default on payments. Firms, however, adopt a different collection policy and procedure for each category of customers. For example, the slow-paying customers who are also permanent customers need to be handled carefully and tactfully. Similarly, some customers may be temporarily in a tight financial position due to some external reasons. Such cases may need special consideration. The firm generally makes a tradeoff between the cost of collection effort and the reduction in bad-debt losses as well as reduction in receivables.

Example 12.2

A U.S.-based affiliate of an MNC currently has annual sales (domestic) of USD 10 million with 60 days credit period. It is expected that sales and bad-debt losses will increase in the following manner if the credit period is extended, as shown in Table 12.2.

Table 12.2 Sales and Bad-debt Losses

Credit policy	*Credit period (days)*	*Sales (USD million)*	*Bad debts as percentage of total sales*
A	60	100	1.0
B	75	130	1.2
C	90	150	1.5

The selling price per unit is USD 20. The average total cost and the variable cost per unit of sale are USD 15 and USD 12, respectively. If the required rate of return on investment is 20 percent, which credit policy the firm should adopt?

Solution

The incremental profit (in USD million) under alternative credit periods is as shown in Table 12.3.

Table 12.3 Incremental Profits Under Alternative Credit Periods

Credit period	*60 days*	*75 days*	*90 days*
Annual sales	100.00	130.00	150.00
Level of receivables (at sales value)	16.67	27.08	37.50
Incremental investment in receivables	—	10.41	20.83
Required incremental profit at 20%	—	2.08	4.17
Contribution	40.00	52.00	60.00
Incremental contribution	—	12.00	20.00
Bad-debt losses	1.00	1.56	2.25
Incremental bad-debt losses	—	0.56	1.25
Incremental profit	—	11.44	18.75
Net gain (incremental expected profit—required incremental profit)	—	9.36	14.58

Thus, the firm can maximize its value if it extends the credit period to 90 days. The firm can further relax credit period until the net gain becomes zero.

Though the relaxed credit period may result in increased sales, there is also a risk of default and increased interest cost on the larger investment in receivables. Further, if the receivables are denominated in a foreign currency, any devaluation of the foreign currency will reduce the home currency value of the receivables. These additional costs need to be taken into account while relaxing the credit period. In other words, the credit terms should be eased only if the incremental profits are greater than incremental credit costs, including the currency value changes.

A firm may also adopt a credit policy similar to that of its competitors to avoid the loss of sales from customers who would buy elsewhere, if they do not receive the expected credit from the firm.

Factoring

One of the major problems faced by MNCs is the collection of receivables. All customers who purchased goods on credit may not pay their dues to the firm in time. Some customers are prompt payers, some are slow payers, and some are non-payers. Firms usually make efforts to accelerate collections from slow payers and to reduce bad-debt losses. A good collection policy makes debtors pay their dues promptly. It need not be overemphasized that prompt collection of receivables leads to fast turnover of working capital. Each firm determines its own collection procedure, keeping in view the characteristics of its customers. For example, some customers may not be able to pay their dues because of factors that are beyond their control. In such cases, the collection procedure of the firm should give special consideration to such customers. The credit management of the firm should aim at reducing bad-debt losses, improving collection efficiency, and ensuring prompt and regular collection—but without antagonizing the customers and losing them to competitors.

Some firms, including affiliates of MNCs, may find it organizationally difficult or expensive to collect receivables. In such cases, factoring is worthwhile. **Factoring** is a financial innovation that helps firms in their collection efforts. It involves the selling of receivables to an organization that specializes in the administration of sales ledgers and collection of receivables. When a firm factors its receivables, it actually sells its receivables to an institution

Example 12.3

The Indian subsidiary of an MNC has annual export sales of USD 10 million with 60 days credit period. The subsidiary expects that its export sales will increase by 10 percent if the credit period is increased to 90 days. The increase in cost of goods sold will be USD 0.60 million. The opportunity cost of funds is 12 percent per annum. The Indian rupee is expected to depreciate 1 percent on average every month.

Should the firm change its credit policy?

Solution

The incremental profit (in USD million) for a 60-day and 90-day credit period is as shown in Table 12.4.

Table 12.4 Incremental Profit (USD million)

	60-day credit period	*90-day credit period*
Present value of sales of USD 10 million	9.80	9.71
Present value of sales (USD 10 million) with depreciation of INR by 1 percent every month	9.61	9.43
Cost of carrying receivables of USD 10 million	0.39	0.57
Cost of carrying receivables (incremental sales) of USD 1 million		0.057
Incremental credit cost (0.57 + 0.057) *		0.627
Incremental profit (USD 1 million—USD 0.60 million)		0.40

Since the incremental credit cost is more than the incremental profit, it is not profitable to change the credit policy.

called the factor. The sale of receivables may be with or without recourse. If it is without recourse, the factor assumes the loss of bad debts. The credit risk associated with accounts receivables may be lower to the factor than to the selling firm. Commercial banks and other financial institutions are engaged in providing factoring services.

***Factoring** involves the selling of receivables to an organization that specializes in the administration of sales ledgers and collection of receivables.*

There are many types of factoring. One of them is *export factoring,* which is catching on in a big way. In export factoring, an exporter sells or transfers the title of its accounts receivables to a factor. The factor then assumes the responsibility of collection of receivables and also assumes the credit risk. But factors generally avoid business in the countries that do not have economic or political stability. Further, a factor may reject certain receivables accounts that it deems too risky. A factor may not be willing to conduct business with a firm unless the volume of receivables is reasonably large.

Generally, a factor performs three functions: (i) sales ledger administration; (ii) credit collection; and (iii) financial accommodation. In *sales ledger administration,* the factors maintain the accounts of their customers to keep the collections prompt and cost effective. In the *credit collection* function, the factors undertake all collection activity that is necessary. The factors may also provide *financial assistance* to their clients by extending advance cash against receivables. Besides these services, the factors may provide information on prospective buyers and assist the client firm in managing its liquidity.

Factoring involves both costs and benefits. The costs are the factoring commission or service fee and the interest on advance granted by the factor to the firm. Generally, the factoring commission or service fee is around 2 percent of the value of the receivables. Factors that have a well-diversified portfolio of receivables denominated in different currencies may charge a smaller fee as their overall credit risk is lower. The factor may make a cash advance of around 90 percent of the receivables value on which the client firm pays interest. The interest on such an advance is over and above the factor's commission or fee. The firm has to take into consideration both the costs and benefits associated with factoring to find out whether factoring is worthwhile.

Forfaiting

Like factoring, *forfaiting* is also a method of financing trade, but it involves financing the exporter against medium- or long-term promissory notes issued by the importer. In a typical forfaiting arrangement, the importer issues a bill of exchange or promissory note to pay the exporter for the goods imported. The exporter then sells the bills or promissory notes without recourse to a forfaiting bank at a discount. The discount depends on the length of time the bill or promissory note has for maturity as well as the credit risk involved in the transaction. Thus, the forfaiter takes on the responsibility for the collection of dues from the importer, assuming underlying credit risk. Generally, forfaiting transactions are supported by a bank guarantee or letter of credit issued by the importer's bank. Forfaiting facilities are available in many currencies, particularly fully convertible currencies (e.g. USD, euro, and GBP). If the amount involved in a forfaiting transaction is very large, more than one bank may be involved.

The main advantage of forfaiting is that it converts a credit-based transaction into a cash transaction for the exporter. Forfaiting provides greater flexibility to the exporter in structuring a deal. The exporter is relieved from receivables administration and collection. More importantly, the exporter is relieved of the inherent political and commercial risks involved in international trade. Forfaiting provides protection from the risk of interest rate increases and exchange rate fluctuations. This enables the exporter to conduct business even in riskier countries. The documentation is also very simple, requiring evidence of the underlying transaction and certain confirmations from the obligor/guaranteeing bank. Thus, forfaiting not only involves financing but also covers credit risk.

Inventory Management

Firms hold inventory for different purposes, which may be broadly categorized as transaction, precautionary, and speculative purposes. A firm may hold inventory to meet its day-to-day business (production) requirements. The level of such inventory should be large enough to meet the normal business requirements of the firm. It may also maintain some extra stock (more than that required for normal business) to meet unexpected increases in business requirements or any contingency. A firm may also maintain a certain stock to cash in on unexpected opportunities in the future. While deciding on the level of inventory (how much stock of inventory a firm should hold during a particular period), the management of the firm should consider the costs of holding inventory as well as the benefits derived from it.

Inventory is broadly classified as raw materials, work-in-process, supplies, and finished goods. *Raw materials inventory* refers to those items which have been purchased and stored for use in the production process. The firm has to maintain adequate quantities of raw materials inventory to meet production schedules and make the most efficient use of its resources and facilities. It may also derive certain advantages like quantity discounts, and economies in transportation when it purchases large quantities of raw materials. A firm can reduce its raw materials cost by maintaining a large quantity of raw materials inventory, subject to the cost of maintaining the inventory.

Work-in-process inventory refers to those items that are at some intermediate stage of completion in the production cycle. In general, the longer the production cycles of a firm, the larger is the work-in-process inventory. Maintaining larger work-in-process inventory is also an expensive proposition and, therefore, the firm has to minimize it by reducing the production cycle through improved production techniques.

A firm may also maintain a *supplies inventory,* which includes office materials, plant maintenance materials, and those items that do not directly enter production, but are necessary for production and maintenance.

The finished goods inventory is maintained by firms to match the demand for goods and the supply of goods. It is required to meet the regular as well as the unexpected demand for goods. If a firm fails to supply the product as and when demanded by the customers, it can lose its customers. Thus, the firm can minimize or avoid stock-outs and lost sales by maintaining adequate finished goods inventory. The policy of maintaining large quantities of finished goods inventory enables a firm to have large production runs and keep the unit production costs low. However, the firm has to consider both the inventory carrying costs and stock-out costs in maintaining its finished goods inventory.

Inventory management refers to planning, monitoring, and controlling inventory. Inventory forms an important part of current assets. In some firms, inventory constitutes more than 50 percent of current assets. In other words, a large amount of funds are invested in inventory and, therefore, considerable attention needs to be paid to inventory management. As inventory is an asset to which capital is committed, the efficient management of inventory will lower the required investment, and thereby enhance the value of the firm. The goal of inventory management is to ensure that the needed inventory is always available with minimum ordering and carrying costs. By having proper inventory management, a firm can reduce inventory cost to a considerable extent without jeopardizing its profitability. The main decisions of inventory management are with regard to the order quantity, order point, and amount of safety stock.

A firm can realize a number of benefits from holding inventory, but various costs are also associated with holding inventory. These costs are broadly identified as ordering costs, carrying costs, and stock-out costs. *Order costs* are the costs of placing and receiving an order;

carrying costs are the costs of storage and deterioration, obsolescence, insurance, taxes, and the costs of funds locked up in inventory; and *stock-out costs* are the revenues lost due to shortage of goods, costs incurred due to slowdown of production, and so on. Stock-out costs are generally avoided by maintaining safety stock.

Given the benefits and costs associated with holding inventory, a firm should manage its inventory to maintain an optimal level of each item. There are a number of inventory control models that can be used to determine the optimal level of inventory. One such model is the *economic order quantity (EOQ)*. The total cost of inventory broadly consists of order costs and carrying costs. The order costs increase with the number of orders placed. The higher the frequency of orders placed for the inventory, the higher the order costs. A high order quantity leads to higher carrying costs but lower order costs. A low order quantity leads to lower carrying costs but higher order costs. Therefore, there is a need to balance the benefits of increased order size and the associated carrying costs. The EOQ model balances order costs against carrying costs.

In multinational firms, inventory management is very complex because of factors like overseas inventory, variety of transportation costs, tariffs and taxes, import controls, and foreign exchange controls. If a multinational firm uses imported raw materials, it may face supply disruptions and delays in international shipment of goods. In other words, firms producing goods with imported raw materials and components may have to hold a larger quantity of inventory because of long delivery lead times. The MNCs may allow their affiliates to have the raw material supplies from within their country of operation to take advantage of low-wage labour, tax holidays, and other government policies.

The affiliates of MNCs generally hold large amounts of inventory in view of uncertainty and potential disruptions in the international shipment of goods. When the affiliates decide to get the required raw materials from other countries, they may face several kinds of risks including currency risk. For example, if the currency of the importing country depreciates, the imports will become costlier. To counter such currency risks, the firms may opt for inventory stockpiling. But holding a large amount of inventory may be quite expensive because of high cost of financing, insurance, storage, and obsolescence. Therefore, the MNC has to make a decision with regard to inventory stockpiling by taking into consideration the expected increase or decrease in the foreign exchange rates along with other costs like carrying costs, order costs, and stock-out costs.

Further, the reordering point of inventory may also be determined by taking into consideration the long delivery lead times. A firm that is dependent on foreign sources may face a threat of disruption or delay in the supply of raw materials due to transportation problems and export-import controls and formalities. The actual raw material delivery time may be different from the normal lead time in the case of imported raw material. Therefore, to avoid stock-out situations, the firm may maintain safety stock or buffer stock as a cushion against unexpected situations. It should be noted that maintenance of safety stock results in higher inventory carrying costs.

Inflation, foreign exchange rate fluctuations, and supply delays are the major concerns associated with inventory management in MNCs. Though such problems are common to all firms, the MNCs are constrained more by restrictions and controls. The MNCs may, however, take advantage of certain concessions including tax holidays offered by the governments of the countries in which their affiliates operate, and try to manage their inventories by balancing several kinds of inventory costs. They may also adopt more effective hedging techniques, including anticipatory purchase of goods to guard against foreign exchange risk and also purchasing power risk.

Financing Current Assets

The current assets in a business can be financed by different sources of funds. Firms may use *long-term sources* of funds like equity share capital, preference share capital, and long-term borrowings to finance their current assets. But short-term sources are the most commonly used sources of funds to finance working capital requirements. *Short-term sources* include accruals, trade credit, bank credit, and commercial papers.

Firms generally prefer to use long-term sources of funds to finance the permanent portion of their current assets, and short-term sources of funds to finance their temporary current assets. Some aggressive firms may even finance their permanent current assets with short-term sources of funds. In fact, some firms may also finance a portion of their fixed assets besides all the permanent current assets with short-term sources of funds. On the other hand, some firms may adopt a conservative approach and use long-term sources of funds to finance all permanent assets, including permanent current assets and a part of temporary current assets. They may also adopt a moderate current asset financing policy that matches the expected life of the assets with the expected life of the source of funds. In other words, they may try to match asset and liability maturities. Such an approach is also called the *maturity-matching approach* or the *self-liquidating approach.*

Whatever the approach followed by a firm, short-term sources of funds are commonly used to finance current assets. Although short-term sources of funds are generally perceived to be riskier than long-term sources, they have certain advantages such as flexibility, low cost, and speed.

Multinational corporations enjoy certain advantages in financing of their working capital requirements. The affiliates of an MNC have a number of financing options that domestic firms do not have. Apart from the usual sources of short-term funds, such as accruals, trade credit, and bank credit, a subsidiary of an MNC can have access to funds from the parent firm and the other subsidiaries.

Accruals are the expenses a firm has already incurred, but not paid. Accruals thus represent a liability that a firm has to pay. Examples are accrued salaries and wages, and accrued taxes. In certain cases, firms may receive advances for goods and services they have agreed to supply in the future. Such receipts, also known as *deferred income,* constitute an important source of financing. Accrued expenses and deferred income are also known as *spontaneous source of financing.* They are cost free in the sense that no explicit interest is paid on these funds. However, firms do not have control over the levels of these funds.

Trade credit is an important source of short-term funds. It refers to the credit that a firm, as a customer, gets from its suppliers of raw materials and components in the normal course of business. Firms that do not have to pay cash immediately for the purchases made, will have trade credit. Trade credit is also a spontaneous source of financing as it arises from ordinary business transactions. It may appear in the form of sundry creditors, accounts payable, bills payable, or notes payable. Suppliers may offer cash discounts besides extending credit to customers. A cash discount is offered as an incentive to customers to pay their dues early. However, a customer firm can avail the cash discount only, if it pays the dues during the early part of the net period. For example, the term "1/8, net 15" indicates that the supplier offers 1 percent discount, if the dues are paid within 8 days; otherwise, the customer-firm must pay the full amount within 15 days. There are three alternative situations for the customer-firm: (i) it avails the cash discount and forgoes the trade credit facility after the early part of the net period; (ii) it does not take a cash discount but pays the dues on the last day of the net period; and (iii) it pays its dues after the net period. The customer-firm must balance the advantages of trade credit against the cost of forgoing a cash discount. Some firms utilize other sources of financing to take advantage of cash discounts. There are, however, certain advantages associated with trade credit as a form of financing. The major advantages are convenience and flexibility.

Short-term unsecured bank credit is another popular source of working capital financing. Commercial banks, especially, may extend unsecured credit to firms under a line of credit, under a revolving credit agreement, or on a transaction basis. A *line of credit* is an informal agreement between a bank and its customer-firm, and specifies the maximum amount of unsecured credit the bank will permit a customer-firm to owe at any time. A *revolving credit agreement* is a formal line of credit under which a bank has a legal obligation to provide credit to a customer. The agreement may be for one to three years. As long as the agreement is in force, the bank must extend credit to the firm whenever the firm wishes to borrow. The total borrowing of the customer-firm should not, however, exceed the maximum amount specified in the agreement. A revolving credit arrangement is useful for firms at times when they are uncertain about their funding requirements. Note that the firm is required to pay a commitment fee on the unused portion of the credit specified in the agreement.

Firms may also avail *bank credit* in the form of overdraft, cash credit, and discounting of bills. Banks sanction working capital loans on the cash flow ability of the firms to repay the credit. They may also extend term credit for a fixed period of time for a specific purpose with specific conditions. The loan provisions are incorporated in the promissory note that is signed by the firm.

Besides the sources of short-term funds we have just discussed, the MNCs can also raise short-term funds by issuing commercial papers. A *commercial paper* is a short-term unsecured promissory note that is generally issued by large firms to institutional investors and other companies on a discount basis. Although the commercial paper is issued at a discount with its full face value redeemed upon maturity in many countries, in some countries it is issued as an interest-bearing instrument. Commercial papers are one of the most favoured short-term financing methods for MNCs across the world.

Summary

1. Management of working capital is the management of the current assets and current liabilities of a firm.
2. Working capital management involves three major decisions with regard to the appropriate level of current assets, the level of investment in each type of current asset, and the sources of working capital.
3. Cash is the most liquid form of asset. Cash management basically involves cash planning and management of cash flows in the business. Management of cash in multinational firms is very complex in view of the movement of funds across national borders.
4. The efficiency of cash management is reflected in the collection and disbursement of cash, as it is in these two areas that cash holdings can be economized.
5. In multilateral netting, each affiliate nets all its inter-firm receipts against all its disbursements and then transfers or receives the balance. Multilateral netting results in a radical reduction in the number of inter-affiliate transfers and thereby minimizes transaction costs.
6. The main objective of receivables management is to maximize the shareholders' value. The major decisions in receivables management are with regard to credit standards, credit terms, and collection efforts.
7. Factoring is a financial innovation that helps firms in their collection efforts. It involves the selling of receivables to an institution that specializes in the administration of sales ledgers and collection of receivables.
8. Inventory management in MNCs is very complex because of overseas inventory, a variety of transportation costs, tariffs and taxes, import controls, and foreign exchange controls. Firms can increase their profitability through efficient and effective management of their inventories.
9. The current assets in a firm are financed by different sources of funds. Short-term sources of funds such as include accruals, trade credit, bank credit, and commercial papers are the chief sources of working capital financing.

Questions and Problems

1. Define working capital. Discuss the decisions that need to be made in managing working capital.
2. What are the advantages and disadvantages of centralized cash management?
3. What is multilateral netting? How does it help in foreign exchange exposure management?
4. What are the objectives of receivables management? How does an MNC determine its credit policy?
5. What are the costs associated with inventory management? How is the optimum level of inventory determined?
6. What are factoring services? How is factoring different from forfaiting?
7. How are the current assets in a firm financed? What are the merits and demerits of trade credit as a method of financing current assets?
8. An MNC has current sales of USD 30 million. To increase sales, the company is considering a more liberal credit policy. The current average collection period is 30 days. If the credit period is extended, the sales are expected to increase in the manner shown in Table 12.5.

Table 12.5 Increase in Sales with Increase in Credit Period

Credit policy	*Increase in credit period*	*Increase in sales (USD million)*
A	20 days	10
B	30 days	15
C	40 days	20

The MNC is selling its products at USD 10 each. The average cost per unit at the current level of sales is USD 7, and the variable cost per unit is USD 5. If the required rate of return on investment is 15 percent, which credit policy is desirable?

9. A U.S.-based MNC has an affiliate in the United Kingdom. The affiliate company has annual sales of GBP 50 million. It sells 90 percent of its products on a 45-day credit period. However, its average collection period is 60 days. The company's bad debts are 1 percent of credit sales. The company incurs GBP 0.50 million annually on credit administration. It is possible to avoid 50 percent of these costs if the company transfers credit administration to a factor. The factor will charge 2 percent commission for its services. The factor will also extend cash advance against receivables at an interest rate of 6 percent after withholding 10 percent as reserve.
   Advise the company on the services of the factor.
10. A London-based MNC has its operations in India. The Indian subsidiary has lost sales many times in the past due to non-availability of the product. The company's average inventory level is INR 500 million. The inventory's carrying cost is 3 percent per annum. The company has a contribution ratio of 40 percent. The firm expects that it will lose sales if the inventory level is less than INR 600 million per annum. The level of inventory and expected lost sales are:

Expected inventory level (INR million)	500	550	600
Expected lost sales (INR million)	100	50	0

   Which inventory policy should the subsidiary firm adopt? Additional data, if necessary, may be assumed.
11. An MNC in India has annual sales of INR 900 million. It has investment opportunities to earn a return of 12 percent per annum. If the company could reduce its float by three days, what would be the company's return?

Multiple-choice Questions

1. Gross working capital refers to ________.
   (a) All current liabilities
   (b) All current assets
   (c) Cash and receivables
   (d) None of these
2. Net working capital is the difference between ________.
   (a) Current assets and current liabilities
   (b) Cash in hand and cash at bank
   (c) Short-term liabilities and long-term liabilities
   (d) None of these

3. Liquidity refers to ability to meet immediate ________.
   (a) Current assets (b) Current liabilities
   (c) Cash obligations (d) None of these
4. Optimum level of working capital is maintained by balancing ________.
   (a) Current assets and current liabilities
   (b) Profitability and liquidity
   (c) Cash and marketable securities
   (d) None of these
5. ________is the most liquid asset in a business.
   (a) Marketable security (b) Cash
   (c) Inventory (d) None of these
6. Efficiency of cash management is reflected in ________
   (a) Cash collection and disbursement
   (b) Current assets
   (c) Current liabilities
   (d) None of these
7. Difference between cash book balance and bank pass book balance is known as________.
   (a) Overdraft (b) Float
   (c) Error (d) None of these
8. Lockboxes are arranged for acceleration of ________
   (a) Cash disbursement
   (b) Cash collection
   (c) Receivables
   (d) None of these
9. A negative balance in the cash book as against a positive balance in the bank pass book is known as ________.
   (a) Collection float (b) Disbursement float
   (c) Mail float (d) None of these
10. The number of cash transactions between affiliates can be reduced by ________
    (a) Netting (b) Issuing cheques
    (c) RTGS (d) None of these
11. In terms of liquidity, ________ come after cash.
    (a) Receivables
    (b) Marketable securities
    (c) Accruals
    (d) None of these
12. Receivables arise from sale of goods and services on ________.
    (a) Credit (b) Cash
    (c) Cheque (d) None of these
13. A high credit standard means that the firm extends credit to ________.
    (a) Individual customers
    (b) Institutional customers
    (c) Select customers
    (d) None of these
14. A liberal credit period results in ________ in receivables.
    (a) High investment (b) Low investment
    (c) No investment (d) None of these
15. If it is without recourse factoring, the________assumes the credit risk.
    (a) Seller
    (b) Factor
    (c) Both seller and factor
    (d) None of these
16. Forfaiting is a method of ________.
    (a) Financing trade
    (b) Financing receivables
    (c) Financing current assets
    (d) None of these
17. Total cost of inventory can be broadly classified into ________.
    (a) Raw material costs and finished goods costs
    (b) Ordering costs and carrying costs
    (c) Carrying cost and cost of work-in-progress
    (d) None of these
18. Matching of assets and liabilities maturities is known as ________.
    (a) Self-liquidating approach
    (b) Aggressive approach
    (c) Conservative approach
    (d) None of these
19. A revolving credit agreement is also known as ________.
    (a) Formal line of credit
    (b) Trade credit
    (c) Bank overdraft
    (d) None of these
20. A commercial paper is a short-term unsecured ________.
    (a) Promissory note (b) Bank deposit
    (c) Cash credit (d) None of these

Case Study

Sun Electronics International is a U.S.-based multinational company with subsidiaries in more than 20 countries. It has a wholly owned subsidiary called Sun Home Appliances Ltd in India, to market its products in India. The subsidiary has more than 500 employees, with annual sales ranging between INR 2,000 million and INR 2,500 million. For the year 2007–08, the subsidiary recorded total sales of INR 2,200 million. It sells the products to retail stores as well as dealers, and it does not maintain any retail or dealer outlet of its own. The company has employed agents in almost all states of India, and their work is to identify the retailers and dealers in their region and provide information about their creditworthiness, sales effort, and goodwill to the company. The agents are paid commission of 1 percent on sales made in their territory.

Almost 90 percent of the company's sales are on credit and the present credit policy of the company allows 60 days credit. But the customers—retailers as well as dealers—hardly ever pay on time, and therefore the effective average collection period is 75 days. The company has a credit department headed by Anand Agarwal, who is an alumnus of Indian Institute of Management in Bangalore. He supervises about 50 employees. The credit department is responsible for monitoring and following up on debtors and maintaining sales ledgers. All the employees are paid monthly salaries and no commission. However, for outstation trips, they are paid travelling and halting allowances. For the year 2007–08, the company has spent INR 15 million on the credit department. In spite of this hugeinvestment in the credit department, the company faces bad debts, the average of which is 5 percent on credit sales.

In view of high bad-debt percentage and increasing average collection period, the company is thinking of an alternative method of credit administration, which includes sales ledger administration and collection of receivables. At this juncture, Full-fledged Factoring Services offers the following package of services at a certain cost:

- It guarantees receivables payment within 60 days.
- It will pay an advance of 85 percent and 90 percent of receivables at an interest rate of 15 percent in case of recourse and non-recourse factoring, respectively.
- It will charge 3 percent and 5 percent as commission in case of recourse and non-recourse factoring, respectively. The commission is payable upfront.
- It will take care of sales ledger administration as well.

The management of Sun Home Appliances Ltd is seriously considering the package offered by the factoring company. If the package is accepted and the agreement is signed, the entire credit department of the company will become redundant.

Analyse the case and advise the company on the best course of action.

Further Reading

1. Collins J. Markham and Alan W. Frankle, "International Cash Management Practices of Large US firms," *Journal of Cash Management* (1985): 42–48.
2. Bokos W. J. and Anne P. Clinkard, "Multilateral Netting," *Journal of Cash Management* (1983): 24–34.
3. Richard K. Goeltz, "Managing Liquid Funds Internationally," *Columbia Journal of World Business* (July–August 1972): 59–65.

CHAPTER 13 International Trade

CHAPTER OBJECTIVES

After studying this chapter, you should be able to:

1 Understand the basics of international trade.
2 Discuss the evolution and structure of the World Trade Organization (WTO).
3 Analyse the trends in world trade over the years.
4 Gain insights into India's external sector.
5 Gain an overview of modes of payment in international trade
6 Discuss institutional export credit in India.
7 Examine the role of the Export-Import (Exim) Bank and the Export Credit Guarantee Corporation (ECGC).

Introduction

Globalization has become a buzzword all over the world. Today, every country and every institution is talking about globalization. Although globalization means many things to many people, it is often referred to as the process of integrating world economies. When people talk about globalization, they mean globalization of markets, globalization of production, or both. Globalization of markets refers to the integration of national markets into a global market. Similarly, globalization of production refers to the establishment of production facilities across the globe in order to take advantage of national differences in the cost and quality of factors of production.

International trade is one of the vehicles through which globalization can be achieved. Trade, whether domestic or international, was traditionally based on the principles of division of labour and specialization. A country that acquires specialization in the production of a product or a commodity will trade with a country that specializes in the production of some other product or commodity. For example, trade between India and the United Kingdom was based on India's specialization in cotton textiles and the United Kingdom's specialization in steel. Trade between any two countries is based on the same principle, and so is the domestic trade (trade between various regions within a country).

International trade is not a recent phenomenon. People throughout the world have been trading in commodities produced by others since the beginning of civilization. However, globalization has led to an increasing number of countries taking part in the world trade in a large measure. Globalization of trade has facilitated the volume and value of world exports and imports to increase at a phenomenal rate.

Although there are certain basic similarities between the domestic trade and the international trade, international trade is always a complex phenomenon involving many different procedures and risks. In other words, international trade is subject to several rules and restrictions like quota systems and foreign exchange regulations. Further, in international trade, the traders—both the exporters and the importers—have to carry out operations in an alien environment. They may not be familiar with each other, or with the environment in which they have to operate. Therefore, they may have to face several kinds of risks including credit risk, political risk, and currency risk. These risks tend to increase, if the foreign markets are not well developed and the countries don't have political stability.

Theories of International Trade

There are many theories of international trade, and the prominent ones are briefly discussed in this section. The first theory of international trade, which emerged in the sixteenth century, came to be known as *mercantilism*. The doctrine of mercantilism is that gold and silver constitute the national wealth of a country. Therefore, nations should always strive to accumulate as much gold and silver as possible. As gold and silver are also the currency of international trade, export of goods by a country would result in the inflow of gold and silver, and import of goods by a country would cause an outflow of gold and silver from the country. Therefore, a country should always have a favourable balance of trade in order to maintain more reserves of gold and silver. To maintain a favourable balance of trade, which translates into more exports and fewer imports, a country should encourage exports by offering incentives to exporters, and discourage imports by imposing restrictions like tariffs and quotas on imports.

Another theory that came into prominence in the eighteenth century was *the theory of absolute advantage*. Advocated by Adam Smith, the theory of absolute advantage postulates that countries differ in their capacity to produce goods efficiently. This might be due to factors such as better manufacturing processes and favourable climatic conditions. A country can have an absolute advantage in the production of a particular product when it is more efficient than any other country in producing it. According to this theory, a country should specialize in the production of product(s) in which it has an absolute advantage, and trade these products for products produced by other countries. This implies that a country should never produce a product it can buy at a lower price from other countries.

David Ricardo further developed the theory of absolute advantage. Countries basically differ in the availability of resources. No country is rich in every resource, and no country is poor in all resources. Depending on the availability of resources (labour, capital, or natural resources), each country tends to produce those products or commodities that are best suited to its resources. According to Ricardo, a country should specialize in the production of products that it can produce *most efficiently* and trade them for products produced by other countries, even if it could produce these products *more efficiently* itself. This theory came to be known as Ricardo's *theory of comparative advantage* and is regarded in economic literature as a proponent of free trade. Comparative advantage arises not only with factor endowments, but also with efficient use of productive factors. According to this theory, all nations that participate in international trade will realize economic benefits, as trade is a positive-sum game and not a zero-sum game.

The *Heckscher–Ohlin theory* is another international trade theory that argues that a country can have a comparative advantage only with national factor endowments. Nations differ in factor endowments such as land, labour, and capital and, therefore, differ in factor costs too. Hence, the pattern of international trade depends on differences in factor endowments rather than differences in production efficiency (or productivity).

Another international trade theory, known as the *new trade theory,* advocates that countries become specialized in the production of certain products, and thereby attain the economies of scale. This lowers the cost of production. First movers (first to produce that product) will naturally get the advantages of economies of scale. Each country should, therefore, specialize in the production of a small range of products, and buy the other products it requires from other countries. The implication of the new trade theory is that a variety of products will be available to consumers at low prices. Thus, international trade offers an opportunity for mutual gain for nations despite their differences in factor endowments.

The national competitive advantage theory propounded by Michael Porter is the latest in the major theories of international trade. According to Porter, four attributes of a country provide the environment in which firms can have competitive advantage. The four attributes, which form a diamond, are: factor endowments; demand conditions; related and supporting industries; and the firm's strategy, structure, and rivalry. Factor endowments include skilled labour, research facilities, communication infrastructure, and technological know-how. The pattern of international trade is influenced by these four attributes of a nation.

A look at the major theories of international trade reminds us of the following benefits of international trade:

- International trade leads to specialization and division of labour, which confers benefits on all the countries participating in international trade.
- Free international trade always leads to the expansion of the world's supply of goods and services.
- Through international trade, scarce resources can be equitably distributed among all countries.
- International trade leads to reduction in the cost per unit of the output because of economies of scale.
- International trade equalizes the prices of not only final goods and services but also of the factors of production in all countries.

It should, however, be noted that these gains depend on several factors, which include the terms of trade, elasticity of demand, competition in the international market, and the scope for improvement of productivity.

World Trade Organization

The recommendations of the Bretton Woods Conference in 1944 envisaged the establishment of three institutions: the International Monetary Fund, or the IMF (for fiscal and monetary issues); the World Bank (for financial and structural issues); and the International Trade Organization, or the ITO (for international economic cooperation). Accordingly, the World Bank and the International Monetary Fund were established immediately after the Conference. As far as the establishment of the ITO was concerned, the United Nations Economic and Social Council adopted a resolution in February 1946, calling for a conference to draft a charter for an international trade organization. Over 50 countries participated in the conference and decided to create an international trade organization as a specialized agency of the United Nations. The draft ITO Charter extended beyond world trade disciplines, to include rules on employment, commodity agreements, restrictive business practices, international investment, and services. In March 1948, the negotiations on the Charter were completed in Havana. The Charter set out the basic rules for international trade and provided for the establishment of the International Trade Organization. Meanwhile, in December 1945, the United States invited its wartime allies to enter into negotiations to conclude a multilateral agreement for the reciprocal reduction of tariffs on trade in goods. The first round of negotiations resulted in a package of trade rules and tariff concessions. On 30 October 1947, twenty-three countries signed the Protocol of Provisional Application of the General Agreement on Tariffs and Trade (GATT). On 21 November 1947, the Havana conference began and the ITO Charter was finally agreed in the conference in March 1948. But the ITO Charter was not ratified by many countries, including the United States, on the ground that the ITO would be involved in internal economic issues. In other words, the ITO was effectively dead. In the absence of an international organization for trade, GATT functioned as a *de facto* international trade organization, and helped create a strong multilateral trading system.

***Tariffs** are taxes levied on goods moved between nations, and non-tariff barriers are other measures that restrict international trade.*

There are two types of barriers that the governments may impose to restrict foreign trade. These are tariff barriers and non-tariff barriers. **Tariffs** are the taxes levied on goods moved between nations. They are in the form of customs duty, export tax, and so on. Different countries handle tariff barriers differently. *Non-tariff* barriers include quotas, import equalization taxes, laws giving preferential treatment to domestic suppliers, administration of anti-dumping measures, exchange controls, and a variety of invisible tariffs that restrict international trade.

The GATT was an agreement as well as an institution. As an institution, it made several efforts to reduce existing tariffs and trade barriers through a series of multilateral negotiations known as "trade rounds." Between 1947 and 1979, seven rounds of GATT-sponsored negotiations were held. The first round, which was held in Geneva on tariffs, began in April 1947 and lasted for seven months. About 23 countries participated in the multilateral negotiations. The seventh round, known as the Tokyo Round, lasted from 1973 to 1979 with 102 countries participating. It made an attempt for the first time to reduce non-tariff barriers. The first seven rounds of negotiations resulted in average tariffs on manufacturing goods in developed countries being brought down from 40 percent to 5 percent and the volume of trade in manufactured goods multiplied more than twenty-fold. GATT membership also increased. However, it was found that GATT was no longer as relevant to the realities of world trade as it had been in the 1940s. World trade had become far more complex and important than 40 years before the globalization of the world economy was underway. Further, the GATT rules did not adequately cover trading in services, investments abroad, or intellectual property rights, which were of growing importance to many countries. In the textiles and clothing area, negotiations were held outside GATT, leading to the Multi-fiber Arrangement. The GATT was thus found wanting in many respects. It was against this backdrop that 90 countries unanimously agreed to the U.S. proposal to launch a new round of global trade talks, eighth in the negotiations series.

The eighth round of negotiations was held in September 1986 in Punta de Este, Uruguay. This round, with the participation of 123 countries, lasted for 18 months. The main subjects for the Uruguay Round were tariffs, non-tariff measures, rules, services, intellectual property, dispute settlement, textiles, agriculture, and the creation of a World Trade Organization (WTO). In the eighth round of negotiations, many new areas were included. Agriculture, a controversial area mainly due to proposed reductions in agricultural subsidies, was included for the first time in GATT. Other new areas were Trade-Related Aspects of Intellectual Property Rights (TRIPS), Trade-Related Investment Measures (TRIMS), and General Agreement on Trade in Services (GATS). The eighth round also aimed at strengthening GATT by removing ambiguity in the rules and improving the enforcement powers of GATT. The Uruguay Round is historically significant as it culminated in the creation of the WTO. The eighth round also led to major reduction in tariffs (about 40 percent).

The eighth round of multilateral negotiations is characterized by many important events such as the participation of many developing countries in trade negotiations and coverage of many important new areas such as agriculture, textiles, services, TRIMS, and TRIPS. It was in this round of negotiations that a comprehensive view was taken of the tariff and non-tariff barriers to trade, with a view to taking world trade to a free trading environment.

The Uruguay Round, which was supposed to end in December 1990, finally ended in November 1992. However, it was only on 15 April 1994 that the agreements were signed by the ministers from most of the 123 participating governments at a meeting in Marrakech, Morocco. It included about 60 agreements, structured into six parts: the agreement for establishing the WTO; agreements for each of the three broad areas of trade that the WTO covers; dispute settlement; and reviews of governments' trade policies. As per the agreements, the WTO came into being on 1 January 1995, and it has since replaced the GATT.

The WTO is run by its member governments and all major decisions are made by the membership as a whole. The primary objective of the WTO is to expand international trade by liberalizing trade to bring about all-round economic prosperity. The important functions of the WTO are to:

- oversee the implementation, administration, and operation of the covered agreements.
- provide a forum for negotiations and for settling disputes.

The rules of the WTO are known as the agreements that emanate from the negotiations between members. The agreements are essentially contracts, binding governments to keep their trade policies within agreed limits. It is ensured that individuals, companies, and governments know what the trade rules are around the world. They are given confidence that the rules are transparent and predictable. The overriding purpose is to help trade flow as freely as possible—so long as there are no undesirable side effects.

The WTO agreements cover goods, services, and intellectual property. The agreements spell out the principles of liberalization, and the permitted exceptions. They set procedures for settling disputes. The agreements are not static and are renegotiated from time to time. New agreements are also added as required. The next round of multilateral negotiations started in November 2001 at the WTO in Doha, but is yet to be concluded. The major subjects of discussion are tariffs, non-tariff measures, agriculture, labour standards, environment, competition, investment, transparency, and patents. The three mega agreements that are currently being negotiated are the Trans Pacific Partnership (TPP), the Trans Atlantic Trade and Investment Partnership (TTIP) and the Regional Comprehensive Economic Partnership (RCEP). The WTO agreements contain special provision for developing countries, including longer time periods to implement agreements and commitments, measures to increase their trading opportunities, and support to help them build their trade capacity, to handle disputes and to implement technical standards.

In the words of the WTO, "a country should not discriminate between its trading partners and it should not discriminate between its own and foreign products, services, or nationals. Lowering trade barriers is one of the most obvious ways of encouraging trade. Foreign companies, investors, and governments should be confident that trade barriers should not be raised arbitrarily. With stability and predictability, investment is encouraged, jobs are created, and consumers can fully enjoy the benefits of competition—choice and lower prices".

The Structure of the WTO

The organizational structure of the WTO in terms of various levels of authority is briefed here as under:

- *The highest level of authority:* The Ministerial Conference is the highest decision-making body of the WTO. It makes all important decisions, particularly on matters under any of the multilateral trade agreements. It meets at least every two years.
- *The second level of authority:* The General Council, the Dispute Settlement Body, and the Trade Policy Review Body handle the daily work of the Ministerial Conference as

the second level of authority of the WTO. The General Council has representatives (usually ambassadors or equivalents) from all member governments and acts on behalf of the Ministerial Conference on all WTO affairs. The Dispute Settlement Body consists of all member governments, usually represented by ambassadors or equivalents. The General Council of WTO also meets as the Trade Policy Review Body whenever trade policy reviews need to be made.

- *The third level of authority:* There are three trade councils of the WTO—(i) the Council for Trade in Goods, (ii) the Council for TRIPS, and (iii) the Council for Trade in Services—which constitute the third level of authority. Besides these three councils, six other bodies report to the General Council on issues such as trade and development, the environment, regional trading arrangements, and administrative issues.
- *The fourth level of authority:* The fourth level consists of subsidiary bodies under each of the three councils that constitute the third level of authority. The Goods Council is the subsidiary under the Council for Trade in Goods. It has 11 committees consisting of all member countries, dealing with specific subjects such as agriculture, market access, subsidies, and anti-dumping measures. The Dispute Settlement Panels and the Appellate Body are the subsidiaries under the Council for Trade-Related Aspects of Intellectual Property Rights. The Dispute Settlement Panels and Appellate Body are constituted to resolve disputes and to deal with appeals, respectively. The Services Council is the subsidiary under the Council for Trade in Services. It deals with financial services, domestic regulations, and other specific commitments.

Principles of the Trading System

The WTO sets a framework for international trade policies based on the principles of non-discrimination, reciprocity, and transparency:

- *Non-discrimination:* The principle of non-discrimination is the foremost principle on which international trade policies are based. The principle of non-discrimination has two components—the Most Favoured Nation (MFN) rule and the National Treatment Policy. The MFN rule states that no country can normally discriminate between its trading partners. In other words, if a special favour (e.g., lower customs duty rate) is granted by a country to some other country, the same should be extended to all other WTO members. Thus, each member of the WTO treats all the other members equally, as 'most favoured' trading partners. Article 1 of GATT ensures that each country treats all member countries equally. However, some exceptions are allowed. For example, countries can set up a free trade agreement that applies only to goods traded within the group—discriminating against goods from outside. Countries can also give developing countries special access to their markets. A country can also raise barriers against products that are considered to be traded unfairly from specific countries. These exceptions are allowed only under strict conditions. The exceptions are allowed in services too, but in limited circumstances. The MFN rule is also a priority article in the GATS and TRIPS agreements. The National Treatment Policy states that a country should give others the same treatment as it gives its own nationals. According to Article 3 of GATT, foreigners and locals, or imported and locally produced goods should be treated equally. However, national treatment only applies once a product, service, or item of intellectual property has entered the market. For example, charging customs duty on an import is not a violation of national treatment, even if domestic products are not charged an equivalent tax. National treatment is also found in all the three main WTO agreements (Article 3 of GATT, Article 17 of GATS, and Article 3 of TRIPS).

- *Reciprocity:* According to the principle of reciprocity, for a nation to negotiate, it is necessary that the gain from doing so be greater than the gain from unilateral liberalization. Reciprocal concessions intend to ensure that such gains will materialize.
- *Transparency:* The members of the WTO are obliged to maintain transparency in their trade dealings. They are required to publish their trade regulations and also to respond to requests for information by other members.

Trends in World Trade

As a result of an open trading system based on multilateral agreements, world trade has registered a phenomenal growth over the last 25 years. As can be observed from Table 13.1, the value of world total exports increased from USD 6,356,563 million in 2000 to USD 15,098,934 million in 2010 to USD 18,459,279 million in 2013. This is about a three-fold increase in 2013 over the year 2000. The value of world total imports also increased from USD 6,521,536 million in 2000 to 15,166,963 million in 2010 to USD 18,401,453 million in 2013. Thus, there is a 2.8-fold increase in the world total imports in 2013 over the year 2000. It can be further observed that more than 50 percent of the world trade is registered by developed countries. Table 13.2 lists out the leading select exporters and importers in world merchandize trade in 2013. It can be observed from the table that China accounts

Table 13.1 Value of World Trade (USD million)

Area	*Total exports*			*Total imports*		
	2000	*2010*	*2013*	*2000*	*2010*	*2013*
World	6,356,563	15,098,934	18,459,279	6,521,536	15,166,963	18,401,453
Developed countries	4,131,930	7,995,847	9,201,229	4,497,925	8,635,733	9,871,054
Asia-Pacific	557,030	1,014,420	1,008,739	465,262	925,893	1,114,910
Europe	2,515,996	5,314,924	6,154,222	2,533,386	5,345,998	5,961,888

Source: International Trade Statistics Year Book 2013.

Table 13.2 Leading Select Exporters and Importers in World Merchandize Trade 2013 (USD billion)

Country	*Exports*		*Imports*	
	Value	*Share (%)*	*Value*	*Share (%)*
China	2,209	11.7	1,950	10.3
USA	1,580	8.4	2,329	12.3
Germany	1,453	7.7	1,189	6.3
Japan	715	3.8	833	4.4
Netherlands	672	3.6	590	3.1
France	580	3.1	681	3.6
Korea, Republic	560	3.0	516	2.7
UK	542	2.9	655	3.5
Russian Federation	523	2.8	343	1.8

(Continued)

Table 13.2 ***(Continued)***

Country	*Exports*		*Imports*	
	Value	*Share (%)*	*Value*	*Share (%)*
Singapore	410	2.2	373	2.0
Mexico	380	2.0	391	2.1
Brazil	242	1.3	250	1.3
India	313	1.7	466	2.5

Source: International Trade Statistics Year Book 2013.

for 11.7 percent share in the world merchandize exports, followed by the U.S. (8.4%), and Germany (7.7%). As far as merchandize imports are concerned, the U.S. accounts for 12.3 percent share, followed by China (10.3%), and Germany (6.3%).

An overall glance at the figures of the world trade reveals that the liberalization and globalization of trade have enabled many countries to participate in the world trade at an increasing rate. Although the share of India in total world trade has also increased over time, it is minuscule.

India's External Sector

India, though big in size, plays a relatively small role in the world trade. Till 1980s, the Government of India had not considered exports as a priority item of international trade. It believed that trade was biased against developing countries, and the prospects for export trade were limited. Therefore, the Government of India mainly aimed at achieving self-sufficiency in most products through import substitution, with exports covering the cost of residual import requirements. Foreign trade was subjected to strict government controls, which consisted of an all-inclusive system of foreign exchange and direct controls over imports and exports. As a result, India's share in the world trade fell drastically from 2.4 percent in 1951 to 0.4 percent in 1980. During this period, the country also faced serious difficulties in balance of payments. It was during these times that the Government of India revised its foreign trade policy, giving priority to exports. In a bid to improve its commercial presence in the world, India also signed bilateral agreements with many countries. All such policy measures have resulted in an increase in India's share in the world exports.

India's merchandise exports increased from USD 300.4 billion in 2012–13 to USD 312.6 billion in 2013–14. The rise of 4.1 percent can primarily be attributed to the turnaround in the exports of manufactured goods, particularly, engineering goods and textile products. Improved global activity and a rise in the world trade have revived India's export performance in 2013–14. OECD countries are the largest export destination, constituting about 35 percent. The developing countries account for 41.5 percent of India's merchandize exports in 2013–14. India's exports to the U.S. constitute about 12.5 percent of India's merchandise exports in 2013–14.

India's merchandise imports declined from USD 490.7 billion in 2012–13 to USD 450.1 billion in 2013–14. The decline in imports could be attributed to curbs on gold imports and weaker domestic demand for non-oil and non-gold imports in 2013–14. Oil imports constitute about 36 percent of total merchandize imports in 2013–14. India's imports from OECD countries constitute about 25.6 percent of total merchandize imports in 2013–14. China is the main source of imports for India accounting for 11.3 percent of total merchandize imports during 2013–14. Saudi Arabia is the second largest source country for India's imports in 2013–14, followed by UAE, U.S., Iraq, and Switzerland.

Foreign Trade Policy 2009–14 The Foreign Trade Policy of 2009–14 was announced following the global recession which affected the countries across the world in varying degrees, and all major economic indicators like industrial production, trade, capital flows, unemployment, per capita investment, and consumption, which had taken a hit.

The long-term policy objective is to double India's share in global trade by 2020. The short-term objectives are to arrest and reverse the declining trend of exports and to provide additional support especially to those sectors which have been hit badly by recession in the developed world. To meet these objectives, the Government would follow a mix of policy measures including fiscal incentives, institutional changes, procedural rationalization, enhanced market access across the world, and diversification of export markets. The Government would strive to improve the infrastructure related to exports, bring down transaction costs, and provide full refund of all indirect taxes and levies. The other salient features of the Foreign Trade Policy are briefly mentioned as below:

- Initiatives to diversify export markets and offset the inherent disadvantages for exporters in emerging markets.
- Diversifying products and markets through rationalization of incentive schemes including the enhancement of incentive rates.
- New emerging markets are given special focus to enable competitive exports.
- Additional resources are made available under the Market Development Assistance Scheme and Market Access Initiative Scheme.
- Government seeks to promote Brand India through 'Made in India' shows.
- For up-gradation of export sector infrastructure, 'Towns of Export Excellence' and units located therein would be granted additional focused support and incentives.
- The policy is committed to support the growth of project exports.
- The policy would encourage production and export of 'green products' through measures such as phased manufacturing programmes for green vehicles, zero-duty EPCG scheme and incentives for exports.

Foreign Trade Policy 2015–20 The Government of India announced its latest Foreign Trade Policy (2015-20) on 1 April 2015. The focus of the Policy is to provide a framework of rules and procedures for exports and imports and a set of incentives for promoting exports. It seeks to achieve the following objectives.

- To provide a stable and sustainable policy environment for foreign trade in merchandise and services;
- To link rules, procedures and incentives for exports and imports with other initiatives such as "Make in India", "Digital India" and "Skills India" to create an Export Promotion Mission for India;
- To promote the diversification of India's export basket by helping various sectors of the Indian economy to gain global competitiveness with a view to promoting exports;
- To create an architecture for India's global trade engagement with a view to expanding its markets and better integrating with major regions, thereby increasing the demand for India's products and contributing to the government's flagship "Make in India" initiative;
- To provide a mechanism for regular appraisal in order to rationalise imports and reduce the trade imbalance.

The measures envisaged to achieve the objectives are to:

- Help improve India's export competitiveness and deepen engagements with new markets;

- Operationalise institutional mechanisms in existing bilateral and regional trade agreements;
- Deepen and widen the export basket;
- Reduce transaction costs;
- Make efforts to reduce the cost of export credit;
- Help improve infrastructure;
- Promote product standards, packaging and branding of Indian products;
- Rationalise tax incidence - introduce the Goods and Services Tax (GST);
- Help improve manufacturing by mainstreaming exports;
- Incentivise potential winners for promising markets;
- Promote and diversify services exports; and
- Mainstream States and Ministries in India's export strategy.

The Foreign Trade Policy is based on certain principles, such as encouraging the export of labour intensive products, agricultural products, high tech products with high export earning potential and eco-friendly and green products and work on focused market diversification. Technology intensive manufacturing will be supported. Other focus areas are defence, pharma, environment friendly products, products meeting BIS standards and technical textile related products.

The schemes for trade promotion, viz. the Market Access Initiative (MAI) Scheme and the Market Development Assistance Scheme will continue. The new Policy seeks to introduce two new schemes. They are the Merchandise Exports from India Scheme (MEIS) for export of specified goods to specified markets: and the Services Exports from India Scheme (SEIS) for increasing exports of notified services. These would replace multiple schemes earlier in place, each with different conditions for eligibility and usage of scrips.

International Trade Finance

The price of merchandise or services is determined by both the exporter and the importer through negotiations. Once the price is determined, the next issue is how the payment should be made. The exporter and the importer should decide the method that will be used to make the payment for the imports. In general, there are five methods of payment in international trade: (i) advance payment (cash in advance), (ii) letter of credit, (iii) bill of exchange (draft), (iv) consignment, and (v) open account. Each of these methods is discussed here.

Advance Payment

If the importer pays the exporter before the merchandise is shipped or transported, such payment is known as *advance payment* or *cash in advance or prepayment*. This method is particularly used when the creditworthiness of the importer is not known to the exporter. Also, where the goods are made to order, the exporter may demand cash in advance. This method of payment gives full protection to the exporter against risks like credit risk, country risk, and currency risk. However, this is not a common mode of payment as importers may not always be ready to make prepayments. Cash payment upon arrival of the merchandise or upon the submission of certain documents is very common.

Banker's Letter of Credit

In international trade, the parties (exporter and importer) involved are in different countries, and they may not know each other well. So, the exporter normally expects the importer to pay cash on receipt of the goods, if not in advance. On the other hand, the importer usually expects the exporter to extend credit. When extending credit to the importer becomes inevitable, the exporter may wish to have the importer's promise of payment, backed by a bank. In other words, the exporter may like to have an undertaking by a bank for the payment of goods sold on credit to the importer. Such an undertaking is called the banker's letter of credit or simply the letter of credit. A **banker's letter of credit (L/C)** is an instrument or letter issued by a bank on behalf of, and for the account of the buyer or importer of the merchandise. By issuing a letter of credit, the importer's bank (issuing bank) agrees to pay the amount directly to the exporter, provided the bill of lading and other documents (e.g. the commercial invoice) are in order. Such payment is known as payment at sight. The letter of credit also confers on the exporter the right to draw bills of exchange on the issuing bank against shipments made by him. Thus, the issuing bank substitutes its creditworthiness for that of the importer who is its customer.

*A **letter of credit (L/C)** is an instrument or letter issued by a bank on behalf of and for the account of the buyer, or the importer, of the merchandise.*

To understand the procedure involved in issuing a letter of credit, let us consider the following example. Assume that a lesser-known Indian company wants to buy certain goods from a company in the U.S. It places a purchase order with the company. Simultaneously, the Indian company approaches its bank (State Bank of India) in Mumbai for a letter of credit for USD 2 million. The State Bank of India (SBI) issues the letter of credit for USD 2 million to the U.S. company through its local bank (American Express Bank). On notification of the letter of credit, the U.S. company ships the goods to the Indian company. As soon as the exporter has shipped the goods and presented the stipulated documents to the bank, it is entitled to the value of the shipment. The importer who requests a bank to open a letter of credit is known as the *accredited buyer.* The exporter in whose favour the letter of credit is established, is referred to as the *beneficiary* of the letter of credit. The letter of credit is thus the contract between the issuing bank and the beneficiary of the letter of credit (exporter). As the exporter further proceeds through its local bank, it first requests the bank to confirm the letter of credit issued in its favour. Subsequently, the U.S. company makes a draft (bill of exchange) on SBI for USD 2 million, and sends the draft along with shipping documents and the letter of credit to SBI through American Express Bank. The SBI accepts the draft and remits USD 2 million to the U.S. company through American Express Bank. Further, the SBI forwards the shipping documents and other details of the loan to the Indian company. Since ultimately it is the accredited buyer who has to reimburse the amount paid by the issuing bank under the L/C, the Indian company pays the amount to SBI on maturity of the draft. Since the State Bank of India has undertaken to honour the specified liability on presentation of stipulated documents, it has a contingent liability from the time it established the credit. Thus, the letter of credit has assured the U.S. company that it will receive payment for the goods it ships to the Indian company, and thereby facilitated international trade.

The exporter may also approach his bank (correspondent bank or advising bank) for a loan on the letter of credit. If the exporter's bank is satisfied with the creditworthiness of the bank that has issued the letter of credit, it will obligate itself to honour the bills drawn in accordance with the letter of credit arrangement. Sometimes, another bank may also be involved in a letter of credit as the confirming bank. The *confirming bank* is generally a bank situated in the beneficiary's country. The confirming bank adds its confirmation to the letter of credit at the request of the issuing bank and further confirms the obligation to pay or accept or negotiate. The liability of the confirming bank is a primary liability, and it becomes a principal obligator along with the issuing bank.

Generally, the importer must have a running account at the issuing bank, which can be drawn upon for payments against the letter of credit. Even if the bank account does not have enough balance, the issuing bank is obliged to pay the exporter against the letter of credit. But whatever payments the issuing bank makes to the beneficiary of the letter of credit, the importer is responsible for repaying the bank both the principal and the interest.

A letter of credit can be any of the following kinds:

- *Revocable letter of credit:* In the case of a revocable letter of credit, the undertaking given by the bank can be withdrawn or the conditions can be changed at any time unilaterally by the issuing bank, and the exporter can do nothing about it even though he may have shipped the goods in accordance with the terms and conditions of the letter of credit. Therefore, this type of letter of credit is not favoured by the beneficiary.
- *Irrevocable letter of credit:* The irrevocable letter of credit cannot be cancelled unilaterally by the issuing bank, nor can its terms and conditions be varied without the consent of the beneficiary. An irrevocable letter of credit can be considered as a definite undertaking by the issuing bank.
- *Red-clause letter of credit:* A letter of credit may also contain a special clause incorporated in red ink, under which another bank, called the negotiating bank, is authorized to grant an advance to the beneficiary on behalf of the issuing bank. The issuing bank will be liable for such credit extended by the negotiating bank, in case the beneficiary fails to repay or deliver the documents for negotiation. The negotiating bank is the bank that negotiates the documents under the letter of credit. It may be a branch of the issuing bank or the beneficiary's bank. The clause may also stipulate the security required for such advances (e.g. warehouse receipts).
- *Back-to-back letter of credit:* This is a domestic letter of credit issued on the strength of a foreign letter of credit. A back-to-back letter of credit is issued by a local bank in favour of a supplier of the beneficiary. For example, a firm in Chennai is the beneficiary of a letter of credit. It requests the negotiating bank to issue a back-to-back letter of credit in favour of a firm in Delhi, which supplies certain components to it. This is an example of a back-to-back letter of credit. It is important to note that the terms and conditions of the back-to-back letter of credit must match the terms and conditions of the original foreign letter of credit, and the amount of the back-to-back letter of credit must be less than the amount of the original foreign letter of credit.
- *Standby letter of credit:* In case the importer fails to pay the invoice amount to the exporter as agreed, then the standby letter of credit comes into effect. That is, when the importer fails to pay the amount to the exporter as per the terms and conditions of the sale, the exporter may use the letter of credit to obtain payment from the issuing bank. Such a letter of credit is known as standby letter of credit. Thus, a standby letter of credit serves as a performance bond to ensure that the importer will make the payment to the exporter as agreed.

A letter of credit offers certain benefits to the exporter. The important benefits are:

- As the issuing bank generally is a reputed bank, the credit risk for the exporter is taken care of. The letter of credit is as good as cash in advance.
- Country risk or political risk is avoided as the political factors within the country will not deter the issuing bank from honouring its commitment. In other words, the letter of credit protects the exporter from the risk of trade controls or exchange rate controls imposed by the government of the importer.
- There is no uncertainty of payment towards the goods sold to the unknown buyer abroad. So, the exporter can focus on manufacturing the product.
- The exporter can get easy and immediate credit by drawing a bill on the importer's bank that has issued the letter of credit. The exporter's bank may also be more ready to extend credit as the letter of credit assures the ultimate availability of funds for the repayment of the loan. In other words, the letter of credit assures the availability of

Example 13.1

An Indian firm wishes to import machinery from the United Kingdom at a cost of GBP 5 million. The firm can avail a bank loan in India at 12 percent interest rate per annum. There is also a facility to obtain 180-days credit at 3 percent rate of interest per annum by opening an irrevocable letter of credit. The firm is also required to pay a commission of 1 percent for the L/C facility. The current spot rate is GBP/INR 75 and 180-day forward rate is GBP/INR 75.75. Advise the firm on this issue.

Solution

Cost of the machine: GBP 5 million
Bank loan required: GBP 5 million × INR 75 = INR 375 million
Interest for six months: INR 375 million × 0.06 = INR 22.5 million
Total payments after 180 days: INR 375 million + INR 22.5 million = INR 397.5 million

The other alternative for the firm is to avail the irrevocable letter of credit facility. In such a case, the commitments will be:

- Interest: GBP 5 million × 0.015 = GBP 0.075 million
- Commission charges: GBP 5 million × 1 percent = GBP 0.05 million
- Total payment after 180 days: GBP 5.125 million (i.e., GBP 5 million + GBP 0.075 million + GBP 0.05 million)
- Forward rate: GBP/INR 75.75
- Indian currency required after 180 days: GBP 5.125 million × INR 75.75 = INR 388.22 million

Therefore, the firm is advised to opt for the irrevocable letter of credit facility.

funds to the exporter for preparation or purchase of the goods which he has contracted to sell.

- The terms and conditions including the documents required are clearly stated in the letter of credit. This facilitates easy financing for the exporter.

The letter of credit may also benefit the importer on whose behalf the letter of credit is issued by the bank. Without the funds of the importer being locked up as cash in advance, the importer will have all the advantages (e.g. cash discount/price reduction) of having paid cash in advance to the exporter, because the letter of credit is as good as the payment of cash in advance. Even if the importer is required to deposit some money with his bank for issuing letter of credit, that deposit may fetch some return, and is safer than the payment of cash in advance to the unknown exporter.

Bill of Exchange (Draft)

A **bill of exchange**, also known as a *trade draft* or simply a *draft,* is an important and widely used document in trade financing. According to Section 5 of the Indian Negotiable Instruments Act 1881, the bill of exchange is an instrument in writing containing an unconditional order, signed by the maker, directing a certain person to pay a certain sum of money only to, or to the order of, a certain person or to the bearer of the instrument. In international trade, the exporter writes or draws the bill of exchange on the importer for the invoiced amount. By drawing a bill on the importer, the exporter is extending credit to the importer for the period specified in the bill. Once the bill of exchange is signed by both the parties—the exporter and the importer—it becomes an unconditional order for the importer to pay on demand, or at a fixed date, the amount specified in the bill. Usually, there are two

*A **bill of exchange** is an instrument in writing containing an unconditional order signed by its maker, directing a certain person to pay a certain sum of money to, or to the order of, a certain person, or to the bearer of the instrument.*

parties involved in a bill of exchange. They are the drawer and the drawee (the acceptor) of the bill. The *drawer* of the bill is the creditor who writes the bill of exchange on the debtor and puts his signature on it. On the other hand, the *drawee* is the debtor who accepts the bill drawn on him by the drawer. In some cases, there is another party called the *payee*. The payee is a person to whom payment of the bill is to be made on demand or on the maturity date of the bill.

Bills of exchange are of different kinds. One classification divides them into inland and foreign bills of exchange. In the case of an *inland bill of exchange,* both the drawer and the drawee of the bill are within the home country. A bill that is not both drawn and payable within the home country is a *foreign bill of exchange.* Another classification of bills of exchange divides them into a clean bill of exchange and a documentary bill of exchange. A bill of exchange is a *clean bill,* if it is not accompanied by any document such as a bill of lading or an insurance policy. A bill of exchange is referred to as *documentary,* if it is accompanied by such documents as a bill of lading, commercial invoice, consular invoice, or insurance certificate. Foreign bills of exchange are mostly documentary bills. Yet another category of bills of exchange is a *sight bill* and a *time* or *usance bill. Sight bills* of exchange are those that are payable upon presentation, at sight, or on demand. A usance bill refers to a bill that is payable at a fixed future time. When the exporter ships the goods to the importer under a sight bill, the importer's bank will not release the shipping documents to the importer until the bill is paid. This is known as *documents against payment* (D/P). When the exporter ships the goods to the importer under a usance bill, the shipping documents will be released by the buyer's bank on acceptance of the bill of exchange by the importer. This is referred to *documents against acceptance* (D/A). Further, there are two types of acceptances: commercial acceptance and banker's acceptance. A time bill of exchange that is drawn on and duly accepted by a commercial enterprise (individuals or firms) is known as a *commercial acceptance* or *trade acceptance.* When the importer's bank accepts the bill of exchange drawn by the exporter, it becomes a negotiable money market instrument called a *banker s acceptance,* for which there is a secondary market.

Usually, the exporter employs a bank as a collection agent or intermediary. The bank (either directly or through a branch, or correspondent bank) collects on the bill of exchange and remits the proceeds to the exporter. When the bank sends the bill of exchange to its foreign correspondent for collection, the exporter has to wait till the bank realizes the amount and credits the customer's account with the same. However, in some circumstances the exporter may request the bank for an advance against such bills during the intervening period. The bank may also provide immediate finance to the exporter by discounting the bills of exchange. Thus, the exporter may hold the bill of exchange to maturity and collect the bill amount at that time. Alternatively, the exporter may discount the bill with a bank and realize the money, or sell it in the secondary market. Unless the bill is sold, the exporter assumes all the risk involved in honouring the bill of exchange. The payment of the bill on demand or at maturity is mostly dependent on the financial integrity of the importer (drawee of the bill). If the bill is not honoured by the importer, the exporter is left with a bad debt.

Consignment

Consignment is a method of sale, according to which the exporter ships the goods to the importer for sale, but retains the title to the goods until they are sold to a third party. The importer sells the goods to others and remits the sale proceeds to the exporter after deducting expenses, if any, at his level as well as the commission as agreed upon. If any of the goods remain unsold at the level of the importer, the exporter either has to take back the unsold stock or has to find another purchaser. The exporter, thus, bears all the risk in a consignment sale.

Open Account

Open account sale is one method through which the exporter finances the importer (buyer). Where the exporter has much familiarity with the importer after having business dealings for a long time, he may sell the goods to the importer on an open account. In an open account transaction, the exporter ships the goods to the importer, and the importer pays the amount to the exporter some time later as per the understanding between the importer and exporter. No documents like letters of credit or bills of exchange are involved in open account transactions. In other words, the exporter bears all the risks in the open account sale. Generally, this type of sale is made to only the most trustworthy importers. However, open account sales have increased greatly with advances in communication technology, which enable the exporters to establish continuous rapport with the importers, thereby developing mutual trust.

Documents Used in International Trade Finance

International trade involves various formalities that need to be fulfilled. Each formality requires a separate documentation. Therefore, a number of documents are involved in the export and import of merchandise. Some documents may indicate the seller's responsibility as well as ownership, and some documents indicate the buyer's credit-standing. The commonly used documents are briefly described in this section.

Bill of Lading

One of the widely used documents in international trade is the bill of lading. A **bill of lading** is basically a shipping document signed by the master of a ship, by the ship owner, or his agent, acknowledging the receipt of goods from the exporter for transportation from the port of shipment to the port of destination. The document contains full details about the goods, the exporter, the importer, the port of destination, and so on. It is an undertaking by the ship owner (common carrier) to deliver the goods to the named party or to his order upon payment of freight charges. Thus, the bill of lading serves mainly three functions: (i) it is a receipt for shipment of goods; (ii) it is a proof that the goods specified will be transported; and (iii) it is a document of title to the goods. As the bill of lading serves as a document of title, the importer takes title to goods once he receives the bill of lading from the transportation company. Though a bill of lading is not a negotiable instrument, it can be transferred by delivery or endorsement and delivery. In view of these characteristics, banks accept the bill of lading as collateral for lending to exporters. In other words, the exporters can use the bill of lading for getting bank credit. If the goods are sent by air, the equivalent of bill of lading is the air waybill.

*A **bill of lading** is a shipping document that specifies the ports of shipment and destination and a full description of the goods.*

Commercial and Consular Invoice

A **commercial invoice** is a document that contains a detailed description of the goods exported. A commercial invoice is prepared by the exporter indicating the description of the goods consigned, country of origin, price, terms of payment, amount of freight, other shipping information, addresses of the exporter and the importer, export or import permit number, and so on. All these details should match the information in the letter of credit. A **consular invoice** is a special type of invoice required by some countries for goods imported into those countries. The principal function of the invoice is to enable the authorities of the importing country to have an accurate record of the types of goods shipped to the country, their quantity, grade, and value. The invoice is generally required for assessing import duties and for general statistical purpose. A consular invoice neither gives any title to the goods being shipped, nor is it negotiable.

*A **commercial invoice** is a document that contains a detailed description of the goods exported. A **consular invoice** is a special type of invoice required by some countries for goods imported into those countries.*

Marine Insurance Policy

A marine insurance policy is a document arising out of a marine insurance contract. A marine insurance contract is a contract in which the marine underwriter agrees to compensate the insured for any loss or damage to his goods or ship during the period of the policy, in consideration of a sum of money called the premium. The insured can claim compensation only for the loss or damage that is caused directly and naturally by a peril insured against, under the policy of insurance.

Institutional Credit

Export credit consists of pre-shipment credit and post-shipment credit.

Export growth is an essential requirement for the development of any economy. To boost economic development in a country, it is necessary to push for export growth. In order to promote exports, the Reserve Bank of India has designed different kinds of credit schemes for the benefit of exporters. Commercial banks and other financial institutions extend two types of credit to exporters. These are **pre-shipment credit** (commonly known as packing credit) and **post-shipment credit**, the details of which are discussed in the next section. The bank credit may be for short-term or medium-term. The lending institutions can also avail the refinancing facility offered by apex banks such as the RBI and the Export-Import (Exim) Bank.

While extending export credit, banks generally prescribe certain limits. These limits are based on the appraisal made by a bank or a consortium of banks, backed by assets of the borrower as collateral. Export credit limit forms part of the working capital limit of a firm. Banks may grant specific individual limits for packing and post-shipment credit, or they may grant a composite limit. This is at the discretion of individual banks and their internal guidelines. The main considerations in granting export credit limits are genuineness, past experience, and the net worth of the borrower. It is also necessary that the borrowing firm should be a registered exporter with an I-E code. Banks also verify whether the exporter is under the caution list or the goods proposed to be exported are under the negative list. Further, whether the country where the goods are exported is sound economically and politically, is also examined. The utilized portion of export credit also needs to be covered under the Export Credit Guarantee Corporation (ECGC).

Pre-shipment or Packing Credit

Pre-shipment credit is a financial facility extended by banks to exporters from the order stage till the goods are shipped or exported, to procure raw material and to process/manufacture and pack the goods for export.

Pre-shipment credit is an advance granted by a bank to an exporter to procure raw materials and to process/manufacture the goods, and pack them for export. In other words, packing credit (PC) is a financial facility extended by a bank to an exporter from the purchase order stage till the goods are shipped or exported. Thus, the PC facility covers the cost of raw materials and other input components, cost of processing/manufacturing, cost of packing, cost of warehousing and transportation, cost of insurance, export duty, and so on.

The PC facility is a big boon to exporters, particularly small and medium scale enterprises that do not generally possess adequate financial resources to meet pre-shipment expenditure. The credit is extended mainly on the strength of either a letter of credit issued in favour of the exporter or a firm export order. PC is granted on more liberal terms, and such loans are always need-based and not directly linked to the availability of collateral security. Such loans are granted even on the basis of correspondence between the exporter and the importer. Pre-shipment credit may also be extended against duty drawback entitlements, provisionally certified by the customs authority. What is most important in this regard is the exporter's or borrower's track record.

Normally, banks extend PC for a period up to 270 days, depending on the operating cycle of the borrowing firm. There are also banks that fix the credit period on the basis of the delivery date of the export order. Generally, banks are liberal in this regard too. For example, for a firm that is not able to fulfill its export orders for a genuine reason within the stipulated time, causing PC to become overdue, the bank may extend the period of credit for a few more days or months. In such cases, the bank may charge a penal rate of interest for the extended period at its discretion. However, the maximum period for which the banks are allowed to extend pre-shipment credit at *concessional* interest rates is 180 days.

The pre-shipment credit can be availed as either INR PC or PC in a foreign currency. The banks are free to extend PC in foreign currencies (as of now in five major currencies USD, EUR, JPY, CHF, and GBP). If the PC is extended in a foreign currency, the borrower can have the advantage of getting a loan at internationally competitive rates of interest. The banks may also extend pre-shipment credit in a foreign currency by discounting the related export bills in the foreign currency.

Another important aspect with regard to pre-shipment credit is that all advances need to be liquidated from export proceeds. If a PC advance is not liquidated by export proceeds, that particular advance may not be eligible for the concessional rate of interest. Pre-shipment advances may be repaid either on an order-to-order basis or in a running account model. Running account means that there is one single account for all the PCs. Accordingly, as and when a PC is availed, the exporter's account is debited, and when an export document is discounted, the account is credited. This is on a first-in first-out basis. Generally, banks offer running account facilities on PC accounts. Banks may also extend revolving credit to export-oriented units, which means that on repayment of the earlier loan, the exporter is automatically granted a corresponding new loan on the same terms. The main advantage with a revolving credit facility is that the exporter need not go around to different banks for each loan.

Post-shipment Credit

Post-shipment credit is an advance extended by a bank to an exporter from the time goods are shipped/exported till the time bills/export proceeds are realized. In other words, post-shipment credit is an advance extended by a bank to an exporter-firm to meet financial requirements that may arise between the time of the shipment of goods and the time of realization of the export proceeds. Post-shipment credit includes any loan or advance given to an exporter on the security of any duty drawback. Post-shipment credit generally takes the form of bills discounting/purchasing or an advance against bills under collection. In cases where the importer opens a letter of credit in favour of the exporter, the exporter would get the sale proceeds instantaneously. In cases where there is no letter of credit, the bank may either purchase/discount the bills of exchange, or it may send the bills for collection. Banks may also extend post-shipment credit against the security of approved shipping documents such as a bill of lading, commercial invoice, and so on.

***Post-shipment credit** is an advance extended by banks to an exporter of goods to meet financial requirements between the time of the shipment of goods and the time of realization of the export proceeds.*

Post-shipment credit may be a short-term, medium-term, or long-term credit. Medium-term credit (up to five years) is provided in the case of durable consumer goods and light capital goods. Long-term credit is extended in the case of capital goods and turnkey projects. The period for which the post-shipment credit is given is based on the payment terms of the export bill. Post-shipment credit is always maintained on a bill-to-bill basis and not as a running account.

In many a case, PC and post-shipment credit limits are not clearly demarcated. In other words, total export credit means PC plus post-shipment credit. As both PC and post-shipment credit are components of total export credit, the effect of one nullifies the other. That is, post-shipment credit drawal leads to repayment of pre-shipment credit.

In addition to PC and post-shipment credit, banks may also provide finance to exporters against export incentives, either at the pre-shipment or at the post-shipment stage. Export incentives which include cash subsidies, refund of excise and customs duties (duty drawbacks), and reimbursement of the differential between indigenous and international prices of certain raw materials, are provided under the Export Promotion Scheme by the Government of India. In the case of exporters with high credit ratings and proven export capabilities, credit is extended against eligible export incentives at the pre-shipment stage. In all other cases, advances against incentives are given as post-shipment credit.

Line of Credit

Line of credit is an arrangement that permits a business unit to borrow from a bank a maximum amount of money without further sanction or approval. Once a bank sanctions a loan of a certain limit (maximum) to a borrower, the borrower is at liberty to draw any amount within the credit limit at any time during a specified time period. Interest is calculated on the amount actually drawn by the borrower. The line of credit is also called the credit line or credit limit.

The advantage of the line of credit facility is that the borrower, who may have to take several loans over time, need not apply for each loan. For example, a firm may require INR 100 million over a five-year period. It can apply for a loan of INR 100 million that is sanctioned by a bank. The firm can then draw on its line of credit when it wants money for a specific purpose, and then pay it back when it has excess cash. The firm is not required to get an additional approval every time it takes money out from the account. Large companies and companies with high creditworthiness can have a substantial line of credit. The borrower can draw down its line of credit according to his expectation of interest rates in future. For example, if the borrower expects downward changes in interest rates, he may delay the drawing of the loan.

Banker's Acceptance

Banker's acceptance is one of the methods of financing international trade. To create a banker's acceptance, a firm (importer) approaches its bank for a letter of credit to be issued to the exporter. The importer's bank issues a letter of credit authorizing the exporter to write a bill (draft) on the bank in payment for the goods sold to the importer. Based on the letter of credit, the exporter ships the goods to the importer and submits a time draft along with the shipping documents to the importer's bank. The shipping documents are then delivered to the importer to claim the shipment. The importer's bank accepts the time draft which becomes a banker's acceptance. Banker's acceptances are generally for short maturities, ranging from 30 to 180 days. The exporter can either hold the banker's acceptance until payment is due (maturity date), discount it, or sell it in the money market. At maturity of the time draft, the importer's bank makes full payment. The importer is required to pay this amount plus an additional amount as commission to the accepting bank. The commission or fee, which the importer is required to pay for banker's acceptance, varies depending on the maturity period of the time draft and the creditworthiness of the importer. Thus, all the parties—exporter, importer, and bank—are benefited by the banker's acceptance.

Imports into India: Guidelines for Trade Credit

***Trade credit** is a credit extended for imports directly by an overseas supplier, bank, or financial institution, with a maturity of less than three years.*

Trade credit (TC) refers to a credit extended for imports directly by an overseas supplier, bank, or financial institution, with a maturity of less than three years. Depending on the source of finance, a TC may be a suppliers' credit or buyers' credit. Suppliers' credit is a credit for imports into a country (e.g. India) extended by the overseas supplier, while buyers' credit refers to a loan for payment of imports into a country (e.g. India) arranged by the importer from a bank or financial institution outside the country, with a maturity of less than three years. It may be noted that buyers' credit and suppliers' credit for three years and above come under the category of *external commercial borrowings (ECB),* which are governed by ECB guidelines.

Amount and Maturity Authorized dealer (AD) banks are permitted to approve TCs for imports into India up to USD 20 million per import transaction for imports permissible under the current Foreign Trade Policy of the Director General of Foreign Trade (DGFT) with a maturity period up to one year (from the date of shipment).

For the import of capital goods as classified by the DGFT, AD banks may approve TC up to USD 20 million per import transaction with a maturity period of more than one year and less than three years. No rollover/extension is permitted beyond the permissible period. AD banks cannot approve TC exceeding USD 20 million per import transaction.

All-in-cost Ceilings All-in-cost refers to arranger fees, upfront fees, management fees, handling/processing charges, and out-of-pocket and legal expenses, if any. All-in-cost ceilings are

- for a maturity period up to one year: LIBOR plus 50 basis points and
- for a maturity period of more than one year but less than three years: LIBOR plus 125 basis points.

Guarantee AD banks are permitted to issue letters of credit/guarantees/letters of undertaking (LoU)/letters of comfort (LoC) in favour of an overseas supplier, bank, and financial institution, up to USD 20 million per transaction for a period up to one year for import of all non-capital goods permissible under the Foreign Trade Policy (except gold) and up to three years for the import of capital goods, subject to prudential guidelines issued by the Reserve Bank of India from time to time. The period of such letters of credit/guarantees/LoUs/LoCs has to be co-terminus with the period of credit, reckoned from the date of shipment.

Forfaiting

Forfaiting is a method of financing international trade. *Forfaiting* is a French term that means "surrendering something" or "relinquishing a right". In the context of international trade, forfaiting refers to an exporter relinquishing his right to export receivables (medium term) due at a future date in exchange for immediate cash payment at an agreed-upon discount. In other words, the exporter, in return for immediate cash payment, surrenders his right to claim payment for goods delivered to the importer in favour of the forfaiter without recourse. Thus, the forfaiter provides immediate finance to the exporter and takes over the responsibility for claiming the debt from the importer. Banks are the major players in providing forfaiting services to exporters for a charge.

***Forfaiting** refers to an exporter relinquishing his or her right to a receivable due at a future date in exchange for immediate cash payment, at an agreed-upon discount.*

A forfaiting transaction involves the following steps:

- The importer and the exporter agree between themselves on a series of imports to be made over a period of time that generally ranges from 180 days to 10 years.
- The forfaiting bank agrees to finance the imports on the submission of the appropriate promissory notes and other documents.
- The importer issues a promissory note for every import with an endorsement by the importer's bank.
- The bank-endorsed promissory notes are delivered to the exporter.
- The exporter discounts the promissory notes (without recourse to the exporter) with the forfaiter and receives the proceeds. The discount is generally added to the invoice price of the goods, so that it will ultimately be borne by the importer.
- The forfaiter either holds the promissory notes till full maturity or discounts them in the international money market. On the date of maturity, the importer is supposed

to honour the promissory notes issued by him. If the importer is unable to pay, then the forfaiting agency is responsible for payment to those with whom the promissory notes are discounted.

Forfaiting is a complementary method of finance to conventional export credit, and each forfaiting transaction involves a large amount, usually more than USD 5 million. For larger amounts, more than one agency (as a syndicate) may be involved. Forfaiting allows the exporter greater flexibility in structuring a finance deal. As forfaiting is without recourse, the exporter can avoid all types of risks associated with a credit sale. In other words, the forfaiter bears the credit risk and country risk associated with the forfaiting transaction. If the forfaiting transaction is backed by a bank guarantee or a letter of credit, the forfaiter's risk is reduced. In view of several benefits associated with forfaiting that ultimately facilitate international trade, forfaiting as an export financing option has also been approved by the Reserve Bank of India. According to the RBI's Circular No. 42 AD (MA) Series dated 27 October 1997, Exim Bank and authorized dealers are permitted to act as intermediaries between the Indian exporter and the overseas forfaiting agency.

Countertrade

Countertrade has gained momentum with the increase in international trade. Many firms have realized that without countertrade in one form or the other, international business is difficult. In a **countertrade** transaction, the exporter sells goods and services to an importer and is obligated to purchase other goods and services from the importer in return. The purchasing from the importer may take place simultaneously with the original export, or it may take place some time later.

***In countertrade**, an exporter sells goods and services to an importer and is obligated to purchase other goods and services from the importer in return.*

There are various forms of countertrade, such as barter, clearing arrangement, switch trading, buy back, counter purchase, and offset. The *barter* system (swapping goods for goods), which has been in existence for thousands of years, refers to a direct exchange of goods and services between two parties. A *clearing arrangement* is one form of barter system according to which the counterparties agree to purchase a certain quantity of goods and services from one another. Both parties maintain accounts with each other, which are debited whenever one party imports from the other. At the end of the specified period, any account imbalances are settled by the payment of money or by the transfer of goods. If the clearing arrangement imbalance is purchased by a third party, it becomes a *switch trade.* In this case, the third party will purchase the imbalance from the surplus party on behalf of the deficit party, which is then resold. In the case of *buy back arrangement,* which is also known as compensation agreement, an exporter of technology or a plant agrees to accept compensation for the value of the sale in the form of a part of the output of the project (products produced with that technology or plant) over a certain period of time. The compensation may become a partial compensation when the buy-back arrangement is for a fraction of the original sale value. In the case *of counter purchase,* the exporter agrees to buy goods that are unrelated to his business from the importer in return for exports. There are two separate contracts expressed in monetary terms for buying of the products from each other. Generally, the goods involved in counter purchase are those for which the importer does not have a ready market. In fact, the exporter is forced to buy the unrelated goods for resale. Such goods, unless offered at reduced prices, do not have a demand in the international market. In an *offset transaction,* the importer will be assured that his purchase price will be offset in some way (through increasing imports from the importer, transfer of technology, etc.) by the exporter. Offsets are commonly used in the case of defence-related exports.

Despite countertrade being less efficient than using cash or credit, it has increased phenomenally over time. Countertrade transactions are usually large, and involve governments and MNCs. The counterparties can conserve cash and hard currency through countertrade.

Countertrading is common among countries that have inconvertible currencies or limited currency reserves. Countertrade is also used to circumvent foreign exchange controls, if any. Country risk and foreign exchange risk can also be reduced with countertrade transactions.

Export-Import Bank of India (Exim Bank)

The Export-Import Bank of India, popularly known as Exim Bank, is a specialized financial institution established on 1 January 1982 by an Act of Parliament for financing, facilitating, and promoting India's foreign trade. It also coordinates the working of various institutions engaged in financing and promoting foreign trade. It facilitates two-way technology transfer by financing import of technology into India, and investment abroad by Indian companies for setting up joint ventures, subsidiaries, or undertaking overseas acquisitions. The Asian Exim Banks Forum was conceived and initiated by the Exim Bank in 1996. Towards fostering institutional linkages, it has signed MoUs with several key institutions in India and abroad. During the year 2013–14, it floated a joint venture called Bharat Handloom Marketing Company Ltd in association with the National Handloom Development Corporation Ltd and the Association of Corporations and Apex Societies of Handlooms. As on 31 March 2014, it was rated Baa3 by Moody's, BBB– by Standard & Poor's, BBB– by Fitch Ratings, and BBB+ by Japan Credit Rating Agency. It has put in place a Technology and Innovation Enhancement and Infrastructure Development Fund of USD 500 million exclusively for MSMEs by partnering with other banks and financial institutions. During the year 2012–13, it became the first ever Indian entity to be included in the Emerging Market Bond Index. It also became the first Indian organization to tap into the Australian dollar market and Singapore dollar market.

Functions and Services The functions of Exim Bank are carried out by the following operating groups:

- *The Corporate Banking Group:* It handles a variety of financing programmes for export-oriented units, importers, and overseas investment by Indian companies.
- *The Project Finance/Trade Finance Group:* It provides the entire range of export credit services such as suppliers' credit, pre-shipment credit, buyers' credit, finance for export of projects and consultancy services, guarantees, and forfaiting.
- *The Lines of Credit Group:* It provides a safe mode of non-recourse financing to Indian exporters, especially to small and medium enterprises (SMEs), and serves as an effective market entry tool.
- *The Agri Business Group:* It handles agriculture-based projects and export transactions for financing.
- *The Small and Medium Enterprises Group:* It handles credit proposals from SMEs under various lending programmes of the Exim Bank.
- *The Export Services Group:* It offers a variety of advisory and value-added information services aimed at investment promotion.
- *The Fee-based Export Marketing Services Group:* It offers assistance to Indian companies to enable them establish their products in overseas markets.
- *The Support Services Group:* It handles research and planning, corporate finance, loan recovery, internal audit, management information services, information technology, legal affairs, human resources management and corporate affairs.

The various forms of credit services provided by the Exim Bank are as below:

- Pre-shipment credit facility at the manufacturing stage to enable exporters to purchase raw materials and other inputs.

- Suppliers' credit facility to enable Indian exporters to extend term credit to importers (overseas) of eligible goods at the post-shipment stage.
- Credit to meet the costs of mobilization/acquisition of materials, personnel, and equipment in the case of overseas project export contracts.
- Special credit facility to Indian exporters of consultancy and technology services so that they can in turn, extend term credit to overseas importers.
- Guarantee facilities to Indian companies to facilitate execution of export contracts and import transactions.
- Project finance and equipment finance for exporting companies.
- Term finance to exporting companies for importing technology and related services, domestic acquisitions of businesses/companies/brands, export product development/research and development, and so on.
- General corporate finance and working capital finance (funded and non-funded) to exporting companies.
- Provision for equity participation in Indian exporting companies.
- Lines of credit to overseas financial institutions, regional development banks, sovereign governments, and other foreign entities to enable importers to import developmental and infrastructural projects, equipment, goods, and services from India on deferred credit terms.

Under overseas investment finance, the Exim Bank provides the following services:

- Finance for Indian companies' equity participation in overseas joint ventures and wholly owned subsidiaries.
- Direct finance (term and working capital) to overseas joint ventures/wholly owned subsidiaries.
- Finance for acquisition of overseas businesses/companies including leveraged buyouts and structured financing options.

In sum, Exim Bank provides export finance in the form of pre-shipment credit, post-shipment credit, buyers' credit, suppliers' credit including deferred payment credit, bills discounting, export receivables financing, warehousing finance, and export lines of credit. It also participates directly in the equity of the overseas joint ventures/wholly owned subsidiaries of Indian companies.

Performance Exim Bank has registered an impressive performance as can be observed from Table 13.3. The total loans disbursed under various schemes stood at INR 40,635 crore

Table 13.3 Financial Performance of Exim Bank (INR crore)

	31 March 2011	*31 March 2012*	*31 March 2013*
Loans sanctioned	47,798	44,412	41,919
Loans disbursed	34,423	37,045	40,635
Total resources (paid-up capital and reserves)	54,751	63,673	76,118
Profit after tax	583.6	675.1	742.3
Capital to risk asset ratio (%)	17.0	16.4	15.30

Source: Exim Bank Annual Report 2012–13.

as against the sanctions of INR 41,919 crore on 31 March 2013. The bank could increase its resources from INR 54,751 crore as on 31 March 2011 to INR 76,118 crore by 31 March 2013. The bank made a profit after a tax of INR 742.3 crore during the year ending 31 March 2013. But the capital to risk asset ratio has declined from 15.28 percent as on 31 March 2013 to 14.32 percent as on 31 March 2014. Return on assets also declined from 1.05 percent as on 31 March 2013 to 0.86 percent as on 31 March 2014.

The Export-Import Bank of India plays an active role in providing value-added services, which include export marketing services, information and advisory services, consultancy support, and so on. Global Procurement Consultants Ltd, a joint venture of Exim Bank, provides procurement-related advisory and auditing services, primarily for projects funded by multilateral agencies in various developing countries. Through its Grassroots Business Initiative, the Exim Bank supports globalization of rural industries. It also promotes export of rural Indian technology to other developing countries under the umbrella of South–South cooperation.

Export Credit Guarantee Corporation (ECGC)

Exporters face several kinds of risks, and these risks have assumed large proportions with the political and economic changes that are sweeping the world. Besides political risks or country risks, exporters are faced with credit risk. It is in this context that the Export Credit Guarantee Corporation has come into existence. The ECGC was established in the year 1957 by the Government of India for the purpose of strengthening export promotion. It is the fifth largest credit insurer in the world in terms of coverage of national exports. The main objectives of ECGC are to:

- provide credit risk insurance covers to exporters against loss in export of goods and services;
- offer guarantees to banks and financial institutions to enable exporters to obtain better facilities from them; and
- provide overseas investment insurance to Indian companies investing in joint ventures abroad in the form of equity or loan.

The ECGC offers the following services:

- It provides insurance protection to exporters against credit risks, and provides guidance in export-related activities.
- It makes available information on different countries with its own credit ratings.
- It makes it easy to obtain export finance from banks/financial institutions.
- It assists exporters in recovering bad debts, and provides information on the creditworthiness of overseas buyers.

The specific products and services of ECGC are classified as credit insurance policies, guarantees to banks, and special schemes. The credit insurance policies include the Shipments (comprehensive risks) Policy, Specific Shipment Policy (short term), Export (specific buyers) Policy, Specific Policy for Supply Contract, Service Policy, Construction Works Policy, Export Turnover Policy, and Buyer Exposure Policy. The guarantees to be given by ECGC include Overseas Investment Guarantee, Packing Credit Guarantee, Post-shipment Export Credit Guarantee, Export Production Finance Guarantee, and Export Finance (overseas lending) Guarantee. Exchange Fluctuation Risk Cover is a special scheme operated by ECGC.

The Shipments (Comprehensive Risks) Policy Among the credit insurance policies, the Shipments (Comprehensive Risks) Policy is very popular, and it is commonly known as the Standard Policy. It covers risks in respect to goods exported on short-term credit, that is, credit not exceeding 180 days. This policy covers both commercial and political risks from the date of shipment. Only those exporters who have an anticipated export turnover of more than INR 5 million in the next 12 months, are eligible to avail of this policy. The risks covered under the Standard Policy are broadly classified into the following categories:

- *Commercial risks,* or the risks arising on insolvency of the buyer; failure of the buyer to make the payment due within a specified period; and buyer's failure to accept the goods, subject to certain conditions.
- *Political risk,* or the perceived risks arising from imposition of certain restrictions by the government of the importer's country or on any other action of the importer's government that may block or delay the transfer of payment from the importer to the exporter. Wars, including civil war or civil disturbances, in the buyer's country may also affect the flow of goods and funds between the exporter and importer. This will also cause political risk to the exporter. Any other cause of loss occurring outside India, not normally insured by general insurers, and beyond the control of both the exporter and the importer, is also perceived as a political risk.

Packing Credit Guarantee The ECGC extends guarantees to banks with regard to their advances to exporters (pre-shipment credit). This scheme is called the PC guarantee scheme. The pre-shipment advances given by banks to parties who enter into contracts for export of services or for construction works abroad to meet preliminary expenses in connection with such contracts are also eligible for cover under the Guarantee Scheme. The Scheme assures the banks that, in the event of an exporter failing to discharge his liabilities to the bank, the ECGC would make good a major portion of the bank's loss. The bank is required to be co-insurer to the extent of the remaining loss.

Exchange Fluctuation Risk Cover The ECGC also offers a special scheme called Exchange Fluctuation Risk Cover to provide a measure of protection to exporters of capital goods, civil engineering contractors and consultants who often wait years to receive payments for their exports or services. They are exposed to foreign exchange risk because of volatile exchange rates. The Exchange Fluctuation Risk Cover takes care of such a risk. It is available for payments scheduled over a period of 12 months or more, up to a maximum of 15 years. The Cover can be obtained from the date of bidding right up to the final installment. The basis for Cover is a reference rate that is agreed-upon. The reference rate can be the rate prevailing on the date of bid, a rate approximating it, or a rate prevailing on the date of contract.

Summary

1. The basis of international trade lies in differences in relative product prices, which, in turn, depend upon differences in the relative scarcities or costs of the factors of production in different countries.
2. There are two types of barriers that governments impose to restrict foreign trade: tariff barriers and non-tariff barriers.
3. The important functions of the World Trade Organization (WTO) are to oversee the implementation, administration, and operation of the covered agreements, and to provide a forum for negotiations and settling disputes.
4. The WTO is structured into the Ministerial Conference, the second level of authority, the third level of authority, and the fourth level of authority.

5. The main principles of international trading are non-discrimination, reciprocity, and transparency.

6. The value of world exports and imports increased from USD 6,356,563 million and 6,521,536 million, respectively, in 2000 to USD 18,459,279 million and 18,401,453 in the same order in 2013.

7. China is the most leading exporter in 2013 with a share of 11.7 percent of the world total exports, followed by the U.S. (8.4%). The U.S. is the most leading importer in 2013 with a share of 12.3 percent of the world total imports followed by China (10.3%).

8. India recorded a 1.7 percent share in the world merchandize exports and a 2.5 percent share in the world merchandize imports in the year 2013.

9. In general, there are five methods of payment in international trade: advance payment (cash in advance), letters of credit, bills of exchange (draft), consignments, and open accounts.

10. Commercial banks are active players in providing institutional export credit. Banks provide both pre-shipment and post-shipment credit to exporters. Banks may also provide finance to exporters against export incentives.

11. The important documents used in financing foreign trade are bills of exchange, bills of lading, banker's letter of credit, commercial and consular invoice, and marine insurance policy.

12. Forfaiting is a complementary method of finance for conventional export credit, and it eliminates political and commercial risks.

13. Countertrade transaction is a transaction in which an exporter sells goods and services to an importer and is obligated to purchase other goods and services in return from the importer.

14. The main objective of Export-Import Bank of India is to finance, facilitate, and promote India's foreign trade. It provides export finance in the form of pre-shipment credit, post-shipment credit, buyers' credit, suppliers' credit, bills discounting, export receivables financing, warehousing finance, and export lines of credit.

15. ECGC offers insurance protection to exporters against payment risks, provides guidance in export-related activities, and makes available information on different countries.

Questions and Problems

1. What is the law of comparative advantage? How it is relevant to international trade?
2. Discuss the importance of international trade in the economic development of a country.
3. Discuss the genesis of the WTO.
4. Discuss the role of the WTO in the development of international trade. What are its limitations?
5. Describe the structure of the WTO.
6. Explain the principles of the international trading system.
7. Describe the trends in world trade in recent years.
8. Discuss the salient features of India's foreign trade policy.
9. Describe the methods of payment used in international trade.
10. What are the forms of institutional credit available to Indian exporters?
11. Explain different types of documents used in financing foreign trade.
12. What is the significance of banker's letter of credit?
13. What is forfaiting? Discuss its significance.
14. Explain different forms of countertrade.
15. Discuss the functions of Export-Import Bank of India.
16. What are the objectives of ECGC? Discuss the role of ECGC in the promotion of exports.
17. Sri Chakra Ltd is a cement company based in South India. It is planning to import some machinery from the United States at a cost of USD 10 million. It has two options as far as financing is concerned. It can get a foreign currency loan of USD 10 million from the State Bank of India at an interest rate of 15 percent per annum. The company also has an offer from American Express Bank, according to which the company can get a loan at 6 percent per annum by opening an irrevocable letter of credit. The commission charges for the letter of credit are 1.5 percent per annum. The current spot rate is USD/INR 48.50 and the 365-days forward rate is USD/INR 49.75. Which option is beneficial to the company?

Multiple-choice Questions

1. The theory of absolute advantage postulates that the countries differ in their capacity ________.
   (a) To produce more
   (b) To produce goods more efficiently
   (c) To produce all kinds of goods
   (d) None of these
2. According to David Recardo, a country should specialize in the production of goods that it can produce ________.
   (a) More efficiently (b) Most efficiently
   (c) Relatively better (d) None of these
3. International trade is a ________.
   (a) Zero-sum of game
   (b) Positive-sum of game
   (c) Negative-sum of game
   (d) None of these
4. ________functioned as a de facto international trade organization.
   (a) IMF (b) GATT
   (c) World Bank (d) None of these
5. A letter of credit is issued by________.
   (a) Importer (b) Exporter
   (c) Bank (d) None of these
6. The undertaking given by the bank can be withdrawn in the case of________.
   (a) Irrevocable letter of credit
   (b) Revocable letter of credit
   (c) Red-clause letter of credit
   (d) None of these
7. A bill of exchange is also known as a ________.
   (a) Banker's cheque (b) Trade draft
   (c) Promissory note (d) None of these
8. Consignment is a method of________.
   (a) Purchase (b) Sale
   (c) Negotiation (d) None of these
9. Bill of lading is signed by a/an________.
   (a) Master of a ship (b) Importer
   (c) Exporter (d) None of these
10. A commercial invoice is prepared by a/an________.
    (a) Exporter (b) Importer
    (c) Bank (d) None of these
11. Packing credit is also known as a ________.
    (a) Pre-shipment credit (b) Post-shipment credit
    (c) Bank credit (d) None of these
12. Trade credit is a credit extended for ________.
    (a) Imports (b) Exports
    (c) Production (d) None of these
13. Forfaiting is a method of financing ________.
    (a) Domestic trade (b) International trade
    (c) Capital goods (d) None of these
14. A clearing arrangement is a form of a ________.
    (a) Barter system (b) Financing imports
    (c) Financing exports (d) None of these
15. Post-shipment credit is maintained as ________.
    (a) Bill-to-bill (b) Running account
    (c) Cash credit (d) None of these
16. In the open account sale, the ________finances the importer.
    (a) Exporter (b) Bank
    (c) Exim Bank (d) None of these
17. When the importer's bank accepts the bill of exchange, it is known as ________.
    (a) Banker's acceptance (b) Draft
    (c) Trade draft (d) None of these
18. If a bill of exchange is not accompanied by any document, it is called the ________.
    (a) Usance bill (b) Clean bill
    (c) Sight bill (d) None of these
19. Under the Most Favoured Nation rule, a country should treat all other countries ________.
    (a) Equally (b) Discriminately
    (c) As per their strength (d) None of these
20. Non-tariff barriers include ________.
    (a) Quota (b) Customs duty
    (c) Export tax (d) None of these

Further Reading

1. International Monetary Fund, *Balance of Payments Statistics.*
2. Paul R. Krugman and Maurice Obstfeld, *International Economics: Theory and Policy* (Glenview, Illinois: Scott Foresman, 1988).
3. http://www.wto.org/
4. Christopher M. Korth, *International Countertrade* (Westport, Connecticut: Quorum Books, 1987).
5. Michael Porter, *The Competitive Advantage of Nations* (London: Macmillan Press, 1990).
6. *Exporter's Manual* (New Delhi: Nabhi Publications, 2005).
7. http://www.eximbankindia.com/
8. https://www.ecgc.in/Portal/aboutus/aboutus.asp

CHAPTER 14

Foreign Investments

CHAPTER OBJECTIVES

After studying this chapter, you should be able to:

1 Understand the concept of foreign investments and their role in the economic development of a country.

2 Discuss the various forms and theories of foreign direct investments (FDI) and explain the economic advantages of FDI.

3 Discuss the factors that influence FDI.

4 Understand India's foreign investment policy and the regulations that govern foreign investments in India.

5 Have insights into foreign investments made by Indian companies.

6 Discuss the global trends in FDI and look at the causes for low FDI in India.

Introduction

Alongside the globalization of trade, there has been a parallel growth in foreign investments. International investments and international trade are complementary to each other as the development of one facilitates the development of the other. Both are considered to be drivers of globalization and world economic growth.

International trade, which started almost with human civilization, has a significant influence on the world economy. Developed economies largely depend on international trade for their economic growth and development. This dependence is even more in the case of less developed economies, which mostly depend on international trade for their survival. A significant proportion of consumption in less developed countries depends on goods and services produced abroad. As the development of the world economy mostly depends on its performance in the world trade, international trade has a large bearing on the lives of people the world over.

To facilitate and develop international trade, most countries have entered into bilateral or multilateral trade agreements. The free trade pact between the United States and Canada; the North American Free Trade Agreement (NAFTA) between Canada, Mexico, and the United States; and the General Agreement on Tariffs and Trade (GATT) are examples of bilateral and multilateral trade agreements. Many international organizations such as the International Monetary Fund (IMF), the International Bank for Reconstruction and Development (or the World Bank), and the Bank for International Settlements (BIS) have been created to facilitate cross-border investments.

International investments are as essential as international trade for increasing a country's output. Before the first international investments or foreign investments were made in the nineteenth century, it had been believed that capital could be invested only within the borders of a country. After foreign investments started, many nations realized that capital investments abroad would play an important role in their economic development. In fact, the railroads, harbours, factories, and mines in Western Europe, Asia, and North America would not have been constructed had there been no foreign investments. With the exception of some countries that were hostile towards foreign investments, nations all over the world have realized that they would derive enormous advantages from foreign investments. Multinational corporations play a vital role not only in the development of international trade but also in the promotion of international investments. In recent years, corporate investments across borders have grown faster than international trade and global output. The reduction of trade and investment barriers, particularly after the emergence of WTO, has accelerated investment flows across countries. Regional, bilateral, and multilateral trade and investment agreements have also contributed to the phenomenal increase in foreign investments in recent years. Cross-border investments have, therefore, assumed greater importance in the world economy than ever before. Many developing economies in competition with economies in transition (e.g. China, Russia) have also become important destinations for foreign investments. It is observed that 60 to 70 percent of world trade is directly or indirectly connected to foreign investments.

Cross-border investments may take the form of foreign institutional investments (FIIs), also known as portfolio investments, or foreign direct investments (FDIs). FDI includes cross-border mergers and acquisitions. In some cases, foreign investments are made indirectly through loans to foreign governments, which in turn use the loan proceeds for investment in their respective countries. But in this chapter, we shall deal with foreign direct investments and foreign institutional investments without any specific discussion on cross-border mergers and acquisitions.

FDI vs FII

***Foreign direct investment (FDI)** is essentially a long-term investment and is associated with investment in capital assets and creating employment, while **foreign institutional investment (FII)** is inherently short-term investment linked to the financial markets.*

Foreign direct investments and foreign institutional investments have inherently different characteristics, but both contribute to the economic development of the host country. Foreign direct investment is essentially a long-term investment, associated with investment in capital assets and creating employment; while foreign institutional investment is inherently short-term investment linked to the financial markets. FIIs usually take the form of investment in equity and debt markets, and as such they do not directly contribute to the creation of new production capabilities.

FIIs increase liquidity in stock markets and increase price-earnings ratios, thereby reducing the cost of capital for firms in the domestic economy. Even the funds flowing through FIIs may have lower cost of capital than domestic funds, which benefits the host country's economy as a whole. The fast increase in foreign exchange reserves of a country may be attributed to a large inflow of foreign currency through foreign institutional investments. Thus, FIIs may have a positive impact on the stock market and corporate transparency and governance norms. However, a large and sudden FII flows may create more volatility in the economy. Although, both FDIs and FIIs are volatile, higher volatility and risk are associated with FIIs. The volatility of FIIs is influenced by global investment opportunities and flow of funds from one country to another. Further, FII flows are considered to be 'hot money', because FIIs can reverse at any time. That is, investors may suddenly withdraw their investments, which will destabilize the stock market, besides causing fluctuations in foreign exchange rates. FDIs, on the other hand, are relatively more stable and have a higher multiplier effect on the host economy than FIIs.

Foreign Direct Investment

Foreign direct investment entails building productive capacity directly in a foreign country. In the *Balance of Payments Manual* (1993) published by the IMF, foreign direct investment is defined as an investment made to acquire lasting interest in enterprises operating outside of the economy of the investor. The foreign entity or group of associated entities that makes the investment is known as the direct investor. The unincorporated or incorporated enterprise—a branch or subsidiary, respectively—in which direct investment is made is referred to as a direct investment enterprise.

***Foreign direct investment** is as an investment made to acquire long-term interest in enterprises operating outside of the economy of the investor.*

According to the *Detailed Benchmark Definition of Foreign Direct Investment* (1996) published by the Organisation for Economic Cooperation and Development (OECD), a direct investment enterprise is an incorporated or unincorporated enterprise in which a single foreign investor: (a) owns 10 percent or more of the ordinary shares or voting power of an enterprise (unless it can be proven that the 10 percent ownership does not allow the investor an effective voice in the management), or (b) owns less than 10 percent of the ordinary shares or voting power of an enterprise, yet still maintains an effective voice in management. An effective voice in management only implies that direct investors are able to influence the management of an enterprise and does not imply that they have absolute control. The most important characteristic of FDIs that distinguishes them from foreign portfolio investment is that they are undertaken with the intention of exercising control over an enterprise.

The level of participation at or above which the direct investor is normally regarded as having an effective say in the management of the enterprise is known as *threshold equity ownership*. The threshold value usually applied for FDI is 10 percent. Some countries do not specify a threshold point, but rely entirely on other criteria, including companies' own assessments of whether the investing company has an effective voice in the foreign firm in which it has an equity stake. In fact, there are many other ways in which foreign investors may acquire an effective voice in an enterprise. These include subcontracting, management contracts, turnkey arrangements, franchising, leasing, licensing, and production sharing. *Subcontracting* refers to assigning some of the obligations of a prior or main contract to another party. In a *management contract*, another firm—usually a foreign firm—performs the managerial functions of the firm, in return for a fee. The management contract may include functions such as technical operations, management of personnel, accounting, marketing, and training. In a *turnkey arrangement* or contract, a company contracts another company— usually a foreign company—that specializes in design, construction, and start-up to build ready-to-operate facilities in complete form. The contract may cover every aspect of the project including training of operating personnel, and on completion of the contract, the 'key' of the manufacturing plant is handed over to the client for operation. *Production sharing* is an alternative to a joint venture in which two or more firms collaborate on the development and production of a product. *Licensing* refers to a firm granting a right to another firm (licensee) to produce its product, use its production processes, or use its brand name or trademark in return for a royalty fee. *Franchising* is essentially the same as licensing, but it is used with reference to services. *Leasing* is a contract in which the owner of an asset grants to another party the right to use the asset for a certain period in return for payment of rent. The financial leases (long-term leases) between direct investors and their branches, subsidiaries, or associates are also included in the definition of FDI.

Foreign direct investment may take the form of either greenfield investment or investment in cross-border mergers and acquisitions. When a multinational corporation (MNC) makes an investment in new production facilities or new operations in a foreign country, such investment is known as greenfield investment. A majority of FDIs in developing countries is greenfield investment. MNCs can also make investments in overseas mergers

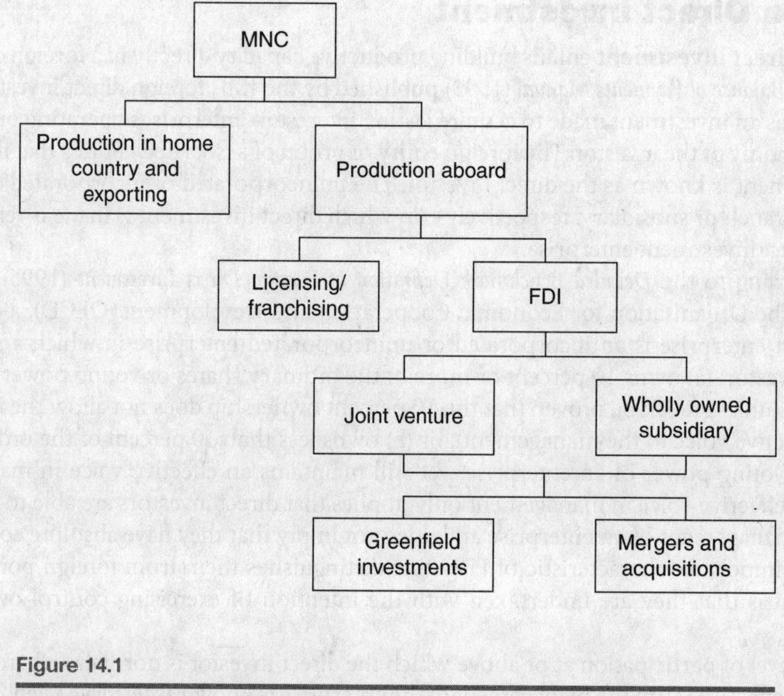

Figure 14.1

The FDI Sequence

and acquisitions in order to have controlling interests in foreign companies. A majority of FDIs in developed nations is in the form of investment in cross-border mergers and acquisitions.

The FDI sequence, as discussed here, is illustrated in Figure 14.1.

Horizontal and Vertical FDI

If an MNC makes an FDI in the same industry in which the MNC does business in its home country, it is called *horizontal FDI*. MNCs undertake horizontal FDIs mainly to reduce trade costs and/or to increase foreign sales. *Vertical FDI* is an FDI made by an MNC in an industry that provides inputs for the MNC, or in an industry that sells the products produced by the MNC in its home country or elsewhere. In other words, vertical investment is a foreign direct investment in companies that are related to different stages of production and distribution of a particular product. An MNC may establish different stages of its production process (vertical FDI) in different countries mainly to take advantage of factor cost differentials.

MNCs may undertake FDIs to increase their market power through vertical integration. The integration may be backward or forward. An MNC may invest in the production process that provides inputs for the MNC's domestic operations. This is called *backward integration*. Backward integration ensures stable supply of inputs to the firm. An MNC may also acquire a foreign firm or make a greenfield investment abroad to sell or distribute the output of its domestic production processes. Such integration, known as *forward integration,* ensures product quality, besides increasing distribution efficiency. By internalizing the upstream or downstream activities, the MNC can exploit lower factor costs abroad. This enables the MNC to be more competitive in both the markets (home market and foreign market).

Key Drivers of FDI

Multinational companies are the driving force behind FDIs. They have established brand names and distribution networks spread over several nations. In fact, the sales turnover of some MNCs is larger than the national incomes of some developing countries. There are, of course, many small and medium-sized MNCs too. Most of these small and medium-sized MNCs are from developing countries, which had earlier isolated themselves from international investment. In view of increasing global business opportunities, MNCs find it necessary to invest overseas. With MNCs going global on a large scale, the entire manufacturing scenario in the world has changed. In the words of UNCTAD, there is a shift from standalone, relatively independent foreign affiliates to integrated international production systems relying on specialized affiliates. In the framework of international intra-firm division of labour, any part of the value-added chain of an enterprise can be located abroad while remaining fully integrated in a corporate network. International economic integration encompasses integration of production in all its aspects along with the integration of markets. This shift encourages FDI in countries that can provide the specific advantages sought by MNCs.

Corporations may have many reasons for undertaking FDIs, and these reasons may not be strictly financial. FDIs may also be made for strategic reasons. For example, corporations may enter foreign countries to preserve their market share when they are being threatened by the potential entry of indigenous firms or MNCs from other countries. Some of the driving forces of FDIs are discussed here.

- *Labour costs and productivity*: The labour market is always an imperfect market. Because of immobility of labour from one country to another, labour services are underpriced in some countries and overpriced in others. Immigration barriers imposed by governments prohibit workers from moving freely across countries to seek adequate compensation (wages or salaries) for their productivity. There are perceptible compensation differentials among countries. This makes corporations undertake productive activities where labour services are underpriced. High productivity of the workforce with low cost is the attraction of FDIs. Countries may become attractive FDI destinations even with higher wage norms, if they have high quality and skilled labour. Countries that possess such advantages are able to attract FDIs in large quantities. The best example in this regard is China. The surge in FDI inflows to China can be attributed to the high productivity but relatively low cost of labour there.
- *Commodity markets*: Another reason for FDIs is imperfect commodity markets. The international markets for goods and services have become imperfect with discriminating tariffs, quotas, and so on, imposed by governments. Various restrictive trade practices adopted by governments have hindered the free flow of goods and services across the countries. In view of restrictions on international trade, corporations may decide to establish production facilities through FDI in countries where there is a good market for their products. In other words, the FDI route enables corporations to circumvent trade barriers and ensure good growth of their businesses.
- *Cost and availability of raw material*: The availability of certain raw materials and components at lower costs may become a good attraction for FDIs into some countries. Corporations may establish their production facilities through FDIs in countries where inputs are available at relatively cheaper or stable prices.
- *Portfolio diversification*: Corporations may also undertake FDIs in order to provide portfolio diversification for their shareholders. In other words, FDIs may enable

corporations to diversify their investments internationally and achieve reduction in investment risks. International diversification of investments may also enhance the value of the firm.

- *Transportation cost and proximity to markets*: Transportation costs are also an important consideration in undertaking FDIs. By establishing production facilities close to raw material sources or distribution centres, the costs of transportation of goods can be reduced. Companies may undertake FDIs closer to their markets (input markets and output market) so that they can reduce their transportation costs. MNCs may also make direct investments in countries that have efficient transportation systems so that transportation costs can be minimized.

Theories of FDI

There are many theories of FDI that explain why and how foreign direct investments are undertaken. The earliest theories of FDI (proposed in the 1950s) held that foreign investments take place because of cross-country differences in return on the capital. The marginal return on capital is low in developed economies as capital is abundantly available. Also, the best investment opportunities are already exploited in these countries. The least developed countries, on the other hand, are capital scarce, and they still have unexploited investment opportunities. Therefore, capital would flow from developed countries to less developed countries for a higher return on investment. Subsequently, it has been realized that cross-border capital flows occur because of other factors too. Some of these factors are:

- Advantage of low taxes or generous subsidies offered by host governments;
- Availability of resources such as labour, managerial personnel, and raw materials at relatively low costs;
- Availability of new markets that can be exploited for the firm's products;
- Improved efficiency that can be achieved in operations by rationalizing operations; and
- Availability of R&D opportunities in the host country.

In view of the changing perspectives of MNCs, new theories have emerged to explain the phenomenon of foreign direct investment. The main theories of FDI are the internationalization theory, Knickerbocker's theory of oligopolistic competition, the eclectic paradigm, and the product life cycle theory. Each of these theories is briefly described in this section.

Internalization Theory Internationalization theory is also known as the *market imperfection approach*. There are three choices for an MNC to expand its business overseas: exporting, licensing, and FDI. The internalization theory explains why MNCs prefer FDI to exporting or licensing. The theory suggests that FDIs are preferable to exporting, if market imperfections are severe. Market imperfections refer to the impediments or hurdles in the free flow of products across national borders. In other words, markets are perfect if there are no external economies of production, there is a free flow of information across the markets, and there are no barriers to trade or competition. Currency overvaluation/undervaluation, capital return differences, technology differences, and government-imposed restrictions would contribute to market imperfections. For example, high tariffs on imported goods and services, restrictions or quotas on imports, and transportation costs are some imperfections in the international market. These imperfections restrict the export of goods and services, thereby reducing the profitability of exporting.

The other routes through which MNCs can extend their operations abroad are licensing or franchising. *Licensing*, as explained earlier, refers to an MNC granting a foreign firm the right to produce its product(s), use its production process, or use its brand name or trademark in return for a fee called royalty. *Franchising* is another name for licensing, but the term franchising is used in the case of services. Franchising is a relatively long-term commitment. In the case of franchising, the MNC that grants the right to use its brand name to the foreign company generally asks for a certain percentage of the franchisee's profits. The franchising contract specifies the percentage of profits to be given to the franchiser. The contract also specifies the conditions, if any, to be fulfilled by the franchisee to use the franchiser's brand name. Licensing and franchising are risky because they involve revealing the proprietary information (e.g. technology, skills) of the MNC. The licensee may use such information (when the contract is interrupted) to compete with the MNC. There is a risk in giving away patent rights or know-how to competitors. When an MNC grants a license to a foreign entity, it means that its control over its own know-how gets diluted. In the case of brands, the licensee may damage the brand image and reputation of the MNC. Further, the firm has to cede a portion of its profits to the licensee or franchisee. These are some of the disadvantages of licensing or franchising. Thus, they may not be preferable when an MNC cannot adequately protect its secrets by a contract, or when it wants to retain tight control over foreign operations emanating from its own knowhow. In certain cases, the expertise of the MNC is not amenable to licensing, which will lead to FDI.

In view of the issues discussed as above, MNCs may prefer the FDI route. An MNC would probably opt for FDI, if the host country market is large, the expected profits are less volatile, or the transaction and transportation costs associated with licensing and exporting are prohibitive. Note that, in a perfectly competitive world economy, there would be no foreign direct investments.

Knickerbocker's Theory of Oligopolistic Competition Many MNCs operate in an oligopolistic environment in which a few firms may dominate a particular industry. For example, three or four firms may control 80 to 90 percent of the market for a particular product. In an oligopolistic market, the action of one player has an impact on other players. Unless there is a close and clear understanding among the dominant players, there will be actions and reactions by the major players. For example, if a firm cuts its price by 10 percent to take away market share from its competitors, it will force the other firms (competitors) to react with similar price cuts to protect their market share. Rivals in the market imitate quickly what a firm does in the market. This imitative behaviour characterizes foreign direct investment. If a firm in an oligopoly market establishes its unit in a foreign country, the other firms think that it will take away their export business in that country or it may affect (through cross-subsidization) their domestic business. Therefore, other firms will follow the first mover and establish units in that country. The motive behind each one's move is to hold each other in check, so that no firm can have a commanding position in the market.

Dunning's Eclectic Paradigm Another theory that analyses and explains FDI is the ownership-location-internalization (OLI) framework or paradigm. Popularly known as Dunning's eclectic theory, the OLI approach states that FDI is the outcome of a process in which the advantages of ownership, location, and internalization work together. Every firm enjoys certain ownership advantages that are firm specific. These include technology, patents, brand image, business reputation, and organization and management skills. Capital abundance is also a firm-specific resource. Economies of scale are also part of ownership advantages. All these factors largely determine the competitive advantage of a firm.

A firm can have these ownership advantages (knowledge capital and money capital) transferred (intra-firm) to different countries without losing their value. The transaction costs involved in such transfer may not be significant. That is, the intangible assets of the firm can be transferred to different foreign locations at little or no cost.

A firm can also derive certain advantages from using location-specific resource endowments. Apart from natural resource endowments, a country may have superior knowledge capital. The cultural and political environment may also generate certain locational advantages. Savings in costs (transportation cost, cost of inputs, etc.) may also be location specific. Low taxes and higher subsidies are also considered as location-specific advantages. Firms may thus set up production or distribution facilities where they can have the maximum locational advantages.

By contracting out the ownership advantages to outside agencies, a firm can gain location-specific advantages. But there are problems with such contracting. The main problem is misuse of the firm's knowledge capital by the licensee or franchisee. In some countries, it may also be difficult to find a suitable licensee or franchisee. Some of the knowledge capital of a firm may not be amenable to licensing. Licensing also involves transaction costs such as costs associated with negotiating, monitoring, and enforcing a contract.

In view of problems with contracting, the firm may develop its own organizational structure to exploit its specific intangible assets and also take advantage of location-specific benefits. In other words, the firm may *internalize* the ownership advantages as well as locational advantages by undertaking FDI. By internalizing across countries, a firm becomes an MNC. But there are costs of operating in foreign countries. Mainly, the MNC has to compete with local firms, which have better market knowledge and contacts. Further, in comparison with other options of servicing the foreign market, such as exporting and licensing, FDI is expensive and risky. It is expensive, because a lot of money has to be expended to float a firm on foreign soil. It is risky, because of problems that may arise in a new or foreign environment.

To penetrate into foreign markets through FDI, ownership advantages and location-specific advantages should be adequate to outweigh the disadvantages of internalizing. If the firm cannot expect the desired location-specific advantages, it is better for the firm to opt for exporting rather than FDI or licensing. Similarly, if internalization advantages are not enough, it is in the best interests of the firm to service the foreign market through licensing.

Vernon's Product Life Cycle Theory The product life cycle model developed by Raymond Vernon also explains the growth of FDIs. Every product passes through a cycle with distinct phases. The product is usually pioneered in a developed country, which has a monopoly as the only country able to produce and supply the product. The product is initially available to the people of that country only. But once it becomes successful in the home market, the company that produces the product exports it to other developed countries. As the demand for the product increases, the pioneering firm undertakes FDI in these countries to take production closer to the markets and also to take advantage of lower factor costs. Simultaneously, the local firms in these countries might set up production facilities and start producing the product for their home markets. This puts a limit on the exports from the pioneering country. As the markets mature and the product becomes standardized in developed countries, price becomes the competitive factor. The cost of the product is under tremendous pressure, and it becomes a crucial issue in sustaining the demand for the product. Thus, Vernon's theory explains the relationship of product life cycle and FDI flows. Note that FDI occurs mostly in the maturity and declining stages of a product's life cycle.

Economic Advantages of FDI

Foreign direct investments have several advantages (direct as well as indirect) for the host country. In fact, host countries may not otherwise be able to get these advantages or resources (e.g. managerial resources). The major benefits of FDIs for the host country are:

- *Technology*: Technology plays a crucial role in the economic development of a country. The developed nations have been able to achieve success mainly through technological progress. However, many countries, particularly the less developed nations, are not able to develop indigenous technology due to various reasons. Such countries can gain access to the technology required for their economic development through FDIs. MNCs that enjoy a monopolistic advantage in technology, may transfer their technological expertise by establishing a foreign subsidiary that can utilize technology not available to its competitors. In other words, countries can benefit from the inflow of technology that accompanies the foreign direct investments made by MNCs. Thus the host country can get not only capital but also technology through FDIs. In some cases, the role of FDI is not to transfer capital but to transfer technology.
- *Knowledge capital*: MNCs are also rich with intangible assets such as patents, trade names, brands, organizational and management skills, and so on. When they undertake FDI, the benefits of such intangible assets are also shared with the host country.
- *Money capital*: MNCs, having access to international capital markets, can get funds at low cost, while indigenous firms may not have the same financing opportunities. The cost of equity capital raised by MNCs in the international financial market is perhaps lower than what it would be for domestic firms. Thus, the cost of funds involved in FDI is low. This may ultimately result in production and supply of the products in the host country at lower prices. Another major advantage of FDIs is the flow of investible resources to host countries. Some countries, especially underdeveloped countries, have limited domestic sources and restricted opportunities to raise funds in the international capital markets. Thus, FDIs facilitate transfer of capital from capital-surplus economies to capital-scarce economies.
- *Cost of production*: It is observed that a foreign firm that comes to a country through FDI carries out business more efficiently or economically than an indigenous firm. This is possible because of certain advantages enjoyed by the MNCs. MNCs may take to vertical integration of various stages of production and distribution, thereby reducing the cost of production. With multiple production centres that enjoy globally coordinated allocation of resources by a single centralized management, the MNC can have optimum utilization of resources and derive the advantage of cost reduction. FDIs allow MNCs to make the best use of their patent rights, leading to large scale production that will reduce the cost of production through economies of scale. The superior management skills and efficient management standards of MNCs will also boost overall productivity, leading to a reduction in the cost of production.
- *Creation of jobs*: Another major advantage of FDIs, particularly greenfield investments, is that the host country will see a substantial increase in employment opportunities for the people in the country. Job creation in the host country by FDIs is both direct and indirect. When an investment is made by an MNC, a lot of new jobs may be created for the citizens of the host country. Some people are directly absorbed by the MNC for its operations in the host country. Most importantly, with foreign direct investments, many new jobs are created indirectly as well. For example, with FDIs in a country, the business of local suppliers may increase, resulting in a substantial rise in job opportunities for the citizens of the host country. The jobs created indirectly will

generally be more than the jobs created directly by FDIs. In some cases, the quality of employment (e.g. higher wage rates) created by FDIs may be better than the quality of the jobs created otherwise. Thus FDIs can be used to reduce unemployment in the host countries.

- *Management development*: MNCs encourage local managerial talent and develop local managers, which will result in a vast pool of superior management skills in the country. In a developing country like India where there is a dearth of superior management expertise, FDIs facilitate the development of managers, besides promoting entrepreneurship.
- *Balance of payments*: As MNCs bring investible funds into the host country, the credits of the capital account of the host country will increase. If the FDIs are used to produce import substitutes or to promote exports from the host country, the current account of the host country will have a favourable position. However, when remittances are made to the parent unit of the MNC, the current account of the host country will have debit entries. On the whole, the host country's balance of payments will improve with FDIs. It is observed that inward FDIs are a major driver of export-led economic growth in a number of countries including China.
- *GDP*: Above all, FDIs increase the production or creation of goods and services in the host country. The increased production of goods and services augments the gross domestic product of the host country. A number of countries have registered higher rates of economic growth with FDIs. The best example in this context is China. The heavy investments made by MNCs in China have helped China in achieving higher annual economic growth rate in the recent past, particularly in the present century. Thus, while FDI is not a sufficient factor for economic development of a country, it is a necessary ingredient. For developing countries, FDI is especially important for eradication of poverty through economic growth.
- *Crowding in*: Crowding in takes place when foreign direct investment stimulates investment in downstream and upstream production by other foreign or domestic producers. The MNCs that enter the host country through FDI provide immense business opportunities for other investors and thereby induce higher investments. In other words, the FDI effect on capital formation in the host country may be greater than the amount of the FDI. For example, a USD 1 million increase in the net flow of FDI may result in an increase of more than USD 1 million in the total investment in the host country. This is possible because of the complementary effect of FDI on investments in the host country. With the initiatives of FDI, many domestic firms may step in and invest in the downstream or upstream activities. In other words, FDI may create an initial base for new entrants.
- *Others*: Foreign direct investments also help the host country in diversifying its industrial base. The international competition that FDIs bring into the host country would result in increased productivity and lower prices through improved business systems. The combined effect of all the benefits of FDIs may lead to an overall increase in standard of living of the people, particularly in the host country.

Limitations of FDI

FDIs may have some negative consequences for the economy of the host country. Some of these are briefly discussed here:

- *Competition*: FDIs increase competition in the host country, not only in the product market but also in the financial market. Such increase in competition may adversely affect domestic companies. The MNCs may have greater economic power to withstand the competition, but domestic firms may not. In other words, the competition in the market may gradually increase the dominance of MNCs, which will ultimately go against the interests of domestic firms.

- *National sovereignty*: The MNCs, with their superior economic power and presence in many countries, may monopolize the markets of the host country. Because of the power they enjoy, the MNCs may hold the host country to economic ransom. If the host country's policies do not suit their business interests, the foreign companies may uproot themselves and transfer their investments elsewhere. Sometimes, the government of the host country may lose real control over the economic affairs of the MNCs in its own country and become a silent spectator to what the MNCs do. In order to maintain national sovereignty despite FDIs, many countries have developed statutes and guidelines that may require that a certain proportion of equity ownership of the foreign subsidiary be spun off to indigenous investors. Some countries impose barriers on foreign entry into certain sectors. Restrictions on royalty payments are also enforced. The host government may also discriminate against foreign firms when awarding contracts. The extent of discrimination may reflect the state of political relations between the source and host countries. The assets of MNCs are also prone to expropriation in the host country, often with inadequate compensation. The fixed investments made by MNCs may be held hostage by the host country to get concessions from source countries. All such fears may create a negative impact on the host country.
- *Crowding out*: If FDIs come into sectors in which domestic firms are themselves planning to invest, impliedly the MNCs would take away the investment opportunities that are available to domestic firms. Further, the MNCs may also out-compete domestic firms if they tend to raise additional funds in the financial markets of the host country. Larger inflows of FDI may also lead to fluctuations in the foreign exchange rate, ultimately resulting in an unfavourable balance of trade. All these imperatives may have a *crowding out* effect on domestic firms.

Despite fears that domestic firms will be edged out in the competition and national sovereignty will be at stake, many nations favour inward FDIs for the reasons discussed earlier. Because of several advantages of FDIs, the host governments offer a number of incentives for FDIs. They may offer tax concessions on sales and profits, tariff concessions such as exemption or reduction of tariffs on imported inputs, and financial incentives such as concessional loans and subsidies. Some host governments may also relax their environmental or safety standards in order to attract FDIs.

Implications of Outward FDIs

FDI from the perspective of the home (source) country of an MNC is called *outward FDI*. For example, if Tata Steel establishes a steel manufacturing plant in the United Kingdom, it is an outward FDI for India, and India is the source or home country. Outward FDIs have both benefits and costs for the home (or source) country. The benefits of outward FDI for the home country are as stated below:

- The major benefit of outward FDI for the home country is in the form of earnings repatriated by the foreign subsidiary. This will contribute to a favourable balance of current account for the home country.
- If an MNC of the home country sets up production facilities in a low-cost production location (country), such products can substitute for the high-cost imports of the home country. This will improve the current account of the balance of payments of the home country.

- The home country's balance of payments will also have an advantage with outward FDIs when the foreign subsidiary imports equipment, machinery, and components from the home country. In other words, the foreign subsidiary may create additional demand for the capital goods of the home country and thereby contribute to the economic development of the home country.
- The MNC that has set up foreign subsidiaries may have exposure to management practices at the international level, which will help in effective management of the parent unit too. This may also improve the overall efficiency of resource utilization in the home country.

Despite the advantages associated with outward FDIs for the home country, countries may restrict or discourage outward FDIs. This is because outward FDIs have certain costs for the home country. Some of them are:

- If the products produced by outward FDIs are substitutes for direct exports from the home country, it will have serious implications for the balance of payments of the home country.
- If the outward FDIs are substitutes for the production of goods and services in the home country, the home country will suffer from further aggravation of unemployment.
- The capital account of the balance of payments of the home country will suffer from the outflow of capital. Capital outflow becomes a serious problem when the home country has a low savings rate and is a capital-scarce economy.
- If outward FDIs are aimed at serving the home country from low-cost production in other countries, it will affect the balance of payments of the home country.

In view of the fact that outward FDIs are not always favourable for the home country, investor countries may take certain policy decisions to restrict the outflow of capital. The home country government may thus make it more difficult for local MNCs to undertake FDIs. It may also offer concessions such as tax holidays for local companies to invest at home.

We have seen why the governments of source countries as well as host countries may encourage or discourage FDIs. Economic considerations as well as political ideologies influence decisions on FDIs. On one extreme, governments may feel that FDIs are instruments for imperialist domination and, on the other extreme, they may subscribe to the idea of a free market world economy. In reality, nations take a stand between these two extremes and adopt policies to suit their national needs and political ideology.

Factors Influencing FDI

Before undertaking an FDI, a company would consider the following factors:

- *The growth potential of the host country*: Corporations would study the host country's economy in order to find out the opportunities for business growth. Important variables such as economic growth rate, per capita income, inflation, fiscal and monetary policies, trade deficit, and currency exchange rate are examined by corporations to assess growth potential. Generally, the less developed economies have huge growth potential as compared to developed economies. Therefore, corporations may direct their FDIs into those potentially high-growth economies.
- *Political stability*: MNCs may also examine the political system in the host country. If the host country is politically unstable, the government policies may become inconsistent and discontinuous, adding to political risk. On the other hand, if a country has

a liberal and market-friendly government, corporations may find good opportunities for business growth with lesser political risk. In tune with their political ideology, political parties may influence the economic or industrial policy of the government. This affects the ownership and control of business operations, including cross-border flows of capital.

- *Integration of the economy*: Corporations would also examine how well the host country's economy is integrated with other economies. If an economy is well integrated into the world economic system, it will have stable economic policies, and abide by international rules and standards. This will give a lot of impetus to FDIs.
- *Ethnic and religious factors*: MNCs may also examine the ethnic and religious issues prevailing in the country, because the frequent occurrence of ethnic or religious conflicts in the host country may disturb the whole business environment.
- *Relation between source country and host country*: MNCs may also take into consideration the relationship that exists between the source country and the host country. If the two countries maintain cordial relations, corporations can function smoothly in the host country. The host country's relations with other major countries in the world are also considered in FDI decisions.
- *Exchange rate stability*: More importantly, the exchange rate stability of the host country's currency against the major currencies in the world is also taken into consideration by corporations. The volatility of the host country's currency will have a detrimental effect on FDIs.
- *Transparent investment environment*: FDIs can also be attracted by a transparent investment climate in the country. The host country should have a good regulatory framework for promoting and protecting investments. MNCs generally expect proper contract enforcement machinery and laws that govern property rights. Stable macroeconomic policies in the country will also attract FDIs. Corporate governance, accounting standards, the taxation system, and the competitive environment in the host country are also important considerations for MNCs to undertake FDIs.

Foreign Investments in India

According to IMF World Economic Outlook 2014, India is the tenth largest economy in the world in terms of GDP at current prices, but in terms of GDP based on PPP valuation, it is the third largest economy in the world. India is also the world's most populous democracy. In addition, India has a large pool of skilled and educated workers. It is also endowed with a good natural resources base. The middle income-group population is large and growing. Labour is abundant with relatively low wages. The country's administration operates under the rule of law with a very stable and established judiciary system. In sum, India has vast industrial opportunities with developed political, legal, and corporate institutions.

FDI Policy

The Government of India announces its policy on foreign direct investment from time to time, keeping in view changing circumstances and requirements. As per the latest FDI policy of the government, the following sectors have been prohibited for FDI:

(i) Atomic energy.
(ii) Lottery business.
(iii) Gambling and betting.
(iv) Business of chit fund.

(v) Nidhi company.
(vi) Agricultural (excluding floriculture, horticulture, development of seeds, animal husbandry, pisciculture, cultivation of vegetables, mushrooms, etc. under controlled conditions and services related to agro and allied sectors) and plantation activities.
(vii) Housing and real estate business (except the development of townships, construction of residential/commercial premises, roads, or bridges to the extent specified).
(viii) Trading in transferable development rights (TDRs).
(ix) Manufacture of cigars and other tobacco items.

The approval mechanism for the foreign direct investment has a two-tier system—the automatic approval route and approval through the Foreign Investment Promotion Board (FIPB).

The activities/sectors that would require prior government approval for FDI are:

(a) Where provisions of Press Note 1 (2005 Series) issued by the Government are attracted; and
(b) Where more than 24 percent foreign equity is proposed to be inducted for manufacture of items reserved for the small-scale sector.

In all the sectors/activities not listed in the FDI policy document, foreign direct investment up to100 percent is permitted on the automatic route, subject to sectoral rules/regulations applicable.

The foreign direct investments may take the form of financial collaborations, joint-ventures and technical collaborations, euro issues, or private placements or preferential allotments.

Foreign Portfolio Investment Policy

Foreign institutional investments are the investments made in securities by institutions incorporated outside India, but registered in accordance with SEBI (FII) Regulations 1995. The foreign institutional investors are permitted to subscribe to new issues or trade in already issued securities.

India has adopted a cautious foreign institutional investment policy, right since it first permitted foreign institutional investments. Foreign institutional investors were first allowed in September 1992 to invest in all kinds of securities traded on the primary and secondary markets. The holding of a single foreign institutional investor and of all foreign institutional investors, non-resident Indians, and overseas corporate bodies (OCBs) in any company are subject to the limit of 5 percent and 24 percent of the company's total issued capital, respectively. Further, the funds invested by foreign institutional investors should have at least 50 participants, with no one holding more than 5 percent. In other words, a foreign institutional investor should be a broad-based and diversified fund. NRIs are permitted to invest through the secondary market subject to individual ceilings of 5 percent, to prevent likely takeover.

The Committee on Liberalisation of Foreign Institutional Investments constituted by the Government of India on 13 March 2002 identified the following advantages and disadvantages of FIIs.

Advantages of FIIs

- Investments by foreign institutional investors increase non-debt-creating foreign currency inflows.
- FIIs can help in reducing the yield differential between equity and bonds, thereby improving corporate capital structure.
- FIIs can contribute to bridging the domestic savings–investment gap.

- FIIs promote financial innovation and development of hedging instruments.
- As professional bodies, foreign institutional investors could increase competition in financial markets, thereby improving the alignment of asset prices to fundamentals. When the prices of securities are aligned to fundamentals, the prices will be as stable as the fundamentals themselves.
- Foreign institutional investors have good information and low transaction costs.
- A variety of risk–return preferences of foreign institutional investors also help in reducing volatility in the market.
- As professional asset managers and financial analysts, the foreign institutional investors will increase efficiency of financial markets besides improving corporate governance.
- By increasing the availability of riskier long-term capital for projects, FIIs can accelerate the process of economic development.

Disadvantages of FIIs

- FIIs may facilitate takeovers, especially hostile takeovers. That is, FIIs may come in handy for acquirers in taking over companies.
- FIIs are popularly described as hot money. They may be withdrawn suddenly and flown to other countries when there are better investment opportunities there. This will destabilize the economy of the host country in general, and stock markets in particular.

Recently, the Securities and Exchange Board of India (SEBI) has introduced a new class of foreign investors, known as Foreign Portfolio Investors (FPIs). This class of investors is formed by merging the existing classes of investors through which portfolio investments were previously made in India, i.e. Foreign Institutional Investors (FIIs), Qualified Foreign Investors (QFIs), and sub-accounts of FIIs. Previously, portfolio investment had been governed by SEBI (Foreign Institutional Investors) Regulations, 1995, for FIIs and their sub-accounts. To govern FPIs, the SEBI has issued the regulations by a notification dated 7 January 2014. Accordingly, no person shall buy, sell, or otherwise deal in securities as a foreign portfolio investor unless it has obtained a certificate granted by the designated depository participant on behalf of SEBI. An applicant shall seek registration as a foreign portfolio investor in one of the categories:

(a) Category I: Includes government and government-related investors such as central banks, governmental agencies, sovereign wealth funds, and international or multilateral organizations or agencies;
(b) Category II: Includes (i) appropriately regulated broad-based funds such as mutual funds, investment trusts, insurance/reinsurance companies; (ii) appropriately regulated persons such as banks, asset management companies, investment managers/advisors, portfolio managers; (iii) broad-based funds that are not appropriately regulated but whose investment manager is appropriately regulated; (iv) university funds and pension funds; and (v) university-related endowments already registered with the SEBI as foreign institutional investors or sub-accounts.
(c) Category III: Includes all others not eligible under Categories I and II, foreign portfolio investors such as endowments, charitable societies, charitable trusts, foundations, corporate bodies, trusts, individuals, and family offices.

A foreign portfolio investor shall invest only in the following securities:

- Securities in the primary and secondary markets including shares, debentures and warrants of companies, listed or to be listed on a recognized stock exchange in India;

- Units of schemes floated by domestic mutual funds, whether listed on a recognized stock exchange or not;
- Units of schemes floated by a collective investment scheme;
- Derivatives traded on a recognized stock exchange;
- Treasury bills and dated government securities;
- Commercial papers issued by an Indian company;
- Rupee-denominated credit-enhanced bonds;
- Security receipts issued by asset reconstruction companies;
- Perpetual debt instruments and debt capital instruments, as specified by the Reserve Bank of India from time to time;
- Listed and unlisted non-convertible debentures/bonds issued by an Indian company in the infrastructure sector, where 'infrastructure' is defined in terms of the extant External Commercial Borrowings (ECB) guidelines;
- Non-convertible debentures or bonds issued by Non-Banking Financial Companies categorized as 'Infrastructure Finance Companies' (IFCs) by the Reserve Bank of India;
- Rupee-denominated bonds or units issued by infrastructure debt funds;
- Indian depository receipts; and
- Such other instruments specified by the SEBI from time to time.

In a separate circular, the Reserve Bank of India has stated that all foreign portfolio investors including FIIs and QFIs taken together cannot acquire more than 24 percent of the paid up capital of an Indian company. A Non-Resident Indian (NRI) and Person of Indian Origin (PIO) can purchase or sell shares/fully and mandatorily convertible debentures of Indian companies on the stock exchanges under the portfolio investment scheme. An NRI/PIO can purchase shares up to 5 percent of the paid-up capital of an Indian company. All NRIs/PIOs taken together cannot purchase more than 10 percent of the paid-up value of the company.

Progressive Liberalization for FIIs To fill the domestic savings-investment gap and encourage professional investment in the country, restrictions on FIIs have been progressively liberalized. The initiatives in this regard are briefly discussed here:

- From November 1996, any registered foreign institutional investor willing to make 100 percent investment in debt securities is permitted to do so, subject to specific approval from SEBI, designating it as a separate category of foreign institutional investors or sub-accounts as 100 percent debt funds. However, such investments by 100 percent debt funds are subject to fund-specific ceilings specified by SEBI and an overall debt cap of USD 1 billion to USD 1.5 billion. Further, investments were allowed only in debt securities of companies listed or to be listed on stock exchanges, provided they are free from maturity limitations.
- Since April 1997, the aggregate limit for all FIIs, which was originally 24 percent, has been allowed to be increased up to 30 percent by the Indian company concerned, through a resolution by its board of directors, followed by a special resolution to that effect by its general body.
- From April 1998, FIIs are allowed in dated government securities. Treasury bills were originally outside the ambit of such investments. But, from May 1998, they have been included in the category of dated government securities despite the fact that they are money market instruments.

- From 1998, the aggregate portfolio investment limits of non-resident Indians, overseas corporate bodies (organizations predominantly owned by individuals of Indian nationality or origin resident outside India), persons of Indian origin, and foreign institutional investors have been raised from 5 percent to 10 percent, and their ceilings are independent of each other.
- From March 2000, the aggregate ceiling for FIIs, usually called ceiling under the special procedure, has been increased from 30 percent to 40 percent of the issued and paid up capital of a company. But that (enhanced ceiling) has to be approved by the board of directors as well as the general body of the company concerned through a special resolution.
- From March 2001, the aggregate ceiling has been raised from 40 percent to 49 percent.
- From September 2001, the ceiling under the special procedure has been raised up to the sectoral cap.
- From February 2008, institutional investors—including foreign institutional investors and their sub-accounts—have been allowed to undertake short-selling, lending, and borrowing of Indian securities. To further increase FIIs in the Indian market, the Government of India and the SEBI have allowed foreign individuals, corporations and other investors such as hedge funds to register directly as foreign institutional investors. It is a move designed to increase transparency and reduce transaction costs for these investors.
- In May 2008, the SEBI simplified the registration norms for FIIs and sub-accounts. Significantly, it has allowed investment managers, advisors, or institutional portfolio managers in the NRI category to be registered as FIIs. The SEBI has also hiked the total permissible investment limit in government and corporate debt up to USD 4.1 billion from USD 3.5 billion. While the limit in corporate debt remains unchanged, the FIIs investment limit in government securities has been increased to USD 2.6 billion from USD 2 billion.
- From May 2008, an asset management company, investment manager or advisor, or an institutional portfolio manager set up and/or owned by a non-resident Indian shall be eligible to be registered as a foreign institutional investor, subject to the condition that they shall not invest their proprietary funds.
- Foreign institutional investors have been allowed to purchase, on repatriation basis, dated government securities/treasury bills, listed non-convertible debentures/bonds, commercial papers issued by an Indian company, and units of domestic mutual funds and security receipts issued by asset reconstruction companies, either directly from the issuer of such securities or through a registered stock broker on a recognized stock exchange in India, provided that:
  - (i) the foreign institutional investor shall restrict allocation of its total investment between equity and debt instruments in the ratio 70:30;
  - (ii) if the foreign institutional investor desires to invest up to 100 percent in dated government securities including treasury bills and non-convertible debentures/bonds issued by an Indian company, it shall form a 100 percent debt fund and get such a fund registered with SEBI; and
  - (iii) the total holding by a single foreign institutional investor in each tranche of scheme of security receipts shall not exceed 10 percent of the issue, and the total holdings of all foreign institutional investors put together shall not exceed 49 percent of the paid up value of each tranche of scheme of security receipts issued by the asset reconstruction companies.

- From October 2008, the conditions pertaining to restrictions of the 70:30 ratio of investments in equity and debt has been dispensed with, to give flexibility to foreign institutional investors to allocate their investments across equity and debt instruments.

Because of progressive liberalization of restrictions on FIIs and the fast growth of the Indian economy, there has been a growing demand for Indian stocks by foreign institutional investors. In addition to a substantial increase in the net investment made by foreign institutional investors in Indian stocks over time, the number of foreign institutional investors registered with SEBI has also increased. As can be observed from Table 14.1, the investments in India by FIIs (net) increased from USD 1,847 million in 2000–01 to USD 29,422 million in 2010–11. In 2013–14, the FIIs made investments to the tune of USD 5,010 million.

External Commercial Borrowings (ECB)

External Commercial Borrowings (ECB) are the commercial loans in the form of bank loans, buyers' credit, suppliers' credit, securitized instruments such as floating rate notes and fixed rate bonds availed from non-resident lenders with minimum average maturity of three years. As per the ECB policy of the Government of India, ECB can be accessed under the automatic route and the approved route.

Automatic Route Corporates except financial intermediaries are eligible to raise ECB. Units in the Special Economic Zone (SEZ) are also allowed to raise ECB for their own requirement. Borrowers can raise ECB from internationally recognized sources such as international banks, international capital markets, multilateral financial institutions, export credit agencies, suppliers of equipment, foreign collaborators, and foreign equity holders.

Table 14.1 Investments in India by FIIs (USD Million)

Year	*Investments by FIIs (net)*
2000–01	1,847
2001–02	1,505
2002–03	377
2003–04	10,918
2004–05	8,686
2005–06	9,926
2006–07	3,225
2007–08	20,328
2008–09	(–)15,017
2009–10	29,048
2010–11	29,422
2011–12	16,812
2012–13	27,582
2013–14	5,010

Source: Reserve Bank of India.

The maximum amount of ECB which can be raised by a corporate is USD 500 million or equivalent during a financial year. The utilization of ECB proceeds is not permitted for on-lending or investment in capital market or acquiring a company in India by a corporate. The ECB proceeds cannot be utilized in real estate. The utilization of ECB proceeds is not permitted for working capital, general corporate purpose, and repayment of existing rupee loans. The ECB proceeds for foreign currency expenditure for permissible end-uses shall be parked overseas and not to be remitted to India.

Approval Route The eligible borrowers under the approval route are as follows:

(a) Financial institutions dealing exclusively with infrastructure or export finance.
(b) Banks and financial institutions which had participated in the textile or steel sector restructuring package as approved by the Government.
(c) Non-banking financial institutions for ECB with minimum average maturity of five years.
(d) Housing finance companies satisfying certain criteria.
(e) Special-purpose vehicles, or any other entity notified by the Reserve Bank of India set up to finance exclusively infrastructure companies/projects.
(f) Multi-state cooperative societies engaged in manufacturing activity.
(g) Corporates engaged in the industrial sector and the infrastructure sector in India.
(h) Non-government organizations engaged in micro-finance activities.

Corporates can avail of ECB of an additional amount of USD 250 million with an average maturity of more than 10 years under the approval route, over and above the existing limit of USD 500 million under the automatic route, during a financial year. A corporate in an infrastructure sector can avail ECB up to USD 100 million and a corporate in the industrial sector can avail ECB up to USD 50 million for rupee capital expenditure for permissible end-uses within the overall limit of USD 500 million per borrower, per financial year, under the automatic route. NGOs engaged in micro-finance activities can raise ECB up to USD 5 million during a financial year. Corporates in the services sector, viz. hotels, hospitals, software, etc. can avail ECB up to USD 100 million per borrower, per financial year, for the import of capital goods.

The ECB can be converted into equity subject to the following conditions:

(a) The activity of the company is covered under the automatic route for foreign direct investment, or Government approval has been obtained by the company for foreign equity participation.
(b) The foreign equity holding after such conversion of debt into equity is within the sectoral cap, if any.
(c) Pricing of shares is as per SEBI and erstwhile CCI guidelines/regulations in the case of listed/unlisted companies as the case may be.

Global Depository Receipts (GDRs)/American Depository Receipts (ADRs)

Indian companies can raise foreign currency resources by issuing Global Depository Receipts GDRs)/American Depository Receipts (ADRs). Depository Receipts are defined as negotiable securities issued outside India by a Depository Bank, on behalf of an Indian company, which represent the local rupee-denominated equity shares of the company held as deposit by a custodian bank in India. The Depository Receipts listed and traded in the U.S. financial markets are known as ADRs and those listed and traded elsewhere are known as GDRs.

Indian companies can raise foreign currency resources abroad through the issue of GDRs/ADRs in accordance with the guidelines issued by the Government of India.

A company can issue ADRs/GDRs, if it is eligible to issue shares to persons resident outside India under the FDI scheme. Unlisted companies, which have not yet accessed the ADRs/GDRs route for raising capital in the international market, would require prior or simultaneous listing in the domestic market, while seeking to issue such instruments. Unlisted companies, which have already issued ADRs/GDRs in the international market, have to list in the domestic market on making profit or within three years of such issue of ADRs/GDRs, whichever is earlier.

There are no end-use restrictions except for a ban on deployment/investment of such funds in real estate or the stock market. There is no monetary limit up to which an Indian company can raise ADRs/GDRs. The ADR/GDR proceeds can be utilized for first-stage acquisition of shares in the disinvestment process of public sector undertakings and also in the mandatory second-stage offer to the public in view of their strategic importance.

The pricing of ADR/GDR issues should be made at a price not less than the higher of the following two averages:

(i) The average of the weekly high and low of the closing prices of the related shares quoted on the stock exchange during the six months preceding the relevant date;
(ii) The average of the weekly high and low of the closing prices of the related shares quoted on the stock exchange during the two weeks preceding the relevant date.

A limited two-way fungibility scheme is in place for ADRs/GDRs. Under the scheme, a stock broker in India, registered with SEBI, can purchase shares of an Indian company from the market for conversion into ADRs/GDRs based on instructions received from overseas investors. Reissuance of ADRs/GDRs would be permitted to the extent of ADRs/GDRs which have been redeemed into underlying shares and sold in the Indian market.

Under sponsored ADR/GDR issue, a company can offer its resident shareholders a choice to submit their shares back to the company so that on the basis of such shares, ADRs/GDRs can be issued outside India. The proceeds of such issue is remitted back to India and distributed among the resident investors who had offered their rupee-denominated shares for conversion. These proceeds can be kept in Resident Foreign Currency (Domestic) accounts in India by the resident shareholders who have tendered such shares for conversion into ADRs/GDRs.

Indian Depository Receipts

An **Indian depository receipt (IDR)** is a financial instrument that allows foreign companies to mobilize funds from Indian markets by offering equity and become listed on Indian stock exchanges. In the words of Reserve Bank of India, "an IDR is an instrument denominated in Indian rupees in the form of a depository receipt created by a domestic depository (custodian of securities registered with the SEBI) against the underlying equity of issuing company to enable foreign companies to raise funds from the Indian securities market". This financial instrument is similar to GDRs/ADRs. The actual shares underlying IDRs are held by an overseas custodian, who authorizes the Indian depository to issue the IDRs. The overseas custodian shall be a foreign bank having a place of business in India. The overseas custodian is required to get approval from the Government of India for acting as a custodian, while the Indian depository needs to be registered with the SEBI. The Government of India, as part of its efforts to globalize the Indian capital market, has opened the window (IDRs) for foreign companies to raise funds from India. IDRs allow local investors exposure in global companies.

*An **Indian depository receipt (IDR)** is a financial instrument that allows foreign companies to mobilize funds from Indian markets by offering equity.*

The Government of India has notified the Companies (Issue of Indian Depository Receipts) Rules, 2004 to facilitate overseas companies issuing depository receipts in Indian currency. These rules apply to these companies incorporated outside India, whether they have established any place of business in India or not. An outline of the major points in these rules is provided in this section.

A company may issue IDRs only if it satisfies the following conditions:

(i) Its pre-issue paid up capital and free reserves are at least USD 50 million, and it has had minimum average market capitalization (during the last 3 years) in its parent country of at least USD 100 million.
(ii) It has a track record of distributable profits for at least three out of immediately preceding five years.
(iii) It has a continuous trading record or history on a stock exchange in its parent country for at least three immediately preceding years.
(iv) It has not been prohibited to issue securities by any regulatory body and has a good track record with respect to compliance with securities market regulations.
(v) The size of an IDR issue shall not be less than INR 50 crore.

No company shall raise funds in India by issuing IDRs unless it has obtained prior permission from SEBI. An application seeking permission shall be made to SEBI at least 90 days prior to the opening date of the issue. The draft prospectus or draft letter of offer along with the prescribed form shall also be filed with the SEBI through the merchant banker.

The company shall obtain the necessary approvals or exemption from the appropriate authority from the country of its incorporation, under the relevant laws relating to issue of capital, where required. It shall appoint an overseas custodian bank, a domestic depository, and a merchant banker for the purpose of issuing IDRs. The issuing company shall deliver the underlying equity shares or cause them to be delivered to an overseas custodian bank, and the said bank shall authorize the domestic depository to issue IDRs.

The IDRs issued by a company in any financial year shall not exceed 15 percent of its paid up capital and free reserves. The issuing company seeking permission shall obtain, in principle, listing permission from one or more stock exchanges having nationwide trading terminals in India. The issuing company may appoint underwriters registered with SEBI to underwrite the issue of IDRs.

Only qualified institutional investors are allowed to invest in Indian depository receipts. Non-resident Indians and foreign institutional investors cannot purchase or possess IDRs unless special permission of the RBI is obtained. Indian companies can also invest in IDRs, but it should not exceed the investment limits fixed by its board. The minimum investment in IDRs is INR 20,000. In every issue of IDR, at least 50 percent of the IDRs issued shall be subscribed to by QIBs, and the balance 50 percent shall be available for subscription by non-institutional investors.

On the receipt of dividend or other corporate action on the IDRs as specified in the agreements between the issuing company and the domestic depository, the domestic depository shall distribute the dividend or corporate action to the IDR holders in proportion to their holdings of IDRs.

A resident holder of IDRs may transfer the IDRs or may ask the domestic depository to redeem the IDRs, subject to the provisions of the Foreign Exchange Management Act (FEMA), 1999 and other laws. In case of redemption, the domestic depository shall request the overseas custodian bank to release the corresponding underlying equity shares in favour of the Indian resident. So they may be sold directly on behalf of the Indian resident or be transferred in the books of the issuing company to the name of the Indian resident. A copy of the request shall be sent to the issuing company for information.

The repatriation of the proceeds of issue of IDRs shall be subject to laws in place regarding the export of foreign exchange. IDRs shall not be convertible into the underlying equity shares before one year from the date of issue of the IDRs.

Fungibility As per the circular of SEBI, dated 1 March 2013, all IDRs shall have partial two-way fungibility. It means that the IDRs can be converted into underlying equity shares and vice versa within the available headroom. The headroom for this purpose shall be the number of IDRs originally issued minus the number of IDRs outstanding, which is further adjusted for IDRs redeemed into underlying equity shares. The following are the SEBI guidelines for fungibility of IDR issuance:

- IDRs shall not be redeemable into underlying equity shares before the expiry of one-year period from the date of listing of IDRs.
- After completion of one-year period from the date of listing of IDRs, the issuer shall, provide two-way fungibility of IDRs.
- IDR fungibility shall be provided on a continuous basis.
- The issuer shall provide said fungibility to IDR holders in any of the following ways:
  (a) Converting IDRs into underlying shares; or
  (b) Converting IDRs into underlying shares and selling the underlying shares in the foreign market where the shares of the issuer are listed and providing the sale proceeds to the IDR holders; or
  (c) Both the above options may be provided to IDR holders.

  Provided that the option once exercised and disclosed by the issuer at the time of offering the IDRs to public cannot be changed without the specific approval of SEBI.
- All the IDRs that have been applied for fungibility by the holder shall be transferred to the IDR redemption account at the time of application.
- In case of option of converting the IDRs into underlying equity shares and providing the sale proceeds to the IDR holders is exercised, the issuer shall disclose the range of fixed/variable costs in percentage terms upfront and ensure that all the costs together shall not exceed 5 percent of the sale proceeds.
- Available headroom and significant conversion/reconversion transactions shall be disclosed by the issuer on a continuous basis.

Foreign Investments by Indian Companies

Globalization of trade and investments has offered opportunities for Indian companies to invest overseas. Previously, the stress was on inward FDI flows to accelerate and sustain economic growth. In recent years, however, it has been realized that the country's economic development also lies in overseas investments made by Indian companies. Accordingly, the government has evolved a policy for outward FDI flows.

In 1969, the Government of India, for the first time, issued formal guidelines for overseas direct investment, and permitted Indian firms to participate in turnkey projects involving no cash remittances. As part of the economic reform process, the Government of India liberalized the overseas investment policy on the recommendations of the Kalyan Banerjee Committee (1992). It was felt that Indian industry should have access to new markets and technologies with a view to increasing its competitiveness globally. In 1992, an automatic route for foreign investments was introduced, and cash remittances were allowed for the first time. However, the total value was restricted to USD 2 million, with a cash component not exceeding USD 0.5 million in a block of three years. In 1995, a fast-track route was introduced where limits were raised from USD 2 million to USD 4 million and linked to average export earnings of the preceding three years. For investment above USD 4 million, approvals were considered under the normal route at the special committee level.

The Foreign Exchange Management Act, which came into effect in 1999, has changed the entire perspective on foreign investment in India. The limit for investment up to USD 50 million, which was earlier available in a block of three years, was made available annually without any profitability condition. Indian companies were also permitted to invest

100 percent of the proceeds of their ADR/GDR issues for acquiring foreign companies and for direct investments in joint ventures and wholly owned subsidiaries. In 2002, the automatic route was further liberalized to enable Indian companies to invest in joint ventures and wholly owned subsidiaries for amounts not exceeding USD 100 million, as against the earlier limit of USD 50 million in a year. In 2003, the automatic route was further liberalized, and Indian firms were permitted to invest overseas in any bona fide business to the extent of 200 percent of their net worth as per the last audited balance sheet. No prior approval of the government is required for opening offices abroad by Indian exporters.

The following are the routes through which Indian companies can make overseas investments:

1. *The automatic route*: Indian companies can freely invest up to USD 100 million in a year without prior approval from the Government of India, provided the overseas investment is not real-estate oriented. In the case of investment in SAARC countries (excluding Pakistan and Myanmar) this limit is raised to USD 150 million. Such investments can be funded out of balances held in the Exchange Earners' Foreign Currency Account (EEFC) of the Indian company, or 100 percent ADR/GDR proceeds, or drawal of foreign exchange from an authorized dealer in India up to 100 percent of the net worth of the Indian company. Such investments are to be reported post facto to the RBI. The special-economic-zone (SEZ) units in the country are eligible to make overseas investments up to any amount under the automatic route without being subject to the ceiling of USD 100 million, to be funded out of EEFC balances of the unit. Such investment by SEZ units shall, however, be subject to an overall ceiling of USD 500 million for all SEZ units put together.
2. *The GDR/ADR automatic stock/swap route*: Indian companies can automatically swap their fresh issue of ADRs/GDRs for overseas acquisitions in the same core activity up to USD 100 million or 10 times their export earnings in the last year, subject to post facto reporting to RBI. Within 30 days from the date of issue of ADRs/GDRs in exchange for acquisition of shares of the foreign company, the Indian company shall submit a report in form ODG to the RBI.
3. *Investment by partnership firms*: A partnership firm registered under the Indian Partnership Act, 1932, and engaged in providing specified professional services may, without prior approval of the RBI, invest up to USD 1 million or its equivalent in one financial year in a foreign concern engaged in similar activity, by way of remittance from India and/or capitalization of fees/other entitlements due to it from such foreign concerns, provided the investing firm is a member of the respective all India professional organization/body.
4. *The normal route*: The investment proposals not covered under the automatic route are considered by the Special Committee on Overseas Investments.

Overseas investments can be funded by different sources. Banks in India are also permitted to extend credit/non-credit facilities to Indian joint ventures/wholly owned subsidiaries abroad up to the extent of 20 percent of their unimpaired capital funds, subject to certain terms and conditions. The Overseas Investment Finance Program of Exim Bank seeks to cover the entire cycle of Indian investment overseas including the financing requirements of Indian joint ventures and wholly owned subsidiaries.

Liberalized guidelines and funding by banks for overseas investment have enabled Indian corporations to establish their presence in overseas markets. Many acquisitions have also taken place through an overseas special purpose vehicle (SPV) set up to raise funds from international markets. Through overseas acquisitions, Indian corporations have gained entry into markets of developed countries. Indian corporations have also acquired advanced manufacturing technologies that help reduce the cost of production. The Indian textile industry and the Indian IT industry have a presence across the globe in the form of high-end designing studios and subsidiaries, respectively, to cater to business in particular regions.

Liberalized Remittance Scheme for Resident Individuals The Reserve Bank of India announced in February 2004 a scheme known as the Liberalized Remittance Scheme towards liberalization of the foreign exchange facilities available to resident individuals. Under the scheme, resident individuals can acquire and hold shares or debt instruments or any other assets including property outside India without prior approval of the Reserve Bank of India. Individual residents can also open, maintain, and hold foreign currency accounts with banks outside India for carrying out transactions permitted under the scheme. Under the scheme, resident individuals including minors are allowed to freely remit up to USD 125,000 per financial year (April–March) for any permissible current or capital account transaction or a combination of both. On a subsequent review of the scheme, it is decided that the scheme should no longer be used for acquisition of immovable property, directly or indirectly, outside India. The scheme shall not be used for making remittances for any prohibited or illegal activities such as margin trading, lottery, etc. Resident individuals are, however, allowed to set up joint ventures/wholly owned subsidiaries outside India for bonafide business activities outside India within the limit of USD 125,000.

The facility under the scheme is in addition to those already available for private travel, business travel, studies, medical treatment, etc., as described in Schedule III of Foreign Exchange Management (Current Account Transactions) Rules, 2000. The scheme can also be used for these purposes. However, remittances for gift and donation cannot be made separately and are subsumed under the limit available under this scheme. Accordingly, resident individuals can remit towards gifts and donations up to USD 125,000 per financial year under this Liberalized Remittance Scheme. All the measures under the scheme are aimed at moderating outflows, but any genuine requirement beyond these limits will be considered by the Reserve Bank of India under the approval route.

India's overseas direct investments can be observed from Table 14.2. There is a spectacular increase in the amount of investment abroad. It increased from USD 1,564.1 million in 2003–04 to USD 30,862.9 million in 2011–12. With the exception of the years when the world economy faced the financial crisis, India's overseas direct investments were set to increase year after year. Cumulatively, India has invested USD 121,818 million during the period from 2003–04 to 2011–12. Much of the overseas direct investments were in the manufacturing sector. Financial services and real estate are also favourable destinations of India's overseas direct investments. Mauritius, Singapore, the Netherlands, the U.K., the U.S.A., the UAE, and Cyprus are the major investee countries of India.

Table 14.2 India's Overseas Direct Investments

Year	*USD million*
2003–04	1,564.1
2004–05	1,991.8
2005–06	7,834.6
2006–07	13,236.8
2007–08	18,446.7
2008–09	16,327.7
2009–10	12,303.6
2010–11	16,402.7
2011–12	30,862.9

Source: Reserve Bank of India.

The Bilateral Investment Promotion and Protection Agreement

The developing countries including India are capital scarce and technology deficient. So they have opened up their economies to attract foreign capital through liberalized investment policies. There is no denying the fact that the developed countries also compete with the developing countries to attract foreign resources to further develop their economies. As investors seek those investment destinations which provide most protective and profitable climate for their investments, the countries, whether they are developed or underdeveloped, have taken several measures to encourage resource flows into their own countries. One such measure is the Bilateral Investment Promotion and Protection Agreement (BIPA). The BIPA is European in origin as the first of its kind was signed between the Federal Republic of Germany and Pakistan in November 1959. By definition, BIPA is a treaty which seeks to promote bilateral investment flows by assuring fair and equitable treatment to investments on post-establishment basis through reciprocal provisions like most favoured nation status, national treatment status and mechanism for dispute resolution, etc. The purpose of BIPA is to create such conditions that are favourable for encouraging investments by the investors of one country in the territory of the other country. The encouragement and reciprocal protection under BIPA will stimulate individual business initiatives for increasing prosperity in both the countries. The BIPA and Double taxation Avoidance Agreement (DTAA) are the policy tools used by the Government of India for the promotion of foreign investments.

As a part of economic reforms, the Government of India liberalized its foreign investment policy and undertook negotiations with a number of countries leading to Bilateral Investment Promotion and Protection Agreements with more than 80 countries. India has signed 83 BIPAs, of which 72 are in force currently. The countries with which India has a BIPA include the United Kingdom, Russia, Germany, Malaysia, Denmark, the Netherlands, Italy, Israel, South Korea, Egypt, Switzerland, France, Vietnam, Spain, Thailand, Taiwan, Australia, Sweden, Mongolia, Portugal, and Argentina.

The legal text of BIPA contains as many as 16 Articles, and each one deals with an aspect of foreign investment. For example, Article 1 defines investment; Article 4 provides for extending National Treatment and Most Favoured Nation Treatment to foreign investments; Articles 9 and 10 provide elaborate dispute resolution mechanisms to resolve disputes between an investor and a host government as well as between the two governments; and Article 16 provides that the Agreement shall remain in force initially for a period of 10 years. However, various clauses in the BIPR are increasingly interpreted in more liberal ways than expected, leading to many disputes. There are many treaty claims against India. One of the recent cases is Vodafone B. V. which filed a notice of dispute in 2012 under the India–Netherlands BIPA. It claimed that the Indian Government's decision to enact the Indian Finance Bill 2012, which sought to retroactively tax the 2007 share–purchase agreement between Hutchinson Telecommunications International Ltd and Vodafone would be a failure to accord fair and equitable treatment. In the same year (2012), the Children's Investment Fund filed a notice of dispute, invoking both the India–UK BIPA and the India–Cyprus BIPA, with regard to its investment in Coal India.

Trends in FDI

According to the World Investment Report 2014, the world's foreign direct investment inflows rose to a level of USD 1,452 billion in the year 2013 from USD 1,330 billion in the year 2012. The world's FDI outflows also increased from USD 1,347 billion in the year 2012 to USD 1,411 in the year 2013. As can be observed from Table 14.3, the developing economies and transition economies are the major destinations of FDI inflows.

Table 14.3 FDI Flows (USD Billion)

Region	*FDI inflows*			*FDI outflows*		
	2011	*2012*	*2013*	*2011*	*2012*	*2013*
World	1,700	1,330	1,452	1,712	1,347	1,411
Developed economies	880	517	566	1216	853	857
Developing economies	725	729	778	423	440	454
Transition economies	95	84	108	73	54	99

Source: World Investment Report 2014.

The FDI flows into India can be observed from Table 14.4. India received USD 4,029 FDI inflows in 2000–01, which rose to USD 22,826 million in 2006–07 and further to USD 36,396 million in 2013–14. India recorded a huge amount of FDI inflow of USD 46,556 million in 2011–12. Cumulatively, India received USD 323,912 million (equity inflows, reinvested earnings, and other capital) from 2000–01 to 2013–14. The cumulative amount of FDI equity inflows was to the tune of USD 217,581 million from 2000–01 to 2013–14.

The FDI equity inflows to India come from different sources. As can be observed from Table 14.5, Mauritius is the largest source, followed by Singapore and the U.K. The countries such as Japan, the U.S.A., the Netherlands, Cyprus, Germany, and France have also contributed in a significant measure to FDI equity inflows into India. Services sector is the major destination of FDI equity inflows, followed by construction development, which includes

Table 14.4 FDI Flows into India (USD Million)

Year	*Total FDI Flows*
2000–01	4,029
2001–02	6,130
2002–03	5,035
2003–04	4,322
2004–05	6,051
2005–06	8,961
2006–07	22,826
2007–08	34,843
2008–09	41,873
2009–10	37,745
2010–11	34,847
2011–12	46,556
2012–13	34,298
2013–14	36,396

Source: Fact Sheet on Foreign Direct Investment, Reserve Bank of India.

Table14.5 FDI Equity Inflows to India by Investing Country (USD Million)

Country	*2011–12*	*2012–13*	*2013–14*
Mauritius	9,942	9,497	4,859
Singapore	5,257	2,308	5,985
U.K.	7,874	1,080	3,215
Japan	2,972	2,237	1,718
U.S.A.	1,115	557	806
Netherlands	1,409	1,856	2,270
Cyprus	1,587	490	557
Germany	1,622	860	1,038
France	663	646	305
Switzerland	353	180	341

Source: Reserve Bank of India.

townships, housing, etc. Telecommunications and computer software and hardware also attract a sizable proportion of FDI equity inflows.

Bottlenecks in FDI Flows to India

After independence, India adopted an economic policy known as the socialistic pattern of society, with central planning and tight government regulations, permits, licences, and controls. The tight government regulations and controls on the start-up as well as expansion of businesses resulted in the slow growth of the economy. A continuous increase in population has also added to both social and economic problems in the country. Rigid economic policies almost brought the country to economic ruin, and India thus nearly reached a state of bankruptcy in 1991. It was at this point that India embraced economic liberalization and started opening its markets to foreign investments. The Indian economy, however, has not been opened up to global investors with full-scale economic reforms. Though there have been vibrant changes across all sectors of the economy following liberalization, the country is still bogged down with several problems, some of which are mentioned below:

- *Infrastructure bottlenecks*: Globalization and economic liberalization have stepped up many economic activities in the Indian economy, putting heavy stress on the available infrastructure. The government has taken certain steps to increase facilities like transport, power, and telecommunications, but these efforts have not yielded the desired results. The growth in infrastructure has not matched the demand. Thus, the inadequate infrastructure has become a major hurdle for inward FDI flows. The poor infrastructure facilities in the country have discouraged foreign investors from investing their money in India.
- *Bureaucratic hurdles*: The government has initiated several measures for smooth flow of FDI into the country. The Companies Act has been amended to ease restrictions on corporate investments. There are provisions in the relevant acts for automatic approvals in many cases and for easy establishment of business units. Nevertheless, investors have to deal with inefficient and slow-moving bureaucracy for several things.

Although the economy is progressing towards liberalization and globalization, the process of economic reforms is very slow. The complex approval procedures confronting foreign investors also discourage FDIs.

- *Taxes and tariffs*: India follows a complex tax and tariff structure, which makes it difficult for potential investors to project their returns. The individual state governments in the country have their own tax and tariff structures. Besides confusion, this adds to uncertainty of returns for investors.
- *Labour laws*: The labour laws in India are highly complex and inflexible. Existing Indian labour laws forbid layoffs of workers and, therefore, even legitimate attempts to restructure business are thwarted. The lack of an exit policy is also responsible for India's poor performance in the area of FDIs.
- *Political instability and corruption*: In recent years, the government at the Centre has become shaky with a multiplicity of political parties having formed ruling coalitions. As the political parties in the coalition government have divergent political agenda, it has become highly difficult to push for sustained economic reforms and growth in India. Moreover, the political system in general is highly corrupt. Corruption is noticed in nearly every public service. The misuse of public office for private gain has become a common phenomenon in India. This has also added to the problems of foreign investors.

Summary

1. Foreign investments and foreign trade are drivers of world economic growth. They are complementary to each other as the development of one facilitates the development of the other.
2. The drivers of foreign direct investments are many, and they may not be strictly financial. Factors like imperfect labour markets, imperfect commodity markets, and inter-national portfolio diversification do influence foreign direct investments.
3. Foreign direct investment is essentially a long-term investment and is associated with investment in capital assets and creating employment, while foreign institutional investment is inherently short-term investment linked to the financial markets.
4. There are many advantages of foreign direct investments. The major advantage is the flow of investible resources to host countries. Foreign direct investments facilitate transferring capital from capital-surplus countries to capital-scarce countries. Foreign direct investments may also stimulate investments in downstream and upstream production by other foreign or domestic producers.
5. If foreign direct investments come into sectors in which domestic firms are themselves planning to make investment, the foreign direct investments may knock away the investment opportunities that are available to domestic firms.
6. Growth potential, political stability, and ethnic and religious factors would influence foreign direct investments.
7. According to the latest FDI policy of India, FDI is not permitted in atomic energy, lottery business, and gambling and betting. In many sectors, the FDI is permitted up to 100 percent on the automatic route, subject to applicable sectoral restrictions.
8. The restrictions on FIIs have been progressively liberalized in India. Equity shares, convertibles debentures, and dated government securities are available for purchase by FIIs subject to certain ceilings.
9. ECB and ADRs/GDRs are other routes through which the Indian corporates can raise foreign funds.
10. Indian companies are also allowed to invest abroad through the automatic route and the approval route.
11. The world foreign direct investment inflows rose to a level of USD 1,452 billion in 2013 from USD 1,330 billion in 2012. Developing economies and transition economies received a substantial part of FDI inflows.
12. Although the share of India in inward and outward global FDI flows is miniscule, the FDI flows into India increased

from USD 4,029 million in 2000–01 to USD 36,396 million in 2013–14.

13. Infrastructure bottlenecks and bureaucratic hurdles are the major discouraging factors of FDI flows into India.

Questions

1. How are foreign trade and foreign investments interrelated?
2. Define FDI, and state the drivers of FDIs.
3. What is the product life cycle model?
4. Discuss the economic advantages of FDIs.
5. Distinguish between crowding-in and crowding-out.
6. Discuss the factors that influence FDIs.
7. Bring out the salient features of the Indian FDI policy.
8. Discuss the policy of the Indian Government on investments by foreign institutional investors.
9. Critically evaluate the SEBI guidelines with regard to foreign portfolio investors.
10. Discuss the factors responsible for low FDI in India.
11. Evaluate the policy of the Indian Government on the foreign investments made by Indian companies.
12. Critically comment on the Bilateral Investment Promotion and Protection Agreement.

Multiple-choice Questions

1. An investor who makes FDI is known as a/an__________.
   (a) Indirect investor (b) Direct investor
   (c) Domestic investor (d) None of these
2. __________ will have control over the direct investment enterprise.
   (a) FDI (b) FII
   (c) Portfolio investment (d) None of these
3. Investment in new production facilities is known as __________.
   (a) Greenfield investment
   (b) Brownfield investment
   (c) Indirect investment
   (d) None of these
4. If an MNC makes FDI in the same business, it is called __________.
   (a) Horizontal FDI (b) Vertical FDI
   (c) Lateral FDI (d) None of these
5. MNCs may also make FDIs to have __________.
   (a) Portfolio diversification
   (b) Higher return
   (c) More profits
   (d) None of these
6. Internationalization theory is also known as __________-.
   (a) Market imperfection approach
   (b) Perfect theory
   (c) Oligopoly theory
   (d) None of these
7. According to Dunning's eclectic theory, firms set up their businesses where they can have __________.
   (a) Lower risk
   (b) Higher revenues
   (c) Locational advantages
   (d) None of these
8. As per product life cycle theory, FDI happens when a product is in its __________.
   (a) Introduction stage (b) Growth stage
   (c) Maturity stage (d) None of these
9. FDI is a major driver of __________economic growth.
   (a) Export-led (b) Import-led
   (c) Agriculture-led (d) None of these
10. The assets of MNCs are also prone to __________in the host country.
    (a) Expropriation (b) Deceleration
    (c) Increase (d) None of these
11. Political instability is a __________factor for FDI.
    (a) Deterrent (b) Favourable
    (c) No-effect (d) None of these
12. __________ is in the prohibited list of FDI in India.
    (a) Retail trade (b) Atomic energy
    (c) Railways (d) None of these
13. If depository receipts are listed on U.S. stock exchanges, they are known as __________.
    (a) ADRs (b) GDRs
    (c) IDRs (d) None of these

14. ________ is the major source of foreign investment in India.

(a) Singaporer (b) Mauritius
(c) U.K. (d) None of these

15. ________ is the major sector in India which attracts FDI inflows.

(a) Manufacturing (b) Services
(c) Real estate (d) None of these

Further Reading

1. John Doukas and Nickolaos G. Travelos, "The Effect of Corporate Multinationalism on Shareholders' Wealth: Evidence from Investment Acquisitions," *Journal of Finance* (December 1988): 1161–1175.
2. E. Han Kim and Vijay Singal, "Are Open Markets Good for Foreign Investors and Emerging Nations?" *Journal of Applied Corporate Finance* (Fall 1997): 18–33.
3. Wi Saeng Kim and Esmerelda O Lyn, "FDI Theories and the Performance of Foreign Multinationals Operating in the US," *Journal of International Business Studies* (First Quarter 1990): 41–54.
4. W.Y. Lee and K.S. Sachdeva, "The Role of the Multinational Firm in the Integration of Segmented Capital Markets," *Journal of Finance* (May 1977): 479–492.
5. Stephen Hymer, *The International Operations of National Firms*: A Study of Foreign Direct Investment (Cambridge, MA: MIT Press, 1976).
6. C. Roy Smith and Ingo Walter, *Global Financial Services* (New York, NY: Harper Business, 1990).
7. Giorgio Ragazzione, "Theories of Determinants of Direct Foreign Investment," *IMF Staff Papers* 20 (1973): 471–98.
8. Richard Caves, *Multinational Enterprise and Economic Analysis* (Cambridge, MA: Harvard University Press, 1982).

CHAPTER

15

Portfolio Theory: An International Perspective

CHAPTER OBJECTIVES

After studying this chapter, you should be able to:

1 Define risk and return.

2 Describe the Markowitz portfolio model.

3 Define the concepts of portfolio return and portfolio risk.

4 Determine market portfolio and optimal portfolio.

5 Discuss the capital asset pricing model (CAPM).

6 Analyse the relationship between the capital market line (CML) and the security market line (SML).

7 Distinguish between systematic risk and unsystematic risk.

8 Gain insight into international portfolio diversification.

Introduction

Return and risk are the two fundamental factors that govern every investment decision. Several factors influence the investment decisions of individuals or organizations, but all of them ultimately get culminated into return and risk. Investments are undertaken in order to have more money in the future than what one has at present. This difference between present money and future money is known as the *return,* which, in pure terms, becomes the rate of return. Future money, however, is not certain. It is the uncertainty of future money that creates *risk.* Although risk is defined in several ways, it is defined in financial literature as the variability around the expected value. Investors always like return and dislike risk. Every rational investor seeks to maximize the return and minimize the risk. However, the higher the rate of return, the larger is the amount of risk involved. So, investors always have to make a tradeoff between the return and the risk.

*The **risk of a security** refers to the dispersion or variability of a security's expected return. A security with more variability of expected return is riskier than one with less variability.*

The **risk of a security** refers to dispersion or variability about a security's expected return. A security with greater variability of expected return is riskier than one with lesser variability. Securities with different levels of variability of their expected return carry different degrees of risk. The standard deviation around the expected return of a security is a risk surrogate. The variance or standard deviation of possible returns is one of the most widely used measures of risk.

In spite of the notion that higher rates of return are accompanied by greater risk, there are methods by which one can minimize the risk for a given level of return, or maximize the rate of return for a given level of risk. That is, the risk in investment can be reduced without sacrificing the return. One such method is *portfolio diversification*. Financial pundits have empirically observed that *a portfolio*, which is a combination of individual assets/securities, may not possess the risk–return characteristics of the individual assets/securities that comprise it. Therefore, an investor can reduce risk by diversifying his investment across securities through a combination of securities. But, mere holding of some securities in the portfolio may not yield the desired result. Only the right kind of diversification will minimize the risk. The best diversification usually comes through holding a large number of securities scattered across industries.

The Markowitz Portfolio Model

Harry Markowitz first developed a portfolio model in 1950s. Markowitz's portfolio theory was the first formal attempt to measure the risk of a portfolio and develop a procedure for determining the best portfolio. The model predicts the expected rate of return for a portfolio of assets or securities along with a measure of expected risk. Markowitz derived a formula for computing the variance of a portfolio. To build a basic model, he made certain assumptions, the most important of them being:

- Each investment alternative is represented by a probability distribution of expected return over some holding period.
- Investors maximize one-period expected utility, and their utility curves demonstrate diminishing marginal utility of wealth.
- Investors estimate the risk of the portfolio on the basis of the variability of expected returns.
- Investors base decisions solely on expected return and risk, so their utility curves are a function of the expected return and the expected variance (or standard deviation) of returns only.
- For a given risk level, investors prefer higher returns to lower returns. Similarly, for a given level of expected return, investors prefer low risk to high risk.

The methodology for determining the optimal portfolio according to the Markowitz model is explained in the following sections.

Return on Individual Security Investment

The expected rate of return for an individual investment can be calculated by using the following formula:

$$\overline{R} = \sum_{i=1}^{n} R_i P_i$$

where

$\overline{R}$ = Expected return on investment in a security or asset

R_i = Outcome of i

P_i = Probability of occurrence of i

n = Total number of outcomes

Example 15.1 shows how the expected rate of return for an individual investment can be calculated.

Example 15.1

An investor holds a security for one year. The probability distribution of possible returns of the investment is given here. Calculate the expected rate of return for the investment.

Probability of occurrence	*Possible rate of return (%)*
0.04	0.10
0.05	0.02
0.10	0.08
0.25	0.12
0.30	0.15
0.26	0.20

Solution

The expected return ($\bar{R}$) on the investment can be computed as follows:

$$\begin{aligned}\bar{R} &= \sum_{i=1}^{n} R_i P_i \\ &= (0.10\times 0.04)+(0.02\times 0.05)+(0.08\times 0.10)+(0.12\times 0.25)+(0.15\times 0.30) \\ &\quad +(0.20\times 0.26) \\ &= 0.14 \text{ or } 14 \text{ percent}\end{aligned}$$

Risk of Individual Security Investment

The standard deviation of the returns (σ), a measure of risk of an investment, can be calculated as follows:

$$\sigma = \sqrt{\sum_{i=1}^{n} (R_i - \bar{R})^2 P_i}$$

Using the data given in Example 15.1, the standard deviation can be calculated as

$$\begin{aligned}\sigma &= (0.10\times 0.14)^2 0.04 + (0.02\times 0.14)^2 0.05 + (0.08\times 0.14)^2 0.10 \\ &\quad + (0.12\times 0.14)^2 0.25 + (0.15-0.14)^2 0.30 + (0.20-0.14)^2 0.26 \\ &= 0.047\end{aligned}$$

Portfolio Return

The expected return on a portfolio is the weighted average of the expected returns of the individual assets in the portfolio. This can be expressed as follows:

$$R_P = \sum_{i=1}^{n} X_i R_i \qquad (15.1)$$

where

R_p = Expected return on portfolio
X_i = Proportion of total portfolio invested in asset/security i
R_i = Expected return on asset/security i
n = Number of assets/securities in the portfolio

Example 15.2 shows the calculation of the expected return on a portfolio of three securities.

Example 15.2

A portfolio consists of three securities, X, Y, and Z, with expected returns of 10 percent, 15 percent, and 20 percent, respectively. The proportions of portfolio value invested in these securities are 0.30, 0.50, and 0.20, respectively. What is the expected return on the portfolio?

Solution

The expected return (R_p) according to Eq.15.1 will be:

$$R_P = (0.30 \times 0.10) + (0.50 \times 0.15) + (0.20 \times 0.20)$$
$$= 0.145 \text{ or } 14.5 \text{ percent}$$

Portfolio Risk

The risk of a portfolio is measured by the variance (or standard deviation) of its return, which can be calculated as follows:

$$\sigma_p \sqrt{\sum_{i=1}^{n}\sum_{j=1}^{n} X_i X_j \sigma_{ij}} \tag{15.2}$$

where

σ_p = Standard deviation of the portfolio
n = Total number of assets/securities in the portfolio
X_i = Proportion of total portfolio value invested in security i
X_j = Proportion of total portfolio value invested in security j
σ_{ij} = Covariance between returns for securities i and j

It is evident that portfolio risk is not a simple weighted average of the standard deviations of the individual assets. The portfolio risk depends on not only the risk of the individual assets constituting the portfolio but also the relationship among these assets.

The Role of Covariance in Portfolio Risk

The ***covariance of the returns of two securities*** *is a measure of the extent to which the returns of the two securities move together.*

The **covariance of the returns of two securities** is a measure of the extent to which the returns of the two securities move together. A positive covariance means that the returns of the two securities move in the same direction, while a negative covariance means that the returns of the two securities move in opposite directions. The magnitude of the covariance depends on the variances of the individual returns as well as the relationship between them. The covariance is given by the following equation:

$$\sigma_{ij} = r_{ij}\sigma_i\sigma_j$$

where

r_{ij} = Expected correlation coefficient between returns of securities i and j
σ_i = Standard deviation of the returns for security i
σ_j = Standard deviation of the returns for security j

The formula for portfolio risk consists of n variance terms and $n(n-1)$ covariance terms. As the number of securities held in a portfolio increases, the number of covariance terms will become much larger. For example, if the number of securities in a portfolio is 100, only 1 percent of the cells of the variance-covariance matrix are variances, and 99 percent of the cells are covariances. Therefore, in the computation of the standard deviation of the portfolio, the covariance terms become dominant, and the portfolio risk is largely determined by the number of securities in the portfolio and the covariance terms.

The Role of the Correlation Coefficient in Portfolio Risk

The expected return on a portfolio is the weighted average of the expected returns of its component securities. The standard deviation (a risk measure) of a portfolio with perfectly positively correlated (+1) returns of the assets is just the weighted average of the standard deviations of the component securities. If the correlation coefficient is less than +1, the portfolio standard deviation will be less than the weighted average of the standard deviations of the component securities. Thus, it is not enough to have many securities in a portfolio, but it is necessary to have securities whose returns are not closely correlated. The lower the correlation coefficient of the returns of the securities in a portfolio, the smaller is the risk of the portfolio. Therefore, the investor has to deliberately select a security that has a low correlation or negative correlation with the other assets in the portfolio.

The lower the correlation coefficient of the returns of the securities in a portfolio, the smaller is the risk of the portfolio. A portfolio with perfectly negative correlation coefficient (–1.00) of returns gives maximum advantage to the investor. Such a portfolio is also called a ***risk-free portfolio***.

For example, let us assume that a portfolio consists of two securities, A and B, in the proportions 0.30 and 0.70. The standard deviations of returns of these two securities are 15 and 25, respectively. The correlation coefficient between the returns of the two securities is 0.40. Using Eq. 15.2, the standard deviation of the portfolio return can be calculated as follows:

$$\sigma_p = \sqrt{0.30^2 \times 0.15^2 + 0.70^2 + 0.25^2 + (2\times 0.30 \times 0.70 \times 0.40 \times 0.15 \times 0.25)}$$
$$= \sqrt{0.002025 + 0.030625 + 0.0063} = \sqrt{0.03895} = 0.1974$$

Suppose the correlation coefficient between the returns of the two securities is –1.00 (i.e. they are perfectly negatively correlated). The standard deviation of the portfolio (σ) becomes

$$\sqrt{0.002025 + 0.030625 + 0.01575}$$
$$= \sqrt{0.0169}$$
$$= 0.13$$

The above value can be reduced to zero by choosing the right kind of portfolio proportions.

If, however, the correlation coefficient between the returns of the two securities is +1.00 (i.e. they are perfectly positively correlated), the portfolio risk would become

$$\sqrt{0.002025 + 0.030625 + 0.01575}$$
$$= \sqrt{0.0484}$$
$$= 0.22$$

When the correlation coefficient is perfectly positive (+1.00), the standard deviation of the portfolio is simply the weighted average of the individual standard deviations. In such a case, there are no risk reduction benefits from portfolio diversification.

If the correlation coefficient is less than 1, portfolio diversification results in the portfolio risk being less than the weighted average of the variances of the individual assets in the portfolio. Thus, the Markowitz model involves combining securities with less-than-perfectly-positive correlation in order to reduce risk in the portfolio without sacrificing the portfolio's return. By choosing a right kind of portfolio proportions, the risk of a portfolio with the perfectly negative correlation coefficient (–1.00) of returns can be reduced to zero. Such a portfolio is also called a **risk-free portfolio**. This is because when the correlation coefficient is perfectly negative, the losses on one security can be exactly offset by gains on the other asset through a judicious selection of portfolio weights.

Although a correlation coefficient of less than +1.00 does not yield the same reduction in risk as a perfectly negative correlation, it does provide reduction in the risk of the portfolio without adversely affecting the expected return of the portfolio.

The Efficient Frontier

An investor can combine securities in a number of ways to form different portfolios, each having differing returns and risks. When the return and risk of each portfolio are plotted on a graph, there will be a set of points, where each point represents a portfolio that is attainable. The collection of all attainable portfolios is called the *opportunity set,* as shown in Figure 15.1. The northwest boundary of the opportunity set (feasible region) is known as the **efficient frontier**. The efficient frontier goes from the minimum variance portfolio to the portfolio with the highest expected return. It represents the portfolios that have the maximum rate of return for every given level of risk, or the minimum risk for every given level of return. In other words, the portfolios that lie on the northwest boundary line are efficient portfolios. A portfolio is not efficient, if there is another portfolio with a higher expected return and a lower risk, a higher expected return and the same risk, or the same expected return but a lower risk. All portfolios that can be created with the given number of securities are referred to as *feasible (possible) portfolios,* but only those portfolios that provide the highest return for a given level of risk, or the lowest risk for a certain level of return, are referred to as *efficient portfolios.* Every efficient portfolio has either a higher rate of return for equal risk or lower risk for an equal rate of return than the portfolios beneath the frontier. For example, consider three portfolios, *P*, *Q*, and *R*, in the opportunity set shown in Figure 15.1. Portfolios *P* and *Q* yield the same return, but Portfolio *P* has lower risk, compared to Portfolio *Q*. Similarly, Portfolio *R* and Portfolio *Q* have the same level of risk, but Portfolio *R* yields a higher return than Portfolio *Q*. Thus, Portfolio *P* and Portfolio *R* are dominant

*The **efficient frontier** represents the portfolios of assets that possess the minimum expected risk for each level of expected portfolio return.*

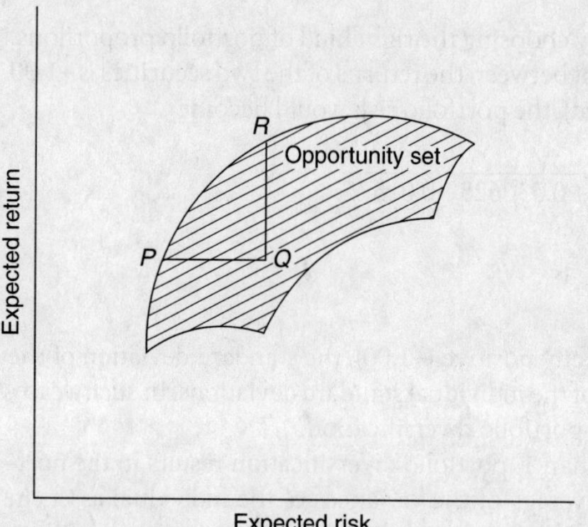

Figure 15.1

Portfolio Opportunity Set

portfolios, as they individually dominate Portfolio Q. The efficient frontier is made up of all such dominant portfolios. Although the portfolios on the efficient frontier have different return and risk, none of the portfolios that make up the efficient frontier can dominate any other portfolio on the same efficient frontier.

The Optimal Portfolio

According to the Markowitz mean–variance maxim, the investor should select a portfolio of securities that lie on the efficient frontier. Although all the portfolios on the efficient frontier are efficient, they are not equally desirable for an investor. There is only one portfolio on the efficient frontier that can satisfy the risk–return preference of an investor. That portfolio is known as the **optimal portfolio**.

The portfolio on the efficient frontier that can satisfy the risk–return preference of an investor is known as the ***optimal portfolio***.

The risk–return preferences of an investor are represented by a set of indifference curves. The rates of return on an indifference curve increase with risk. An investor is indifferent to any combination of expected return and risk on a particular indifference curve. In other words, an indifference curve represents combinations of expected return and risk that result in the same level of expected utility. The steeper the slope of the indifference curves, the greater is the risk aversion of that investor. When there is a set of indifference curves, each successive curve towards the left represents a higher level of expected utility. Given the efficient frontier and the risk–return indifference curves, an investor can find an optimal portfolio. The optimal portfolio is the point of tangency between the efficient frontier and a risk–return indifference curve, as shown in Figure 15.2. The point *T* represents the highest level of utility an investor can reach. At this point, the indifference curve (I_2) touches the efficient frontier.

The Market Portfolio

All portfolios on the efficient frontier are risky. Consider a situation where an investor can lend and borrow at a risk-free rate. To determine the optimal portfolio in such a situation, a line is drawn from the risk-free rate (R_f) on the *y*-axis through its point of tangency, as illustrated in Figure 15.3. This line, which represents the combinations of risk-free and risky securities in the feasible region, is the new efficient frontier. It can be seen from the figure

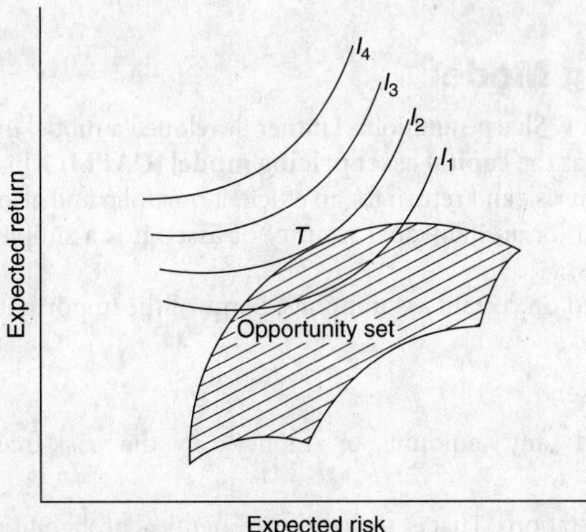

Figure 15.2

Indifference Curves and the Optimal Portfolio

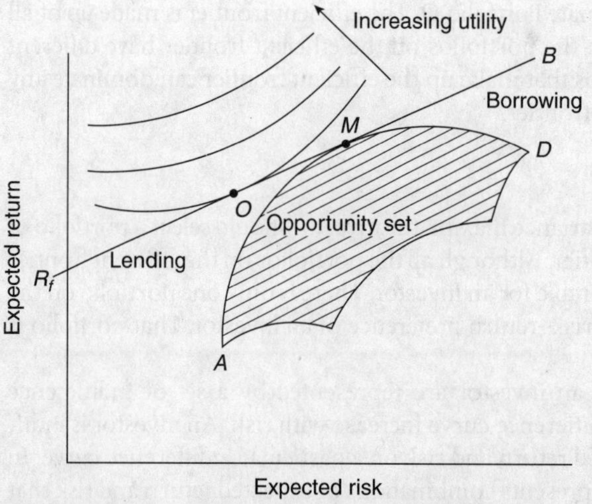

Figure 15.3

Optimal Portfolio With Lending and Borrowing

that only one portfolio of risky securities (*M*) is dominant now. To the left of *M*, an investor can hold the risk-free asset and risky Portfolio M, and to the right, an investor can hold only Portfolio M and must borrow funds to supplement his funds in order to invest further in it. Given the new efficient frontier, the optimal portfolio for an investor is the point of tangency (*O* in Fig. 15.3) between the straight line and the highest indifference curve of the investor. Portfolio *M* is known as the *market portfolio,* and by definition it contains all the securities available in the market.

Although the Markowitz model was the first systematic attempt to delineate the optimal portfolio, it was highly demanding in its data needs and computational requirements. Therefore, William Sharpe, among others, tried to simplify the process of selecting an optimal portfolio. He developed a simplified variant of the Markowitz model, requiring lesser data inputs and with fewer computational requirements. We shall discuss this model—the capital asset pricing model—in the next section.

The Capital Asset Pricing Model

*The **capital asset pricing model (CAPM)** considers the relationship between risk and return for an efficient portfolio and the relationship between risk and return for an individual security or asset.*

Based on the Markowitz model, William F. Sharpe and John Lintner developed a model in the 1960s, which has come to be known as the **capital asset pricing model (CAPM)**. This model considers the relationship between risk and return for an efficient portfolio and also the relationship between risk and return for an individual security or asset. It is a simple model with many real-world applications.

CAPM, like any other model, is based on certain assumptions. Some of the important assumptions are:

- Investors are rational and risk averse.
- Investors can borrow or lend any amount of money at the risk-free rate of return (R_f).
- Investors have homogeneous expectations. That is, they estimate identical probability distributions for future rates of return.
- All investments are infinitely divisible.

- There are no taxes or transaction costs involved in buying or selling assets.
- Capital markets are in equilibrium.

In Figure 15.3, the original efficient frontier is *AMD*. Suppose that an investor can lend at the rate of 6 percent, the rate on Indian Government Treasury bills. Therefore, point R_f represents the return on a risk-free investment. The investor could invest all or part of his funds in this risk-free asset. By investing a part of his funds in the risk-free asset and the rest in one of the portfolios of risky securities along the efficient frontier, an investor can generate portfolios along the straight line segment R_fM. Suppose at point *M*, the return on the portfolio is 0.12, with a standard deviation of 0.05. Further, assume that 50 percent of the funds are placed in the risk-free asset and the remaining 50 percent in the risky portfolio (*M*). The combined portfolio return and risk can be calculated using the following equation:

$$R_p = XR_m + (1-X)R_f \tag{15.3}$$

and

$$\sigma_p = X\sigma_m \tag{15.4}$$

where

X = Proportion of total portfolio value invested in the market portfolio *M*
$(1-X)$ = Proportion of total portfolio value invested in the risk-free asset
R_m = Expected return on the market portfolio
R_f = Risk-free return
σ_m = Standard deviation of the returns on the market portfolio

Substituting numerical values, given in the example, in Eqs. 15.3 and 15.4,

$$R_p = (0.50)(0.12) + (0.50)(0.06)$$
$$= 0.09$$
$$\sigma_p = (0.50)(0.05) + (0.50)(0.00)$$
$$= 0.025$$

Thus, with an investment in a risk-free asset, the overall return and risk of the portfolio have been reduced. By using Eqs. 15.3 and 15.4, the return and risk of all the portfolios between R_f and *M* can be determined, which will form a straight line, as shown in Figure 15.3.

If borrowing of funds at the risk-free rate is allowed in order to increase the total funds to be invested, a new efficient frontier will emerge. An investor borrows the funds at the risk-free rate rather than lending, which makes the following equation:

$$R_P = XR_m - (X-1)R_f$$

For example, if $X = 1.35$, it would indicate that the investor borrows an amount equal to 35 percent of his total investment. So, the return and risk of the investment would be

$$R_p = (1.35)(0.12) - (0.35)(0.06)$$
$$= 0.141$$
$$\sigma_p = (1.35)(0.05)$$
$$= 0.0675$$

Thus, the leveraged portfolio has increased both the return and the risk.

The Capital Market Line

By borrowing varying amounts and investing in the risky portfolio *M*, the investor can generate a number of leveraged portfolios. With risk-free lending and borrowing, a new efficient frontier may emerge, which is shown as R_fMB (a straight line) in Figure 15.3. This straight line is referred to as the *capital market line* (*CML*), and all the investors are expected to end up with portfolios somewhere along the CML. The portfolios that lie below the CML are not efficient portfolios. The CML can be expressed as follows:

$$R_p = R_f + \left(\frac{R_m - R_f}{\sigma_m}\right)\sigma_p \tag{15.5}$$

In Eq. 15.5, the first term on the right side (R_f) is the price of time, and the second term is the market price of risk multiplied by the portfolio risk. For efficient portfolios, the non-systematic risk tends to be zero. In other words, the only risk present in efficient portfolios is the systematic risk, which is denoted by beta (β). Thus, the CML represents the linear relationship between the risk and return of efficient portfolios, including the market portfolio.

The Security Market Line

As stated earlier, the returns of all efficient portfolios will lie on the CML. The returns of inefficient portfolios and individual securities will, therefore, lie below the CML. They, however, have a linear relationship with the expected return and risk of the market portfolio. This relationship forms a line, called the *security market line* (*SML*).The SML is expressed as

$$R_j = R_f + \left(\frac{R_m - R_f}{\sigma_m^2}\right)(r_{jm}\sigma_j\sigma_m)$$

or

$$R_j = R_f + \left(\frac{R_m - R_f}{\sigma_m}\right)(r_{jm}\sigma_j)$$

or

$$R_j = R_f + (R_m - R_f)\beta_j$$

where

R_j = Risk-free rate of return
R_m = Expected overall return for market portfolio
β_j = Beta coefficient for security *j*

$$\beta_j = \frac{(r_{jm}\sigma_j\sigma_m)}{\sigma_m^2}$$

R_{jm} = Expected correlation between possible returns for security *j* and the market portfolio
$(r_{jm}\sigma_j\sigma_m)$ = Covariance of returns for security *j* with those of the market portfolio
σ_j = Standard deviation of the probability distribution of possible returns for security *j*

σ_m = Standard deviation of the probability distribution of possible returns for the market portfolio

$(r_{jm}\sigma_j)$ = Systematic risk (in absolute terms) of security j

β_j = Systematic risk of security j in relative terms $[(r_{jm}\sigma_j)/\sigma_m]$

Thus,

Expected return on security j = Risk-free return + Market risk premium × Beta of security j

The SML (see Figure 15.4) describes the expected return for all assets/securities and portfolios, efficient or not. The relationship between beta and expected return is linear. In other words, the higher the beta for any security, the higher must be its expected return. It should be noted that only that part of the risk of a security that cannot be eliminated by diversification (systematic) can influence the return of a security. Thus, the SML represents the linear relationship between the return of any security or asset and its covariance with the market portfolio.

Systematic Risk and Unsystematic Risk

The total risk involved in holding a security comprises two types of risks: systematic risk and unsystematic risk. Systematic risk is also known as *non-diversifiable risk,* and unsystematic risk is also called *diversifiable risk.* The other names for unsystematic risk are *idiosyncratic risk, asset-specific risk, and company-specific risk.* **Systematic risk** is the risk that arises from changes in macro-level factors like national income, rainfall, monetary policy, and fiscal policy. These factors affect overall investments and, therefore, the risks arising from changes in these factors cannot be avoided through portfolio diversification. Even investors who hold a well-diversified portfolio may be exposed to this type of risk. **Unsystematic risk**, however, is specific to a particular security. For example, a labour strike or a technological breakthrough in a company is unique to the company and occur independently. They are independent of economic, political, technological, and other factors that affect investments in general. Further, the proportion of systematic risk in the total risk of an individual security's return depends on the correlation and covariance of the security's return with that of the return of other securities in the portfolio.

***Systematic risk** is the risk that arises from changes in macro-level factors like national income, rainfall, monetary policy, and fiscal policy, whereas **unsystematic risk** is specific to a particular security.*

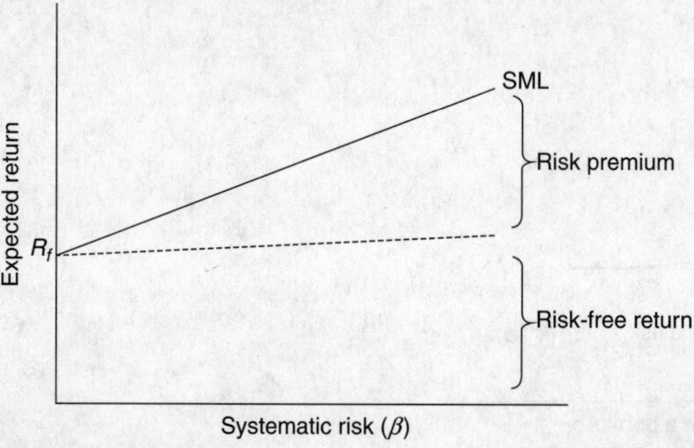

Figure 15.4

The Security Market Line

Diversification of investments can reduce or even eliminate the unsystematic part of the risk. Unsystematic risk is the amount of total risk that can be eliminated by diversification (Figure 15.5). In a portfolio, the values of some securities will go up as a result of good news specific to the companies that issued those securities, whereas the values of other securities will go down as a result of unexpected company-specific unpleasant events. If one investment creates a loss, it may be offset by profit of another investment. Therefore, as a portfolio becomes well-diversified, its unsystematic risk becomes smaller. Efficient diversification of investment can even reduce the unsystematic risk to zero. In other words, the risk of a well-diversified portfolio closely approximates the risk of the market. A portfolio is said to be well diversified, if it spreads out over many securities in such a way that the proportion of investment in any security is small. However, beyond a finite number of securities, adding more to a portfolio is expensive in terms of the time and money spent on identifying and monitoring performance. Sometimes, this cost may not be balanced by any benefit in the form of additional reduction of risk. CAPM assumes that all risk other than systematic risk is diversified away.

When an investor acquires assets outside the domestic market, he may be acquiring foreign currency-denominated assets for portfolio construction. This gives rise to two types of risks: country risk and foreign exchange risk. These risks can also be reduced by international diversification.

Country risk, also known as *political risk,* arises due to unexpected political events in thehost country. The important political risk variables are government stability, law and order, ethnic tensions, religious tensions, and internal conflicts. The most extreme consequence of political risk is expropriation, which occurs when the government seizes foreign assets within its borders. Thus, a major change in the political or economic environment in a country will increase the risk of investment in that country. Country risk is generally at higher levels in developing countries as they do not have stable economic or political systems.

Foreign exchange risk arises due to exchange rate fluctuations. For example, let us assume that an Indian investor wants to invest in U.S. Government bonds that carry an interest rate of 6 percent. This investment is risk-free for the U.S. investor. But the same is not the case for the investor from some other country. Suppose an Indian investor wants to invest INR 10 million in U.S. Government bonds. This amount is exchanged for USD 232,558 at an exchange rate of USD/INR 43, and invested at an interest rate of 6 percent. This will become USD 246,512 in a year. During the year, the INR appreciates to USD/INR 42. Thus, USD

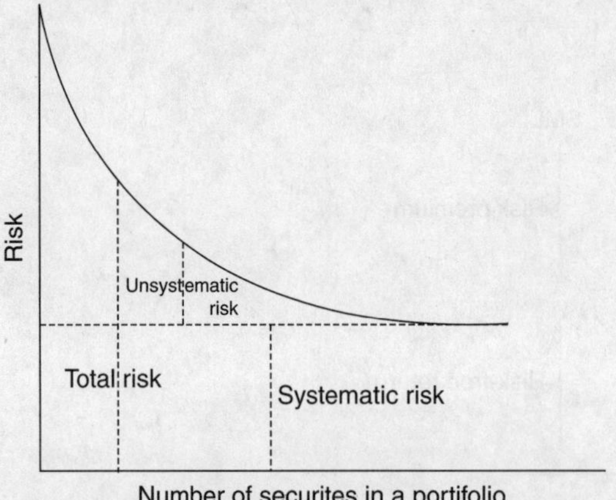

Figure 15.5

Systematic and Unsystematic Risk

246,512 can be exchanged for only INR 10,353,482, resulting in a return of 3.54 percent. Despite a 6 percent USD-denominated return, the INR-denominated return is only 3.54 percent. The INR-denominated return on the U.S. investment can be expressed as

$$1+r_d=(1+r_f)[1+(S_1-S_0)/S_0]$$
$$\Rightarrow r_d=(1+r_f)[1+(S_1-S_0)/S_0]-1$$

where

r_d = Domestic rate of return
r_f = Foreign rate of return
S_1 = Spot exchange rate at the end of the year
S_0 = Current spot exchange rate

It is evident that the domestic currency-denominated return equals the foreign currency-denominated return multiplied by the exchange rate ratio and, therefore, exchange rate fluctuations have large effects on domestic currency- denominated returns. Investors should take into account the potential influence of exchange rate changes on the returns of foreign assets, before making foreign investments. Much in the same way, *currency risk* is also a factor to be reckoned with in financing (i.e. while raising funds from abroad). The financing cost will come down, if the foreign currency depreciates, and go up if the foreign currency appreciates against the borrower's home currency over the financing period.

Systematic risk in the international environment includes economic risk, inflation risk, interest rate risk, exchange rate risk, and political risk. But these risks are not entirely systematic. Some portion of these risks can be diversified away, which means the premium for only a fraction of these risks is added to the risk-free rate.

Example 15.3

An Indian investor invested in the stock of a U.S. company a year back. The stock has increased in value by 30 percent over the year. Over the same period, the Indian rupee has depreciated by 25 percent against the U.S. dollar. What is the effective rate of return to the Indian investor?

Solution

The effective rate of return (R_e) is as follows, assuming that R is the rate of return on the stock, and *e* is the percentage change in the exchange rate:

$$R_e=(1+R)(1+e)-1$$
$$=(1+0.30)(1+0.25)-1$$
$$=0.625,\ \text{or } 62.5 \text{ percent}$$

Example 15.4

A firm in India has borrowed a certain amount in U.S. dollars for one year at an interest rate of 8 percent. The U.S. dollar has depreciated against the Indian rupee by 1 percent over this one-year period. What is the effective financing cost for the firm?

Solution

The financing cost (R_f) is as follows, assuming that K is the interest rate and e is the rate of change in the exchange rate:

$$\begin{aligned} R_f &= (1+K)(1+e)-1 \\ &= (1+0.08)[(1+(-0.01)]-1 \\ &= 0.0692, \text{ or } 6.92 \text{ percent} \end{aligned}$$

International Portfolio Diversification

Empirical studies have pointed out that about 70 percent of the total risk of a portfolio can be eliminated through diversification within the domestic economy. But with the expansion of a domestic portfolio to an internationally diversified portfolio, systematic risk can also be brought down.

Domestic investors in any country have several avenues through which they can invest internationally. Some of these avenues are:

- *Direct purchase of securities in foreign markets*: Investors can directly purchase securities in the capital markets of other countries through brokerage firms. But the lack of information about foreign assets is often a problem. Direct purchasing of securities may involve transaction costs and information costs. Moreover, securities trading and settlement systems are different in different countries. In some countries, custodial or depository facilities are not available. All of these are problems international investors face while buying securities directly in foreign markets.
- *Purchase of foreign securities listed on domestic stock exchanges*: In view of the problems associated with buying securities directly in foreign markets, domestic investors may as well buy foreign securities listed on domestic stock exchanges. Since the early 1990s, a growing number of foreign securities have begun to trade in domestic stock markets. These carry the same transaction costs as domestic securities. The information cost in such cases is also not problematic, because the foreign companies that list their securities on domestic stock markets are required to meet the same disclosure requirements as domestic companies. Thus, investors can buy foreign securities in their domestic market.
- *Investment in MNCs*: A multinational corporation may maintain operations in many countries, and, therefore, the sales revenues of an MNC are well-diversified. In other words, the variability (risk) of the net cash flows of an MNC is lower. Investors can achieve international diversification by buying the stocks of MNCs.
- *Purchase of depository receipts in the home market:* Investors can also acquire foreign stocks by buying depository receipts in the home market. For example, American Depository Receipts (ADRs), which represent ownership of foreign stocks, are traded on the U.S. stock markets. Investors can invest in ADRs which are U.S. dollar-denominated, and derive the advantages of direct investment in foreign stocks. Similar to ADRs are global depository receipts (GDRs). GDRs are traded on many markets outside the issuer's home country. Investors can trade GDRs on any market in the world where they are listed and in the local currency. GDRs are less expensive to trade than ADRs.
- *Purchase of shares of internationally diversified mutual funds*: Another avenue for investors to achieve internationally diversified portfolios is to buy units (shares) of internationally

diversified mutual funds. These would reduce risk better than a purely domestic mutual fund, because international mutual funds invest in well diversified foreign portfolios. In recent years, internationally diversified mutual funds such as global funds, international funds, regional funds, and single-country funds have become more attractive investments. *Global funds* can invest in any market in the world, including their home market. *International funds* can invest in any market in the world outside their home market. *Regional funds* focus on specified regions of the world for their investment. *Single-country funds* can invest only in one specified country. Exchange-traded funds (ETFs) also provide international diversification for investors. *Exchange-traded funds* are open-end companies that seek to achieve the same return as a particular market index. They are available on major stock indices such as the Dow Jones Industrial Average, S&P 500 Composite Index, and the NASDAQ Composite Index. For example, SPDR ETF invests in all the stocks contained in the S&P 500 Composite Stock Price Index. An ETF can invest in either all of the securities or a representative sample of the securities included in the index.

Investors make foreign investments not only to diversify their investments and reduce risk but also to get higher returns. Emerging economies have been experiencing above-average economic growth and have high growth potential. Developed countries as well as emerging economies have good debt and equity markets, which provide greater opportunities for investors to diversify across national markets and reduce portfolio risk.

With globalization of trade and investments, and the increasing integration of world economies, the domestic stock markets are increasingly driven by global factors rather than domestic factors. The liberalization of regulations governing the listing and trading of securities on foreign stock markets has increased cross-border trading of securities. Many companies are now listed on more than one stock market. Cross-border mergers and acquisitions have also brought the stock markets closer to a global equity market.

The International CAPM

According to the *classical portfolio theory,* the efficient frontier represents the portfolios that possess the minimum expected risk for each level of expected return. An individual investor seeks a portfolio on the efficient frontier that satisfies his risk–return characteristics. This portfolio, called a *domestic optimal portfolio,* provides the maximum return for the risk that an investor is prepared to bear. However, with international stocks in the portfolios, the efficient frontier shifts left of the purely domestic efficient frontier (Figure 15.6). The curvature of the efficient frontier with an internationally diversified portfolio opportunity set would increase. The greater the curvature of the efficient frontier, the larger is the risk reduction for the given levels of return. So, an efficient frontier for internationally diversified portfolios provides lower risk for each level of expected portfolio return. The new CML starts from the same risk-free return (R_f) and goes through the point of tangency along the internationally diversified efficient frontier, as shown in Figure 15.6. The new CML has a steeper slope and provides higher expected portfolio return for given the portfolio risk than the purely domestic portfolio-based CML. The global market portfolio (M) is superior to the domestic market portfolio. An investor, who wants to borrow at a risk-free rate and invest, can invest in the market portfolio. With international securities being included in the efficient frontier, CAPM becomes the international CAPM (ICAPM) with a different expected market return and beta estimate. Further, the investor's portfolio expectations are represented by a global market index rather than a purely domestic market index. The classical CAPM, which

An efficient frontier for internationally diversified portfolios provides lower risk portfolios for each level of expected portfolio return.

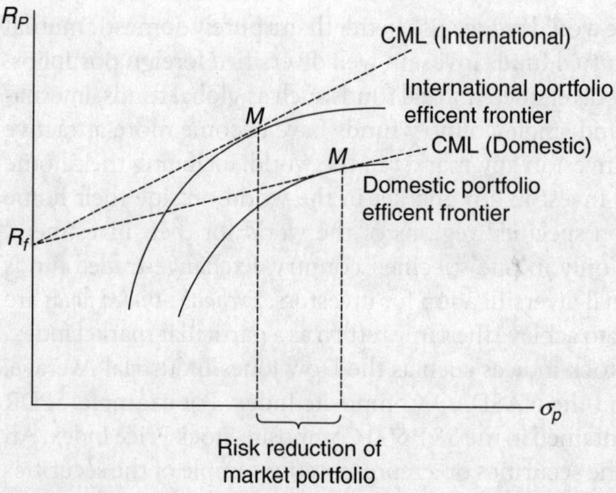

Figure 15.6

International CML

is known as domestic CAPM, thus becomes the international CAPM when a global market portfolio is built into the model.

Researchers in recent years have observed that the CAPM as developed by William Sharpe and John Lintner is appropriate only for a closed economy. In other words, the domestic CAPM is not appropriate when there are interactions among the financial markets of various countries. When funds flow across countries, the market portfolio under CAPM cannot capture all the systematic risk, because the foreign exchange risk, which is an important factor in international investments, is not built into the model. Therefore, the international CAPM has been developed to take into account all systematic risk. The international CAPM may be the *single-factor international CAPM* or the *multiple-factor international CAPM*.

The single-factor international CAPM for asset *j* can be expressed as

$$R_j = R_f + \beta_j^w (R_w - R_f)$$

where

R_j = Expected rate of return on asset *j*

R_f = Risk-free return (nominal) denominated in the pricing currency

β_j^w = Sensitivity of asset *i* to world market portfolio (index), which is defined as

$$\frac{\text{Cov}(R_j, R_w)}{\text{Var}(R_w)}$$

$(R_W - R_f)$ = Difference between real return on the world market portfolio and the risk-free interest rate

The single-factor ICAPM is based on the following assumptions:

- The world market portfolio is unhedged.
- Purchasing power parity holds at any point in time.
- Investors all over the world have the same consumption baskets.
- Investors hold a combination of the risk-free asset in their own currency and the unhedged world market portfolio.
- Investors are homogeneous and they hold every security in the market portfolio.

The model implies that an investment in a foreign asset as measured in the home currency is subject to two sources of risk: (i) the sensitivity of the country's index to a global market portfolio and (ii) the performance of the domestic currency relative to the foreign currency.

As the domestic market portfolio does not move in line with the world market, the beta of the domestic CAPM will be different from the beta of the international CAPM. In fact, the international CAPM establishes the conditions under which completely integrated financial markets in the world are in equilibrium. If the world's capital markets are not integrated (i.e., they are segmented), the world market portfolio will not exist. The world market portfolio is the portfolio that fully explains the risk–return relationship of assets in different capital markets. The markets are said to be integrated, if assets with the same risk are priced equally in different markets.

When an investor holds a foreign security, the return of the security in domestic currency depends on the exchange rate. If purchasing power parity holds, a percentage depreciation of the domestic currency is offset by an equivalent percentage increase in domestic prices. In such a case, the return of a foreign asset is not exposed to foreign exchange risk. Therefore, the return of a foreign asset is subject solely to global market risk, and the asset is priced accordingly.

If purchasing power parity does not hold, investors in different countries expect different rates of return for the same asset. In equilibrium, the expected return on any asset in the economy, denominated in the investor's currency, is equal to the risk-free domestic return plus the risk premium for exposure to global market risk and specific currency risk. Further, if purchasing power parity does not hold, investors can hedge their foreign assets against currency risk. In such a case, the exposure to the currency risk should not be priced.

The multiple-factor international CAPM for asset *j* is given by the following equation:

$$R_j = R_f + \beta_j^w (R_w - R_f) + \gamma_{j1} R_{p1} + \gamma_{j2} R_{p2} + \cdots + \gamma_{in} R_{pn}$$

where

γ_{j1} to γ_{jn} = Sensitivities of asset *j* to the currencies 1 to *n*

R_{p1} to R_{pn} = Risk premia on currencies 1 to *n*

It may be noted that the number of exchange rate factors can be as many as the number of currencies other than the numeraire currency (or the currency in which portfolio returns are reported), because the investors can theoretically bear exchange risks from all currencies.

The basic assumptions of the multiple-factor international CAPM are as follows:

- Investors throughout the world have different consumption baskets.
- Purchasing power parity does not hold.
- There is no inflation.
- There are no institutional barriers to investment.
- Investors hold securities from around the world in proportion to market capitalization.

Thus, the multiple-factor international CAPM does not assume that purchasing power parity holds. There can also be variations in consumption baskets across countries. With different consumption baskets, investors can invest in foreign goods. They can also hedge against foreign exchange risk.

Note that the international CAPM is appropriate when financial markets are completely integrated. When financial markets across countries remain segmented, the domestic CAPM is appropriate. The asset pricing varies from one country to another, and domestic risk factors determine the expected return of an asset. That is, in the segmented market, the expected return of an asset depends on its location. If the markets are partially integrated, investors face global risk as well as country-specific risk. In this case, the expected return of an asset is determined by a combination of country-specific risk factors and global risk factors. When financial markets are fully integrated, country-specific risk is fully diversified away internationally. The expected return of an asset is determined solely by global risk factors. Thus, in the integrated world market, an asset has the same expected return irrespective of where it is traded.

Financial markets are said to be integrated when there are no barriers to foreign investments, and investors can access freely financial markets worldwide. The country funds and domestic stocks can be listed on international stock markets. Integrated financial markets would provide capital at a lower cost, and there would be greater investment opportunities. The more integrated the market, the lower is the required risk premium. It means that the corporations can have a lower cost of capital. In fact, many domestic financial markets in the world are between the theoretical extremes of segmentation and complete integration. That is, they are partially integrated. The degree of integration depends on a set of variables related to national and international market structures. Legal restrictions on cross-border investments, foreign exchange regulations, taxes, transaction costs, and information costs, affect the ability of global investors to invest in the assets of a particular country. In recent years, many barriers or restrictions have been liberalized in the process of globalization of economies. In some cases, especially in developed countries, the barriers to financial integration are completely eliminated. The markets of emerging economies are becoming integrated with the markets of developed nations. It should be noted that the economic conditions in a country may also influence the integration of financial markets. For example, recession in a country may drive investors to foreign countries in search of higher returns, which would lead to the integration of markets. Closed-end country funds and international cross listings play an important role in global market integration. For example, ADRs are the negotiable certificates listed on U.S. stock exchanges but they confer ownership of shares in foreign companies. Depository Receipts (GDRs and ADRs) are examples of cross-listed securities.

Portfolio of Currencies

As discussed earlier, financing cost or return on investment is also influenced by exchange rate fluctuations. The financing cost will be low, if the foreign currency depreciates against the firm's domestic currency, and it will be high, if the foreign currency appreciates against the domestic currency. The same is the case with foreign investments. Appreciation of the foreign currency would yield high effective returns for the investor, and depreciation of the foreign currency would yield low effective returns for the investor.

A portfolio of currencies, or a combination of several currencies, can be used to reduce currency risk. Such a portfolio can be used for financing as well as investment. Suppose that the interest rate in a foreign country is lower than the domestic interest rate. A firm that borrows from abroad may not benefit from the lower foreign interest rate, if the foreign currency appreciates. This is because appreciation of the foreign currency may more than offset the advantage of a lower foreign interest rate. The firm can, however, achieve lower financing costs (cost of capital) without excessive risk in this situation by raising funds in different foreign currencies (i.e. by financing with a portfolio of foreign currencies). Foreign financing with a highly diversified portfolio of currencies may be less costly than financing with a single currency or a few currencies. As different currencies may not move in tandem, it is unlikely that the foreign currencies will simultaneously appreciate enough to offset the advantage of their lower interest rates. However, if the currencies in the portfolio have a high positive correlation with each other, financing with a portfolio of currencies may not yield any benefit.

A portfolio of currencies can be used for investment as well. Investment in a single foreign currency (e.g. U.S. dollar deposits) may yield a lower effective return, if the foreign currency depreciates against the domestic currency over the investment period. Investment in a diversified portfolio of currencies would therefore be more rewarding than investment in a single foreign currency. As different foreign currencies may not depreciate simultaneously to offset the advantage of their higher interest rates, the investor can benefit more by investing in a portfolio of currencies than in a single foreign currency. However, as in the case of financing, investment in a portfolio of currencies that are highly positively correlated with each other may not be very different from investment in a single foreign currency. The degree of correlation between the currencies is an important consideration, if one wants to benefit from a portfolio of currencies. The characteristics of the component currencies in the portfolio will determine the variance (i.e. risk) in the return of the portfolio.

International Diversification: Challenges and Opportunities

Now national economies are fast becoming closely linked if not closely integrated. The main drivers of this closeness are the development of transnational companies and organizations, advances in computing and communication technology, deregulation of financial markets and institutions, cross-border investment flows, significant growth of international trade, and convertibility of currencies. The closeness of economies is also strengthened by their growing interdependence. With the integration of financial markets, the benefits of international diversification decrease. This is because international diversification results in risk reduction for a given return of an asset when the correlation coefficient between the domestic market and foreign market is very low. The lower the correlation coefficient, the higher is the risk reduction. For example, let us assume that the U.S. and Japanese markets are highly positively correlated. So, the U.S. investors having a portfolio of U.S. stocks will not experience significant diversification benefit by investing in Japanese stocks. When the markets of any two countries are highly integrated, the prices of assets in the markets of the two countries move together. In other words, the investors cannot diversify risk by investing in different markets. Market integration, therefore, reduces the advantage of international diversification.

Integration of markets can be viewed differently as well. In the integrated global market, the returns of the securities of companies located in different countries may not be too closely correlated as different economies do not follow the same business cycle. Various research studies have pointed out that, despite markets being increasingly integrated, the relatively low correlation coefficients among the returns of securities of different countries indicate great potential for international diversification.

Although there are increasing opportunities for international diversification of investments, there are certain hurdles in international portfolio diversification. Many countries have not yet eased the regulations governing the free flow of capital across national boundaries. Direct or indirect capital inflow and capital outflow controls and the various forms of taxes imposed by the governments of many countries are also impediments to forming internationally diversified portfolios. In addition, transaction costs, unequal access to information, and cross-cultural differences pose real barriers to international portfolio diversification.

Summary

1. The price of an asset or security should be such that its expected return is in excess of the risk-free return and is an increasing function of risk.

2. *Portfolio* refers to a combination of securities or assets. An investor can reduce investment risk without sacrificing return's by holding a portfolio.

Holding a combination of securities is also known as *diversification.*

3. The *Markowitz portfolio theory* was the first formal attempt to measure the risk of a portfolio and develop a procedure for determining the best portfolio.

4. The expected return of a portfolio is the weighted average of the expected returns of the individual assets in the portfolio. Portfolio risk is largely determined by the number of securities or assets in the portfolio as well as the relationship among these assets as represented by their covariance. The lower the correlation coefficient of the returns of the securities in a portfolio, the smaller is the risk of the portfolio.

5. When the return and risk of each portfolio are plotted on a graph, there will be an *opportunity set,* and the northwest boundary of the opportunity set is known as the *efficient frontier.* The portfolio that satisfies the risk–return characteristics of an investor is called the *optimal portfolio.*

6. The *capital asset pricing model (CAPM)* deals with (i) the relationship between risk and return for an efficient portfolio, and (ii) the relationship between risk and return for an individual security or asset.

7. The *capital market line (CML)* represents the linear relationship between the risks and returns of efficient portfolios, including the market portfolio. The *security market line (SML)* represents the linear relationship between the expected return of any asset or portfolio and its covariance with the market portfolio.

8. The total risk involved in holding a security or asset is comprised of two types of risk: systematic risk and unsystematic risk. *Systematic risk* arises because of changes in macro-level factors, and *unsystematic risk* is specific to a particular asset or a particular company. By diversification of investments one can reduce or even eliminate completely the unsystematic part of the risk. The CAPM assumes that all risk other than systematic risk is diversified away.

9. The internationally diversified portfolios-based efficient frontier provides lower risk portfolios for each level of expected portfolio return. In other words, an investor holding foreign securities or assets in his or her portfolio may have lower risk for the given expected return as compared to a pure domestic-securities portfolio.

10. Country risk and foreign exchange risk are the main hurdles in international diversification. Various forms of taxes and other regulations that restrict foreign investments are also impediments to forming internationally diversified portfolios.

Questions and Problems

1. Explain the basic assumptions of the Markowitz portfolio model.
2. Define return and risk of a portfolio according to the Markowitz model.
3. What is the relationship between correlation coefficient and covariance? State the importance of the covariance factor in portfolio selection.
4. Define efficient frontier. Explain the process of selecting the optimal portfolio.
5. All optimal portfolios are efficient but all efficient portfolios are not optimal portfolios. Comment.
6. How do you derive the capital market line?
7. Explain the basic assumptions underlying the capital asset pricing model.
8. What is the relationship between the risk and return for efficient portfolios?
9. How is the beta of a security measured?
10. How is the price of a security determined according to the security market line?
11. What do you understand by international diversification?
12. How is the market portfolio on the domestic efficient frontier different from the market portfolio on the international efficient frontier?
13. How can risk be reduced with international diversification?
14. Distinguish between systematic risk and unsystematic risk. How one can eliminate unsystematic risk?
15. How can an investor achieve international diversification of his or her investment?
16. What are the opportunities and challenges associated with international diversification?
17. The following stocks are available to an investor:

Year	Return on Stock X	Return on Stock Y
2012	12%	15%
2013	18%	14%
2014	17%	!6%

a. What is the expected return on a portfolio made up of 30 percent X and 70 percent Y?
b. Calculate the standard deviation of each stock.
c. What is the portfolio risk of a portfolio made up of 30 percent X and 70 percent Y?

18. The following data are available to you as a portfolio manager:

	Expected return (%)	Beta	Standard deviation (%)
Stock A	20	1.50	35
Stock B	32	1.75	35
Stock C	50	1.80	40
Stock D	15	1.20	15
Market index	13	1.00	10
Treasury bills	8	0	0

In terms of the security market line, which of the securities are undervalued? How?

Multiple-choice Questions

1. The difference between present money and future money is known as________.
   (a) Return (b) Cost
   (c) Profit (d) None of these
2. It is the uncertainty of future money that creates________.
   (a) Risk (b) Return
   (c) Profit (d) None of these
3. One of the measures of risk is________.
   (a) Standard deviation (b) Uncertainty
   (c) Mean (d) None of these
4. Expected return on a portfolio is the________of expected returns on the individual assets that form the portfolio.
   (a) Simple average (b) Weighted average
   (c) Median (d) None of these
5. A portfolio of________perfectly correlated assets always offers better risk–return opportunity.
   (a) Less than (b) More than
   (c) None of these
6. The collection of all attainable portfolios is known as________.
   (a) Opportunity set (b) Efficient frontier
   (c) Efficient portfolios (d) None of these
7. A portfolio that gives a maximum return for the given risk is known as ________.
   (a) Efficient portfolio (b) Feasible portfolio
   (c) Inefficient portfolio (d) None of these
8. A portfolio that can satisfy the risk–return preference of an investor is known as a/an________.
   (a) Optimal portfolio (b) Efficient portfolio
   (c) Feasible portfolio (d) None of these
9. A portfolio with all the securities is known as a/an ________.
   (a) Market portfolio (b) Efficient portfolio
   (c) Inefficient portfolio (d) None of these
10. CAPM is the relationship between________.
    (a) Return and risk
    (b) Risk and uncertainty
    (c) Return and profit
    (d) None of these
11. Portfolios below the CML are known as________.
    (a) Efficient portfolios
    (b) Inefficient portfolios
    (c) Infeasible portfolios
    (d) None of these
12. Return of a security is influenced by________.
    (a) Systematic risk (b) Unsystematic risk
    (c) Total Risk (d) None of these
13. Unsystematic risk is also known as________.
    (a) Diversifiable risk
    (b) Un-diversifiable risk
    (c) Total risk
    (d) None of these

14. The most extreme consequence of political risk is__________.

    (a) Expropriation

    (b) Increase in costs

    (c) Losing profitable opportunities

    (d) None of these

15. The CAPM becomes international CAPM when the__________is built into the model.

    (a) Market portfolio

    (b) Global market portfolio

    (c) International portfolio

    (d) None of these

Further Reading

1. Richard A. Brealey, "Portfolio Theory versus Portfolio Practice," *Journal of Portfolio Management* (Summer 1990): 6–10.
2. Donald E. Fischer and Ronald J. Jordan, *Security Analysis and Portfolio Management* (New Delhi: Prentice-Hall, 2002).
3. David J. Denis, Diane K. Denis, and Keven Yost, "Global Diversification, Industrial Diversification, and Firm Value," *Journal of Finance* (October 2002): 1951–79.
4. Roy C. Smith and Ingo Walter, "Risks and Rewards in Emerging Market Investments," *Journal of Applied Corporate Finance* (Fall 1997) 8–17.
5. Michael Adler and Bernard Dumas, "International Portfolio Choice and Corporation Finance: A Synthesis," *Journal of Finance* (June 1983): 925–84.
6. Rene M. Stulz, "On the Effects of Barriers to International Investment," *Journal of Finance* (Sept 1981): 923–33.
7. Rene Stultz, "A Model of International Asset Pricing," *Journal of Financial Economics* (December 1981): 383–406.

CHAPTER 16

The Indian Accounting and Taxation System

CHAPTER OBJECTIVES

After studying this chapter, you should be able to:

1 Understand the international accounting system.

2 Discuss the salient features of AS 11.

3 Highlight the major provisions of income tax in India.

4 Understand the concept of double-taxation relief.

5 Know the salient features of DTAA.

Introduction

Accounting is a system of recording that helps the organization communicate its performance or its activities to its stakeholders. It facilitates the preparation of financial statements such as the profit and loss account, the balance sheet, and the cash flow statement meant for various stakeholders of the business. Accounting is rightly considered as the language of business. The organization can speak to its stakeholders through its accounting. The businesses have a statutory responsibility to provide truthful, relevant, and timely information to the stakeholders. Basically, accounting provides information to the stakeholders to take informed decisions. The accounting information can be used by the stakeholders for various purposes. For example, the investors can use the accounting information to identify better investment opportunities. The accounting information can also enable the investors to decide the timing of their purchase or sale of their investments. The lenders might also use the accounting information to determine the financial status of the firm that approaches them for funds. The internal management of the firm may use the accounting information for planning and controlling operations, besides other purposes. The employees of the firm may be interested in the accounting information to know the stability and profitability of their employer. Much in the same way, the other stakeholders such as customers, security analysts, business analysts, rating agencies, regulatory authorities, political parties, environment protection groups, anti-business activists, etc. may use the accounting information for their specialized or specific purposes.

The accounting information is the basis for financial reports which the organization prepares and publishes periodically. The preparation of financial reports is guided and governed by a set of conventions, rules, and procedures, popularly known as Generally

Accepted Accounting Principles (GAAP). Put differently, the GAAP is a framework of accounting principles, standards, and procedures as established by the accounting bodies. The accounting bodies differ from one country to another. For example, the Institute of Chartered Accountants of India (ICAI) prescribes the GAAP for India. Similarly, the Financial Accounting Standard Board sets the accounting standards in the U.S.A. The International Accounting Standards Board (IASB), head-quartered in London, is an independent accounting standard setter. It was established on 1 April 2001 to replace the International Accounting Standards Committee (IASC). The IASC was established in June 1973, following an agreement by accounting bodies of Australia, Canada, France, Germany, Ireland, Japan, Mexico, the Netherlands, U.K., and U.S.A.

Each country has evolved its own accounting system on the basis of which financial statements are prepared. The accounting system of a country lays down accounting standards and conventions. As the countries differ in their accounting systems, each country has its own accounting standards and conventions. For example, the U.S.-based companies charge pension costs against earnings, but Japanese companies do not impose any such charge. Countries also differ on disclosure practices. Such differences may not matter, if the firms are purely domestic and stakeholders do not want to make any international comparisons. Differences in accounting do, however, result in a lack of comparability in the financial reports of companies located in different countries. The differences in accounting systems among countries matter a lot when firms opt for cross-border financing and cross-border investments. *Cross-border financing* refers to the raising of capital in another country's capital market by a firm based in one country. An Indian firm raising funds in the U.S. capital market by issuing ADRs is an example of cross-border financing. *Cross-border investment,* on the other hand, refers to an investment by a domestic entity in a foreign country. Cross-border financing and cross-border investments, which have been on the rise in recent years (the 2000s), have necessitated common (international) accounting standards. Adoption of international accounting standards facilitates the development of international capital markets, the end result of which will be a lower cost of capital and efficient use of capital funds. In this context, the International Accounting Standards Board (IASB) has emerged to prescribe common accounting standards to be adopted by companies. The basic objective of the IASB is to develop international accounting standards for worldwide acceptance and observance so that the accounting standards in different countries are harmonized. The IASB issues new international accounting standards as and when required. Although every country is free to choose its accounting standards, many countries have adopted the accounting standards developed by the IASB. The accounting bodies of some countries are also working with the IASB to harmonize accounting standards. Companies that want to get their capital issues listed on European stock exchanges are required to prepare their accounts to conform to IASB standards. As the latest initiative, the IASB has developed a set of high-quality accounting standards known as International Financial Reporting Standards (IFRS). The IFRS provides consistency in matters like revenue recognition, measurement of costs, balance sheet classification, fair value measurement, etc.

An MNC that conducts its operations in many countries is confronted with a problem of consolidation of financial statements of subsidiaries located in different countries having different accounting standards. The MNC may need to translate the financial statements of its affiliates into its reporting currency in order to have meaningful financial statements. Further, an MNC that enters into transactions denominated in a foreign currency (e.g. exports, imports, lending, investing, and borrowing) may have to express these transactions in its reporting currency. Thus, there is a need for two types of accounting: (i) accounting for foreign currency transactions and (ii) accounting for foreign operations. The major accounting issues are with regard to the choice of exchange rate and the treatment of exchange rate differences (exchange gain or loss). As there is a great diversity in accounting standards practiced in different countries, the MNCs find it hard to have effective financial reporting.

The Accounting Standards Board

The Institute of Chartered Accountants of India (ICAI) is a premier accounting body in India that provides leadership in matters of accounting. It became an associate member of the International Accounting Standards Committee in April 1974, and set up the Accounting Standards Board (ASB) in April 1977. The main objective of the ASB is to develop accounting standards for economic entities in India, keeping in view the realities in the international arena. The composition of the ASB is broad-based, with representatives from various interest groups in industry, government departments, regulatory authorities, financial institutions, and academic and professional bodies. The wide representation ensures participation of all interest groups in the accounting standards-setting process. The accounting standards issued by the ASB have legal sanction and recognition. According to the Companies Act, 1956, every company is required to comply with the accounting standards issued by the ASB. The statutory auditor of the company is required to report whether the accounting standards have been complied with or not. The report of the board of directors of the company should also include a Directors' Responsibility Statement indicating that, in the preparation of the annual accounts, the applicable accounting standards have been followed along with proper explanations for material departures.

Accounting standards are developed on the basis of certain accounting principles. When they are applied in the preparation and presentation of financial statements, the users of the financial statements can have a true and fair view of the performance and financial status of the company, which will enable them to make informed economic decisions. Accounting standards would ensure comparability of financial statements of different enterprises. To ensure international harmonization of accounting standards, India is committed to converge its accounting standards with IFRS. The ICAI issued a timetable for the transition to IFRS, from accounting periods commencing on or after 1 April 2011. Accordingly, the corporates are expected to shift to IFRS in a phased manner beginning with large and listed companies. As the capital markets are increasingly becoming global markets, the investors would see the need for a common set of international accounting standards. Shifting to IFRS would enable Indian companies to have easy access to international capital markets without having to go through the conversion and filing process that is currently required. The IFRS can also enable Indian companies to assess their relative strength or standing, by looking beyond the country. In other words, Indian companies can benchmark their performance with global standards by having financial reports based on the IFRS. Nevertheless, adoption of the IFRS is not a mere technical exercise limited to change from one set of accounts to another set of accounts. The consequences are far more than financial reporting issues, and extend to significant business and regulatory matters including implications on performance indicators, compliance with debt covenants, changes in IT systems, etc. The IFRS also requires significant additional disclosures, particularly in the areas of enterprise risk management, asset liability matching, management commentary on profitability drivers and sensitivity thereof. To comply with the disclosure requirements, many changes are required for IT systems to capture additional information.

Accounting Standard 11*

Accounting Standard 11 (AS 11), entitled "Accounting for the Effects of Changes in Foreign Exchange Rates", was originally issued in 1989 by the Council of the Institute of Chartered Accountants of India. It was revised in 1994 and then in 2003. The revised version of AS 11

* Based on AS 11, "Accounting for the Effects of Changes in Foreign Exchange Rates," The Institute of Chartered Accountants of India (ICAI).

came into effect from 1 April 2004. It is mandatory for all enterprises that engage in activities involving foreign exchange transactions to comply with AS 11. All enterprises must follow AS 11 while accounting for transactions in foreign currencies, and while translating the financial statements of foreign branches for inclusion in the financial statements of the enterprise. AS 11 is also applicable to exchange differences on all forward exchange contracts to hedge the foreign exchange risk of existing assets and liabilities. The major points of AS 11 are discussed in this section.

Recording Transactions on Initial Recognition

According to AS 11, a transaction in a foreign currency should be recorded in the reporting currency by applying to the foreign currency amount the exchange rate between the reporting currency and the foreign currency at the date of the transaction (spot rate). **Reporting currency** is the currency used in presenting financial statements, and the **foreign currency** is a currency other than the reporting currency of an enterprise. If two or more transactions take place simultaneously and can be set off against one another, such transactions are considered interrelated. For example, receivables can be used to settle payables directly. In such cases, the receivables and payables are reported at the exchange rate as applicable to the net amount of receivables or payables. Where realizations are deposited into and disbursements made out of a foreign currency bank account, all the transactions during a period (e.g. week or month) are reported at a rate that approximates the actual rate during that period. If the transactions cannot be interrelated by setoff or otherwise, the receivables and payables are reported at the rates applicable to the respective amounts, even where these are receivables from or payables to the same foreign party.

***Reporting currency** is the currency used in presenting financial statements, and **foreign currency** is a currency other than the reporting currency of an enterprise.*

Subsequent Reporting

A foreign currency item may be monetary or non-monetary. **Monetary items** are those that represent a claim to receive or an obligation to pay a fixed amount of foreign currency units (e.g. accounts receivables and payables), while all other items are non-monetary (e.g. inventory and fixed assets). At each balance sheet date, the foreign currency monetary and non-monetary items are recorded in the reporting currency. AS 11 has the following standards for reporting monetary and non-monetary assets:

***Monetary items** are those that represent a claim to receive or an obligation to pay a fixed amount of foreign currency units, while all other items are non-monetary.*

(i) Monetary items denominated in a foreign currency (e.g. foreign currency notes; balances in bank accounts denominated in a foreign currency; and receivables, payables, and loans denominated in a foreign currency) should be reported using the closing rate. However, in certain circumstances, the closing rate may not reflect with reasonable accuracy the amount in reporting currency that is likely to be realized from, or required to disburse a foreign currency monetary item at the balance-sheet date. In such circumstances, the relevant monetary item should be reported in the reporting currency at the amount which is likely to be realized from, or required to disburse such item at the balance-sheet date.

(ii) Non-monetary items other than fixed assets, which are carried in terms of historical cost denominated in a foreign currency, should be reported using the exchange rate at the date of the transaction.

(iii) Non-monetary items other than fixed assets, which are carried in terms of fair value or other similar valuation (e.g. net realizable value, denominated in a foreign currency), should be reported using the exchange rates that existed when the values were determined.

Recognition of Exchange Differences

An exchange difference arises when there is a change in the exchange rate between the transaction date and the date of settlement of any monetary items arising from a foreign currency transaction. When the transaction is settled within the same accounting period as that in which it occurred, the entire exchange difference arises in that period. However, when the transaction is not settled in the same accounting period as that in which it occurred, the exchange difference arises over more than one accounting period. When the exchange rate on the date of the transaction and on the date of settlement/record is different, it results in exchange gain or loss.

According to AS 11, exchange differences arising on the settlement of monetary items or on reporting an enterprise's monetary items at rates different from those at which they were initially recorded during the period, or reported in previous financial statements, should be recognized as income or expenses in the period in which they arise. However, exchange differences arising from a monetary item that, in substance, forms part of an enterprise's net investment in a non-integral foreign operation should be accumulated in a foreign currency translation reserve in the enterprise's financial statements until the disposal of the net investment, at which time they should be recognized as income or expenses. On the disposal of a non-integral foreign operation, the cumulative amount of the exchange differences that have been deferred and that relate to that operation should be recognized as income or expenses in the same period in which the gain or loss on disposal is recognized.

Forward Exchange Contracts

A *forward exchange contract* is a legally enforceable agreement to deliver or receive a specified quantity of a foreign currency at a fixed forward rate on a specified date in future. The forward rate is usually different from the spot rate. AS 11 states that an enterprise may enter into a forward exchange contract, or another financial instrument that is in substance a forward exchange contract, to establish the amount of the reporting currency required or available at the settlement date of a transaction. The difference between the forward rate and the exchange rate on the date of the transaction should be recognized as income or expense over the life of the contract, except in respect of liabilities incurred for acquiring fixed assets, in which case, such difference should be adjusted in the carrying amount of the respective fixed assets. Any profit or loss arising on cancellation or renewal of a forward contract should be recognized as income or expense for the period, except in case of a forward contract relating to liabilities incurred for acquiring fixed assets, in which case, such profit or loss should be adjusted in the carrying amount of the respective fixed assets.

Translation of the Financial Statements of Foreign Affiliates

The financial statements of foreign affiliates, which are usually stated in foreign currency, need to be translated into the parent firm's reporting currency while preparing the consolidated financial statements. The restatement of the financial statements of subsidiary units into a single common denominator of one currency facilitates inter-firm comparison. The restated financial statements are also used by the management to evaluate the performance of foreign subsidiaries. If the exchange rates change, the value of the assets and liabilities of a foreign subsidiary denominated in a foreign currency change when they are viewed from the perspective of the parent firm. There are different methods of translation of financial statements. Depending on the nature of assets and liabilities and the method of translation, the parent firm may have an exchange gain or loss.

The foreign operations of an enterprise can be classified as either integral foreign operations or non-integral foreign operations. If the foreign operation is carried on by an enterprise as if it were an extension of its business, it is called an integral foreign operation. Non-integral foreign operations are carried out with a significant degree of autonomy from the reporting enterprise. They are also financed mainly from their own operations or local borrowings rather than by the reporting enterprise. Further, costs of labour, material, and other components of the foreign operation's products or services are primarily paid or settled in the local currency rather than in the reporting currency, and the sales are mainly in currencies other than the reporting currency.

The financial statements of an integral foreign operation should be translated as if its transactions had been undertaken by the reporting enterprise itself. In translating the financial statements of a non-integral foreign operation for incorporation in its financial statements, the reporting enterprise should use the following procedure:

(i) The assets and liabilities, both monetary and non-monetary, of the non-integral foreign operation should be translated at the closing rate.

(ii) Income and expense items of the non-integral foreign operation should be translated at the exchange rates prevailing on the dates of the transactions.

(iii) All resulting exchange differences should be accumulated in a foreign currency translation reserve until the disposal of the net investment.

Disclosures

As far as disclosure is concerned, AS 11 mentions that an enterprise should disclose the following information:

(i) The amount of exchange differences included in the net profit or loss for the period.

(ii) The net exchange differences accumulated in a foreign currency translation reserve as a separate component of shareholders' funds, and a reconciliation of the amount of such exchange differences at the beginning and end of the period.

(iii) When the reporting currency is different from the currency of the country in which the enterprise is domiciled, the reason for using a different currency should be disclosed. The reason for any change in the reporting currency should also be disclosed.

(iv) When there is a change in the classification of a significant foreign operation, the enterprise should disclose the reason for and nature of the change, the impact of the change in classification of shareholders' funds, and the impact on net profit or loss for each prior period presented had the change in classification occurred at the beginning of the earliest period presented.

Tax Rates in Select Countries

Tax systems influence investments, particularly foreign investments. In order to attract more investments, many developed and developing countries have lowered their corporate income tax rates. The tax rates of some select countries are presented in Table 16.1. As can be observed from the table, the tax rate for individuals is higher than that for corporates. The tax rates vary from country to country. There are countries with zero tax on income. They include Saudi Arabia, Qatar, Oman, Kuwait, Cayman Islands, Bermuda, Bahrain, and Bahamas. Many developed countries levy taxes at higher rates than the developing countries.

In the U.S., federal income tax applies to bands of taxable income at rates between 15 percent and 35 percent. In other words, the marginal federal corporate income tax rate on the highest income bracket of companies is 35 percent. Branch profit tax is imposed at 30 percent on foreign companies engaged in the U.S. The U.S. also has an alternate minimum tax system. In addition, state and local governments may impose income taxes ranging from

Table 16.1 Income tax rates by select countries (2014)

Country	*Individual tax rate (%)*	*Corporate tax rate (%)*
Argentina	35	35
Australia	45	30
Belgium	50	33
Brazil	27.5	34
Canada	29	15
China	45	25
Egypt	25	25
France	45	33.33
Mauritius	15	15
Mexico	30	30
Japan	50.84	25.5
Germany	45	15
South Africa	40	28
Russia	13	20
UK	45	21
US	39.6	35

0 percent to 12 percent. The companies are, however, allowed to deduct their state and local tax expenses when computing their federal taxable income. Thus, the effective tax rate may vary depending on the locality in which a company conducts its business.

The corporate income tax rate in the U.K. has been reduced in recent years to 21 percent. The U.K. has a small companies rate system which is at 20 percent. Small companies rate applies to companies with taxable profits of up to GBP 300,000 with a marginal relief up to GBP 1.5 million. It means that a company with a taxable profit of GBP 1.5 million or more pays tax at the main rate.

The corporate tax rate in Japan is 25.5 percent. This rate is applicable to ordinary companies with share capital exceeding JPY 100 million. Surtax is imposed at 10 percent for three years for fiscal years beginning on or after 1 April 2012, so the national corporate tax rate will be 28.5 percent for the first three years, and 25.5 percent thereafter. Companies also pay local tax, which varies depending on the location and the size of the company. Thus, the effective tax rate for companies in Japan is about 36 percent.

The corporate tax rate in Germany is at 29.58 percent, which includes corporate income tax at a rate of 15 percent, solidarity surcharge at a rate of 5.5 percent of the corporate income tax, and local trade tax, which varies between 7 percent and 17.15 percent. The effective tax rate varies from business location to business location in the country. The local trade tax is not deductible from the taxable corporate income.

The corporate income tax rate in Brazil is 25 percent, which is a combination of 15 percent basic rate and 10 percent surtax on income that exceeds BRL 240,000 per year. In addition, a social contribution tax at 9 percent (15 percent for financial institutions) is levied on adjusted net profits of companies.

The Taxation System in India

The Constitution of India confers the sovereign powers on the State, under Article 265, to levy taxes and to enforce collection and recovery thereto. No taxes shall be levied or collected except by authority of law. India is a federal republic comprising the union government, 29 self-governing states, and six union territories. The power to levy taxes is conferred on the Union of India in respect of matters falling within its domain (list 1, Schedule VII of the Constitution). The Union Government is empowered to levy almost all direct taxes in addition to some indirect taxes. Power to levy taxes is conferred on the state legislatures with regard to matters falling within their domain (list 2 of Schedule VII of the Constitution). The state governments are authorized to levy some indirect taxes. Thus, taxes are levied in India by both the Union Government and the state governments through their respective legislatives.

The principal taxes levied by the Union Government on the companies are the corporate income tax, minimum alternate tax, capital gain tax, dividend distribution tax, wealth tax, and indirect taxes such as value-added tax, central sales tax, securities transaction tax, customs duty, excise duty, and service tax. The taxes levied by the state governments include sales tax, profession tax and real estate tax. However, tax incentives are provided for establishing new industries and encouraging investments in undeveloped areas, infrastructure, and promoting exports.

Income Tax

Income tax is levied in accordance with the provisions of the Income Tax Act, 1961, as amended from time to time. The Central Board of Direct Taxes (CBDT) is the apex tax authority, which administers and implements the direct tax laws. The Income Tax Act, 1961, also empowers the CBDT to make rules for implementing various tax provisions. To deal with certain specific problems, the CBDT issues circulars from time to time.

The Union Finance Minister presents the union budget every year, which reflects the fiscal policy of the government. To give effect to the various proposals contained in the union budget, the parliament passes the Finance Bill, which eventually becomes the Finance Act of that year. The Finance Act consists of rates of income tax and various amendments to the Income Tax Act, besides many others.

Income tax is levied on taxable income, which is classified into five heads: (i) salaries, (ii) income from house property, (iii) profits and gains of business or profession, (iv) capital gains, and (v) income from other sources. The incidence of tax depends on the residential status of the assessee as well as the place and time of accrual or receipt of income. Accordingly, the income is classified into Indian income and foreign income.

Indian Income and Foreign Income Any of the following is an *Indian income:*

(i) If income is received (or deemed to be received) in India during the previous year, and at the same time it accrues (or arises or is deemed to accrue or arise) in India during the previous year.

(ii) If income is received (or deemed to be received) in India during the previous year, but it accrues (or arises) outside India during the previous year.

(iii) If income is received outside India during the previous year, but it accrues (or arises of is deemed to accrue or arise) in India during the previous year.

Income is *foreign income* if it is not received (or not deemed to be received) in India and if the income does not accrue or arise (or does not deemed to accrue or arise) in India. Income that is deemed to accrue or arise in India includes the following:

- Income arising from a business connection, property, asset, or source of income in India;
- Capital gains from the transfer of capital assets situated in India; and

- Interest, royalties, and technical service fees paid by an Indian resident, non-resident or the Indian government.

Payments made to a non-resident for the provision of services are taxable in India even if the services are rendered outside the company. Where the fees are payable in respect of services used in a business or profession carried on by such a person outside India or for the purpose of making or earning income from a source outside India, they are not taxable in India.

Residential Status According to the Income Tax Act, 1961, the assessees are classified into:

- An individual;
- A Hindu undivided family (HUF);
- A firm or an association of persons;
- A joint stock company; and
- Every other person.

An individual and an HUF can either be resident and ordinarily resident in India, resident but not ordinarily resident in India, or non-resident in India. All other assessees can either be resident in India or non-resident in India.

Indian income is always taxable in India irrespective of the residential status of the taxpayer. Foreign income is taxable in the hands of resident (in case of a firm, an association of persons, a joint stock company, and every other person) or resident and ordinarily resident (in case of an individual and a HUF) in India. Foreign income is not taxable in the hands of non-residents in India. In the case of the resident but not ordinarily resident, foreign income is taxable only if it is (a) business income where the business is controlled from India or (b) professional income from a profession that is set up in India. In any other case, foreign income is not taxable in the hands of resident but not ordinarily resident taxpayers.

Thus, nonresidents are liable to pay tax on India-source income, which includes interest, royalties, and fees for technical services paid by an Indian resident. Remuneration received by foreign expatriates working in India is subject to tax under the head 'salaries' and is deemed to be earned in India. In other words, irrespective of the residential status of the expatriate employee, the salary or any remuneration paid for services rendered in India is liable to tax in India. Where salary is payable in foreign currency, it is converted to INR at the rate of exchange as adopted by the State Bank of India on the last day of the month immediately preceding the month in which the salary is due or paid.

There are no special exemptions or deductions available to non-residents working in India. However, a non-resident who comes to India on short-term business visits can claim an exemption under the domestic tax law or a relevant tax treaty.

According to the Income Tax Act, 1961, an Indian company is a company that is formed and registered under the Companies Act, 1956. Any company that is not a domestic company is a foreign company. A company's tax liability under the Act is determined in accordance with the residential status of the company in the relevant *previous* year. A company is said to be resident in India in any previous year if it is an Indian company or if during that year the control and management of its affairs is situated wholly in India. The expression 'control and management' means *de facto* control and management and not merely the right to control and manage. The year in which income is earned is known as *the previous year* and the next year in which income is taxable is known as the *assessment year.*

Business Income Chargeable to Tax *Business* is defined to include any (i) trade, (ii) commerce, (iii) manufacture, or (iv) any adventure or concern in the nature of trade, commerce, or manufacture. The term *profession* implies professed attainments in special knowledge as distinguished from mere skill. Many vocations may fall within the ordinary and accepted use of the term *profession* (e.g. accountants, architects, engineers, journalists).

Under Section 28 of the Income Tax Act, 1961, the following incomes are chargeable to tax under the head 'Profits and Gains of Business or Profession':

- Profits and gains of any business or profession;
- Any compensation or other payments due to or received by any person specified in Section 28 (ii);
- Income derived by a trade, professional, or similar association from specific services performed for its members;
- The value of any benefit or perquisite, whether convertible into money or not, arising from business or the exercise of a profession;
- Any profit on transfer of the Duty Entitlement Pass Book Scheme;
- Any profit on the transfer of the duty free replenishment certificate;
- Export incentive available to exporters;
- Any interest, salary, bonus, commission, or remuneration received by a partner from the firm;
- Any sum received for not carrying out any activity in relation to any business or not to share any knowhow, patent, copyright, trademark, etc;
- Any sum received under a Keyman insurance policy including bonus;
- Profits and gains of managing agency;
- Any sum received or receivable in cash or kind, on account of any capital asset being demolished, destroyed, discarded or transferred, if the whole of the on such capital asset has been allowed as a deduction under section 35 AD; and
- Income from speculative transactions.

Deductible Losses While determining the actual profits or losses of a business, the assessees are allowed to deduct certain trading losses incurred in business, provided they are incidental to the operation of business. The following losses are generally deductible from business income:

(a) Loss of stock-in trade as a result of enemy action, or arising under similar circumstances.

(b) Loss of stock-in trade due to destruction by an act of God.

(c) Loss arising on account of failure on the part of the assessee to accept delivery of goods.

(d) Depreciation in funds kept in a foreign country for purchase of stock-in-trade.

(e) Loss due to exchange rate fluctuations of foreign currency held on revenue account.

(f) Loss arising from sale of securities held in the regular course of business.

(g) Loss of cash and securities in a banking company on account of dacoit.

(h) Loss incurred on realization of amount advanced in connection with business.

(i) Loss of security deposited for the purposes of acquisition of stock-in trade.

(j) Loss due to forfeiture of a deposit made by the assessee for properly carrying out of contract for supply of commodities.

(k) Loss on account of embezzlement by an employee.

(l) Loss incurred due to theft or burglary in factory premises during or after working hours.

(m) Loss of precious stones or watches of a dealer while bringing them from business premises to his house.

(n) Loss arising from negligence or dishonesty of employees.

(o) Loss incurred on account of insolvency of banker with which current account is maintained by the assessee.

(p) Loss incurred due to freezing of the stock-in-trade by enemy action.

(q) Loss incurred by a sugar manufacturing company by foregoing the advance made to sugarcane growers who used to sell sugarcane crop exclusively to the company.

(r) Loss on account of non-recovery of advances given by the assessee to a 100 percent subsidiary company.

(s) Loss incurred by a holding company that has guaranteed a loan taken by its subsidiary company.

The following are the losses that are not deductible from business income:

(a) Loss that is not incidental to the trade or profession carried on by the assessee.

(b) Loss incurred due to damage or destruction of capital assets.

(c) Loss incurred due to the sale of shares held as investment.

(d) Loss of advances made for setting up of a new business that ultimately could not be started.

(e) Depreciation of funds kept in foreign currencies for capital purposes.

(f) Loss arising from non-recovery of tax paid by an agent on behalf of the non-resident.

(g) Anticipated future losses.

(h) Loss relating to any business or profession discontinued before the commencement of the previous year.

Allowable Deductions The following expenses are expressly allowed under the Income Tax Act, 1961, as deduction against profits and gains of business or profession, subject to certain conditions as stated under respective sections of the Income tax Act:

- Rent, rates, taxes, repairs, and insurance for building (Sec. 30).
- Repairs and insurance for machinery, plant, and furniture (Sec. 31).
- Depreciation allowance (Sec. 32).
- Investment deposit account scheme (Sec. 32AB).
- Tea/coffee/rubber development account (Sec. 33AB).
- Site restoration fund (Sec. 33ABA).
- Reserve for shipping business (Sec. 33AC).
- Expenditure on scientific research (Sec. 35).
- Expenditure on acquisition of patent rights and copyrights (Sec. 35A).
- Expenditure on know-how (Sec. 35AB).
- Amortization of telecom licence fees (Sec. 35ABB).
- Expenditure on eligible projects or schemes (Sec. 35AC).

- Payment to associations and institutions for carrying out rural development programmes (Sec. 35CCA).
- Payment for carrying out programmes of conservation of natural resources (Sec. 35CCB).
- Amortization of preliminary expenses (Sec. 35D).
- Amortization of expenditure on prospecting, and so on, for development of certain minerals [Sec. 35E]
- Insurance premium [Sec. 36 (I) (i)].
- Insurance premium paid by a federal milk cooperative society [Sec. 36 (1) (ia)].
- Premia for insurance on health of employees [Sec. 36 (1) (ib)].
- Bonus or commission to employees [Sec. 36 (1) (ii)].
- Interest on borrowed capital [Sec. 36 (1) (iii)].
- Discount on zero-coupon bonds [Sec. 36 (1) (iiia)].
- Employer's contribution to recognized provident fund and approved superannuation fund [Sec. 36 (1) (iv)].
- Contribution towards approved gratuity fund [Sec. 36 (1) (v)].
- Employees' contribution towards staff welfare schemes [Sec. 36 (1) (va)].
- Write-off of allowance for animals [Sec. 36 (1) (vi)].
- Bad debts [Sec. 36 (1) (vii)].
- Provision for bad and doubtful debts relating to rural branches of scheduled commercial banks [Sec. 36 (1)].
- Transfer of special reserve [Sec. 36 (1) (viii)].
- Family planning expenditure [Sec. 36 (1) (ix)].
- Contribution towards exchange risk administration fund [Sec. 36 (1) (x)].
- Revenue expenditure incurred by entities established under any central, state or provincial Act [Sec. 36 (1) (xii)].
- Banking cash transaction tax [Sec. 36 (1) (xiii)].
- Advertisement expenses [Sec. 37 (2B)].
- General deduction [Sec. 37 (1)].

There are also certain specific disallowances, the details of which are provided in Sections 40, 40A, and 43B of the Income Tax Act. Further, no deduction is permissible under Section 28 to 44D with respect the income referred to in Sections 115A, 115AB, 115AC, 115AD, 115BBA, and 115D.

A special mention may be made of the following deductions:

- A 100 percent deduction for interest payments on capital borrowed for business purposes.
- Capital expenditure on research conducted in-house and for payments made for payments made for scientific research to specified companies or specified organizations.
- Investment-linked incentives (a 100 percent deduction for capital expenditure other than expenditure incurred on the acquisition of land, goodwill, or financial instruments) for setting up and operating cold chain facilities, warehousing, and laying and operating cross-country natural gas or crude or petroleum oil pipeline networks for

distribution, including storage facilities that are an integral part of such networks. This incentive is also available on investment made in housing projects under a scheme for affordable housing, building and operating two-star hotels, building and operating a hospital with 100 beds, and for the production of fertilizers in India.

- Interest, royalties, and fees for technical services paid outside India to overseas affiliates or in India to a non-resident provided tax is withheld.
- Capital assets purchased for scientific research may be written off in the year the expenditure is incurred.

Indian branches of foreign companies can claim limited tax deduction for general administrative expenses incurred by the parent firm. These expenses should not exceed 5 percent of the annual income or the actual payment of the parent firm's expenditure attributable to the Indian business during the year, whichever is lower.

Taxing of Capital Gains Under Section 45 of the Income Tax Act, any gain arising from the transfer of a capital asset is chargeable to tax under the head "capital gains." *Capital asset* refers to property of any kind, whether fixed or circulating, movable or immovable, tangible or intangible. However, the following assets are excluded from the definition of capital asset:

(a) Any stock-in trade, consumable stores, or raw material held for the purposes of business or profession.

(b) Personal effects of the assessee.

(c) Agricultural land in India, provided it is not situated in an area within the territorial jurisdiction of a municipality or a cantonment board, having a population of 10,000 or more, or in any notified area.

(d) Six and half percent Gold Bonds, 1977, or 7 percent Gold Bonds, 1980, or National Defence Gold Bonds, 1980, issued by the central government.

(e) Special Bearer Bonds, 1991 and Gold Deposit Bonds, issued under the Gold Deposit Scheme, 1999.

Capital assets are classified as short-term capital assets and long-term capital assets. Short-term capital assets refer to a capital asset held by an assessee for not more than 36 months immediately preceding the date of its transfer. In the case of a financial asset, short-term capital asset means a share, security, unit, or zero-coupon bond held by an assessee for not more than 12 months instead of 36 months as in case of other assets. Long-term capital asset is a capital asset, which is not considered as a short-term capital asset.

Capital gain is computed by deducting the cost of acquisition, cost of improvement, and any expenditure incurred in connection with the transfer from the sale consideration. Thus, a gain arising on the transfer of a capital asset is known as capital gain. In this context, transfer means sale, exchange, or relinquishment of the asset, the extinguishment of any rights therein, or the compulsory acquisition thereof under any law. The Income Tax Act also specifies certain transactions that are not considered transfers. Thus, one may derive short-term capital gain or long-term capital gain on transfer of short-term capital asset or long-term capital asset as the case may be.

Capital Gains Exempt from Tax Any gains arising on transfer of the following assets are exempt from tax on certain conditions:

- Capital gains in case of liquidation of companies [Sec. 46 (1)].
- Capital gains arising from the transfer of property used for residence (Sec. 54).
- Capital gains arising from the transfer of land used for agricultural purpose (Sec. 54B).

*Any gain arising from the transfer of a short-term capital asset (asset held by an assessee for not more than 36 months immediately prior to its date of transfer) is a **short-term capital gain**, and any gain arising from the transfer of a long-term capital asset (asset held by an assessee for more than 36 months) is known as a **long-term capital gain**.*

- Capital gains on compulsory acquisition of lands and buildings (Sec. 54D).
- Capital gains arising from the transfer of a specified long-term capital asset (Sec. 54EC).
- Long-term capital gains on investment of the consideration in residential house (Sec. 54F).
- Capital gains on transfer of assets in cases of shifting of industrial undertaking from urban area to rural area (Sec. 54G).
- Capital gains on transfer of assets in cases of shifting of industrial undertaking from an urban area to any special economic zone (Sec. 54GA).
- Capital gains on transfer of residential house property if transfer takes place during 1 April 2012–31 March 2017 (Sec. 54GB).
- If long-term capital gain arises from the transfer of equity shares or units of equity-oriented mutual fund, and the transaction is covered by securities transaction tax, such capital gain is exempted under Section 10(38).

Tax Rates Applicable to Capital Gains There is no special tax rate applicable for short-term capital gains and they are taxed normally based on the applicable slab rate. However, if the sale of a company's equity shares is subject to the securities transaction tax (STT), the short-term capital gains are taxed at a rate of 15 percent.

Long-term capital gain is chargeable to tax at a flat rate of 20 percent plus surcharge and education cess. In the case of capital gains on transfer of equity shares or units of equity-oriented mutual funds, the tax rates are as follows. The surcharge and education cess are also levied wherever applicable:

- 15 percent on short-term capital gains, if the STT is paid.
- Short-term capital gains shall be part of another income, if the STT is not paid.
- Long-term capital gains are exempted from tax, if the STT is paid.
- 10 percent on long-term capital gains on listed securities without indexing the cost of acquisition, if the STT is not paid.
- 20 percent on long-term capital gains on listed securities after indexing the cost of acquisition, if the STT is not paid.

Income from Other Sources Income from other sources is the residual head of income, and an income that does not specifically fall under any one of the other heads is to be computed and brought to charge under the head 'income from other sources'.

The following incomes are taxable under the head 'income from other sources':

(a) Dividend.

(b) Any winnings from lotteries, crossword puzzles, races including horse races, card games and other games of any sort, or from gambling or betting of any form or nature whatsoever.

(c) Any sum received by the assessee from its employees as contributions to any staff welfare scheme.

(d) Interest on securities, if not charged to tax under the head 'Profits and gains of business or Profession'.

(e) Income from machinery, plant, or furniture let on hire (if it is not taxable under the head 'profits and gains of business or profession').

(f) Income from letting of plant, machinery, or furniture, along with the building and letting of building, is inseparable from the letting of plant, machinery, or furniture (if it is not taxable under the head 'Profits and gains of business or profession').

(g) Any sum received under a Keyman insurance policy including bonus, if not taxable as salary or business income.

(h) Where any sum of money exceeding INR 25,000 is received without consideration by an individual or HUF from any person, the whole of such a sum.

Treatment of Dividend According to Section 2 (22) of the Income Tax Act, the following payments or distributions by a company to its shareholders are deemed as dividend to the extent of accumulated profits of the company. It may be noted that these payments may not be dividend according to the Companies Act:

(a) Any distribution entailing the release of the company's assets;

(b) Any distribution of debentures, debenture-stock, deposit certificates, and bonuses to preference shareholders;

(c) Distribution on liquidation of company;

(d) Distribution on reduction of capital; and

(e) Any payment by way of loan or advance by a closely held company to a shareholder holding substantial interest, provided the loan was not made in the ordinary course of business and money lending is not a substantial part of the company's business.

Dividend (including deemed dividends) received from a domestic company is not taxable in the hands of the shareholders u/s 10(34). However, the company declaring the dividend will pay dividend distribution tax u/s 115-O. A domestic company is required to pay dividend distribution tax at 15 percent plus a surcharge of 5 percent and 3 percent cess on any amount declared, distributed, or paid as dividend. From the assessment year 2015–16, the dividend distribution tax is to be levied on the gross amount of dividends. So the effective dividend distribution tax may come to 20.47 percent. Indian holding company is allowed to set off the dividends received from its Indian subsidiary against dividends distributed in computing the dividend distribution tax, provided certain conditions are satisfied. Dividends paid to the New Pension Scheme Trust are exempt from the dividend distribution tax.

The dividend received from a company other than a domestic company, is included 'net' in the income. However, where the assessee claims double taxation relief, the gross amount shall be included in the income. Where the total income of an Indian company includes any income by way of dividends paid by a specified foreign company, the Indian company shall be liable to pay tax on such income.

Investment Allowance To encourage capital investment, the Government of India offers an investment allowance to companies so that they can deduct a specified percentage of capital costs from their taxable income.

A new Section 32 AC was inserted in the Finance Act, 2013, to provide a tax incentive by way of investment allowance to encourage huge investments in plants or machineries. Under this new Section 32AC, a manufacturing company is entitled to an investment allowance at a rate of 15 percent of the actual cost of the new plant and machinery acquired and installed during the financial years 2013–14 and 2014–15, provided the actual cost of the new plant and machinery exceeds INR 100 crore. But as per the Finance Act, 2014, the applicability of this section is extended till the assessment year 2017–18. A provision is also made in the Finance Act, 2014, to include medium-size investments in plant and machinery also as eligible for deduction. Thus, the deduction shall be allowed, if the company invests more than INR 25 crore on or after 1 April 2014 in plant and machinery in a year.

Taxable Income and Tax Liability of Companies The total income computed as per the various provisions of the Income Tax Act under different heads is the gross total income. From the gross total income, the following deductions are permissible:

(a) Donations to charitable institutions and funds (Sec. 80G).

(b) Donations for scientific research for rural development (Sec. 80GGA).

(c) Contributions given to political parties (Sec. 80GGB).

(d) Profits and gains by an undertaking or enterprise engaged in infrastructure (Sec. 80IA).

(e) Profits and gains by an undertaking or enterprise engaged in development of a special economic zone (Sec. 80-IAB).

(f) Profits and gains from certain industrial undertakings other than infrastructure development undertakings (Sec. 80-IB).

(g) Profits and gains of certain undertakings in certain special category of states (Sec. 80-IC).

(h) Profits from the business of collecting and processing biodegradable waste (Sec. 80-JJA).

(i) Employment of new workmen (Sec. 80-JJAA).

The income tax is levied on the chargeable income at tax rates listed hereunder (applicable for Assessment Year 2015–16). Note that companies and firms are subject to tax at flat rates, whereas individuals and specified taxpayers are subject to progressive tax rates.

Income tax rates for general individual assessee

Net income range	*Income-tax rates*	*Surcharge*	*Education cess*	*Secondary and higher education cess*
Up to ₹250,000	*Nil*	*Nil*	*Nil*	*Nil*
₹250,000 – ₹500,000	10% of (total income *minus* ₹250,000)	*Nil*	2% of income tax	1% of income tax
₹500,000 – ₹1,000,000	₹25,000 + 20% of (total income *minus* ₹500,000)	*Nil*	2% of income tax	1% of income tax
₹1,000,000 – ₹10,000,000	₹125,000 + 30% of (total income *minus* ₹1,000,000)	*Nil*	2% of income tax	1% of income tax
Above ₹1,00,00,000	₹28,25,000 + 30% of (total income *minus* ₹10,000,000)	10% of income-tax	2% of income tax and surcharge	1% of income tax and surcharge

Rates of Corporate Income Tax

I. In the case of a domestic company — 30 percent of the total income;

II. In the case of a company other than a domestic company—

(i) on so much of the total income as consists of—

(a) royalties received from the Government or an Indian concern in pursuance of an agreement made by it with the Government or the Indian concern after the 31st day of March, 1961, but before the 1st day of April, 1976; or

(b) fees for rendering technical services received from the Government or an Indian concern in pursuance of an agreement made by it with the Government or the Indian concern after the 29th day of February, 1964, but before the 1st day of April, 1976, and where such agreement has, in either case, been approved by the Government of India. — 50 per cent;

(ii) on the balance, if any, of the total income — 40 percent

While delivering the budget speech on 28 February 2015, the Union Finance Minister said that the basic rate of corporate tax in India at 30 percent is higher than the rates prevailing in the other major Asian economies, making the domestic industry uncompetitive. Therefore, as a part of Union Budget 2015, he announced that the basic rate of corporate tax will be reduced from current 30 percent to 25 percent over the next four years, accompanied by fewer exemptions. This will lead to higher level of investment, higher growth and more employment.

Surcharge on Income Tax The amount of income tax computed in accordance with the provisions shall, in the case of every company, be increased by a surcharge.

(i) in the case of every domestic company—

(a) having a total income exceeding INR 1 crore, but not exceeding INR 10 crore, at the rate of five percent of such income tax; and

(b) having a total income exceeding INR 10 crore, at the rate of ten percent of such income tax;

(ii) in the case of every company other than a domestic company—

(a) having a total income exceeding INR 1 crore but not exceeding INR 10 crore, at the rate of two per cent of such income tax; and

(b) having a total income exceeding INR 10 crore, at the rate of five percent of such income tax.

Provided that in the case of every company having a total income exceeding INR 1 crore but not exceeding INR 10 crore, the total amount payable as income tax and surcharge on such income shall not exceed the total amount payable as income tax on a total income of INR 1 crore by more than the amount of income that exceeds INR 1 crore.

Provided further that in the case of every company having a total income exceeding INR 10 crore, the total amount payable as income tax and surcharge on such income shall not exceed the total amount payable as income tax and surcharge on a total income of INR 10 crore by more than the amount of income that exceeds INR 10 crore.

Minimum Alternate Tax Some companies may not be required to pay income tax in spite of the fact that they have earned substantial book profits and have paid dividends. In order to make such zero-tax companies pay tax, the government has introduced the *minimum alternate tax (MAT)*. In the case of a company where the income tax payable on the total income by a company is less than 18.5 percent of its book profits, the book profits are deemed to be the total income of the company on which tax is payable at a rate of 18.5 percent, plus applicable surcharge and education cess. MAT is applicable both for domestic companies as well as foreign companies. The tax paid under MAT may be carried forward to be set off against income tax payable in the next 10 years, subject to certain conditions.

Indirect Taxes

The major indirect taxes in India are value-added tax (VAT), securities transaction tax (STT), customs duties, central sales tax, service tax, and central excise duty. A brief note on each of them is provided in the following paragraphs.

Value-added Tax (VAT) was introduced in India on 1 April 2005. Now, India is among the 124 countries in the world that have a value-added taxation system. VAT is a centrally administered tax system with a revenue-sharing mechanism. It has replaced the single-point system of tax levy known as sales tax. Value-added tax is a multi-point levy on each of the entities in the supply chain with the facility of set-off of input tax. In other words, only the value addition in the hands of each of the entities in the supply chain is subject to tax. For example, a dealer has purchased goods for INR 100 million from a manufacturer and a tax of INR 10 million (input tax) has been charged in the bill. The dealer sells the goods for INR 120 million on which the dealer charges a tax of INR 12 million (output tax). According to the new system, the tax payable by the dealer is only INR 2 million, being the difference between the tax collected (INR 12 million) and the tax already paid (INR 10 million) on purchase of these goods. Thus, the dealer pays the tax at 10 percent on INR 20 million, reflecting the value addition by his hands. The VAT system thus permits the dealer to set-off the input tax against the output tax.

***Value-added tax** is a multi-point levy on each of the entities in the supply chain with the facility of set-off of input tax.*

There are three methods by which VAT can be computed:

(a) *The subtraction method:* In this method, the tax rate is applied to the difference between the value of output and the cost of input.

(b) *The addition method:* As per this method, the value added is computed by adding all the payments that are payable to the factors of production or by adding all the payments that are payable at a point in the supply chain.

(c) *The tax credit method:* In this method, the tax paid on inputs is set off against tax collected on sale.

The major advantage of VAT is that it has no cascading effect. But VAT is levied on all goods and services, while central sales tax is levied on goods only. Presently, VAT is applicable only to sales within a state. The sales that take place outside the state, interstate sales, and the sales made in the course of export or import shall continue to be liable under the Central Sales Tax Act, 1956.

Securities Transaction Tax (STT) is levied on the purchase or sale of an equity share, derivative, or unit of equity-oriented fund listed on a recognized stock exchange. The tax at the prescribed rates (varies from 0.017% to 0.125%) is paid by the seller of the security. The STT paid in respect of taxable securities transactions made in the course of business is allowed as a deduction, if income from the transaction is included in the businessincome.

Customs duties are levied by the Government of India generally on the import of goods into India. In certain cases, exported goods are also liable for customs duties. The rates of customs duties vary depending on the classification of the goods under the Customs Tariff Act, 1975.

The Government of India levies the **central sales tax** (CST) on the interstate movement of goods, but the tax is collected and retained by the origin state. CST is levied at a rate of 2 percent on the movement of such goods from one state to another provided specified forms are submitted. The CST paid on interstate purchases is not allowed as a set off or as a credit against VAST/CST payable in any state.

Service tax is levied on a broad range of services which include advertising, credit rating, banking and financial consulting, financial leasing, storage and warehousing, and renting of commercial property. Credit for inputs, capital goods, and input services used in the provision of taxable output services is available, subject to specific conditions.

Central excise duty is levied by the Government of India on the production or manufacture of goods in India. The producer or manufacturer is liable to pay the central excise duty. The rates of the central excise duty vary depending on the classification of goods under the Central Excise Tariff Act, 1985. Credit for inputs, capital goods, and input services is available subject to specific conditions.

Withholding Tax for NRIs and Foreign Companies

The withholding tax rates for payments made to non-residents are determined by the Finance Act passed by the parliament every year. These rates are general and with respect to the countries with which India does not have a double-taxation avoidance agreement. The current rates are:

- Interest from infrastructure debt fund: 5 percent
- Income in respect of units: 20 percent
- Interest from companies: 5 percent
- Income on Government securities: 5 percent
- Income from units: 10 percent
- Income from foreign currency bond or shares of Indian companies: 10 percent
- Income of FIIs from securities: 20 percent

To achieve closer economic integration and investment protection, many countries have entered into investment treaties. These investment treaties may be bilateral investment treaties (BITs), double-taxation treaties (DTTs), or international investment agreements other than BITs and DTTs. These agreements establish binding obligations on the contracting parties concerning the admission and protection of foreign investment in addition to establishing a framework on investment promotion and cooperation.

Double-taxation Avoidance Agreement (DTAA)

Double taxation may arise when a person earning any income has to pay tax in the country (source country) in which the income is earned as well as in the country (residence country) in which the person is domiciled. As such, the said income is liable to tax in both the countries. To avoid the hardship of double taxation, the governments may enter into a Double-taxation Avoidance Agreement (DTAA). It is essentially a bilateral agreement to promote and foster economic relations between two countries by avoiding double taxation. DTAA typically provides relief from double taxation of incomes by providing exemption and also by providing credits for taxes paid in one of the countries.

The Income Tax Act, 1961, has conferred powers on the Government of India to enter into an agreement with the government of any country:

(i) for the granting of relief with respect to income on which both income tax under the Income Tax Act, 1961 and income tax in the foreign country have been paid; or

(ii) for the avoidance of double taxation of income under the Income-Tax Act, 1961 and under the corresponding law in force in the foreign country; or

(iii) for recovery of income tax under the Income Tax Act, 1961 and under the corresponding law in force in the foreign country.

It may be noted that the Government of India is also empowered to enter into agreements for avoidance of double taxation in the levy of other taxes as well.

As far as India is concerned, DTAA covers only residents of India and the other contracting country that has entered into the agreement with India. In other words, a person who is not a resident either of India or of the other contracting country, cannot claim any benefit under the DTAA. The DTAA allocates jurisdiction between the source and the residence country. Wherever such jurisdiction is given to both the countries, the agreements prescribe maximum rates of taxation in the source country, which is generally lower than the rate of tax under the domestic laws of that country. The double taxation in such cases is avoided by the residence country agreeing to give credit for tax paid in the source country, thereby reducing tax payable in the residence country by the amount of tax paid in the source country. The source country is also given this right, but such taxation in the source country has to be limited to the rates prescribed in the agreement. It may be noted that DTAAs mostly follow a uniform pattern in as much as India has guided itself by the UN model of double-taxation avoidance agreements.

The DTAAs shall have clear provisions to deal with specific items of taxable income. For example, the income derived from the operation of air transport in international traffic by an enterprise of one contracting country will not be taxed in the other contracting country and income earned from the operation of ships in international traffic will be taxed in that contracting country wherein the place of effective management of the enterprise is situated. Capital gains are taxed in the country where the capital asset is situated at the time of sale. Income from professional services will be taxed in the country where the person is a resident. However, if he has a fixed base in the other contracting country, the income attributable to the fixed base will be taxed in the other contracting country. With regard to income from royalties, some DTAAs provide for taxation in the other contracting country, and some agreements provide for taxation in the contracting country. However, some DTAAs contain provisions to tax the income in the other contracting country also, although at reduced rate. For example, interest paid in a contracting country to a resident of the other contracting country is chargeable in both the countries.

The DTAA can have the following benefits:

- Facilitates investment and trade flow by preventing discrimination between tax payers.
- Removes tax obstacles that inhibit trade.
- Facilitates movement of capital and people across countries.
- Avoids undue tax burden on persons earning income in the source country.
- Adds fiscal certainty to nations.
- Reduces evasion and avoidance of tax.
- Promotes cooperation between the nations.
- Facilitates mutual exchange of information.
- Reduces international-level litigations.
- Facilitates mutual resolution of issues as per the Law of Treaties.

In accordance with the general principles laid down in the model draft of the Organization for Economic Cooperation and Development (OECD), the Government of India entered into double-taxation avoidance agreements with more than 80 countries by the end of 2014. The countries include the United States, United Kingdom, Japan, France, Germany, Singapore, The Netherlands, Malaysia, Italy, Egypt, Denmark, Spain, Vietnam, Australia, New Zealand, Brazil, Syria, Switzerland, Canada, China, Kenya, Portugal, Romania, Korea, Sweden, Sri Lanka, Ukraine, UAE, Uzbekistan, Russian Federation, and Romania.

The format of DTAAs is explained with two examples—the Indo-Mauritius DTAT and the Singapore–India DTAT.

The Indo-Mauritius Double-taxation Avoidance Treaty

The Indo-Mauritius Double-taxation Avoidance Treaty was first signed in 1983 by the Government of the Republic of India and the Government of Mauritius for the avoidance of double taxation, prevention of fiscal evasion with respect to taxes on income and capital gains, and encouraging mutual trade and investment. One of the main provisions of the Treaty stipulates that the profits of an enterprise in a contracting Government are to be taxed only in that country, unless the enterprise carries on business in the other contracting country through a permanent establishment situated there. If a permanent establishment has been created, the profit may be taxed in the other country only to the extent that is attributable to that establishment. *Permanent establishment* is defined as a fixed place of business through which the business of the enterprise is wholly or partly carried out. It is also stated that the income from immovable property will be taxed in the contracting country in which the property is situated. Thus, the gains derived by a resident of a contracting country from the alienation of any property will be taxable only in that country. For example, if a Mauritian company earns capital gains in India, then such income is not taxed in India. Also, capital gains arising from the sale of securities in India by a Mauritian resident are taxable only in Mauritius. The dividend income of a Mauritian resident derived from India is liable to be taxed in Mauritius.

The Indo-Mauritius Double-taxation Avoidance Treaty has played an important role in facilitating foreign investment in India. Many venture capital investors have structured investments in India through Mauritius, taking advantage of the beneficial provisions of the Indo-Mauritius DTAA. As a result, Mauritius has emerged as the largest source of foreign direct investment in India.

Though the Indo-Mauritius DTAA was signed in 1983, for almost 10 years the treaty existed only on paper as foreign investors were not allowed to invest in Indian stock markets. It was only around 1992 that FIIs were allowed to invest in Indian stock markets. At the same time, the Government of Mauritius passed the Offshore Business Activities Act, which allowed foreign companies to register in Mauritius for investing abroad. A company can enjoy benefits like total exemption from capital gains tax, and completely convertible currency, if it is registered in Mauritius. Therefore, for foreign investors who wish to invest in India, it makes sense to set up a subsidiary in Mauritius and route their investments through that country.

The Indo-Mauritius DTAA lays down certain rules when an entity has income arising both in Mauritius and in India. If the entity is a resident of India, it will be taxed under Indian tax laws. On the other hand, if the entity is a resident of Mauritius, it will be taxed under Mauritian tax laws. Mauritius, and other 41 nations across the world including the Bahamas, Bermuda, Barbados, Luxembourg, Ireland, Malta, the Virgin Islands, the Canary Islands, the Cayman Islands, the Isle of Man, and Switzerland, are known as *tax haven countries* as they have zero to negligible rates of tax.

In recent years, the treaty between India and Mauritius has come under criticism for encouraging round tripping and treaty shopping of investments, resulting in losses to the Government of India. *Round tripping* of investments occurs when an investment that originates in one country goes through another country—usually an offshore tax haven such as Mauritius—and then re-enters the first country as "foreign investment". *Treaty shopping* is an expression used to describe the act of a resident of a third country taking advantage of a bilateral treaty between two contracting countries.

Investments routed through Mauritius enjoy the best tax rates. For example, let us assume that a London-based firm wants to invest directly in India. It would be subject to more than 40 percent corporate tax rate, inclusive of surcharge. However, if it invests in India as a resident—foreign companies incorporated in India are considered residents of

India for tax purposes—it would be taxed on a par with a domestic company, at less than 40 percent inclusive of surcharge. Alternatively, if the same investment is brought in to India through Mauritius, it would be subject to a negligible tax rate. The same is true of portfolio investments. Foreign investments routed via Mauritius are exempt from tax. If there is direct foreign investment in India, the transfer of capital assets is subject to capital gains tax. But Mauritius has abolished capital gains tax, so that there are effectively no taxes on Mauritius-based foreign institutional investors investing in India. Further, Mauritius laws permit a company registered in Mauritius with incomes in other countries to claim 100 percent credit for tax paid on that income abroad. Even if the company cannot furnish proof of the tax payment, it would be permitted to claim 90 percent credit against the sum it claims it has paid as tax in another country. The net result is an effective rate of corporate tax of a very negligible percentage. Because of such tax benefits, foreign companies prefer to route their investments through Mauritius. It is for this reason that Mauritius tops India's list of sources of foreign direct investments and foreign portfolio investments.

If a foreign company wants to invest in India and claim tax treatment under Mauritius law, it would need to fulfill two requirements: (i) it should have income arising in both countries, and (ii) it should prove that it is managed from Mauritius. An entity would be considered a domicile of Mauritius so long as it is registered there and holds a substantial number of board meetings there. Because of laws where firms can become residents merely by registering, the potential for abuse is immense. It is reported that some Indian entities use Mauritius-registered firms and Mauritius offshore trusts to hold assets abroad, beyond the reach of Indian tax laws. Many Indians re-route funds stashed abroad through Mauritius. In other words, entities are using 'notional residence' in Mauritius to avoid paying taxes in India. It has even been claimed that tax losses to India are more than incoming investments.

In spite of the controversies generated, the Government of India has not revised the treaty because of larger economic, political, and diplomatic considerations. The Government of India feels that any move to tax Mauritius-registered FIIs will lead to huge capital outflows, simultaneously bringing about a crash in the stock market and hurting India's image. This stand of the Indian government attracted public interest litigation in the Delhi High Court, claiming that the Government of India may actually be shielding tax evaders by refusing to act against investors who are operating through Mauritius solely to save tax. In this context, the Supreme Court of India in the Union of India versus Azadi Bachao Andolan (2003) case observed that "many developed countries tolerate or encourage treaty shopping even if it was unintended, improper and unjustified for non-tax reasons, unless it leads to a significant loss of revenue. The court cannot judge the legality of treaty shopping merely because one section of thought considers it improper; neither can it characterize the act of incorporation under the Mauritian law as a sham or a device actuated by improper motives."

The Singapore–India Double-taxation Avoidance Agreement

The Government of Singapore and the Government of India signed a Comprehensive Economic Cooperation Agreement (CECA) on 29 June 2005. The agreement has a protocol that improves certain provisions in the existing tax treaty between the two countries. The most important improvement is in the taxation of capital gains. Under the protocol, capital gains from disposal of property will now be taxable only in the country of residence of the seller. However, this does not apply to capital gains from disposal of immovable property or movable business property that is attributable to a permanent establishment or a fixed base, for the purpose of performing independent personal services. According to the Agreement, gains derived from disposal of equity investments in India by a Singapore resident will not be subject to tax in India. As Singapore does not tax capital gains, the gains will also not be taxed in Singapore, if the investments are held for long-term investment purposes. This means that the gains will be entirely tax free.

The Agreement has certain provisions to prevent treaty shopping. First, the capital gains tax exemption is not available to those who arranged their affairs with the primary purpose of taking advantage of this treaty benefit. This aims at preventing anyone from enjoying the benefit simply by holding its Indian investment through a Singapore-resident company. Second, a shell or a conduit Singapore company will not enjoy this treaty benefit. A company is considered a shell or a conduit, if it has negligible or no business operations in Singapore and no real and continuous business activities are carried out in Singapore. A Singapore-based company is deemed not to be a shell or a conduit, if it is listed on a recognized stock exchange of Singapore, or its total annual expenditure on operations in Singapore is at least SGD 200,000 in the 24 months immediately preceding the date the gains arose.

The protocol also amends the withholding tax rate for royalties and fees for technical services to a single reduced tax rate of 10 percent. Earlier, the withholding tax rate was 10 percent or 15 percent, depending on the nature of the payment.

Thus, the Singapore–India Double-taxation Avoidance Agreement opens up an option for investments into India for businesses with substantial operations in Singapore.

Summary

1. Two types of accounting are required for foreign currency transactions and for foreign operations. The major accounting issues are with regard to choice of exchange rate and the treatment of exchange rate differences.

2. Companies in India are required to follow the provisions of AS 11, issued by ICAI in accounting for transactions in foreign currencies and in translating the financial statements of foreign branches for inclusion in the financial statements of the enterprise.

3. According to AS 11, a transaction in a foreign currency should be recorded in the reporting currency by applying to the foreign currency amount the exchange rate between reporting currency and foreign currency on the date of the transaction.

4. AS 11 states that *monetary items* should be reported using the closing rate; *non-monetary items* other than fixed assets should be reported using the exchange rate on the date of the transaction, and the carrying amount of fixed assets should be adjusted differently.

5. According to AS 11, exchange differences arising on foreign currency transactions should be recognized as income or expenses in the period in which they arise, except in certain cases. The difference between the forward rate and the exchange rate on the date of the transaction should be recognized as income or expenses over the life of the contract, except for liabilities incurred in acquiring fixed assets, in which case such differences should be adjusted in the carrying amount of the respective fixed assets.

6. AS 11 states that the revenue items, except opening and closing inventories and depreciation, should be translated into the reporting currency of the enterprise at the average rate. Monetary items should be translated using the closing rate, and non-monetary items other than inventories and fixed assets should be translated using the exchange rate on the date of the transaction.

7. In India, taxes are levied by the central government as well as state governments. Income tax is levied by the central government in accordance with the provisions of the Income Tax Act, 1961. The incidence of tax depends on the residential status of the assessee as well as the place and time of accrual or receipt of income.

8. Companies and firms are subject to tax at flat rates, while individuals and specified taxpayers are subject to progressive tax rates.

9. *Value-added tax* is a multi-point levy on each of the entities in the supply chain with the facility of set-off of input tax.

10. The Indian government has entered into *Double Taxation Avoidance Agreements* (DTAAs) with more than 80 countries. A typical DTAA states that if a resident of India becomes liable to pay tax in the foreign country for income from any source, he shall be allowed credit against the Indian tax payable with respect to that income. The amount of relief shall not exceed the tax borne by him in the foreign country on that portion of the income that is taxed in the foreign country.

11. India has entered into a treaty with Mauritius for the avoidance of double taxation, prevention of fiscal evasion with respect to taxing of income and capital gains, and encouraging mutual trade and investment.

12. The Government of Singapore and the Government of India have signed an agreement to improve certain provisions in the existing tax treaty between the two countries.

Questions

1. Explain the need for accounting for the effects of changes in foreign exchange rates.
2. What are the important provisions of AS 11?
3. Why do the financial statements of foreign affiliates need to be translated? How they are translated?
4. How are exchange gains/losses recorded?
5. Briefly explain the taxation system in India.
6. How is Indian income defined as per the Income Tax Act?
7. What are the incomes chargeable to tax under the head 'Profits and Gains of Business or Profession'?
8. What are deductible losses?
9. What are the allowable deductions under the head 'Profits and Gains of Business or Profession'?
10. How are capital gains taxed according to the Income Tax Act?
11. How are dividends treated under the Income Tax Act?
12. What are the permissible deductions available to companies under U/S 80 of the Income tax Act?
13. How is VAT computed? What are the advantages of VAT?
14. What do you understand by double-taxation relief? Comment on the Indo-Mauritius Double-taxation Avoidance Treaty. Also, highlight the salient features of Singapore–India Double-taxation Avoidance Agreement.

Multiple-choice Questions

1. Stakeholders of a company include ———.
   (a) Creditors (b) Employees
   (c) Customers (d) All the above
2. Accounting standards would ensure ——— of financial reports prepared by different enterprises.
   (a) Comparability (b) Consistency
   (c) Equality (d) None of these
3. Shifting to IFRS would enable Indian companies to have easy access to ———.
   (a) International trade
   (b) International capital markets
   (c) Foreign exchange market
   (d) None of these
4. Reporting currency is a currency used in preparing ———.
   (a) Financial Reports
   (b) Balance sheet
   (c) Profit and loss account
   (d) None of these
5. ——— is an example of a monetary item.
   (a) Inventory (b) Bank deposit
   (c) Fixed asset. (d) None of these
6. ——— is not a direct tax.
   (a) Wealth tax (b) Service tax
   (c) Income tax (d) None of these
7. Taxable income is classified into ——— heads.
   (a) Two (b) Three
   (c) Five (d) None of these
8. Indian income is taxable, irrespective of the ——— of recipient.
   (a) Residential status (b) Country of origin
   (c) Economic status (d) None of these
9. The year in which the income is earned is known as the ———.
   (a) Previous year (b) Assessment year
   (c) Financial year (d) None of these
10. Foreign income is not taxable in the hands of a ———.
    (a) Non-resident
    (b) Resident
    (c) Not ordinarily resident
    (d) None of these
11. Income from speculation is ———.
    (a) Taxable (b) Not taxable
    (c) Exempted from tax (d) None of these
12. Zero-tax companies may be required to pay ———.
    (a) Special tax
    (b) Minimum Alternate Tax
    (c) Wealth tax
    (d) None of these
13. VAT is a ——— levy.
    (a) Multi-point (b) Single-point
    (c) Zero-point (d) None of these
14. VAT can eliminate ———.
    (a) Cascading effect (b) Tax burden
    (c) Corruption (d) None of these

15. ———————— is liable to pay central excise duty.
    (a) Manufacturer. (b) Distributor
    (c) Consumer (d) None of these

16. DTAA is a ———————— agreement.
    (a) Multilateral (b) Bilateral
    (c) Three-party (d) None of these

Case Study

Ravi Nikethan is a Mumbai-based tax consultant and his customers are mostly multinational firms. A London-based MNC has its subsidiary unit in Mumbai, engaged in manufacturing textiles. The subsidiary unit has earned a net profit of INR 130 million for the financial year 2013–14.

The company has requested Ravi to assist the subsidiary unit to compute its taxable income after taking note of the following:

1. Other income credited to profit and loss account includes the following:
   - INR 3 million received on termination of a contract entered into in the ordinary course of business.
   - INR 2 million realized as penalty from a supplier of raw material whose supply fell short of the quantity contracted to be supplied by him.
   - INR 5 million being dividends received from a foreign company on shares allotted in pursuance of a collaboration agreement.
2. Interest debited to the profit and loss account is inclusive of the following:
   - Payment of interest for late filing of return of income for the last assessment year: INR 50,000.
   - Payment of interest on money borrowed from the bank for the purchase of land for construction of administrative offices: INR 1 million.
   - Payment of interest on overdraft utilized for payment of dividend: INR 1 million.
3. Repairs and maintenance include the following:
   - Expenditure incurred on replacement of worn out asbestos sheets of the factory shed with new sheets: INR 50,000.
   - Repairs to the compound wall that collapsed due to heavy rain: INR 0.5 million.
4. Salaries and staff welfare expenses include the following:
   - Expenditure of capital nature incurred for the purpose of promoting family planning amongst its employees: INR 0.75 million.
   - Contribution to Government of Maharashtra for construction of health centre adjacent to the company's factory where its employees are treated along with the members of public: INR 0.85 million.
   - Salary of foreign technicians retained on contract basis to study and suggest improved method of production: INR 1 million.
5. The company decided to close one of the divisions of the subsidiary unit and accordingly retrenched employees working in that division by paying retrenchment compensation and notice pay of INR 10 million, which is separately debited to the profit and loss account.

Questions

Ravi seeks your help for this case. How would you deal with each of the issues mentioned above and what provisions of the Income Tax Act would you consider?

Further Reading

1. Vinod K. Singhania and Monica Singhania, *Income Tax* (New Delhi: Taxman Publications, 2014).
2. H.C. Mehrotra and S.P. Goyal, *Income Tax—Law & Practice* (Agra: Sahitya Bhawan Publications, 2014).
3. David K. Eitemen, Michael H. Moffett, and Arthur I. Stonehill, *Multinational Business Finance* (Delhi: Pearson Education, 2007).
4. Gilbert E. Metcalf, "Value Added Taxation: A Tax Whose Time Has Come?," *Journal of Economic Perspectives* (1995), 121–40.
5. Jon E. Bischel and Robert Feinscheiber, *Fundamentals of International Taxation* (New York: Practising Law Institute, 1985).
6. PricewaterhouseCoopers, *Corporate Taxes: Worldwide Summaries* (New York: John Wiley and Sons, 2002).

CHAPTER 17

Multilateral Financial Institutions

CHAPTER OBJECTIVES

After studying this chapter, you should be able to:

1 Highlight the role of the International Bank for Reconstruction and Development (IBRD) in the development of the world economy.

2 Discuss the economic and social functions of the International Development Association (IDA).

3 Present a brief sketch of the International Finance Corporation (IFC).

4 Discuss the role of the Asian Development Bank (ADB) as a multilateral financing agency.

5 Describe the role of the International Monetary Fund (IMF) in promotinga stronger international monetary system.

Introduction

*The World Bank is made up of the **International Bank for Reconstruction and Development (IBRD)** and the International Development Association (IDA). IBRD assumes the responsibility of providing finance and advice to countries for the purpose of economic development and elimination of poverty.*

To focus on the overall development of the world economy, many institutions of multilateral character have sprung up over time. Each of these institutions has a different organizational set-up, resource base, and functions to meet specific requirements of different regions and different target groups. However, these institutions work together and complement each other to achieve the common goal of improving the living standards of people. In this era of globalization, multilateral financial institutions, along with the World Trade Organization (WTO), have become a unifying force that integrates several economies in the world. The performance of various multilateral institutions also reflects how well the "haves" (developed economies) could support and develop the "have-nots" (less developed economies).

Following the collapse of the gold standard, representatives of 44 countries met at Bretton Woods, New Hampshire, in July 1944 to design a new international monetary system. After a prolonged discussion, the representatives signed the Articles of Agreement of the International Monetary Fund. They also decided to create the **International Bank for Reconstruction and Development (IBRD)** to help in the reconstruction and development of countries that suffered in World War II. Accordingly, IBRD came into formal existence on 27 December 1945. On 9 May 1946, it approved its first loan of USD 250 million to France for postwar reconstruction. In real terms, this loan is considered to be the largest loan issued by IBRD to date.

The IBRD, which was originally conceived to help in the postwar reconstruction and development of nations ravaged by World War II, has subsequently assumed the responsibility of providing financial support and advice to countries in their economic endeavours for faster growth and development, including poverty elimination. In order to facilitate and support development of poor nations in all spheres, the representatives of the member countries also decided to create four more institutions—the International Finance Corporation (IFC), the International Development Association (IDA), the Multilateral Investment Guarantee Agency (MIGA), and the International Centre for Settlement of Investment Disputes (ICSID). These four multilateral agencies along with IBRD constitute the World Bank Group. In the words of past president of World Bank, Robert B. Zoellick, "it is the vision of the World Bank Group to contribute to an inclusive and sustainable globalization—to overcome poverty, enhance growth with care for the environment, and create individual opportunity and hope".

The IBRD, established in 1945, provides debt financing to the member countries on the basis of sovereign guarantees. The *International Finance Corporation (IFC)*, established in 1956, provides various forms of financing, primarily to private sector entities without sovereign guarantees. *The International Development Association*, established in 1960, provides concessional financing (interest-free loans or grants), usually with sovereign guarantees. The *Multilateral Investment Guarantee Agency (MIGA)*, established in 1988, provides insurance against certain types of risk, including political risk, primarily to the private sector. The *International Centre for Settlement of Investment Disputes (ICSID)*, established in 1966, works with governments to reduce investment risk.

Each institution of the World Bank Group is owned by its member governments which subscribe to its basic share capital, with votes proportional to shareholding. Membership in the institution gives certain voting rights that are the same for all countries. But there are additional votes that depend on financial contributions to the organization. By virtue of them being the major financial contributors, the developed nations obviously become the controlling group of these organizations. In other words, the developing nations are the major clients of these organizations. The clients can have access to capital on favourable terms in larger volumes, with longer maturities, and in a more sustainable manner than the financial markets typically provide. The mission of the World Bank Group is to:

- fight poverty with passion and professionalism for lasting solutions; and
- help people help themselves and their environment.

According to the World Bank, about 1.2 billion people live in extreme poverty (FY 2013), which constitutes about 21 percent of the population in the developing world. In view of these bare facts, the World Bank Group has redefined its strategy that is grounded in two goals. They are:

- ending extreme poverty by reducing the percentage of people living on less than USD 1.25 a day to 3 percent by 2030 and
- promoting shared prosperity by fostering income growth for the bottom 40 percent of the population in every country.

In simple terms, the goals are to end extreme poverty and promote shared prosperity. The new strategy outlines how the World Bank Group will partner with clients to help them achieve these goals through economic growth, inclusion, and sustainability.The areas of assistance and support include education, health, public administration, infrastructure, financial and private sector development, agriculture, and environmental and natural resource management. In October 2014, the World Bank Group launched Global Infrastructure Facility (GIF) that has the potential to unlock billions of dollars for infrastructure in the developing world. The world's largest asset management and private equity firms, pension and insurance funds, and commercial banks have also joined as partners in this new initiative.

The World Bank Group endeavours to achieve its mission and goals by providing resources, sharing knowledge, building capacity, and forging partnership in the public and private sectors. However, each of the institutions of the World Bank Group is governed by its Articles of Agreement that serves as the legal and administrative framework for its functioning. The International Bank for Reconstruction and Development in conjunction with the International Development Association is popularly known as the World Bank.

The International Bank for Reconstruction and Development

The mission of IBRD is to reduce global poverty and improve the living standards of people in the world in general and in developing countries in particular by building a climate suitable for investments, jobs, and sustainable growth. The activities of IBRD are mainly focused on achievement of the millennium development goals (MDGS) that call for the elimination of poverty and sustained development.

The major functions of IBRD are as follows:

- Support long-term human and social development needs that private creditors do not finance.
- Preserve borrowers' financial strength by providing support in crisis periods, which is when poor people are more adversely affected.
- Use the leverage of financing to promote key policy and institutional reforms.
- Create a favourable investment climate in order to catalyze the provision of private capital.
- Provide financial support in areas that are critical to the wellbeing of poor people all over the world.

Although poverty has declined over the last three decades, more than 1 billion people live in destitution. At the same time, inequality is rising in many developing nations. Thus, it is this realization that made the Bank redesign its business lines which embrace strategy and coordination services, financial services, and knowledge services. The latest commitment of IBRD is also to meet the increasingly sophisticated demands of middle-income countries.

Membership and Organization

The International Bank for Reconstruction and Development was established in 1945 with 38 members. Currently, it has 188 member countries, so almost all countries of the world are members. These countries have become members by subscribing to the share capital of IBRD. To become a member of IBRD, a country must first join the International Monetary Fund (IMF). Membership in IBRD is open to all members of the IMF. IBRD has adopted a weighted system of voting. Accordingly, each new member country is allotted 250 votes plus one additional vote for each share it holds in the Bank's capital stock. The countries that have a substantial proportion of voting rights are the United States (15.63%), Japan (7.81%), China (5.04%), Germany (4.38%), France (4.10%), and the United Kingdom (4.10%). India has 3.18% of the total voting power in IBRD. As major decisions require an 85 percent supermajority, the United States can have a say in every major decision of IBRD. Having more than 15 percent of voting rights, the United States can even block any major change in IBRD.

The Board of Governors is the highest authority and thus the ultimate policy making body of IBRD. Each member nation appoints one governor and one alternate governor in accordance with the Articles of Agreement. Generally, the ministers of finance/ministers of development represent members on the Board of Governors. The governor and alternate governor each would serve a five-year term and may be reappointed. No alternate governor can vote, except in the absence of his principal. The Board meets once a year at annual meetings, held in Washington every two consecutive years and in a member country every third year. On a daily basis, the Bank is run by the Board of Executive Directors, consisting of 25 members to whom the Board of Governors delegates certain powers. Of the 25 executive directors, five are appointed by the five largest shareholders and 20 are appointed by the remaining member countries through an election process conducted every two years. The Board of Executive Directors usually meets at least twice a week to oversee the Bank's operations and take certain decisions.

The Bank has a president, who is elected by the Board of Governors for a five-year, renewable term. The president of IBRD chairs the meetings of the Board of Governors, which meets once a year. The president is responsible for overall management of the Bank. The day-to-day operations of IBRD are looked after by the vice presidents and other managers under the leadership and direction of the president of the Bank.

Resources

The main resource strength of IBRD is its share capital, contributed by its 188 member countries. The authorized capital stock of the Bank shall be USD 10,000,000,000. The capital stock is divided into 100,000 shares having a par value of USD 100,000 each. The Bank also raises funds by issuing AAA-rated bonds in international financial markets. Although the Bank does not operate for profit, it does earn a small margin on lending. The Bank has also built up its reserves over the years.

Operations

The operations of IBRD are broadly classified as investment operations and development policy operations. IBRD provides investment loans to finance goods, works, and services in support of economic and social development projects in a broad range of sectors. The projects range from urban poverty reduction to rural development, water and sanitation, natural resources management, post-conflict reconstruction, education, and health. In the form of development policy loans, IBRD provides quick-disbursing external financing to support policy and institutional reforms. These loans have evolved to focus on structural, financial sector, and social policy reform and on improving public sector resource management.

The IBRD operates some active trust funds supported by donors. They are accounted separately from the Bank's own resources. This has led to grant funding of high-priority development needs, including technical assistance and advisory services, debt relief, and post-conflict transition. IBRD also offers different kinds of guarantees and risk-management tools to protect commercial lenders from risks associated with investing in developing countries.

The Bank helps the governments of developing countries take the lead in preparing and implementing development strategies to shape the future of their economies. For example, in the case of poverty reduction strategies, a government identifies the country's priorities and aims at reducing poverty over a three-tofive-year period. IBRD and other multilateral agencies then align their assistance with the country's own strategy. On the same lines, the Bank approved a new five-year Country Partnership Strategy for India in April 2013. The strategy sets specific goals for reducing poverty and increasing prosperity for the poorest people. The strategy shifts the Bank's support significantly to low-income states, where many of India's 400 million poor people live.

According to the Articles of Agreement, except in special circumstances, IBRD loans are for specific projects of reconstruction or development. The projects selected should be those most useful and urgent for increasing the productive capacity of borrowing countries.

For this, IBRD studies the entire economy and investment programme of the prospective borrower extensively. It believes that the borrowing country should hold some financial stake in the project. Accordingly, it is the general policy of the Bank not to finance the entire cost of the project.

The International Development Association

The initial purpose of IBRD was to help nations recover from the devastation of World War II. Later, IBRD turned its attention to helping the countries come out from poverty and underdevelopment. But very soon, it was realized that the poorest developing countries needed loans on softer terms than those that were offered by IBRD. It was this realization that brought the **International Development Association** into existence on 24 September 1960. In fact, IDA was established as a conduit for the haves (rich countries) to help the have-nots (poor countries), but on the principles of banking. It was made a part of the World Bank so that it could complement the efforts of IBRD. Both IBRD and IDA share the same staff and headquarters.

*The **International Development Association** strives to reduce inequalities, both across and within countries, by reducing poverty and promoting equal access to the opportunities created by economic growth.*

Mission and Goal

The mission of IDA is to help the world's poorest countries reduce poverty by providing interest-free loans and grants for programmes aimed at boosting economic growth and improving the living standards of people. Its goal is to reduce inequalities, both across and within countries, by reducing poverty and promoting more equal access to the opportunities created by economic growth.

Organization

The International Development Association has a Board of Governors and Executive Directors at the top of the administration. All the powers of IDA are vested in the Board of Governors. Each governor and alternate governor of IBRD, appointed by member countries, is governor and alternate governor, respectively, of IDA. The chairman of the Board of Governors of IBRD is the ex-officio chairman of the Board of Governors of IDA. Most of the powers of the Board of Governors are delegated to the executive directors. The executive directors are responsible for the conduct of the general operations of IDA. The president of IBRD is the ex-officio president of IDA. The president is the chairman of the Board of Executive Directors of IDA.

Resources

IDA gets the funds it needs through subscriptions and contributions from the governments of its richer member countries on the principle that the haves should help the have-nots. IBRD also supplements the resources of IDA. The representatives of the donor nations meet every three years to replenish IDA funds and review policies. Donor contributions account for more than half of IDA resources. A notable feature in this context is that the representatives of borrower countries are also invited to take part in the replenishment negotiations. The United States, Japan, Germany, the United Kingdom, and France are the major donor countries of IDA.

Deployment of Resources

IDA lends funds to eligible borrower countries. The criteria used to determine the eligibility of countries for assistance from IDA are:

- Relative poverty, defined as GNI per capita below an established threshold.

- Lack of creditworthiness to borrow on market terms and therefore a need for concessional resources to finance the country's development programme.
- Good policy performance, defined as the implementation of economic and social policies that promote growth and poverty reduction.

Thus, IDA assists three categories of countries. They are

- the countries that are the earth's poorest (77 countries in FY 2014);
- the countries that are above the operational poverty cut-off but lack the creditworthiness needed to borrow from IBRD and other agencies (59 countries in FY 2014); and
- the countries that are eligible to seek assistance from IDA based on their per capita income levels but are also creditworthy for borrowing from IBRD and other agencies. They are referred to as 'blend' countries (18 countries in FY 2014).

Countries such as Vietnam, Pakistan, etc. are referred to as 'blend' countries because they are IDA eligible, based on per capita income levels and are also creditworthy for some IBRD borrowing. India receives transitional support as it has graduated from IDA at the end of FY 2014 but will receive transitional support on an exception basis through the IDA 17 period (FY 2015–17).

Long-term loans are granted by IDA after evaluating projects with rigorous standards. They are interest free, but carry a small service charge of 0.75 percent on funds disbursed. The first IDA loans were approved in 1961 to countries such as Chile, Honduras, India, and Sudan. Since then many countries have received assistance from IDA.

Eligibility for IDA support depends first and foremost on a country's relative poverty, defined as GNI per capita below an established threshold and updated annually (USD 1,215 in fiscal year 2015). Seventy-seven countries (plus India) are currently eligible to receive IDA resources. Together, these countries are home to 2.8 billion people, half of the total population of the developing world. An estimated 1.8 billion people there survive on incomes of USD 2 or less a day.

The main consideration in allocating resources among eligible nations is the performance of the country in implementing policies that promote economic growth and poverty reduction. Every year, the quality of each borrower's policy performance is assessed by IDA. Sixteen performance criteria, grouped into four clusters (economic management, structural policies, policies for social inclusion/equity, and public sector management and institutions), are used in the assessment. The performance assessment also takes into account the performance of the country's active project portfolio performance.

Thus, the allocation of IDA's resources primarily depends on the borrower country's rating in the annual country performance and institutional assessment. The link between allocation and performance has resulted in an increasing concentration of lending to countries where policy performance is most conducive to effective resource use.

IDA extends loans to eligible borrower countries for a period of 20, 35, or 40 years with a 10-year grace period before repayment of principal starts. The loans are mainly for the purposes of primary education, basic health services, clean water and sanitation, environmental safeguards, business climate improvements, infrastructure, and institutional reforms. They are expected to pave the way towards economic growth, job creation, higher incomes, and better living conditions. In addition, IDA coordinates donor assistance to provide relief for poor countries that cannot manage their debt service burden.

Countries such as Pakistan, Vietnam, Ethiopia, India, Bangladesh, Nigeria, Congo, Ghana, and Afghanistan are the major beneficiaries of IDA's assistance. Although all the regions of the world have received assistance from IDA, sub-Saharan Africa has got the lion's share, followed by South Asia. Sector-wise, the social sector has received a substantial share of IDA's assistance, closely followed by public administration and law.

IDA-supported countries are subject to a variety of crises and emergencies that can undermine their economic and social development efforts. These include economic shocks such as food, fuel and financial crises, and natural disasters, such as droughts, earthquakes, floods, tsunamis and storms. But these countries have limited capacity to address the impact of such crises given their limited resources, infrastructure gaps, limited economic diversification, environmental vulnerabilities, widespread poverty, and often poorly developed formal safety nets. The long-term development effects of the crises often include lower growth, destruction of infrastructure assets, and declines in government revenues and resources for core development spending. To improve IDA's capacity to respond in the immediate aftermath of a crisis or emergency, the Immediate Response Mechanism (IRM) was adopted in 2011 which allows the crises-ridden countries to have immediate access to a portion of the undisbursed balances of their IDA project portfolio in the event of an eligible crisis or emergency. At the same time, the countries are also encouraged to proactively prevent and prepare to respond to crises in a rapid and effective manner.

IDA also carries out analytical studies to build a sound knowledge base and advises governments of member countries on ways to broaden the base of economic growth, thereby eliminating poverty and inequalities in the income and asset distribution among the people.

The International Finance Corporation

The **International Finance Corporation** was established in 1956 as a member of the World Bank Group to promote sustainable private-sector investment in developing countries. It is believed that private-sector investment is also a way to reduce poverty and improve the living standards of people. As a member of the World Bank Group, the International Finance Corporation, hereinafter called the Corporation, shares the primary objective of the World Bank Group: to improve the living conditions or standards of the people in developing countries. Given the immense need for private sector development, the Corporation works in partnership with other international development institutions such as IBRD, IDA, Multilateral Investment Guarantee Agency, International Centre for Settlement of Investment Disputes, African Development Bank, Asian Development Bank, European Bank for Reconstruction and Development, European Investment Bank, Inter-American Development Bank, International Monetary Fund, and Islamic Development Bank.

*The **International Finance Corporation** aims at improving the living conditions or standards of the people in developing countries.*

Mission and Objectives

The mission of the Corporation is to promote private sector investment in developing countries, which will reduce poverty and improve the lives of people.

Objectives:

- To finance private sector projects located in the developing countries that are members of the Corporation;
- To help private companies in the developing countries mobilize funds in international capital markets; and
- To provide advice and technical assistance to businesses and governments.

Strategic Priorities:

- Strengthening the focus on frontier markets;
- Addressing climate change and ensuring environmental and social sustainability;
- Addressing constraints to private sector growth in infrastructure, health, education, and the food supply chain;

- Developing local financial markets; and
- Building long-term client relationships in emerging markets

Membership and Resources

As of January 2015, the IFC had 184 member countries, which provide its authorized share capital of USD 2.4 billion. The five largest shareholders are the United States, Japan, Germany, the United Kingdom and France. The United States is the single largest shareholder with voting rights exceeding 23 percent. The member countries of the Organization for Economic Cooperation and Development (OECD) hold more than 70 percent of the voting rights in IFC. The Corporation has another category of countries, called donors,which support its activities. Donors are important partners for the Corporation, backing much of its technical assistance and advisory services that aim at promoting sustainable private sector development. To supplement its own resources (share capital and reserves) the Corporation also raises funds for its investment activities through the issuance of notes, bonds, and other debt securities in the international financial market.

Organization

Although the Corporation is in the World Bank Group, it is legally, financially, and organizationally independent. Corporate powers are vested in the Board of Governors. Each member country appoints one governor and one alternate governor. Usually the minister of finance or an equivalent represents the member country on the Board of Governors of the Corporation. The Board of Governors delegates most powers to the Board of Directors, which looks after the routine operations of the Corporation. The Board of Directors is assisted by standing committees such as Audit Committee, Budget Committee, and so on.

Products and Services

The main aim of the Corporation is to foster private sector investment in the developing nations of the world by providing investment, advice, and asset management. In order to help private sector companies in developing countries, Corporation has pioneered many credit products and services. The financial products of Corporation include loans for IFC's own account, syndicated loans, equity finance, quasi-equity finance, structured finance, risk management products, trade finance, and sub-national finance, among others.

The loan commitments to the target group include funds to be provided by the Corporation for its own account, funds to be provided by the participants through the purchase of an interest in the Corporation's investment, and funds to be provided by other financial institutions in association with the Corporation. Thus, the Corporation provides financing and financial services to the private sector in member countries, in partnership with other investors and lenders. The Corporation seeks partners for joint ventures and raises additional financing by encouraging other institutions to invest in the Corporation's project. The term 'Corporation's project' refers to a commercial investment that may involve a loan, equity investment, guarantee, or other financial product. The portfolio of the Corporation's own account is composed of loans, equity, guarantee, and risk management products. The loans for the Corporation's own account are called A-loans. The Corporation offers fixed and variable rate loans on its own account to private sector projects.

The Corporation does not lend directly to micro, small, and medium enterprises or individual entrepreneurs. But it lends to other financial intermediaries which in turn lend to the small business groups. That is, the Corporation makes loans to intermediary banks, leasing companies, and other financial institutions through credit lines for further on-lending.

The Corporation's investments generally range from USD 1 million to USD 100 million. But there are also cases in which the Corporation has lent in the range of USD 100,000 to USD 1 million. To ensure participation of other financial agencies, the Corporation typically finances no more than 25 percent of the total estimated project cost. Generally, the Corporation charges market-based rates for its loans and seeks market returns on its equity investment.

Apart from its core investment activities, the Corporation carries out technical assistance and advisory services programmes. Funded mainly by donor countries, these programmes complement Corporation's mainstream business (commercial investments), and they differentiate the Corporation from other financiers. The Corporation designates a certain percentage of its net income to fund its technical assistance and advisory services.

The Corporation focuses on the sectors that have a high impact on the economies of developing countries. The sectors that are given emphasis include the financial sector, small and medium enterprises, infrastructure, information and communication technologies, and health and medium enterprises. The Corporation believes that increasing access to finance for poor people and the businesses they create is the key to sustainable economic growth. Accordingly, it helps strengthen the financial markets in developing countries. The Corporation and IBRD launched the Strengthening Grassroots Business Initiative, which works with organizations that help poor, marginalized people expand revenue-generating activities that bring them into the market economy. The Corporation also advises the governments of member countries on how to create an environment suitable for the growth of private enterprise and foreign investment.

The Corporation has developed new approaches that increase private sector participation in infrastructure, health, and education. For example, to support biotechnology and pharmaceuticals, which are potentially major growth sectors in India, the Corporation has invested in the APIDC Biology Fund. The Fund will, in turn, make equity and equity-related investments in early-stage life science businesses. The Corporation also makes efforts to integrate environmental, social, and corporate governance issues with financial and economic factors so that private sector development will have a positive and long-term contribution to the economy.

It may also be mentioned that the International Finance Corporation is the largest multilateral source of equity and loan financing for private-sector businesses in developing and emerging countries. It fosters economic growth in these countries by financing private sector investments, mobilizing capital in the international financial markets, and providing technical assistance and advice to governments and businesses. In response to the global financial crisis following the subprime crisis in the United States, the Corporation has launched or expanded four facilities: the Expanded Trade Finance Program, Bank Recapitalization Fund, Infrastructure Crisis Facility, and IFC Advisory Services. These facilities are aimed at addressing the problems of the private sector during the global financial crisis.

The IFC holds USD 49.6 billion portfolio by the end of the FY 2014, touching almost every major industry. It has reached millions of people in more than 100 countries, creating jobs, raising living standards, and building a better future to support the World Bank Group's two goals: ending extreme poverty and boosting shared prosperity.

The Asian Development Bank

The **Asian Development Bank (ADB)** was established in 1966 to promote economic and social development in Asian and Pacific countries through loans and technical assistance. On the lines of IBRD, the Asian Development Bank aims at improving the living conditions of the people in Asia and the Pacific, which is home to two-thirds of the world's poor.

*The mission of the **Asian Development Bank (ADB)** is to help its developing member countries reduce poverty and improve the quality of life of people.*

In addition to the hundreds of millions who survive on less than USD 1 a day, some 1.7 billion people live on less than USD 2 a day in the countries of Asia and Pacific.

The mission of ADB is to free the Asia and Pacific region from poverty by helping its developing member countries reduce poverty and improve the quality of life of their people. ADB has its headquarters in Manila and 27 other offices around the world.

Objectives

- To extend loans and make equity investments in its developing member countries for their economic and social development;
- To provide technical assistance for the planning and execution of development projects and programmes;
- To promote and facilitate investment of public and private capital for development; and
- To coordinate the development policies and plans of its member countries.

Membership and Organization

The Asian Development Bank is a multilateral development financial institution with 67 member countries, of which 48 countries are from the region, and 19 are from other parts of the world. Japan and the United States have the largest shareholdings, each with 12.8 percent of total voting power. While the regional members have 65 percent of total voting power, the non-regional members have 35 percent.

Each member country appoints one governor and one alternate governor to represent the country on the Board of Governors. The Board, which is the highest policy-making body, meets once a year at an annual meeting held in a member country. Most of the powers of the Board of Governors are delegated to the 12-person Board of Directors. Eight of the 12 directors represent countries within the Asia Pacific region and four representing countries outside the region. The day-to-day business of ADB is managed by the president, assisted by four vice-presidents and a managing director general. The president of ADB is elected by the Board of Governors for a term of five years, with the possibility of re-election. The president chairs the meetings of the Board of Directors.

Resources

The financial resources of ADB consist of subscribed capital, reserves and surpluses, and borrowed funds. ADB raises funds through bond issues in the international capital markets. It has issued a variety of debt instruments, which include liquid benchmark bonds, plain vanilla bonds, emerging market currency bonds, and investor-specific structured notes. It is an AAA- credit rating borrower in international and domestic capital markets. It undertakes most of its borrowings through its global medium-term notes. For its short-term funding needs, ADB operates its Euro-commercial Paper Programme. The borrowing policy of ADB is to avoid becoming dependent on any one currency or market for funding. Accordingly, it borrows in a broad range of currencies, instruments, markets, and maturities.

Operations

The Asian Development Bank provides loans, technical assistance, grants, guarantees, and equity investments to governments and private enterprises in its developing member countries. Since its inception, ADB has supported projects in agriculture and natural resources, energy, finance, non-fuel minerals, social infrastructure, transport and communications, besides disaster and emergency assistance. ADB works in partnership with governments, public and private enterprises, non-government organizations, multilateral and bilateral agencies, community-based organizations, and foundations to support projects and programmes that will contribute to economic and social development.

In 2008, ADB adopted a long-term strategic framework called Strategy 2020 in compliance with its vision of "Asia and Pacific Region Free of Poverty by 2020". The three strategic agendas set out in Strategy 2020 are inclusive growth, environmentally sustainable growth and regional integration. In this context, ADB will focus on five core areas, namely, infrastructure, environment including climate change, regional cooperation and integration, finance sector development, and education.

ADB has some special funds, which are mostly contributions of members for ADB's concessional loan and technical assistance programmes. The special funds are the Asian Development Fund, Japan Fund for Poverty Reduction, the Poverty Reduction Cooperation Fund, and the Cooperation Fund in Support of the Formulation and Implementation of National Poverty Reduction Strategies. The Asian Development Fund was instituted in 1973 for extending concessional finance in support of equitable and sustainable development of the region. The most recent replenishment (ADF IX, 2005–2008) was negotiated between ADB and donors for USD 7 billion; at least USD 3.7 billion was to be provided from internal resources and the remaining USD 3.2 billion was to be provided by new donor contributions on a burden-shared basis. There were also some additional voluntary contributions. Since 2000, the Asian Development Fund has transformed the region with the construction of thousands of schools, bridges, health clinics, and roads, providing opportunities for people to lift themselves out of poverty. The Japan Fund for Poverty Reduction was instituted in 2000 with USD 90 million, initially contributed by Japan. The Poverty Reduction Cooperation Fund was established in 2002 with an initial grant of USD 75 million from the United Kingdom and Northern Ireland. The Cooperation Fund was established in 2001 as a multi-donor fund with an initial contribution of 15 million Dutch guilders by the Government of Netherlands.

Millennium Development Goals

The world leaders at the UN Millennium Summit held in September 2000 agreed on the Millennium Declaration for accelerating democratization and securing peace, scaling up development and poverty reduction, ensuring environmental sustainability, and promoting global partnerships. These were translated into the Millennium Development Goals in 2001. MDGs are time-bound measurable targets for combating certain problems. The eight MDGs are to:

1. Eradicate extreme poverty and hunger;
2. Achieve universal primary education;
3. Promote gender equality and empower women;
4. Reduce child mortality;
5. Improve maternal health;
6. Combat HIV/AIDS, malaria, and other diseases;
7. Ensure environmental sustainability; and
8. Develop a global partnership for development.

The goals are, however, adjusted according to the specific country context. There are one or more targets for each goal, and the year 1990 is the benchmark. The targets are set mostly for 2015. Indicators are also identified to measure progress against each target.

For achieving the MDGs in Asia and the Pacific, ADB is engaged in a regional MDG partnership with the United Nations Development Programme (UNDP) and the United Nations Economic and Social Commission for Asia and the Pacific (ESCAP).

*The **International Monetary Fund** has been established to help the world economy by promoting international monetary cooperation.*

The International Monetary Fund

On the recommendations of the Bretton Woods conference, the **International Monetary Fund** was established in 1945 to help promote the world economy on sound lines. The Articles of Agreement of the IMF, signed by the representatives of 44 nations, form its constitution and set out several aspects for smooth and effective functioning of the IMF. The IMF shall be guided in all its policies and decisions by the Articles of Agreement. As per Article I, the main purposes of the IMF are:

- To promote international monetary cooperation;
- To facilitate the expansion and balanced growth of international trade;
- To promote exchange stability and maintain orderly exchange arrangements among members;
- To assist in the establishment of a multilateral system of payments with respect to current transactions between members; and
- To give confidence to members by making the general resources of the Fund temporarily available to them.

Membership and Organization

The original members of the IMF are those countries represented at the United Nations Monetary and Financial Conference whose governments accepted membership before 31 December 1945. For other countries, the membership is open at such times and in accordance with such terms as may be prescribed by the Board of Governors. The current membership of the IMF is 185 countries.

The Board of Governors is the highest policy-making body of the IMF. The board consists of one governor and one alternate governor appointed by each member of the IMF. The Board of Governors selects one of the governors as chairman. The Board of Governors holds meetings as may be provided for by the Board of Governors or called by the Executive Board. The Board normally meets once a year at the annual meeting. Twenty-four of the governors are on the International Monetary and Finance Committee, and meet twice a year.

The day-to-day work of the IMF is conducted by the Executive Board, supported by more than 2,700 professional staff from 165 countries. The Executive Board consists of 24 members, with the managing director as Chairman. Of the executive directors, five are appointed by the five members having the largest quotas, and fifteen are elected by the other members. Election of executive directors is conducted at intervals of two years. The executive board functions in continuous session at the principal office of the IMF and meets as often as the business of the IMF may require.

Special Drawing Rights

Every country has to maintain official foreign exchange reserves that can be used to purchase the domestic currency in the foreign exchange market to maintain at a certain level the exchange rate of its domestic currency against foreign currencies. Before the Bretton Woods System came into being, the U.S. dollar was the only currency that was fully convertible into gold. As countries could use not only gold but also the U.S. dollars as international means of payment, they accumulated U.S. dollars as reserves. When the United States experienced huge trade deficits with many countries in the world, and the total value of the U.S. gold stock fell short of foreign USD holdings, particularly in 1960s, there was a concern over the viability of the USD-based system. Further, the two principal reserve assets (gold and USD) proved inadequate for supporting the expansion of world trade and cross-border investments. Therefore, to ease the pressure on the U.S. dollar as the reserve currency, the IMF created an artificial international reserve asset called the *special drawing right (SDR)*. As SDRs were basically created to replace gold in large international transactions, they are also referred to *as paper gold*. SDR is neither a currency nor a claim on the IMF which has created it. It is, rather, a potential claim on the freely usable currencies of IMF members. In other words, the holders of SDRs can obtain these currencies in exchange for their SDRs. The SDR is also used as a unit of account by the IMF and many other international organizations. A few countries do peg their currencies against the SDR. Many believed that the use of the SDR as a reserve asset was the prelude to the creation of a single world currency.

The special drawing rights (SDRs) were initially created by the IMF in 1969 to support the Bretton Woods exchange rate system. According to the Bretton Woods system, each country had to establish a par value of its currency in relation to the U.S. dollar, which was pegged to gold at USD 35 per ounce. The price of gold at USD 35 per ounce continued until 18 December 1971. The U.S. dollar was pegged to gold at USD 38 per ounce between 18 December 1971 and 11 February 1973; and at USD 42.22 per ounce between 12 February 1973 and 30 June 1974. Since July 1974, the SDR has been defined in terms of a basket of currencies. Initially, the basket consisted of 16 currencies but was reduced to five in 1981. Before the emergence of the euro in 1999, the Deutsche mark and the French franc were included in the basket of currencies.

SDR Basket Composition and Value The basket composition is reviewed by the IMF Executive Board every five years, and the currencies in the basket and their values are determined to ensure that the SDR reflects the relative importance of the currencies in the world's trading and financial system. The weight of each currency in the basket is based on the value of the exports of goods and services of the respective countries and the amount of reserves held by other IMF members that are denominated in the respective currencies. In the most recent review in November 2010, the weights of the currencies in the SDR basket were revised based on value of the exports of goods and services and the amount of reserves denominated in the respective currencies that were held by other members of the IMF. The revision became effective on 1 January 2011. According to the latest revision, the initial weights of the currencies in the basket are: USD (41.9%), EUR (37.4%), JPY (9.4%), and GBP (11.3%). The next review will take place in 2015. The weights are subject to change with the fluctuations of the exchange rates of the constituent currencies. The value of SDR in terms of USD is determined daily by the IMF, based on the exchange rates of the currencies making up the basket. The value of SDR as on 30 January 2015 is presented in Table 17.1. As it can be seen from the table, one USD is equivalent to SDR 0.709319.

Allocation of SDRs The IMF allocates SDRs to member countries in proportion to their quotas. If a member's SDR holdings rise above its allocation, it earns interest on the excess, and if it holds fewer SDRs than allocated, it pays interest on the shortfall. The Articles of Agreement have also empowered the IMF to cancel the SDRs allocated to any country.

There are two types of SDR allocations to countries: general allocation and special allocation. The *general allocation* of SDRs is based on a long-term global need to supplement existing reserve assets. The first allocation was for a total amount of SDR 9.3 billion, distributed in 1970–1972. The second allocation was to the cumulative total of SDR 21.4 billion, distributed in 1979–1981. To mitigate the effects of the financial crisis, a third general SDR allocation of SDR 161.2 billion was made in August 2009.

A proposal for a *special one-time allocation* of SDRs was approved by the Board of Governors in September 1997 through the Fourth Amendment of the Fund's Articles of Agreement to correct the imbalances in the allocation and to enable members to participate in the SDR system on an equitable basis. The Fourth Amendment became effective for all

Table 17.1 Currency Amounts in New Special Drawing Rights (SDR) Basket

		30 January 2015		
Currency	*Currency amount under Rule O-1*	*Exchange rate*[1]	*U.S. dollar equivalent*	*Percent change in exchange rate against U.S. dollar from previous calculation*
Euro	0.4230	1.13380	0.479597	0.239
Japanese yen	12.1000	117.71000	0.102795	0.246
Pound sterling	0.1110	1.50820	0.167410	−0.317
U.S. dollar	0.6600	1.00000	0.660000	1.409802
		USD1.00 = SDR	0.709319[2]	−0.061[3]
		SDR1 = USD	1.409800[4]	

Source: www.imf.org/external/np/exr/facts/sdr.htm.

[1] The exchange rate for the Japanese yen is expressed in terms of currency units per U.S. dollar; other rates are expressed as U.S. dollars per currency unit.

[2] IMF Rule O-2(a) defines the value of the U.S. dollar in terms of the SDR as the reciprocal of the sum of the equivalents in U.S. dollars of the amounts of the currencies in the SDR basket, rounded to six significant digits. Each U.S. dollar equivalent is calculated on the basis of the middle rate between the buying and selling exchange rates at noon in the London market. If the exchange rate for any currency cannot be obtained from the London Market, the rate shall be the middle rate between the buying and selling exchange rates at noon in the New York market or, if not available there, the rate shall be determined on the basis of euro reference rates published by the European Central Bank.

[3] Percent change from previous calculation.

[4] The reciprocal of the value of the U.S dollar in terms of the SDR, rounded to six significant digits.

members in August 2009 when IMF certified that at least three-fifths of the IMF membership (112 members) with 85 percent of the total voting power accepted it. Thus, the special allocation was implemented in September 2009.

The IMF members may buy or sell SDRs to adjust the composition of their reserves. In such cases, the IMF may act as an intermediary between members and prescribed holders to ensure that SDRs are exchanged for freely usable currencies.

Resources

Most resources for the IMF are provided by the member countries, primarily through their payment of quotas. Each member is assigned a *quota* expressed in special drawing rights, based on its relative size in the world economy. A member's quota determines its maximum financial commitment to the IMF and its voting power. On joining the IMF as a member, a country normally pays up to a quarter of its quota in the form of widely accepted foreign currencies or SDRs. The remaining three quarters are paid in the country's own currency. Total quotas at the end of August 2008 were SDR 217.4 billion, equivalent to USD 341 billion. Quotas are reviewed at least every five years, and adjustment of the quotas may be made by the Board of Governors. Any changes in quotas require broad support, as they must be approved by an 85 percent majority.

The largest member of the IMF is the United States, with a quota of SDR 42,122.4 million, and the smallest member is Tuvalu with a quota of SDR 1.8 million. It may be noted that the quota largely determines a member's voting power in IMF decisions. A member's share of general SDR allocations is in proportion to its quota. Further, the amount of financing a member country can obtain from the IMF is based on its quota.

The IMF can also borrow when required through supplementary borrowing arrangements. The first and principal resort is the *new arrangements to borrow (NAB),* which was established in 1998. The NAB are a set of credit arrangements between the IMF and 38 member countries and institutions to provide supplementary resources to the IMF to forestall or cope with an impairment of the international monetary system or to deal with an exceptional threat to the stability of that system. So far, the NAB has been activated eight times, starting from December 1998 when the IMF called on funding of SDR 9.1 billion. Most recently, the NAB has been activated six times commencing on 1 October 2011, 1 April 2012, 1 October 2012, 1 April 2013, 1 October 2013, and 1 April 2014.

The IMF can also borrow specified amounts of currencies from 11 industrial countries through the *general arrangements to borrow (GAB)* under certain circumstances at market-related rates of interest. The GAB was established in 1962 and expanded in 1983 to SDR 17 billion from about SDR 6 billion. It has been activated ten times, the last time in 1998. The GAB and the associated credit arrangement with Saudi Arabia were renewed for a period of five years from 26 December 2013.

The G-20 nations agreed in April 2009 to increase the resources available to the IMF by up to USD 500 billion to support growth in emerging markets and developing countries in the post-global financial crisis.

The IMF is one of the largest official holders of gold in the world, but it is prohibited from buying gold or engaging in other gold transactions except accepting gold as payment by member countries.

Operations

The IMF is primarily responsible for ensuring the stability of the international monetary and financial system. The IMF has three objectives in this regard:

- To promote economic stability and prevent financial crises;
- To help resolve financial crises; and
- To promote economic growth and alleviate poverty.

To meet these objectives, the IMF employs three functions: *surveillance, technical assistance,* and *lending.* The surveillance may be multilateral and bilateral. Under multilateral surveillance, the IMF provides periodic assessments of global and regional developments and prospects, which are published twice each year in the *World Economic Outlook.* Bilateral surveillance refers to the regular dialogue and policy advice that the IMF offers to each of its member countries on a one-on-one basis. The IMF conducts an in-depth study of each member country's economic situation and offers advice on several policy issues. It also assists member countries in identifying and diagnosing financial system problems and designing strategies for systemic reforms and bank restructuring. Thus, the IMF keeps track of the economic health of its member countries through its economic surveillance and helps countries make informed decisions. In fact, the IMF drew attention to growing risks in the U.S. mortgage market well before the subprime crisis erupted in the United States in August 2007.

The IMF also provides technical assistance to member countries to implement specific measures that will strengthen their financial infrastructure. The technical assistance may include training and advice on improving monetary and fiscal management, foreign exchange and capital market development, and strategies for systemic bank restructuring. Through the Financial Sector Assessment Program (an IMF–World Bank initiative), the IMF alerts countries to likely vulnerabilities in their financial sectors—whether originating from inside the country or from outside sources—and assists them in the design of measures that would reduce these vulnerabilities. The technical assistance is mostly provided free of cost.

The IMF gives special treatment to poor countries. It provides financial support to low-income countries through its concessional lending facilities—the Poverty Reduction and Growth Facility and the Exogenous Shocks Facility. The interest rate levied on these types of loans is only 0.5 percent, and they are to be repaid over a period of 5 to 10 years. Financial support is also provided to low-income countries through debt relief under the Heavily Indebted Poor Countries Initiative and the Multilateral Debt Relief Initiative. In collaboration with the World Bank, the IMF has been working to reduce to sustainable levels the debt burdens of heavily indebted poor countries. The IMF also helps low-income countries by encouraging aid effectiveness, promoting social spending, providing policy framework for good performers, and expanding regional technical assistance.

Non-concessional loans are provided by the IMF through standby arrangements to help countries address short-term balance of payment problems. The IMF also provides loans under the Extended Fund Facility to help countries address long-term balance of payments problems requiring fundamental economic reforms. To meet a need for very short-term financing on a large scale, the IMF provides loans to member countries under the Supplemental Reserve Facility. To assist member countries experiencing either a sudden shortfall in export earnings or an increase in the cost of cereal imports, often caused by fluctuating world commodity prices, the IMF provides financial assistance to countries under the Compensatory Financing Facility. The IMF also has a provision for emergency assistance to countries that have experienced a natural disaster or are emerging from conflict. The IMF does not lend for specific projects.

Often, countries (especially developing nations) face a situation where sufficient financing on affordable terms cannot be obtained to meet international payment obligations. In the worst case, balance of payments difficulties can build into a crisis. In such a situation, the country's currency may be forced to depreciate rapidly, making international goods and capital more expensive. In other words, the domestic economy may experience a painful disruption. These problems may also spread to other countries. In this context, the IMF plays a vital role. It extends financial assistance to member countries to rebuild their international reserves, stabilize their currencies, continue paying for imports, and restore the environment for strong economic growth. The IMF works in partnership with other international organizations to promote economic growth and reduce poverty in the world. The IMF also plays an important role in the fight against money laundering and terrorism.

The Purchase–Repurchase Mechanism

The IMF extends financing by providing reserve assets (foreign currencies acceptable to the IMF or SDRs) to the borrower from the reserve asset subscription of members or by calling on countries that are considered financially strong to exchange their currency subscriptions for reserve assets. Repayment of the loan is achieved by the borrower "repurchasing" its currency from the IMF with reserve assets. A country that provides reserve assets to the IMF as part of its quota subscription or through the use of its currency, receives a liquid claim on the IMF, which can be encashed on demand to obtain reserve assets to meet a balance of payments financing need. As IMF loans are repaid (repurchased) by the borrower with reserve assets, these funds are transferred to the creditor countries in exchange for their currencies, and the creditor's claim on the IMF is extinguished. Although the purchase–repurchase mechanism is not technically or legally a loan, it is the functional equivalent of a loan.

The IMF and the WTO

One of the objectives of the IMF is to facilitate the expansion and balanced growth of international trade. Accordingly, the IMF works in close liaison with the World Trade Organization (WTO) to ensure a sound financial system for global trade and payments. In fact, the functions of the IMF and the WTO are complementary. A sound international financial system would ensure vibrant international trade, while a smooth flow of goods and services across countries helps reduce the risk of payments and financial crisis. To enable the IMF and the WTO to work together, a cooperation agreement between the two organizations covering various aspects of their relationship is also signed. According to the agreement, the WTO is required to consult the IMF when it deals with issues concerning monetary reserves, balance of payments, and foreign exchange arrangements. Having an observership status at the WTO, the IMF participates actively in many meetings of WTO committees, working groups, and bodies. Similarly, the WTO Secretariat attends meetings of the IMF Executive Board.

Informal consultation between IMF staff and the WTO Secretariat takes place regularly regarding trade policy developments and advice for individual countries. The Managing Director of the IMF and the Director General of the WTO consult regularly on a wide range of trade-related issues. The IMF, the WTO, and other international organizations and donors often work together to help countries improve their ability to trade.

Summary

1. Multilateral financial institutions have assumed a special role in reducing the gap between the 'haves' and the 'have-nots' by supporting and assisting developing nations in their development endeavours.
2. The *World Bank Group* consists of the International Bank for Reconstruction and Development (IBRD), the International Development Association (IDA), the International Finance Corporation (IFC), the Multilateral Investment Guarantee Agency (MIGA), and the International Centre for Settlement of Investment Disputes (ICSID).
3. *IBRD,* which was originally conceived to help in the postwar reconstruction and development of countries ravaged by World War II, has subsequently assumed the responsibility of providing finance and advice to countries for the purpose of economic development and eliminating poverty in the world.
4. IBRD helps the governments of underdeveloped countries take the lead in preparing and implementing development strategies to shape the future of their economies.
5. IBRD offers loans and grants to developing nations. IBRD-financed projects cover urban poverty reduction, rural development, water and sanitation, natural resources management, post-conflict reconstruction, education, health, and so on.
6. The mission of the *International Development Association* is to help the world's poorest countries reduce poverty by providing interest-free loans and grants for programmes aimed at boosting economic growth and improving living standards of the people.
7. The *International Finance Corporation* was established to promote sustainable private sector investment in developing countries. It is believed that private sector investment is also a way to reduce poverty and improve the living standards of people.
8. The *Asian Development Bank (ADB)* was established to promote economic and social development in Asian and Pacific countries through loans and technical assistance. ADB provides help to its developing member countries through loans, technical assistance, grants, guarantees, and equity investments. It lends to governments and to public and private enterprises in its developing member countries.
9. The *International Monetary Fund (IMF)* is primarily responsible for ensuring the stability of the international monetary and financial system. The IMF employs three functions, namely, surveillance, technical assistance, and lending to meet its objectives. The main objective of the IMF is to promote economic stability and prevent financial crises. In collaboration with the World Bank, the IMF has been working to reduce the debt burdens of heavily indebted poor countries.
10. The Special Drawing Right (SDR) is an artificial international reserve created by the IMF. It represents a basket of currencies, and presently the basket consists of the euro, the Japanese yen, the British pound, and the U.S. dollar. The weight of each currency in the basket is based on the value of the exports of goods and services of the respective country and the amount of reserves denominated in the respective currencies by other members of the IMF.

Questions and Problems

1. Discuss the role of multilateral financial institutions in the development of low-income countries.
2. Explain the origin and development of IBRD.
3. Describe the organizational structure of the World Bank.
4. Evaluate the operations and performance of IBRD in recent years.
5. What is the mission of the International Development Association? Evaluate its performance vis-à-vis its mission.
6. What are the objectives of IFC? Explain the products and services of IFC.
7. Critically evaluate the performance of the Asian Development Bank in the last five years.
8. Explain the special funds of the Asian Development Bank.
9. What are the purposes of the IMF? How is it serving these purposes?
10. Explain the membership and organization of the IMF.
11. What are the objectives of SDRs? Comment on the SDR allocation policy of the IMF.
12. How is the IMF collaborating with other multilateral financial institutions in promoting economic development and reducing poverty in the world?
13. To what extent have the poorest nations of the world benefited by multilateral financial institutions? Discuss.

Multiple-choice Questions

1. ________ is not part of the World Bank Group.
   (a) Asian Development Bank
   (b) IFC
   (c) Multilateral Investment Guarantee Agency
   (d) None of these
2. ________ is the latest addition in the World Bank Group.
   (a) Multilateral Investment Guarantee Agency
   (b) IFC
   (c) International Centre for Settlement of Investment Disputes
   (d) None of these
3. According to the World Bank, ________ billion people live in extreme poverty.
   (a) 2.1 (b) 1.2
   (c) 3.1 (d) None of these
4. The World Bank Group aims at reducing the percentage of people living on less than USD 1.25 a day to ________ percent by 2030.
   (a) 2 (b) 0
   (c) 3 (d) None of these
5. Country Partnership Strategy for India is the idea of ________.
   (a) IMF (b) IBRD
   (c) IFC (d) None of these
6. ________ is considered to be a conduit for the haves (rich countries) to help the have-nots (poor countries).
   (a) IDA (b) IBRD
   (c) IFC (d) None of these
7. According to IDA, ________ countries constitute the earth's poorest.
   (a) 77 (b) 59
   (c) 18 (d) None of these
8. ________ is an example of blend countries.
   (a) Vietnam (b) Sri Lanka
   (c) India (d) None of these
9. ________ specifically aims at promoting the private sector investment.
   (a) IFC (b) IDA
   (c) IMF (d) None of these
10. The Strengthening Grassroots Business Initiative was launched by ________.
    (a) IFC and IBRD (b) IBRD
    (c) IAD (d) None of these
11. ADB aims at improving the living conditions of people in ________.
    (a) Asia (b) Asia and Pacific
    (c) Asia and Europe (d) None of these

12. Millennium Development Goals include _________.
    (a) Achieving universal primary education
    (b) Achieving computer literacy
    (c) Achieving zero population growth
    (d) None of these

13. SDR is known as _________.
    (a) Paper gold (b) Paper currency
    (c) Claim on IMF (d) None of these

14. The SDR basket contains _________.
    (a) INR (b) USD
    (c) AUD (d) None of these

15. The largest voting rights in IMF are held by _________.
    (a) USA (b) UK
    (c) Germany (d) None of these

Further Reading

1. The World Bank, *World Development Report 2014* (Washington DC: World Bank and Oxford University Press).
2. The Asian Development Bank, *Annual Reports* (Manila: ADB).
3. International Finance Corporation, *Annual Reports* (Washington DC: IFC).
4. The World Bank, *Annual Reports* (Washington DC: World Bank).
5. www.imf.org.
6. www.worldbank.org.

Index